DETROIT IS NO DRY BONES

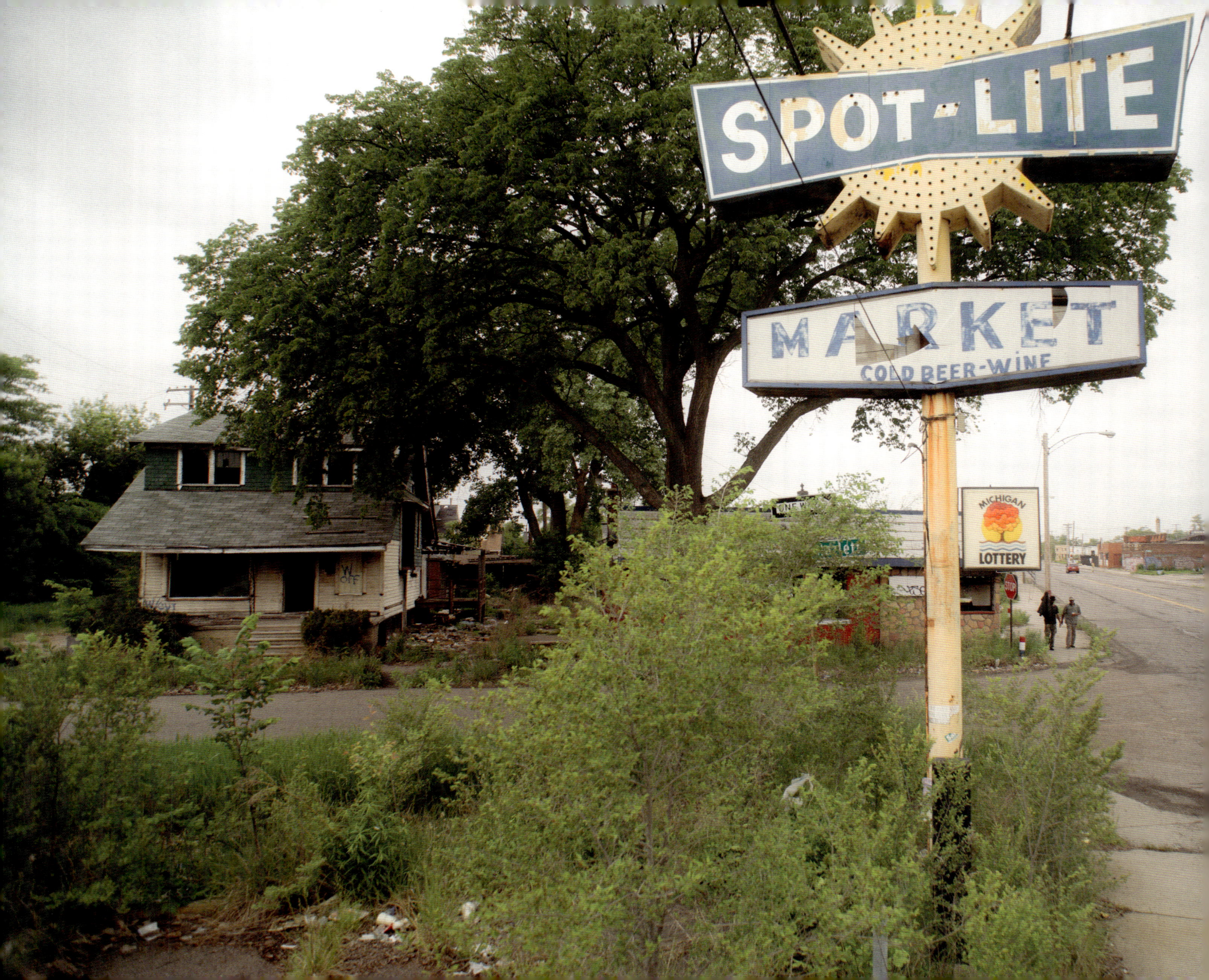
SPOT-LITE
MARKET
COLD BEER-WINE
MICHIGAN
LOTTERY

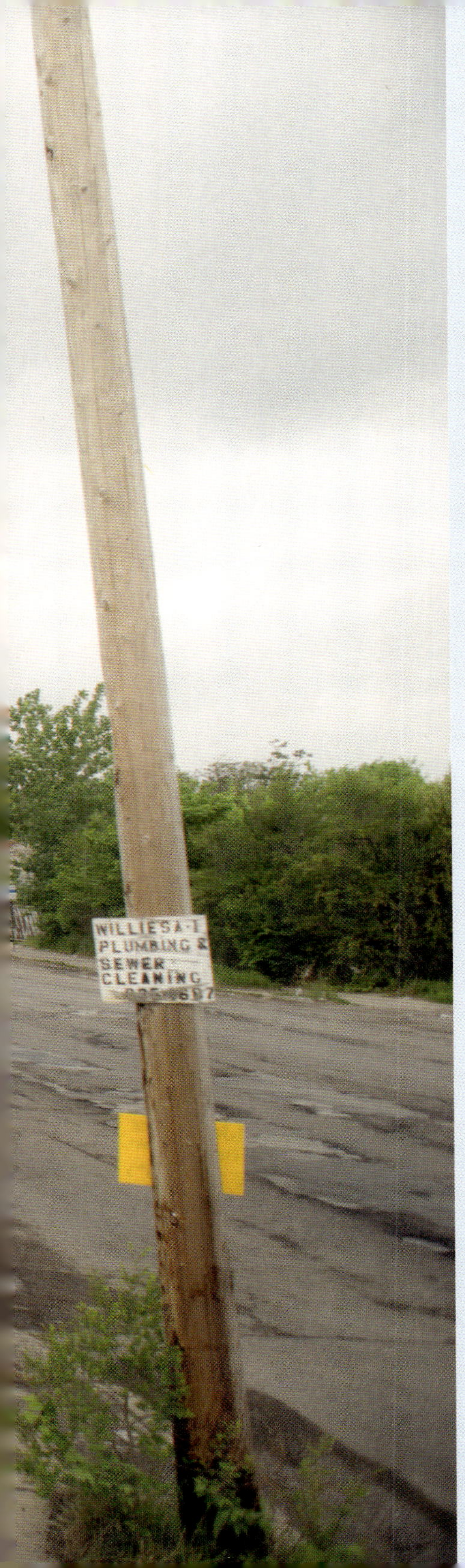

DETROIT IS NO DRY BONES

THE ETERNAL CITY OF THE INDUSTRIAL AGE

CAMILO JOSÉ VERGARA

University of Michigan Press Ann Arbor

CONTENTS

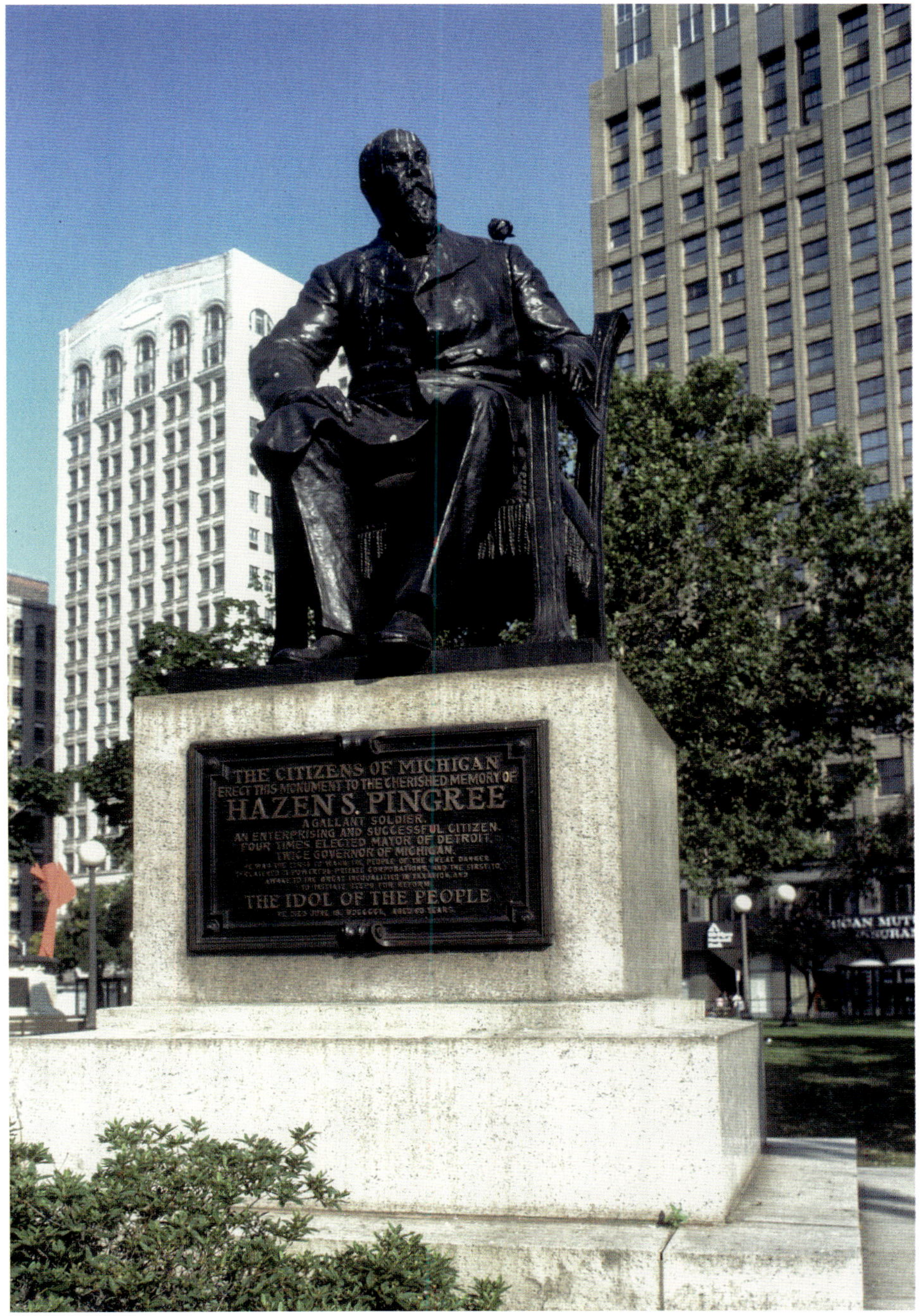

Hazen S. Pingree (1841–1901), "The Idol of the People," elected Mayor of Detroit four times. Grand Circus Park, Woodward Ave., Detroit, 1995

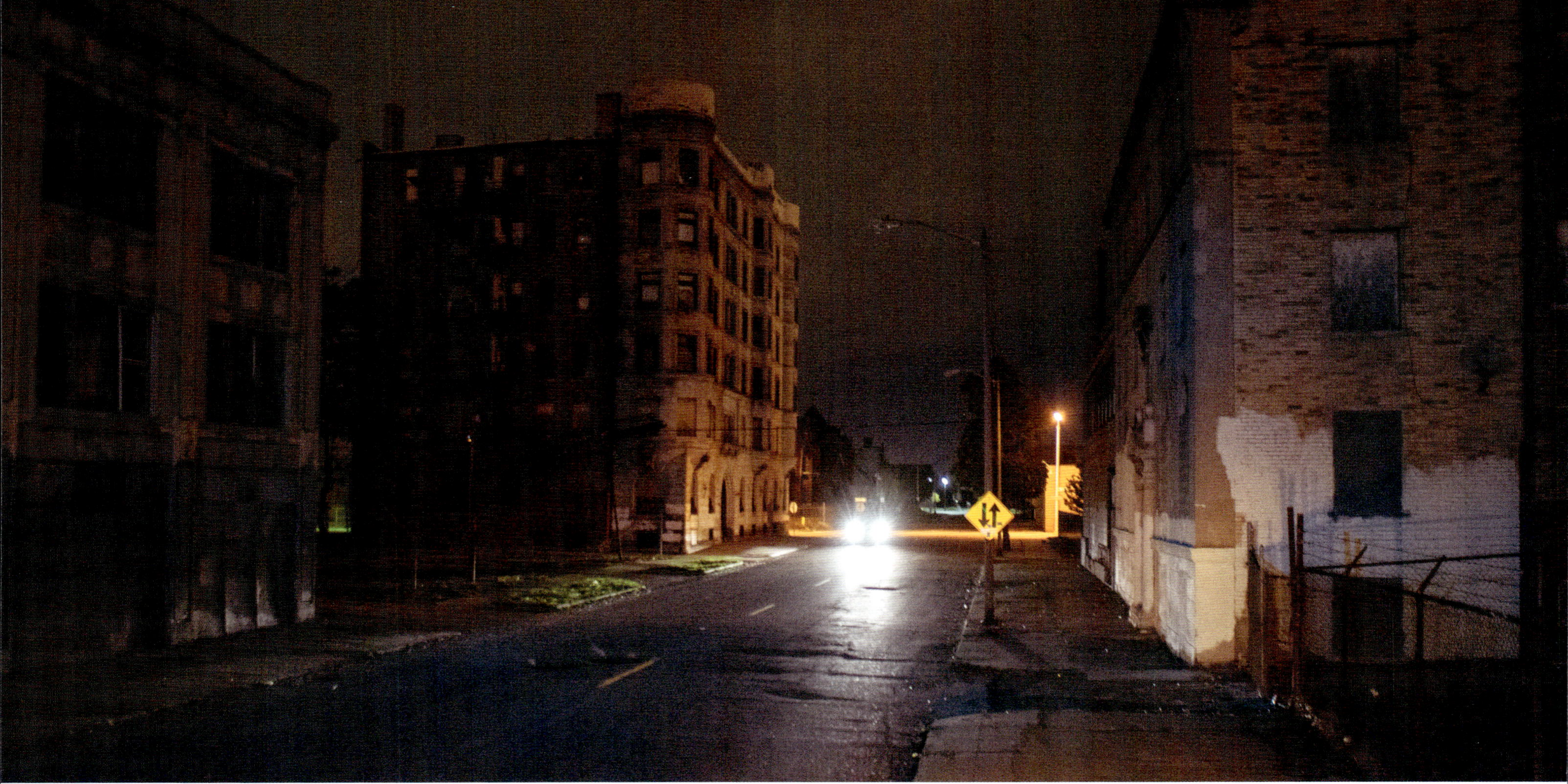

Former Alhambra Flats (originally Alhambra Hotel) at far right. The new Red Wings Stadium being built in this area will completely change the streetscape. View east along Temple Street from Cass Avenue, Detroit, 2013.

INTRODUCTION

MY LOVE OF RUINS FIRST ATTRACTED ME TO DETROIT, to a city far removed from its golden age. Unexpectedly, this passion led me to the wider culture that had developed over several decades in extremely segregated areas of the city. I had visited the ruins of Gary, Chicago, Newark, the Bronx, and Camden, New Jersey, and each one had impressed me in its own way. But none had anything like the effect of Detroit's abandoned skyscrapers, derelict industrial plants, and avenues of faded grandeur. I wanted to follow the trajectory of these urban leftovers—toward greater decay, disappearance, or revival—and to see where the new crop of ruins would emerge. That is, I went from regarding ruins as spectacle to noticing the elements of the declining city: small-scale inventions, additions, recycling of materials, signage, murals, and other components that make up the urban fabric. The ruins led me to an entire ghetto culture within the postindustrial city.

People in the future, I believe, will want to know about the evolution of postindustrial Detroit in terms of the visual forms of everyday life. But there are disincentives to probing this subject. Scholars interested in Detroit and other cities undergoing depopulation, disinvestment, and dereliction are eager to find ways to return them to prosperity—usually, however, at the cost of ignoring the physical adaptations and new beginnings made by locals in their struggle to survive. At times I have also felt discouraged by the guardians of Motor City's reputation, who complain that photographic documentation of decay makes the city look "grotesque, ugly, and bad." An interest in urban decline and deterioration clashes with the prevailing cult of hope that favors such dictums as "Nothing Stops Detroit," "Don't Dump on Detroit," "Speak Positively About Detroit," "Detroit vs. Everybody," and "If You Can't Say Something Nice About Detroit, Don't Say Anything At All." My view is that grand ruined buildings, and a green, largely vacant city, can coexist with economic development.

Emphasizing achievements such as the new restaurants, entertainment venues, high-tech ventures, and incoming businesses has led the world media to report extensively on the revival of a small, safe, lively, and predominantly white core of Detroit. Contrastingly, the African American community believes that a revival is taking place elsewhere in the city, but may not reach their communities in their lifetimes. Meanwhile, the progress of decline and the local residents' efforts to mitigate the effects of extreme inequality are left unmentioned. And as Detroit's downtown and midtown grow stronger, representations of the neighborhoods grow weaker. In trying to mitigate this, I persist in documenting the neighborhoods. My research relies on what my eyes see, what my camera can record, and the answers to my questions that people from all over the city have given during unstructured interviews. When initiating conversations, I bring with me my whole sensual memory of the place as well as my collection of images, and these shape the questions I ask.

Detailed locations, street names, and precise urban descriptions have been a feature of all my work. My notebook is as much a part of my equipment as is my camera. I also take frequent time-travel trips through the streets using Google Street View investigating changes and collecting images as I go along. And I have searched online for additional information about every place mentioned in this book. I contact people whose names and numbers appear on buildings. I go to the websites of restaurants, churches, and businesses. I follow how the city is being discussed online by looking up "Detroit," followed by keywords such as authenticity, God, ruins, crime, soul food, symbols, and folk art. In a continuous loop, field searches followed by online searches enrich my observations and insights and provide me with with new and more refined questions to ask on return visits.

I am always eager to return and find out what the next step will be in the life of a derelict building, city lot, or vacant land on which life once thrived. For example, I returned to the desolate block on Detroit's east side where the church of St. Cyril and St. Methodius and its adjacent Catholic school once stood. I could remember looking through books left in the abandoned library and passing by the dusty old pews, the broken columns, and the remains of the organ, and smelling the odor of wet plaster. Then, walking across the empty lot, I felt astonished at how this erasure could have come about. I imagine a Mass in progress, hear the choir singing, and smell incense, all the while being intensely aware of the absence of these things. But then I move on, my interest now piqued by some mounds made of discarded building materials on nearby vacant land, and in a parking lot, broken pieces of floats from The Parade Company.

I follow developments—sometimes pathetic, sometimes encouraging—that take place adjacent to derelict landmarks. For example, in 1943 the Packard plant employed 36,000 people; now, in the immense parking lot there stands a social services building that houses Operation Get Down, an alcoholism treatment center. By contrast, the Michigan Central Station has attracted a vibrant complex of restaurants, music venues, and hotels, and the neighborhood is now a magnet for tourists.

I see my role as an informed, stubborn witness. The humble ways in which people in inner-city neighborhoods shape their surroundings deserve to be recorded and understood—even if this may appear insignificant when compared to the ways the rest of the nation is being shaped. In the process, my photographs are a record of evolving relationships between the city and its suburbs, of relations between blacks and whites, and of the residents' beliefs, their sense of aesthetics, and their successes and failures in making do. I follow the way people from all over the nation and the world flock to the city, leaving their mark. At the same time, in tracking the way Detroit is recreated in cyberspace, I find how the virtual city shapes the "real" city.

Every year, starting a quarter century ago, I have spent at least a week, and often more, in Detroit. During my visits to the city, I always stay downtown on Bagley Avenue at The Michigan Building, one of the city's landmarks. (In 1896, Henry Ford built his first automobile, the "quadricycle," in a small garage at the site. The former Michigan Theater, built inside it in 1926, was turned into an equally famous parking garage in the late 1970s.) Upon my return to New York, I caption and organize the images, researching issues that come up, and conducting telephone interviews.

From Bagley Avenue I have traveled as far as the city limits, taking such commercial thoroughfares as West Front Street, Michigan Avenue, Grand River Avenue, Woodward Avenue, Jefferson Avenue, and Gratiot Avenue. To survey the city's downtown, I walked or used the People Mover. My yearly visits, which continue, have included over 500 miles of driving through streets and alleys, surveying the entire city at a cruising speed of 12 miles per hour. Driving along the main commercial and residential streets, I visit the city's landmarks, parks, and cemeteries, taking numerous detours into residential streets and alleys. I have explored inside abandoned buildings and photographed panoramas from their rooftops. Now Google Maps influences where I visit, the photographs I take, and the conversations I have with residents.

The way I came to the title of this book exemplifies a situation in which Detroit, as it evolves, draws together a surprising conjunctions of elements. In this case, the following came into alliance: the former Missionary Baptist Church's 1928 brick building, now housing the small Ruth Chapel congregation headed by Pastor Diane Chapelle, and a secularist, all-woman Dutch design group called the Pink Pony Express. Four of its members came up with the idea of asking pastors to replace the word "God" with "Detroit" on their signboards. They thought that interventions like this, in hundreds of churches throughout the city, would help lift the spirits of the residents. Pastors were not very receptive to the idea of sponsoring announcements such as "Detroit Is Love," "What About Detroit Coming," and "Detroit Cares for You." While attending a service at Ruth Chapel AME Church, on Kirby Street in a poor, depopulated neighborhood, Pink Pony Express was inspired by the sermon given by Pastor Chapelle, who quoted from the Book of Ezekiel about new life being given to "dry bones." After the service the designers got permission to paint a text adapted from this scripture on the side of the church, and they rendered it as "Detroit Is No Dry Bones." I mistakenly took this evocative phrase, written neatly in all caps, for an example of religious folk art. Pastor Chapelle, though, told me about Pink Pony Express and put me in touch with Annemarie van den Berg, a member of the team, who explained that the purpose of their project was "to flood the city with strong messages of OPTIMISM . . . to boost the city's weary image, and that of all its people."

In this book I pay heed to this trend in Detroit's evolution, namely the ways in which the local culture has garnered the attention of global culture, leading to imaginative interventions and creating new opportunities.

> It is an Isle under Ionian skies
> Beautiful as a wreck of Paradise . . . .
>
> —Percy Bysshe Shelley, *Epipsychidion*, 1821

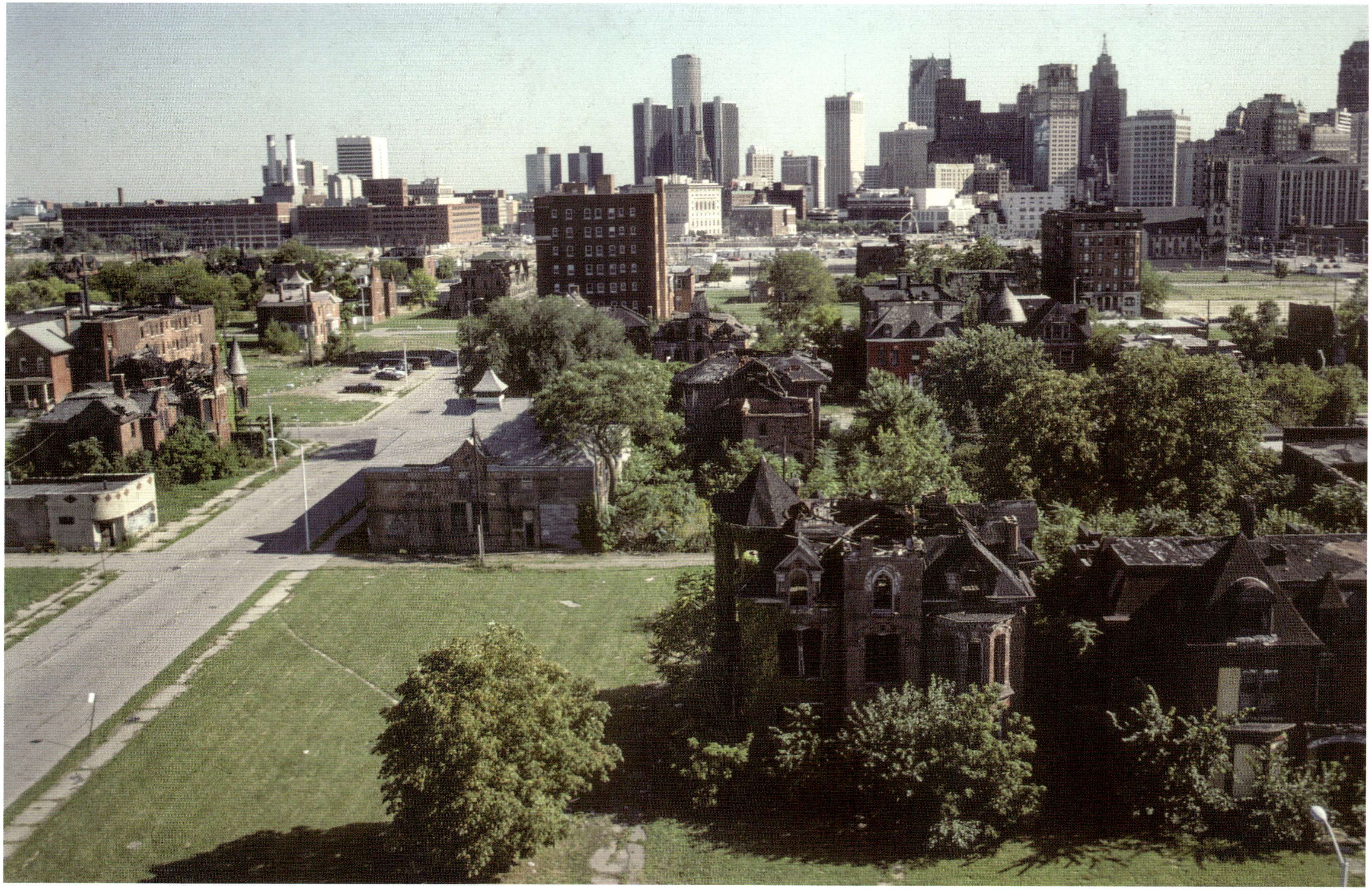

View of Brush Park from Edmund Pl. along John R Street, 1998

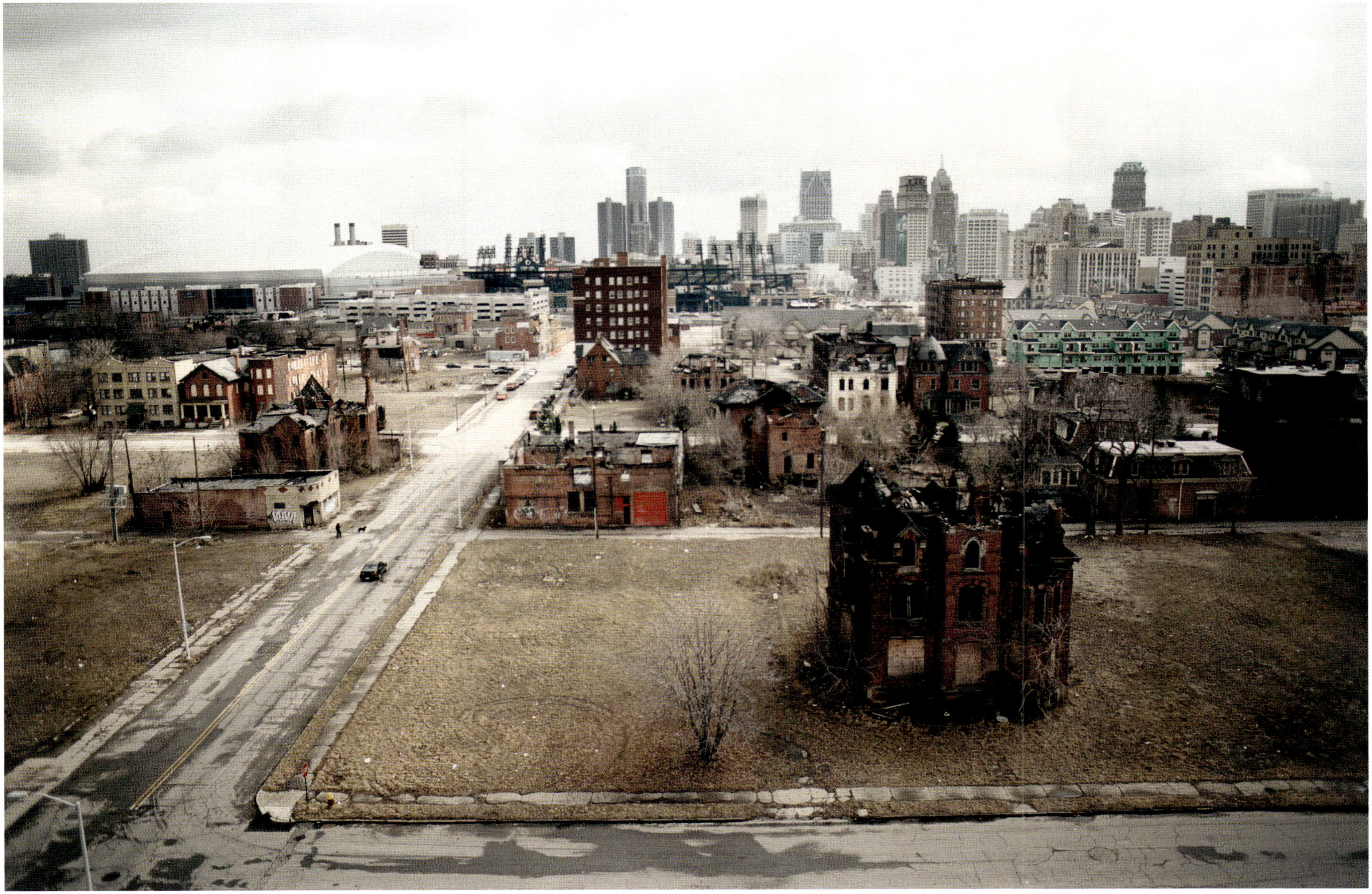

During the past twelve years, several Brush Park mansions have been rehabilitated, including the Edmund, here seen as a ruin in the foreground. View south from the roof of the former Carlton Plaza Hotel. John R Street at Edmond Place, Detroit, 2003.

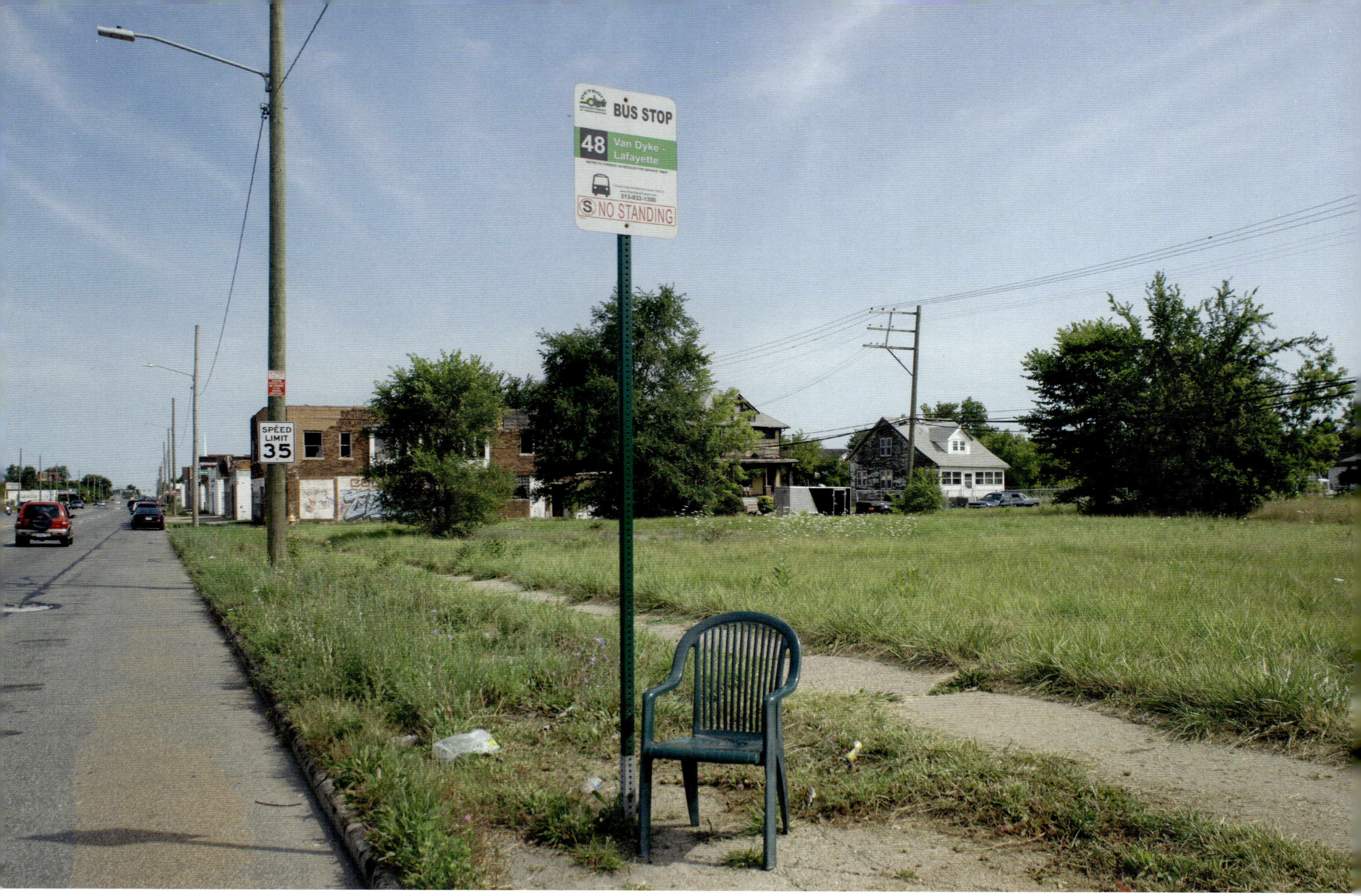

Bus Stop with “No Standing” sign. Someone put a plastic chair there for the long wait. Van Dyke Road at Badger Street, Detroit, 2015.

ROBERT FISHMAN

CAMILO VERGARA'S DETROIT

IN THE LATE 1970S, CAMILO JOSÉ VERGARA set out to reinvigorate the tradition of critical urban photography that dates back to Jacob Riis's *How the Other Half Lives* (1890) and to adapt it to what he called "the new American ghetto." Like Riis, he wished to combine image and text into a synthesis that would both shock and educate. Like Lewis Hine, who carried on Riis's work into the Progressive Era of the early twentieth century, Vergara sought to foreground the endurance and dignity of the poor in a degraded environment. Like the social photographers of the Great Depression, he wished to show an America that most Americans did not wish to see. In the forty years since he began his work, Vergara's images have come to define the inner city in the era of the urban crisis.

His main achievement in my view has been to find a photographic language that captured what was *new* about "the new American ghetto." When he began his work, the idea of "slum" was still dominated by images that date back to Riis on Manhattan's Lower East Side and that emphasized above all density and overcrowding. Although the specifics might vary from the brick tenements of the Lower East Side or Harlem to the frame structures of Chicago's South Side in the 1940s, the slum was all about crowded streets, tiny airless apartments, and dark filthy courtyards. The old slum was, if nothing else, visually *dramatic* in the intensity of its overcrowding; the bustling street-life of these districts was a sign of their residents' position at the heart of the low-wage economy that dominated the rapidly expanding immigrant cities.

But by the 1960s such slum districts were emptying out, and the "new American ghetto" was now increasingly characterized by isolation and abandonment. In response, Vergara has attempted to make visible the process of disinvestment that was creating a landscape of empty lots, deserted storefronts, and closed factories in what had only recently been among the most densely populated and productive urban districts in the world. But the meaning of these landscapes can be grasped only by comparison with what had existed before; whereas, as Susan Sontag has observed, a photograph can never be anything more than a "neat slice of time." But how can one photograph what was no longer there? How, in other words, can one photograph the abstract process of disinvestment and make it as visually compelling and as humanly powerful as the classic urban social photography of the past?

Born in Santiago, Chile in 1944 and raised in the small town of Rengo, Vergara brought to this challenge an outsider's eye for the realities of American life and a boundless energy to seek out precisely those parts of urban America that the rest of American society was increasingly shunning. He came to this country in 1965 to study sociology at Notre Dame University, attracted by America's reputation for "innovation and resilience, modernity and progress." But he found, first in the Midwest rustbelt cities and then in New York City, some of the poverty and decay that he thought he had left behind. Latin America, as the anthropologist Claude Levi-Strauss has observed, is the global heartland of urban abandonment, as each successive wave of plunder and development (gold, silver, diamonds, coffee, rubber, and so on) threw up a network of cities that burned themselves out when their particular boom evaporated. Vergara's photographs have always had a touch of "magic realism" derived perhaps from his reading of, for example, the Argentinian poet Evaristo Carriego or the Colombian poet Jose Asuncion Silva, with their deep understanding of decay and degeneration and the bizarre incongruities that emerge when ideals of growth and progress meet the reality of decline.

But if one source of Vergara's photographic imagination was Latin American magic realism, another was the New York City street photographers who were his most immediate influences. Vergara in fact began in the 1970s photographing the New York street scene, and his work can perhaps be best understood as both a development of and a reaction against such figures as Helen Leavitt, Diane Arbus, or Garry Winogrand. Compared to the Riis/Hine tradition of urban social photography, the street photographers of the 1950s and 1960s were aggressively apolitical and nonjudgmental. As Holland Cotter characterized Winogrand's approach, "Photographs don't change anything . . . and shouldn't try. They're not about morality. They're about recording what's passing by."

Yet precisely because the street photographers refused to edit their work to fit a preconceived agenda—either a critical social message or the celebration of the glamour and excitement of New York—their photographs captured so much that was unexpected, unsettling, and bizarre about city life. Vergara in fact began photographing New York City street scenes in the early 1970s, and it was only when he despaired of finding his own vision as a photographer that he temporarily abandoned photography for graduate studies in sociology at Columbia University. When he returned to the streets in the late 1970s, it was with a much greater theoretical sophistication about what was happening to American cities. He realized that the urban crisis of his own time required a new photographic language precisely in order to maintain its links with the older tradition of socially committed work. The results as we see them in this book represent a unique synthesis of the humanistic values of the urban photographers of the past with a cool aesthetic that captured the strangeness and surrealism of these voids opening up in the American city: a "magic realism" for the age of the urban crisis.

Vergara had learned from his sociology studies to understand the devastated landscape of the "new American ghetto" as the result of a long process of disinvestment. But how to show that process when the photograph is necessarily, as Susan Sontag defined it, a "neat slice of time"? Vergara solved this problem through the seemingly simple expedient of returning to the same sites year after year to document the changes. We literally see vibrant neighborhoods turning into wastelands; cherished family homes abandoned and collapsed; solid and well-maintained apartment houses losing their tenants and their solidity until they are nothing but ruins; massive factories transformed into vast wastelands; once-dignified bank buildings and other commercial structures become empty and forlorn; schools, libraries, hospitals, courthouses, and other embodiments of solid civic virtue and responsibility reveal in their increasingly ruinous state the decay of the larger social contract.

Through these time sequences the urban crisis becomes visible, and we glimpse the human tragedy behind the abstract process of urban disinvestment. Yet however precise and analytical these sequences might be as a record of the disinvestment process, they have the strangeness of a bad dream where expectations of stability are constantly disrupted and familiar building types (the single-family home, the apartment house, the commercial strip) turn into grotesque fantasies. This is even truer of Vergara's extensive photography of the end-results of so many of these time-sequences: the ruin.

What the crowded slum dwelling was to Riis or child labor was to Hine, the urban ruin is for Vergara. The ruin is the characteristic image that exhibits with unique clarity the deeper destructive

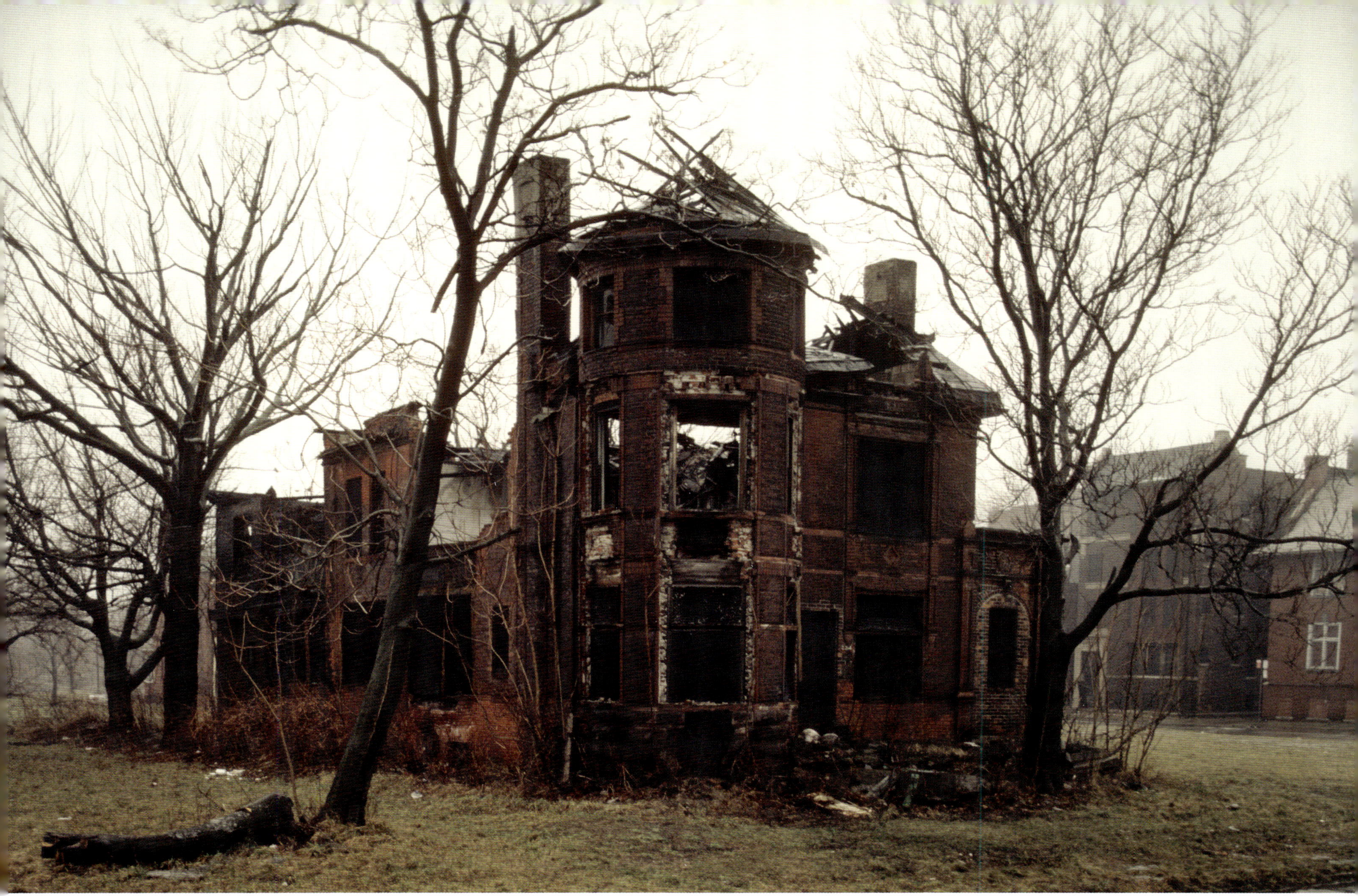

Ruins of a mansion in winter, so bleak that can lift one's spirits.
Erskine St. at John R., Detroit, 1998

processes at work within the new American ghetto. Not only was he the first to practice what is now the popular genre of "ruin photography," but his Detroit photographs especially have helped to make some of the more monumental sites as famous and as integral to the worldwide identity of the city as the automobile assembly plants had once been. One thinks especially in this book of the ruins of the once-grand Brush Park district; the Michigan Theatre downtown whose ruined auditorium now houses an indoor parking lot; the abandoned Packard Plant, a mile-long complex of buildings which epitomize the rise and fall of manufacturing in the city; and the monument of monuments, the abandoned Michigan Central Railroad Station, whose ruined high-vaulted classical interiors from 1913 designed by the architects of Grand Central Terminal in New York seem to announce literally a Roman scale of decline and fall.

Detroit is the ruins capital of the United States, so it was inevitable that America's most prominent photographer of the urban crisis would make this city a principal focus of his work. Perhaps equally inevitable, some Detroiters, ranging from municipal officials to neighborhood activists, have criticized Vergara's portrayal of their city. These disparate groups are united in insisting that the abandoned structures that dot the Detroit landscape are not fit subjects for dissemination, and the only attention paid to them should be to knock them down. Even when Detroit lacked money to keep its streetlights working, the city nevertheless devoted scarce resources to finance the bulldozers and wrecking crews for "blight busters." Almost all the more monumental ruins in this book have been targeted for demolition during the period that Vergara photographed them, and those that remain owe their survival to the high costs of demolition that the city could not afford.

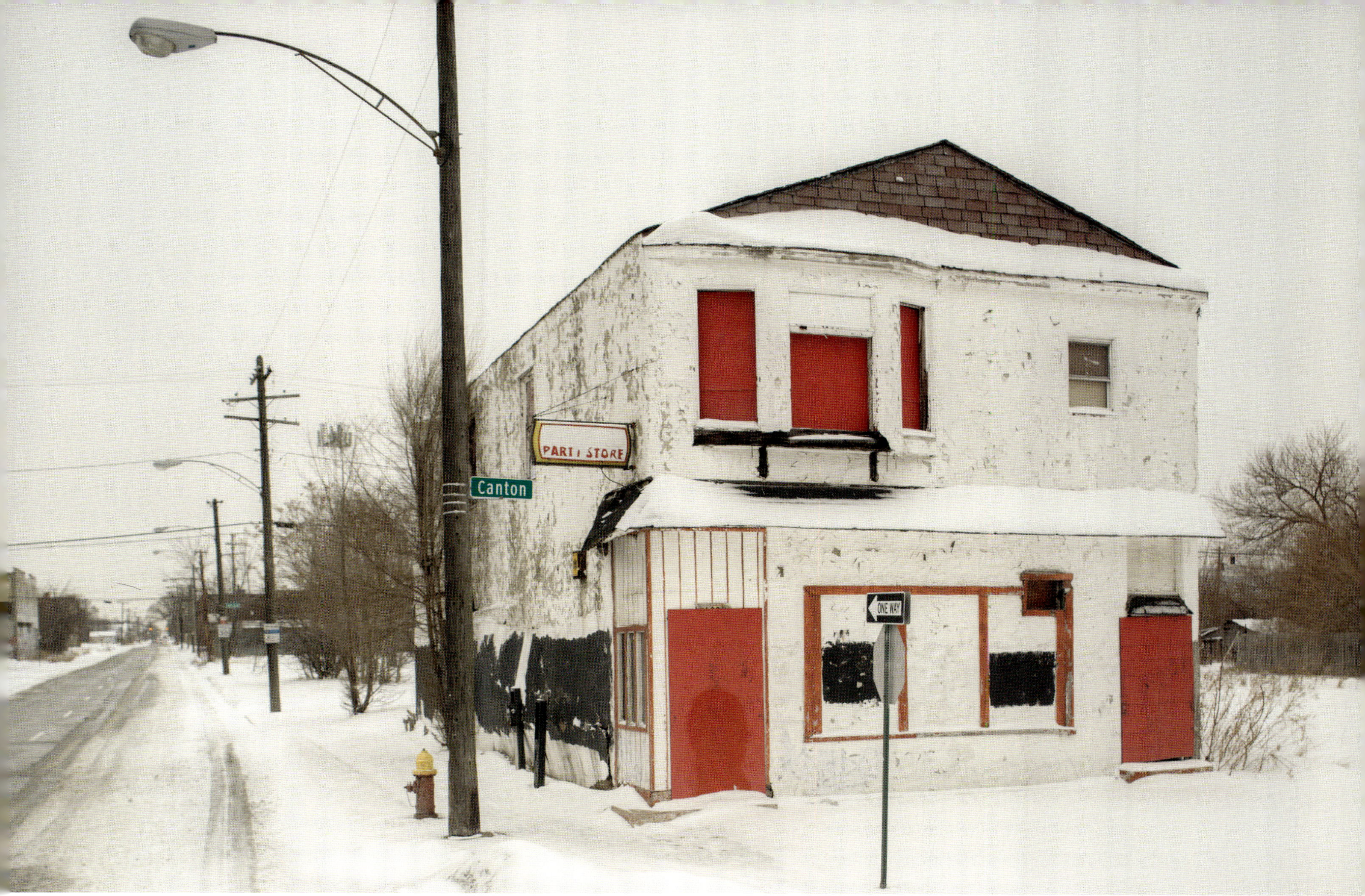

Former party store. Canton St. at East Warren Avenue, Detroit, 2014

Vergara's ruin images have in my view a complexity that is rarely captured either by his many imitators or by his critics, and they reflect the complex condition of Detroit itself. "Detroit," we must remember, refers to both the central city and its metropolitan area. The central city has indeed experienced a radical depopulation and deindustrialization matched only among major American cities by Cleveland and St. Louis. But the Detroit metropolitan area as a whole has remained surprisingly stable in population, reaching almost five million people in 1970 and maintaining that population through 2010. Despite the extremes of concentrated poverty in its core, the region as a whole is also surprisingly prosperous. Median household income for the metropolitan area (which in this US Census statistical measure includes not only the city of Detroit and its suburbs but also such struggling neighboring cities as Pontiac and Flint) is close to the high-tech Austin, Texas, metropolitan region; it is also higher than Portland, Oregon, and Los Angeles, and especially higher than Cleveland or St. Louis. The overall decline of the Big Three automakers often meant a reconcentration of their highest-skilled manufacturing operations back to new factories in the Detroit suburbs. With its corporate headquarters, suppliers, and consultants, the Detroit metro area remains the most important single center of the world's most important manufacturing industry.

In this respect, the Detroit metro area as a whole represents a relatively successful transition to a diversified regional economy. The ruins in this book nevertheless convey an important reality, namely that of a "divided metropolis" where the costs of regional economic transition were concentrated in the central city and the very substantial economic benefits were bestowed on the suburbs. Despite the boom-and-bust cycle of the Big Three automakers, the Detroit suburbs have seen more than a half-century of solid growth of both population and jobs, while the central city has been mired in radical decline and depression. In the classic postwar national pattern, suburban municipalities used their increased revenues from property taxes to increase their funding for local schools and other services, while the shrinking central city was forced to cut back on vital services; until recently this division, moreover, followed very strict racial lines, with only whites able to benefit directly from suburban prosperity. The well-publicized bankruptcy of Detroit in 2013, the largest municipal bankruptcy in American history, concealed the fact that the region as a whole and its many suburban municipalities were far from bankrupt, but the artificial boundary line between city and suburb had almost surgically separated the central city from the real wealth of the metropolitan region.

One might argue, paradoxically, that the overall prosperity of the region contributed directly to the extreme (and extremely racialized) poverty in its inner city. In other metro areas a slowing manufacturing economy meant that industries were trapped in older inner-city plants, and their employees, white as well as black, lacked the income to move to the suburbs. But in Detroit during the crucial years from 1945 to the 1970s, both the automobile industry and the well-paid white working class had ample resources to quickly and completely abandon the central city for new plants and new tract houses in the suburbs.

The "ruins of Detroit" thus have a very different meaning from any general decline of the region than one might assume. It took tremendous *prosperity* to finance this extreme form of abandonment, and the Detroit region's overall statistical stability masked a destructive "zero-sum game" where growth in the suburbs necessarily meant ruin in the 139-square miles of the municipality of Detroit.

Once the pattern of white flight became almost universal, there were not enough black migrants from the South to fill up the hundreds of thousands of bungalows, two-family houses, and apartments that the city contained, so rents and property values in the older districts plummeted to near zero. By the 1980s, virtually the whole city met the economic definition of a slum: a place where a dollar spent on basic maintenance yielded less than a dollar in increased property value. So little or nothing was spent, and homes turned into ruins. Even the downtown, which in the 1910s and 1920s had been among the fastest-growing in the country, was not exempt from this capital flight. Some of the nation's proudest skyscrapers built during the 1920s when Detroit was the third major skyscraper city in the world (behind New York and Chicago) now stood abandoned in a dying downtown.

The divided metropolis implicitly frames Vergara's ruin photography, which conveys the painful irony of poverty and decay in the midst of (regional) plenty. He takes pains to show us the abandoned skyscraper and the ruined homes for precisely the same reason that the "blight busters" wish to demolish them. They are the visible signs of a deep disorder in our society. Hence his emphasis on the ruin of those structures whose design once betokened Progress: not only the ornate downtown skyscrapers but the modest art deco stores and workshops in the neighborhoods and, above all, the still-visible symbols of domesticity that somehow cling to the most ruined bungalows.

But at the same time, Vergara is clearly attracted to the strange beauty of these structures. He was certainly not the first to notice the aesthetic power of ruins, disturbing precisely because it rests on decline and defeat. That tradition goes back to the Renaissance depictions of the Roman Forum and continues through Walker Evans's 1930s photographs of deserted plantation houses and ruined mansions reduced to crumbling boarding houses. But such images traditionally had an elegiac quality, a lament for a vanished era that has nevertheless been necessarily relegated to the past. Vergara's images by contrast have the rawness of recent decay: the nightmare/fantasy of magic realism that defamiliarizes the once-solid urban environment into empty vistas of rubble-strewn vacant lots.

Yet those who stigmatize Vergara's work as "ruin porn" tend to miss a very important theme in his photographs. The economic forces that created an economic desert in the heart of the Detroit metro area not only isolated the people left behind but forced them to rely on their own resources. Vergara's ruins are inhabited by some very resourceful people, who continually reshape their environment. The time-sequences of the former bank buildings often reveal a whole series of enterprises that successively occupy the space. The struggle of the storefront churches, which occupy every possible site from the former banks to vacant lots, tell a similar story. And then there is the resourcefulness of individuals: the people who adapt their motorized wheelchairs as substitutes for the bus that never comes, or the man who made his own bus shelter out of discarded tires and a plank.

For me, some of the most moving images of strength and resilience in this book show isolated meticulously maintained houses in the midst of abandoned and decayed structures. Although each has its own story, the general narrative is clear. Many of these houses were first bought in the 1970s when blacks began to move in significant numbers to formerly white neighborhoods within the city of Detroit. Such black purchasers often paid relatively high prices for these houses, but as white flight to the suburbs emptied these temporarily integrated neighborhoods, their homes became impossible to sell, and the homeowner was more or less trapped in decline. While some gave up, others responded by keeping their homes in top condition, and the house became a kind of ark in a sea of abandonment, often for an extended family. (By a particularly cruel irony, many of these homeowners were enmeshed in the predatory lending scams of the early 2000s, and wound up losing their homes in the Great Recession.)

Isolation, as Vergara shows, can produce a unique culture that has had its impact far beyond the new American ghetto. This is especially true for music, both historically in Motown and even today as Detroit's techno-music continues to have a worldwide impact. But Vergara is especially attentive to visual culture, and he has uniquely recorded and celebrated the otherwise lost world of local sign painters and muralists. Located somewhere between folk and commercial art, these painters introduce moments of intense color into an otherwise drab environment. They celebrate not only a particular enterprise but the "black metropolis" itself and its heritage and heroes. Often the murals and make-shift memorials mourn the victims of Detroit's drug trade and endemic violence. Often they proclaim a religious faith that contrasts strongly with the ruined structures on which they are painted. In these images Vergara captures the soul of the new American ghetto.

Vergara has won many honors during his career, including the MacArthur Foundation "genius" award, the 2012 National Humanities Medal (the first ever awarded to a photographer), and the accession and digitalizing of his photographic collection by the Library of Congress. Nevertheless, his work refuses to fit neatly into anyone's social or aesthetic agenda. He is far too genuinely political for the superficially "engaged" art world, but he is too aesthetically complex for those seeking reassuring images of neighborhood or community. He marches to a different drummer.

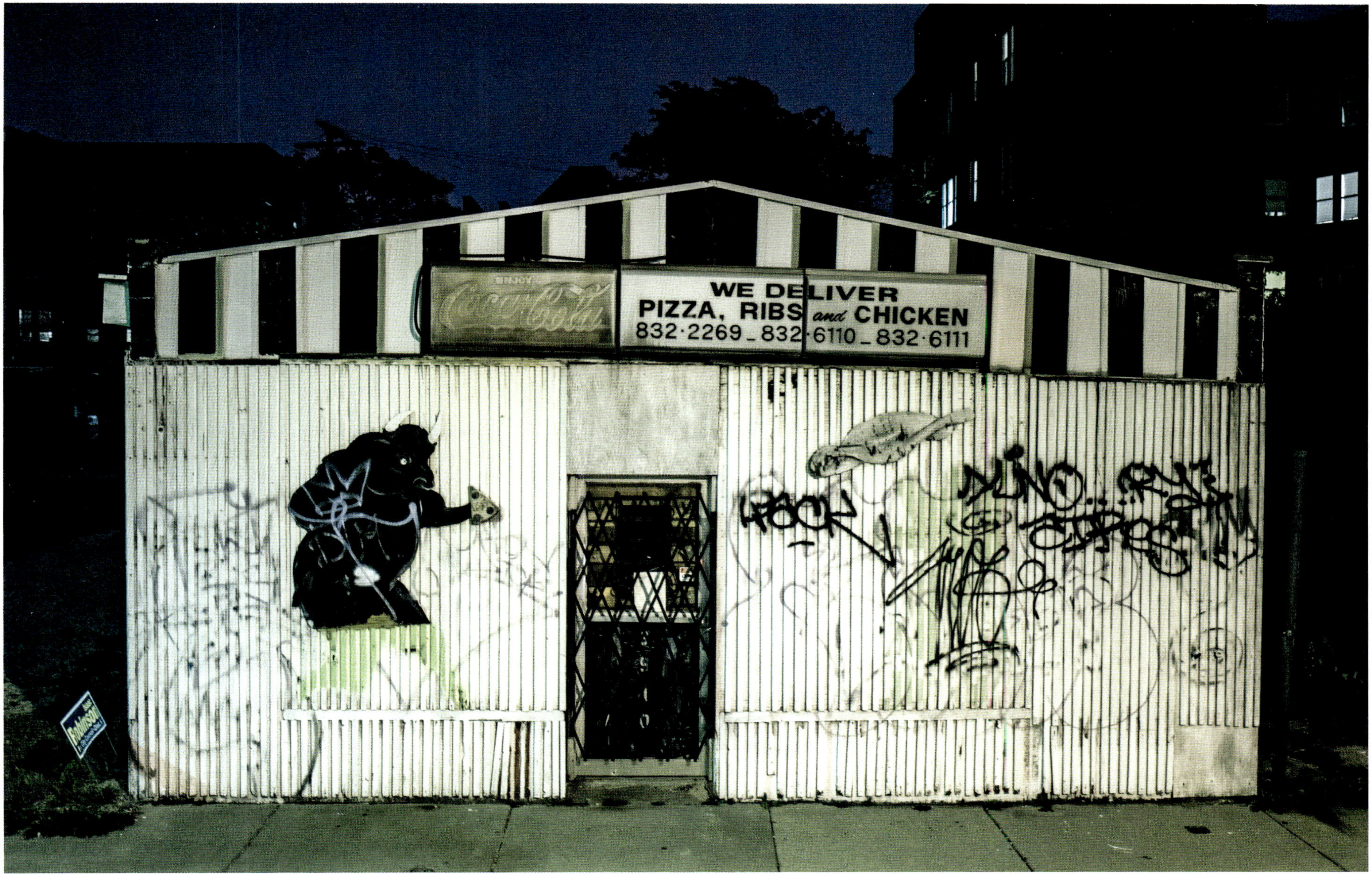

Sign showing a bull holding a slice of pizza. 3940 Third Ave., Detroit, 2013

The relationship of Vergara's Detroit to the present moment of national recovery of the American city is similarly complex. His most recent book, *Harlem: The Unmaking of a Ghetto* (2013), brought his time-sequences into the era of gentrification, as sites that he shows being emptied and abandoned during the 1980s and 1990s are now being occupied with upscale development. But Detroit is not New York, and its trajectory will almost surely be unique among American cities. In 1994, Vergara wrote a controversial set of articles calling for a national "ruins park" in downtown Detroit where the empty skyscrapers could be preserved and stabilized until new uses could be found, and visitors could wander in this memorial to a once-great downtown much as they would wander around the Civil War battlefields. The response was scathing, but Vergara was at least half-right in his vision. For the next decade more downtown buildings were demolished than reoccupied, and downtown did seem like a kind of eerie Acropolis of abandonment. But starting with the renovation of the Book Cadillac Hotel in 2008 and the capital intensive intervention of two billionaires, Dan Gilbert of Quicken Loans and the Ilitch family of Little Caesars Pizza, downtown has seen the beginning of an extensive renovation that promises to restore its position as the historic core of a major American region.

Indeed, so many old buildings are being renovated and new ones constructed that one might predict that, only a decade from now, downtown Detroit will be a thriving, seamless blend of old and new structures. For example, Brush Park, the old residential neighborhood just outside the downtown, is slated for a complete renovation. The surviving mansions whose extravagant ruins engulfed in lush foliage represent some of the most telling images in this book, will soon be tastefully restored and surrounded by a new neighborhood of well-designed townhouses and condominiums. Visitors unacquainted with Brush Park's recent history will never suspect the devastation recorded in this book.

But if the seven to eight square miles of Detroit's downtown and midtown neighborhoods seem destined for conventional redevelopment, the fate of the other 130 square miles of the city of Detroit remains uncertain. Here Vergara's imagery can have a unique and unexpected impact. Although the Detroit "boosters" had feared that merely photographing the ruins would retard Detroit's recovery, in fact Vergara and other photographers, such as Julia Taubman and Yves Marchand and Romain Meffre, have made Detroit a vital international presence on the Internet. These images are now among Detroit's most powerful exports, attracting a steady stream of visitors and potential residents from around the world. The magic realism of Vergara's photographs with their strange mixture of the raw and the empty, combined with ultra-cheap real estate, seem to promise a challenging and authentic setting for creative outsiders seeking what the *New York Times* has called "the next Brooklyn."

Detroit may never become a hipster's paradise, but its recovery outside downtown will necessarily take a form radically different not only from its own past but from any other American city. As Vergara's photographs show, there is simply too much emptiness to refill with conventional in-fill development. With abundant—indeed over-abundant—space for both new residents and old, there is at least the possibility of a uniquely positive interaction between the special creativity and resilience of black Detroit as shown in this book, and the international hipster culture attracted by low rents and authenticity.

The landscape will continue to be raw and unresolved as Vergara shows it, neither urban nor rural nor suburban in any traditional sense. But the emptiness will be mitigated by urban farming; homeowners will be officially encouraged to take over (as they in fact do now unofficially) vacant land on their blocks for extensive lawns and gardens; the empty storefronts along the main transportation corridors will refill with a host of small businesses, a creative economy run by both new and old residents. The city will combine an intense urban diversity with an almost bucolic setting. From this (no doubt utopian) perspective, the images in this book will take on yet another meaning. They are both profound records of one of the worst urban catastrophes in American urban history and prophecies of a new Detroit to come.

January 2016

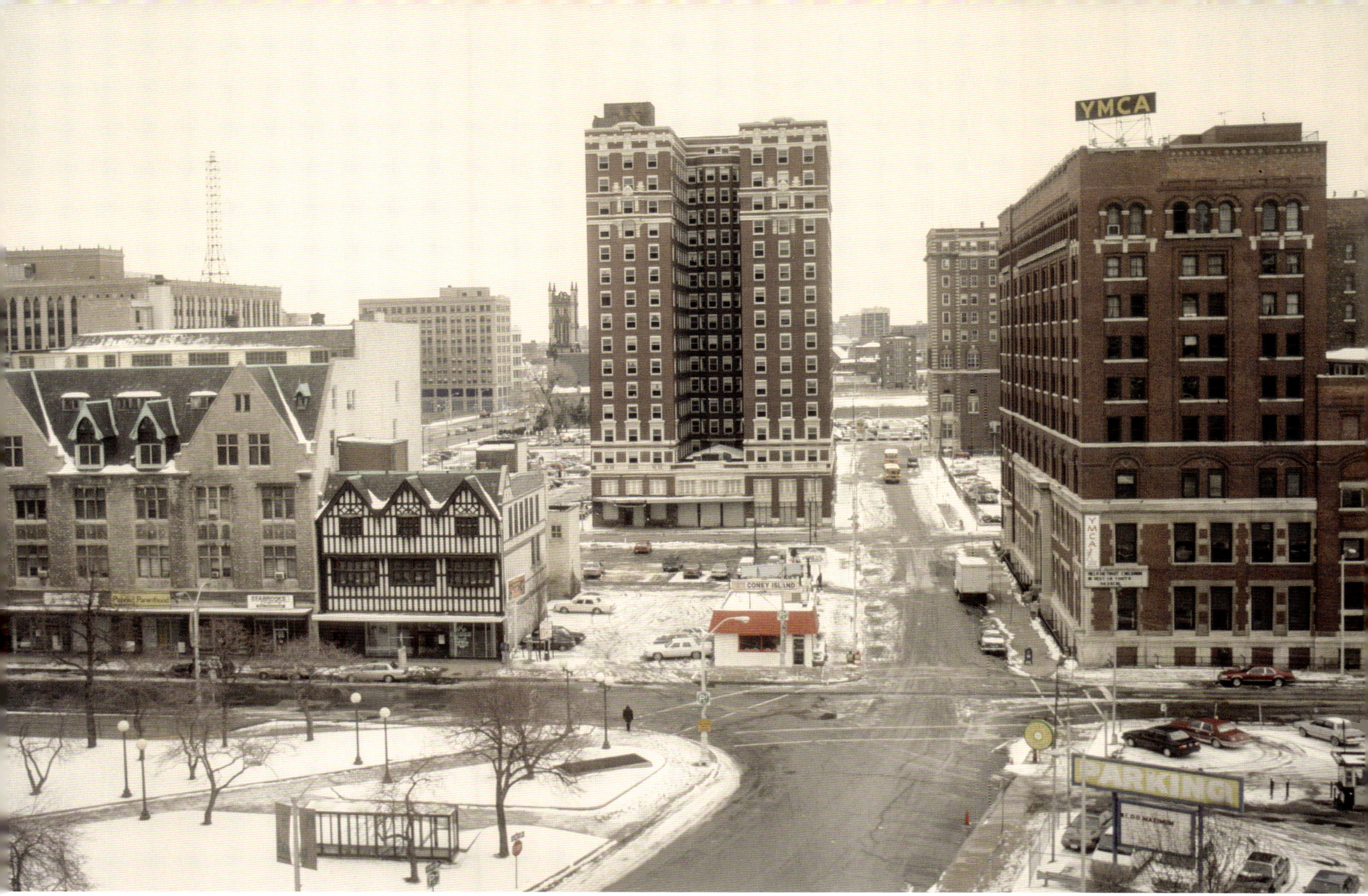

View north of downtown Detroit seen from the roof of the former Paramount Theater. Broadway at Grand Circus Park, 1995

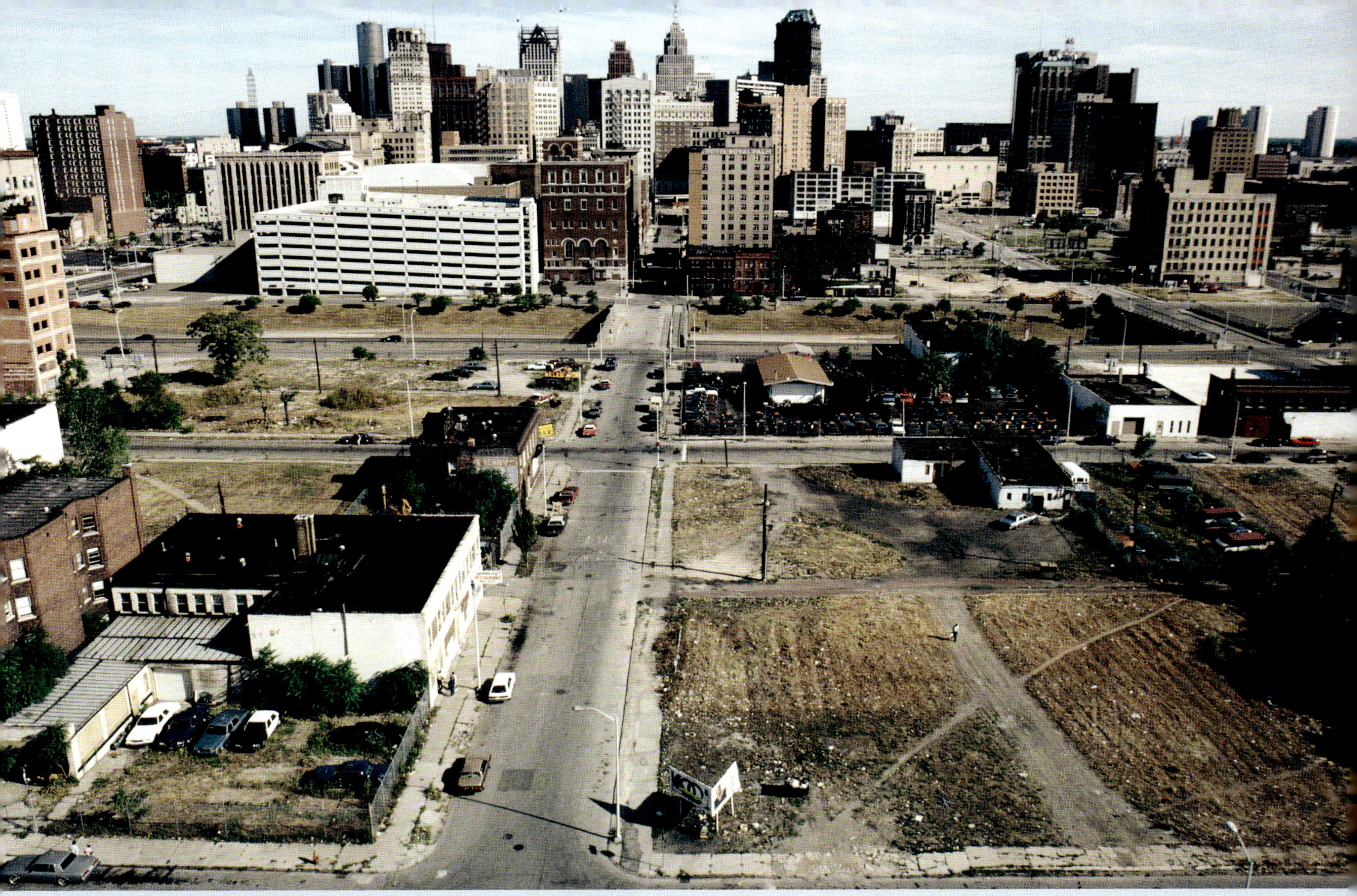

At the time of this photograph, Detroit had the largest concentration of vacant skyscrapers in the world. "Splendid is this masonry—the fates destroyed; the strong buildings crashed, the work of giants molders away." Thus "The Ruin," a late medieval poem about Roman remains, probably from Bath, England. View south from Sibley Street along Park Avenue, downtown Detroit, 1991.

GAME CHANGERS

DETROIT, ONCE THE HEART OF THE INDUSTRIAL UNITED STATES, is now its greatest ruin, with at least 78,000 vacant buildings, a resident population less than 40 percent of its peak, and the highest homicide rate among large American cities. Thirty-eight percent of the local residents live below the poverty line, and among children more than fifty-nine percent live in poverty. The city's unemployment rate is more than two and a half times the national average.

Through neglect and disinvestment, Detroit became a city of unique environments, characterized by such words as "blighted," "edgy," "authentic," and "cool." This Detroit attracts adventurous tourists, generous urban gardeners, enthusiastic volunteers, rebellious artists, and global media attention. The city is now being shaped by investors, artists, and entrepreneurs from as far away as China and Peru. Their growing activity in Detroit's center recreates lifestyles that approach those found in gentrified Brooklyn, albeit in far grittier surroundings. There are fine restaurants offering a large variety of cuisines, drinks, gourmet coffee, and an entertainment center with theaters, sports arenas, and an opera house, all this on newly safe, clean streets. But the city is also being shaped by its overwhelming majority of poor residents living in desolate neighborhoods untouched by development. An evolving urban utopia of idealistic young people, following their dreams, coexists with the grim reality of thousands of families having their water shut off for nonpayment, losing their homes to foreclosure, and living in fear of violence. Success for poor black residents generally means moving out, increasing depopulation and leaving behind empty shells of neighborhoods.

The leaders of the downtown and midtown revival are white and, in addition to three billionaires, include a handful of high-profile young entrepreneurs united in the belief that they can both altruistically and profitably rebuild the city. These entrepreneurs regard doing business in Detroit as an opportunity to become wealthier and more renowned in the service of good. "Anything can be created in Detroit," claims Dan Gilbert, the Quicken Loans tycoon, who also put up signs in the city center saying "Opportunity Detroit." Gilbert, a relative latecomer, presides over the transformation of downtown where his company owns 14 million square feet of property, and his enterprises continue to expand. At his headquarters stands a model of the center city in which the ninety buildings he owns have orange tops that light up. In 2014, Brent Ryan of MIT explained that Gilbert's plans "amount to one of the most ambitious privately financed urban reclamation projects in American history." Through his umbrella company, Rock Ventures, Gilbert employs an armed security force working around the clock as well as 500 video cameras linked to a control center that monitors his properties. As a result, aggressive panhandlers, muggers, and "outlaw" graffiti artists have disappeared. According to Gilbert, once the derelict structures are cleared the city will have open land and, more importantly, "hope and optimism." He has declared blight to be a cancer. Since 2013 his struggle has extended to the entire 139 square miles of the city and to the estimated 78,000 buildings in need of demolition. Altruistic as his vision is, its impact was not being felt in the most blighted areas of Detroit in 2015.

Then there is Mike Illitch of Little Caesars Pizza who with his wife Marian controls the Detroit Tigers, the Detroit Red Wings, and Motor City Casino. The couple is building a $650 million hockey stadium for the Red Wings south of downtown in a desolate area of the Cass Corridor. In the process, the elegant ruins of former hotels and apartment buildings along Temple Street, including the Alhambra, will be demolished.

Away from the business center, standing in isolation, is the former Michigan Central Station, America's most famous ruin, owned by Matty Moroun, who also owns the Ambassador Bridge to Canada. The station's monumental lobby was inspired by the Baths of Caracalla in Rome. In 2015, the old depot has been fitted with a new elevator, new windows, and a huge new American flag. In front, rose bushes have been planted. But now half-ruined and half-rehabilitated, it lacks the stirring grandeur of a full ruin.

Corktown, a former Irish neighborhood regarded as an oasis, a safe area, is a well-known meeting place for hipsters and the college crowd. They patronize Slows BBQ, begun by Phil Cooley, and St. CeCe's Pub and Astro Coffee. Bakeries, coffee shops, refurbished buildings, murals, music venues, and startups, as well as the people who make them possible, are often celebrated for making a difference. Yet the online images of the patrons posted by these trendy spots underscore the segregated character of the city.

In forums discussing Detroit, Kresge Foundation president Rip Rapson is one of the most visible presences. Rapson proudly told the *Chronicle of Philanthropy* in 2013 that philanthropy designed to revive a city "has never been attempted at the scale it's being attempted in Detroit. Without being grandiose about it, there's nothing even close."

Among media favorites is Phil Cooley, a former fashion model and now a successful Detroit restaurant owner and businessman sometimes referred to as "the prince of the city." Cooley has become living proof that taking a chance on investing in the city can get you respect and celebrity and make you rich.

Locally famous, but not among those struggling to bring new life to the city, is Joumana Kayrouz, a personal injury attorney ready to come to the defense of desperate people. On billboards and buses throughout Detroit, huge portraits of Kayrouz, arms crossed, are placed next to the question, "Injured?" In some of the advertisements she asks, "Auto Accident? Truck Accident? Motorcycle Accident?" and in others she offers people a chance to get some money, promising "settlement for your pain and suffering." In September 2013, Google Street captured on the side of a red bus a giant portrait of Kayrouz as it stopped on the corner of Mack Avenue and McClellan Avenue, next to a large vacant lot. In another example of Detroit's creepy surrealism, the bus was headed to St. John Hospital as the young, blond figure Kayrouz asked, "INJURED?" and offered to fight for "1–866 YOUR RIGHTS."

Urban gardeners are a different breed. While the artists, entrepreneurs, and business people wind up in safe places, gardeners need to go where devastation has been total, where white people don't normally go, and where open land is available. Working with local residents to grow food, theirs is an idealistic mission. People working in the gardens include a mix of minorities who live in the neighborhoods and whites who volunteer their time. Unlike billionaires, young entrepreneurs, and personal injury attorneys, urban gardeners do not become celebrities.

Two decades ago, Detroit civil-rights luminary Arthur Johnson saw the city "facing problems springing from white hostility, going at it alone." He stood with a group of African American sports figures, doctors, and lawyers, militantly presenting their views and questions in a city otherwise "scarred by the media to an unprecedented scale." He told me, "I do not know a community I would want to go to outside of Detroit." When Johnson died in 2011, the precipitous decline of the black population of Detroit was already acknowledged, its militancy a memory, and the city was becoming the Promised Land for young, white pioneers. Now, with a new white elite speaking for Detroit, and the city-suburb hostility gone, I am grateful to Arthur Johnson for his passionate description of his home city; his voice is missed. If he were alive, what would he say to me, I wonder, in 2016?

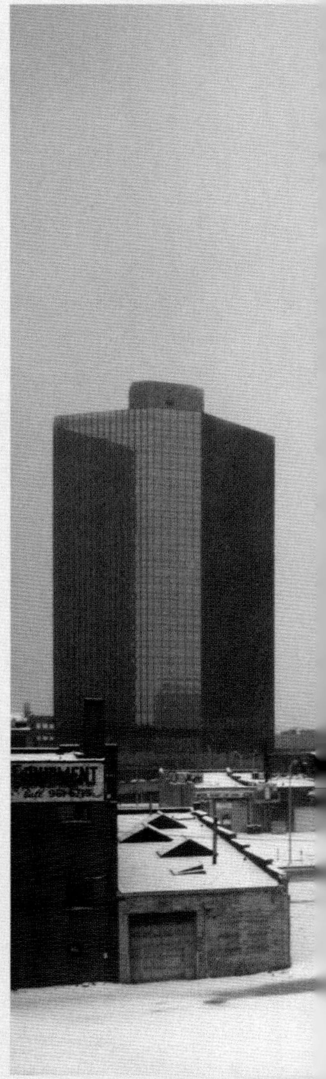

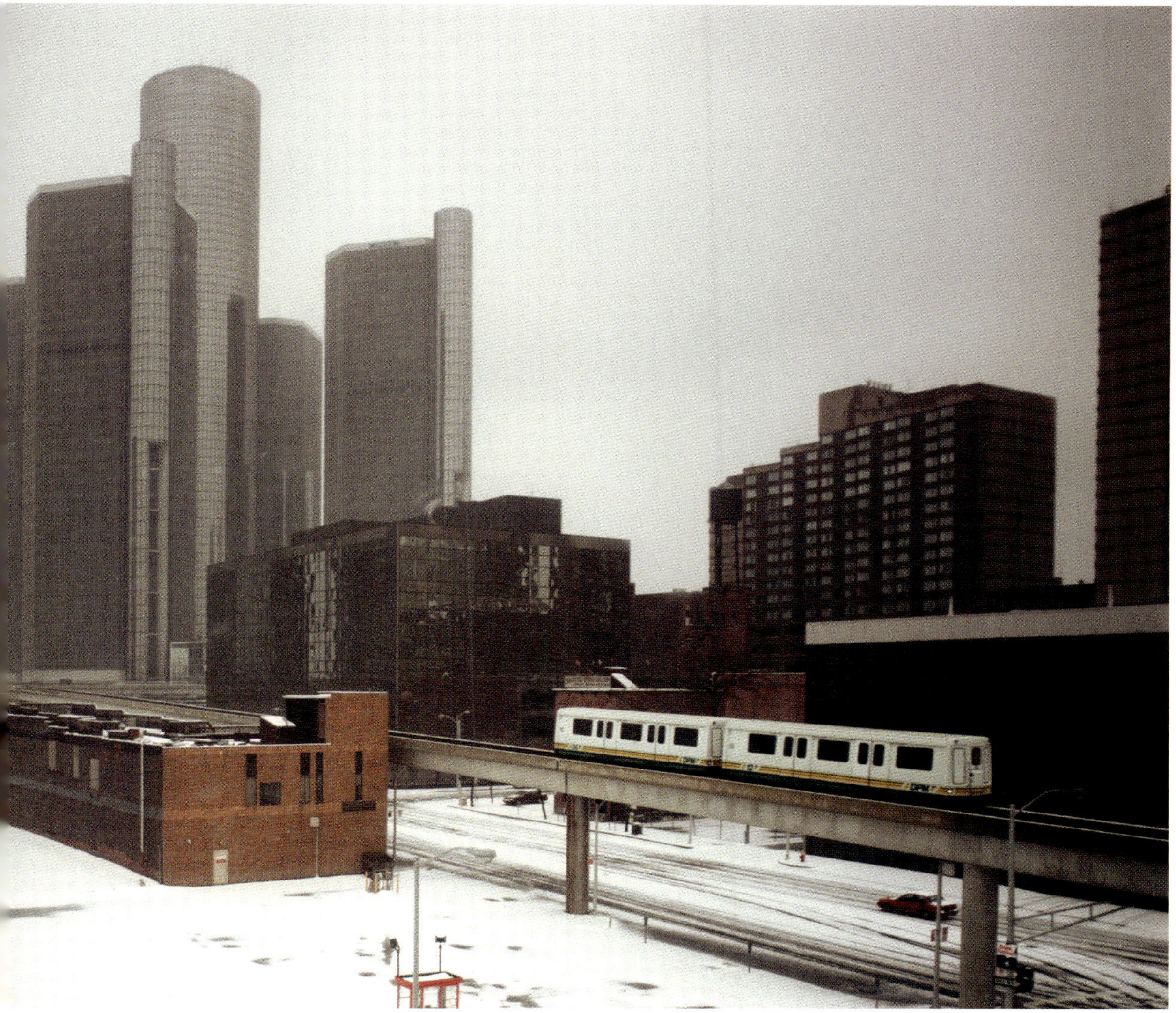

The Renaissance Center, built in 1977, and the People Mover, which went into operation in 1987. The Renaissance Center was designed by John Portman, who associated the building with, as he phrased it, “Movement... Excitement... Life.” Designed to kick-start the city, the isolated waterfront complex was called “a city within a city” and a place that said to those afraid of Detroit: “come in and be safe.” Completed during the Coleman Young administration as part of an urban renewal effort, it is one of the most popular symbols of the city among African Americans. The Renaissance Center is now the site of the General Motors world headquarters. East Congress Street at Beaubien Street, Detroit, 1995.

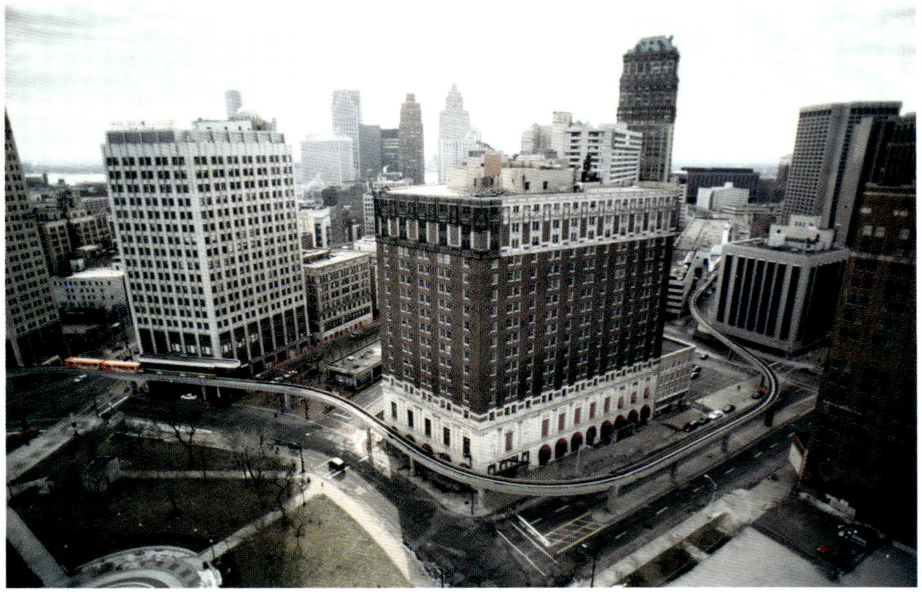

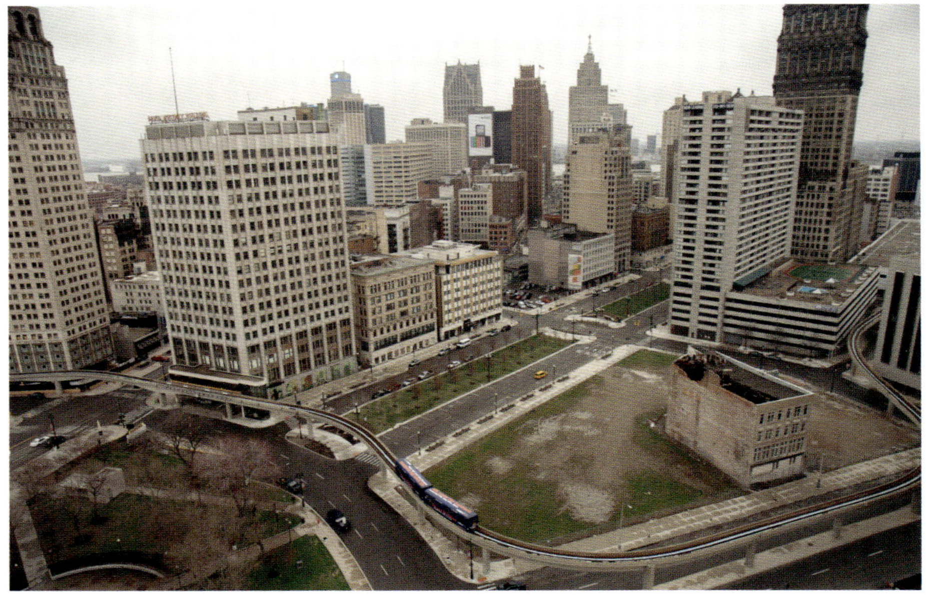

Former Statler Hilton Hotel at center, David Whitney Building at left. Completed in 1915, the hotel stood empty for thirty years before being demolished in 2005. View southwest from the roof of the Kales Building, Park Avenue at Grand Circus Park, 2001.

Empty lot where the former Statler Hilton Hotel stood, David Whitney Building on the left. View southwest from the roof of the Kales Building, Grand Circus Park, Detroit, 2011.

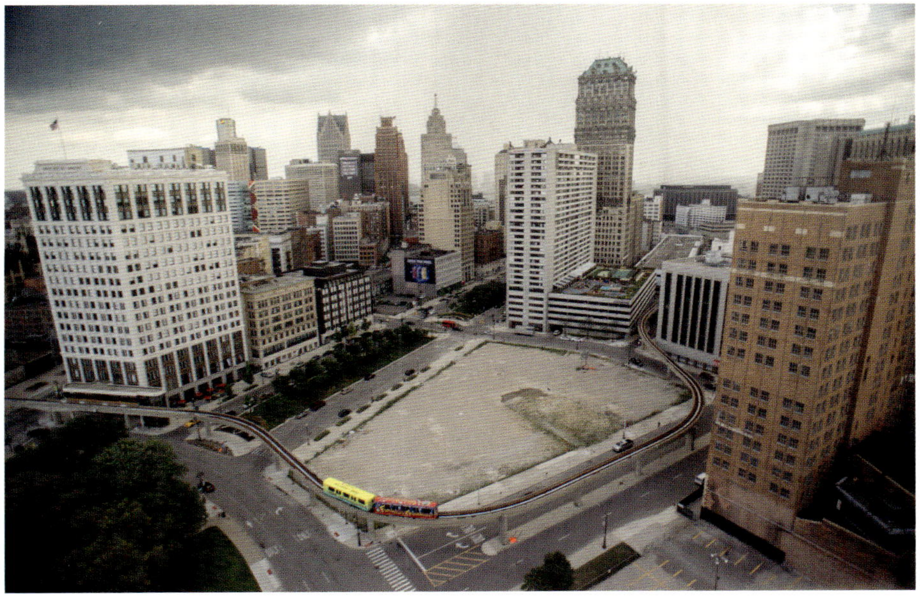

The space occupied by the Statler Hilton Hotel remains an empty lot. The David Whitney Building on the left has been refurbished. View southwest from the roof of the Kales Building, Grand Circus Park, Detroit, 2015.

AMERICAN ACROPOLIS: THE END OF AN IDEA

I propose that as a tonic for our imagination . . . as a call for renewal, as a place within our national memory, a dozen city blocks of pre-Depression skyscrapers be stabilized and left standing as ruins: an American Acropolis. We could transform the nearly 100 troubled buildings into a grand national historic park of play and wonder.

—Camilo José Vergara, *New York Times*, December 10 1995

. . . Vergara is not immune to the pleasures and instruction found in decay . . . In 1995, he proposed that Detroit set aside twelve blocks downtown as a "skyscraper ruins park." With almost a quarter of these buildings 'nearly empty and several in advanced states of ruin,"' he believed a radical rethinking of the area was needed. 'The place that invented planned obsolescence has itself become obsolescent,' he wrote. Had the authorities heeded his suggestion instead of scorning it, they might have created a tourist attraction to rival New York's High Line.

—Richard Woodward, "Disaster Photography: When Is Documentary Exploitation?" *Art News*, February 6, 2013

Until two decades ago an area of three blocks surrounding Grand Circus Park, once the city's business center, contained the world's largest concentration of abandoned skyscrapers. Built mostly before the Great Depression, these grand buildings, once symbols of progress and ambition, were prosperous until the mid-1950s, when they fell out of fashion, deteriorated, and were left to the elements. The sheer number and size of these abandoned structures, rising within a subsequently near-lifeless environment, turned Detroit's old downtown into a surreal place. In the early 1990s, these behemoths became the dregs of history, enormous shadows lined up along deep canyons. Their awesome presence convinced me that they should be preserved as an American

Acropolis, a ruined skyscraper park. Even now, for me, Detroit is a unique and much needed place of peregrination that renews my spirit, a realm where I can escape the prison of capitalism.

Anchoring the unique park that I envisioned was the huge Hudson's Department Store, occupying an entire city block, the second-largest such store in the nation, a massive, misshapen fortress that had grown through a series of asymmetrical additions. However, Hudson's was imploded in 1998 as Detroit mayor Dennis Archer proclaimed, "Let the Future Begin." There was also the Book Cadillac Hotel, which once rivaled New York's Waldorf Astoria in elegance. I once explored its darkened Florentine grand ballroom, the huge chandeliers still in place but the floor covered with debris. The Book Cadillac has now been restored as an apartment building and Westin Hotel. The Statler Hilton Hotel, where Franklin Delano Roosevelt stayed, was demolished in 2005 to make downtown attractive for the 2006 Super Bowl. Among the last remaining abandoned skyscrapers is the gritty Book Tower, its green roof favored by peregrine falcons for nesting and by cell phone companies for their antennas.

People willing to visit a ruined skyscraper had to search the perimeter for an entrance, sometimes a plywood-covered hole in the wall. Climbing over piles of trash leading to dark rooms, they would look for an unblocked set of stairs to climb to the roof. Ascending the stairs, they would be put on guard by the masses of debris, old mattresses and sleeping bags, pigeons flying overhead, water dripping from the ceiling, occasional homeless men, and the expectation of dangerous encounters. More recently, due to heightened security, it has become almost impossible to enter these buildings.

Left with most of their contents intact, the vacant buildings were time capsules of the Motown of half a century ago: storehouses of people's dental and medical histories, divorce papers, tax forms, and real estate investments. Inside were beauty salons adorned with pictures of popular hairstyles and travel agencies with fading posters of warmer destinations. One could peek into a dozen dentists' offices with their drills, dental chairs, and file cabinets covered with fallen plaster. The office of Jessie Willie, the elderly caretaker at the David Broderick Tower, was decorated with objects that former tenants had left behind, including an idyllic picture of Portofino.

From the roofs of the skyscrapers one can see a great city spreading far to the north with the wide radial avenues meeting the horizon, the slow Detroit River to the south, and the Ambassador Bridge to Canada to the west. I often tagged along with Peter Zeiler, a planner who worked for the Downtown Development Authority and had access to the vacant buildings. Peter carried a machete to cut down trees growing on the roofs, believing that vegetation would discourage investors. I, on the other hand, hoped for nature to take over, creating many secret gardens. Green moss would spread, frogs would populate the pools of accumulated water, and the graceful alder trees and cell phone antennas would become a thick forest. Surely owls, terns, and geese would follow, and storks would come to eat the frogs. On summer nights the skies would fill with bats and swallows.

On the ground, nine vintage trams imported from Portugal and Switzerland, part of a 1976 bicentennial project, began operating within a ghost town atmosphere. Until 2003, the tinkling of the trams' bells filled the air as they moved from their station on Washington Boulevard toward the Renaissance Center and back again in a strange ritual. The tram cars were colorful, charming, and mostly empty. They bore the names of exotic cities such as Lisbon, Montreaux, and Vevey. Watching them inch past the derelict grey skyscrapers, along the vacant streets, felt like a hallucination. These trams that once gave life to the ruins have been forgotten along with other perceived failures of the Coleman Young era. Now, the People Mover, a clean, screechy, well-lit monorail, circles downtown. It is mostly empty at night, throwing light at the dark hulks of ruins as it glides by. The sides of the cars carry advertisements, such as the one in 2009 with the Pepsi symbol followed by the word OPTIMISMMMMMMMMMMMM in giant letters against a pink background.

Late in the last century, downtown Detroit became a sports and gambling center with new stadiums and casinos. Suburban families discovered that the city could be a fun place to watch baseball and hockey games, throw tailgate parties, attend conventions, and enjoy the theater. Although Detroit's population is seventy-nine percent African American, on game days the downtown population is predominantly white.

It was once common to hear members of the African American elite complain angrily that whites had drained capital out of the city, leaving behind derelict buildings that city residents were expected to maintain. They asked, "If people in the suburbs liked these buildings so much, why didn't they take them with them?" Sandra Hines, a community activist, called Hudson's a "significant and magical store," adding that blacks, though, "unless they were very light skinned, could not aspire to become a doorman or elevator operator; it wasn't for us." Arthur Johnson, a vice president of Wayne State University, felt no love for the booming city that had excluded him in his youth. He told me, "I wasn't in the robust thriving Detroit of the 1950s." Many other black leaders feel the same.

Nowadays, Detroit's downtown blight has been greatly diminished. People's Outfitters, a once-celebrated then abandoned Albert Kahn building, has been replaced by a multilevel parking garage. The site of the old Statler Hilton is a vacant lot, and Hudson's footprint is a field of concrete above an underground parking garage. The Metropolitan,

United Artists, Book, and Wurlitzer buildings and many empty storefronts, however, still remind us of the abandonment that was once the norm. Several survivors have been rehabilitated and made into apartment buildings by members of a new generation who appreciate their craftsmanship and design. The CompuServe Building, now the headquarters of Quicken Loans, together with the Ernst and Young Building, represent something different—modern, glitzy high rises.

Admittedly, allowing the old downtown to safely descend into further ruin would have been expensive, requiring frequent inspections and maintenance. Unlike ancient ruins that were built brick upon brick or stone upon stone and can last for thousands of years, modern ruins are supported by steel armatures that can rust, and water infiltration will corrode the clips that hold the cladding. When water freezes between the cladding and frame, the resulting expansion loosens the coverings and they collapse. Yet as preservationist Daniel Bluestone has observed, "There is something definitive and authentic about these places. . . . You can literally see the play of time on those surfaces."

I was one of the few who loved the "enchanted world" of derelict skyscrapers. This caused me to be characterized as an outsider, an aesthete. My proposal for a ruins park—the core of the old downtown preserved as an acropolis—involved far less than one percent of the city's surface. More than the cost of preserving the ruins, the chief criticism of my proposal was its perceived attempt to reduce Detroit to a hopeless reminder of its former greatness. As Wayne State University planner Gary Sands put it in 1997: "The very concept that this city should have produced a 'magnificent ruin' that others would come to marvel at is considered to be an embarrassment to city residents. After all, Detroit prides itself on producing things that are useful and stylish, not things that are abandoned and decayed." It took more than a decade for the beauty of derelict Motown to be more widely acknowledged, first in Europe and later, begrudgingly, as "ruin porn" in the United States. But by then the ruins park had been reduced by demolition and rebuilding.

Downtown has lost so much of the mystery and strangeness of its ruins that I hardly recognize it. Yet in the 1990s I was there walking the streets and alleys, looking for ways to enter vacant buildings with names like Wurlitzer, Lafayette, and David Stott while trying to avoid being mugged. Sometimes, though, I believe that the whole place was the creation of my imagination.

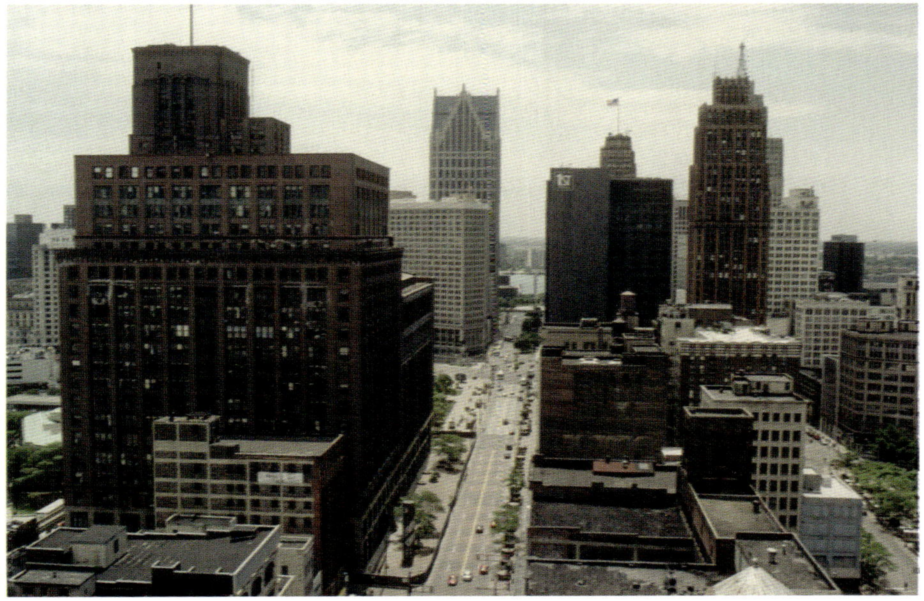

The massive reddish-brown building on the left is the J. L. Hudson's Department Store, which opened in 1927. View south from the David Broderick Building along Woodward Avenue, Detroit, 1998.

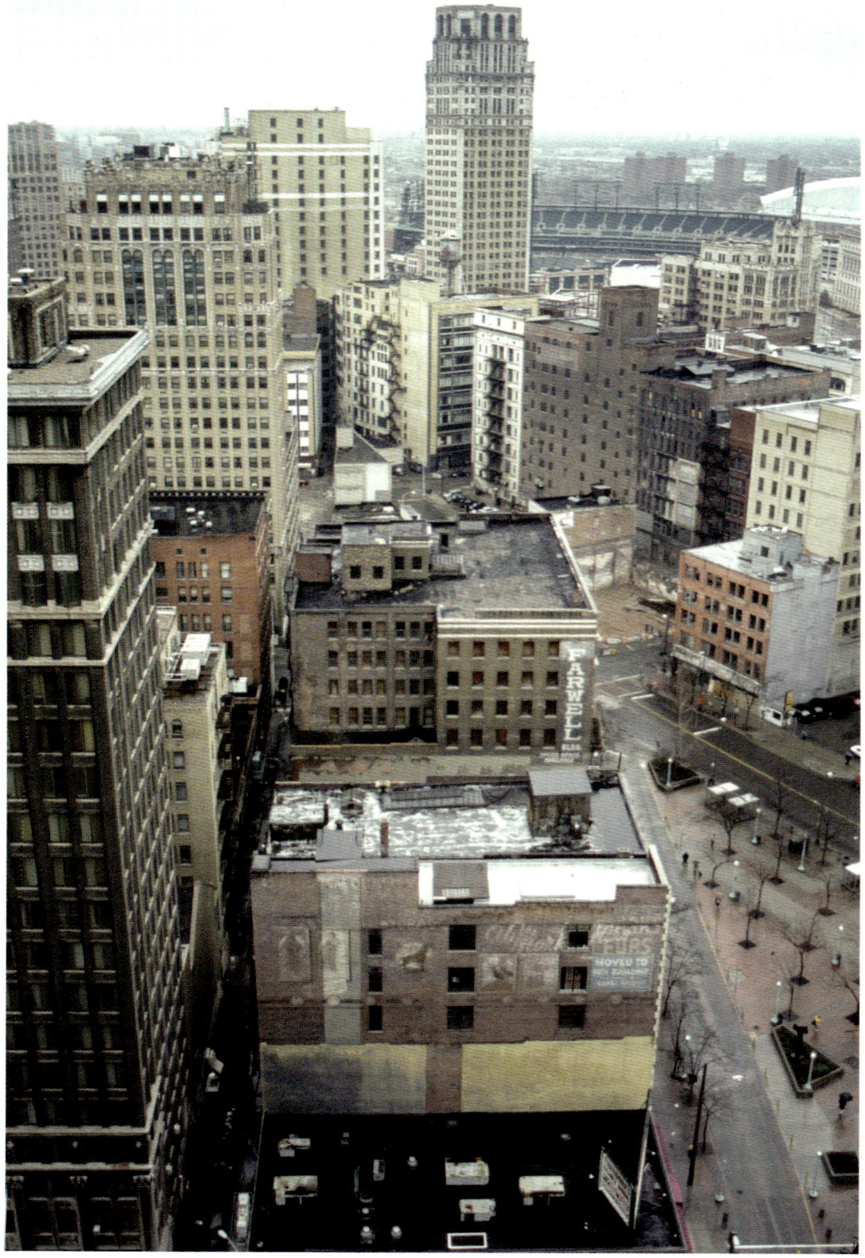

A 2013 booklet entitled "A Placemaking Vision for Downtown Detroit" says of Capitol Park that it "is envisioned to be the center of a new arts district with galleries and cafes on the ground floors and residential apartments above.... It will provide a venue for emerging artists to display or perform their work and a welcome green refuge for residents who live around the park. It will be a pedestrian-friendly district and conducive to walking." View northeast from Washington Boulevard and Michigan Avenue, Detroit, 2003.

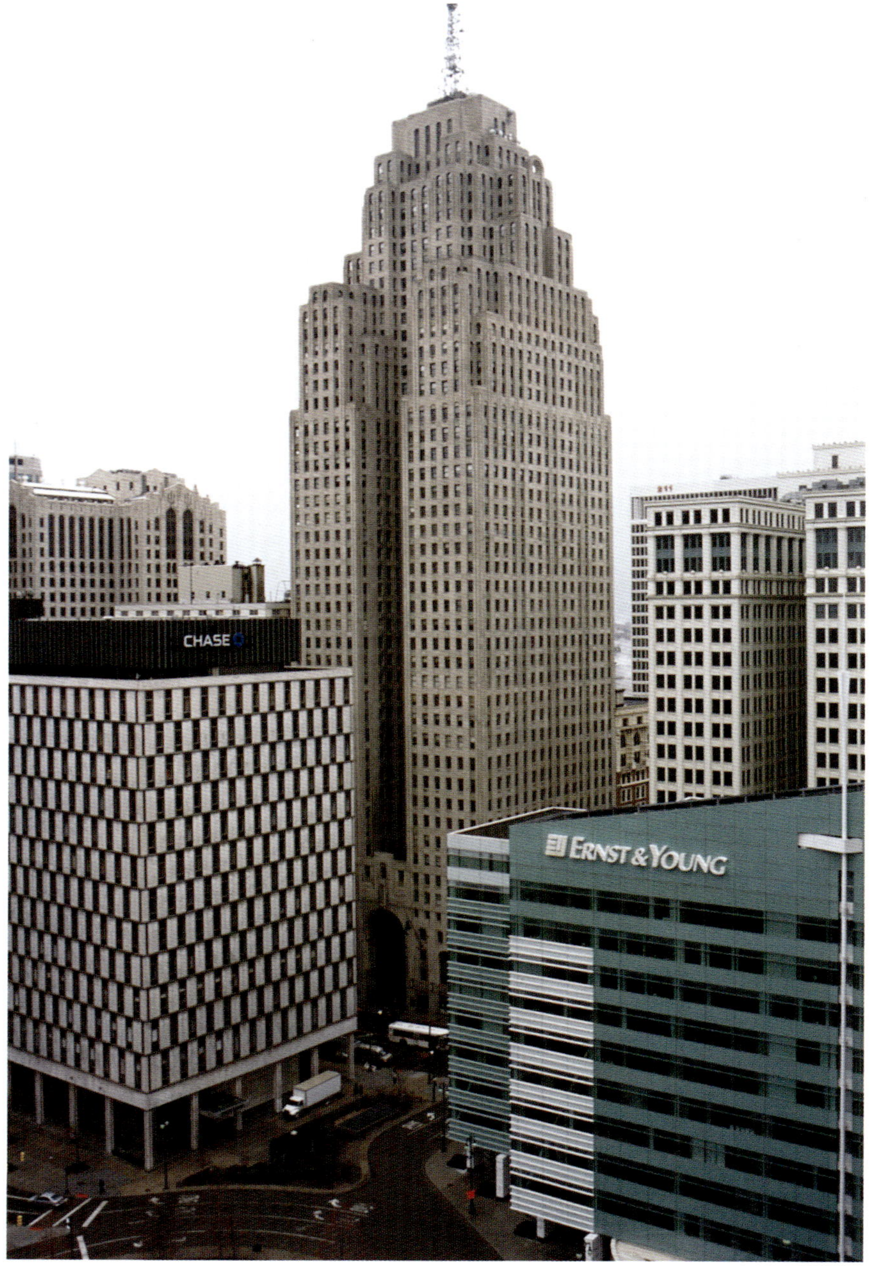

View southwest from the roof of the Compuware Building toward the Penobscot Building (1928) at center. Woodward Avenue at Campus Martius, Detroit, 2011.

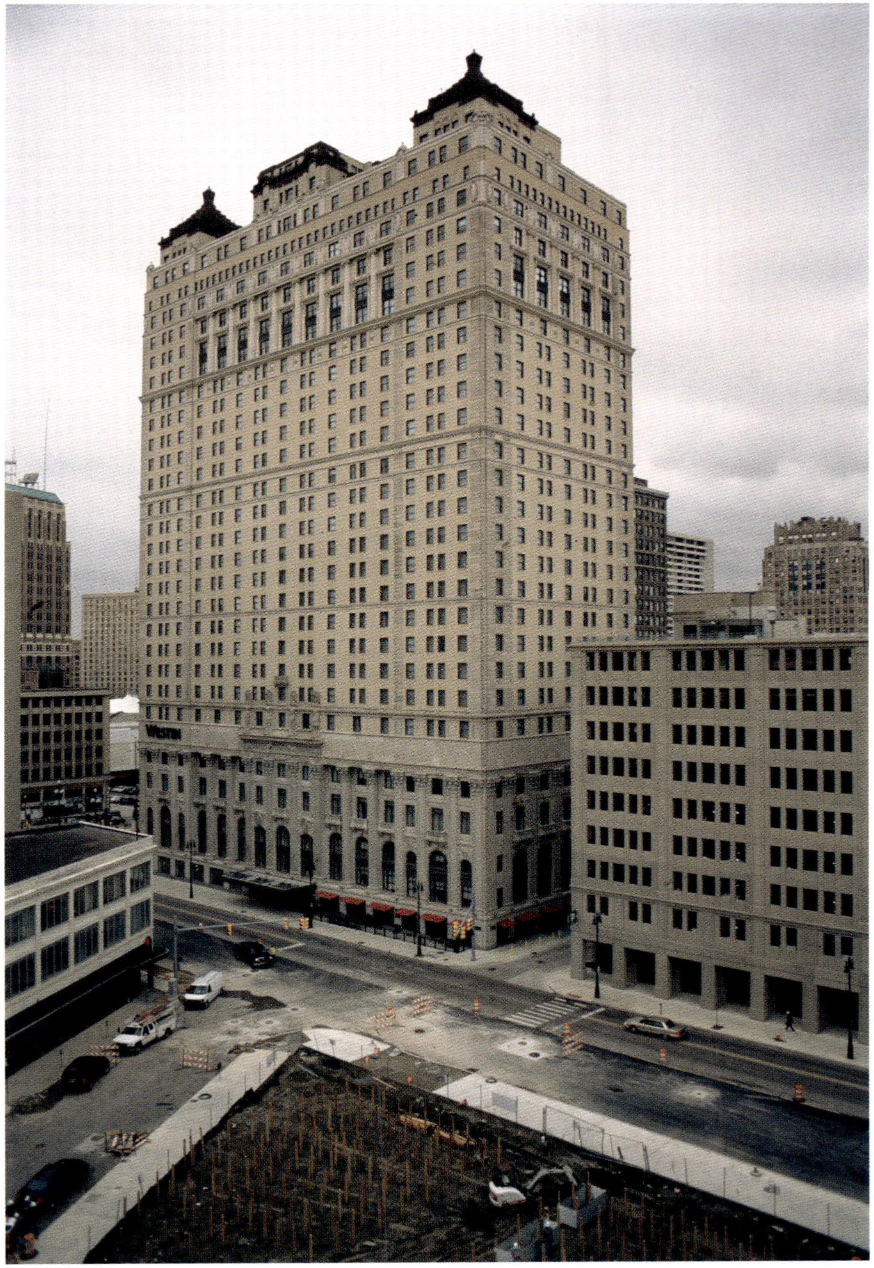

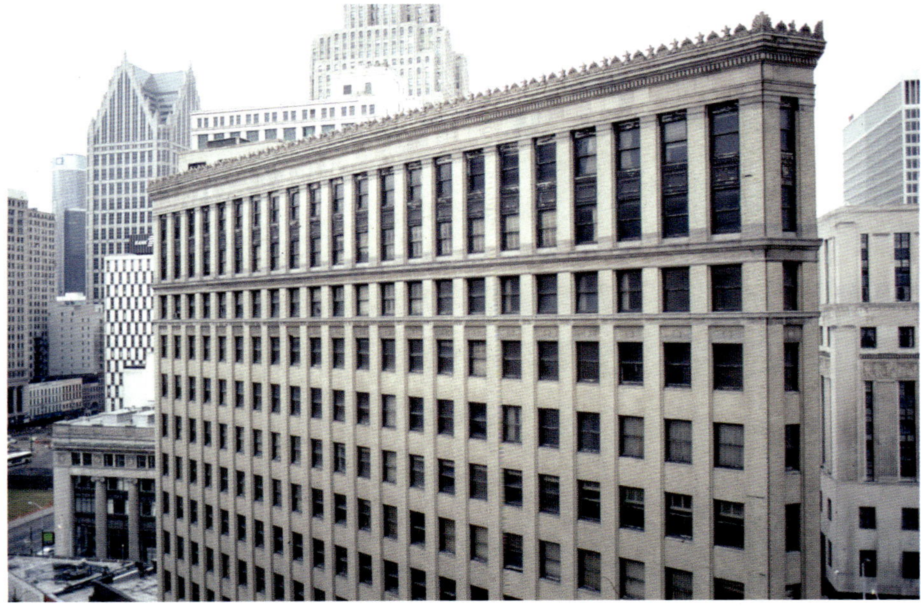

The Book Cadillac, built in 1924, was once the tallest hotel in the world, Detroit's answer to New York's Waldorf Astoria. Renovated at a cost of $190 million and reopened in 2008 after being closed for 24 years, the Book Cadillac became a test case in investing in historic architecture. Today the Book Cadillac is part of the Westin chain. 1114 Washington Boulevard, Detroit, 2011.

The Lafayette Building (1923), with its streamlined classicism, was demolished in 2010. View from Michigan Avenue at Shelby Street, Detroit, 2003.

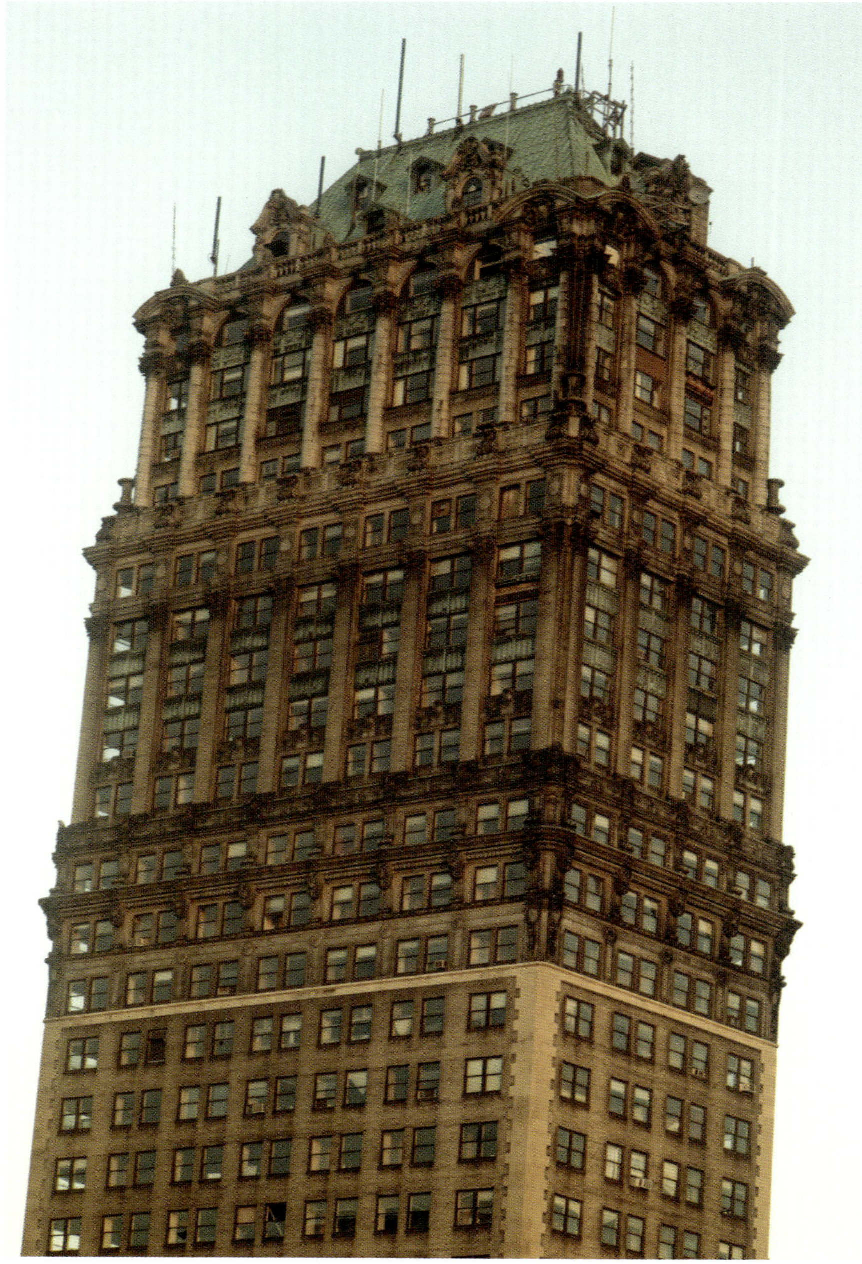

The craftsmanship and engineering that went into the vacant thirty-eight-story Book Tower, designed by Louis Kamper in 1926, remains impressive, a symbol of the power and wealth of an era. 1255 Washington Boulevard, Detroit, 2014.

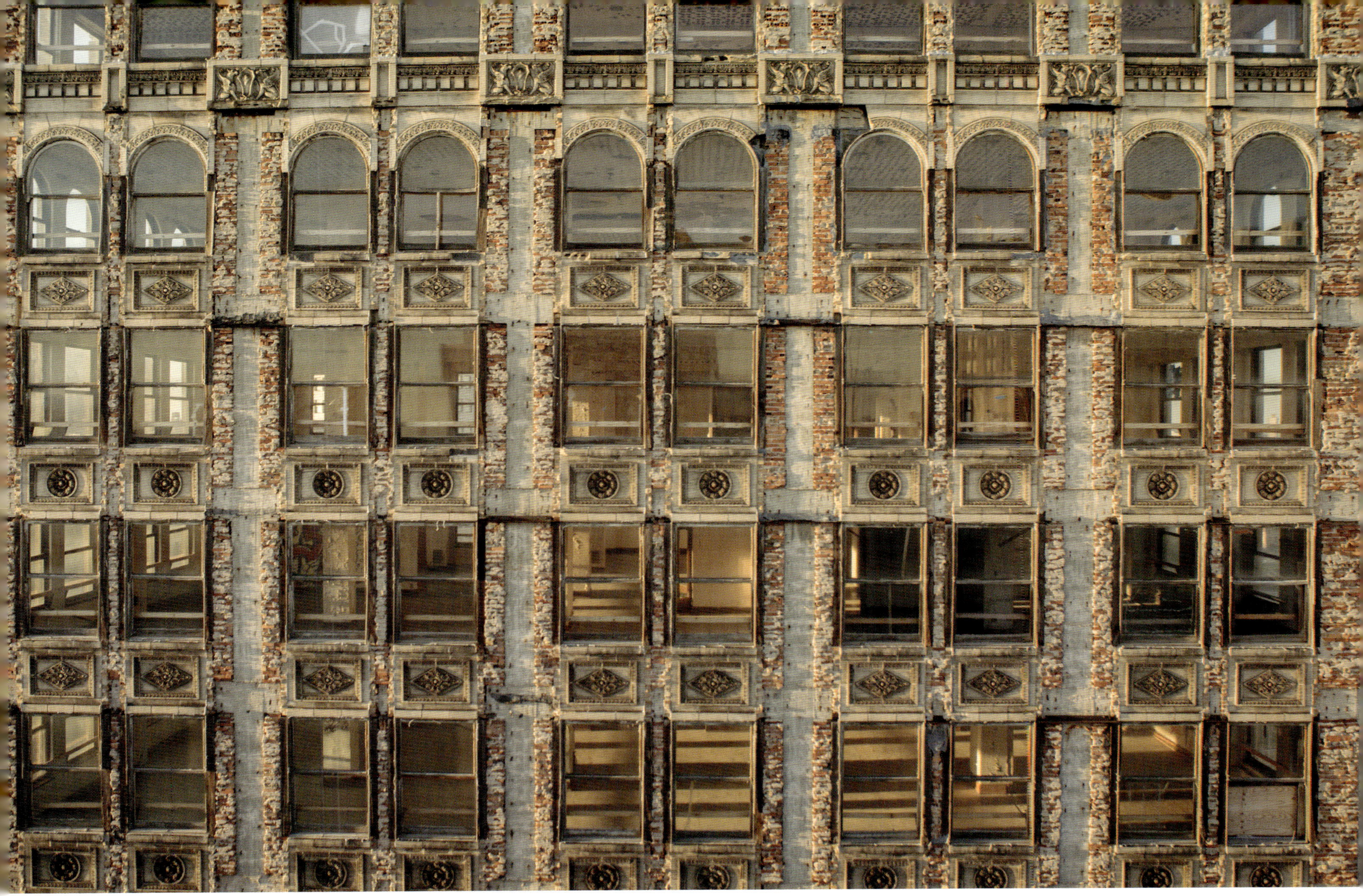

Low evening light reveals the flayed exterior of the United Artists Building of 1928. View east from the roof of 220 Bagley Avenue, Detroit, 2014.

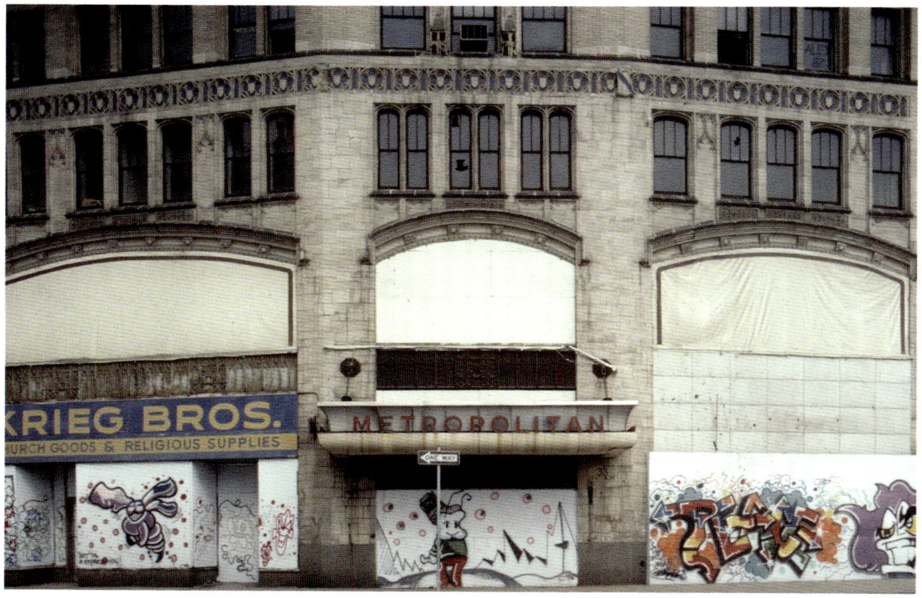

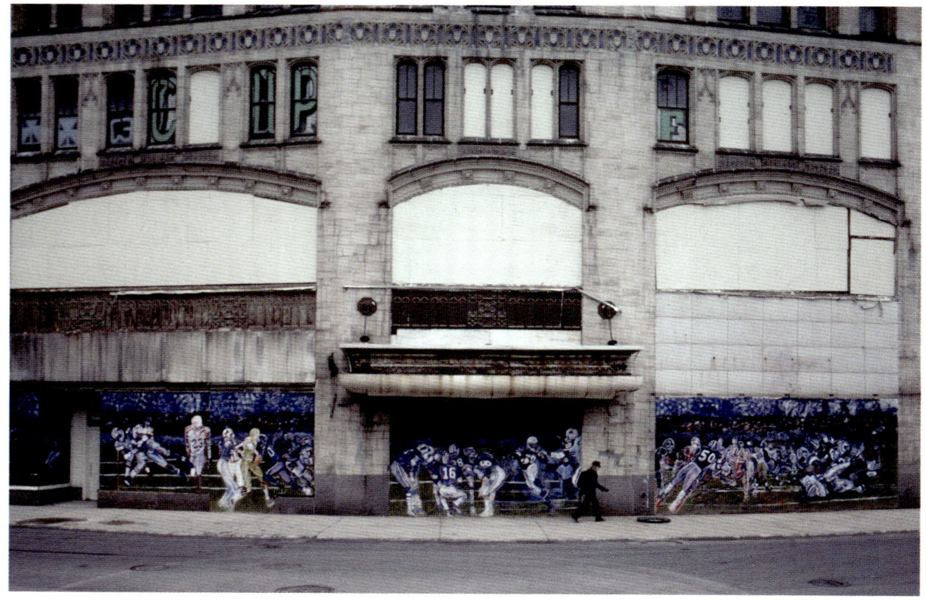

Former Metropolitan Building, built in 1924 and closed in 1977. The Metropolitan was known as the Jewelers Building. John R Street at Farmer Street, Detroit, 1993.

Former Metropolitan Building, detail. The mural on the façade was painted on the occasion of the Super Bowl held in Detroit in 2006. Farmer Street at John R Street, Detroit, 2006.

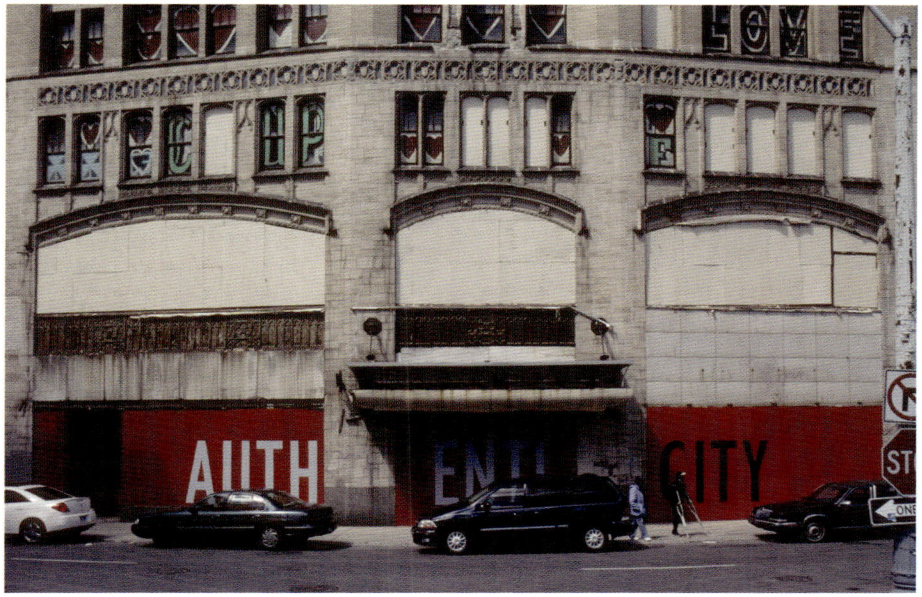

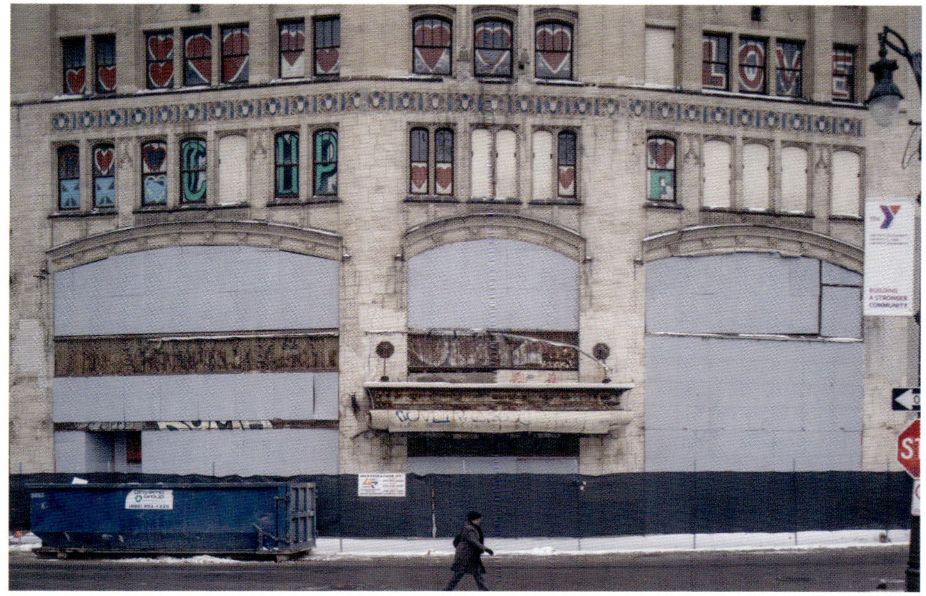

Former Metropolitan Building. “Detroit’s brand has become authenticity, a key component of which has to do with the way the city looks,” wrote Mark Binelli in the *New York Times* in 2012. Farmer Street at John R Street, Detroit, 2009.

Former Metropolitan Building, detail. Farmer Street at John R Street, Detroit, 2015.

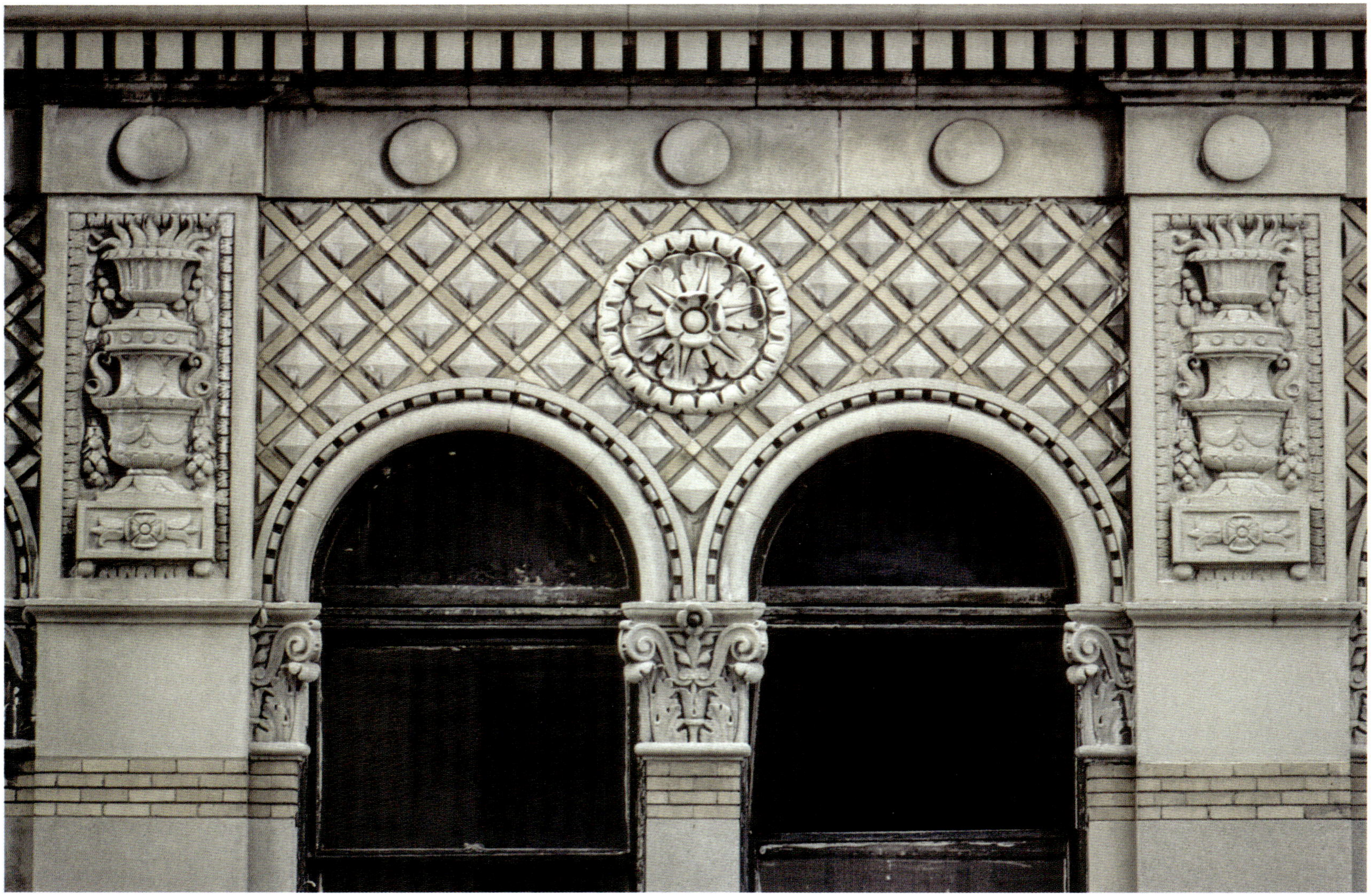

Classical ornament, Park Avenue Building, built in 1923 by Albert Kahn.
Park Avenue at West Elizabeth Street, Detroit, 2001.

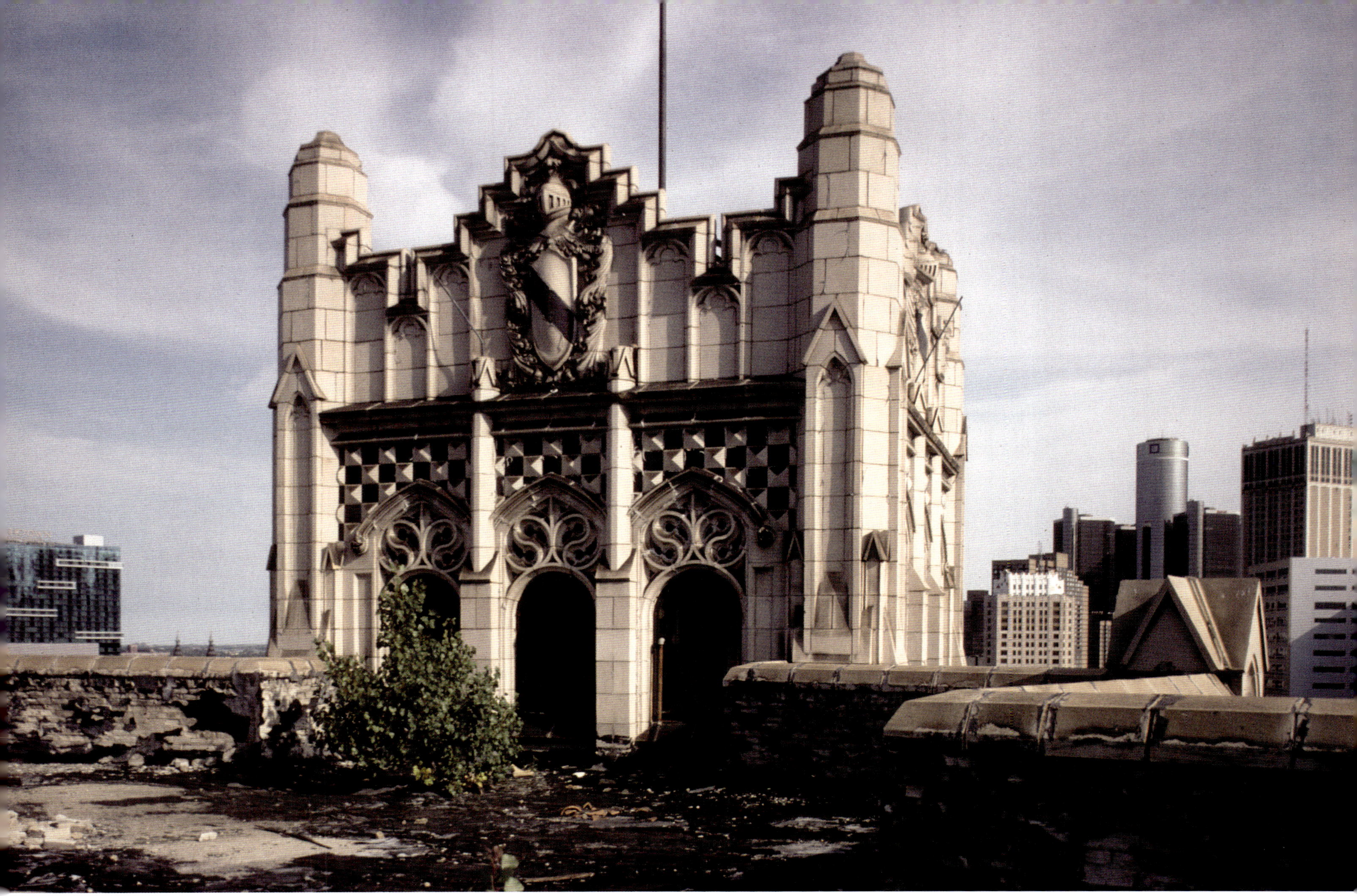

Top of the Metropolitan Building of 1924, recalling a Gothic chapel.
Farmer Street at John R Street, Detroit, 2009.

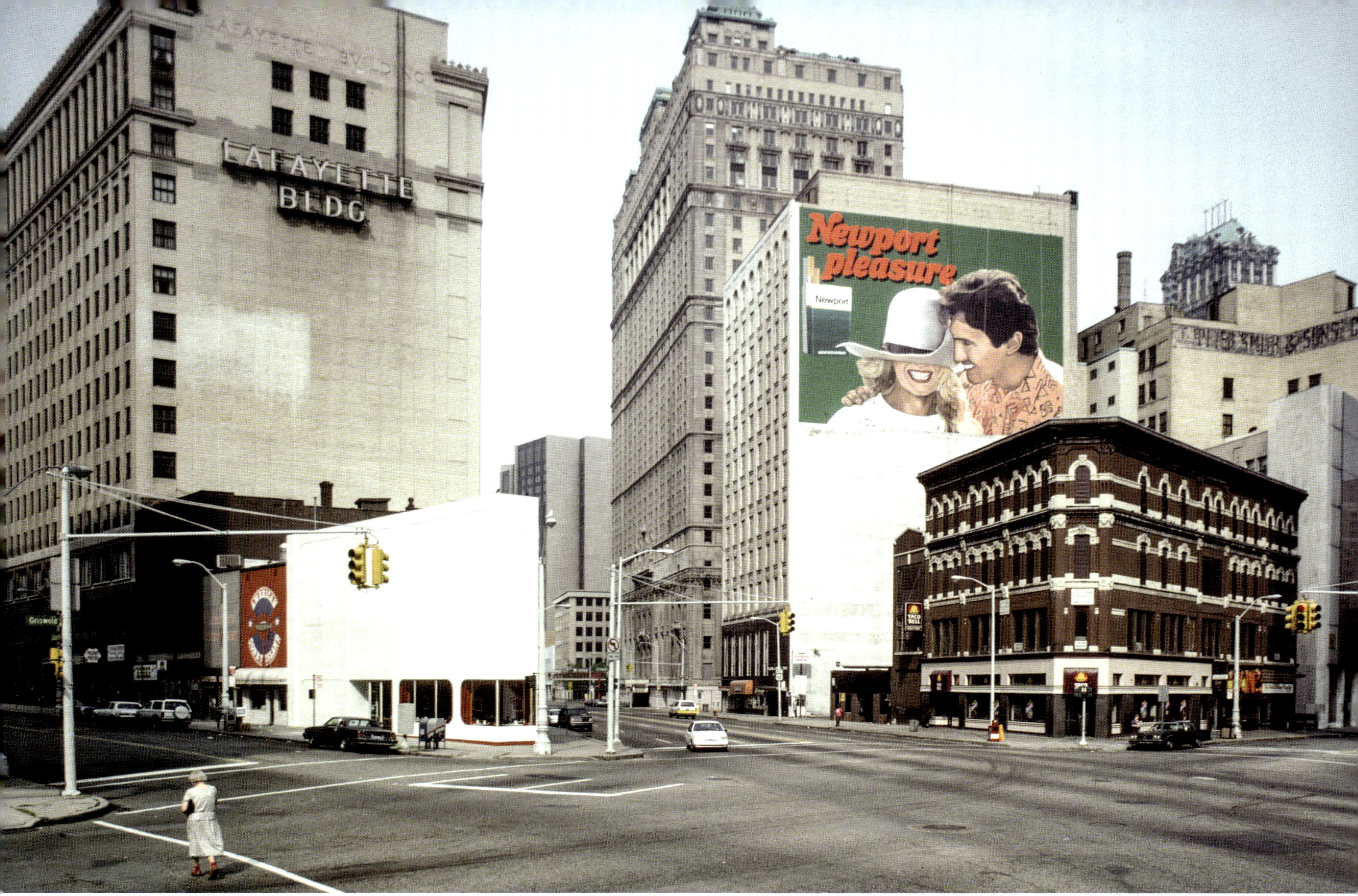

On the right is the Book Cadillac Hotel and on the left the Lafayette Building. View west from the corner of Michigan Avenue and Lafayette Boulevard, Detroit, 1993.

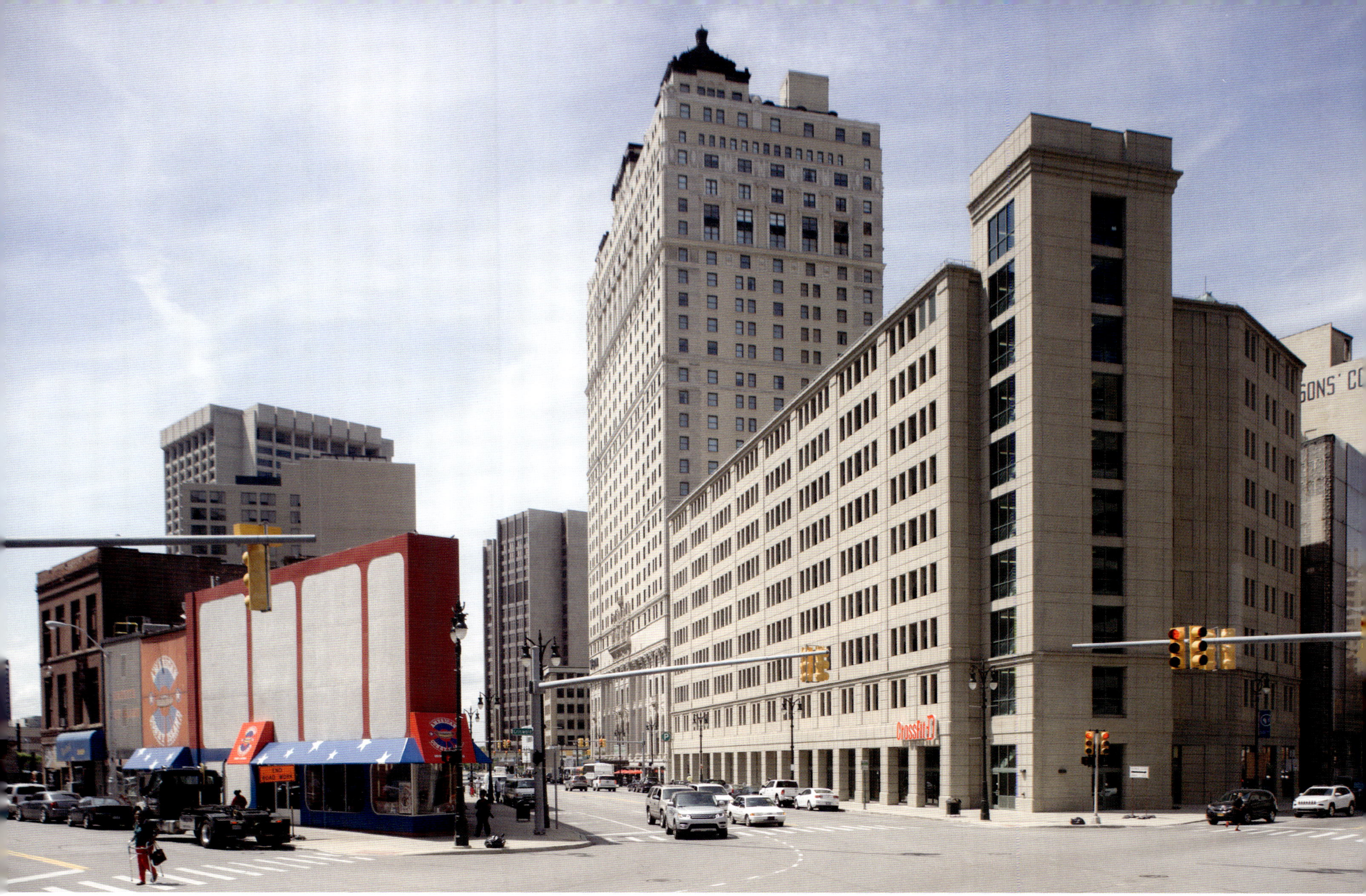

Two of the oldest, most well-known Coney Island restaurants in Detroit, the Lafayette Coney Island and the American Coney Island, seen on the left next to each other. View west from the corner of Michigan Avenue and West Lafayette Boulevard, Detroit, 2015.

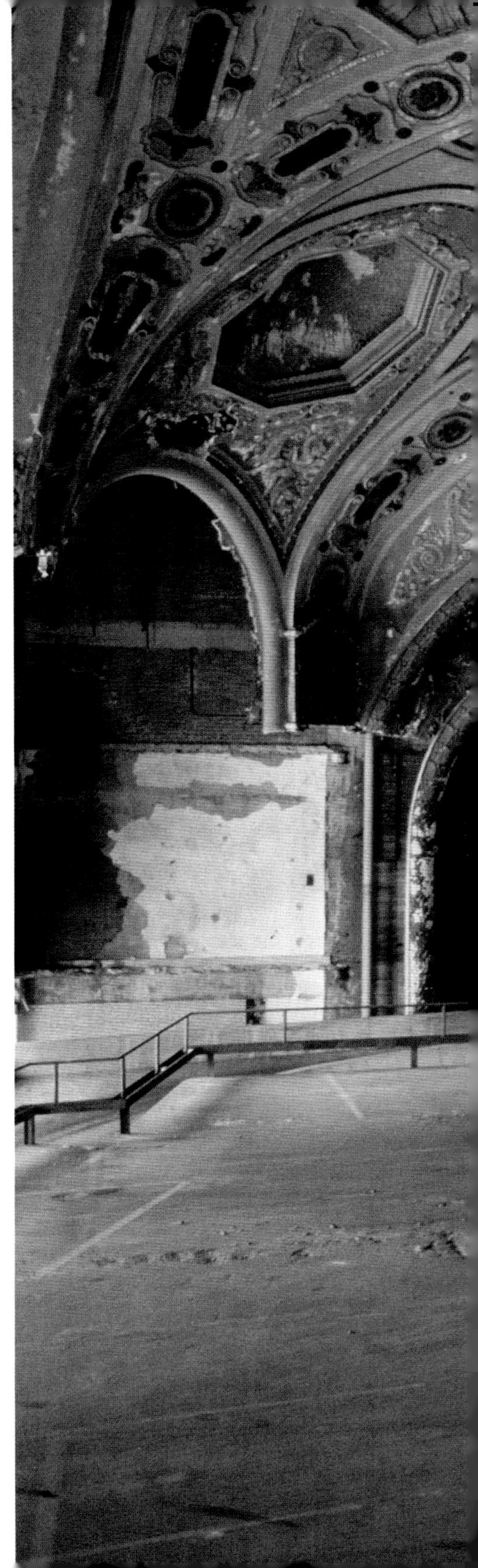

Former Michigan Theater, now a parking garage. The theater was completed in 1926 and closed in 1976. This garage, carved out of the 4,050-seat movie palace, provides safe downtown parking for tenants and for people attending sports events.
220 Bagley Avenue, Detroit, 1995.

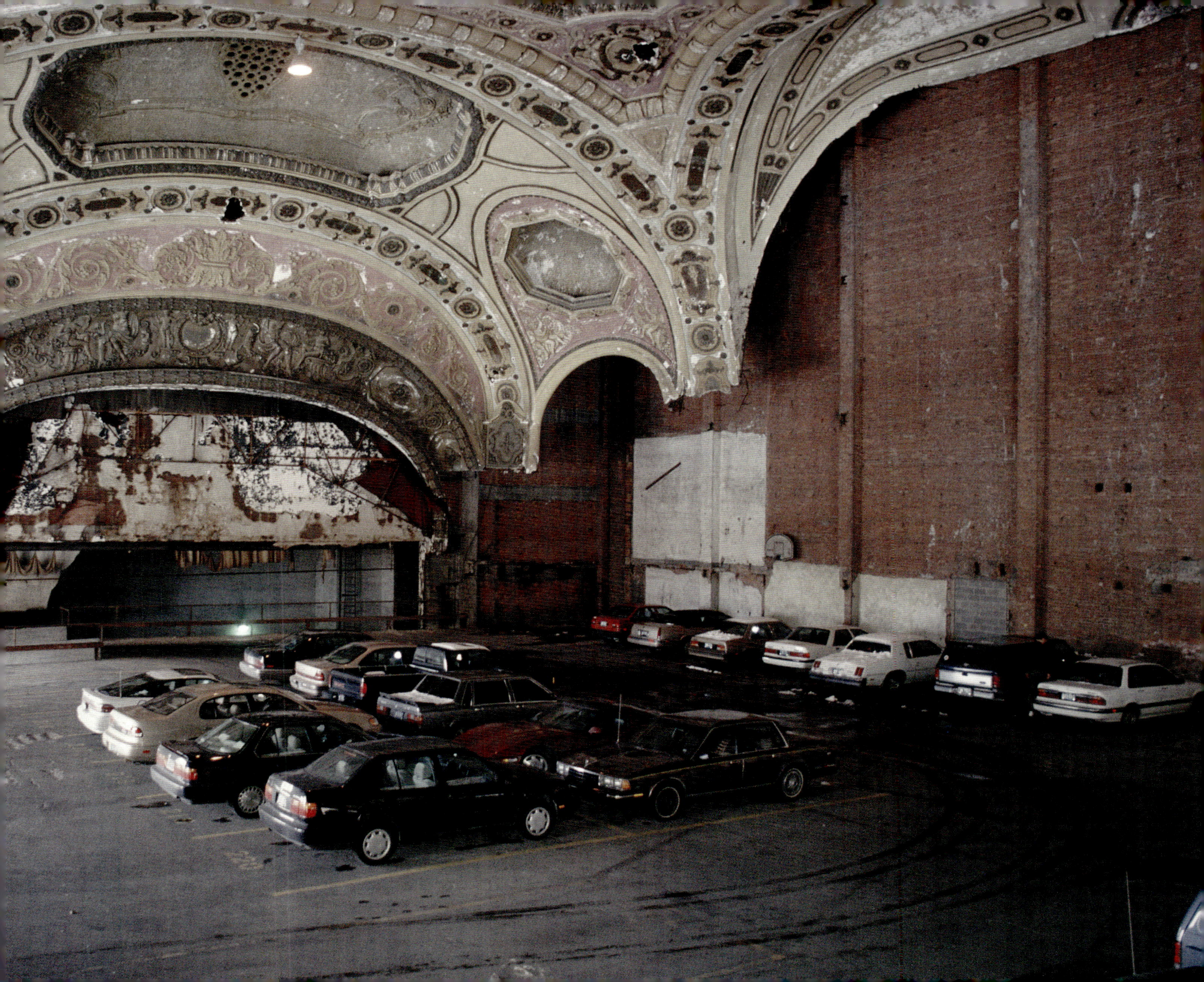

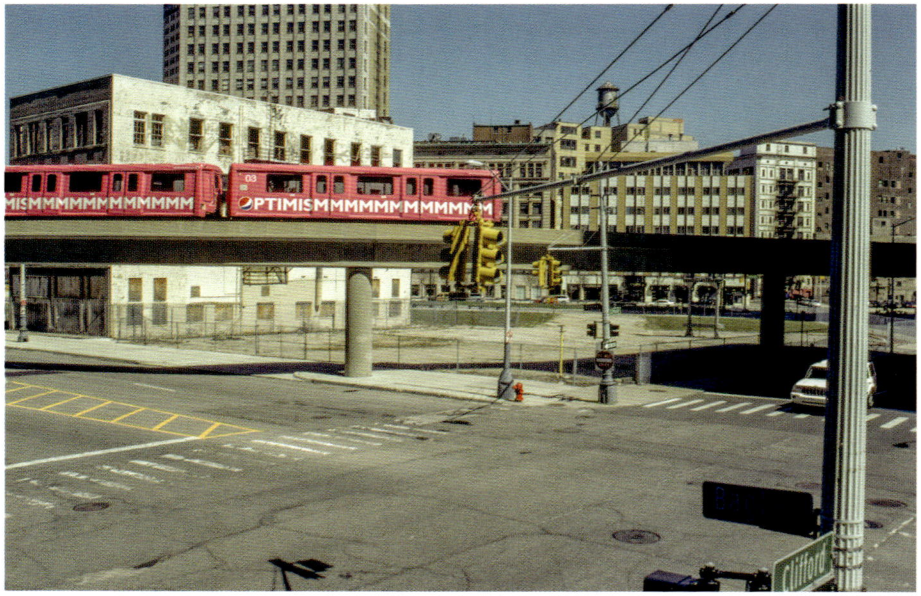

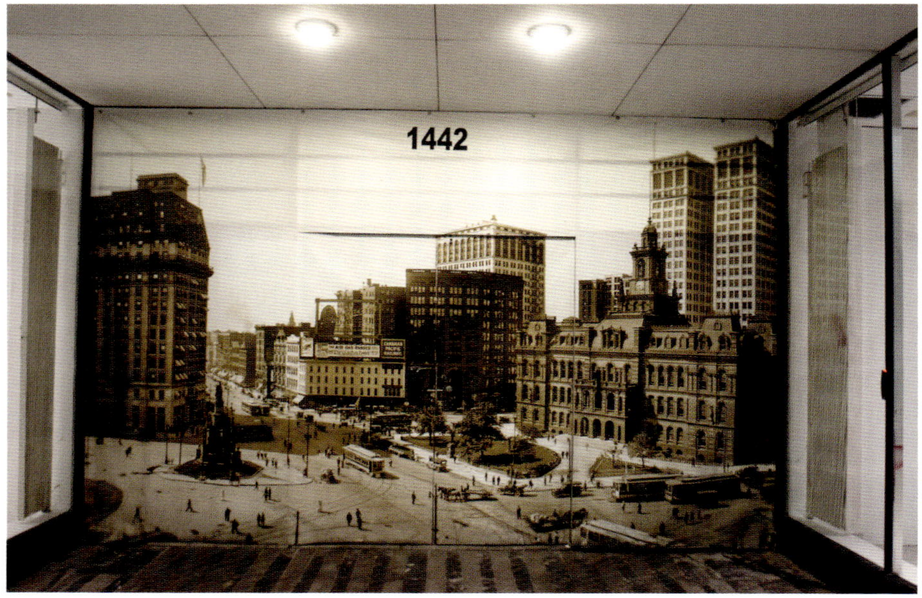

"OPTIMISMMMMMMMMMMMMM," written on the People Mover. View from the Michigan Building, Bagley Avenue at Clifford Street, Detroit, 2009.

Pop-up store with an image of downtown Detroit in its "white golden age." As David Segal commented: "It is a huge, sepia-toned shot of Campus Martius, snapped in 1917. Looking at the picture, you realize that it includes the neighborhood where you are standing, though at a time when it bustled with men and women in hats, strolling amid billboards, retailers and a lineup of trolley cars" ("A Missionary Quest to Remake Motor City," *New York Times*, April 13, 2013). 1442 Woodward Avenue, 2014.

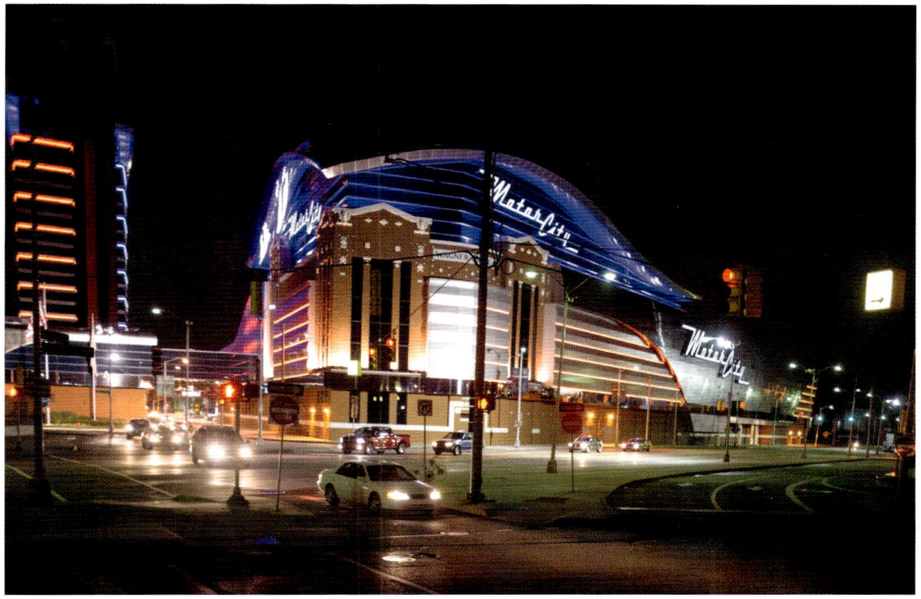

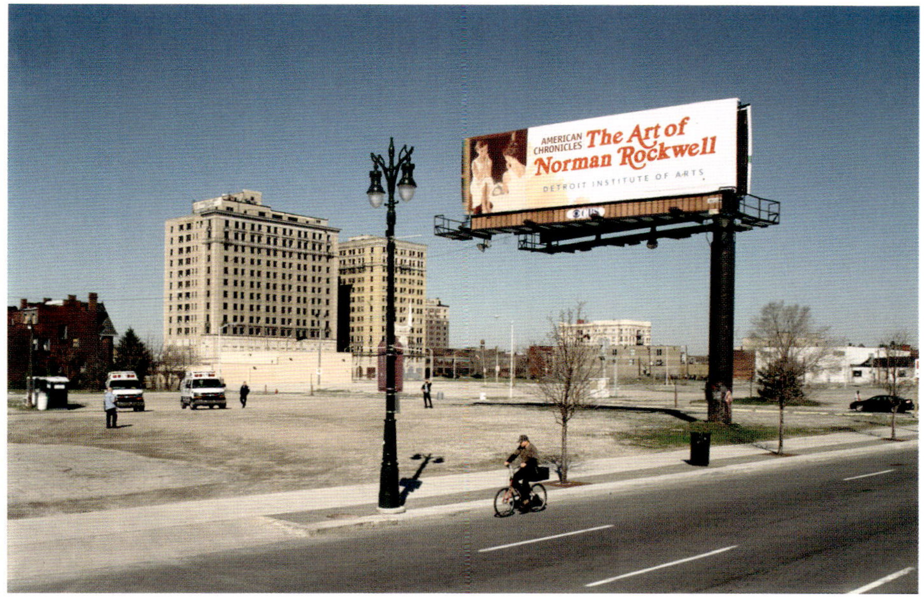

Motor City Casino, a Las Vegas style casino incorporating in its design the 1915 Wagner Bread building by Walter W. Ahlschlager, Here a beautifully designed industrial building accommodates attention-getting glitz. 2901 Grand River Avenue, Detroit, 2013.

Ambulance workers playing baseball against the ruins. A billboard at top right advertises the art exhibit: "American Chronicles: The Art of Norman Rockwell." View northwest from Woodward Avenue at Sibley Street, Detroit, 2009.

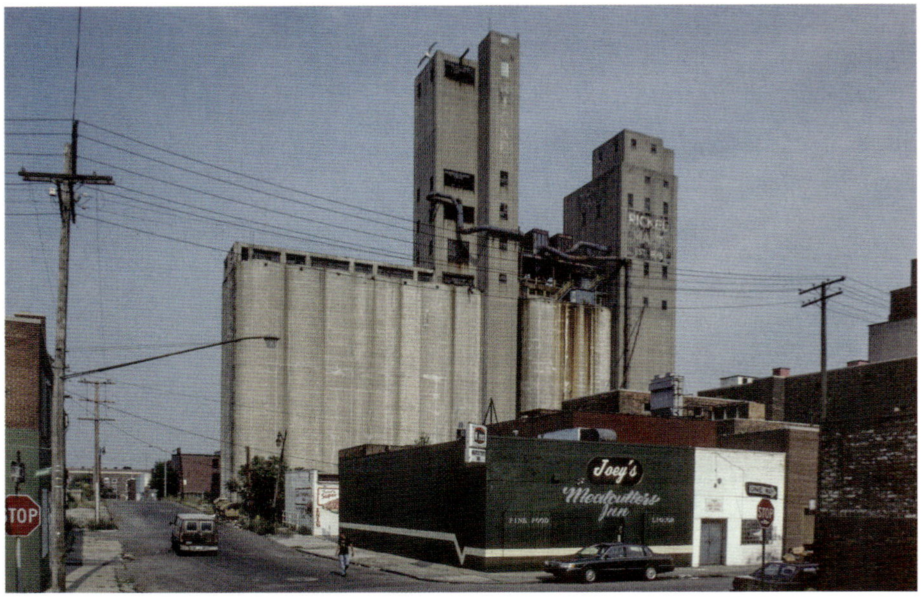

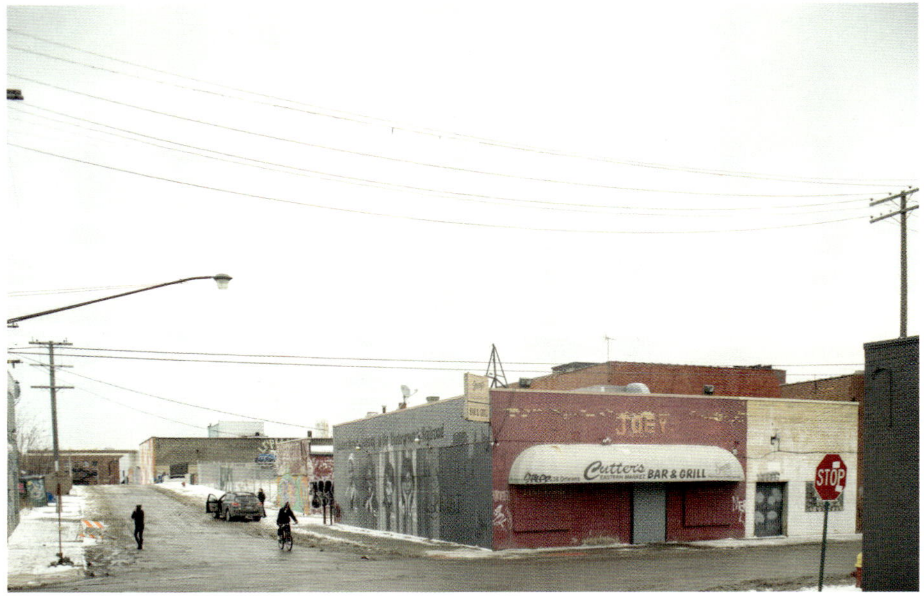

Eastern Market; in the background, Rickel Malt, established in 1876.
Division Street at Orleans Street, Detroit, 1994.

Eastern Market, two decades after the demolition of Rickel Malt,
Division Street at Orleans Street, Detroit, 2015.

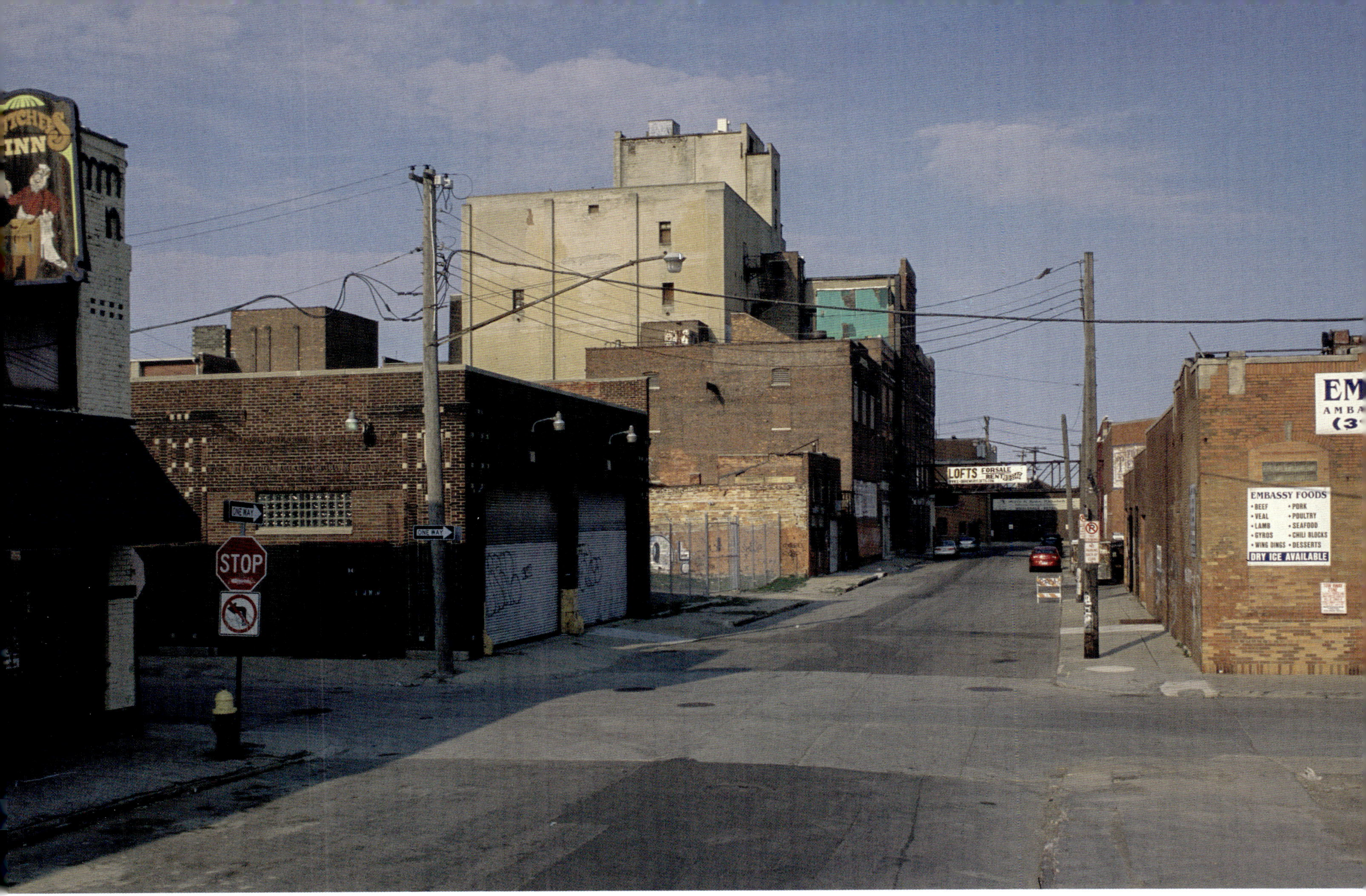

An advertisement for Eastern Market lofts calls the area "vibrant with culture" and an "unparalleled urban living experience." View along Winder Street toward Riopelle Street, Detroit, 2011.

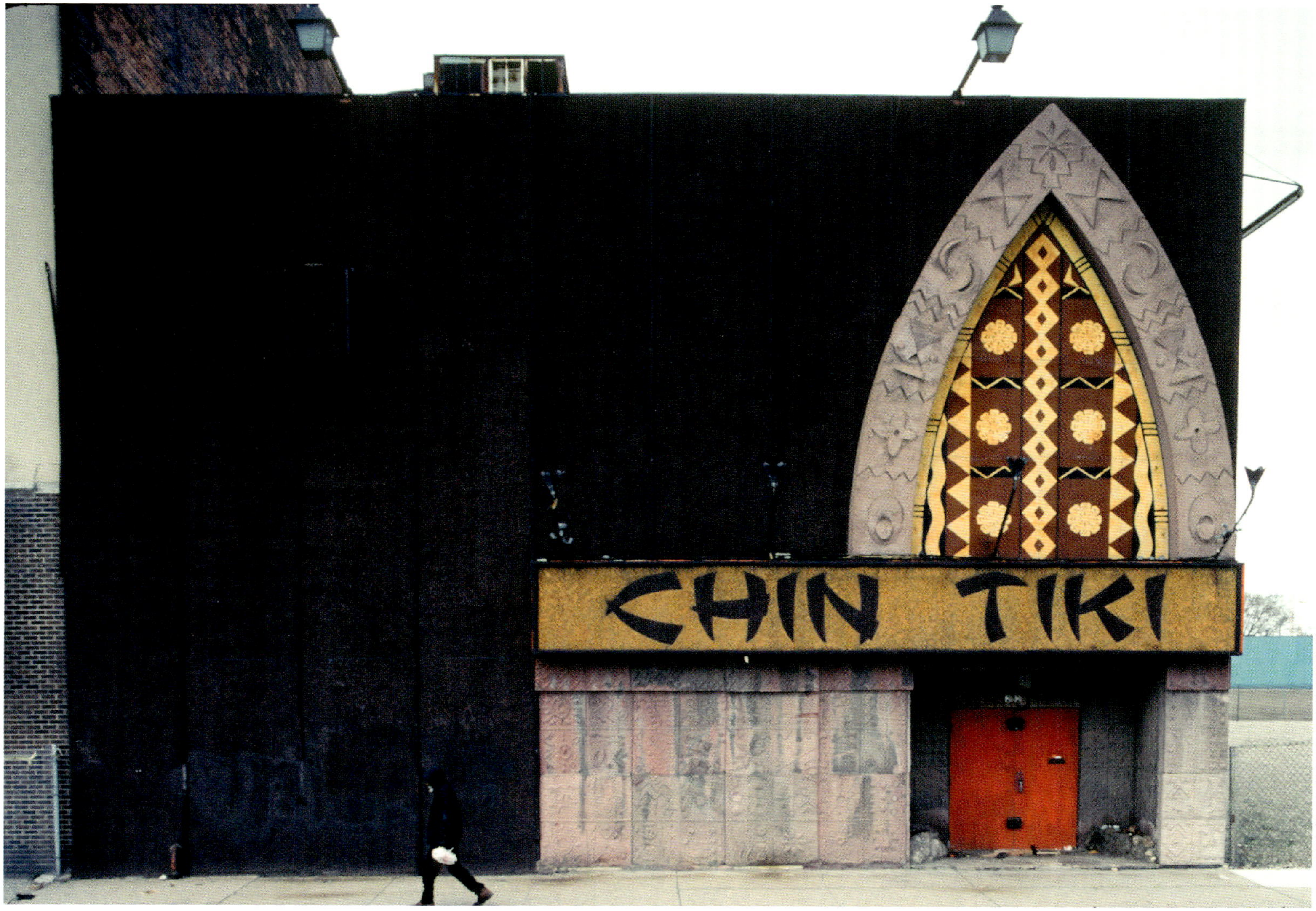

Chin Tiki, "Island Style Dining," demolished in 2009. Chin Tiki was featured in the movie *8 Mile*. 2121 Cass Avenue, Detroit, 2006.

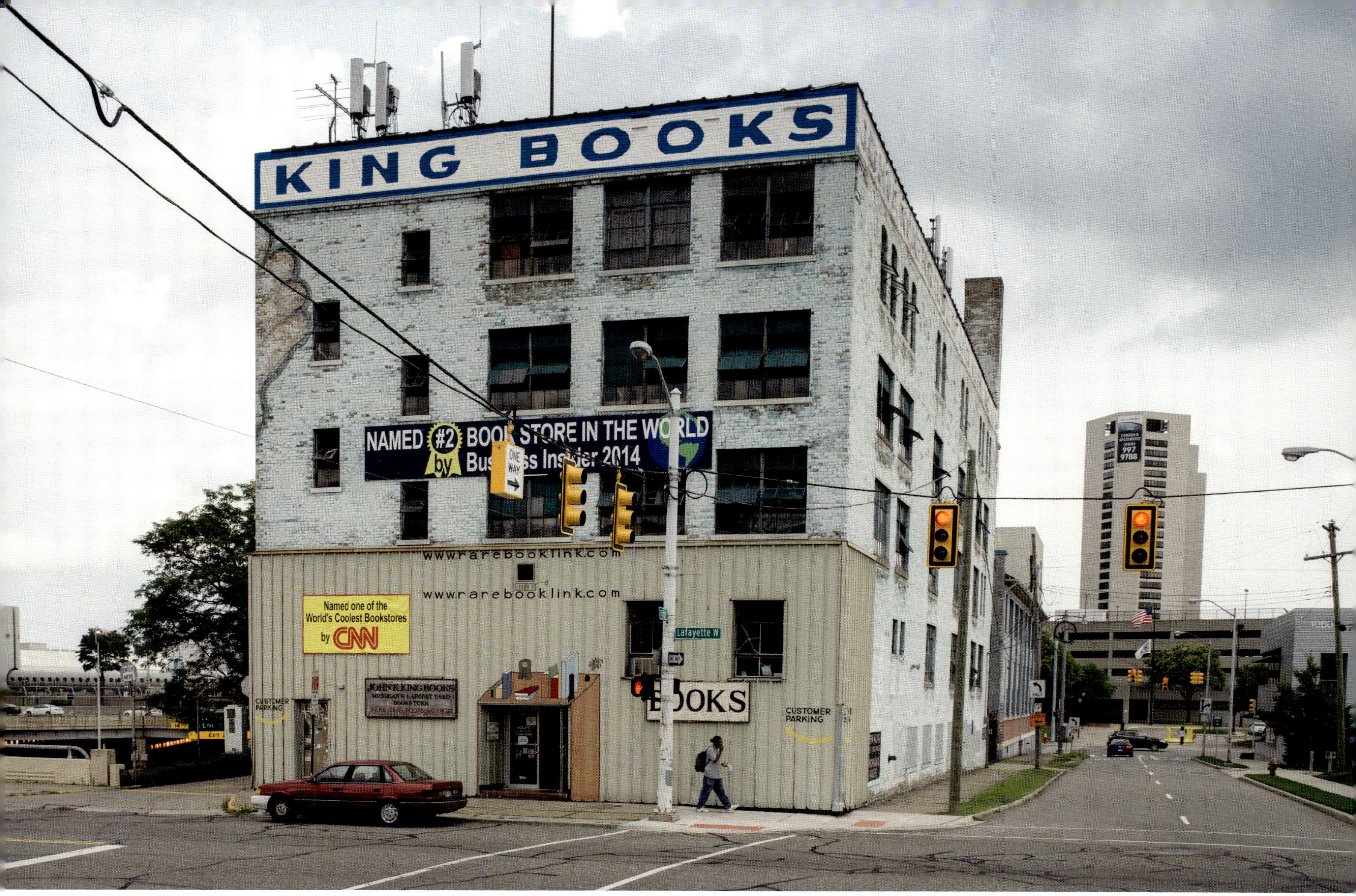

John K. King Books, advertising "rare used books," located in the former Advance Glove Factory Building. West Lafayette at Fifth Street, Detroit, 2015.

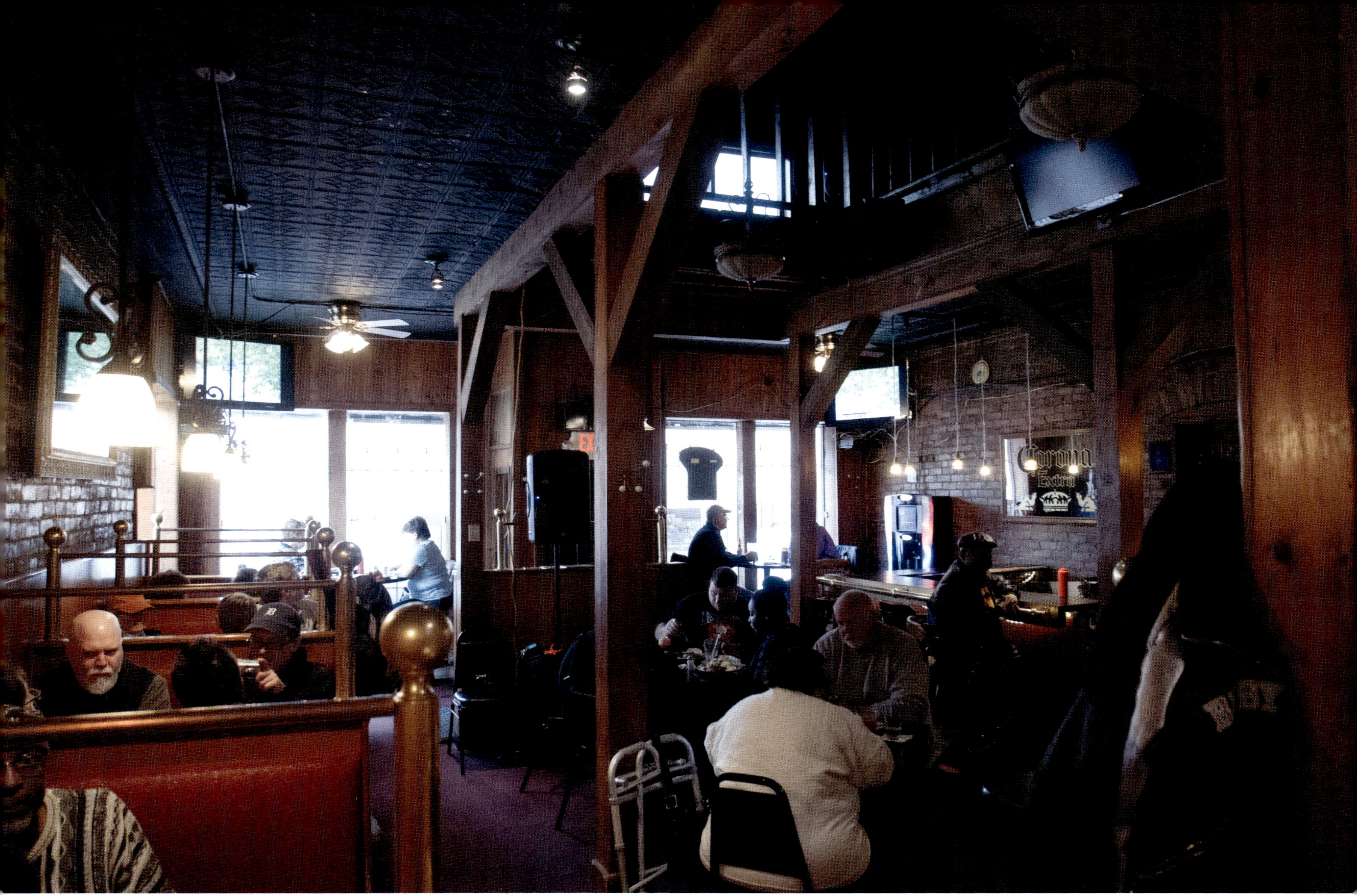

The Butcher's Inn (1890) reopened in fall 2010 after being closed for five years.
1489 Winder Street, Eastern Market, Detroit, 2011.

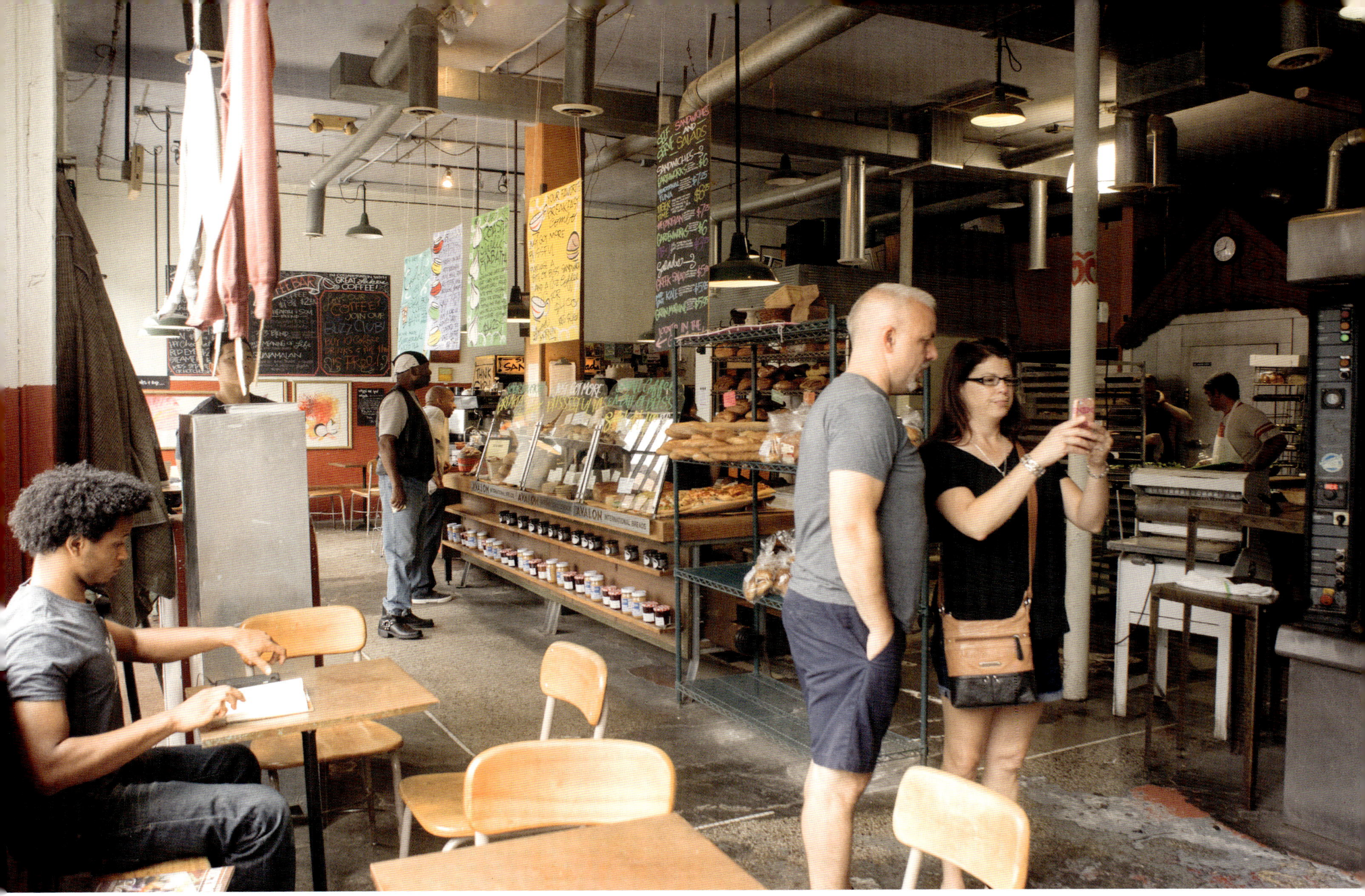

Avalon Bakery was established in 1997 in a former furniture store that then became the Willis Art Gallery. The floor and walls are exactly as the owners found them, and the interior is carefully curated using random fragments of the past. Chairs come from empty Detroit public schools and copper tables are from another coffee shop. An elegant architectural detail from a mansion in Brush Park seems to float above an industrial refrigerator. The baked goods are artisanal, the menu boards handwritten. Ava on, a comfortable and unpretentious place to relax, exemplifies the interest in the past among trendy venues. 422 West Willis Street, Detroit, 2015.

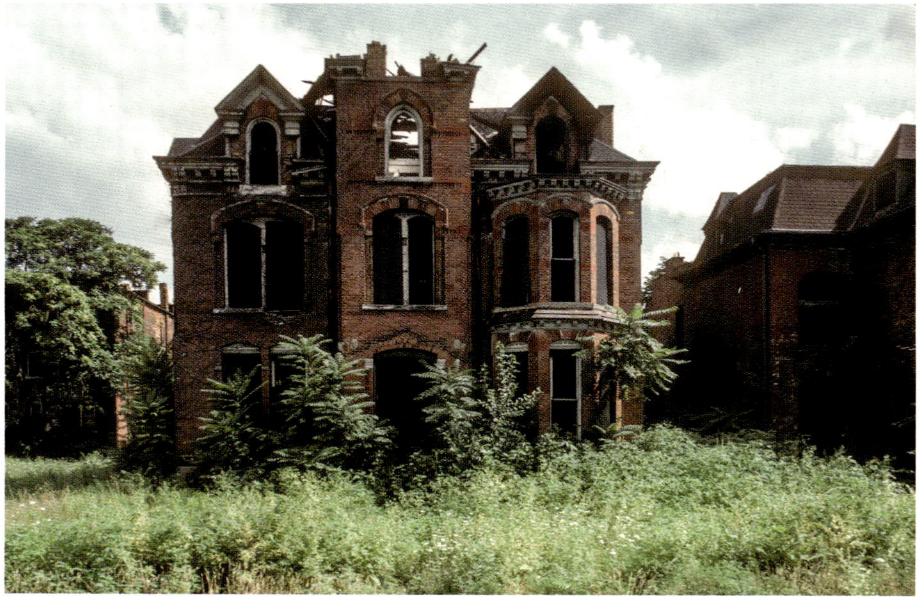

The Edmund in ruins. It was built in 1885 for a lumber baron named Lucien Moore. Edmund Place west of John R Street, Detroit, 1987.

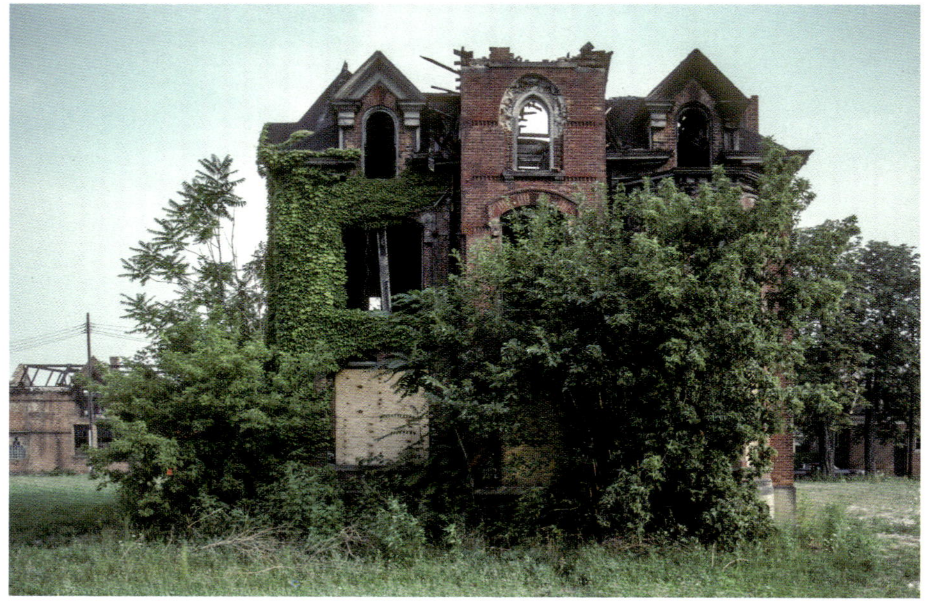

The Edmund overgrown by trees. Edmund Place west of John R Street, Detroit, 2000.

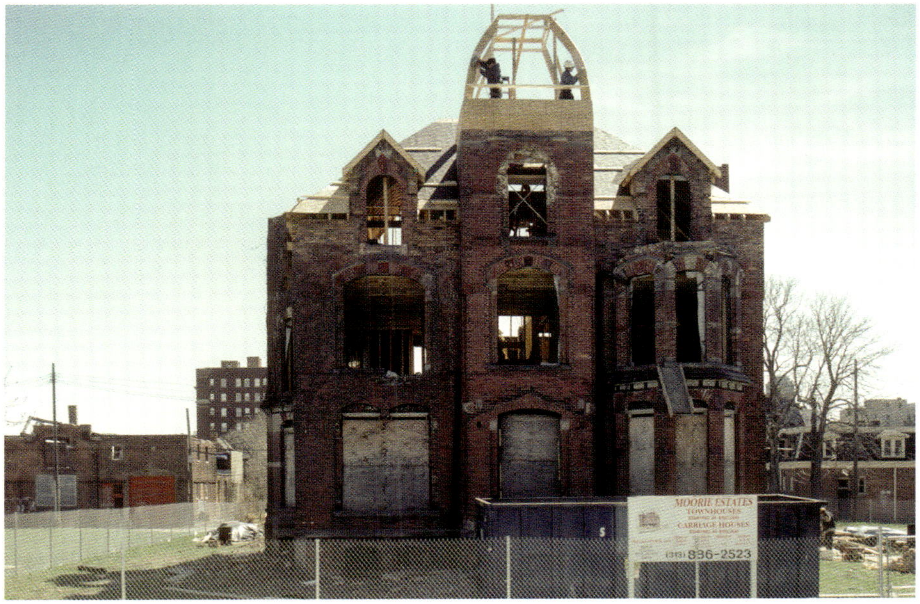

The Edmund being rehabilitated. Edmund Place west of John R Street, Detroit, 2005.

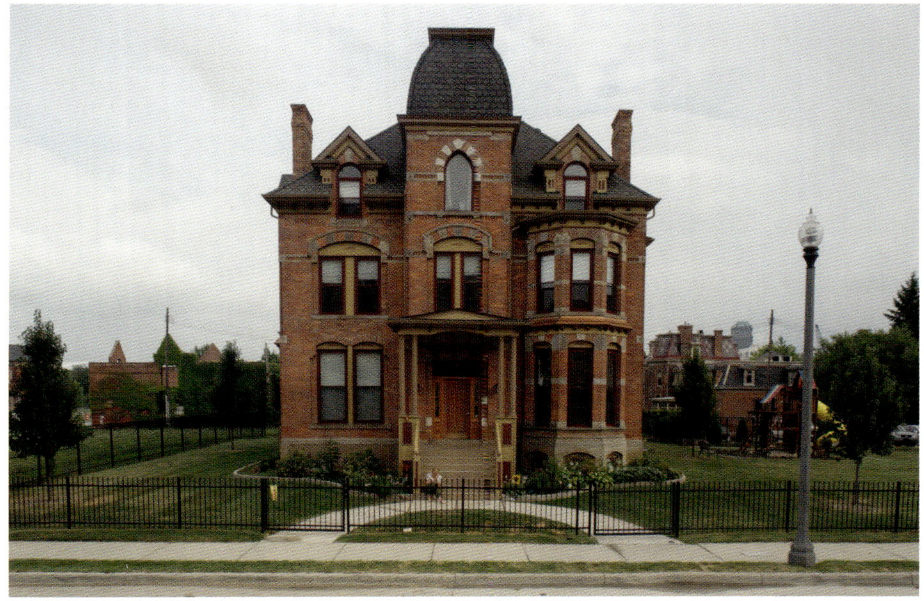

The Edmund. Edmund Place west of John R Street, Detroit, 20ˉ5.

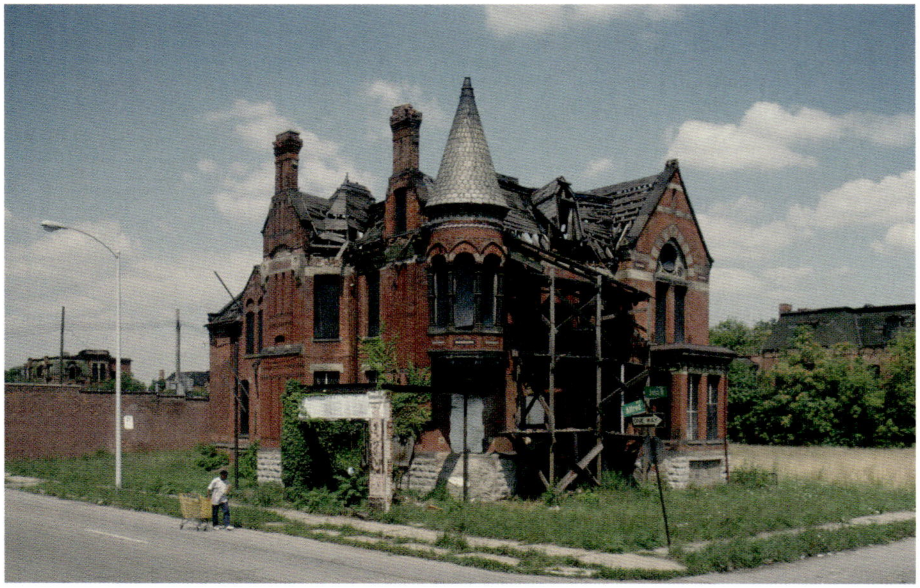

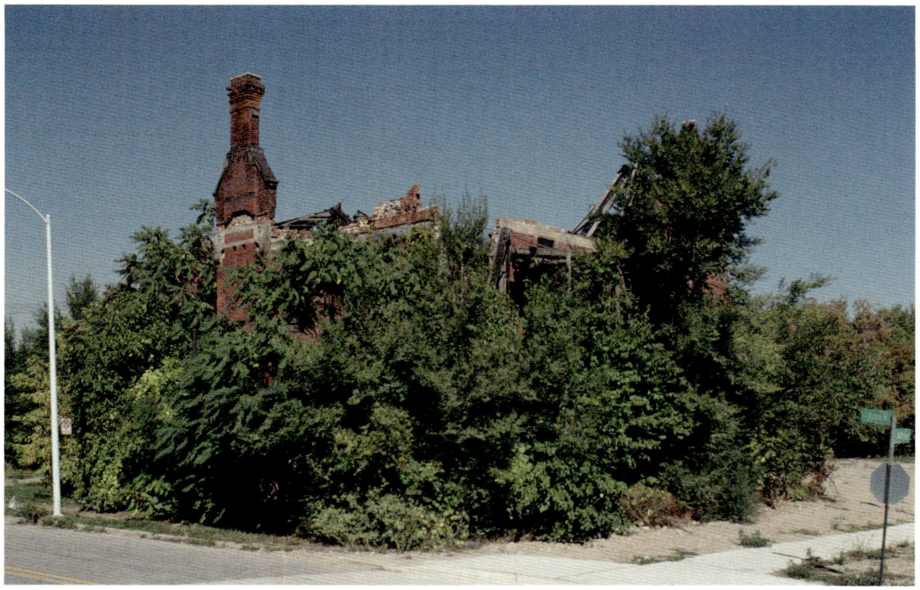

Above Ransom Gillis Mansion. Alfred Street at John R Street, Detroit, 1993.
Below Ransom Gillis Mansion. Alfred Street at John R Street, Detroit, 2002.

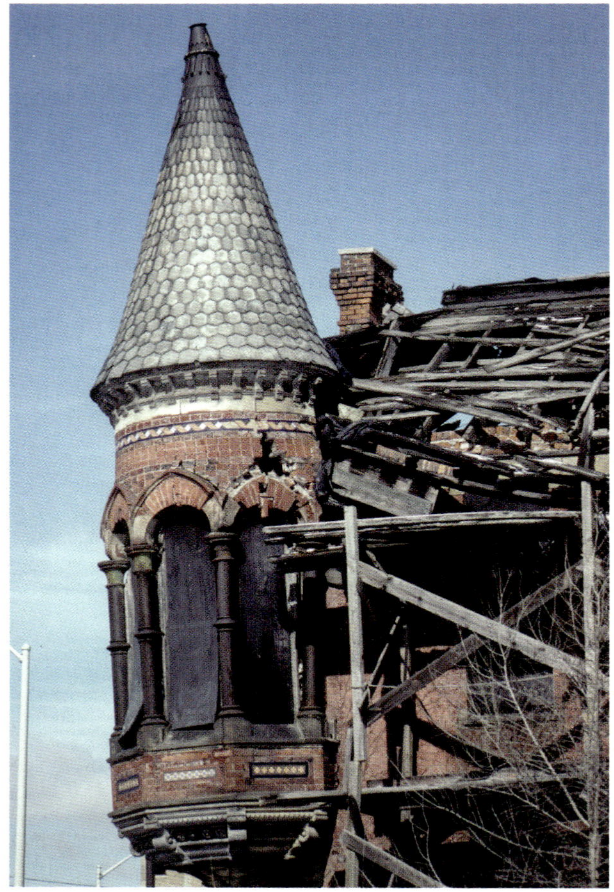

This photograph of a ruined, picturesque turret has been frequently posted online by viewers. The turret was replaced twice, the second time faithfully to the original. Ransom Gillis Mansion, Alfred at John R Streets, Detroit. 1998

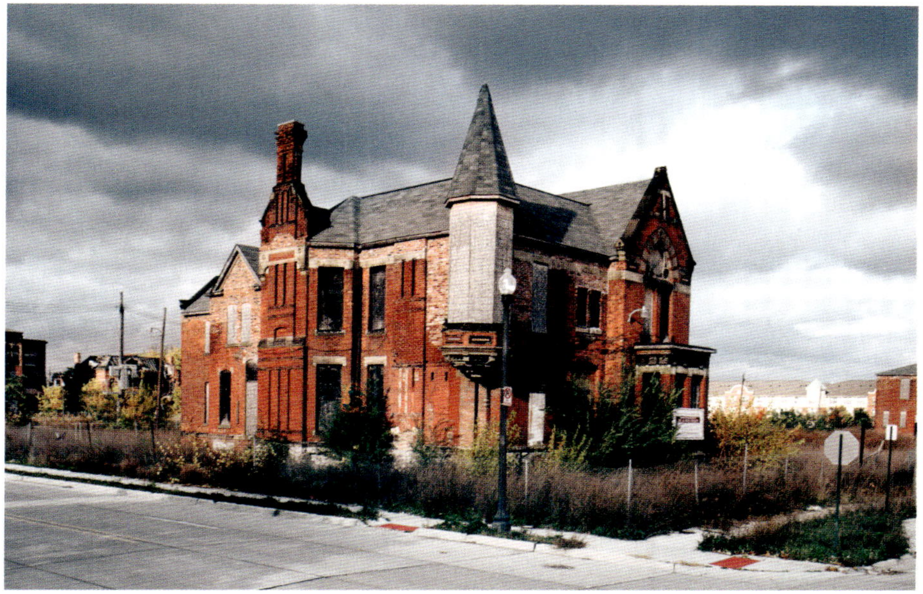

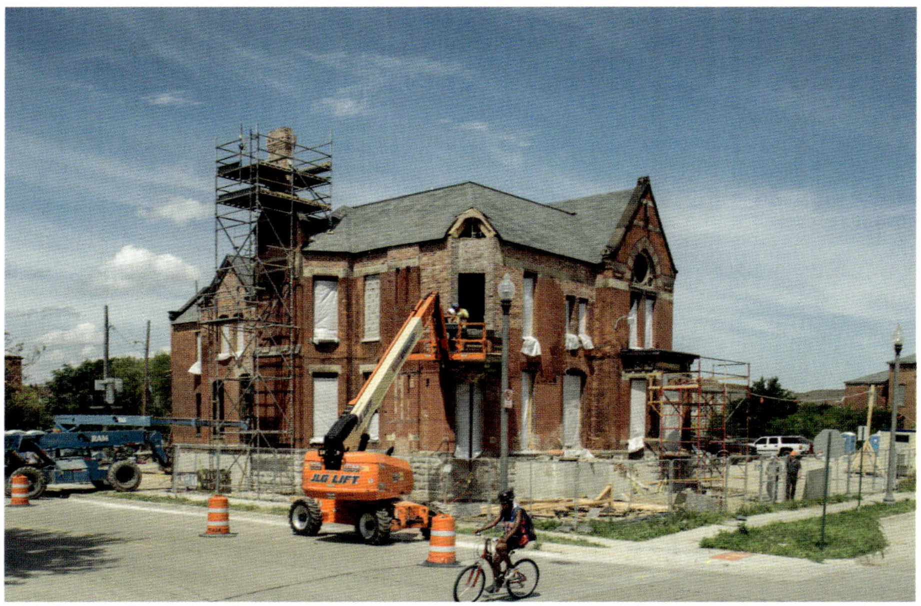

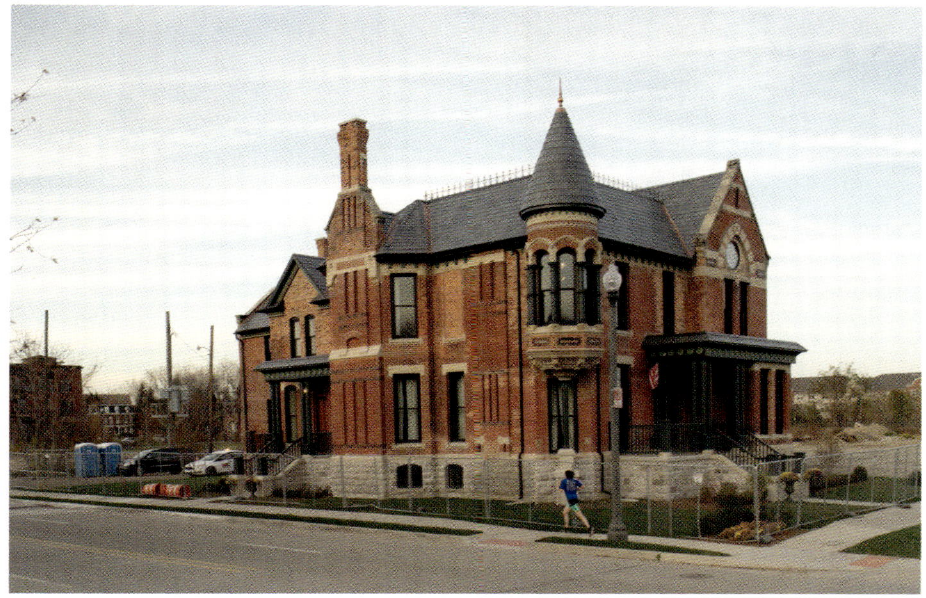

Above Ransom Gillis Mansion. The city partially refurbished the mansion with a simplified tower, and then it stood empty for eight years. Alfred Street at John R Street, Detroit, 2007.

Opposite below Ransom Gillis Mansion. When the rehabilitation was taken over to show on a television program, the decision was made to bring back the building to its original form, which meant tearing down the replacement tower that the city had built in 2007. Alfred Street at John R Street, Detroit, August 2015.

Above Restored Ransom Gillis Mansion: the rehabilitation comes close to the original, minus one window and a chimney. Alfred Street at John R Street, Detroit, November 2015.

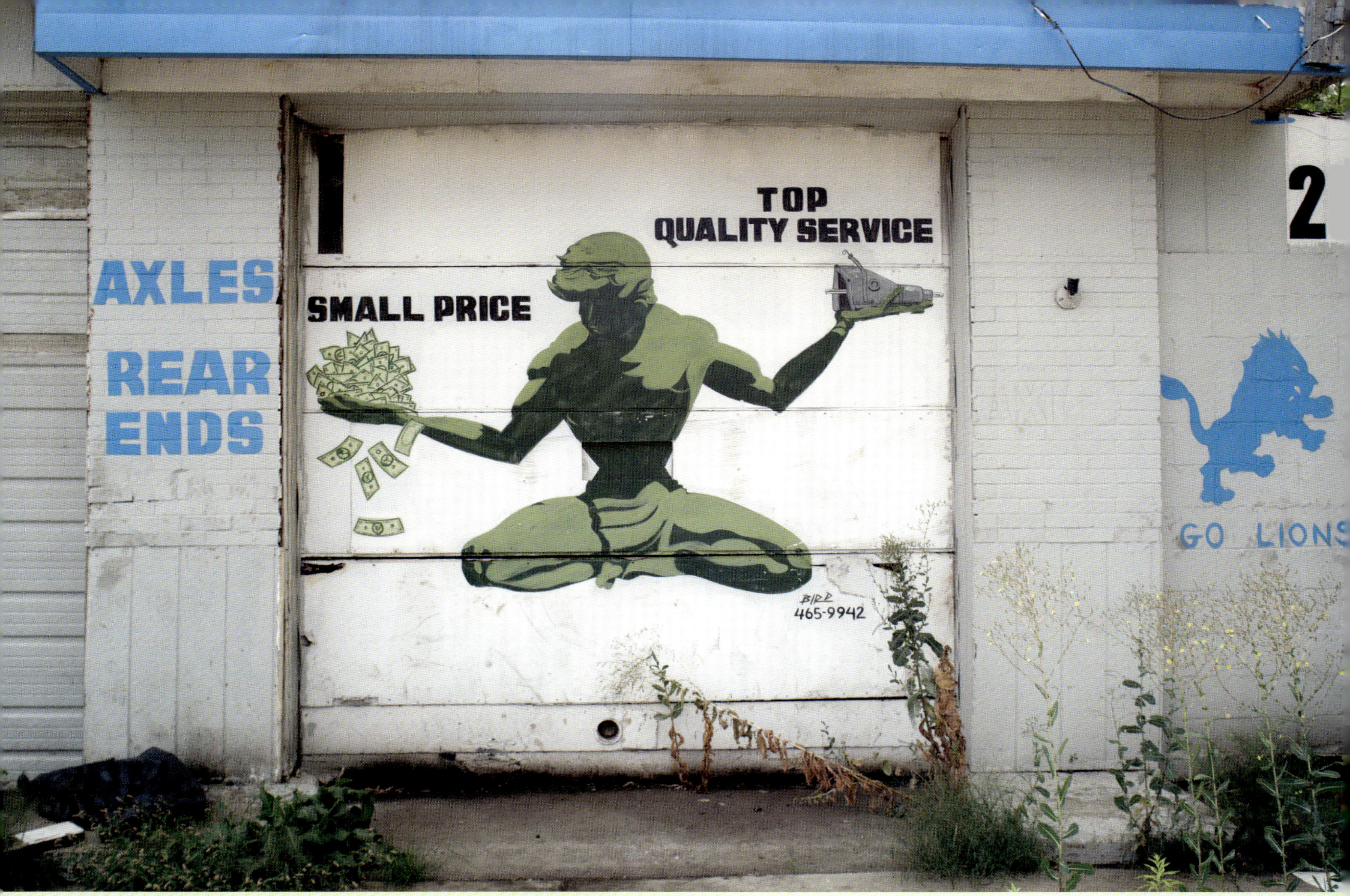

Painting advertising the former Rob's Makin' It Happen Transmissions. Bird, a local artist, painted this sign using the *Spirit of Detroit* statue as a model. In the sign, instead of the human family, the right hand holds dollar bills, and instead of a symbol of God, the left hand holds a transmission. Bird charged $450 for this work.
12930 McNichols Road, Detroit, 2015.

URBAN FABRIC

TRACES OF PAST GRANDEUR Detroit was built with pride and to last. In its libraries, schools, police stations, mansions, and many other buildings, statues commissioned by the German and Italian communities pay tribute to Schiller and Dante, and impressive civic monuments celebrate locally born heroes and politicians. Beaux arts mansions often stand precariously in neighborhoods such as Boston Edison and Indian Village, their new owners lacking the resources to properly maintain them. Even when these opulent buildings seem well-kept, there is always a derelict mansion nearby. Some impressive commercial buildings, fountains, mausoleums, libraries, and greenhouses have been continually funded and remain in good condition. But in the four decades since the completion of the Renaissance Center, nothing reminiscent of Detroit's golden age of grandeur has emerged.

In 1993, Arthur Johnson, a Wayne State University official, used the struggle of a poor family to maintain a palatial dwelling as a metaphor for Detroit. For Johnson, the city was a prize and a burden, "a big mansion, left for a poor family to keep. They cannot heat it, they cannot provide air conditioning, they cannot paint it or keep up the grounds because they don't have the means to do so. As long as they stay they prevent the fixtures from being stolen, the pipes from freezing; they are the ones who keep the water running and put out the fires. If they manage to preserve it, it would be for those who stay."

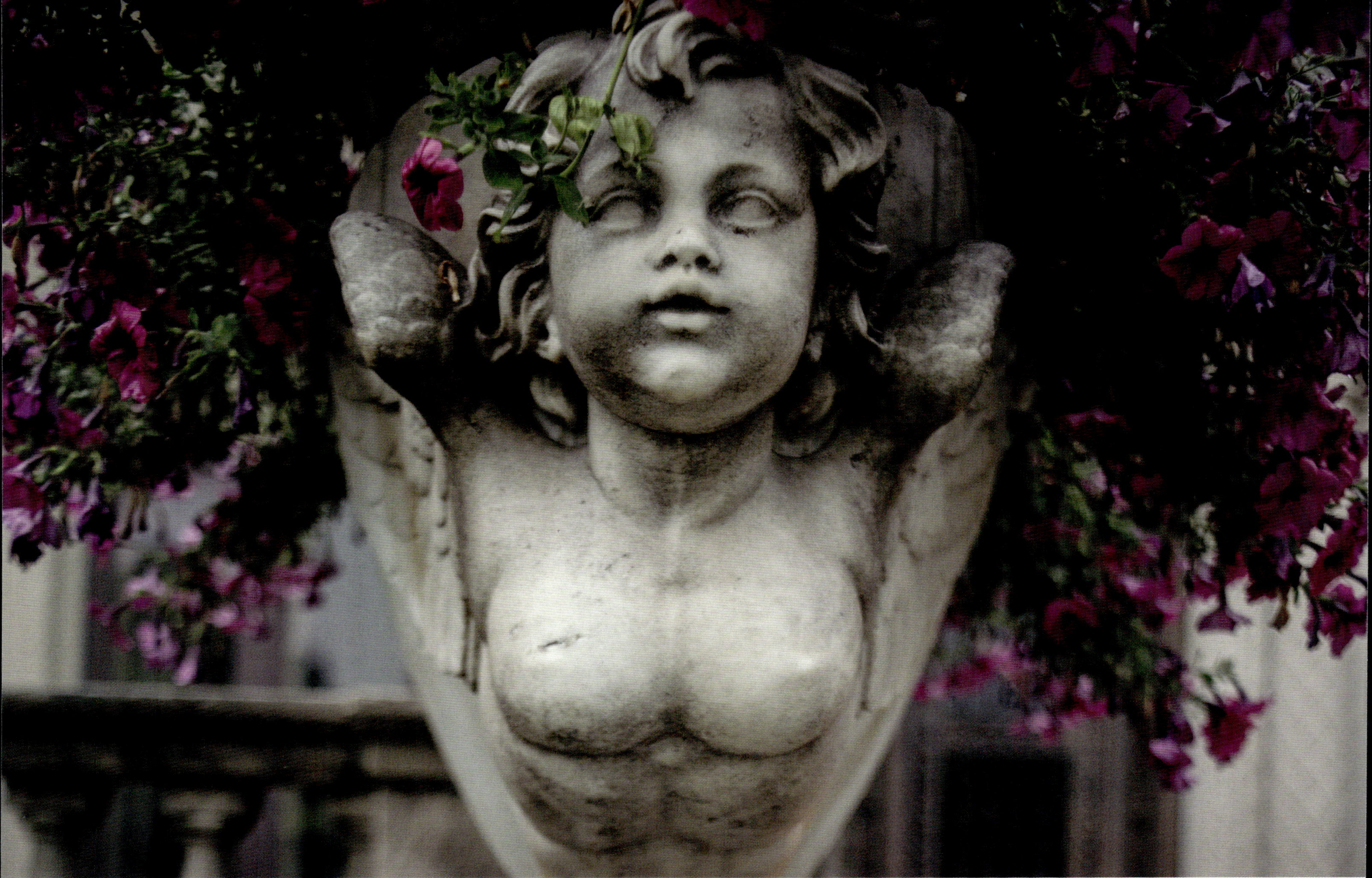

Classical statuary planter at the former Barry Gordy Motown Mansion.
918 West Boston Boulevard, Detroit, 2015.

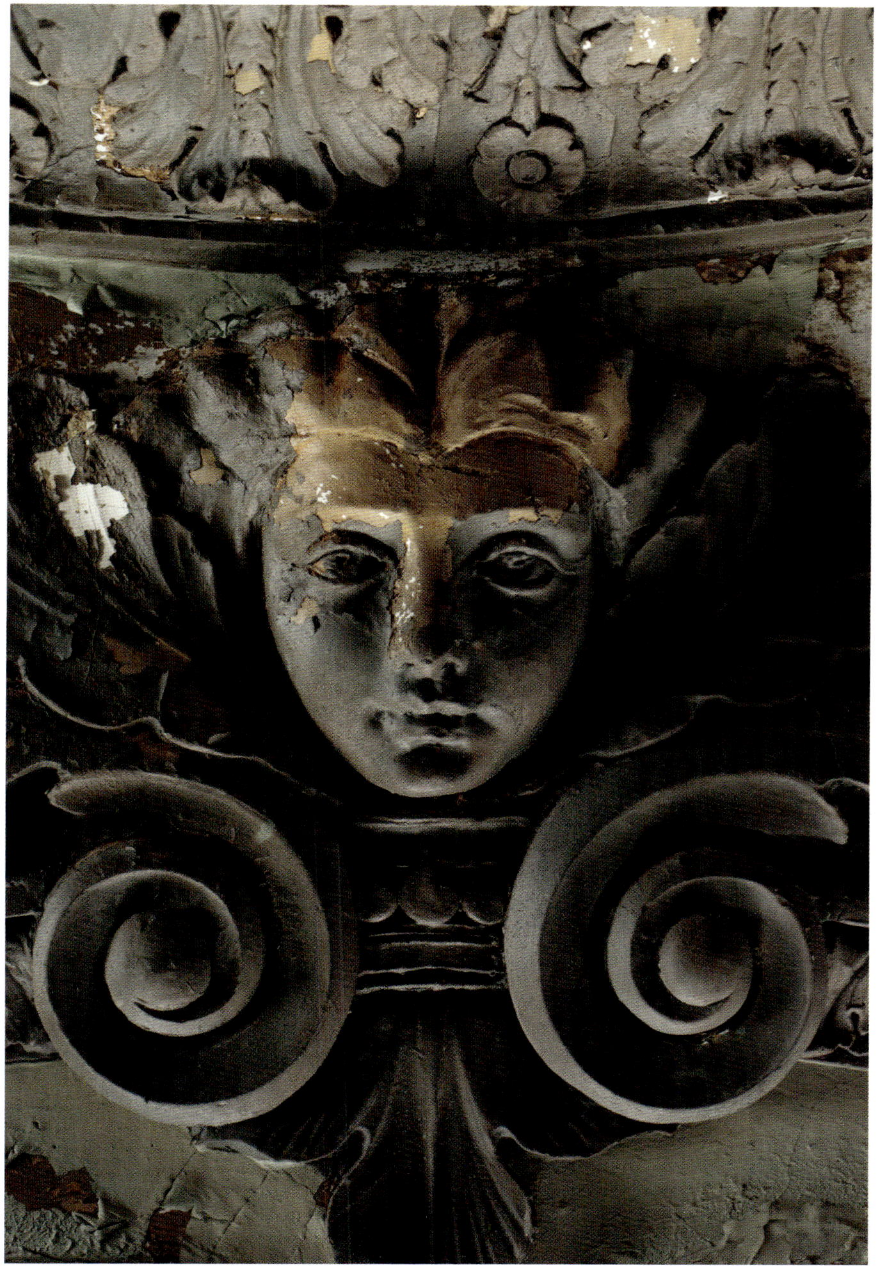

Decorative face, lobby of former Michigan Theater. 220 Bagley Avenue, Detroit, 2014.

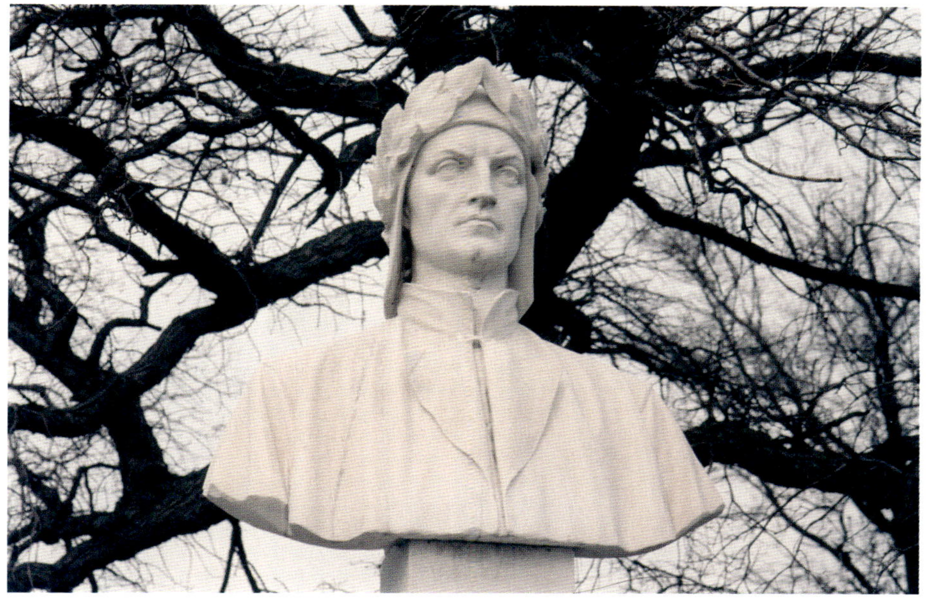

Bust of Dante Alighieri, its majesty enhanced by the surrounding trees. The inscription reads: "Raffaelo Romanelli, Erected by the Italian Community of Detroit in 1927." Belle Isle, Detroit, 2009.

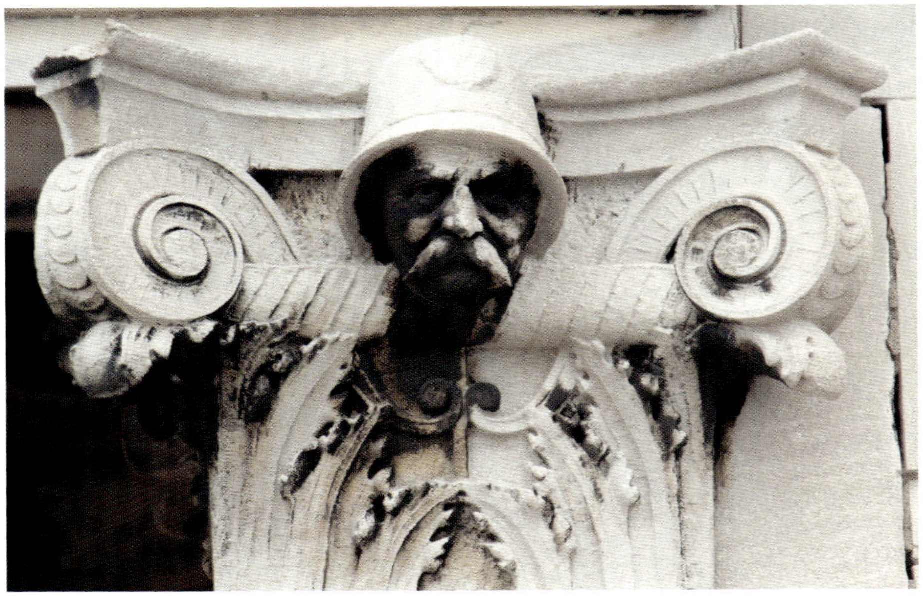

In this classical pilaster, the hyper-realistic head of a police officer is organically integrated into the capital. Former Third Precinct Police Station, DuBois Street at Hunt Street, Detroit, 2011.

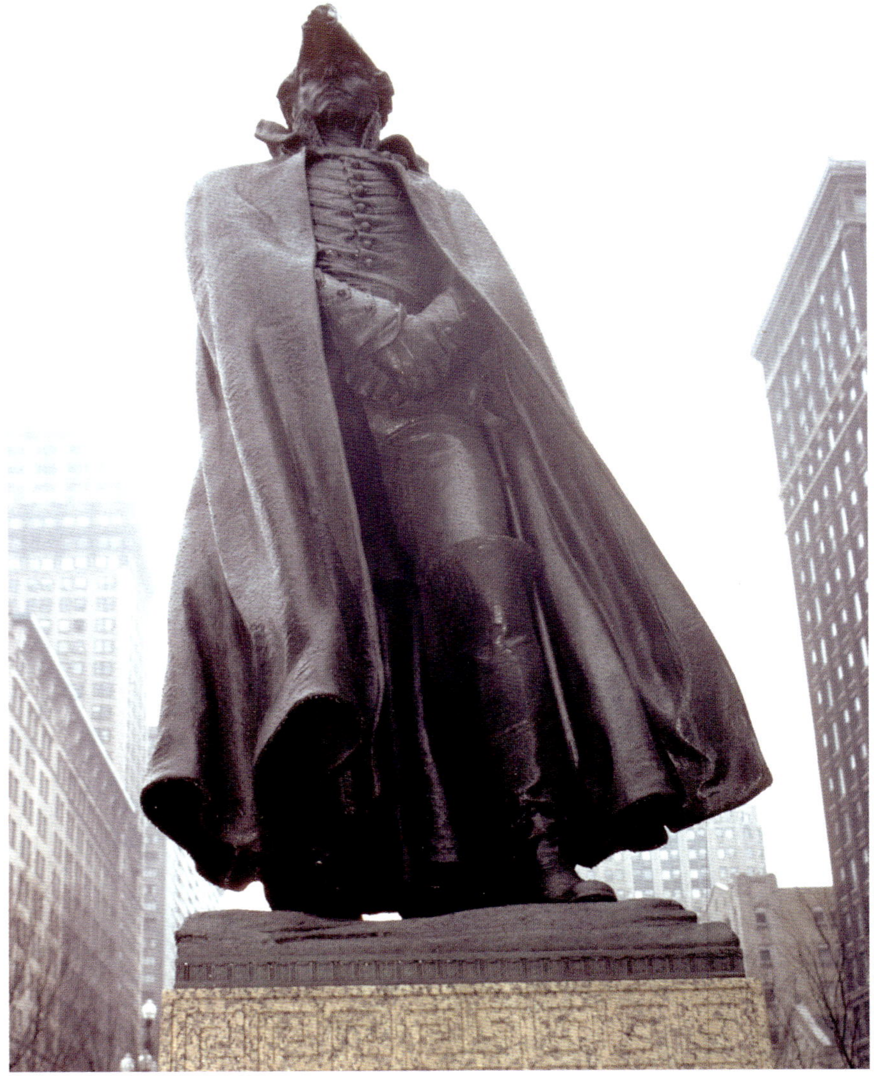

Alexander Macomb, a hero in the War of 1812, was born in Detroit. The sculptor Adolph Alexander Weinman "portrayed Macomb as a dashing officer whose vitality is suggested by the slightly off-center stance of the figure and furl of the wind-blown cape," wrote Dennis Alan Nawrocki in his book *Art in Detroit Public Places*. Washington Boulevard at Michigan Avenue, Detroit, 2006.

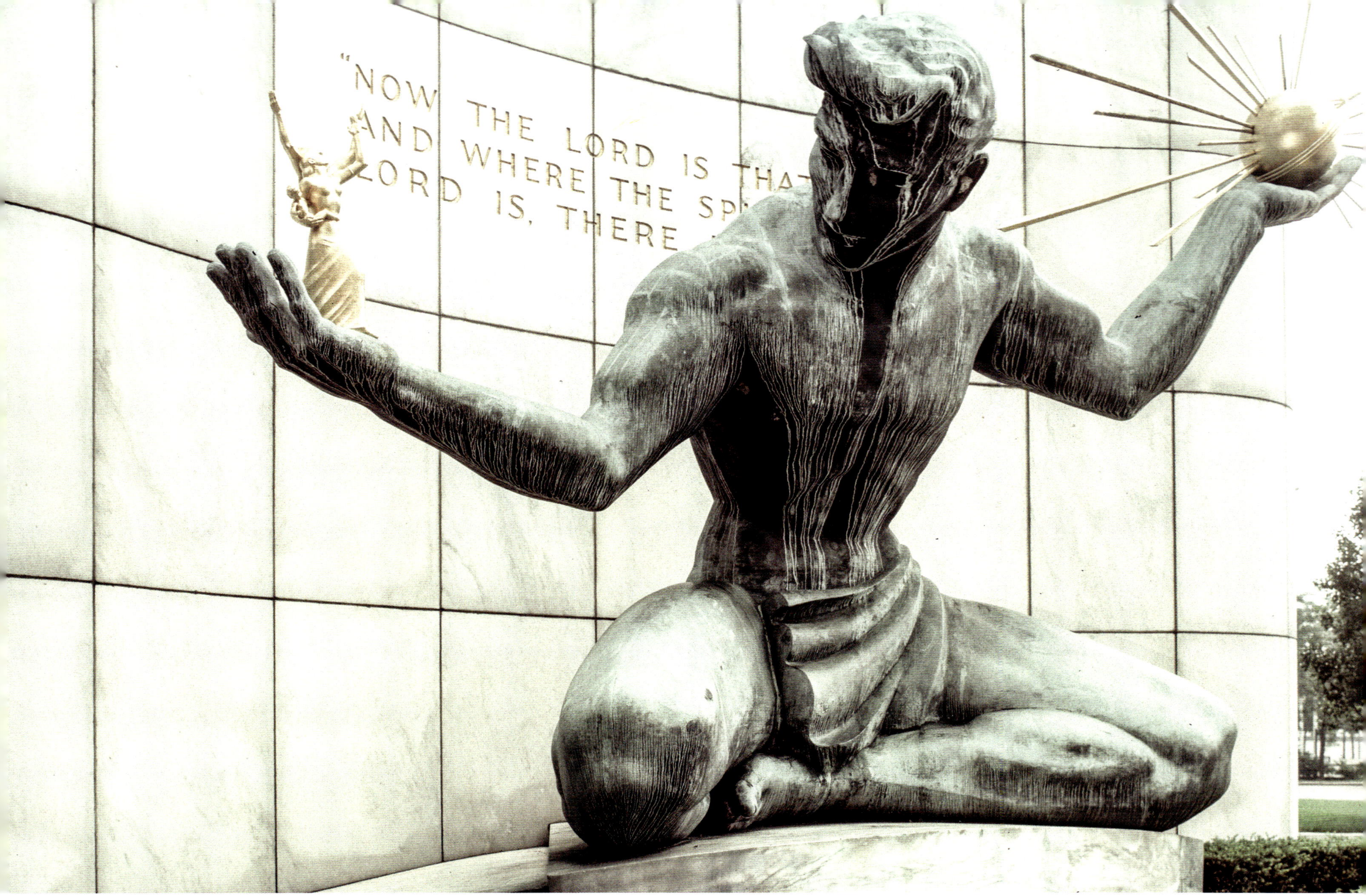

Spirit of Detroit, by Marshall Fredericks, unveiled in 1958. The dated imagery and the green patina earned it the nickname "The Jolly Green Giant." Woodward Avenue at East Jefferson, Detroit, 1993.

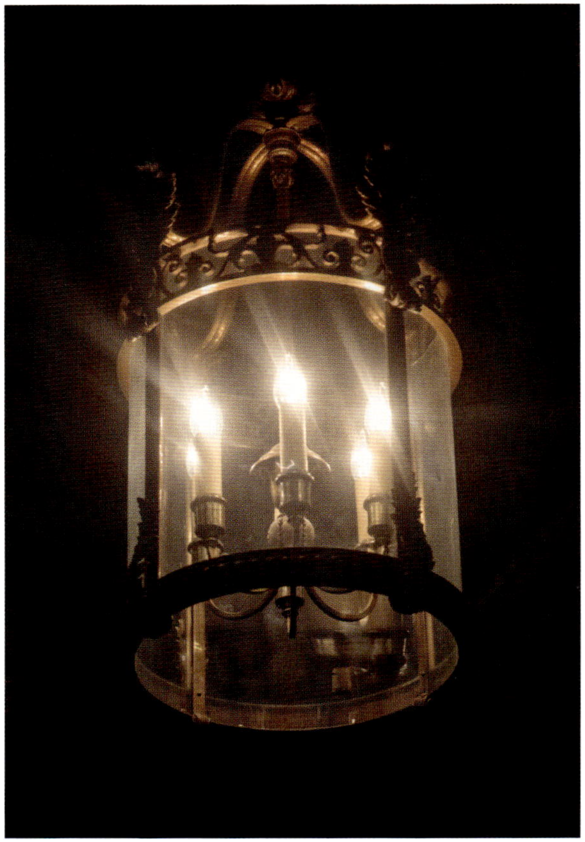

Light fixture, Detroit Public Library. 5201 Woodward Avenue, Detroit, 2014.

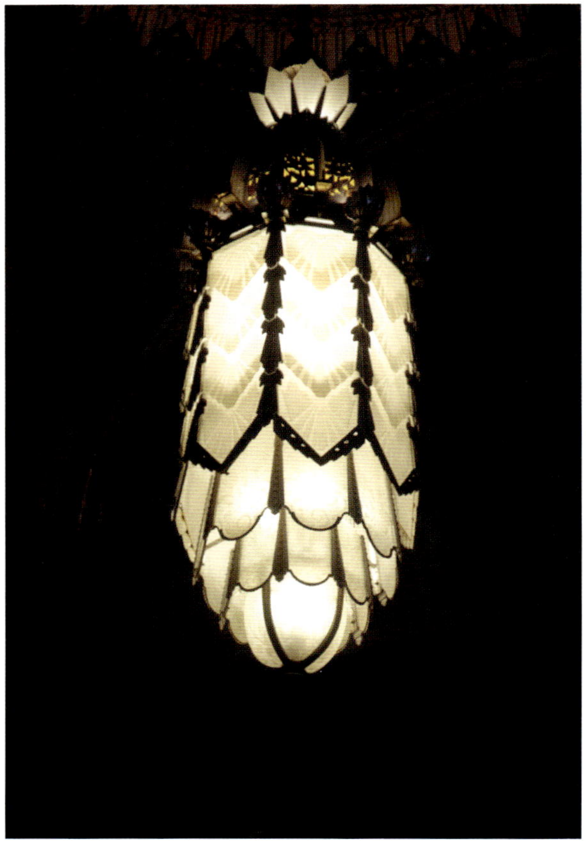

Art deco light fixture in the lobby of the Fisher Building. 3011 West Grand Boulevard, Detroit, 2012.

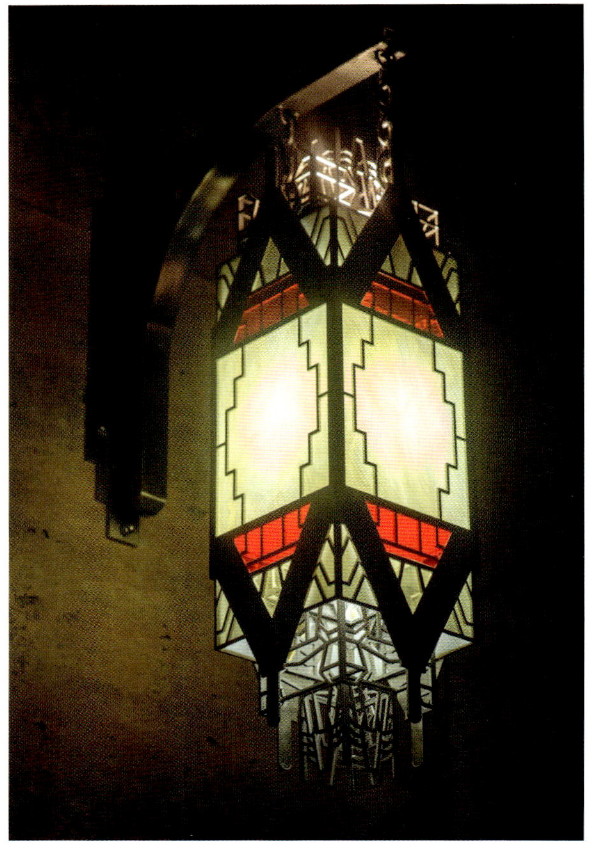

Art deco light fixture made of amber glass imported from Czechoslovakia; Guardian Building, completed in 1929. Griswold Street at West Congress Street, Detroit, 2014.

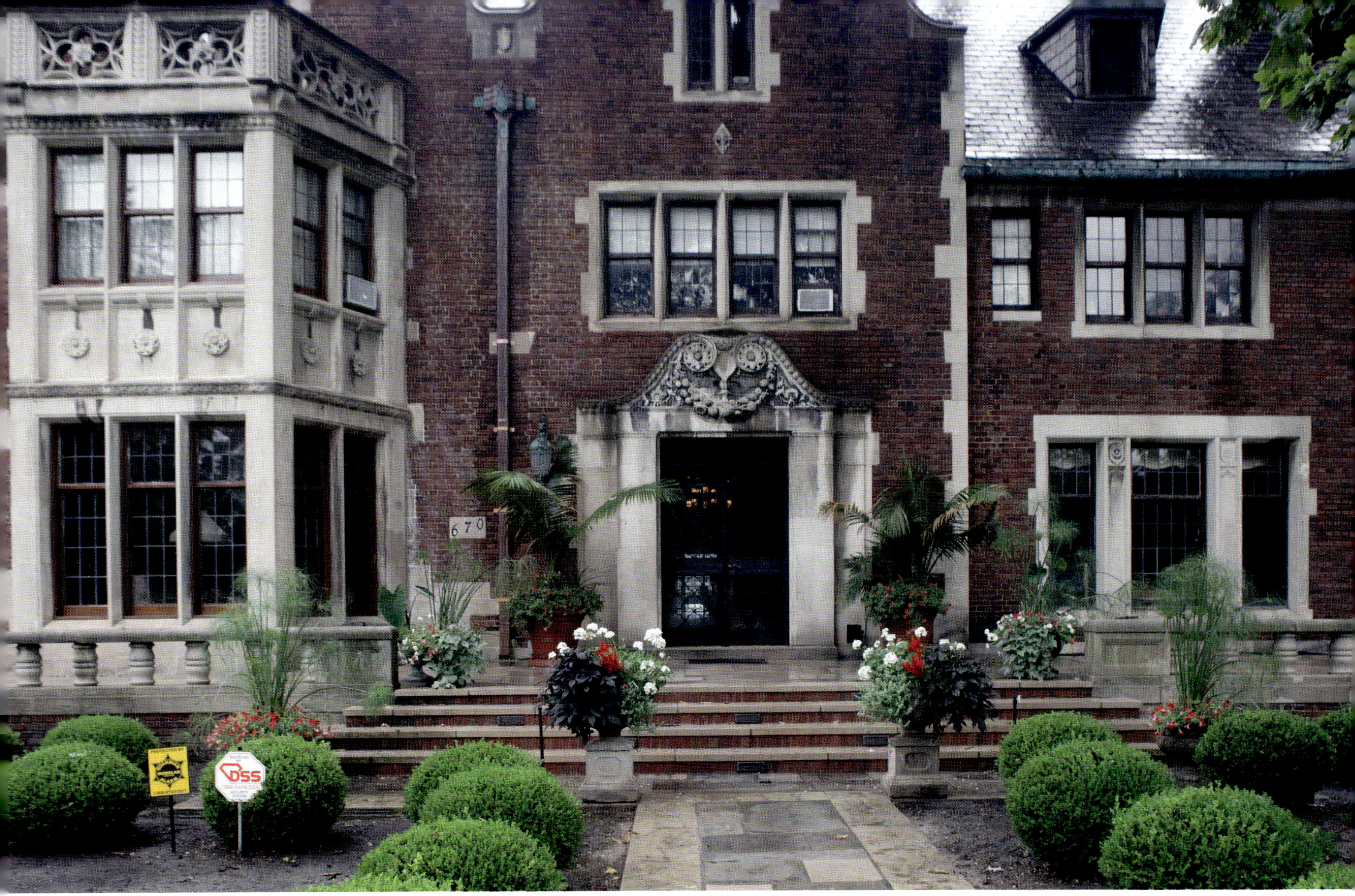

Magnificent Tudor-style mansion built in 1915 for Charles Fisher.
670 West Boston Boulevard, Detroit, 2015.

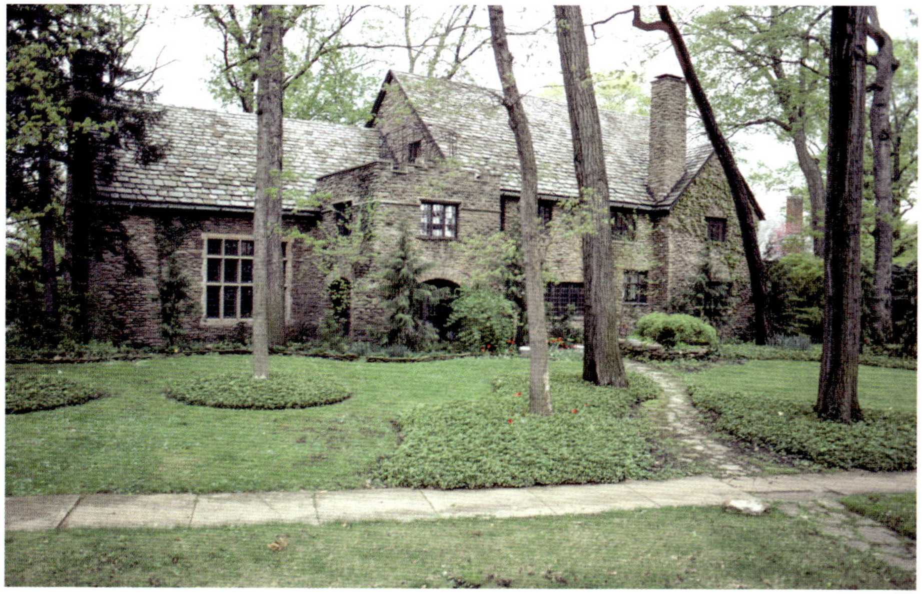

Mansion. Burlington Drive at Strathcona Drive, Palmer Woods, Detroit, 2008.

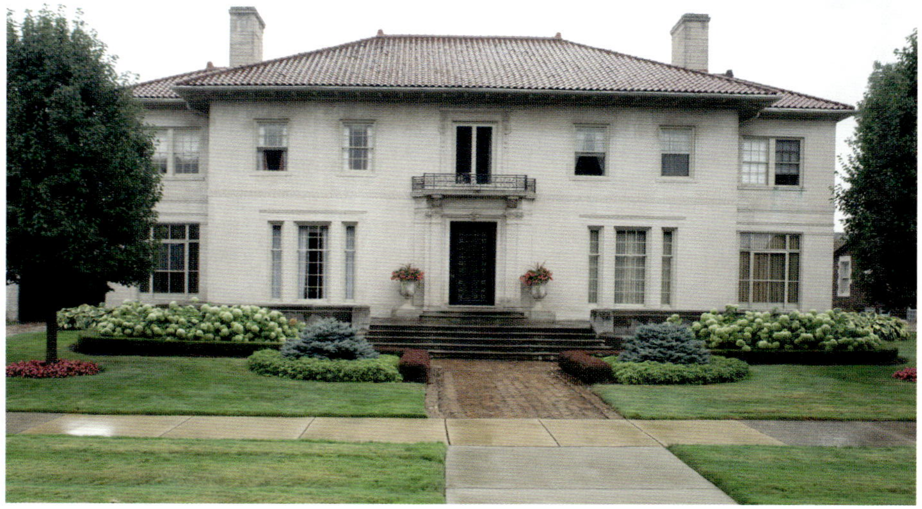

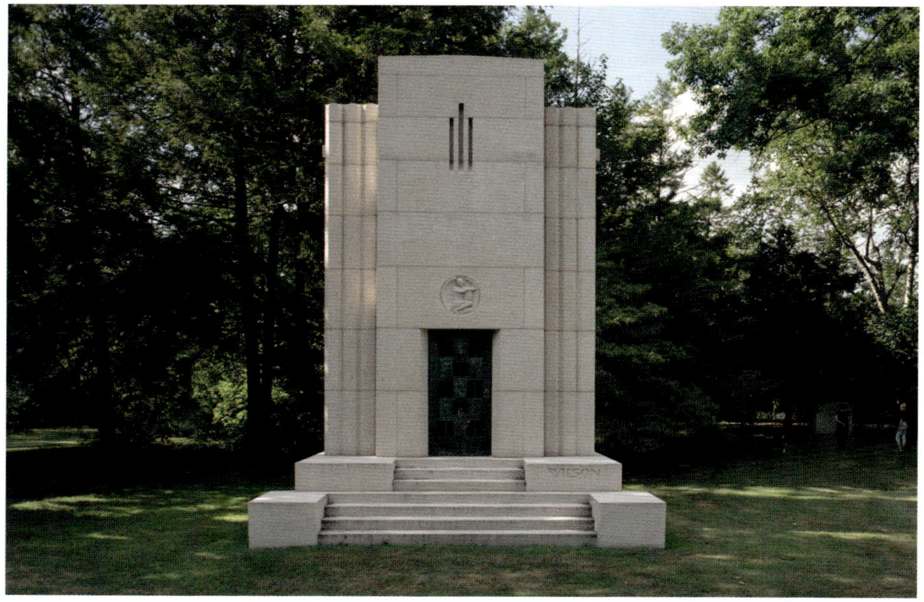

Above Italianate mansion built for Fred Fisher in 1917. 54 Arden Park Boulevard, Detroit, 2015.

Below Wilson mausoleum, an art deco-style gem designed in 1939 by architect William Henry Deacy. Woodlawn Cemetery, Detroit, 2015.

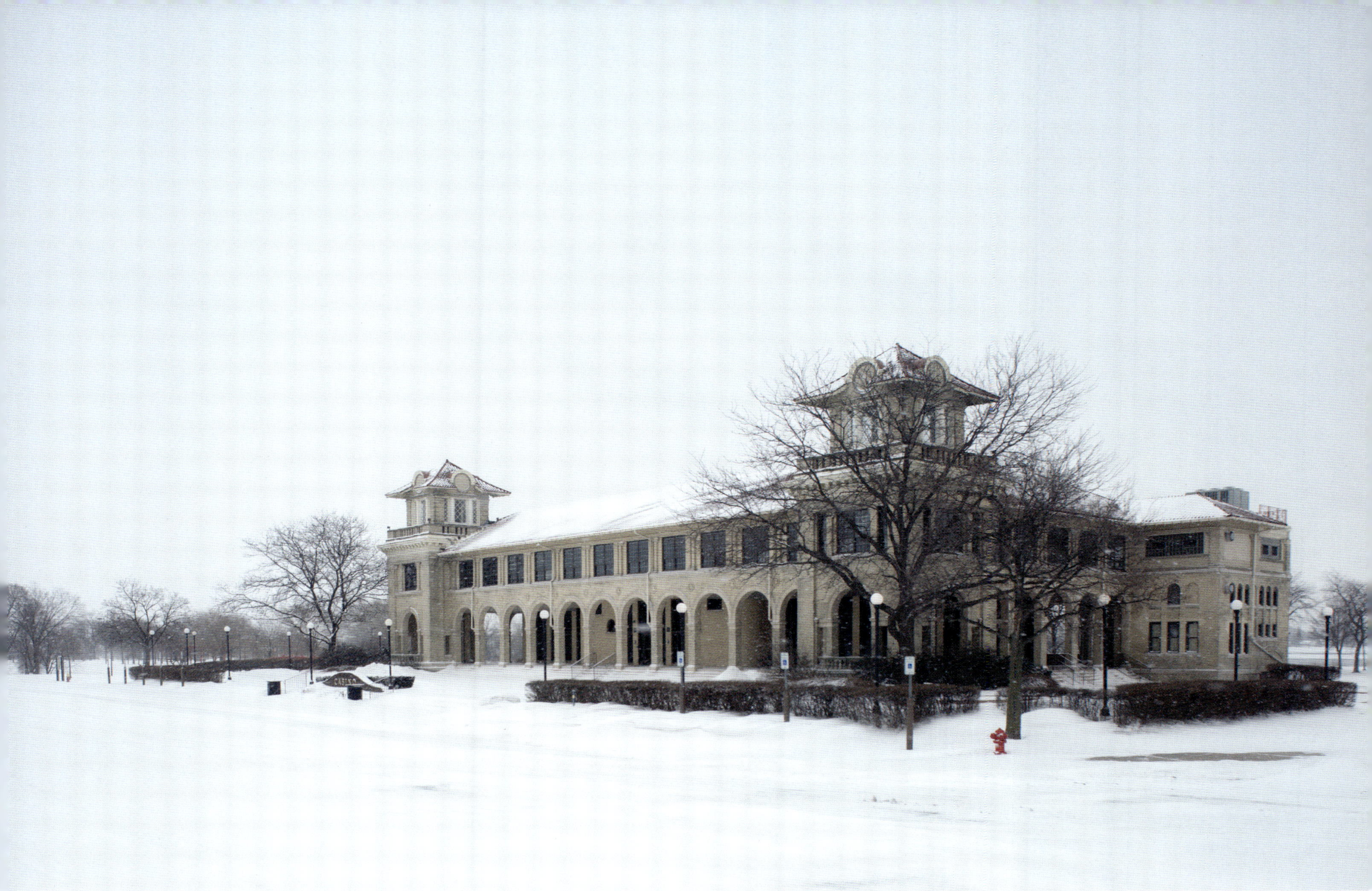

Belle Isle Casino, completed in 1908 by the firm Van Leyen and Schilling. Detroit, 2014.

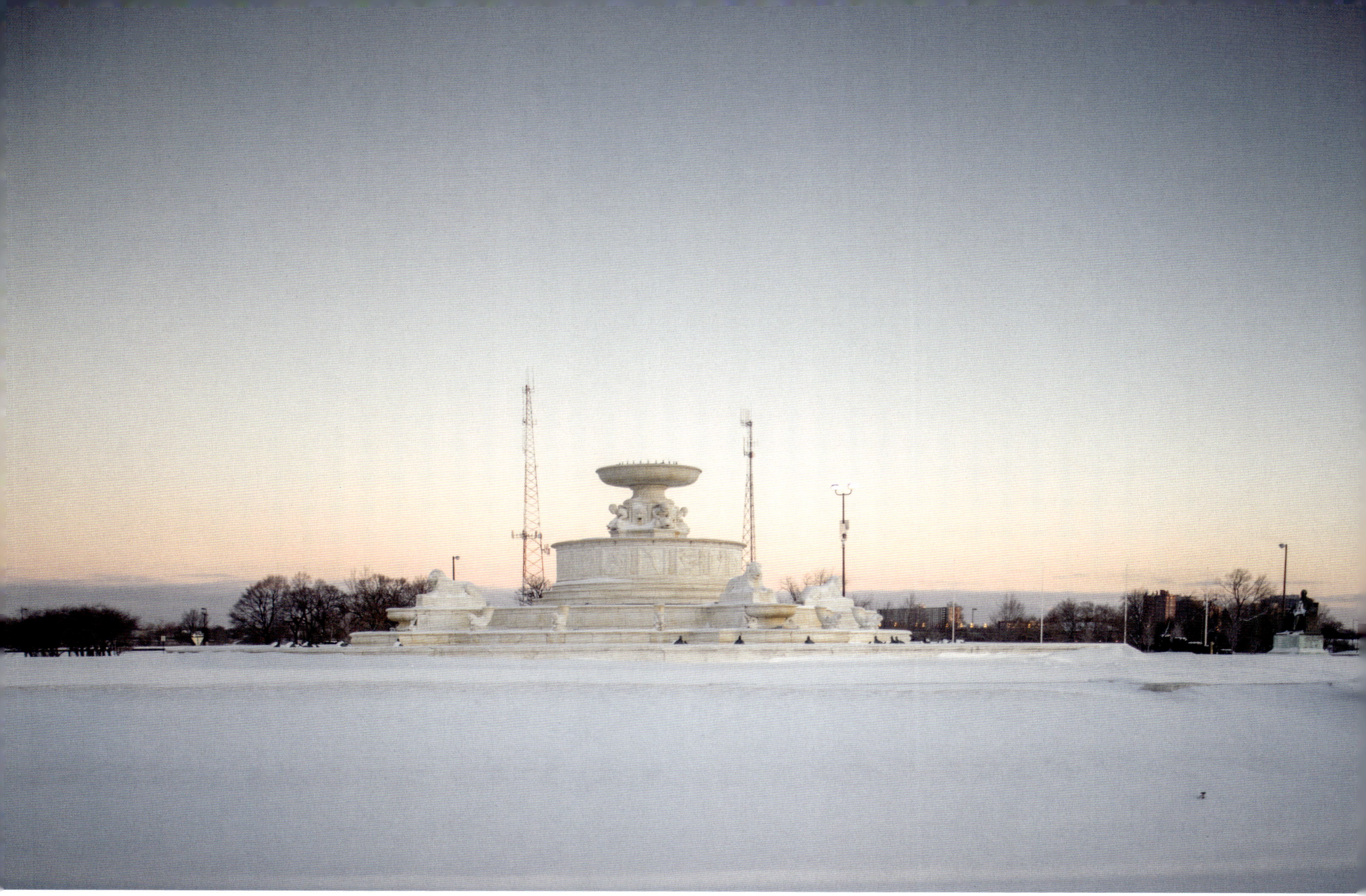

James Scott Fountain, in the beaux arts tradition, designed by Cass Gilbert and completed in 1925. Belle Isle, Detroit, 2015.

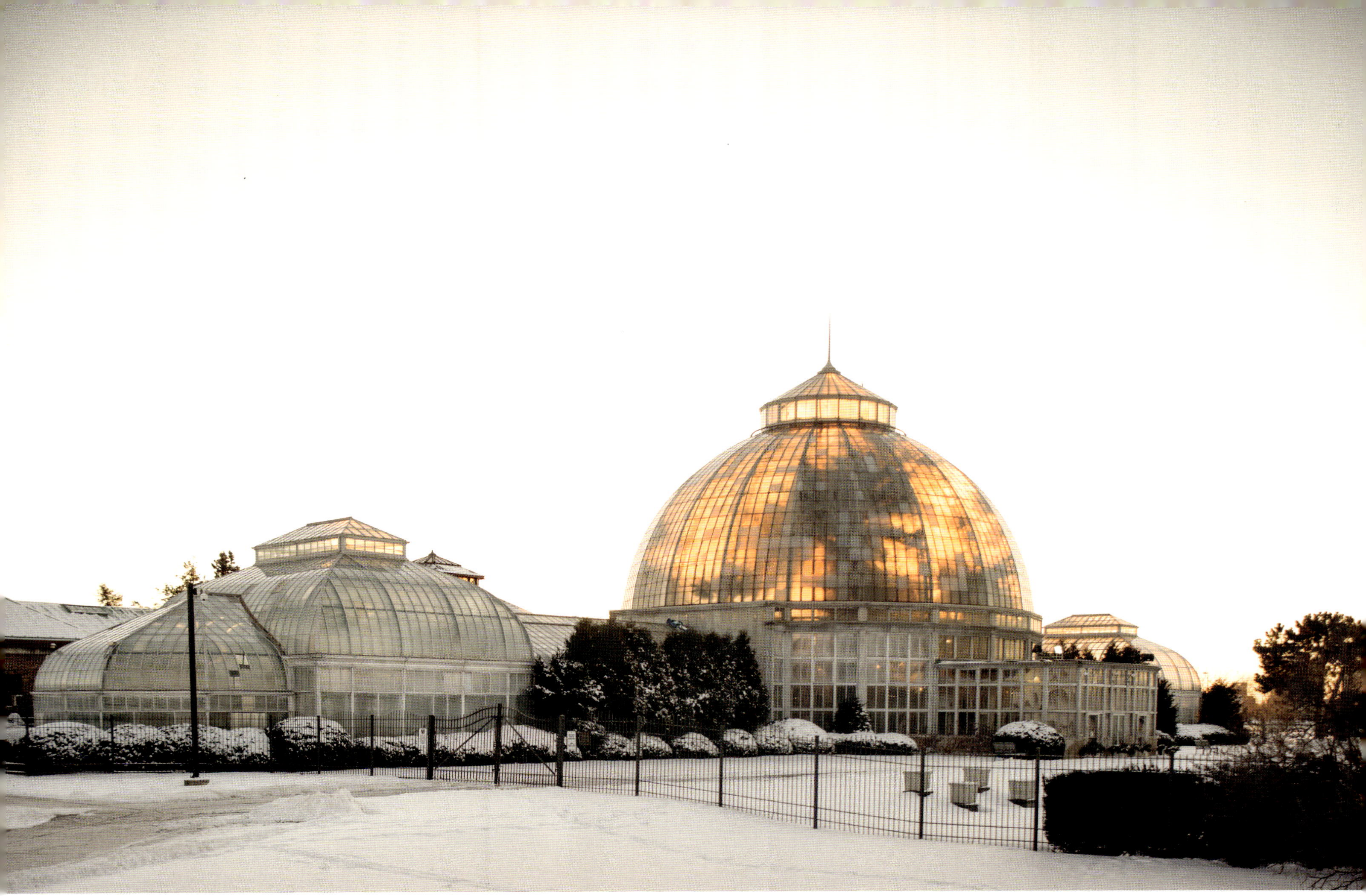

Anna Scripps Whitcomb Conservatory, designed by Albert Kahn in 1904. The conservatory is famous for its orchids. Belle Isle, Detroit, 2015.

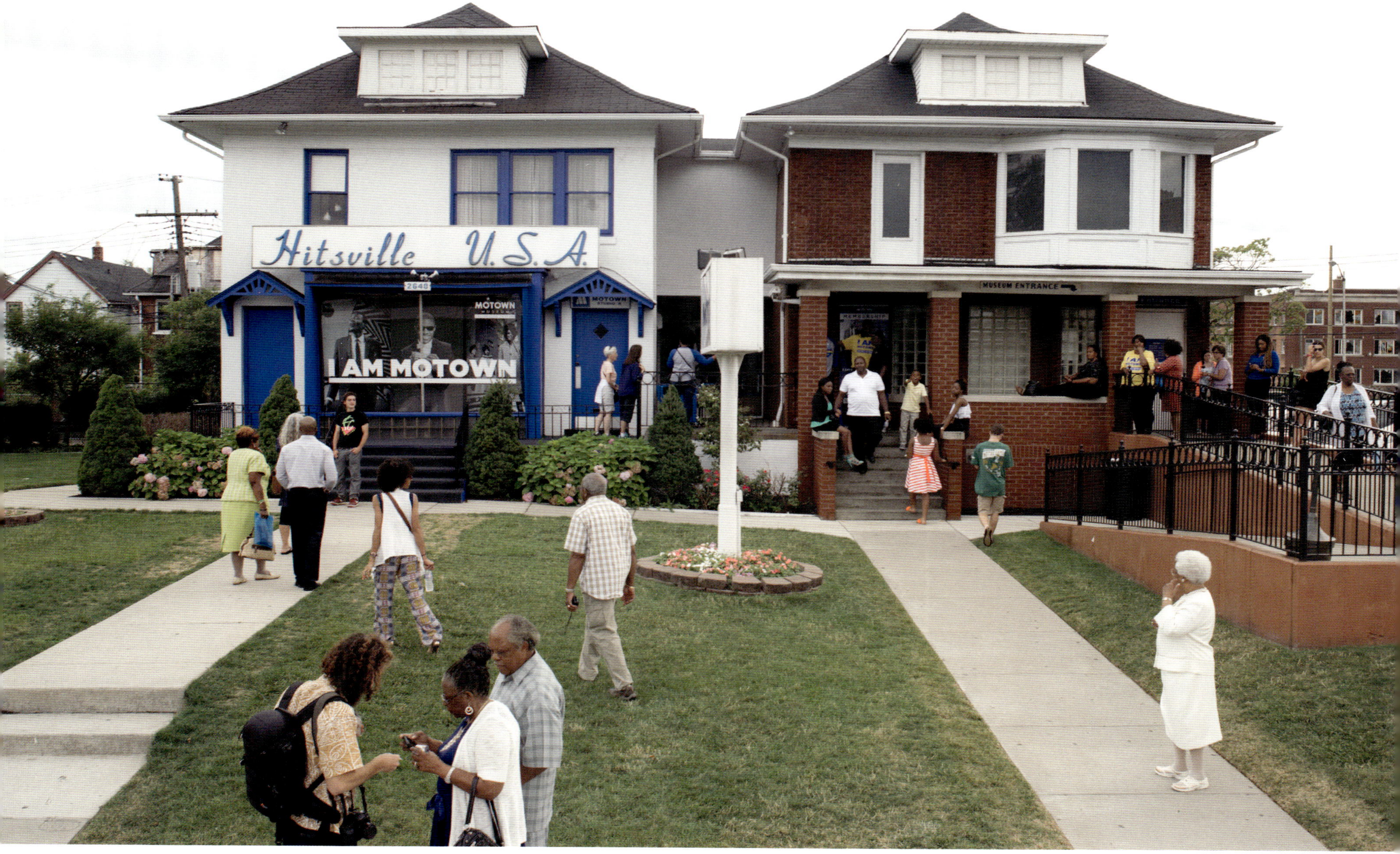

"Hitsville USA," Motown Museum, founded in 1985 by Esther Gordy Edwards. The Supremes, The Temptations, Marvin Gaye, and The Jackson Five recorded their most memorable hits at this modest house. 2648 West Grand Boulevard, Detroit, 2015.

NEIGHBORHOOD LANDMARKS Among the plethora of important buildings in Detroit are impressive synagogues, churches, libraries, schools, and warehouses. The Vanity Ballroom, on the National Register of Historic Sites, was designed in an Aztec Revival style by architect Charles N. Agree in 1929. The dance floor accommodated a thousand couples. Duke Ellington, Benny Goodman, and Tommy Dorsey played there. It is now abandoned and stripped of some of its decoration. The ground floor commercial space was last used as headquarters for voting registration and as a pizza parlor.

Dom Polski (Polish House) of 1913, adorned with the crowned eagle of the Polish Republic, was one of the city's several ethnic halls. Reverend Kevin Dean of the organization Detroit Love told me that the building had been saved because of its constant use as a storage place for salvageable items from houses targeted for demolition. His desire was to give it back "to the true community." "In 2015," he remarked, "the community is not Polish." The community is black, and black artists are trying to make visible the African American contribution shaping the city. For example, folk artist Sylvia Burke, in her now disappeared *The History of Detroit*, painted the white-owned landmarks of the city, such as the former GM Building and the Fisher Building, but she paired them with icons of African American Detroit, including the Motown Museum and the Stinson Funeral Home.

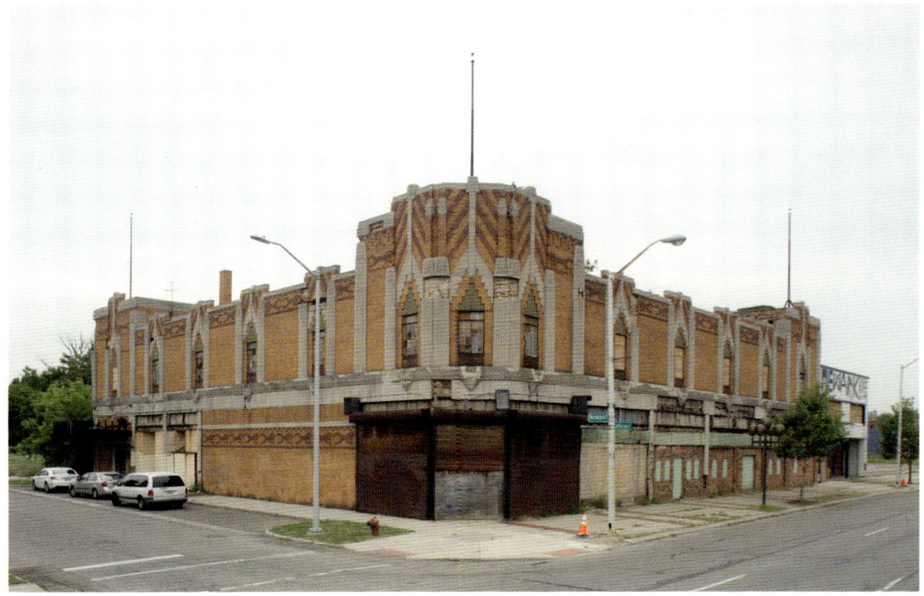

Vanity Ballroom, now abandoned. Newport Street at East Jefferson Avenue, Detroit, 2015.

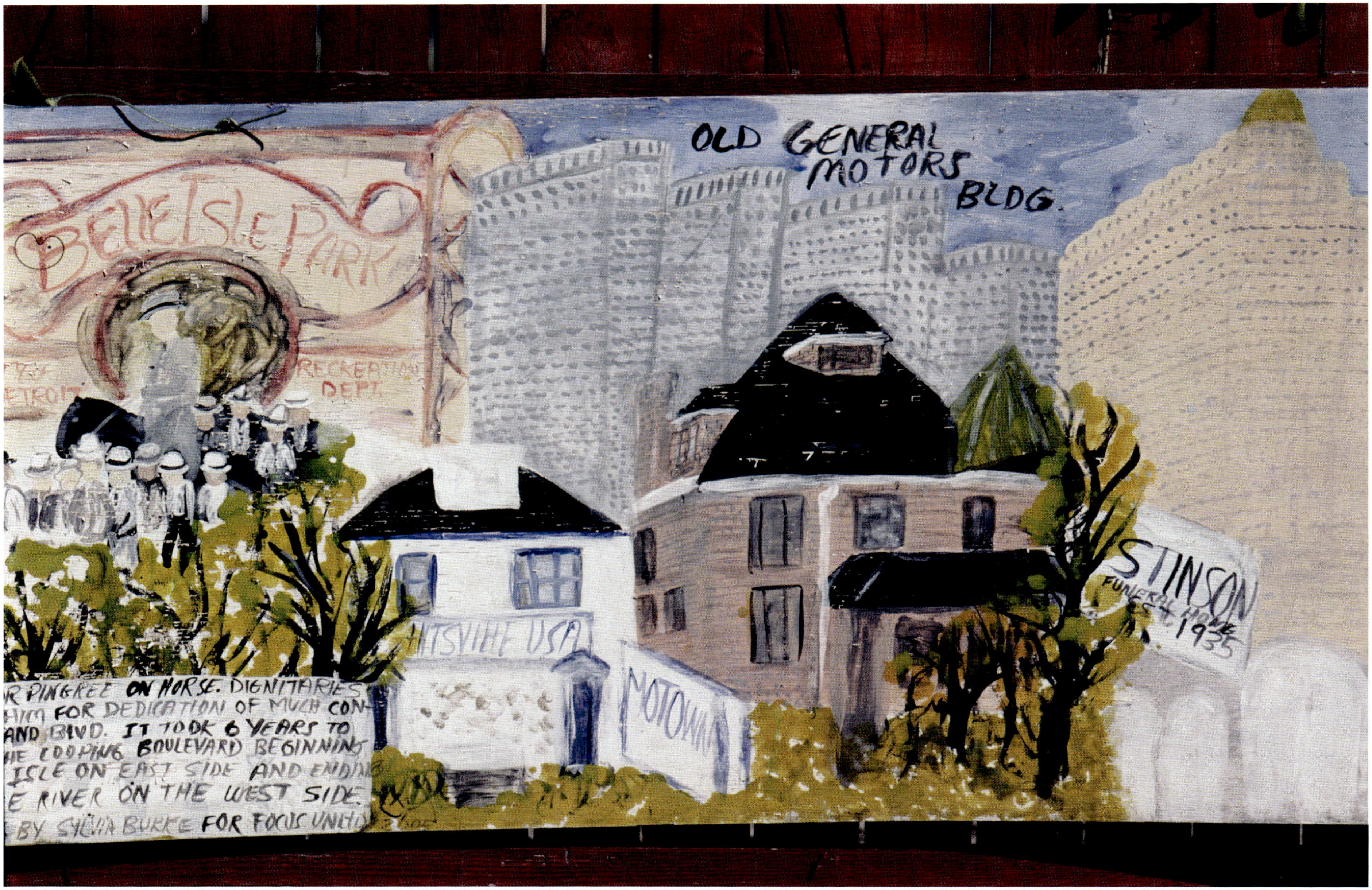

Sylvia Burke, detail of her mural, *The History of Detroit*, showing the Motown Museum and the old GM Building. 1776 West Grand Boulevard, Detroit, 2006.

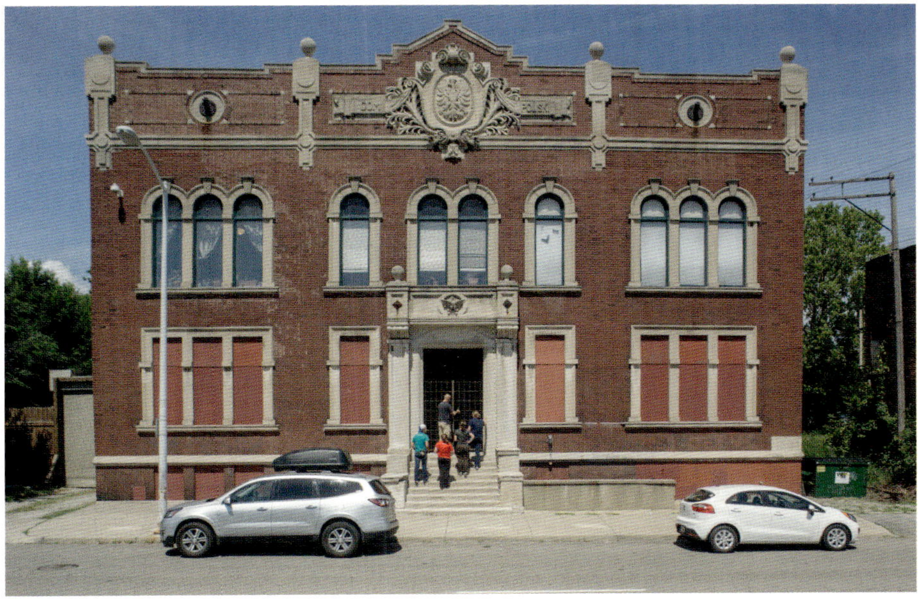

Dom Polski (Polish House, 1913). 2281 East Forest Avenue, Detroit, 2015.

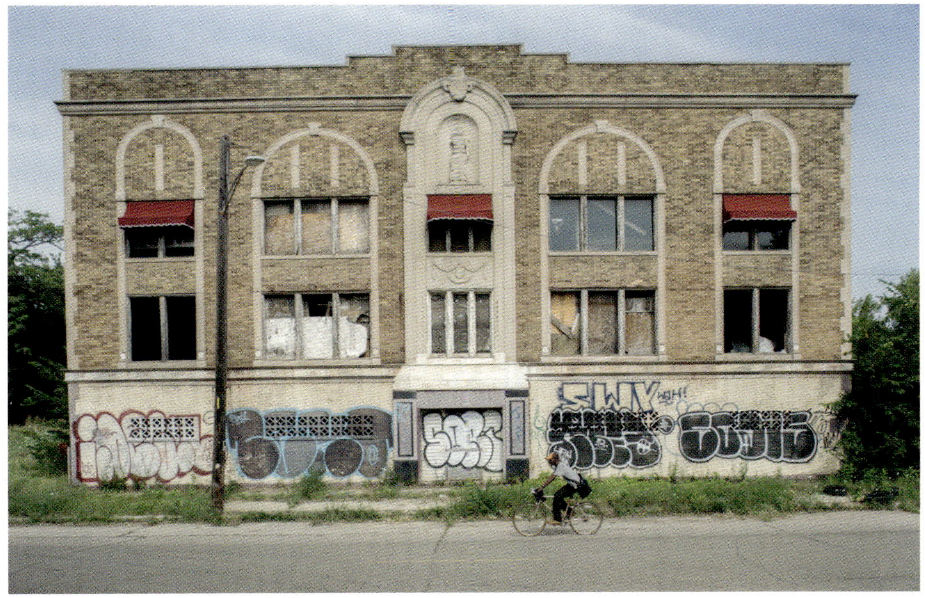

Slovak Home (1922), now in ruins. The words “Everlasting Life” remain from its subsequent use as The Promised Land Missionary Baptist Church. Strong Street at Frontenac Avenue, Detroit, 2015.

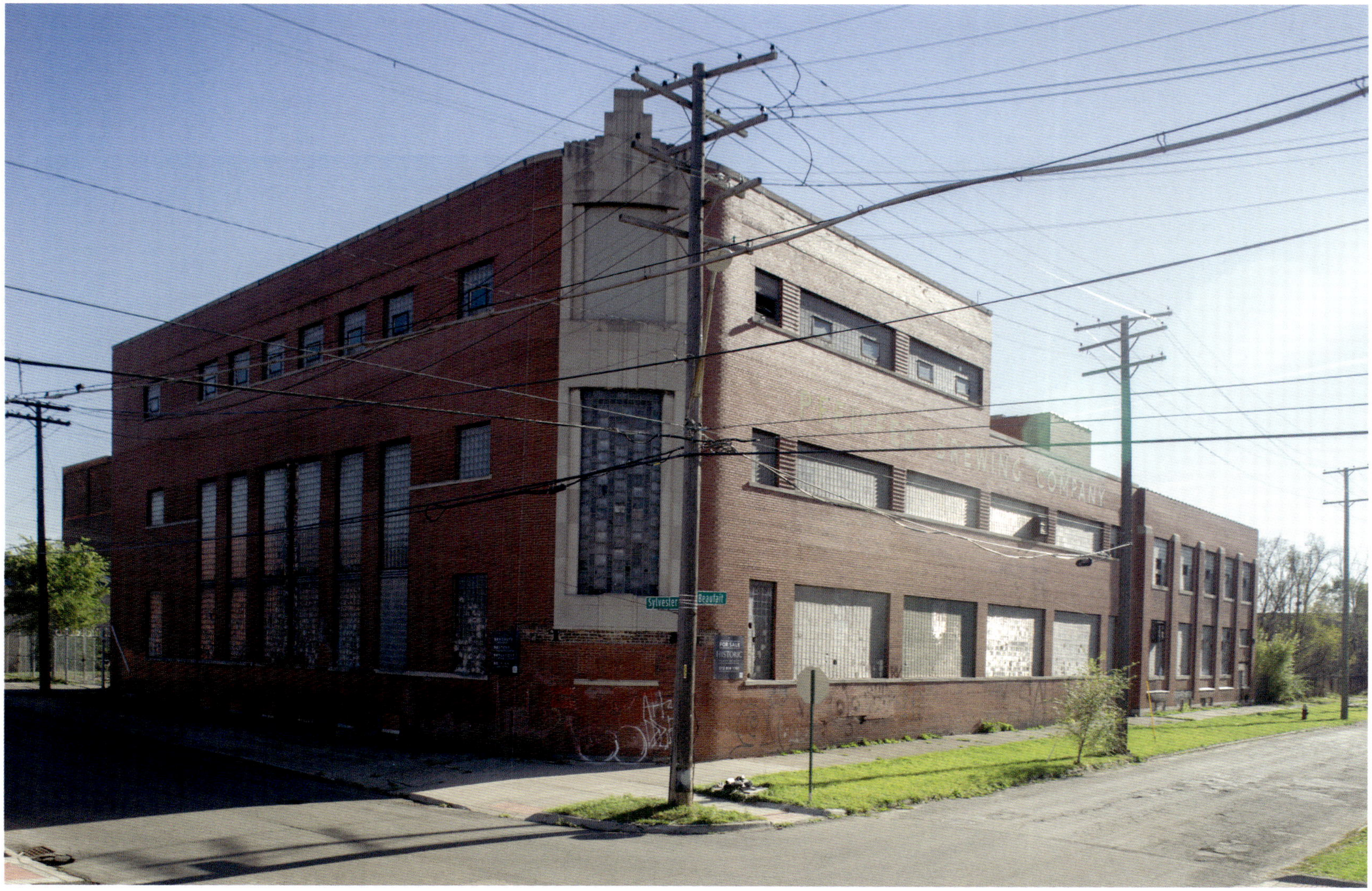

Art deco Pfeiffer Brewing Building, Sylvester Street at Beaufait Street, Detroit, 2015.

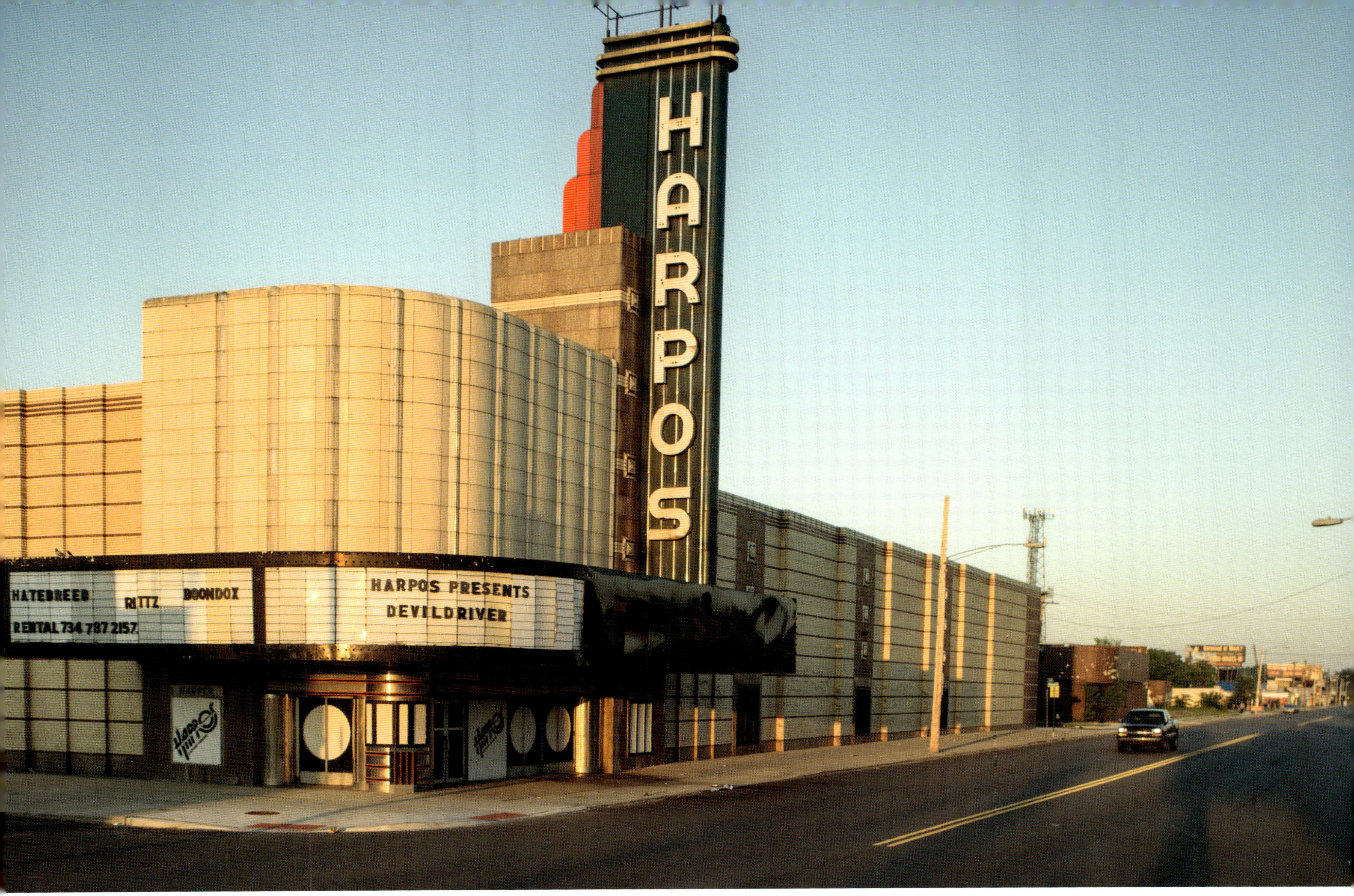

Harpos, an art deco movie theater, is now a venue for heavy metal and industrial rock bands. Designed by Charles N. Agree, 1939. 14238 Harper Avenue, Detroit, 2014.

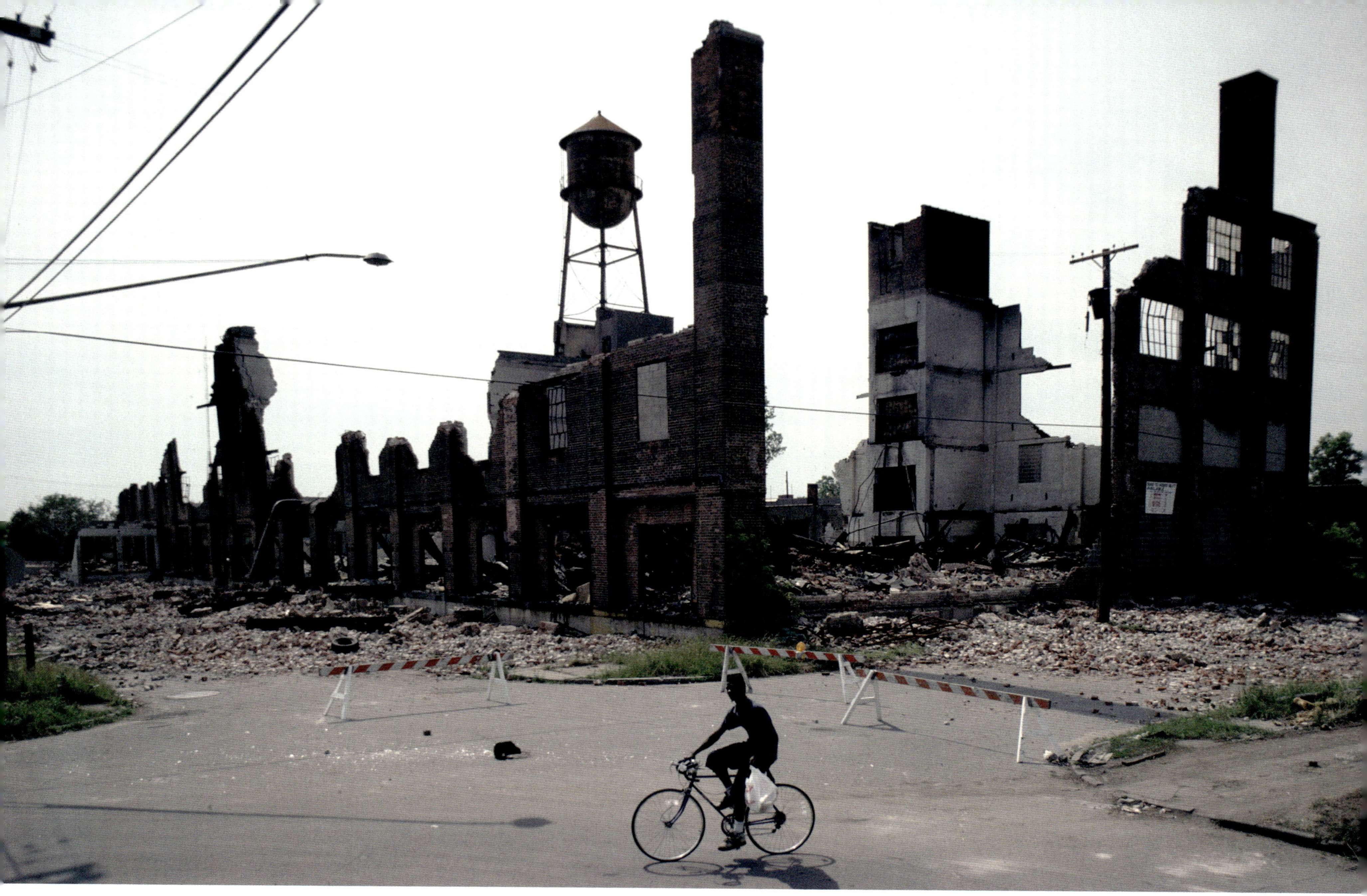

Ruins of Montgomery Ward Warehouse. 17th Avenue at Hancock Street, Detroit, 1996.

THIS IS NO ROME: RUINS AND DESOLATE CITYSCAPES

Detroit is anxious to get rid of its ruins. Instead of widespread pride in their majesty, or a sense that at least the grandest of them should be left as monuments to the city's history, the common belief is that nothing good can come from these open, useless, and dangerous spaces, visible symbols of what is holding the city back. City officials, community organizations, and foundations use the term "blight" as a blanket designation for abandoned industrial buildings, skyscrapers, remains of burnt dwellings, and abandoned cars, boats, and tires.

The significance of the ruins has become irrelevant to most neighborhood residents. They have no knowledge of what the old plants once produced because most of the people who worked in manufacturing have moved away or died. One of these leftover places is the Federal Mogul #1 ball bearings plant. Only two tall smokestacks remain in the middle of vacant land now used as an illegal dump. A local resident told me, "I don't know what that factory used to be because I'm too young. I'm only twenty five." Another neighbor could only observe, "I see they are getting ready to do something. They are putting up new gates."

Although not grand, some significant buildings constructed after the 1967 riots have already become abandoned. Such is the case with the Mannia Cafe, built as a large Chinese restaurant with a strikingly futuristic look that spoke of progress. Coleman Young was present for the opening in 1971, and from the start there was a strong African American presence among the patrons. Later, Mannia Cafe became The Rhythm Kitchen, a reggae and hip-hop dance hall where many well-known performers of the genre appeared. At first a surprising symbol of hope for revival in a landscape of deindustrialization, The Rhythm Kitchen went out of business and became the Grace Fellowship Church in 1999 and then God's Way Church.

The city establishment, in its single-minded battle against ruin and abandonment, does not give collective imagination a chance. But artists and people sensitive to the ongoing transformation are creating rich narratives that transcend the word blight. Artists, filmmakers, lovers of ruins, and skateboarders see visions of the end of the world in Detroit's powerful ruins. To experience them, they trespass, running the risk of being mugged or falling through holes and broken stairs. Excited by their discoveries, these urban explorers share their accounts online. What has been summed up by the word blight became a symbol of authenticity and source of inspiration for such artists as Banksy, Eminem, and Tyree Guyton, and has been seen by millions in videos and movies filmed in ruined cityscapes.

At 2126 Pierce Street, an experimental dwelling built by Cranbrook Academy is one indication of the desire to rebuild the city and to achieve recognition in doing so. As a master's thesis, Cranbrook students Matt Miller and Thomas Gardner with the help of volunteers built this "urban centric" house in 2007, using low-cost materials, for under $60,000. The dwelling was intended for an under-housed family from the east side of Detroit. The little structure, called "One of Detroit's Strangest Houses," seemed to ask "Why am I here?" and to dare people to live in it, surrounded by high crime and empty land. Every time I have visited I have found it empty and unsecured. But in 2013 a sunflower garden appeared, and in 2015 the lawn was mowed and a fanciful mural by Brooklyn-based artist Beau Stanton in his signature style was added. Tyree Guyton's large red dot by the door proudly remains, while GASM's later tag has been painted over.

The Cranbrook team, submitting the house in an architectural competition, wrote: "The project will act as a framework and methodology for thinking and regarding human settlement, domesticity, and modes of living, while serving as a harbinger, a seed-germ for viability. And most importantly, in a modest but significant way, attend to the needs of a city and its citizenry." By all accounts the house did not fulfill these goals. In 2015, empty and having failed as a housing solution it has nevertheless become an outdoor art space and is slated to become a micro-hotel for brave souls. This failed experimental dwelling, once in the middle of nowhere, is now placed in the context of Eastern Market, the Dequindre Cut—Detroit's answer to New York's High Line—and the nearby art lofts and galleries; it has become part of the Detroit that is coming back. The experimental house is emblematic of the unpredictable uses to which buildings are put and an example of the lure that very visible surfaces on vacant buildings exert in Detroit. It also attests to the ability to generate excitement and meaning online. With a strong social media presence, 2126 Pierce has become a magnet for wanderers traveling though Detroit's east side.

Unlike the experimental house, with its touch-and-go but continuing viability, its adaptability to decline, is the steady downfall from prosperity represented by Ned's Firestone Tire dealership. With its clean, streamlined design, Ned's was built for a new world of movement and mid–twentieth-century progress. A great presence, the futuristic-style Ned's once expressed the Motor City's optimistic outlook. I followed the building over time as it fell victim to neglect and vandalism. This place that sold tires became a hardware store, then was eventually left open to the elements, mined by scavengers, and demolished and replaced by a one-story laundromat, now itself in ruins. This building type meant to embody movement and progress turned out to have a very limited future.

In 2012, videographer Insulationking traveled six hundred miles to the abandoned United Community Hospital in southwest Detroit. I have seen dozens of videos made in Detroit by urban explorers, but Insulationking's is for me the most memorable. In the video, we see the interior of the hospital, lit only by his flashlight as he walks alone, slowly, over puddles of water. We hear plaster falling and glass breaking under his feet. Sometimes he turns around as if to make sure he's not being followed. The isolation and vulnerability of the explorer are evident in the sound of his deep breathing, his huffing and puffing, and in the scene ahead coming out of the darkness as light shines through windows, then returning to dark hallways. He seems to be waiting for some nasty surprise: perhaps falling through a hole, being mugged, or encountering the creations of his own nightmares. He stares at operating tables, x-ray machines, syringes, contaminated waste, and piles of old medical records. He walks down dark stairs, looking, as he tells us, for the morgue. Audibly recording his impressions seems a way to calm himself. In one of the managers' offices on the top floor, Insulationking finds a lingerie catalogue with color photographs of semi-naked young women and pictures of contented families. The general tendency would be to regard macabre videos like this as providing cheap thrills. But among the 152 comments that this video has elicited are many addressing such serious, timely issues as how to dispose of medical records and equipment, the need for protection when going to such places, and the obligation to report the water leak to the proper city authorities.

How do places in Detroit die? I repeatedly called businesses that I knew were on the way out, such as West Fort Appliances, whose entrance is a refuge for sex workers seeking protection from rain and sun while soliciting truckers. West Fort's way of holding on to the bitter end, serving some purpose, fascinates me. I knew that there was a slim chance that my calls to such places, when I actually had a phone number, would be answered. Even if unable to talk to the owners and patrons, though, I would have been delighted to visit Ellyn's Soul Food restaurant, just to sit there, before the lights went out in 2013. Then there is the White Grove diner that the elderly owner closed down. Why has it been spared from ransacking? In 2015 the White Grove is vacant, but as if the owner had just walked out. Nobody has broken in despite the many things that could be sold. It remains clean, the lights stay on, sodas are in the cooler. A framed picture of a Detroit patron saint by the name of Solanus Casey, "Detroit Miracle Worker," still hangs on the wall. Only ants in the glass sugar container reveal the restaurant's long vacancy. I want to document and share the transition of such places from moribund to deceased. I am trying to reach the essence of losing, of letting go, of disappearing.

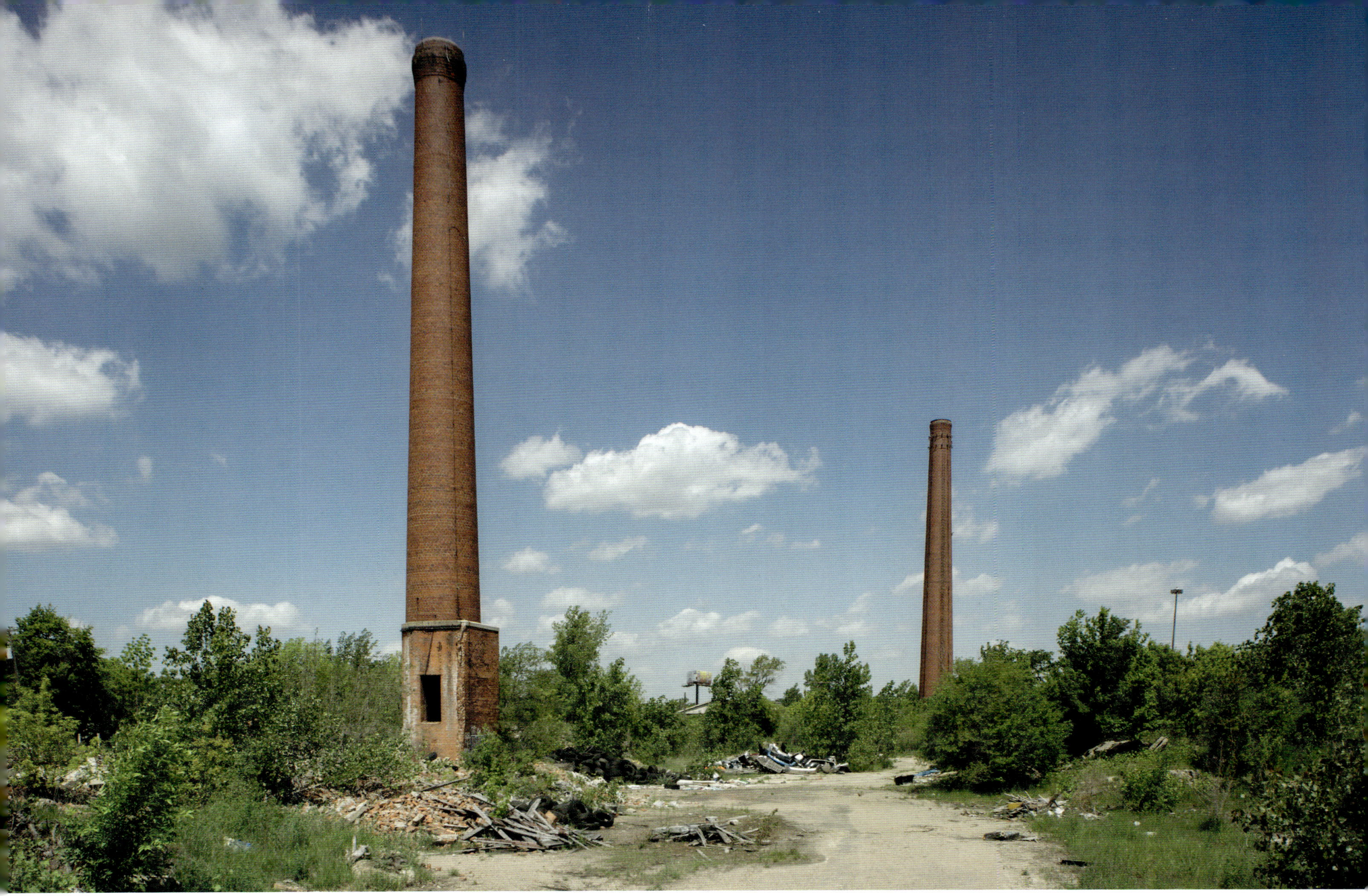

Power plant for Federal Mogul Plant #1. Lillybridge Street at Shoemaker Street, Detroit, 2014.

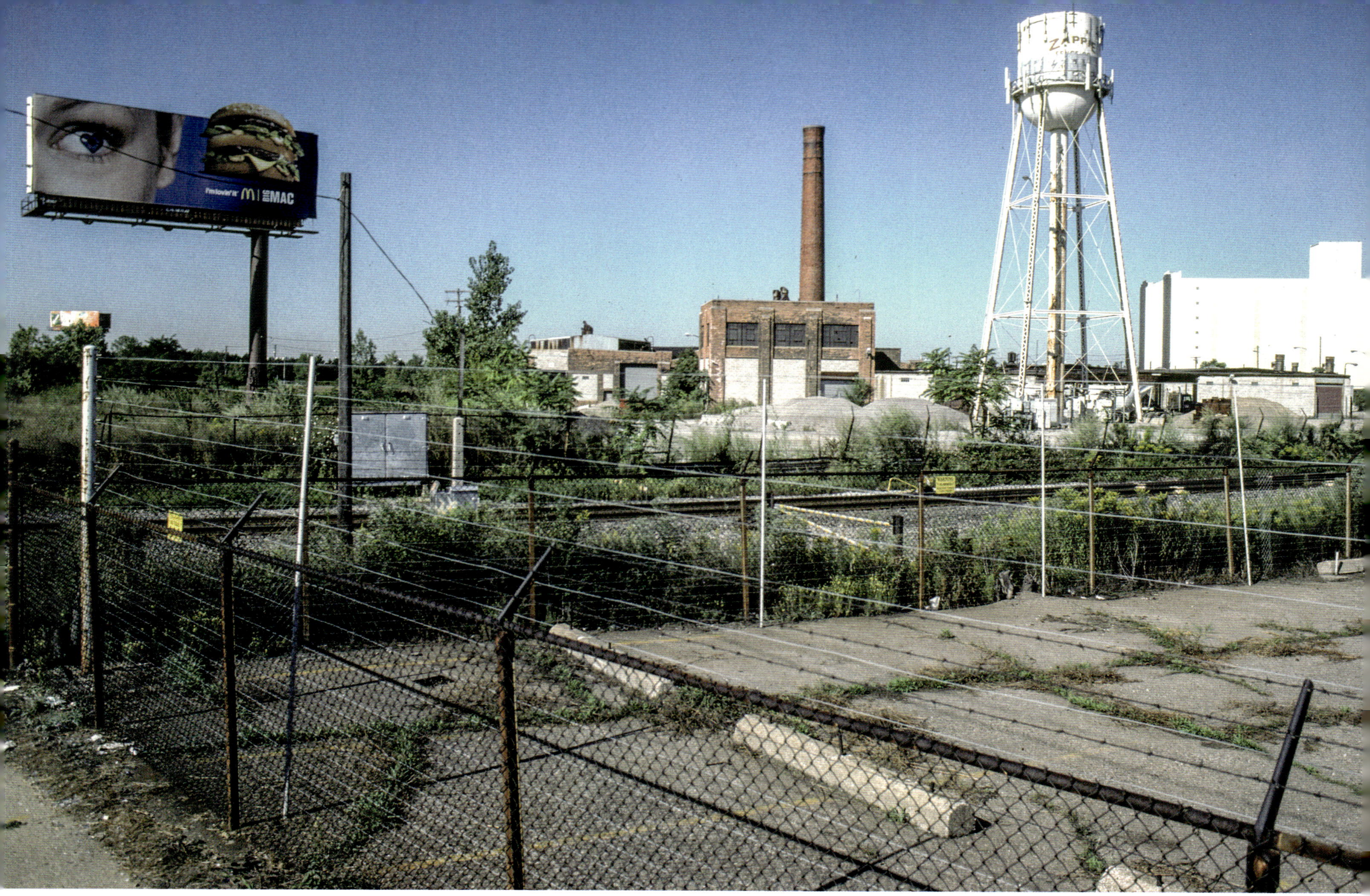

A "brownfield," former industrial land now contaminated, consisting of abandoned factories, junkyards, and railroad tracks, along with an eye-popping ad for McDonald's Big Mac. Harper Avenue at Sherwood Street, Detroit, 2010.

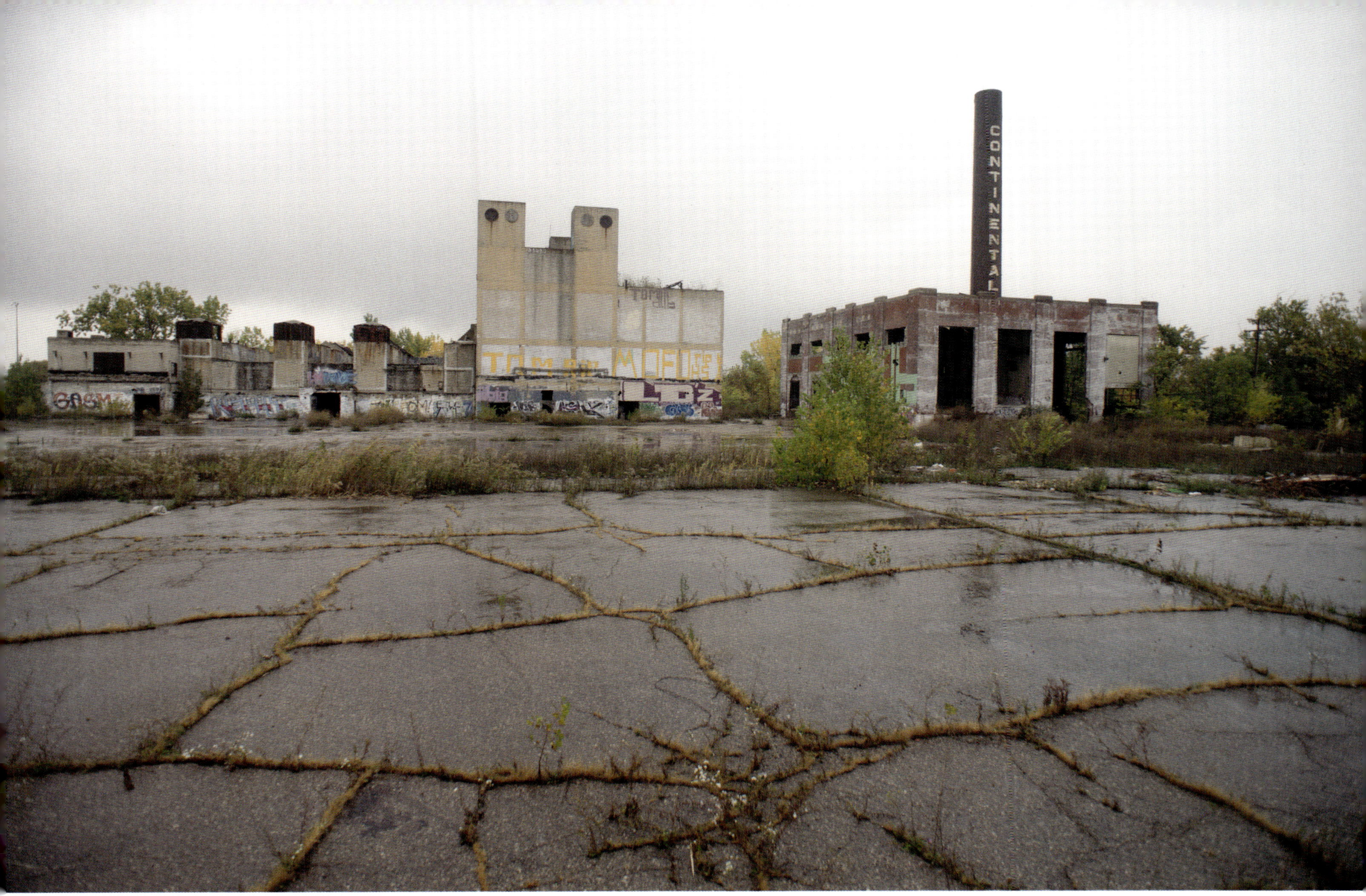

Former Continental Motors plant. Completed in 1912, Continental Motors was one of the largest makers of automotive engines in Detroit. East Jefferson at Algonquin, Detroit, 2013.

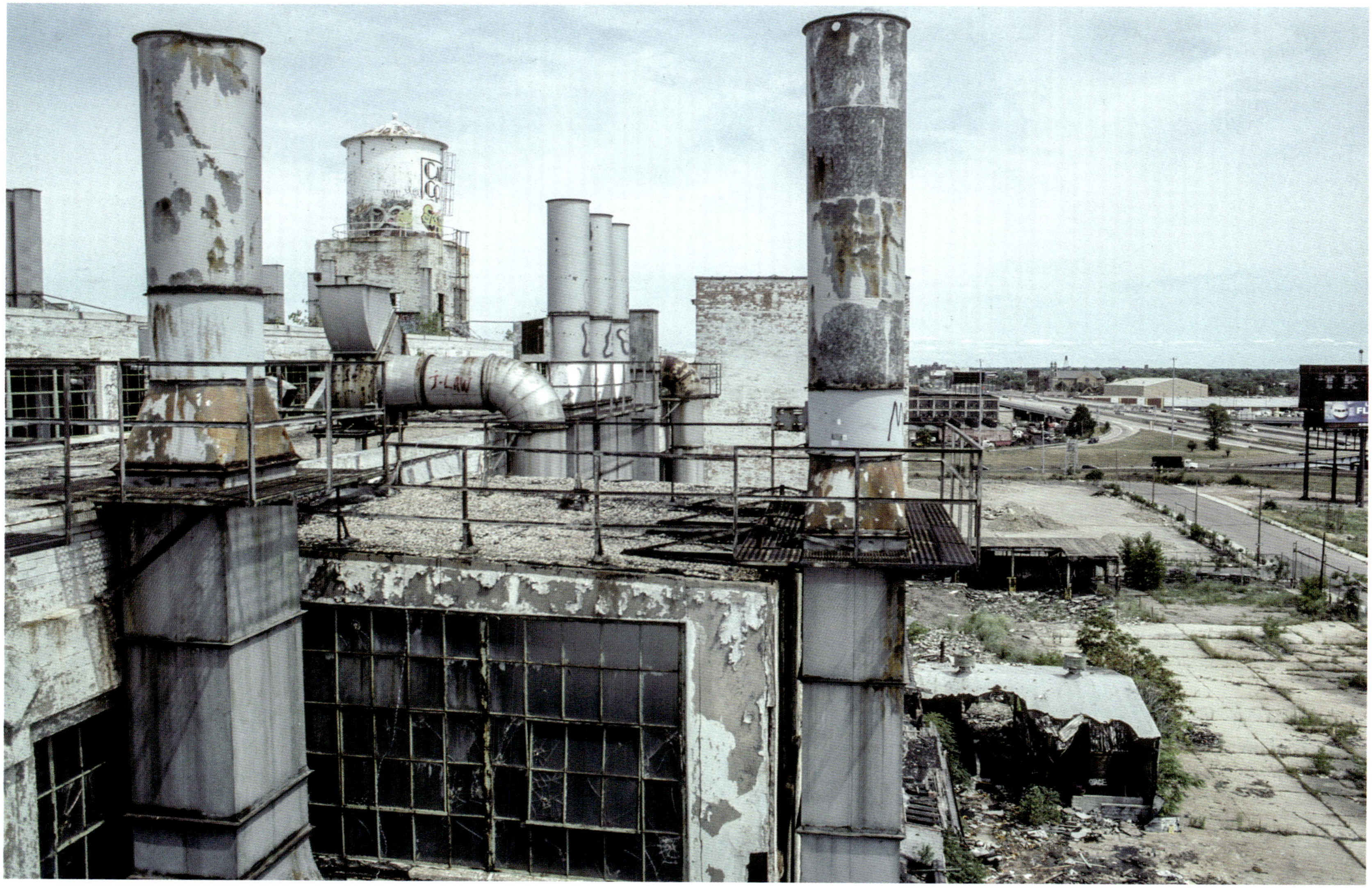

Roof, former Fisher Body Plant 21. Piquette Avenue at Hastings Street, Detroit, 2007.

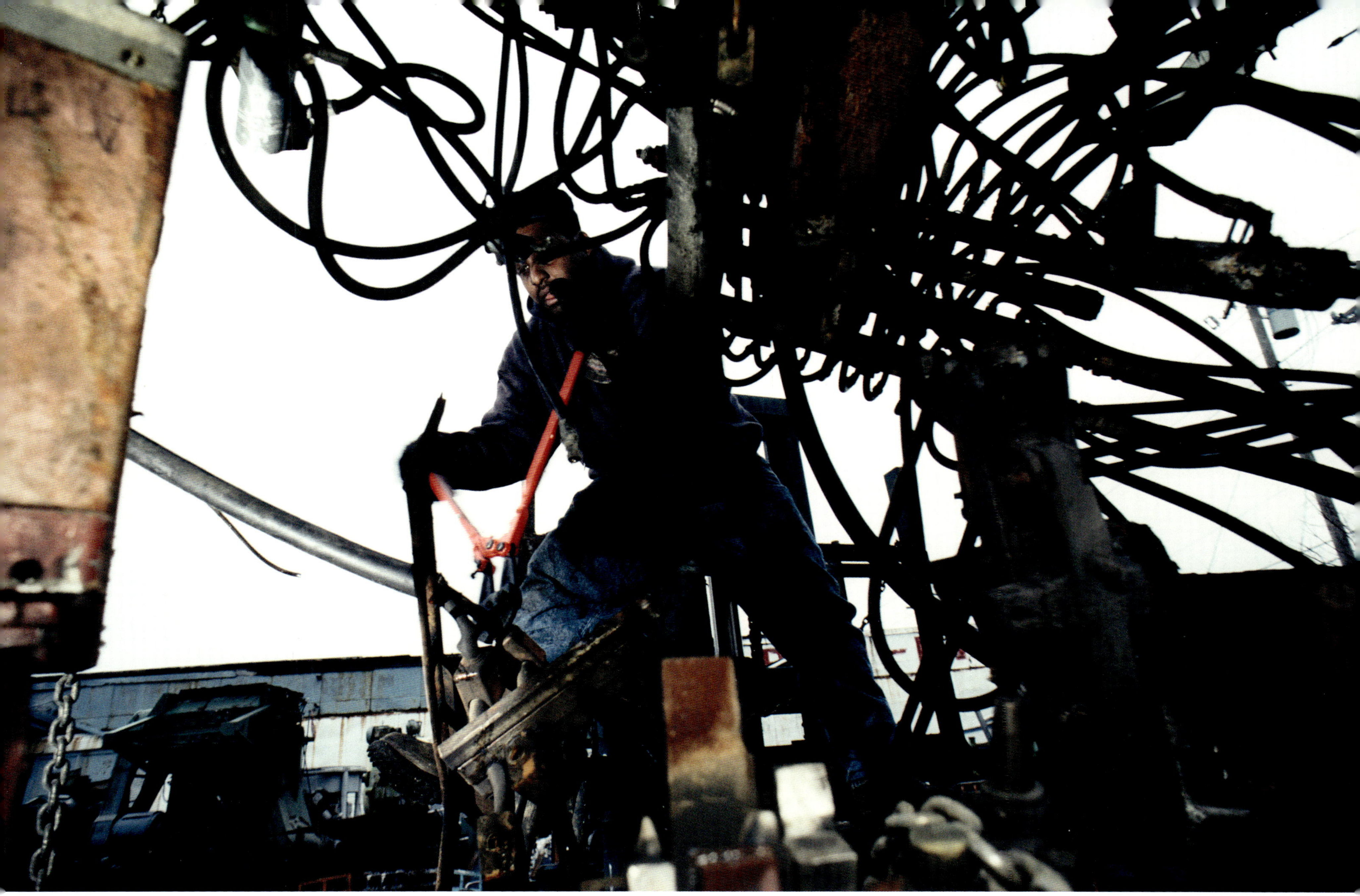

Sarah-Lil, an industrial equipment salvage company; Harvey, a maintenance worker, cutting hoses. 7485 Central Avenue, Detroit, 2001.

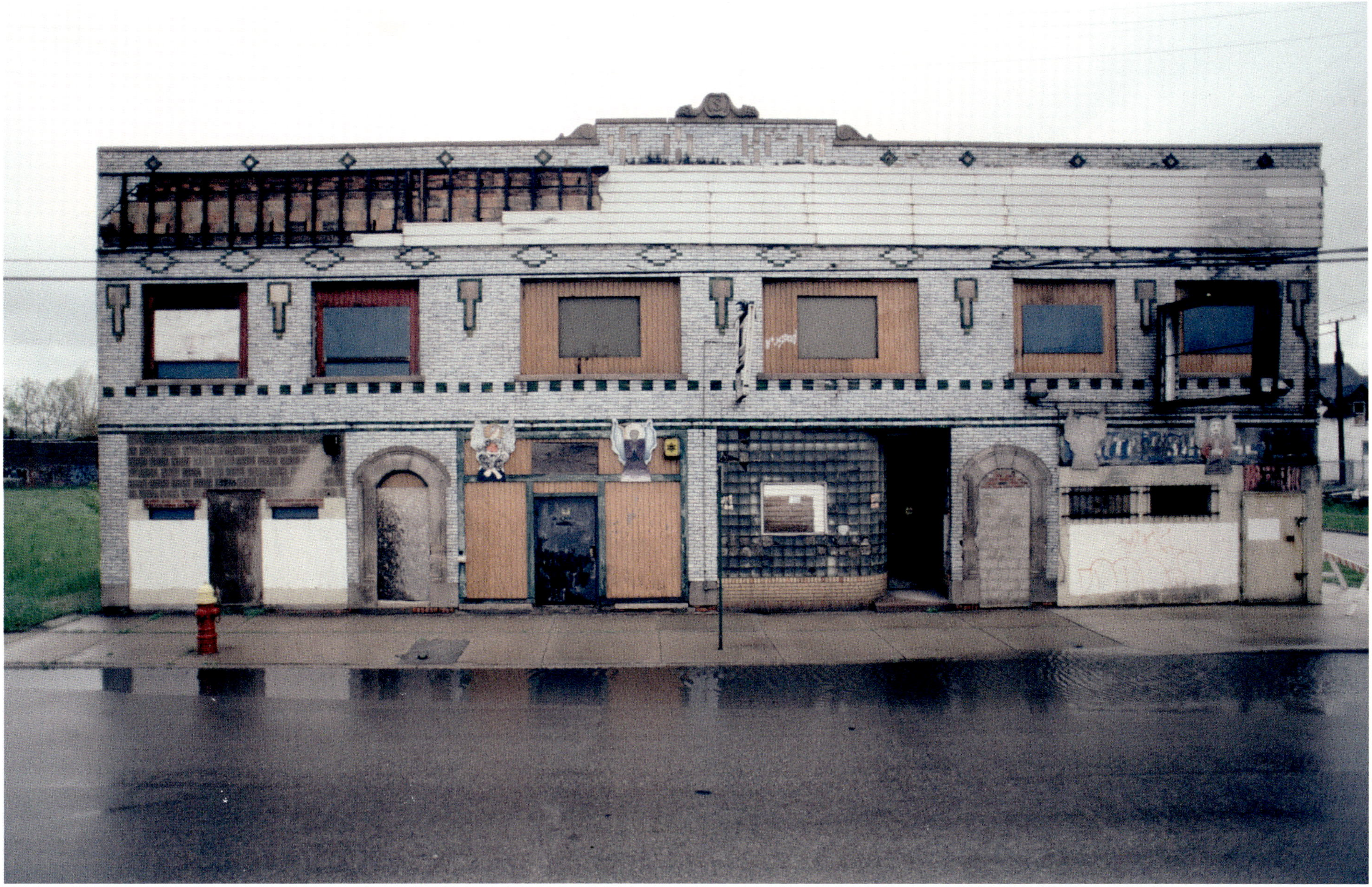

Abandoned building with four plywood guardian angels dedicated to the memory of local residents. 7716 West Jefferson Avenue, Detroit, 2008.

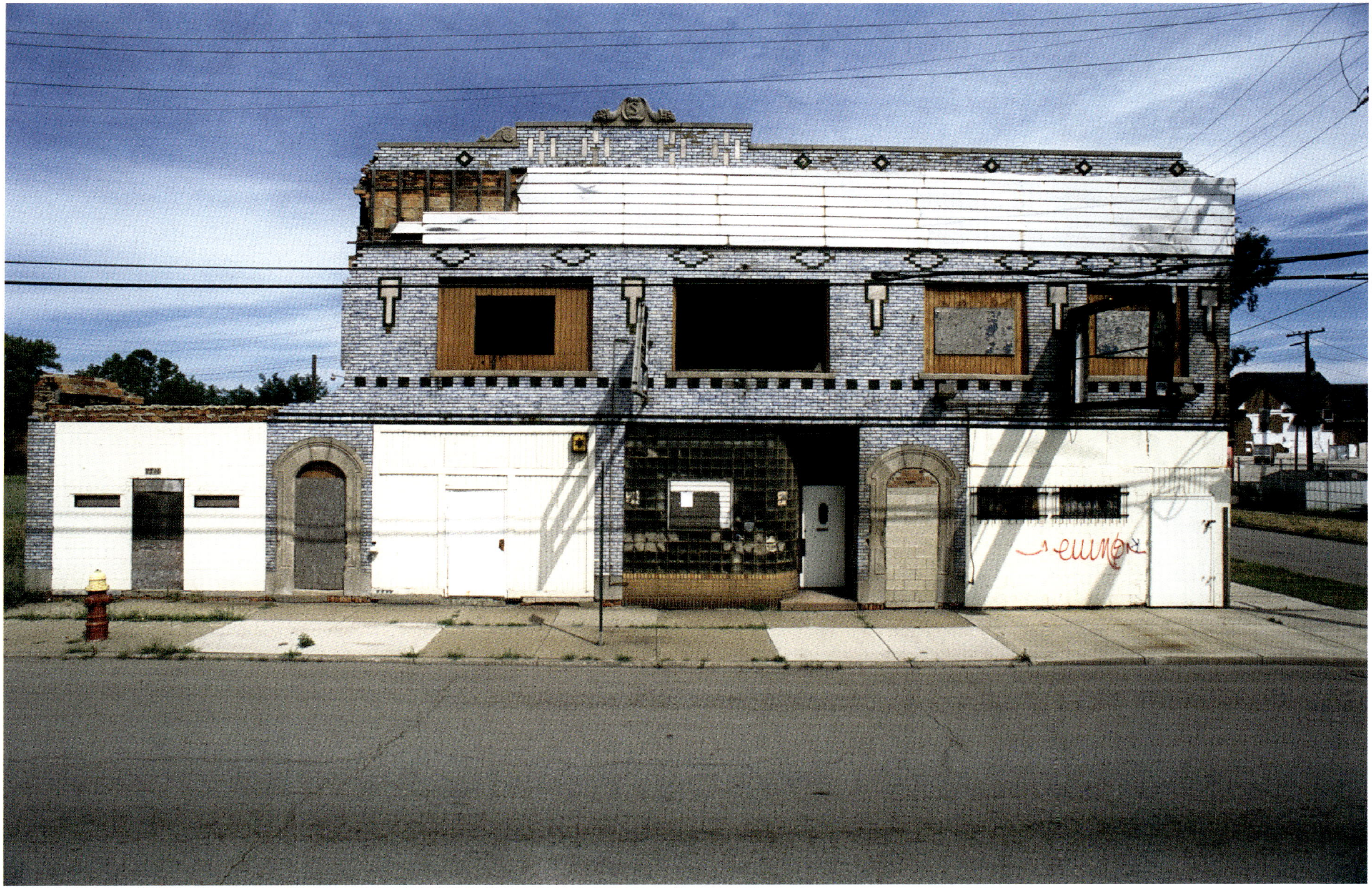

7716 West Jefferson Avenue, Detroit, 2012.

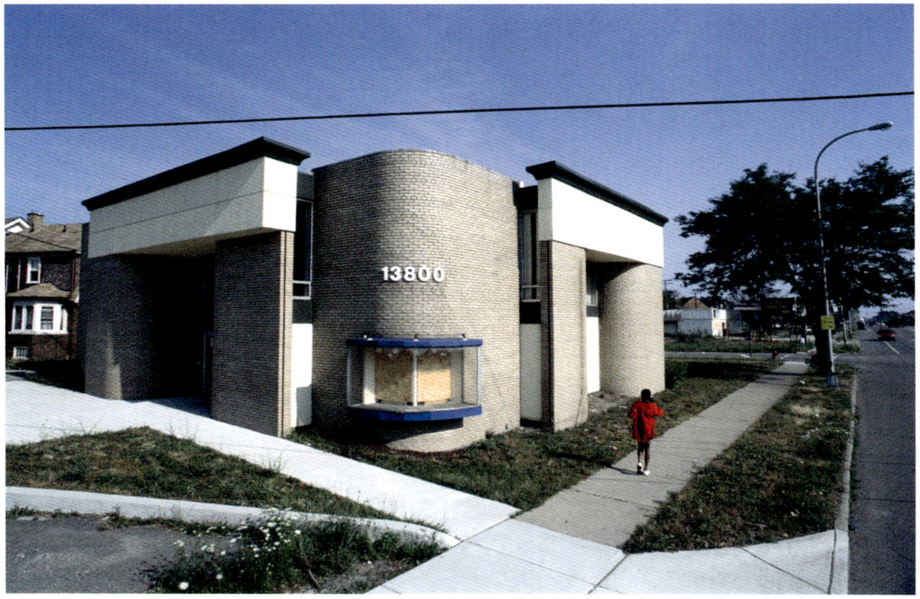

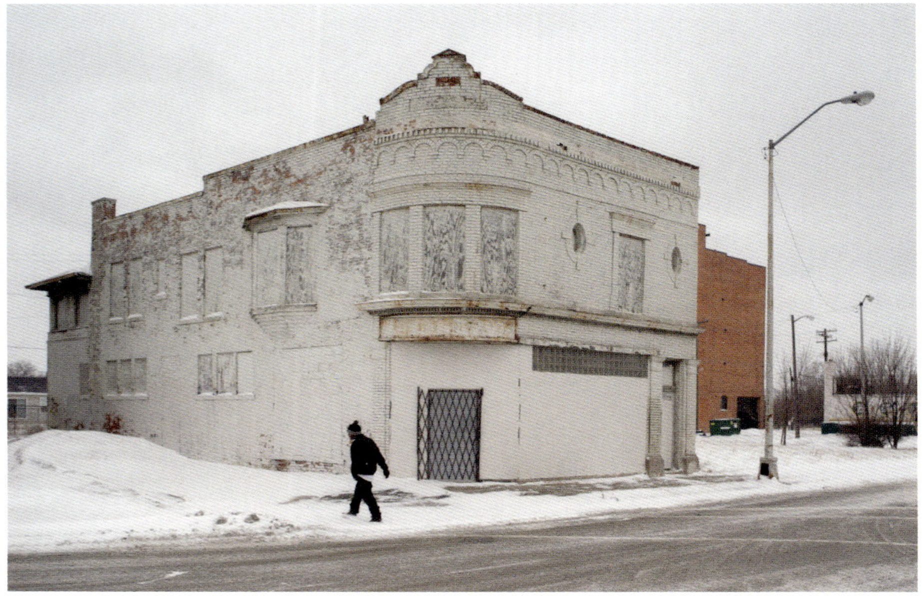

Former Burton Pharmacy and Metrocare Health Service. 13800 Livernois Avenue, Detroit, 2012.

Warehouse for Gardella Furniture. Gratiot Avenue at Chene Street, Detroit, 2014.

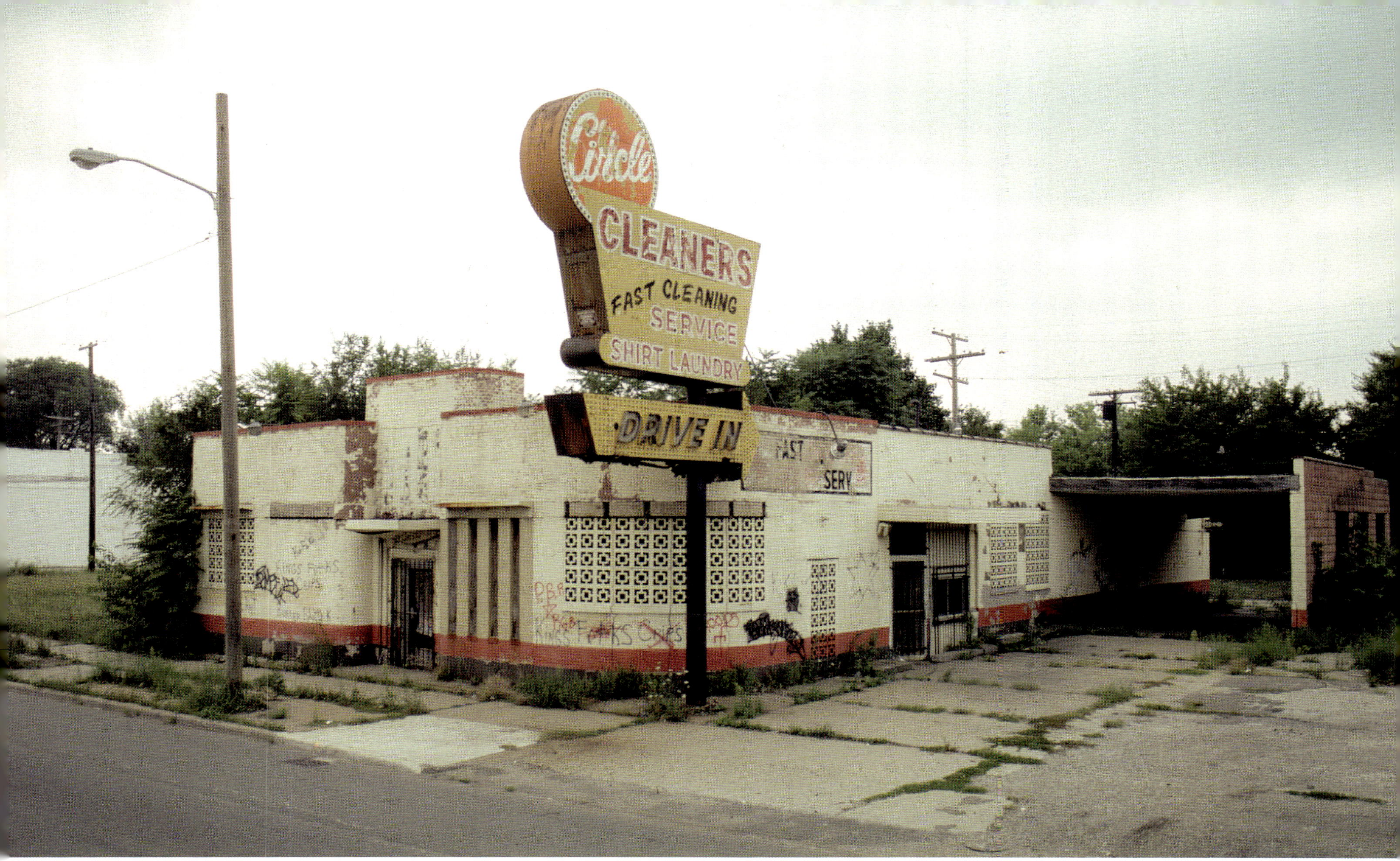

Circle Cleaners. Later, in 2010, the British graffiti artist Banksy painted "the girl with the diamond" on the front of this abandoned building. The painting was removed, leaving a hole in the wall. Buildings like this once represented modernity and commercial prosperity. Van Dyke Road at Palmetto Avenue, Detroit, 2007.

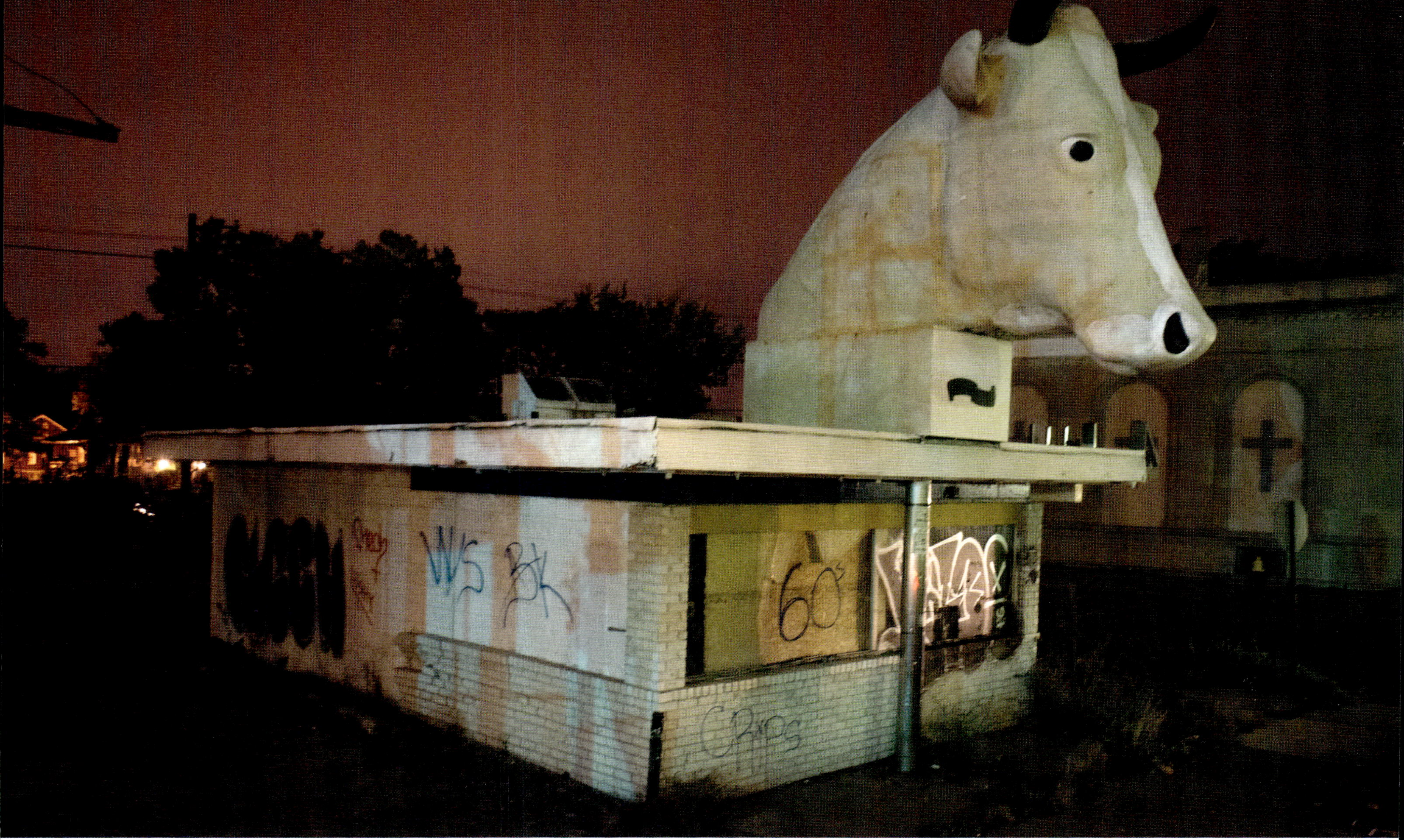

Former Ira Wilson and Sons Dairy. At night, the enormous cow head on the small store creates a scene reminiscent of Goya's "Caprichos." The head was repainted for the movie *8 Mile*. Mack Avenue at Lenox Street, Detroit, 2013.

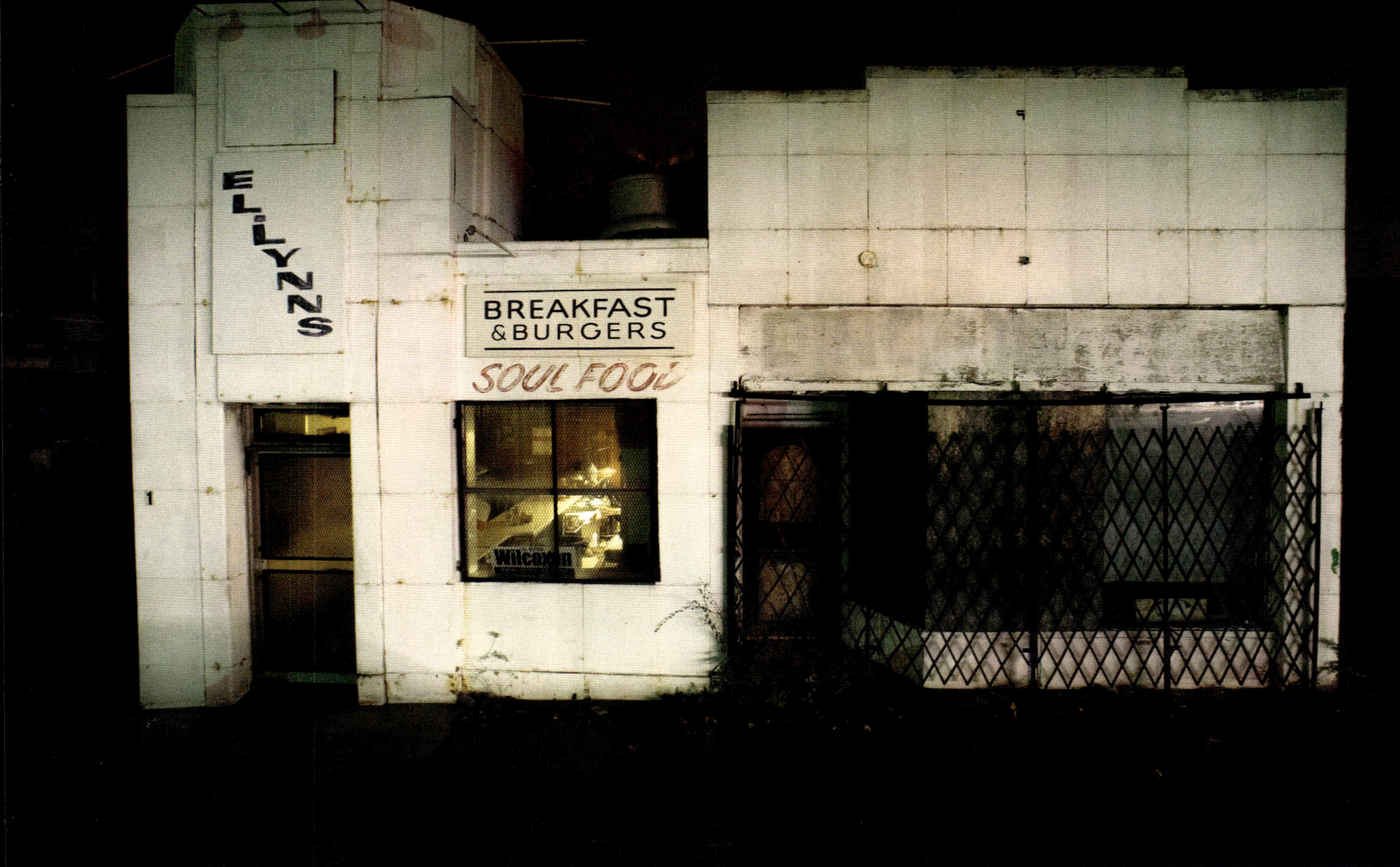

Ellyn's Soul Food, Detroit s Finest. Within a few months of this photograph Ellyn's was abandoned. Livernois Avenue at Ellsworth Street, Detroit, 2013.

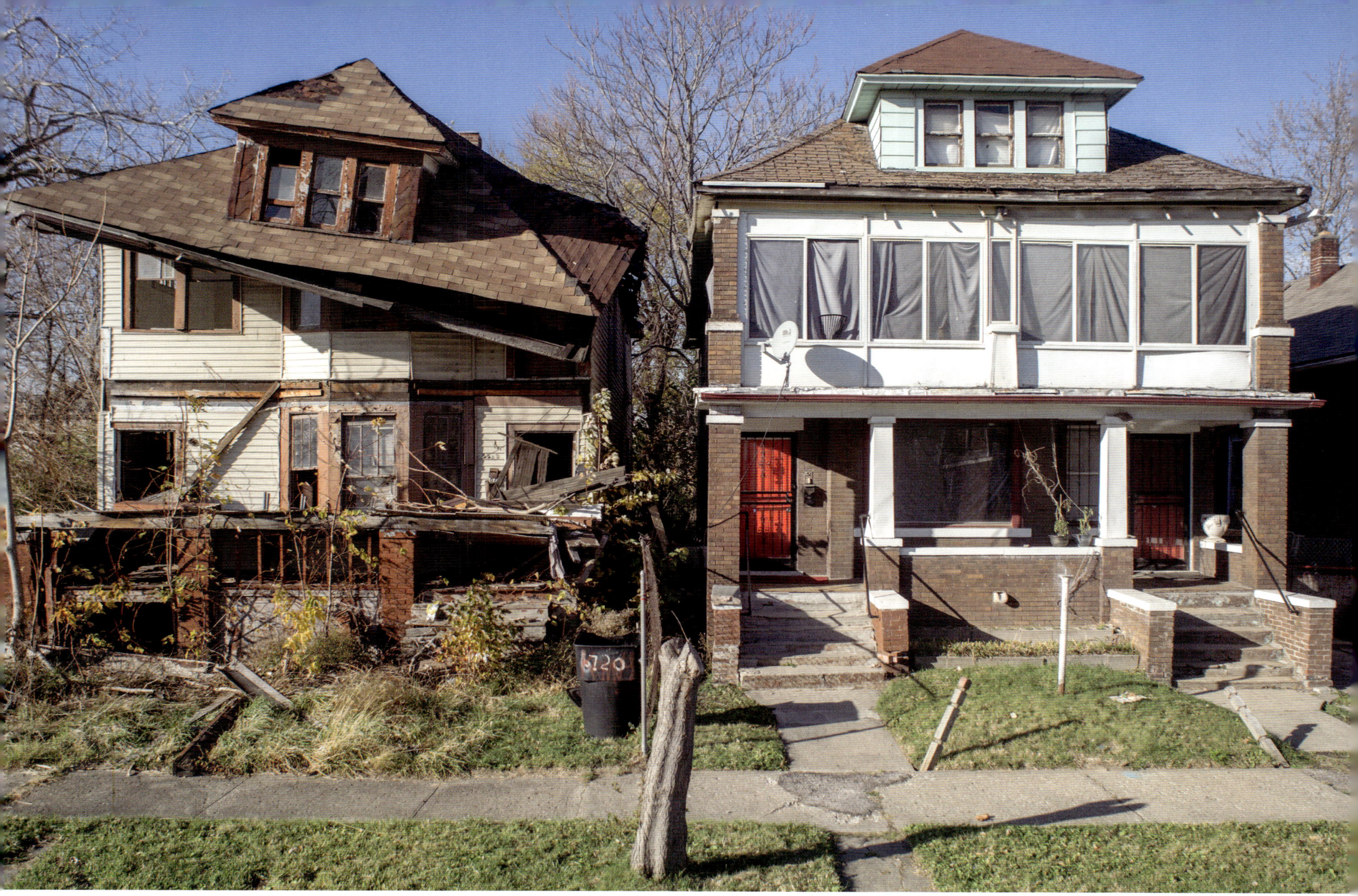

Paired houses, 6726 Sparta Street, Detroit, 2015.

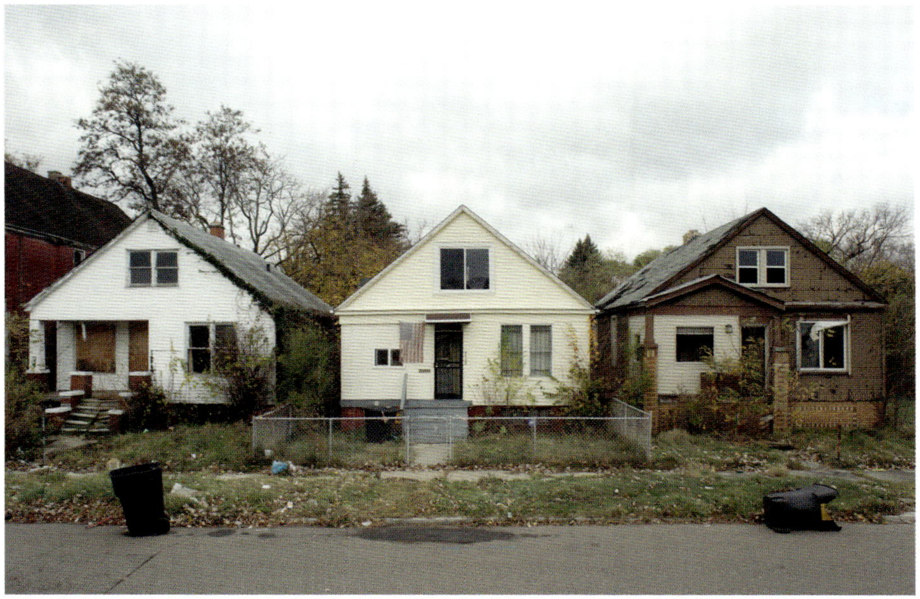

Holding out: a house with a cyclone fence and a faded American flag flanked by two once-similar abandoned houses. 5739 Baldwin Street, Detroit, 2015.

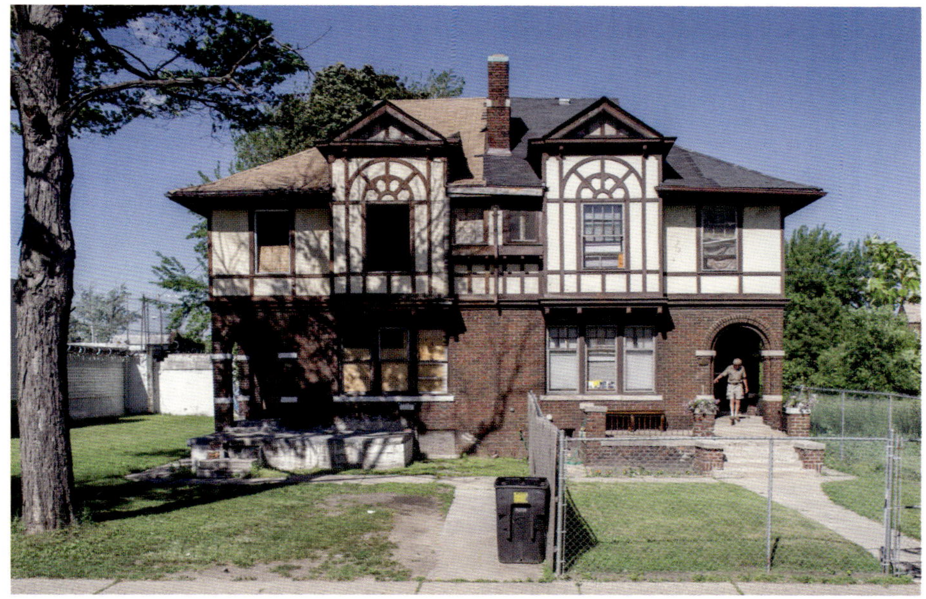

Paired houses. An Austrian engineer lives in the occupied half of the house. He hopes one day to fix the other half. 420 East Grand Boulevard, Detroit, 2014.

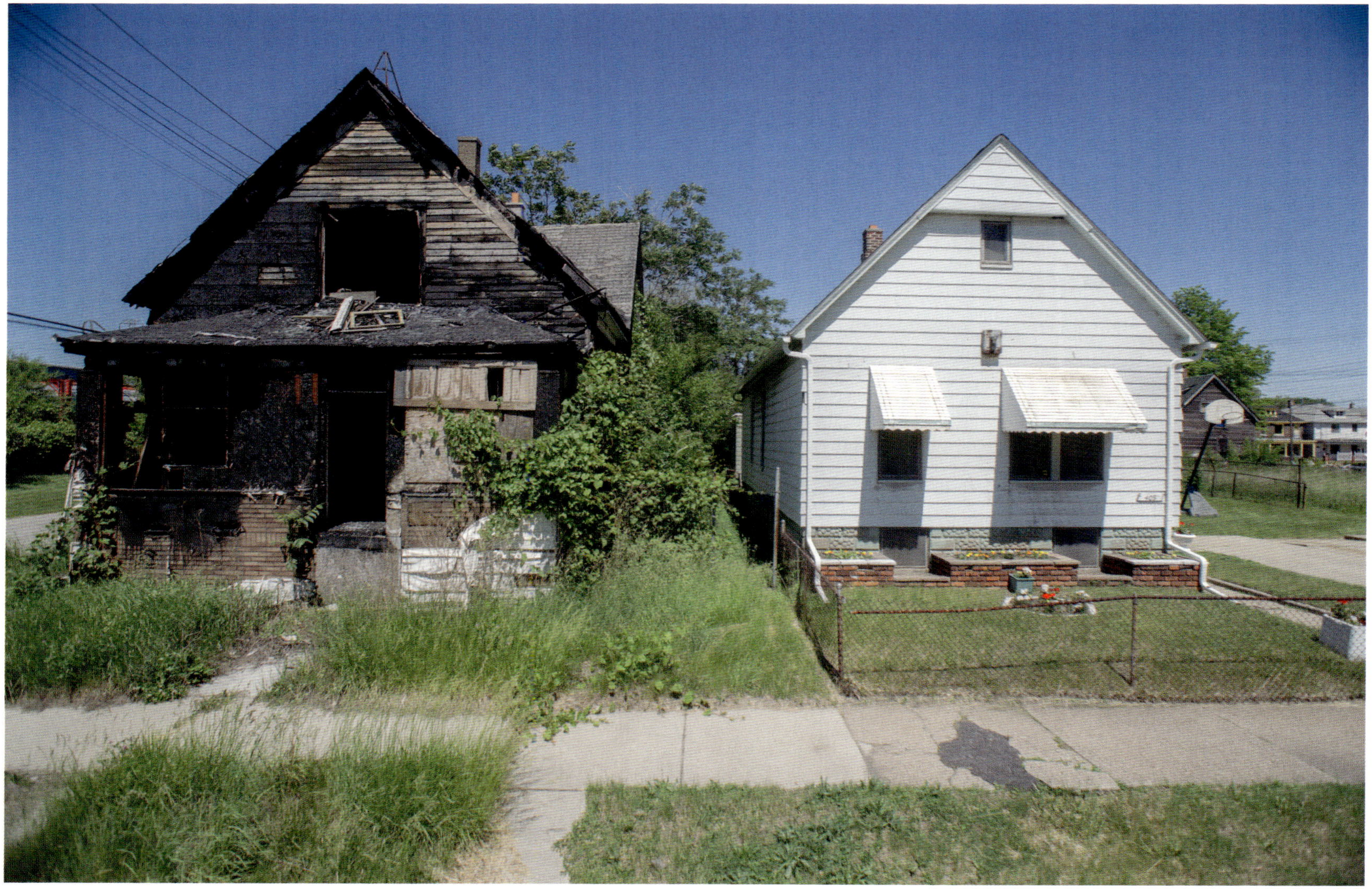

Paired houses, 409 Crossley Street, Detroit, 2014.

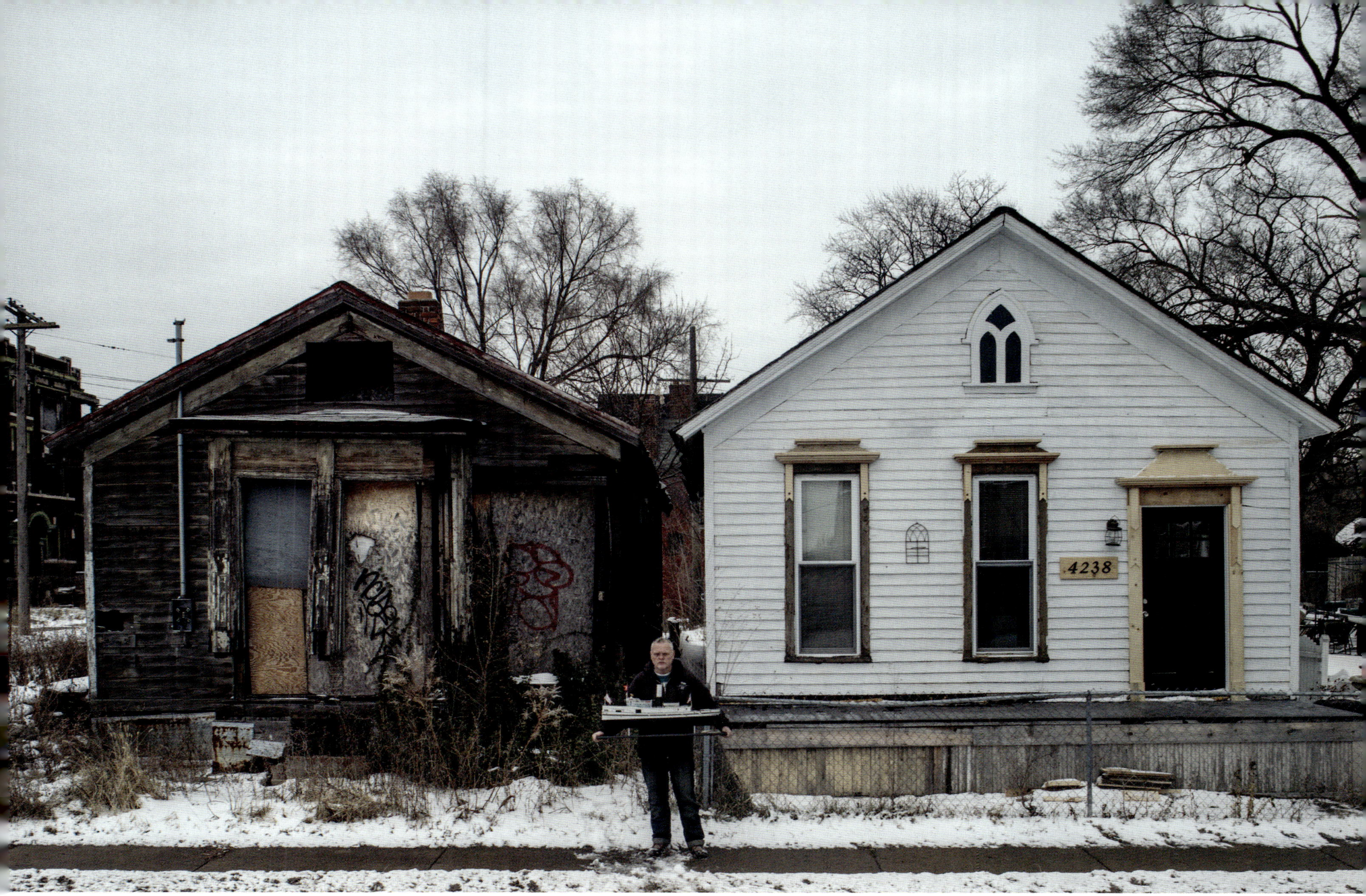

Paired houses. George, a carpenter who makes model ships, stands next to his house. George happily reported that the vacant house next door was soon going to be demolished. 4238 Rosa Parks Boulevard, Detroit, 2015.

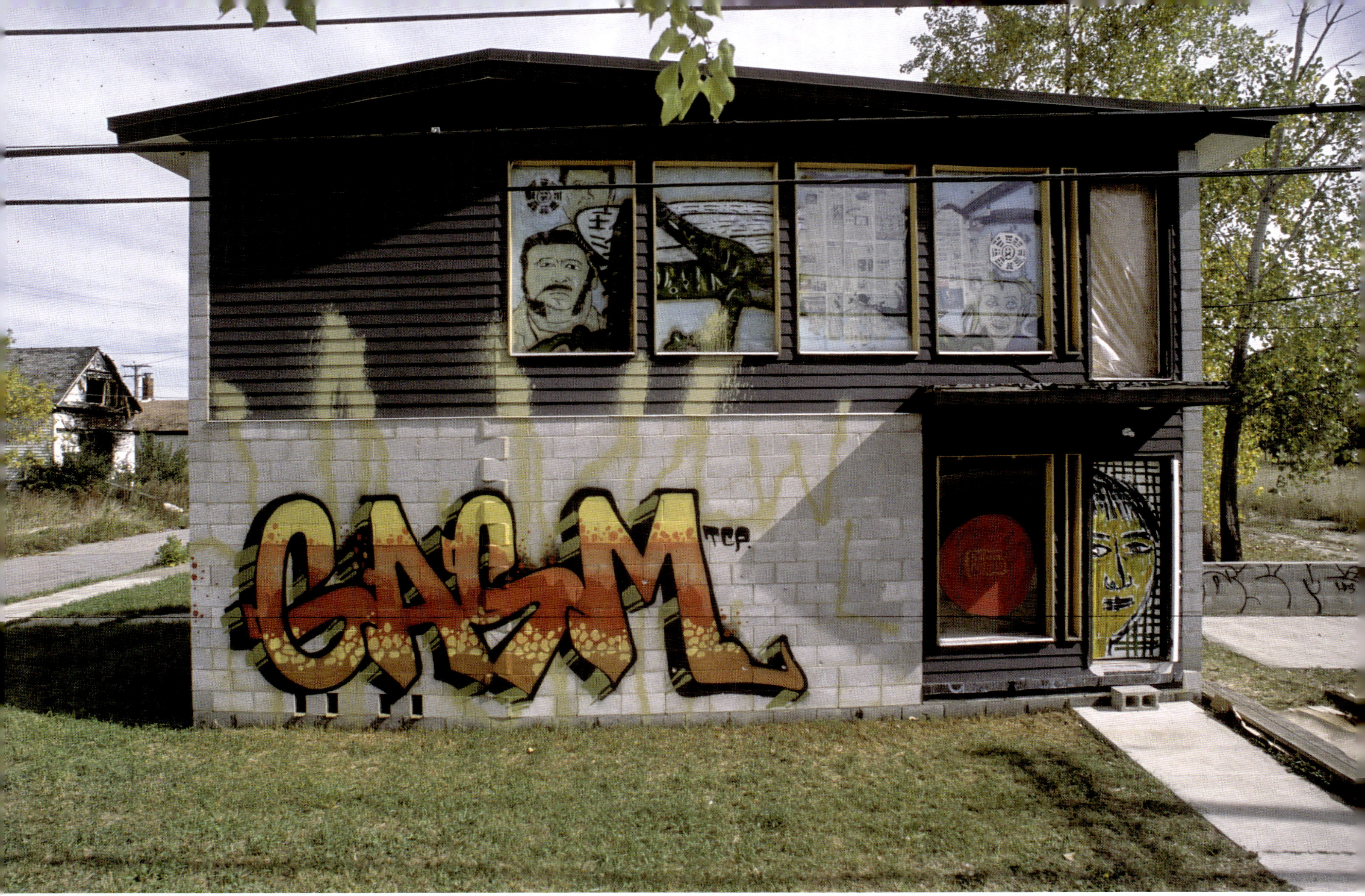

Experimental house. Artist Tyree Guyton painted one of his signature dots at the entrance. A sign at the center of the dot reads: “Botanical Fortress.” 2126 Pierce Street, Detroit, 2012.

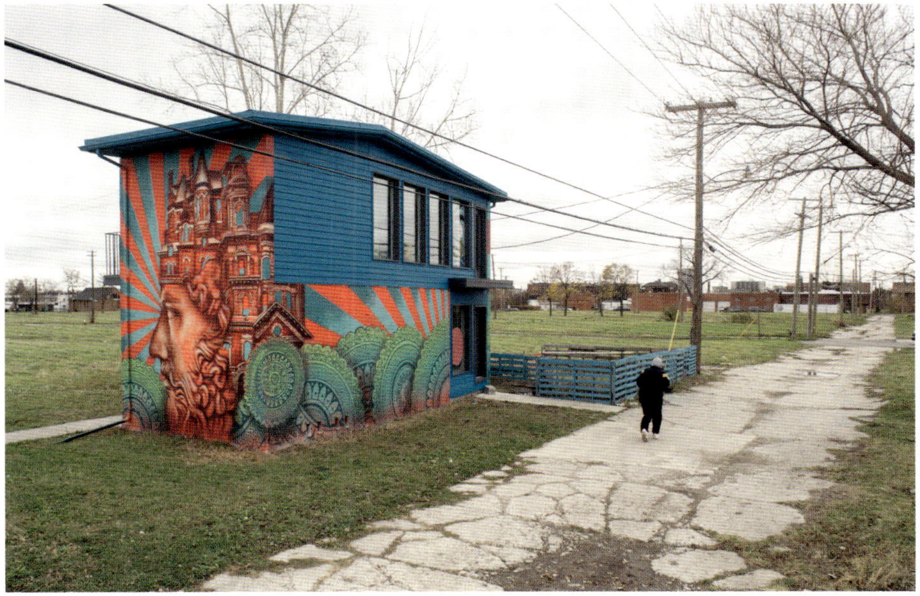

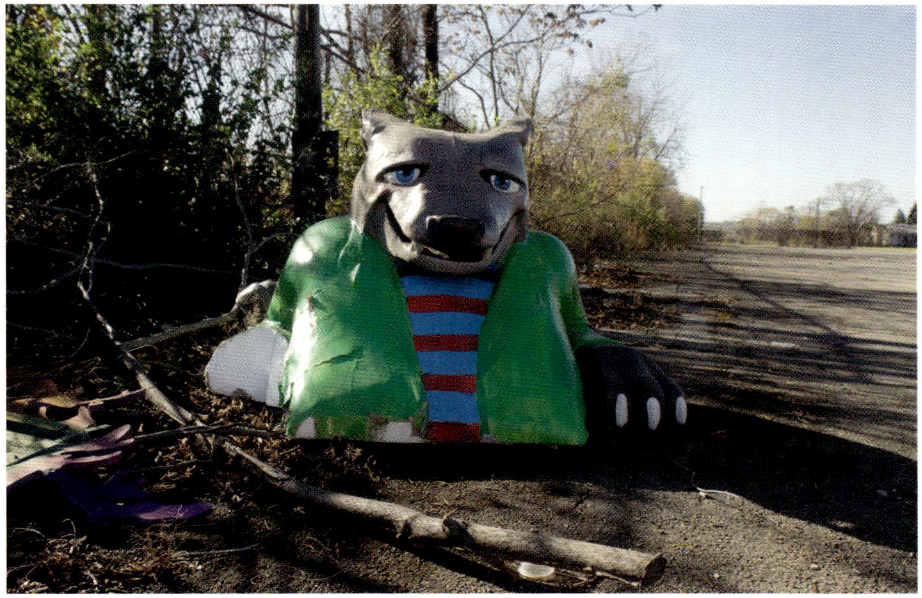

Experimental house. Mural by Brooklyn-based artist Beau Stanton.
2126 Pierce Street, Detroit, 2015.

Discarded animal from a parade float. The wolf-like creature wears a green suit coat and has prominent blue eyes. Parking lot by The Parade Company, Huber Street at Pease Street, Detroit, 2015.

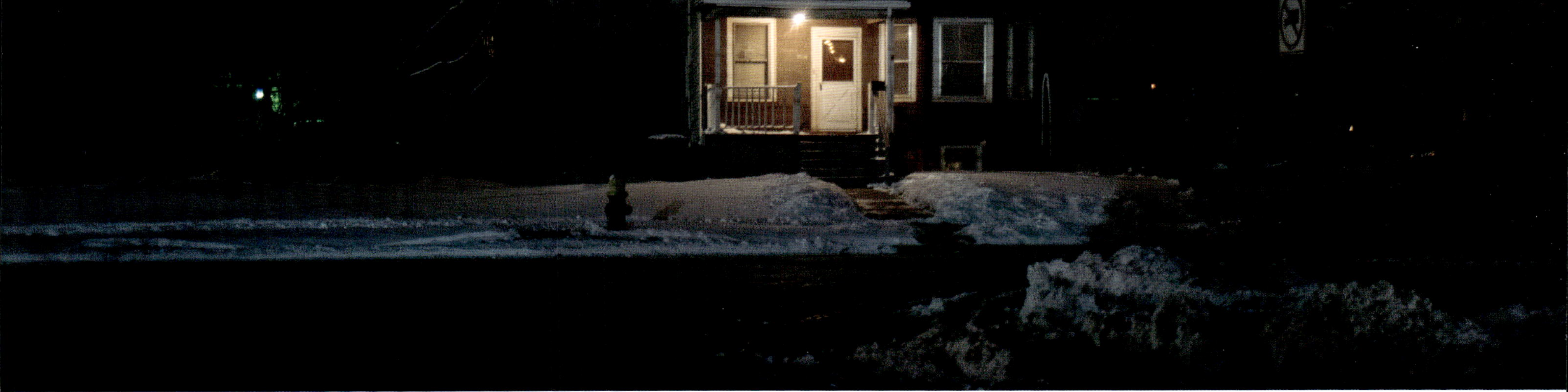

Night view of an isolated house in a former industrial area near Woodmere Cemetery and the Rouge River. 9536 Stone Avenue, Detroit, 2015.

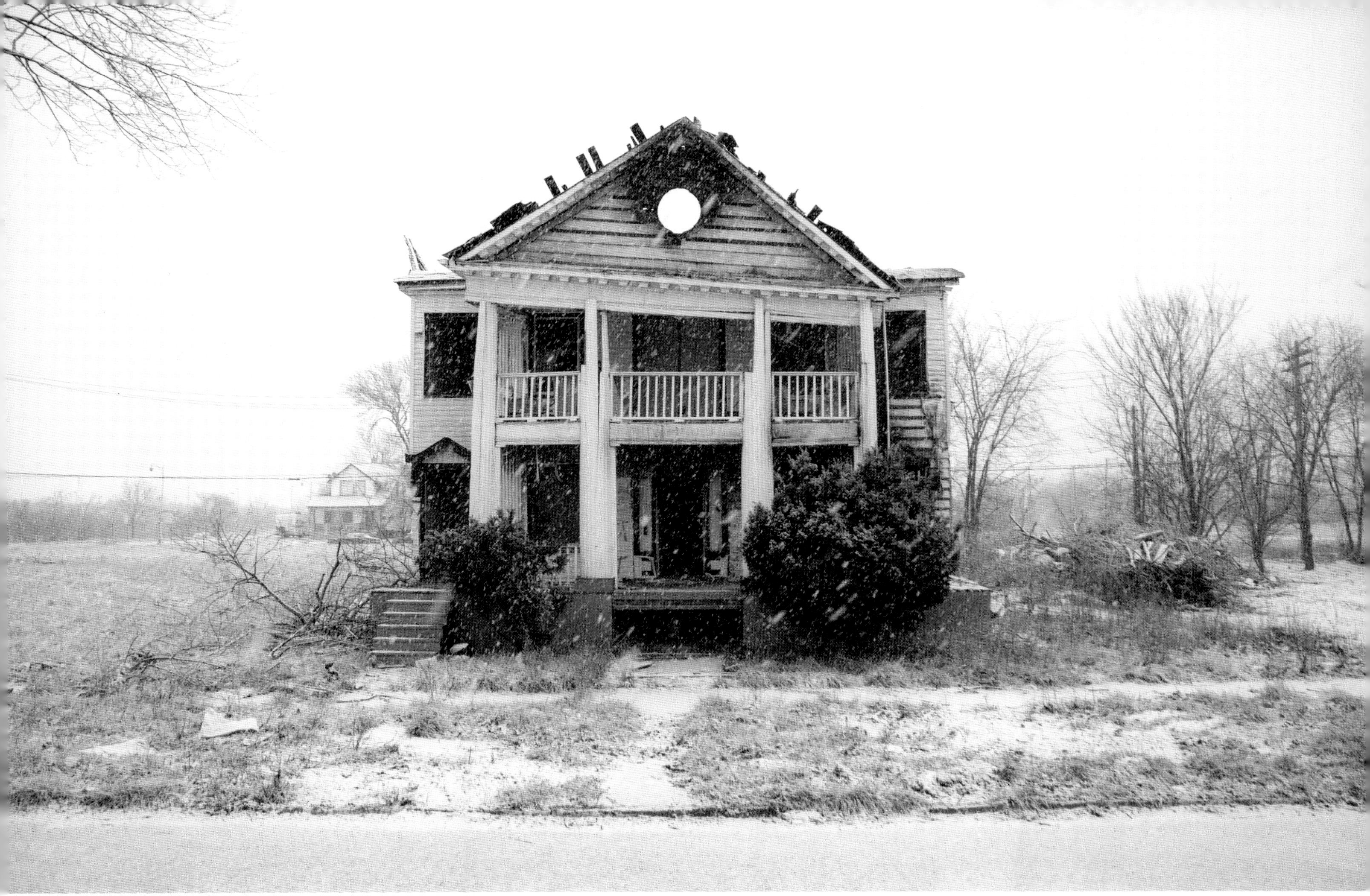

The lopsided remains of a once beautiful house. Grandy Street north of Medbury Street, Detroit, 2012.

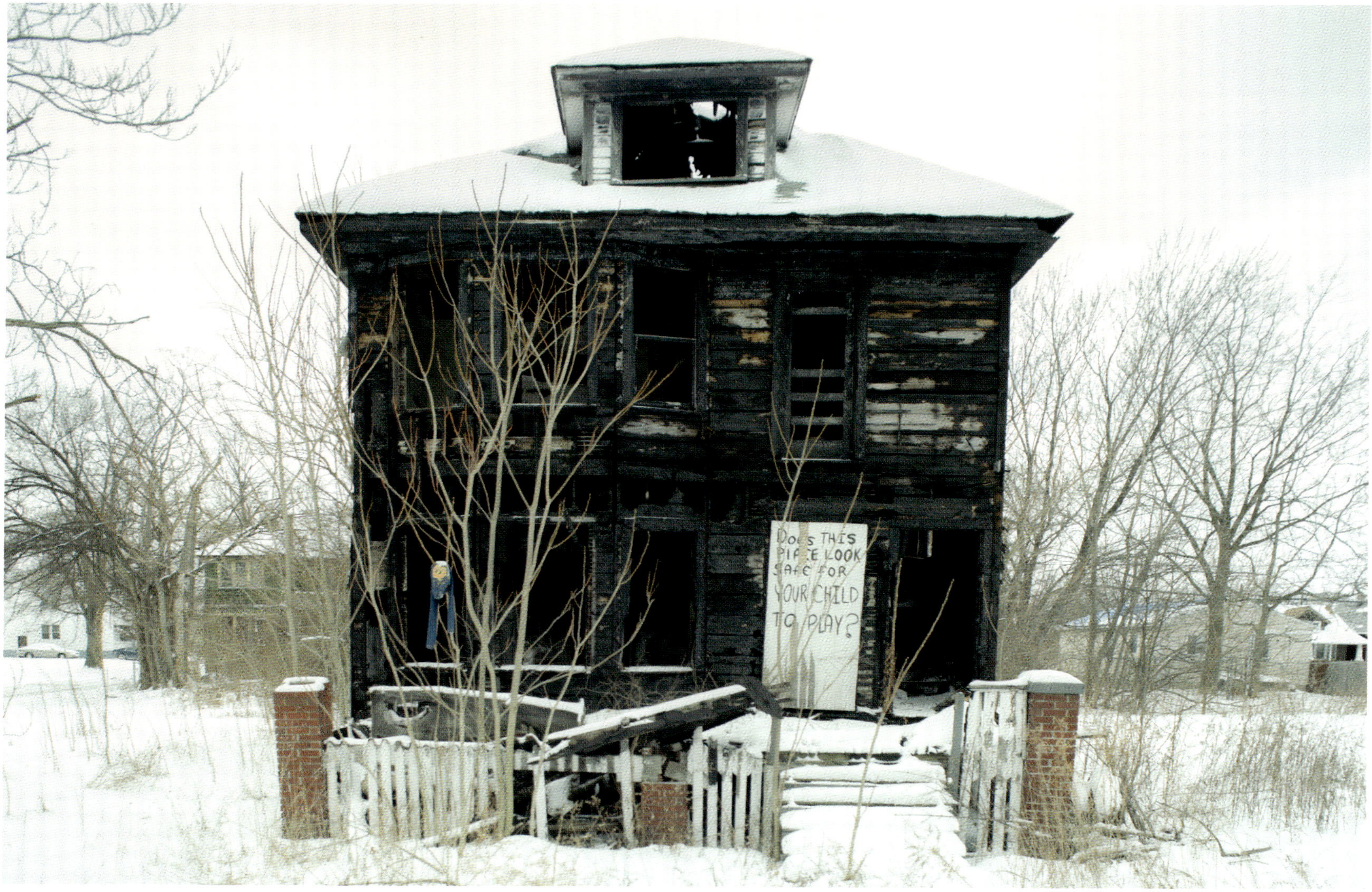

Burnt house with sign. There were other versions of this sign with the same lettering on abandoned buildings on the east side of the city. One asked: "Where are 20,000 troops to protect our own children and communities?" Another asked: *"Look around is this your children's reality?" Millner Street at Georgia Street, Detroit, 2008.

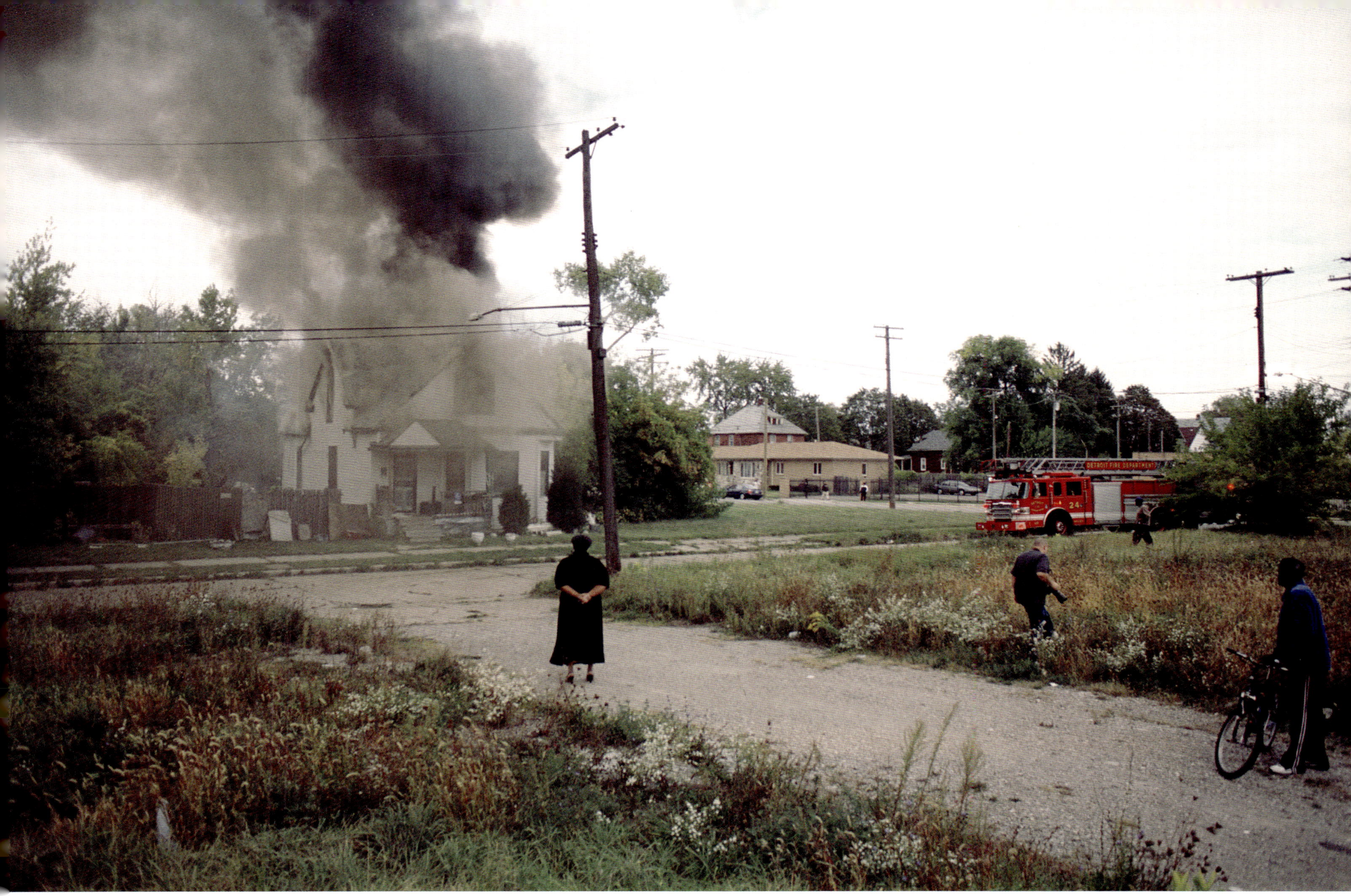

House burns as neighbors look at the destruction.
East Forest Avenue at Moran Street, Detroit, 2012.

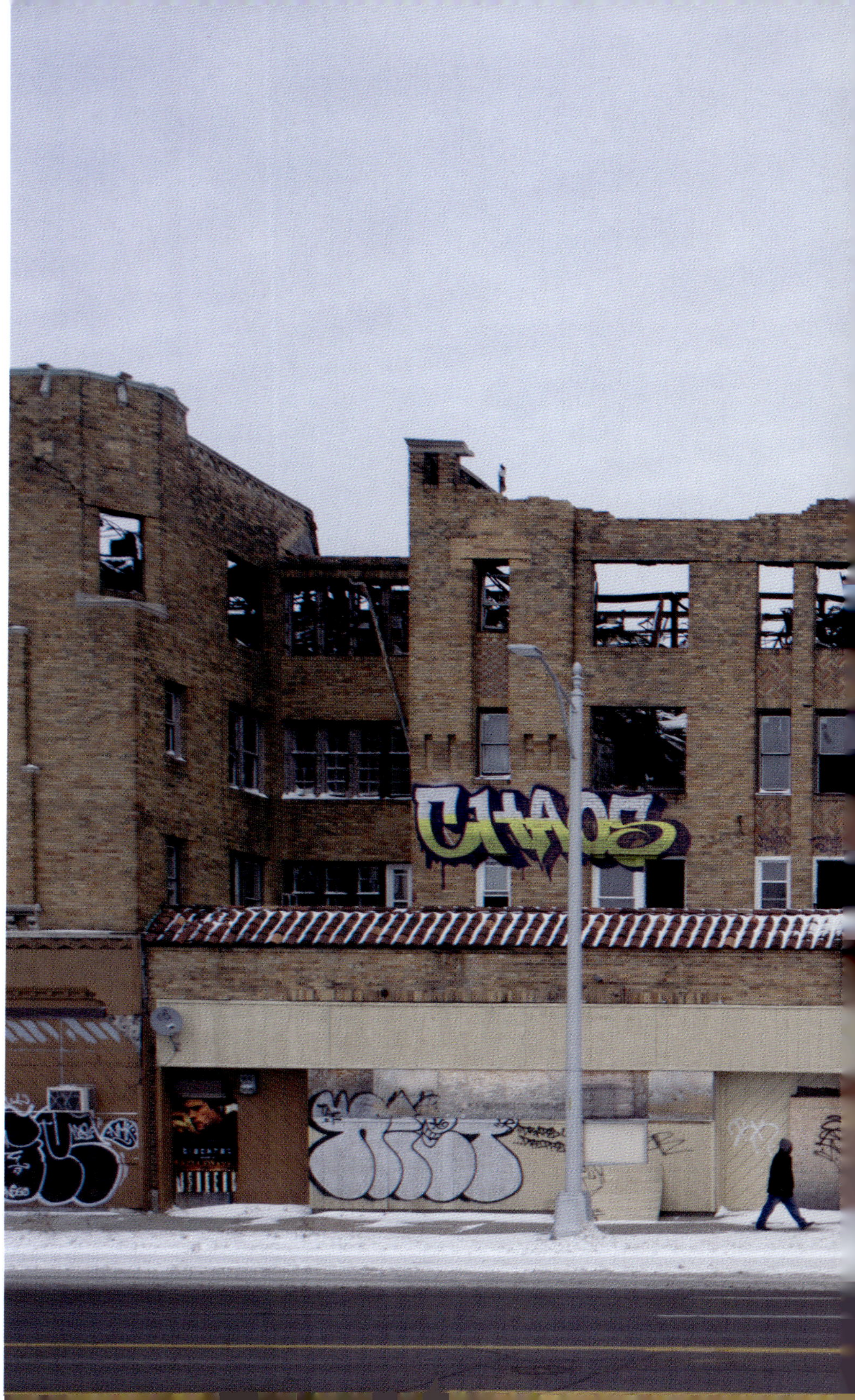

Highland Towers (1932), a former luxury apartment building, takes up an entire block. It has been a ruin since 2009. Tag artists have further defaced the building. Woodward Avenue at McLean Street, Highland Park, 2015.

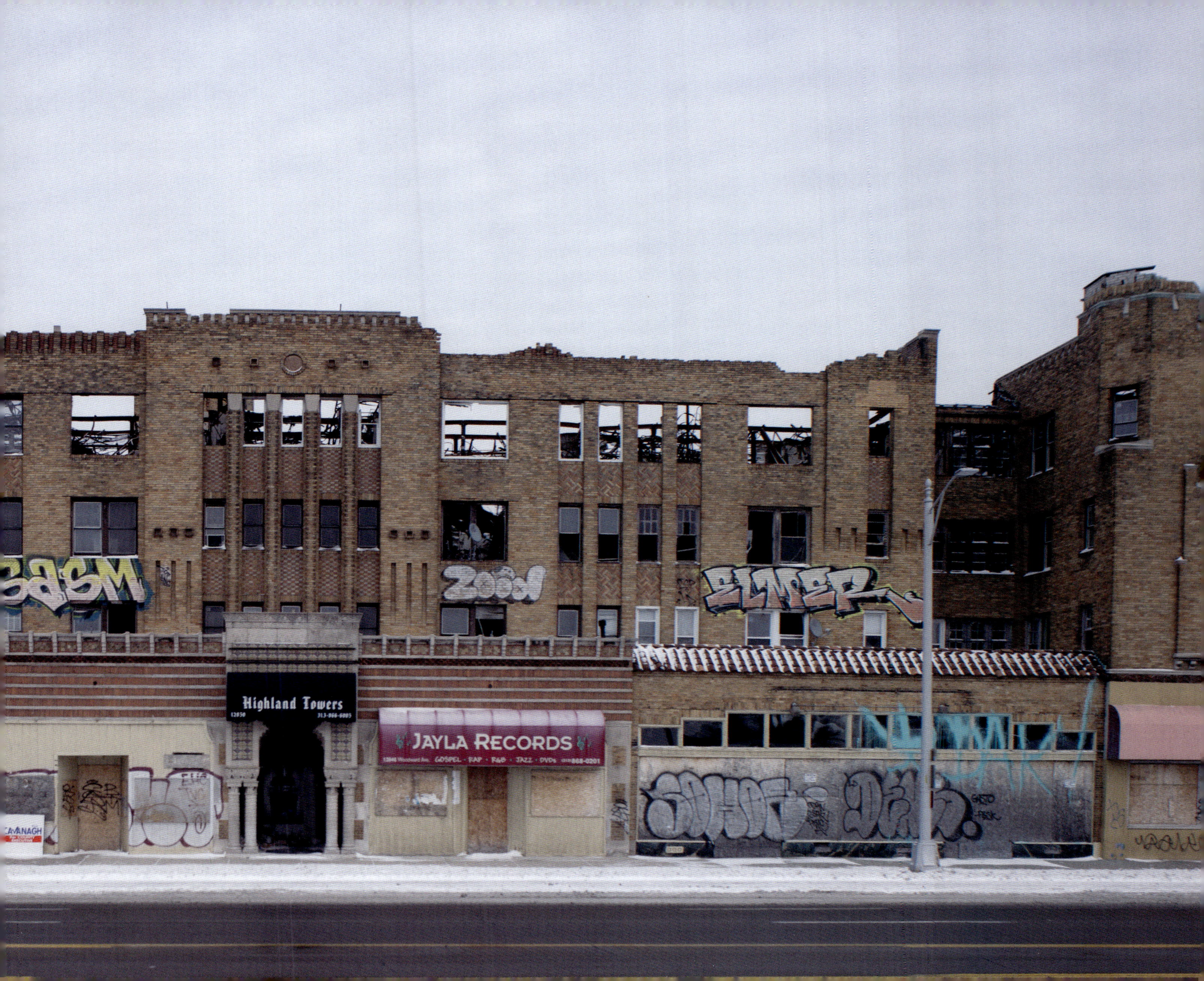
Highland Towers
JAYLA RECORDS
GOSPEL · RAP · R&B · JAZZ · DVDs
CAVANAGH

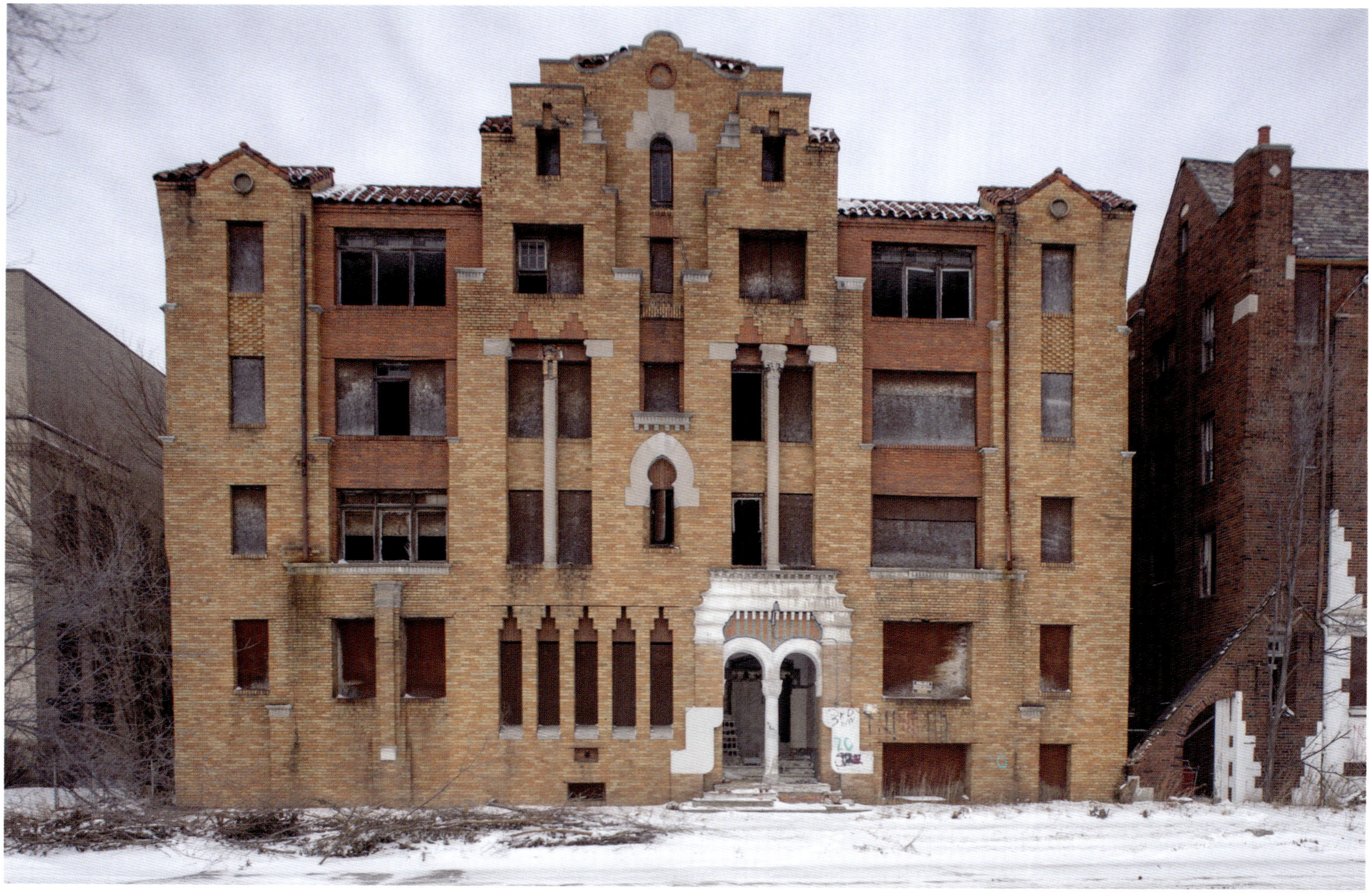

Moorish-style apartment building. 70 Highland Street, Highland Park, 2015.

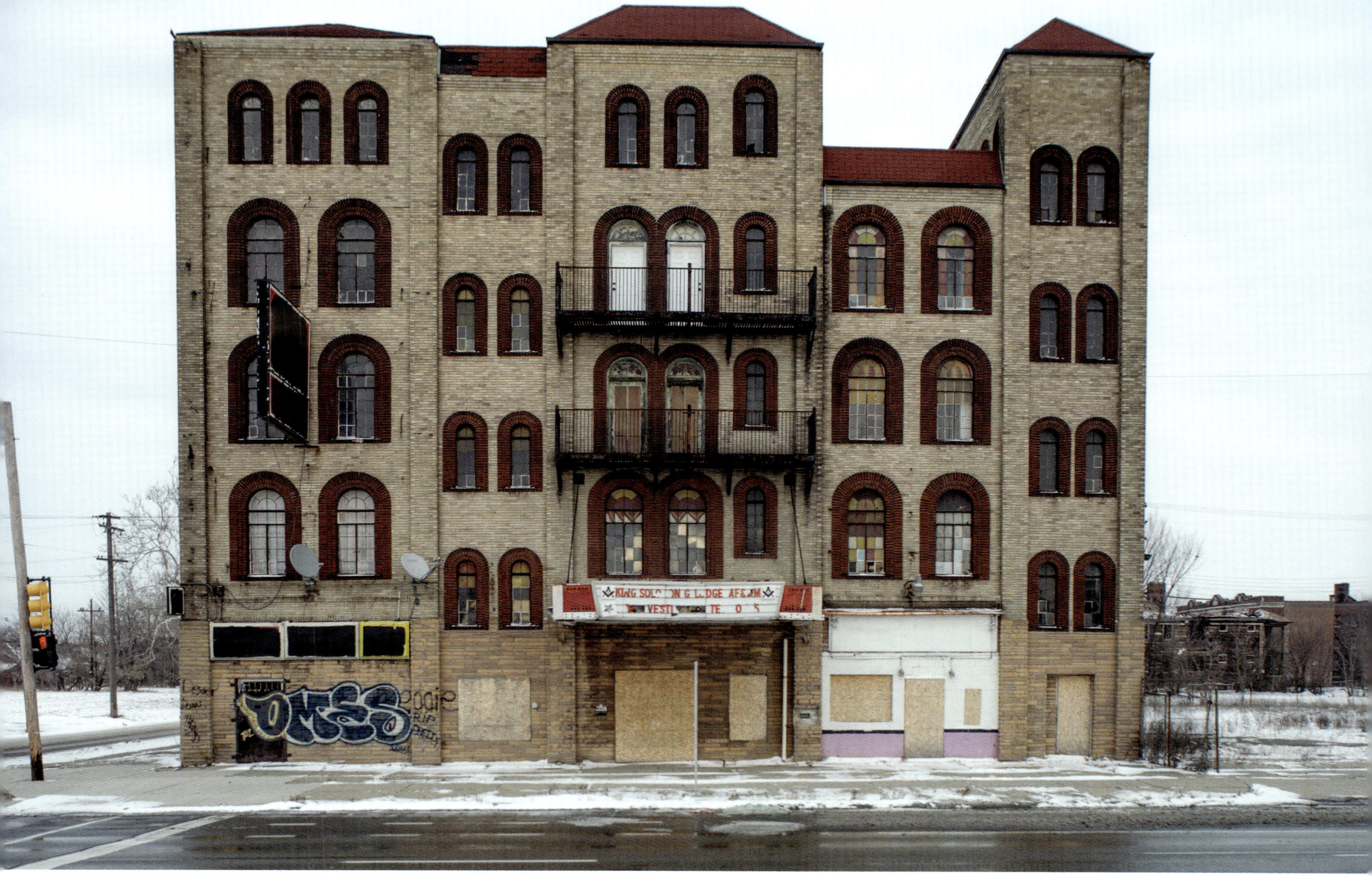

Former King Solomon Lodge. Dexter Avenue at Boston Boulevard, Detroit, 2015.

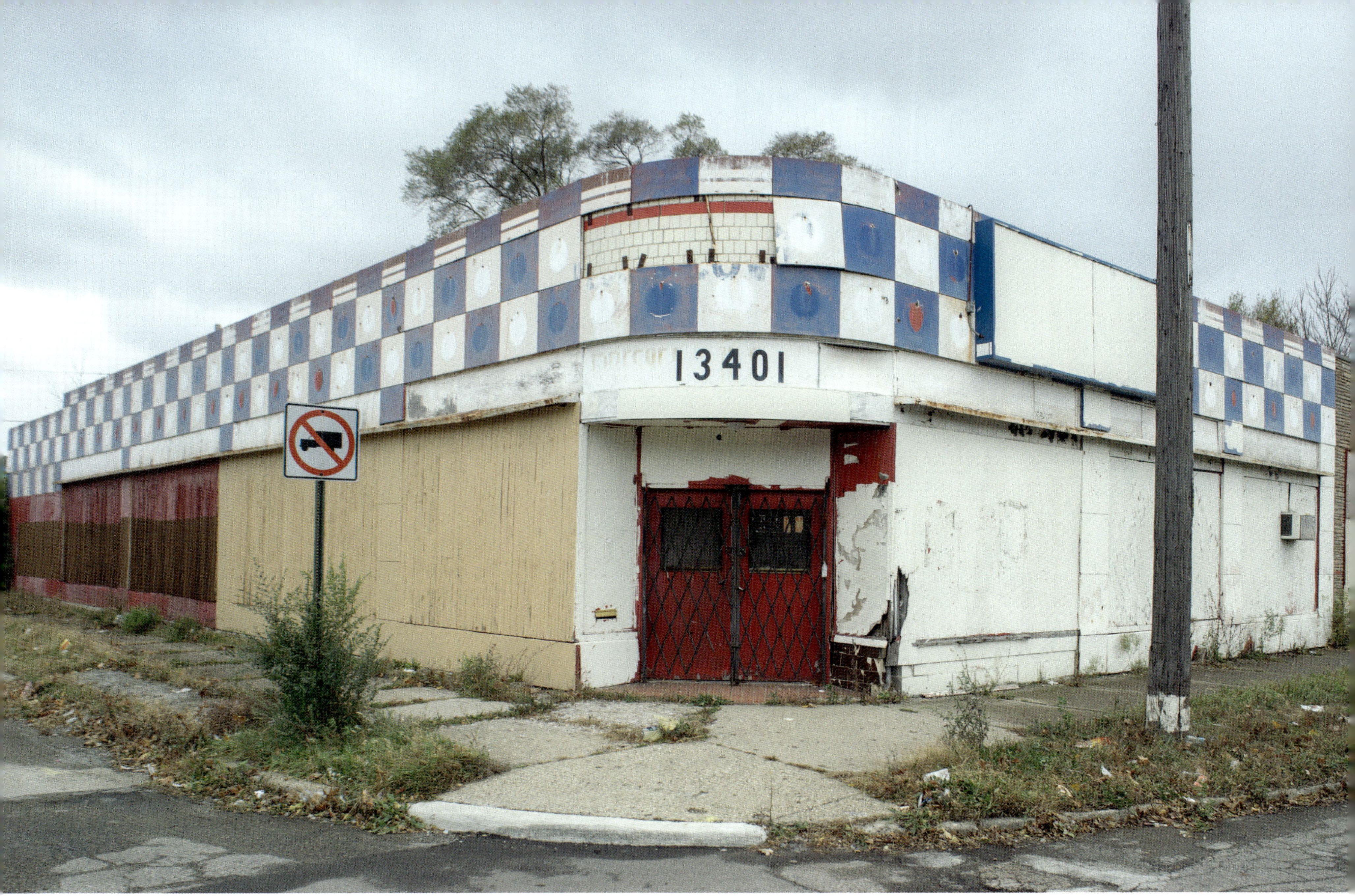

This building was erected in 1937 as a substantial commercial venue but has gone through many permutations since. In 2013, it was a facility managed by "From Felons to Professionals," a mentorship program to help felons return to society. 13401 Fenkell Avenue, Detroit, 2015.

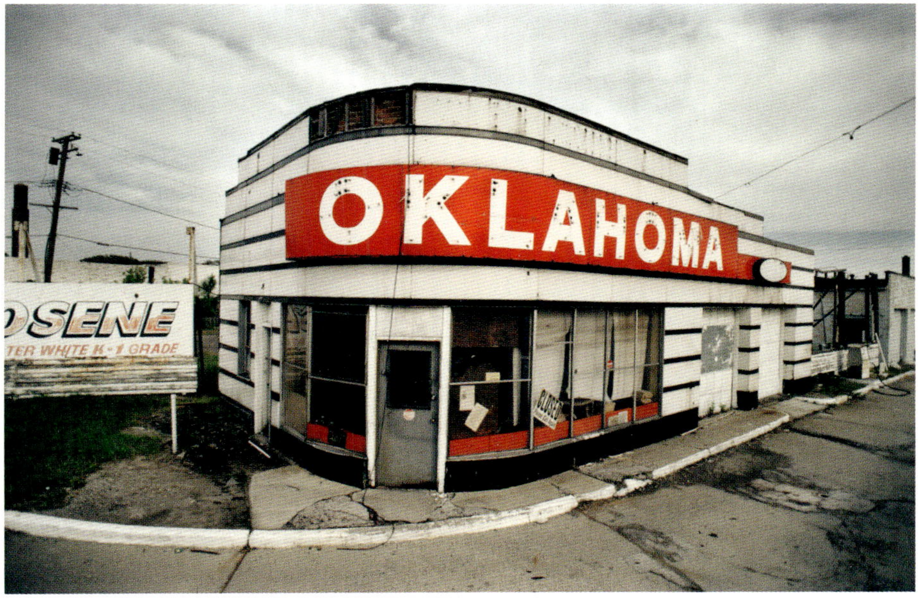

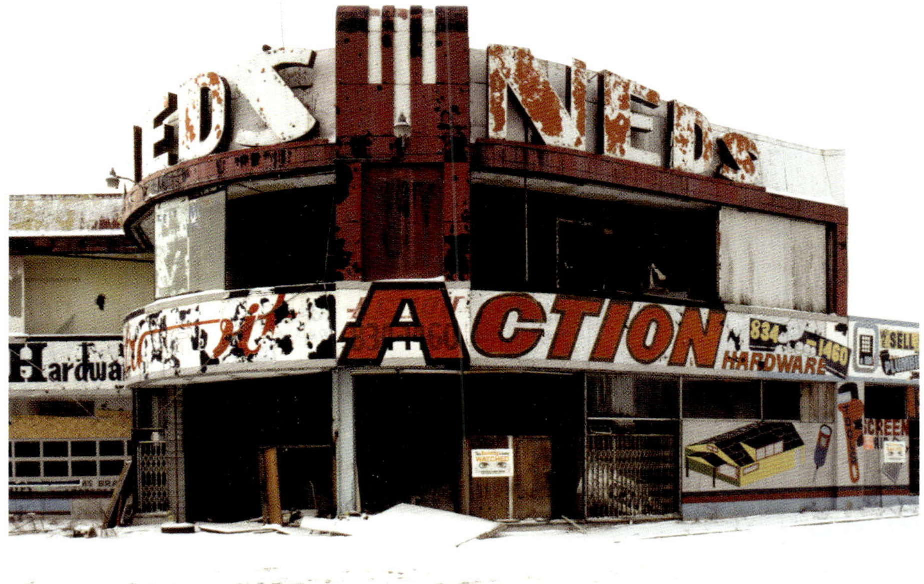

Former Oklahoma Gas Station. This streamlined building, clad with porcelain enamel, was demolished and replaced by a Valero gas station. Livernois Avenue at Joy Road, Detroit, 1998.

Ned's Firestone Tire dealership, now demolished. Contrasting with the bold signage are the familiar "eyes" posters put up by the city to warn arsonists that they are being watched. Grand River Avenue at Chicago Avenue, Detroit, 1997.

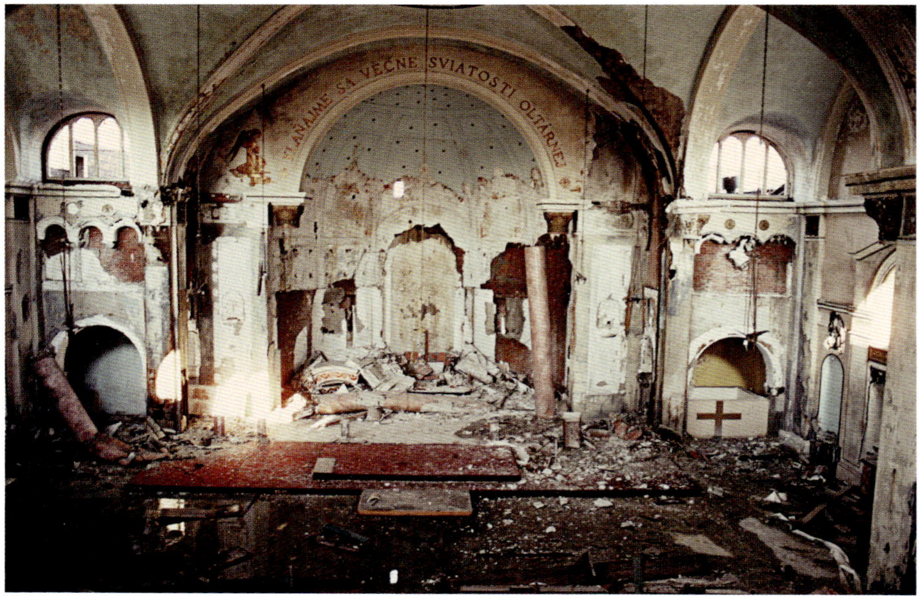

St. Cyril and St. Methodius, a Slovak Catholic Church, was completed in 1929. 9047 Cyril Street, Detroit, 2003.

Former Woodward Avenue Presbyterian Church, built in 1911 in the Gothic revival style, now a ruin. Before being abandoned, the church became the Interdenominational Church. Woodward Avenue at West Philadelphia Street, Detroit, 2013.

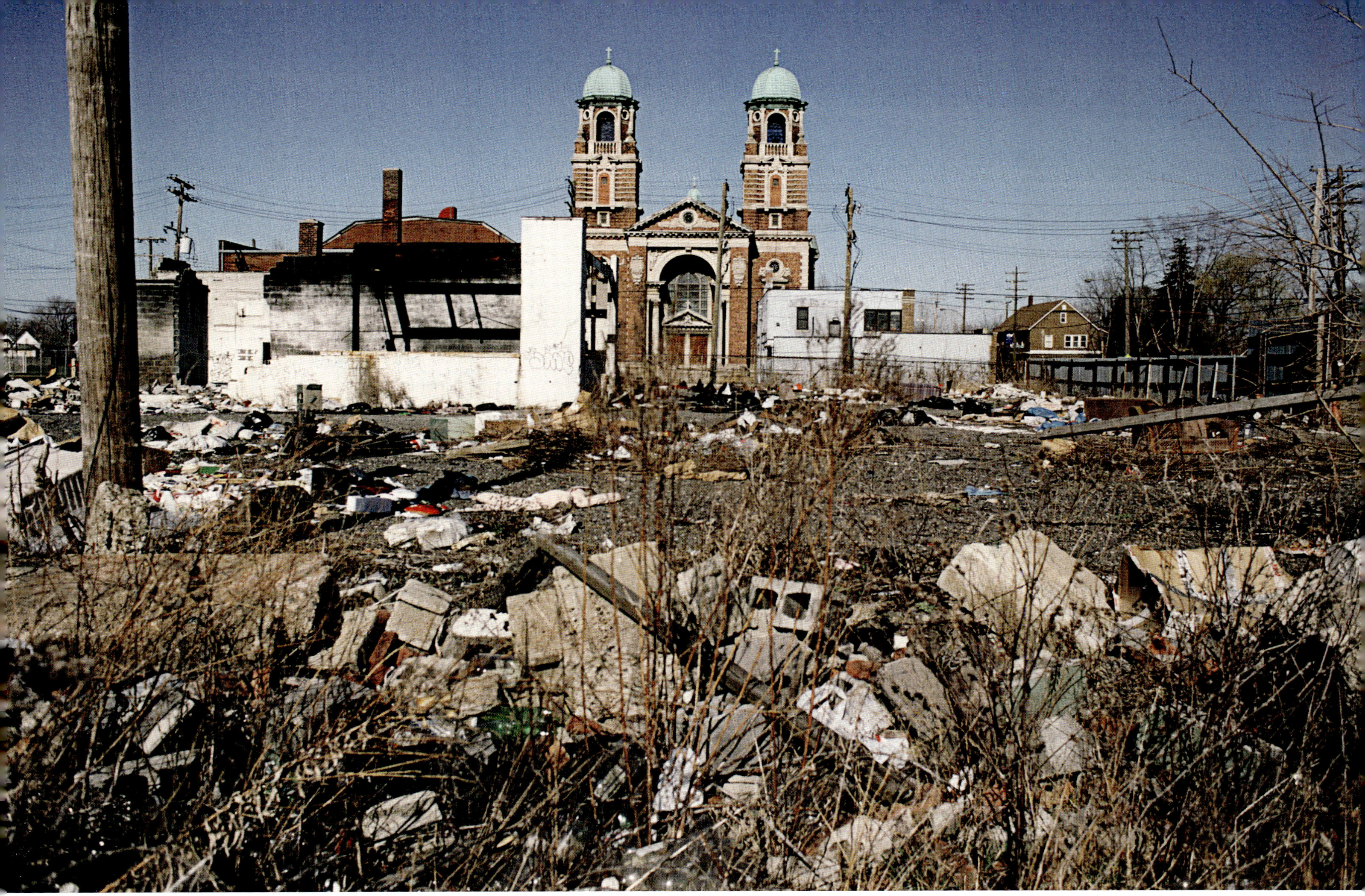

Church of St. Francis of Assisi, 1903. Once a Polish Catholic Church, St. Francis today serves the mostly Latino residents on Detroit's west side. Although the church remains in good repair, it sits amidst industrial ruins. View east from Hammond Street at Buchanan Street, Detroit, 2009.

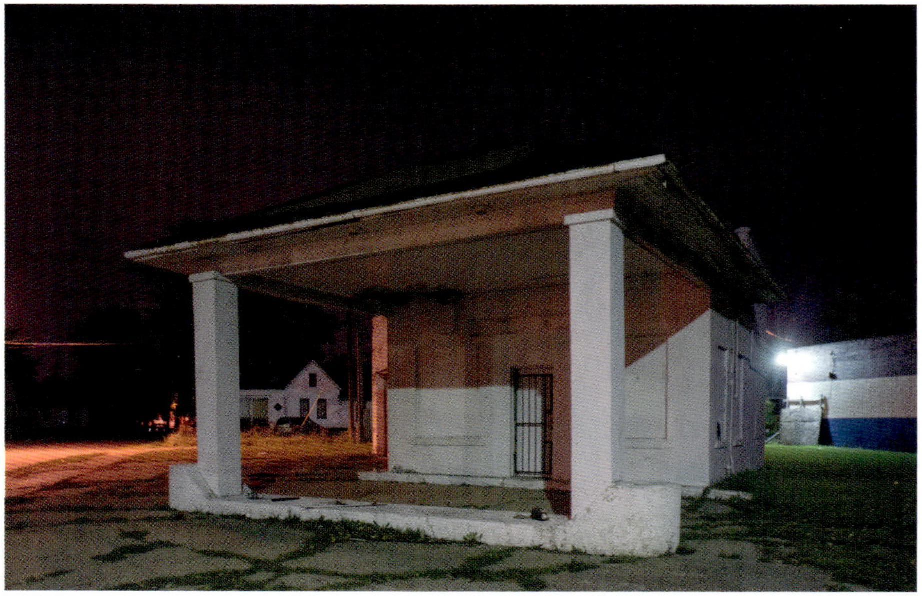

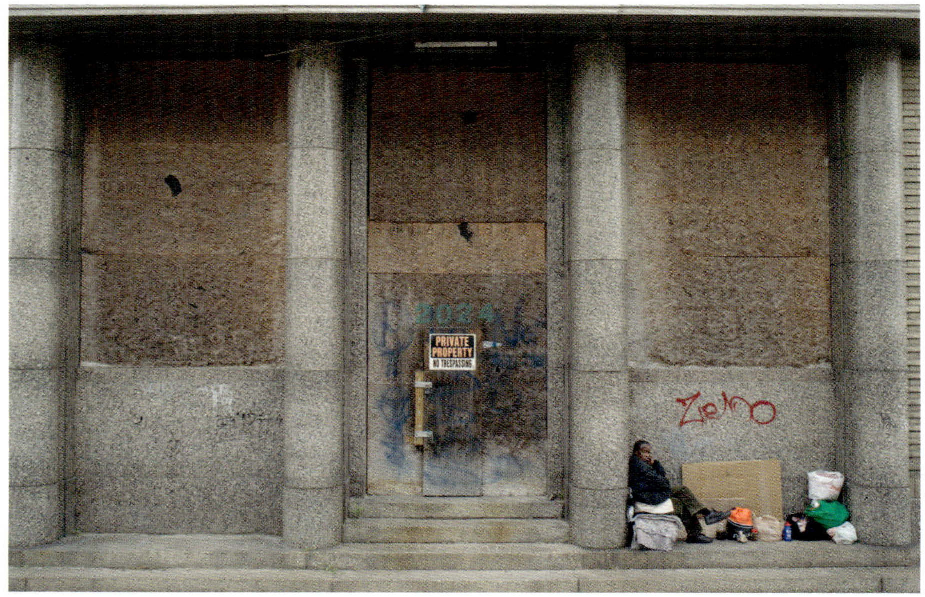

Vintage gas station, transformed into Sweet Kingdom Annex, a storefront church, now abandoned. Chene Street at Superior Street, Detroit, 2013.

Detail, Roosevelt Warehouse, used as a school book depository; abandoned after a fire in 1987. In 2009, the body of a frozen homeless man encased in ice was found in the basement. 14th Street at Marantette Street, Detroit, 2015.

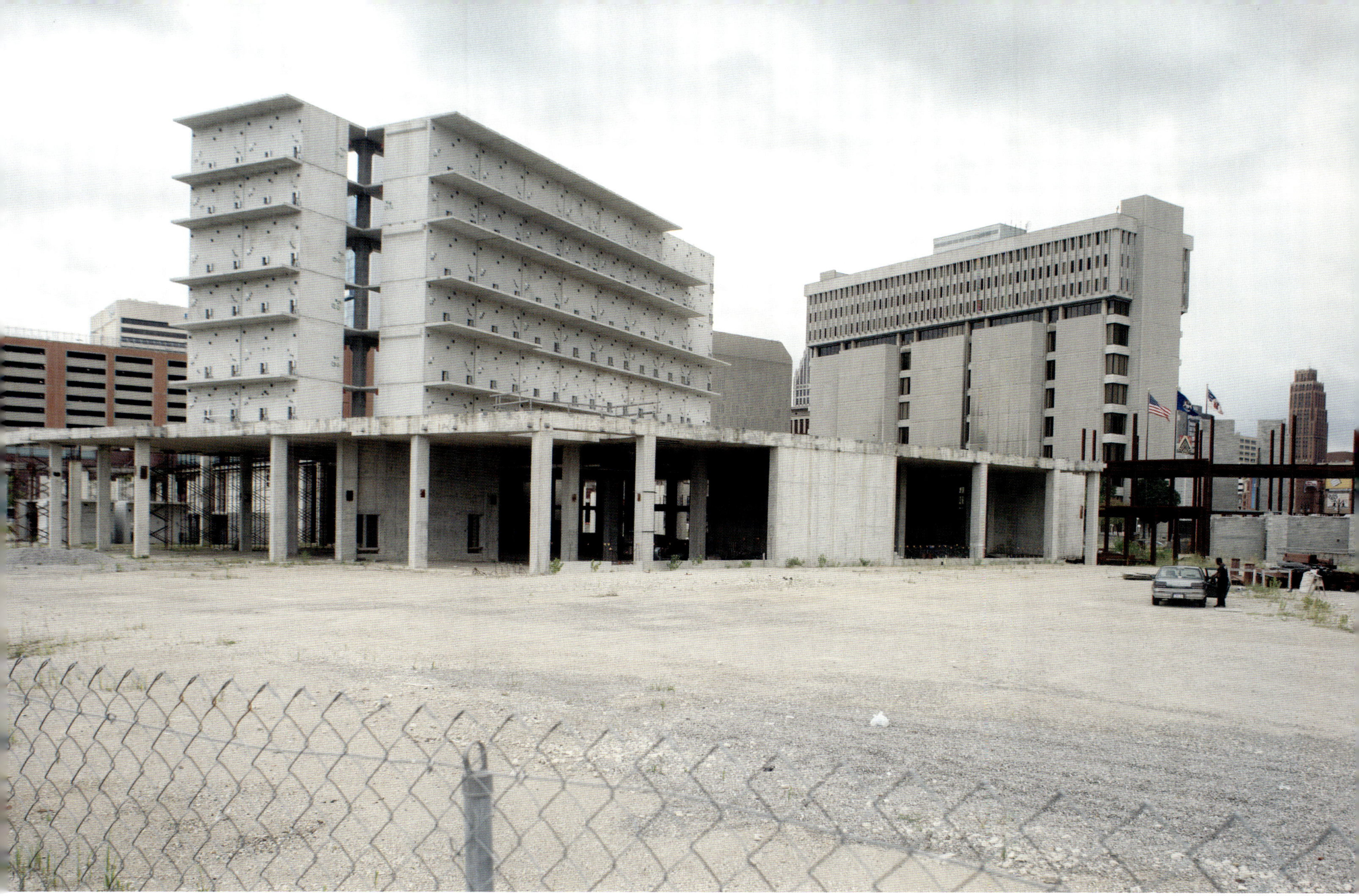

Wayne County Jail, intended as a 715,000 square-foot facility, was left unfinished in 2013. Overruns threatened to almost double the initial cost estimate of $220 million. Gratiot Avenue at St. Antoine Street, Detroit, 2015.

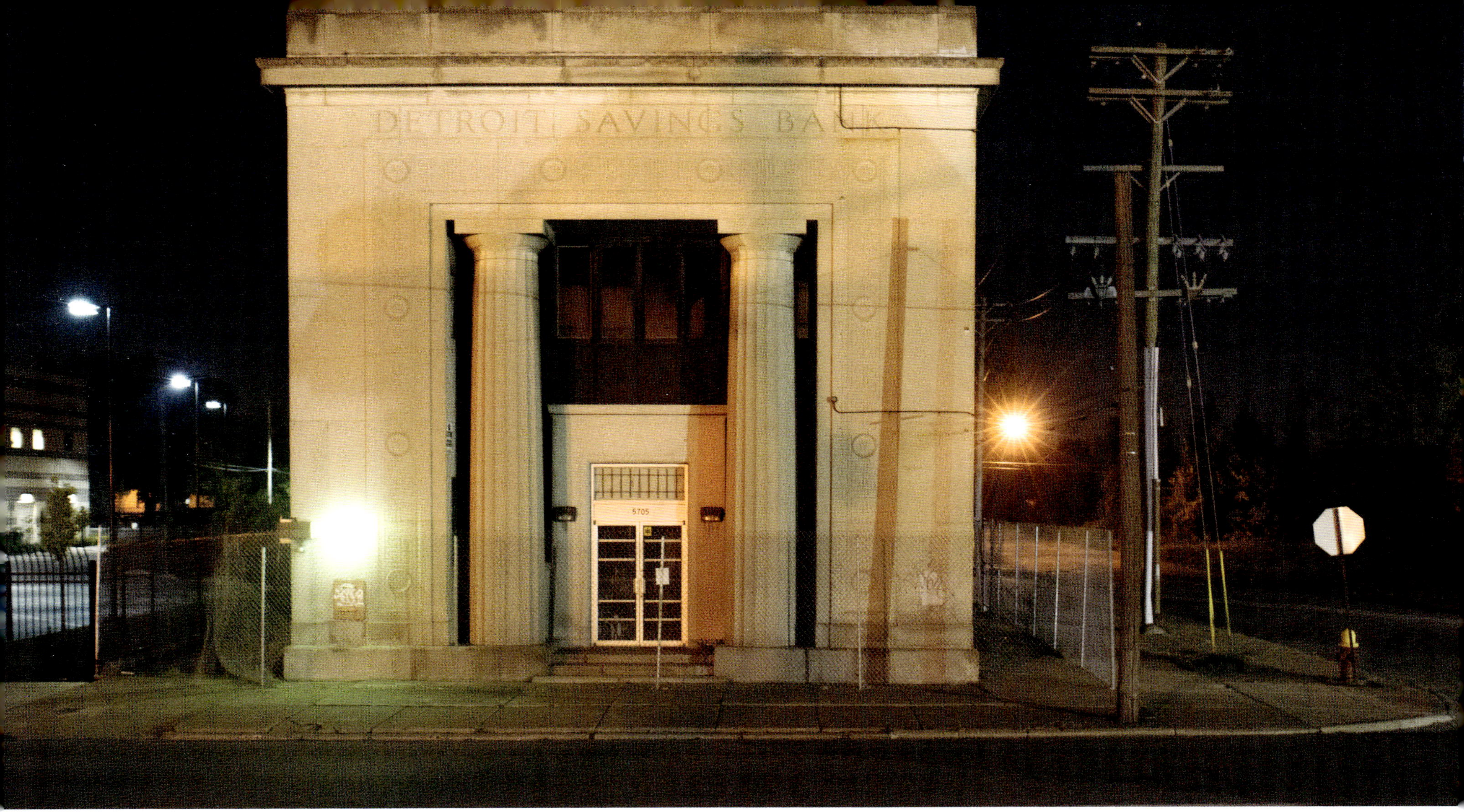

Former Detroit Savings Bank. This neoclassical-style bank, designed by Albert Kahn in the early twentieth century, was nominated to the National Register of Historic Places in 2014. 5705 West Fort Street, Detroit, 2013.

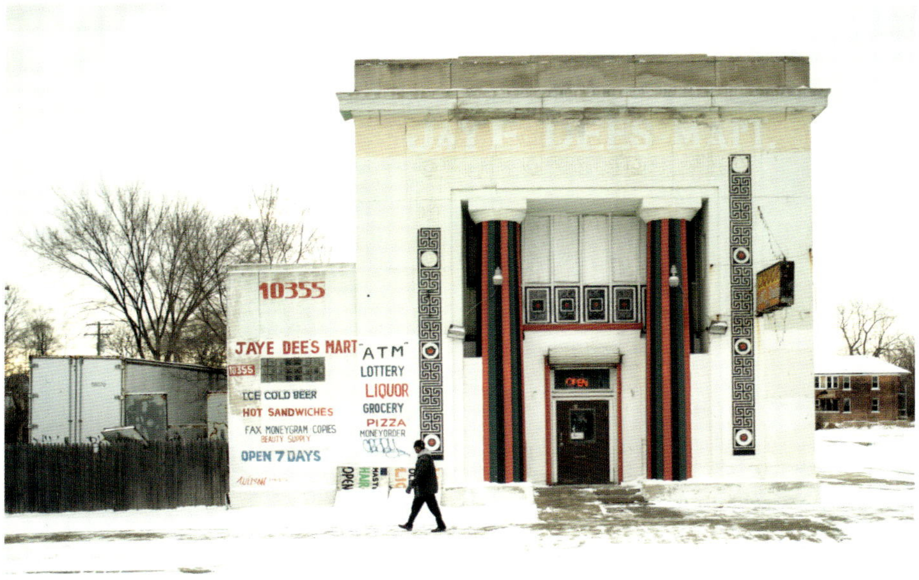

NEW LIFE FOR FORMER BANKS Bank buildings have a distinctive appearance. Often located on a street corner, they are sturdily built, with a flagpole on the roof and on the side wall a safe deposit box and a metal alarm. They outlive the rest of the buildings on the block, going on to become churches, fast food restaurants, community organizations, and even gentlemen's clubs. When abandoned, banks resemble Old World ruins; their prominently displayed clocks have stopped and trees grow on their roofs.

Jaye Dee's Market is a liquor store on Hamilton Avenue, but the building had served as the Detroit Bank and Trust until the early 1980s. I asked Jason, the present owner, what it's like to have a business in a former bank building. He responded by asking, "Do you have a problem with that?" I had to convince him that I had no intention of "demonizing his building." He explained: "My parents needed to move the store to another location, but they didn't want to move out of the neighborhood. The building had been empty for a long time and was a good building so they moved here. The name Jaye Dee's Market comes from my name, Jason Dean. They made the words longer so as to 'give it a swagger.'" He had the columns painted red for the blood of the people, black for their skin color, and green for the land.

Jaye Dee's Market. The former Detroit Bank and Trust was vacant in 1994 when Jaye Dee's Market moved in. The columns are painted in the colors of the Pan-African flag. 10355 Hamilton Avenue, Detroit, 2015.

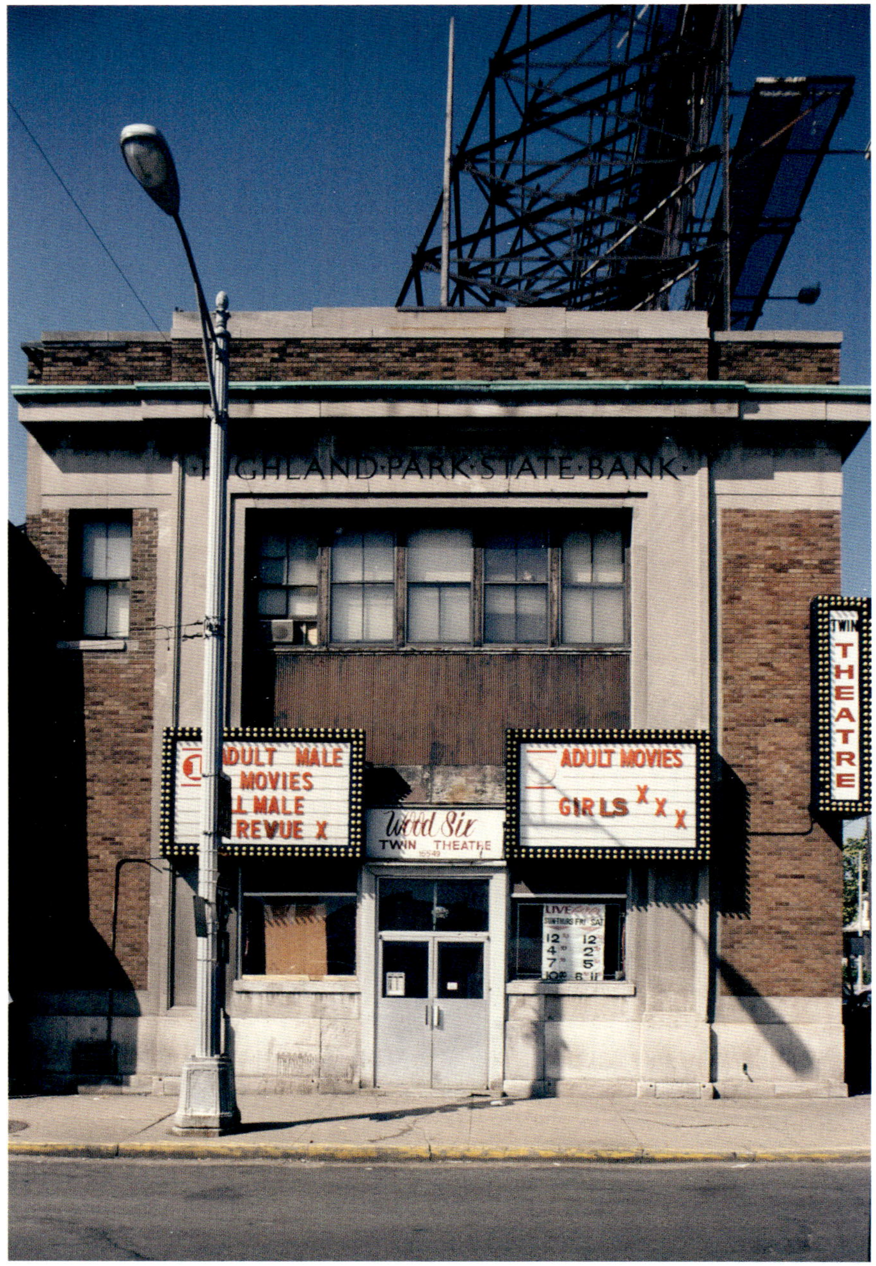

Former Highland Park State Bank, which became the Wood Twin Six adult theater. 16549 Woodward Avenue, Highland Park, 1993.

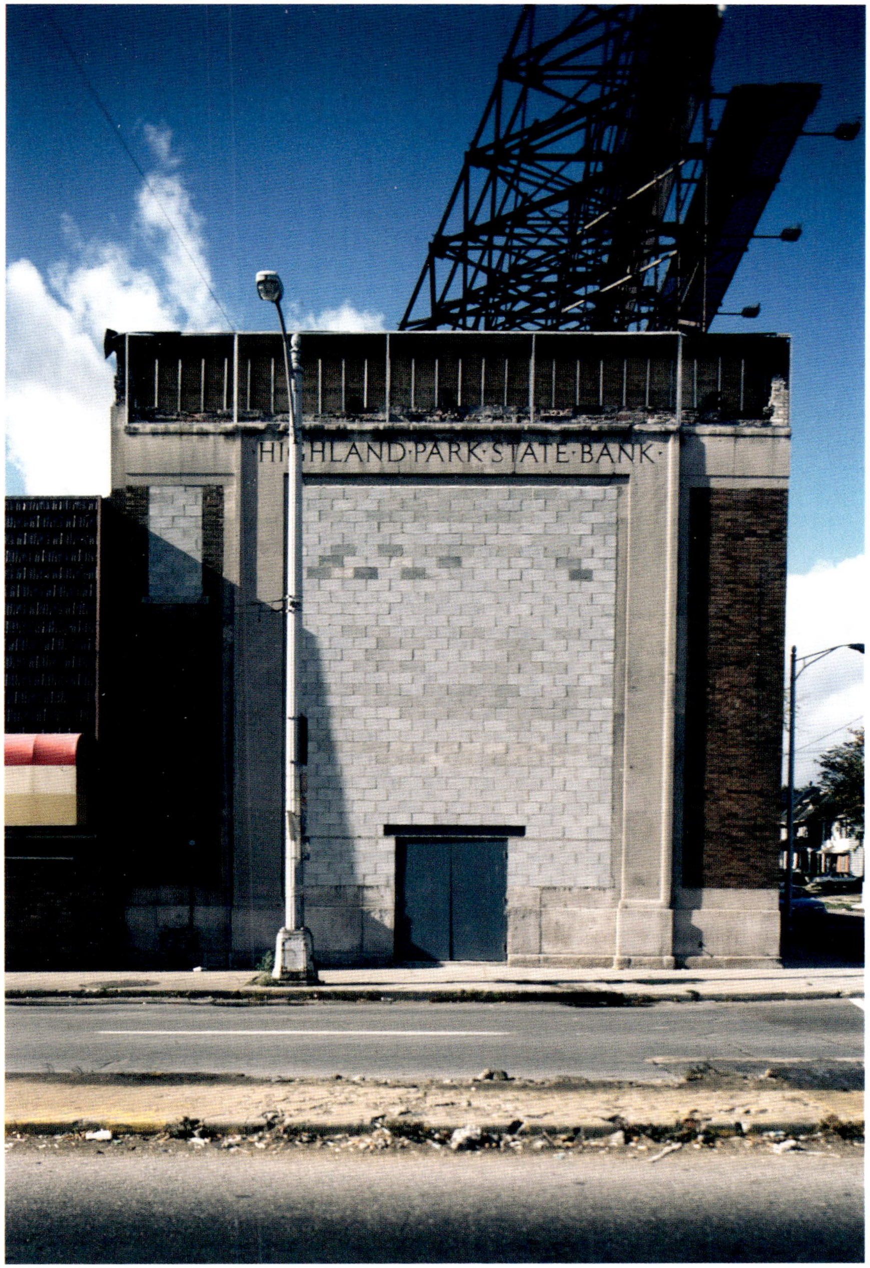

16549 Woodward Avenue, Highland Park, 2002.

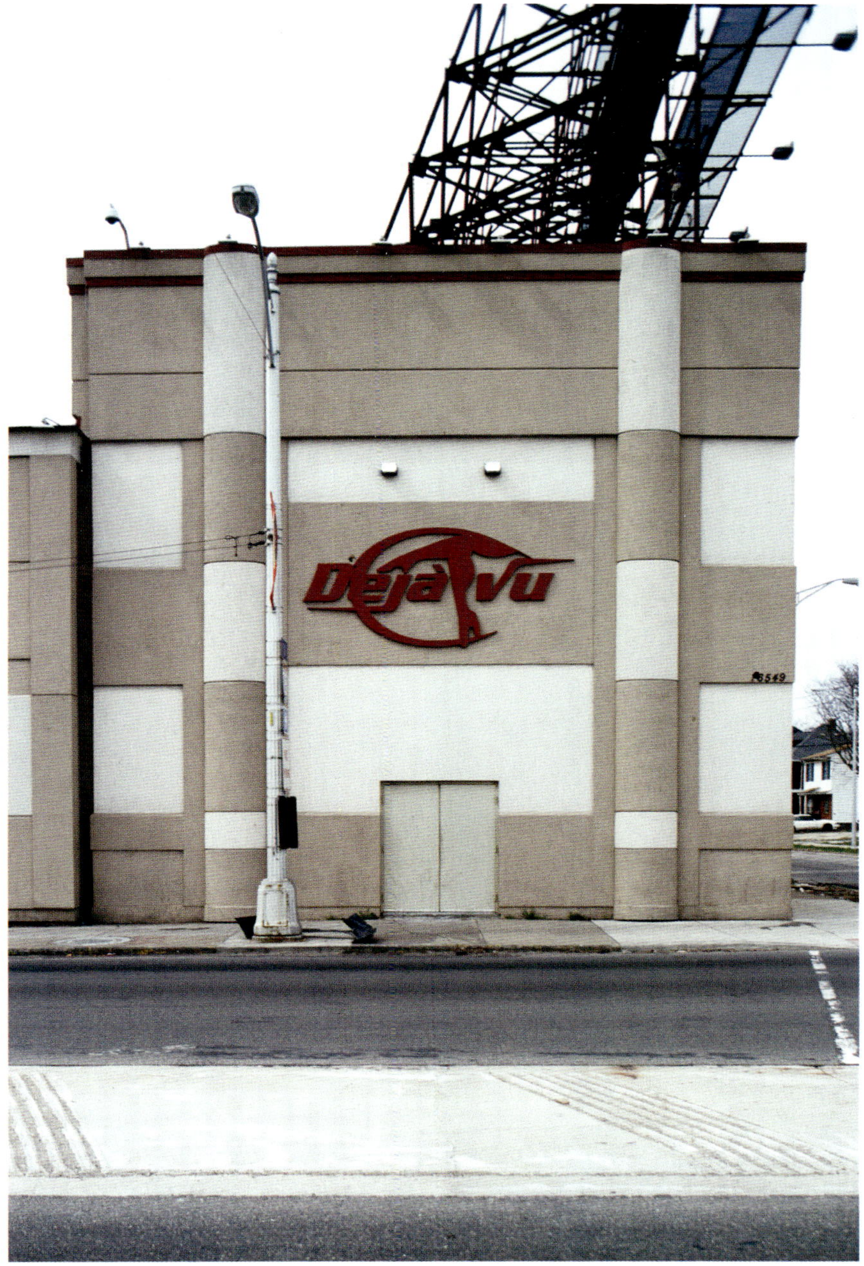

Deja Vu Strip Club, adult entertainment. 16549 Woodward Avenue, Highland Park, 2009.

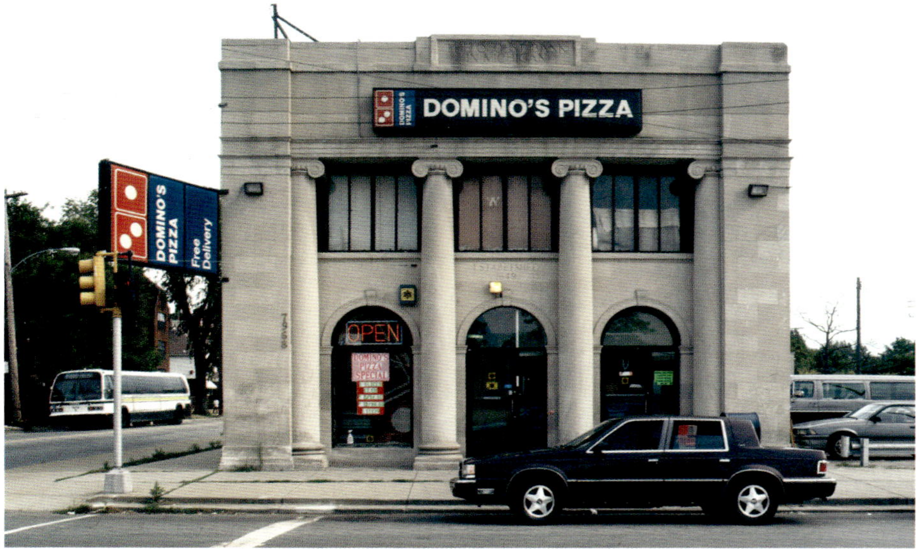

Domino's Pizza. The sign above reads, "The Oldest Bank in Michigan." Kercheval Street at Van Dyke Road, Detroit, 1991.

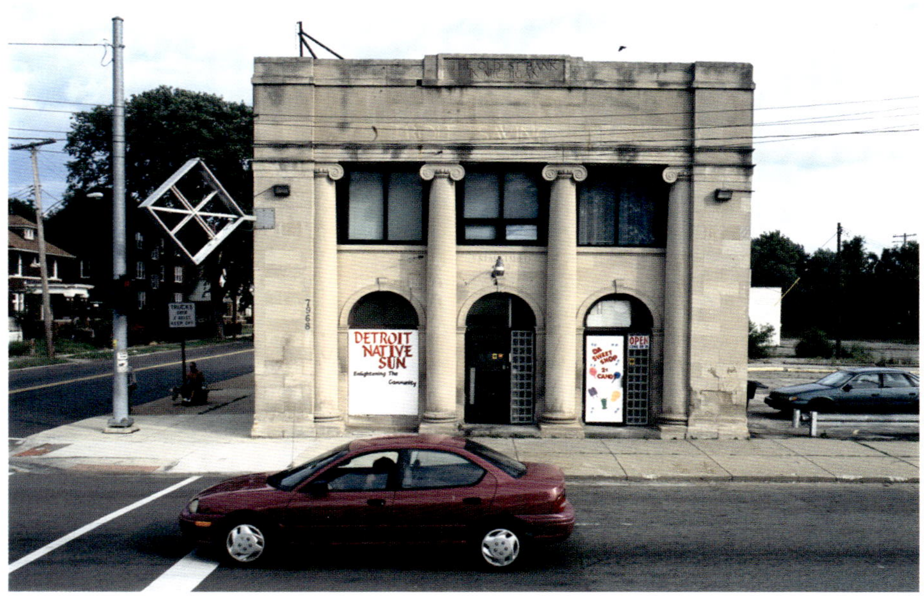

Detroit Native Sun, which produces a free publication of the same name, and Da Sweet Shop share the ground floor of the former bank. Kercheval Street at Van Dyke Road, Detroit, 2011.

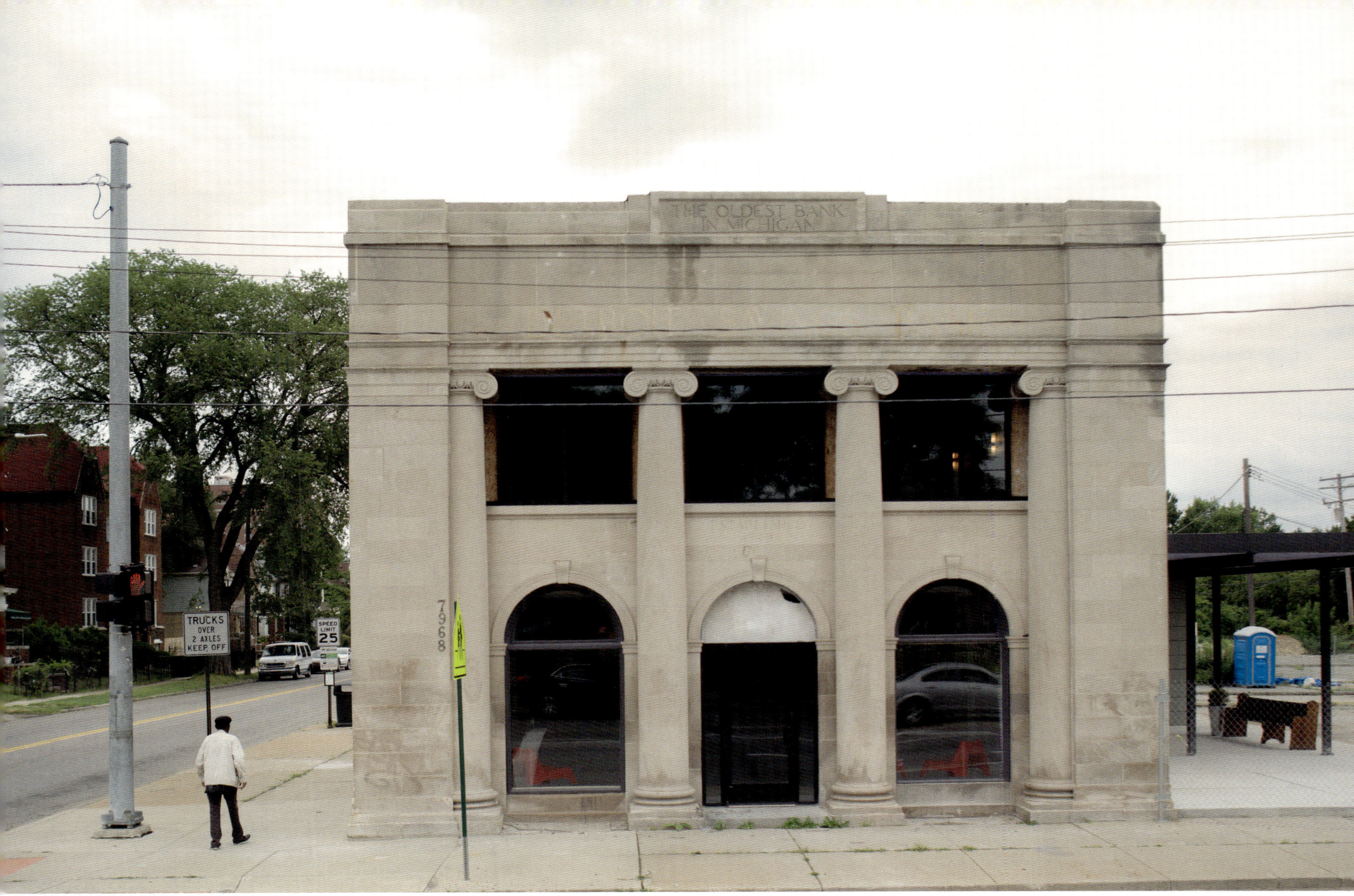

In 2015, the former bank was being rehabbed. There will be a flower shop on the ground floor and apartments on the second floor. Kercheval Avenue at Van Dyke Road, Detroit, 2015.

TO REACH THE LOST: CHURCHES WHERE EVERYBODY IS SOMEBODY

The attitude of many residents of the neighborhoods, who patiently rely on God to intervene, contrasts with the city leaders' sense of urgency for Detroit to "come back." A lady gives testimony at an outdoor service of the Free Indeed Outreach Ministries, while a member of the congregation grills sausages to offer to passersby. Charles, a member of the congregation, told me, "Detroit has been through a lot, but the people of Detroit have not given up.... The city is going to come back, but perhaps not during my lifetime." He warned, "We can't rush God." Charles as well as other religious leaders place their faith in God that things are going to turn around. They are willing to help out, but bringing about a revival is not in their power. The late Pastor Prota Stevan of St. Petka Serbian Orthodox Church similarly was quoted as saying: "The true Builder of the Holy is not man, nor his money and power, but God Himself, Who sanctifies all creation."

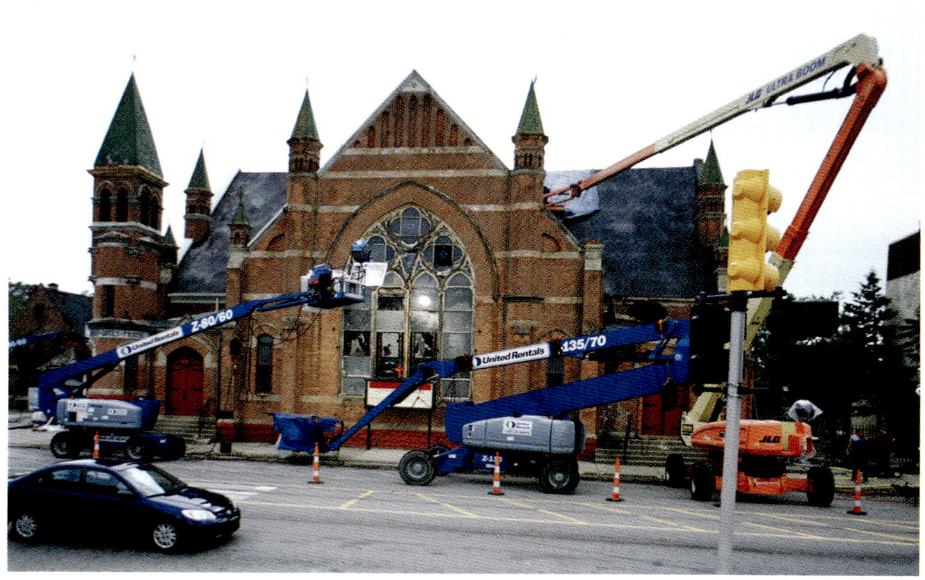

A movie is being filmed at Pilgrim Church, which includes a shelter called I am My Brother's Keeper. The building was completed in 1891 for the Trumbull Avenue Presbyterian Church, changed owners, and was renamed Pilgrim Church in 1992. Grand River Avenue at Trumbull Street, Detroit, 2011.

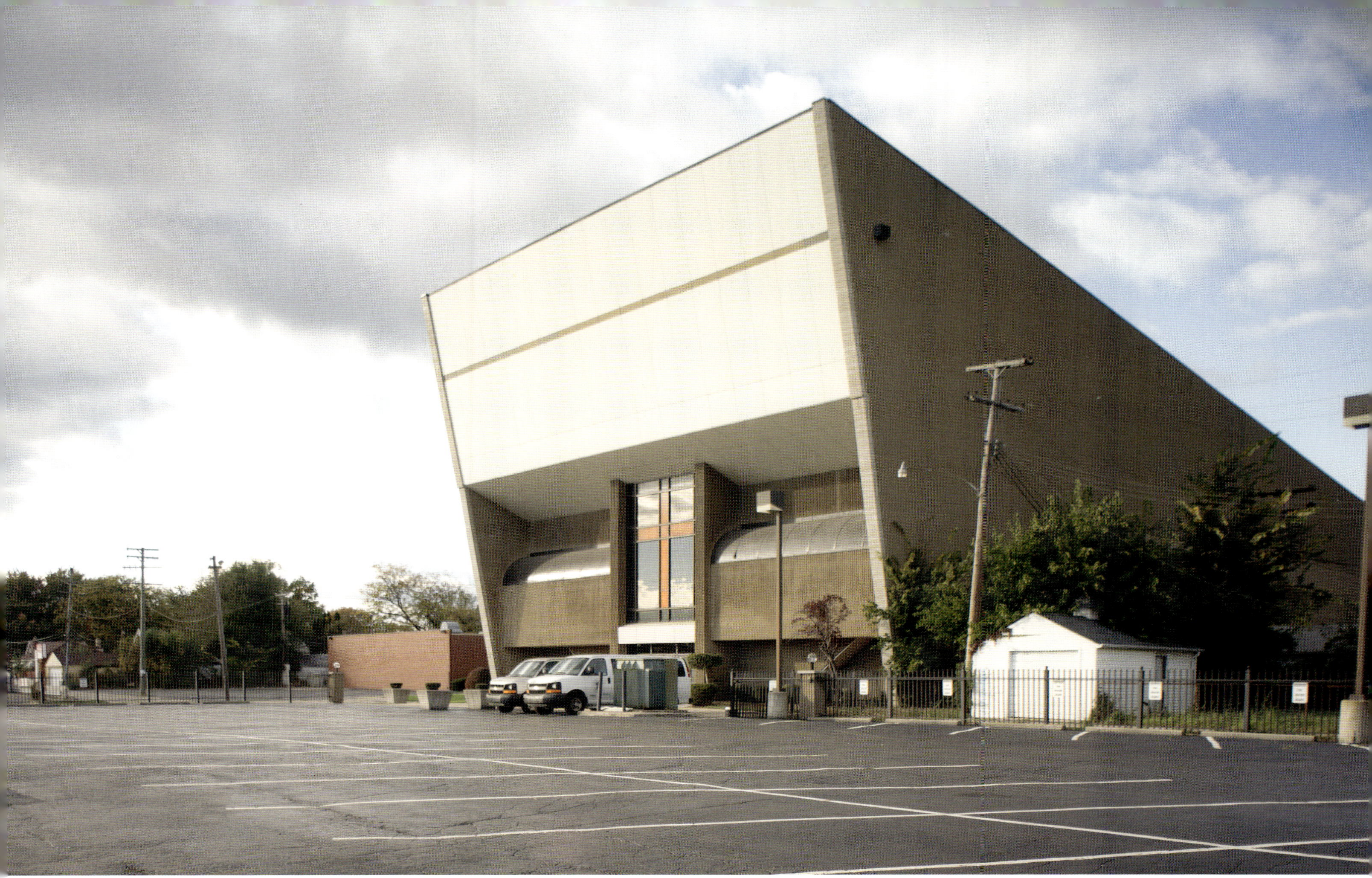

Brutalist-style church built in 1954 by Greater Grace Temple is now Greater Emmanuel Institutional Church of God in Christ, whose motto is "A church that is driven by the cross." West Seven Mile at Schaefer Highway, Detroit, 2013.

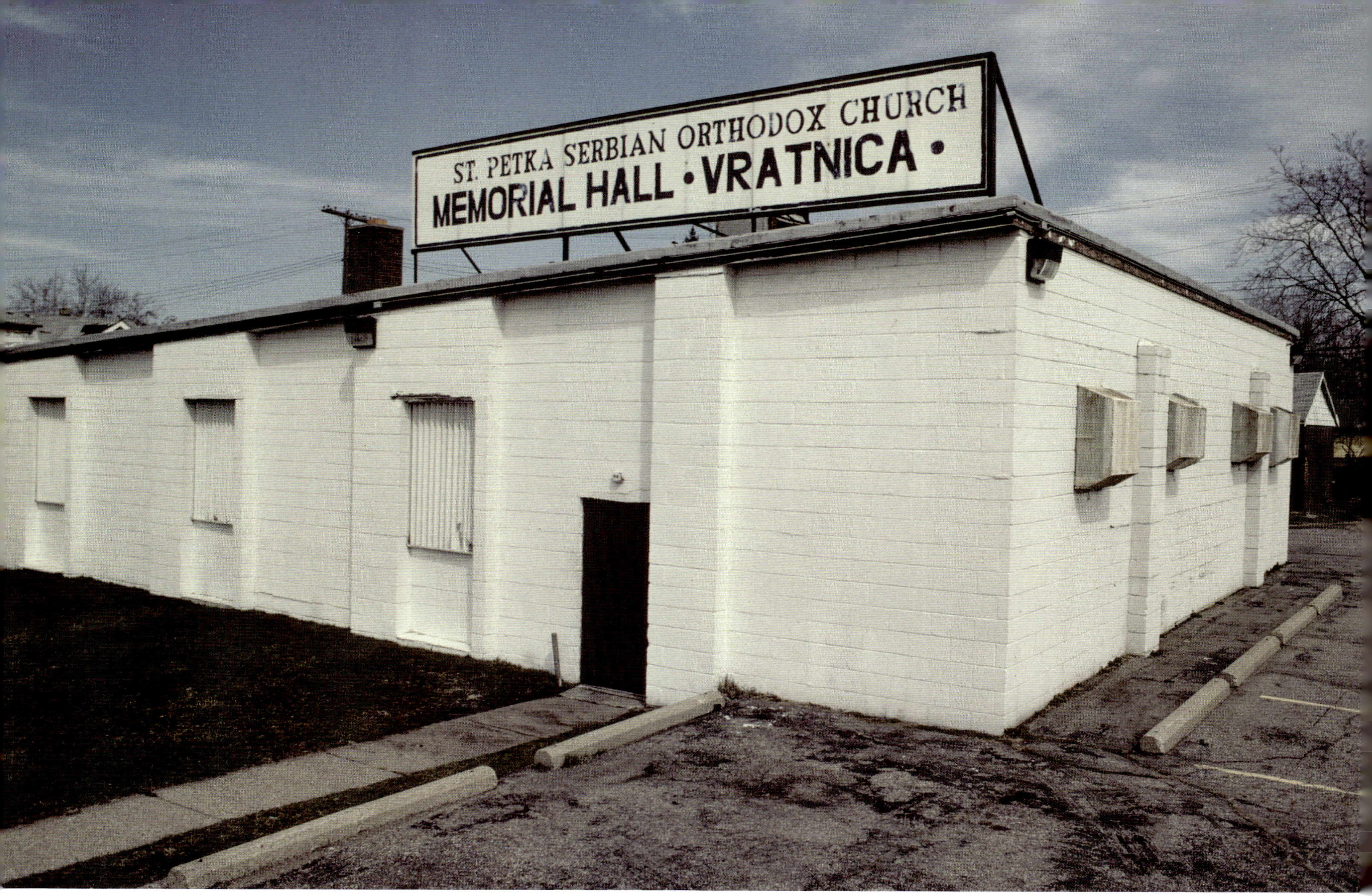

Former Memorial Hall of St. Petka Serbian Orthodox Church, looking like a combination of fortress and shed. Van Dyke Road at Emily Street, Detroit, 2006.

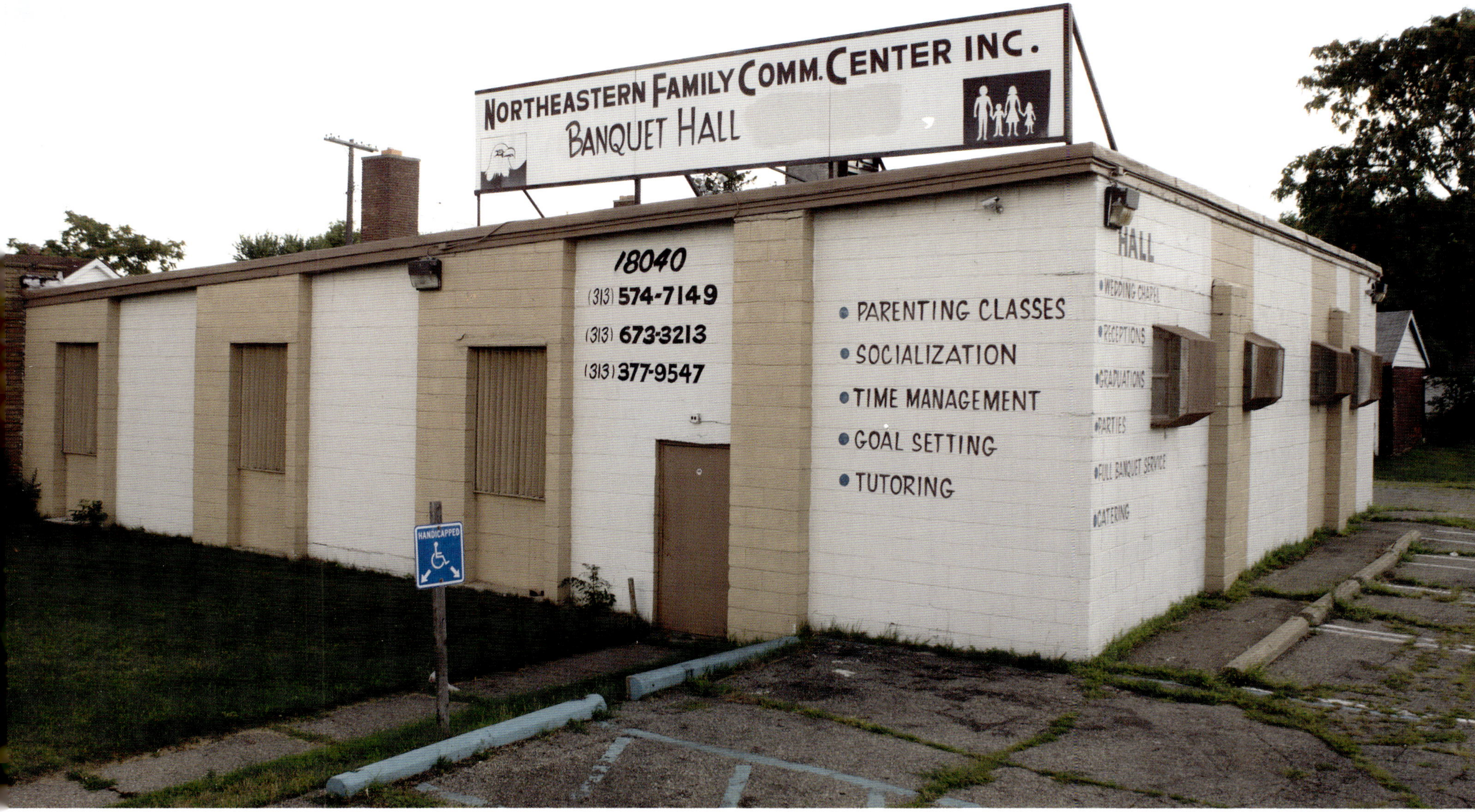

Northeastern Family Community Center, former Memorial Hall of St. Petka Serbian Orthodox Church. Van Dyke Road at Emily Street, Detroit, 2006.

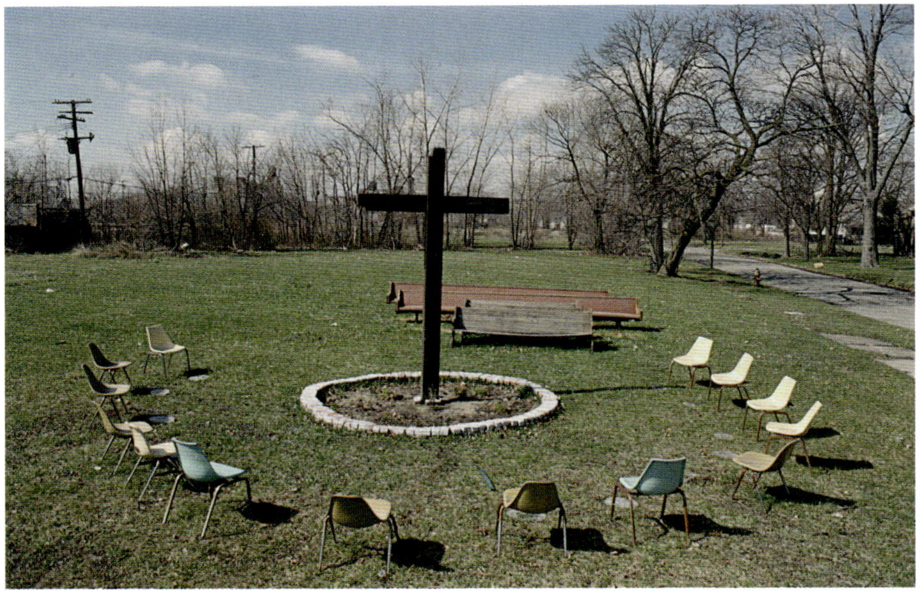

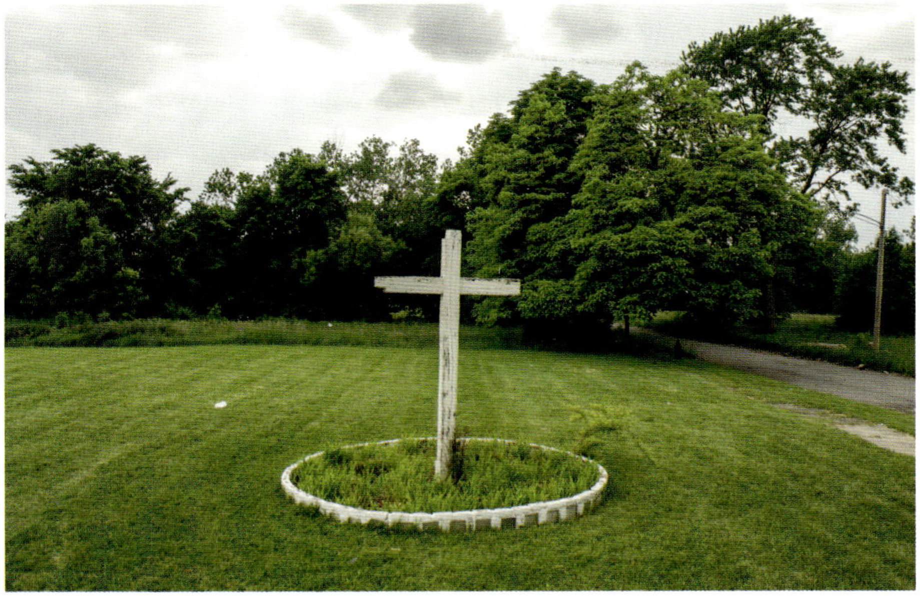

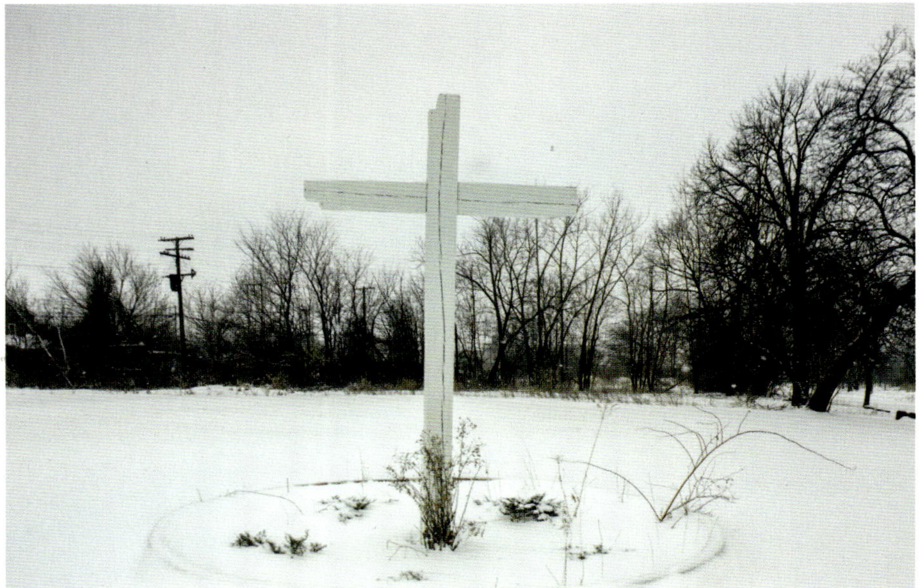

Above Free Indeed Outreach Ministries, makeshift meeting place and outdoor church. Chene Street at Frederick Street, Detroit, 2006.

Below Cross. Chene Street at Frederick Street, Detroit, 2014.

The same cross, in winter. Chene Avenue at Frederick, Detroit, 2014

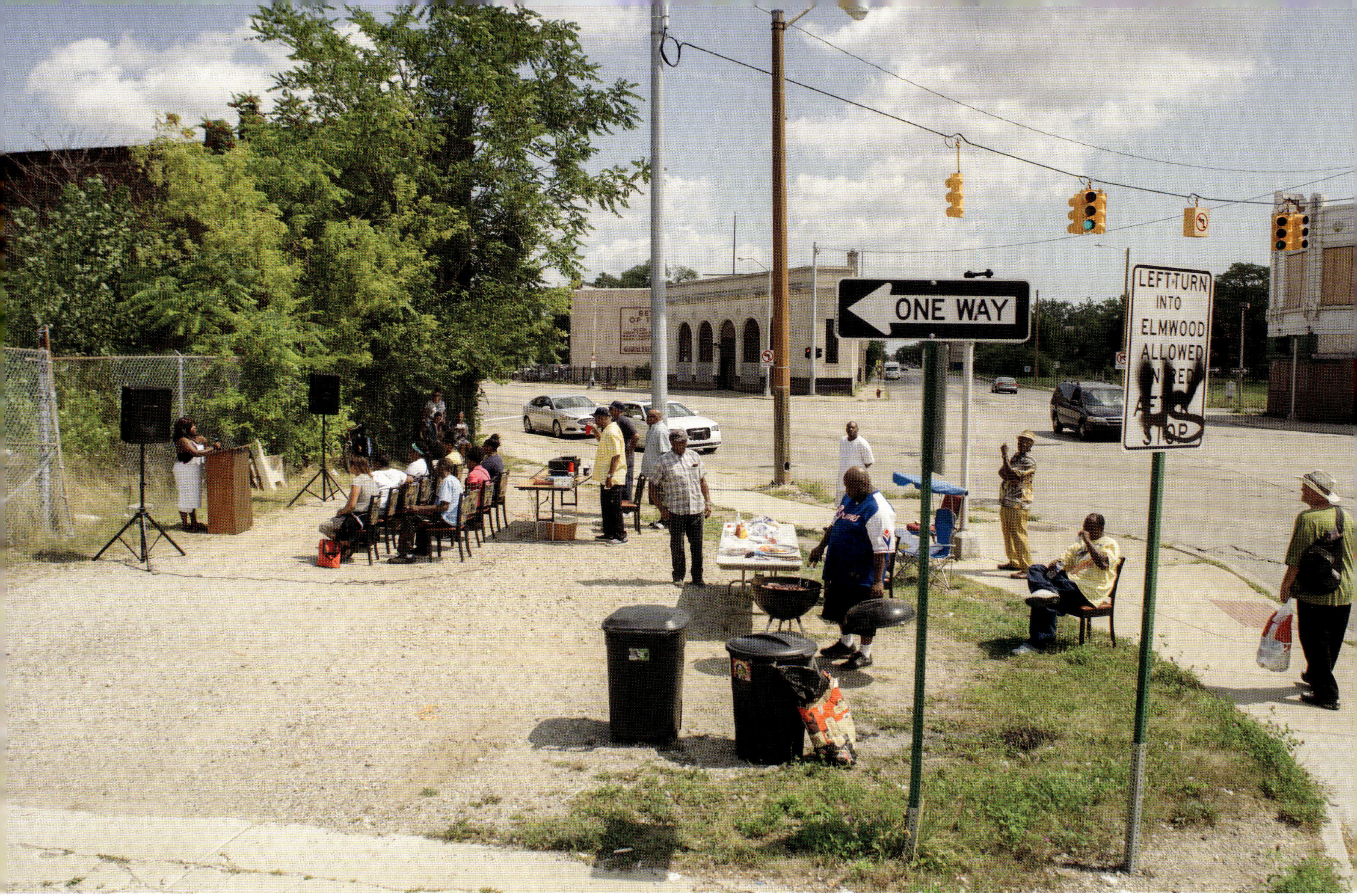

Outdoor service, Free Indeed Outreach Ministries. 3323 Gratiot Avenue, Detroit, 2015.

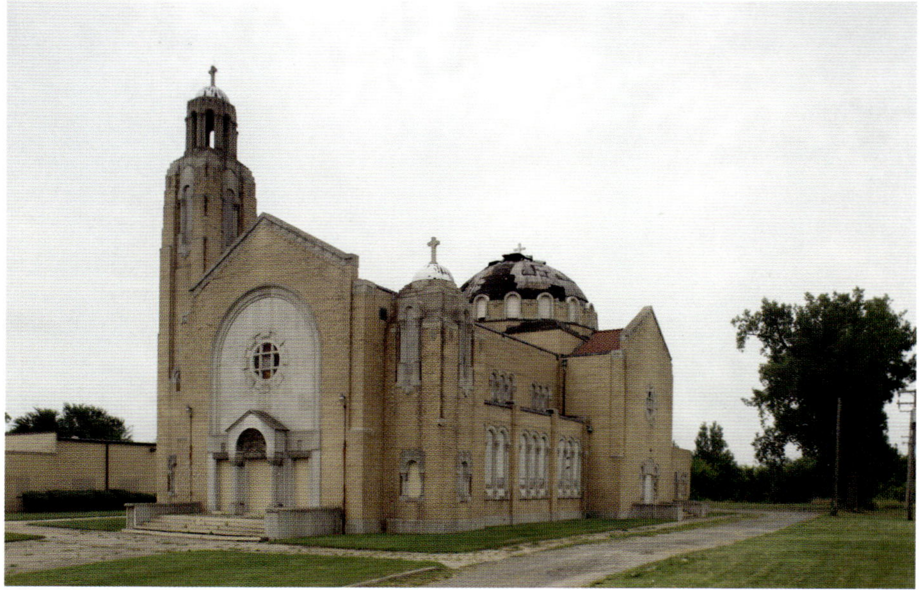

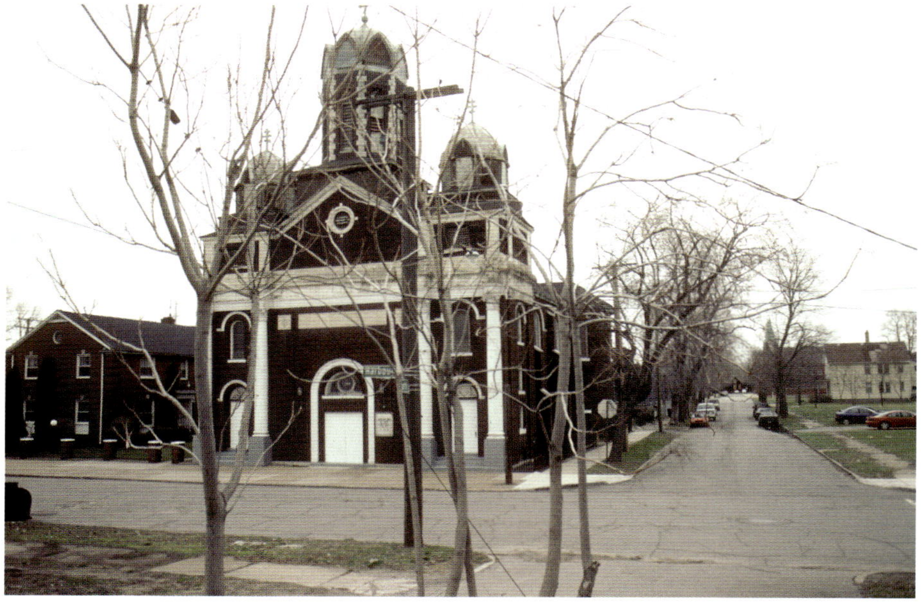

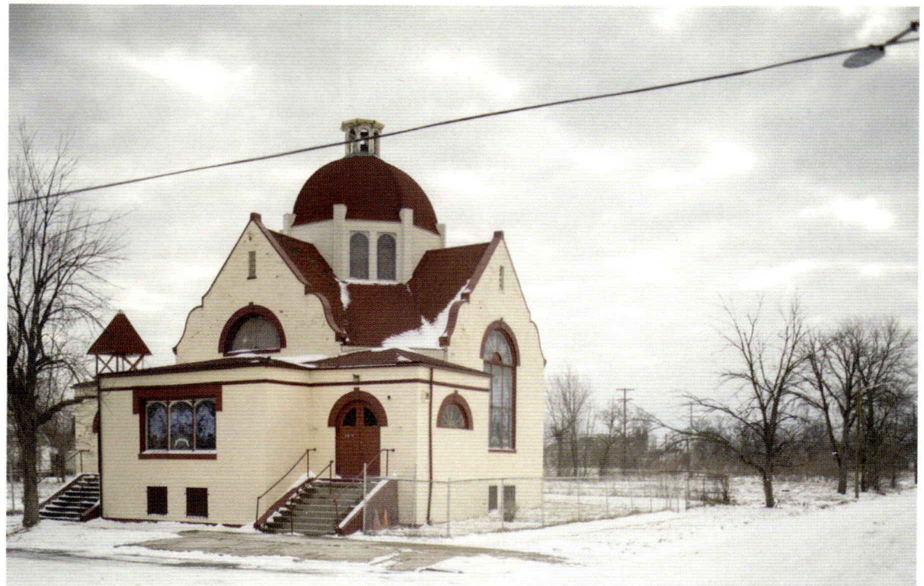

Above left Former Assumption Greek Orthodox Church (1953), once a fine, well-built structure, was sold in the 1970s to the Apostolic Way Church of God. Charlevoix at Fairview, Detroit, 2015.

Below left Jehovah Jireh Full Gospel Church, formerly the St. Janos Catholic Hungarian Church (1911). Harbaugh Street at South Street, Detroit, 2006.

Above "Church on the Move," formerly All Saints Russian Orthodox Church, still evokes an Old World village church. 2918 Hendrie Street, Detroit, 2015.

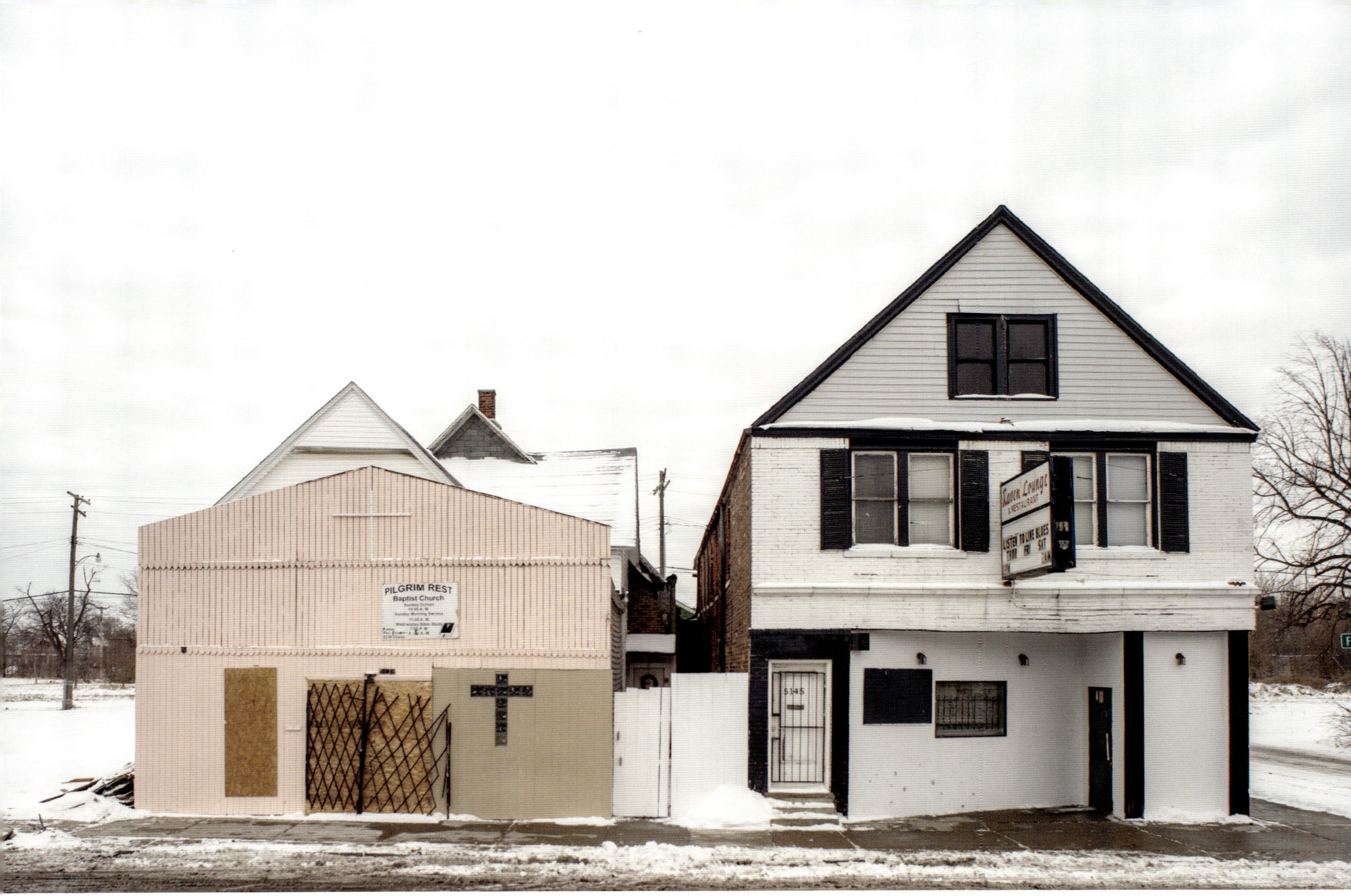

Pilgrim Rest Baptist Church, next to The Raven Lounge (advertised as Michigan's oldest blues bar). 5139 Chene Street, Detroit, 2015.

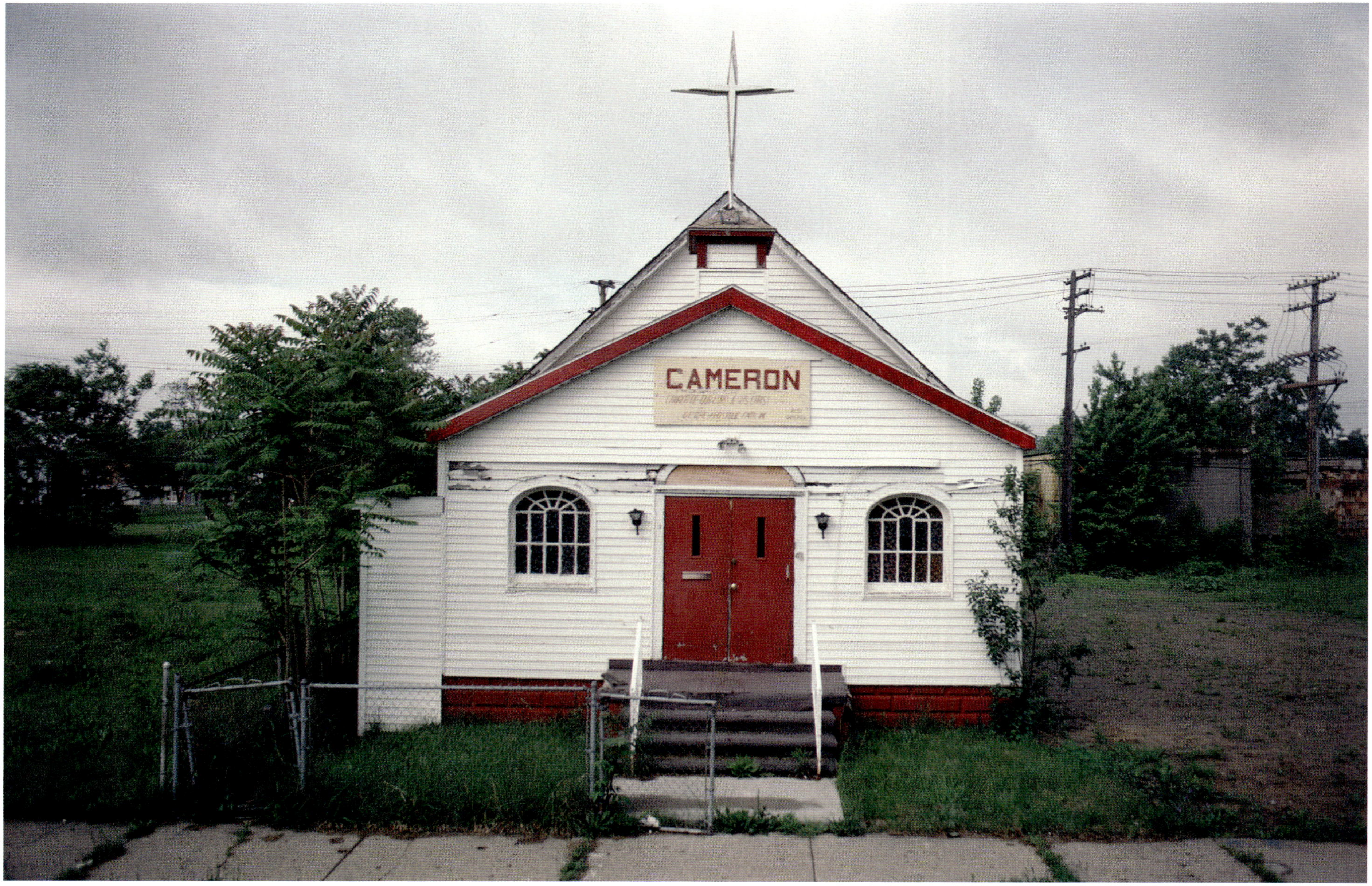

Cameron Church of Our Lord Jesus Christ, formerly Heres Israel Synagogue, built in 1923. 9231 Cameron, Detroit, 2001.

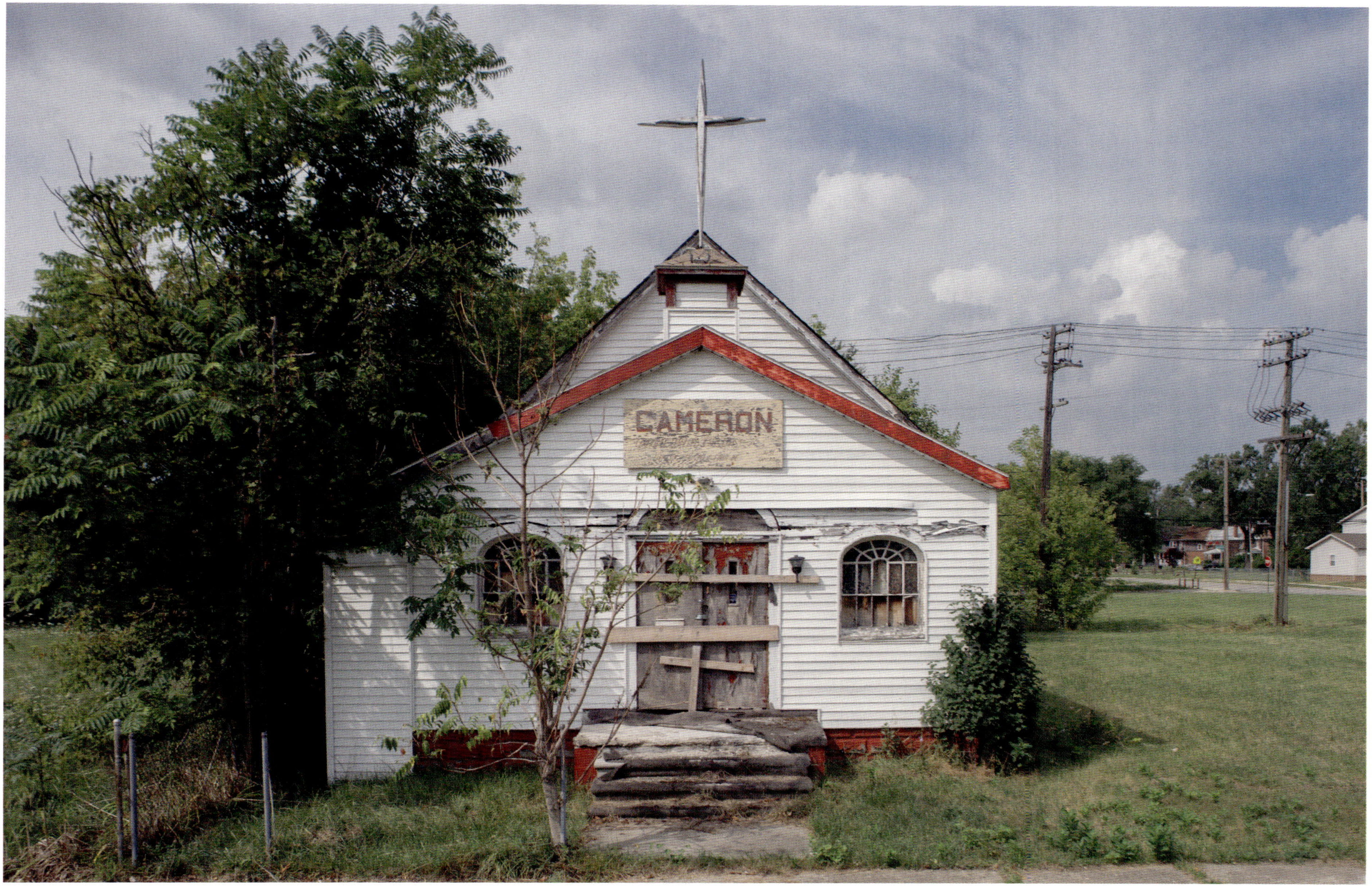

Former Cameron Church of Our Lord Jesus Christ. 9231 Cameron, Detroit, 2015.

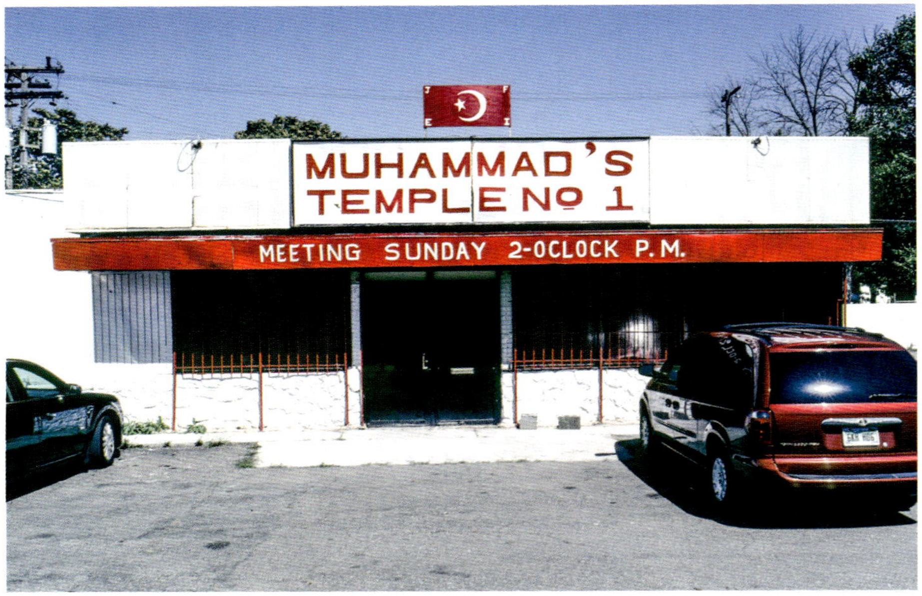

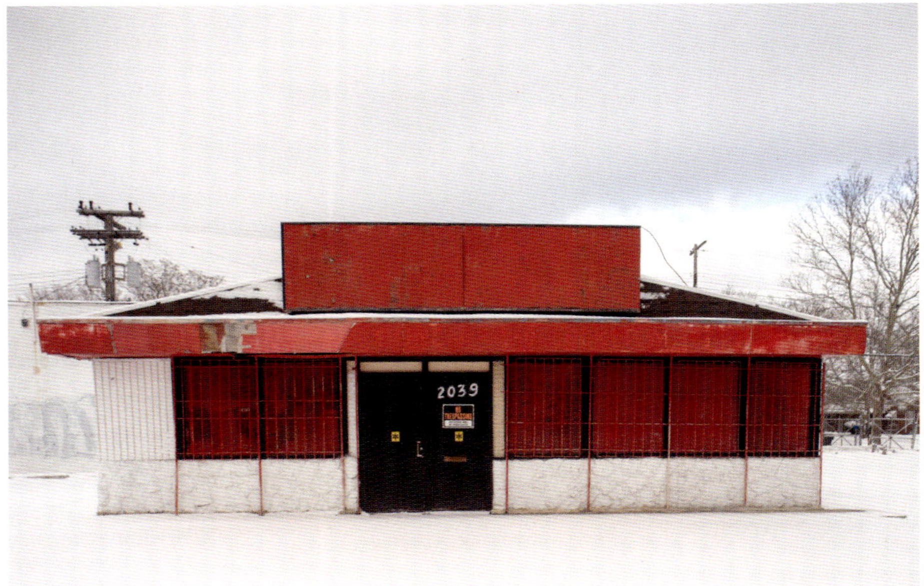

Muhammad's Temple Number 1,
2039 East Seven Mile Rd., Detroit, 2010

Muhammad's Temple Number 1, now vacant.
2039 East Seven Mile Road, Detroit, 2015.

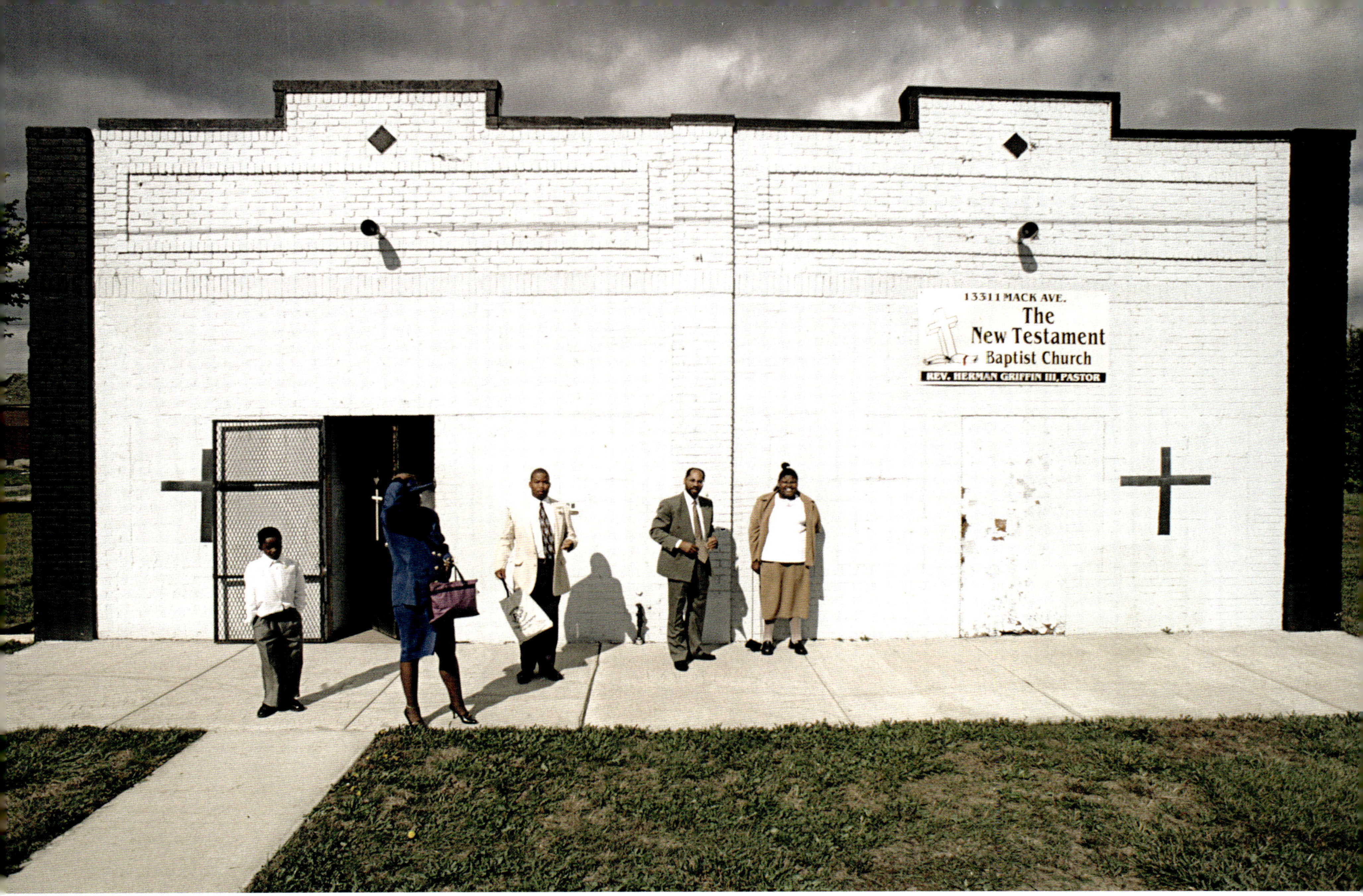

The New Testament Baptist Church. Storefront churches are all that remain on this desolate block of Mack Avenue. 13311 Mack Avenue, Detroit, 2002.

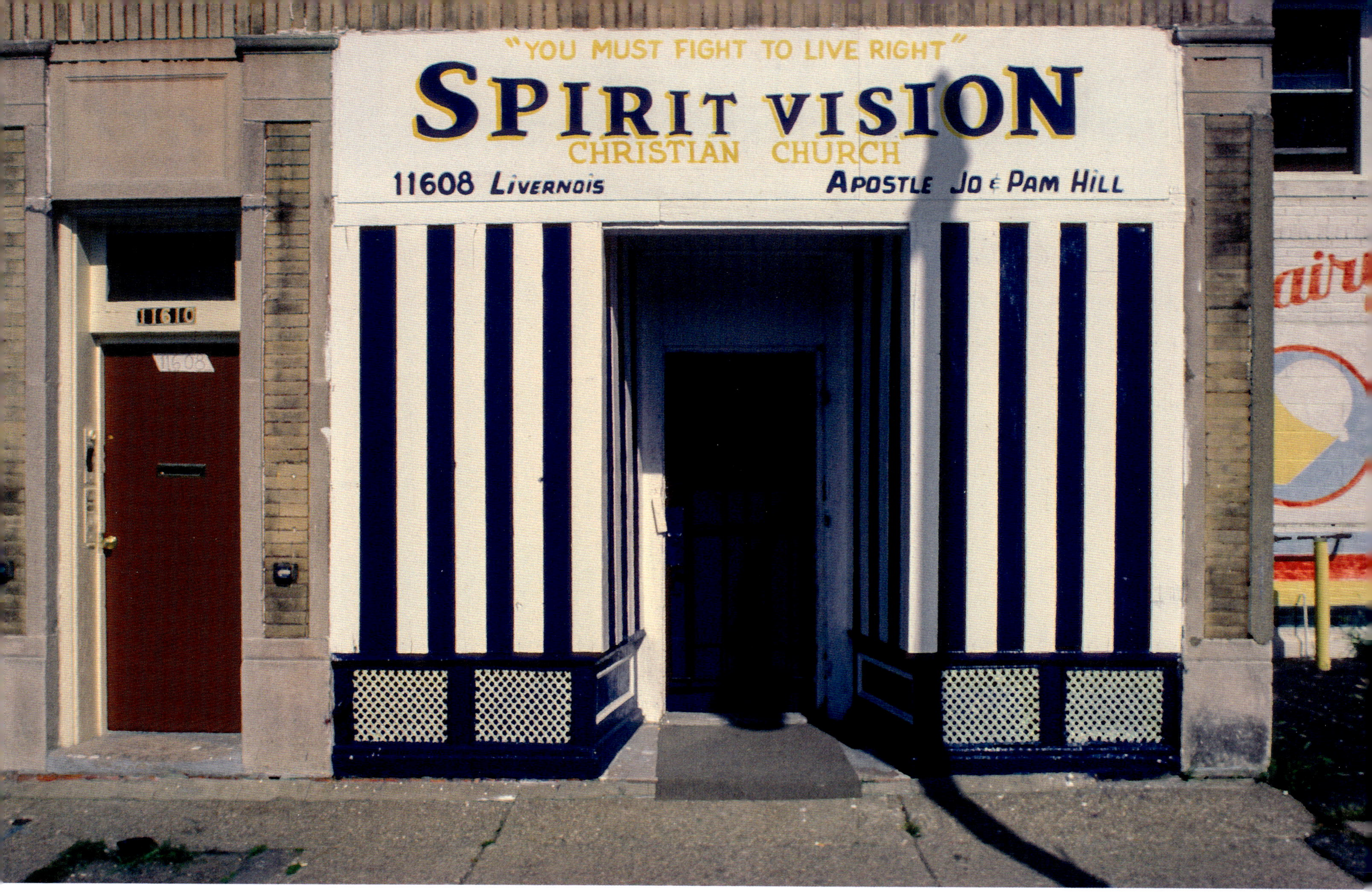

Spirit Vision Christian Church, since demolished. 11608 Livernois Avenue, Detroit, 1987.

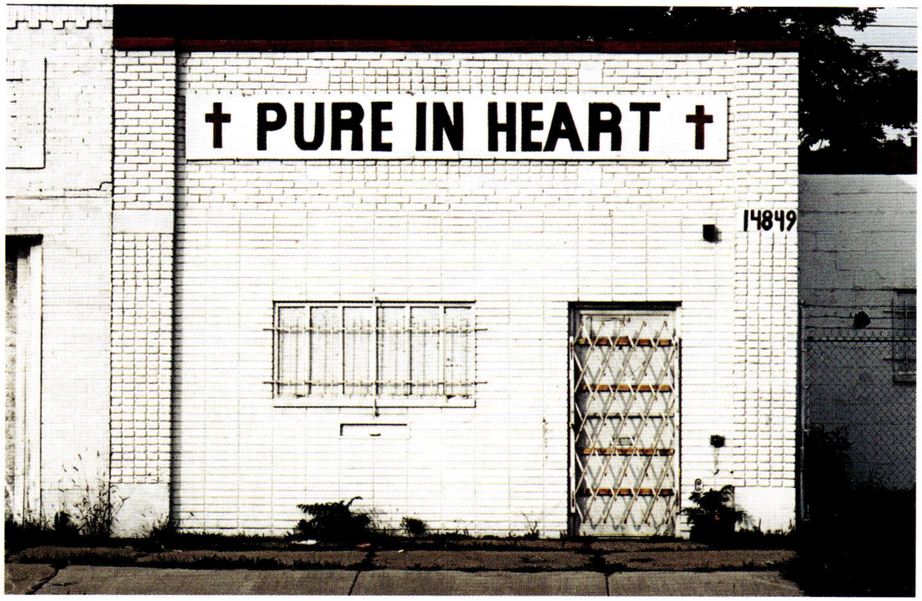

Pure in Heart. 14849 Livernois Avenue, Detroit, 2000.

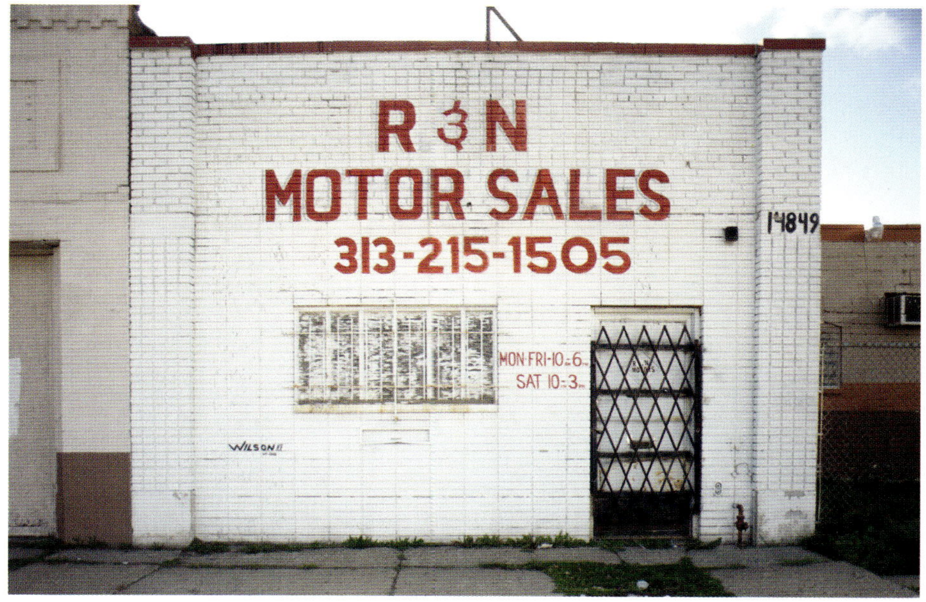

R & N Motor Sales, formerly the Pure in Heart church. 14849 Livernois Avenue, Detroit, 2013.

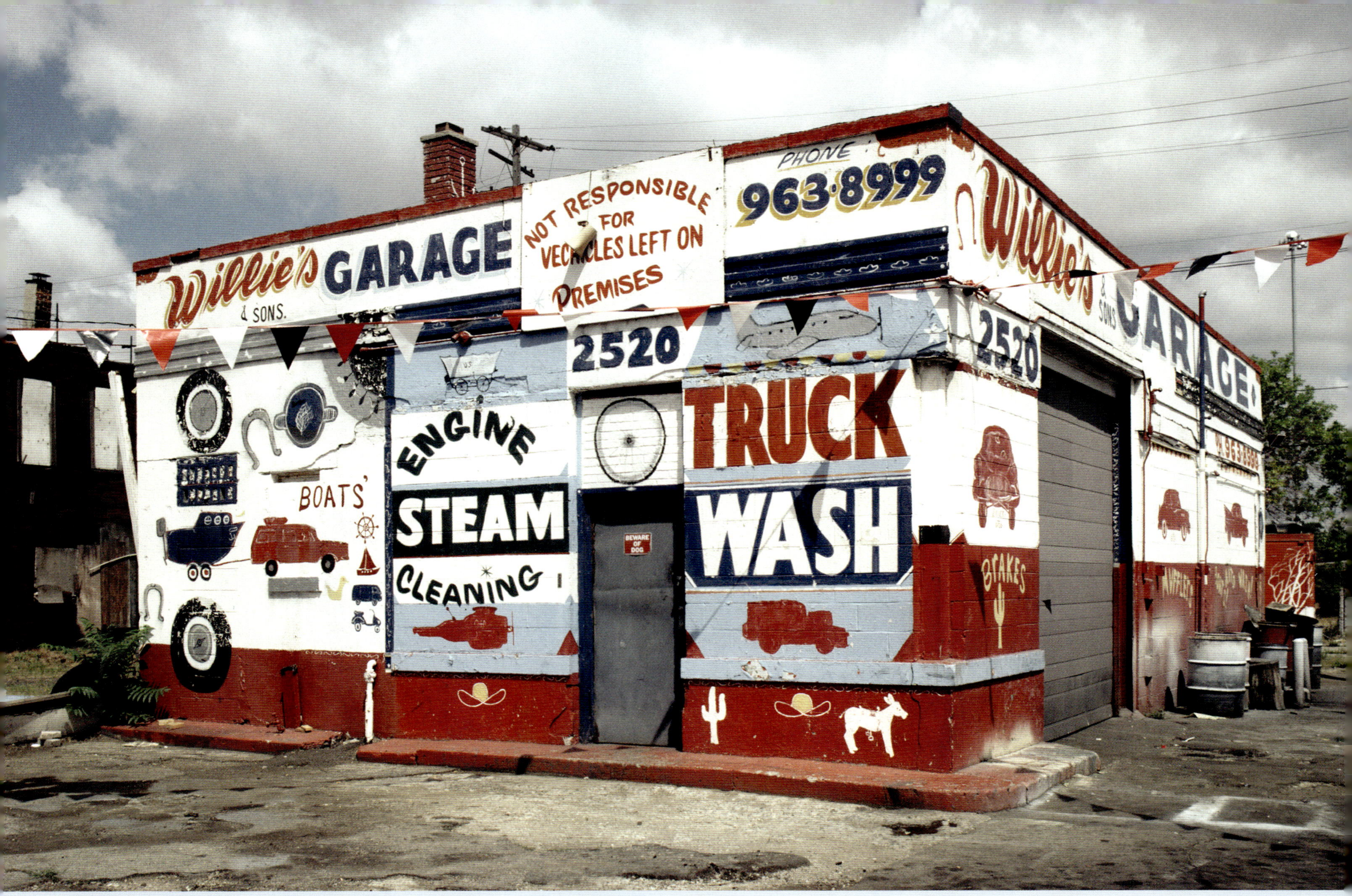

Willie's Garage. 2520 Michigan Avenue, Detroit, 1991.

SPIRITS OF MOTOR CITY

FOLK SIGNS AND MURALS

DETROIT IS OBSESSED WITH ITS HISTORY AND ITS NAME. The Old English D forming the Detroit Tigers logo is ubiquitous on baseball caps and t-shirts and appears in the form of decals on vehicles of all kinds. Filling the walls of trendy restaurants, bars, pop-up stores, and offices in the booming parts of the city are images of Detroit pride: in addition to sports-team logos, the Spirit of Detroit sculpture, street scenes from the 1920s, and knockoffs of Diego Rivera's Detroit Industry murals.

Trained artists seek recognition in Detroit, "a world center of street art," "a city where you can do things you can't do in any other," where walls are easily available and the media receptive. Taggers and muralists are depicted in videos as lonely rebels, risking their lives for their art, walking at night along railroad tracks, abandoned factories, and bridges, and making dangerous climbs to paint billboards next to freeways. Misunderstood by their families for following their call, they form a supportive community with a strong online presence. Being arrested and spending time in jail is a badge of honor.

Matt Eaton, a local art entrepreneur, describes painting tags as "a repetitive task that has nothing to do with anything but ego and destruction." Instead, with the support of the energy drink Red Bull, he is sponsoring "real competent" murals from world-class practitioners that he believes will "add value to the community." Eaton was quoted in an article in the Metro Times: "[We challenged] our-selves to find legal ways to get a bunch of really good talented world-class graffiti art up to, in a weird way, give people some context to judge what they think is beautiful right now, or what they think is ugly." Ordinary tags are seen as part of the blight that Detroit needs to get rid of. But in areas adjacent to neighborhoods showing signs of revival, the work of "the biggest names in street art" is welcomed to spearhead development.

Wanting to get far away from its ruins and desolation, Detroit sponsors upbeat artists. In strategic locations, such as Michigan Avenue and Grand River Avenue northwest of the Michigan Central Station, cheerful murals "change that ruin porn narrative." The murals are made with corporate support and curated by galleries. Challenging decay with images of "magic," flamboyant imagery—such as castles, sharks, and dragons—artists encourage developers to follow their lead and rebuild the city.

In contrast to these commissioned murals are the folk images that I collect from the distinct culture of black, segregated Detroit. In no other large American city has segregation been so extreme and lasted for so long. Nowhere else is the black population so homogenous. As a result, struggling neighborhoods here contain a concentration of Afrocentric commercial and religious imagery, naive folk signs that are simple and impervious to fashion. This huge body of street art constitutes, I believe, the purest expressions of what it is like to be African American, segregated, and poor.

Art museums and other cultural institutions now collect data about official murals created by trained artists and sponsored by city officials and foundations, but they often overlook the more organic forms of street art. Galleries and museums of folk art, on the other hand, are attracted to these works in their original form. Walls crumble, colors fade, youths cover up previous murals with their spray-painted names and tags. With each year that passes, less of the earlier generations of painting on city walls survives.

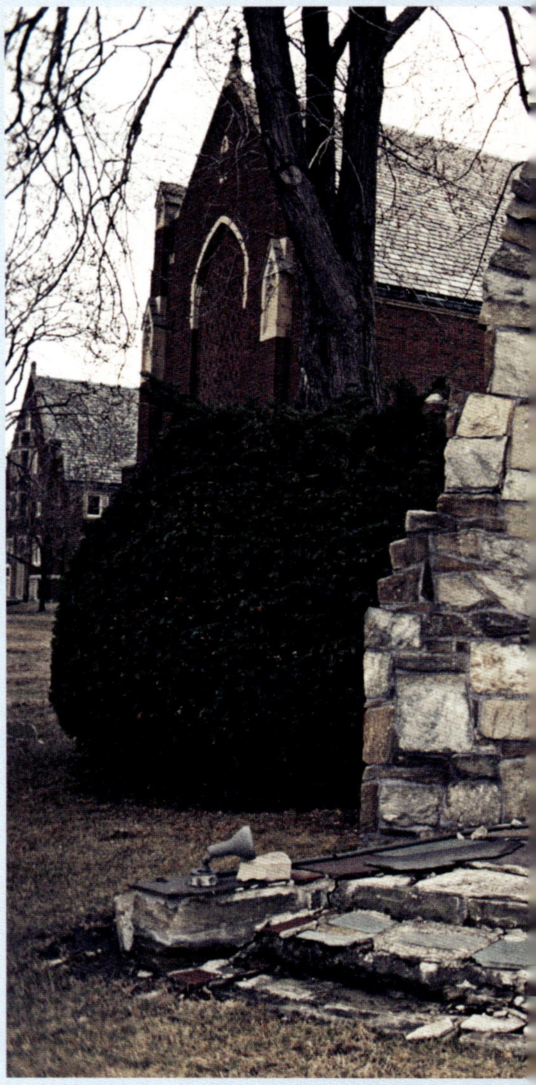

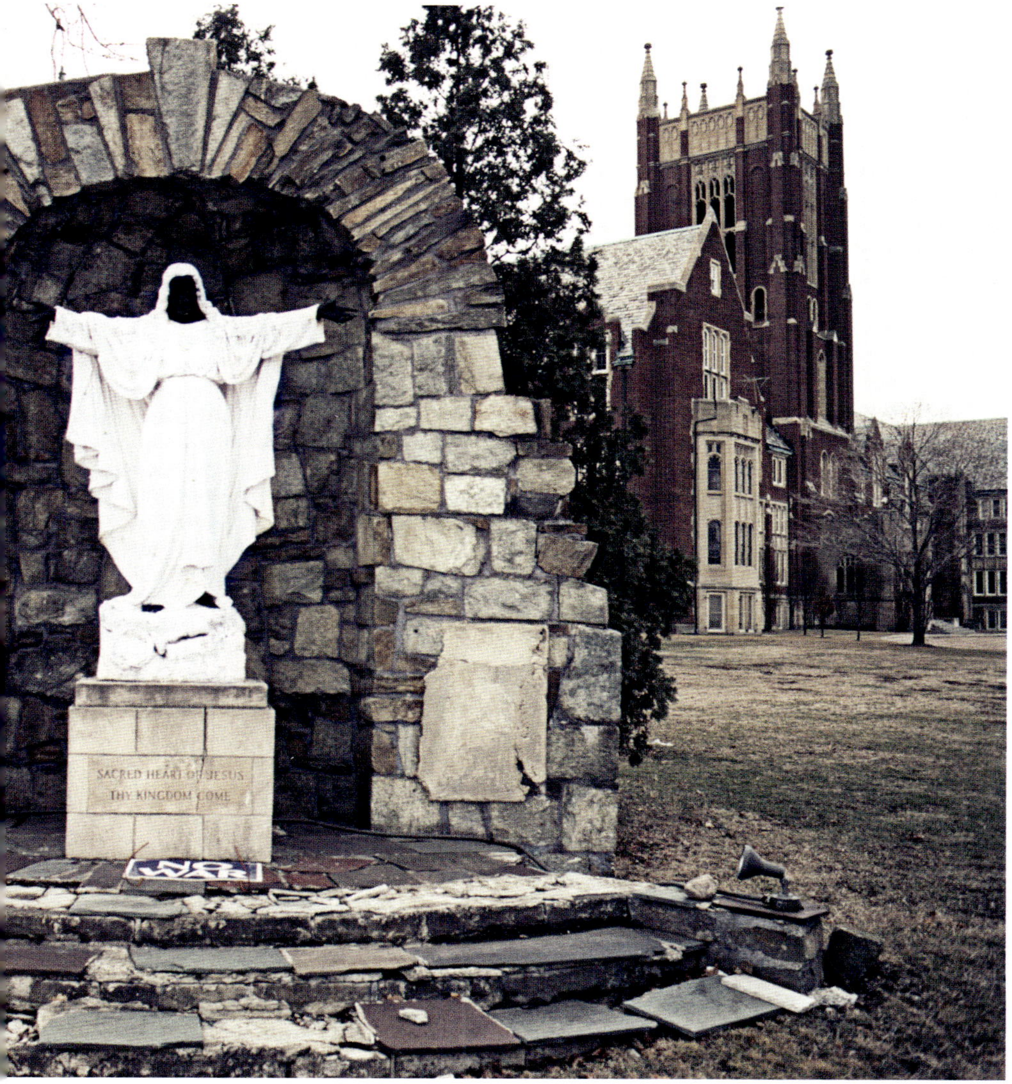

Sacred Heart Seminary. 2701 Chicago Avenue, Detroit, 2003.

IN DETROIT, JESUS IS THE ONLY STAR

In Detroit's neighborhoods references to God are as common as the words food, gas, and liquor, and faith is manifested everywhere in the inner city. A famous example is the statue of Jesus at Sacred Heart Seminary on Chicago Avenue. The statue was once all white. Then, during the riots of 1967, someone painted the face, hands and feet pitch black using tar. At first this was regarded as an act of vandalism, and so someone restored the whiteness. But soon, as a friendly gesture to the neighborhood, the seminary authorities repainted the skin black.

Kat, who lives across the street from the Goethe Building on the city's east side, hired a sign painter to enliven the building with religious imagery. The postman, named Berry, commenting on the art work, remarked to me, "The neighborhood is being blessed. The area is so bad that they could use a blessing. The murals on it are about faith." He added that the building was not "so much the eyesore that it used to be." In the wider world, perhaps the most popular expression involving divinity in the city can be seen scribbled on the wall of the ruined Arnold Nursing Home, which reads, "God Has Left Detroit." By the time I visited the hospice in 2009 somebody had inserted "Not" in the sentence. When I asked Deacon Jacob Smith of the Heavenly Mission Baptist Church if God had left Detroit, he answered by asking: "Has God left Heaven?"

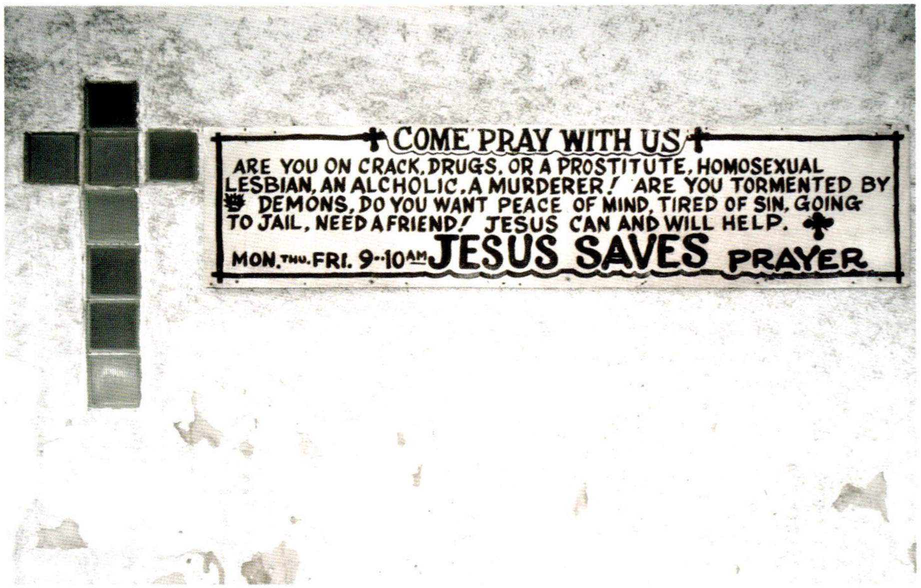

Pentecostal Outreach Church of God in Christ. 3871 West Warren Avenue, Detroit, 2002.

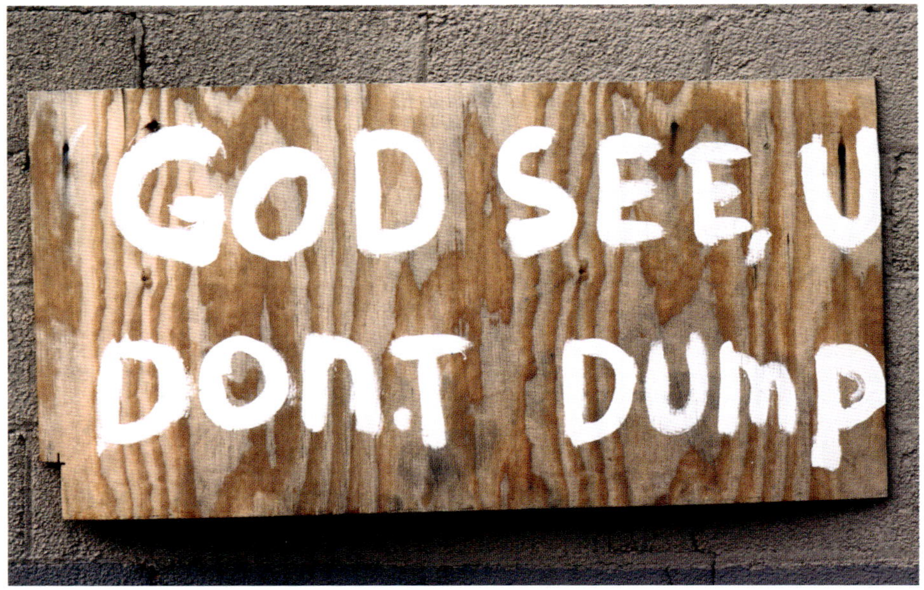

Church sign, removed in 2012. Pastor Clyde M. Tyus remarked that the sign's warning had worked. Livernois Avenue at Northfield Street, Detroit, 2006.

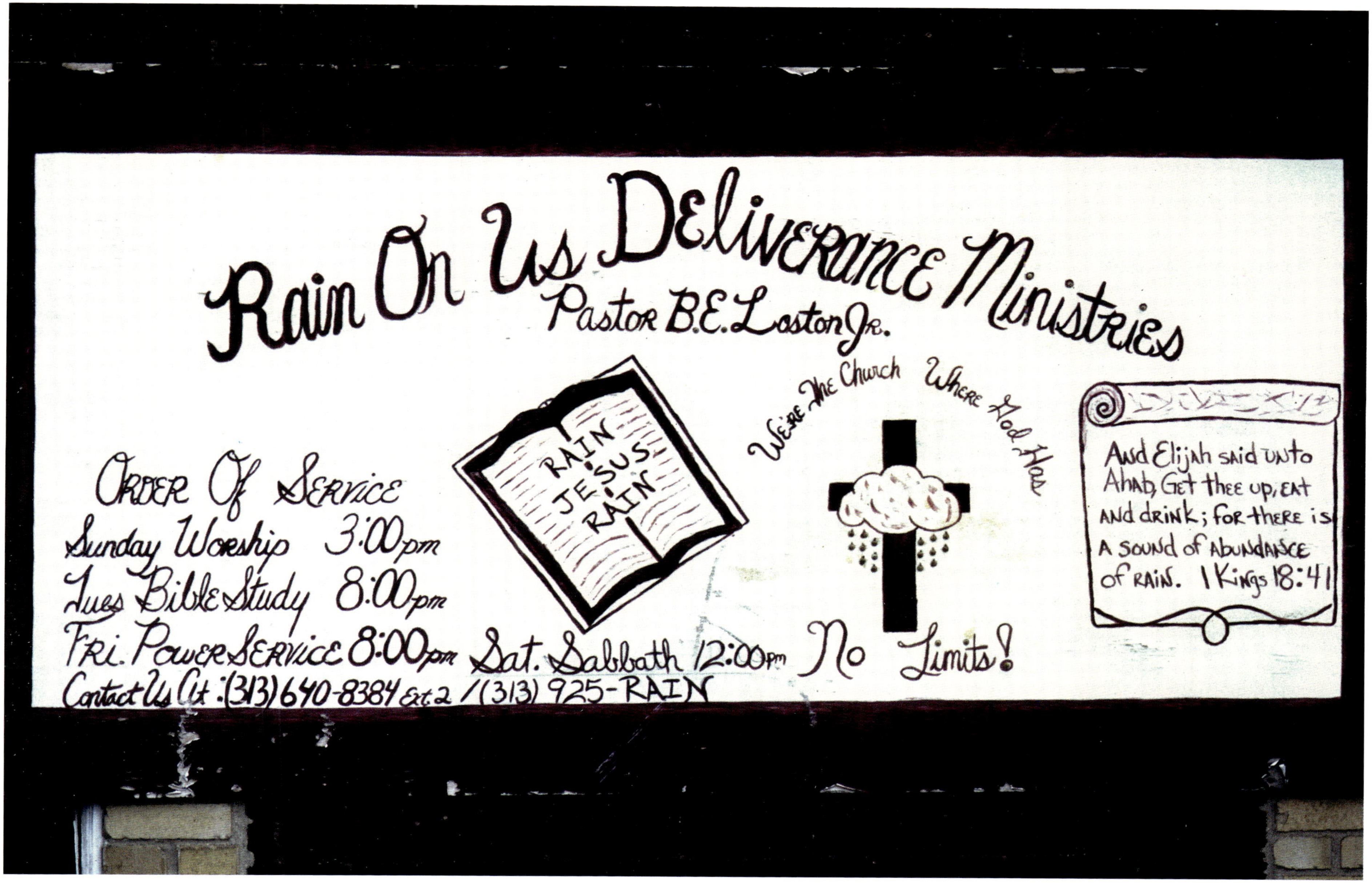

Rain On Us Deliverance Ministries, We're the Church Where God Has No Limits! This church was still operating in 2013. Its name had changed to Prophetic Ministries but the minister's name remained the same. 4256 Mitchell Street, Detroit, 2003.

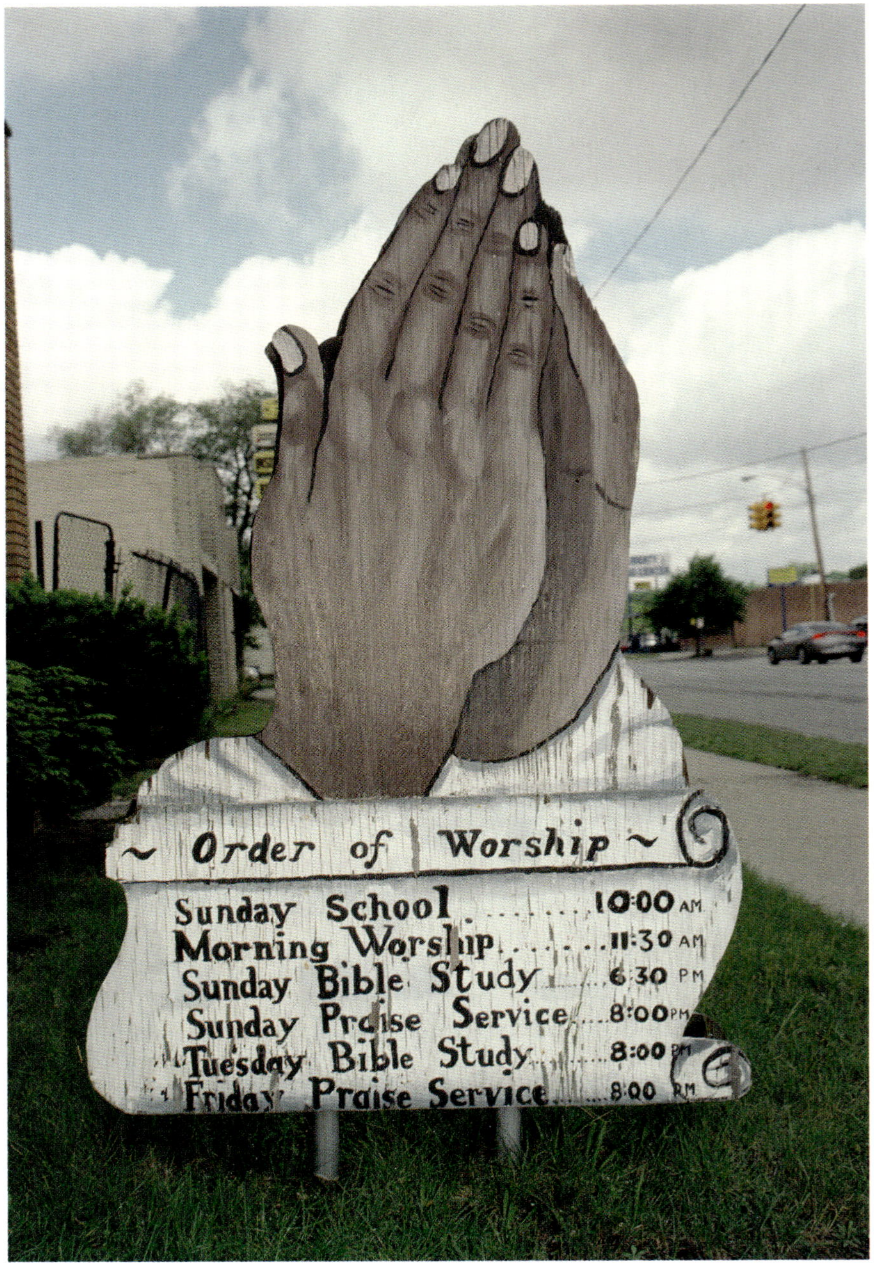

Praying hands, Tehillim Church of God in Christ. West McNichols Road at Mendota Street, Detroit, 2001.

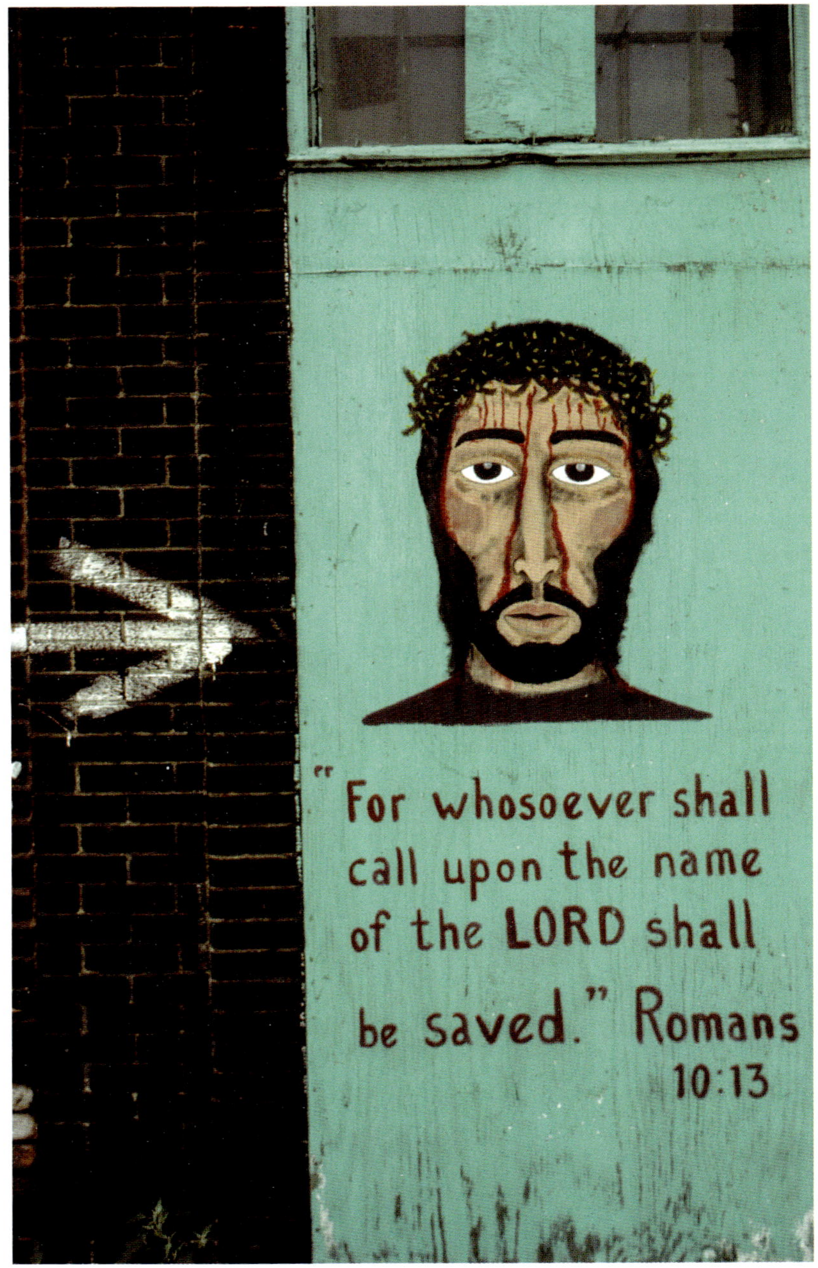

Suffering Christ painted by an ex-convict, Crossover Inner City Gospel Ministry. Cass Avenue at Temple Street, Detroit, 1994.

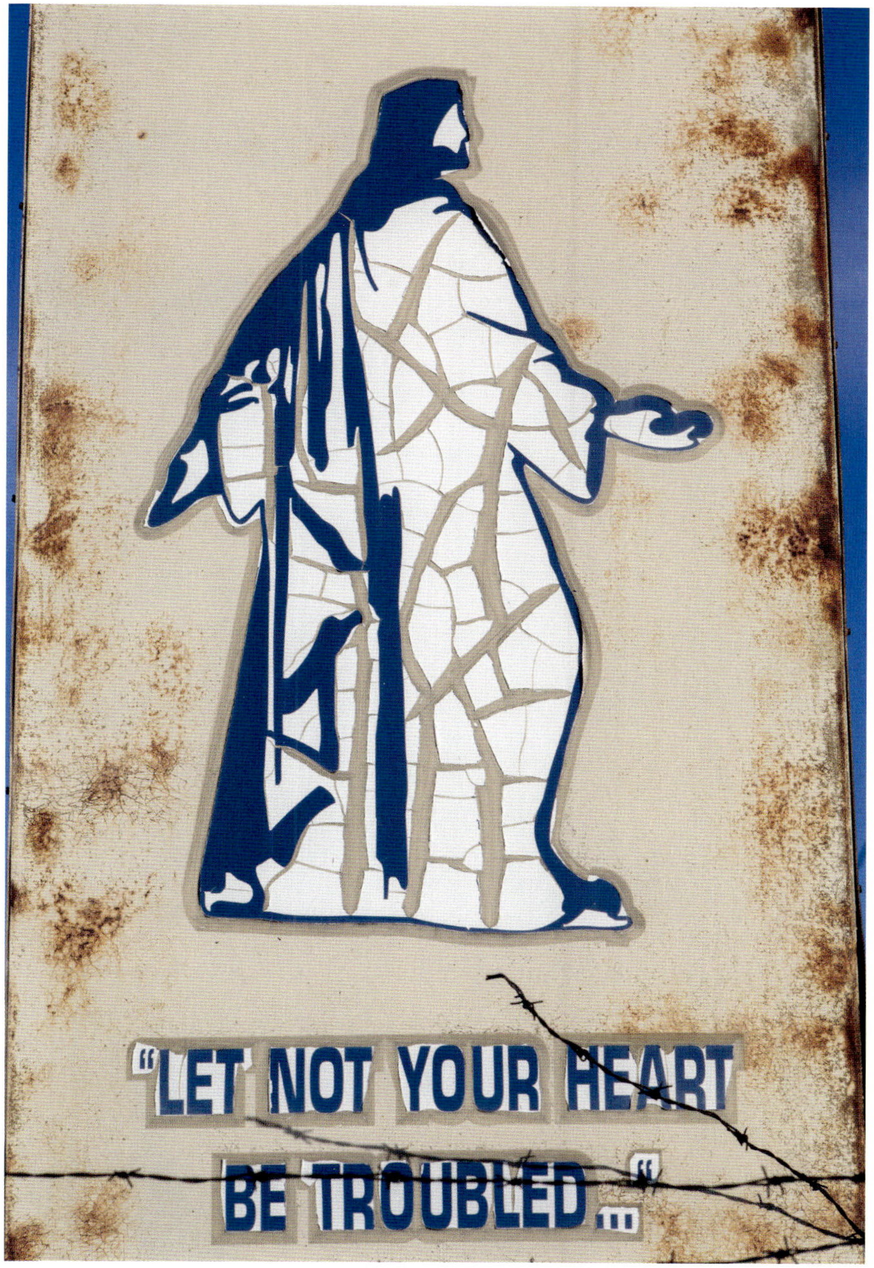

Decayed image of Jesus, True Holiness Church. 7326 Tireman Avenue, Detroit, 2015.

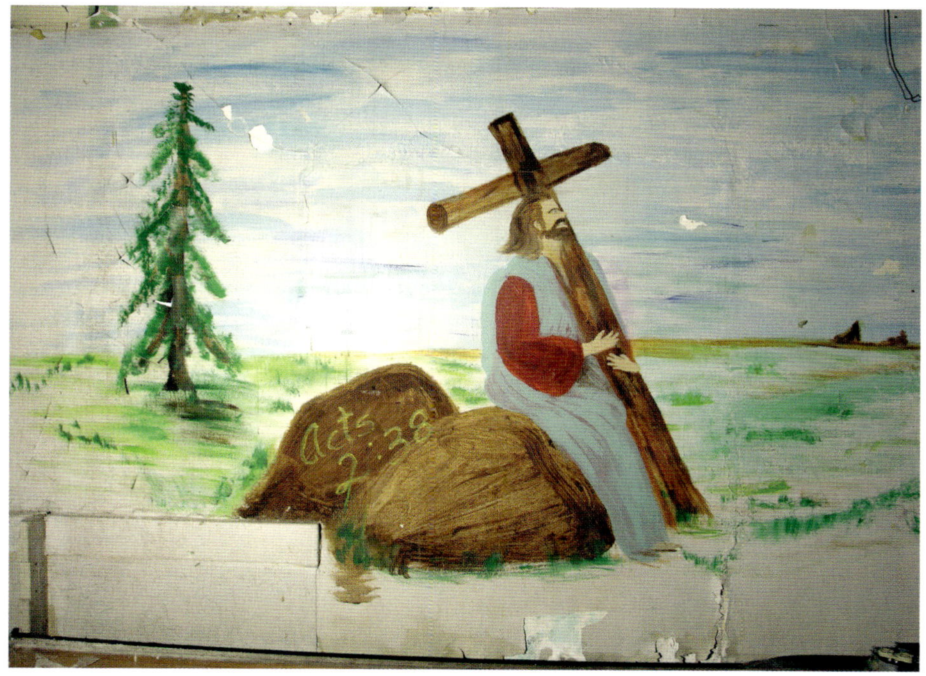

Mural of Christ behind the altar of the former Shiloh Temple Apostolic Faith. Christ is depicted alone in a bleak northern landscape. Linwood Street at Richton Street, Detroit, 2005.

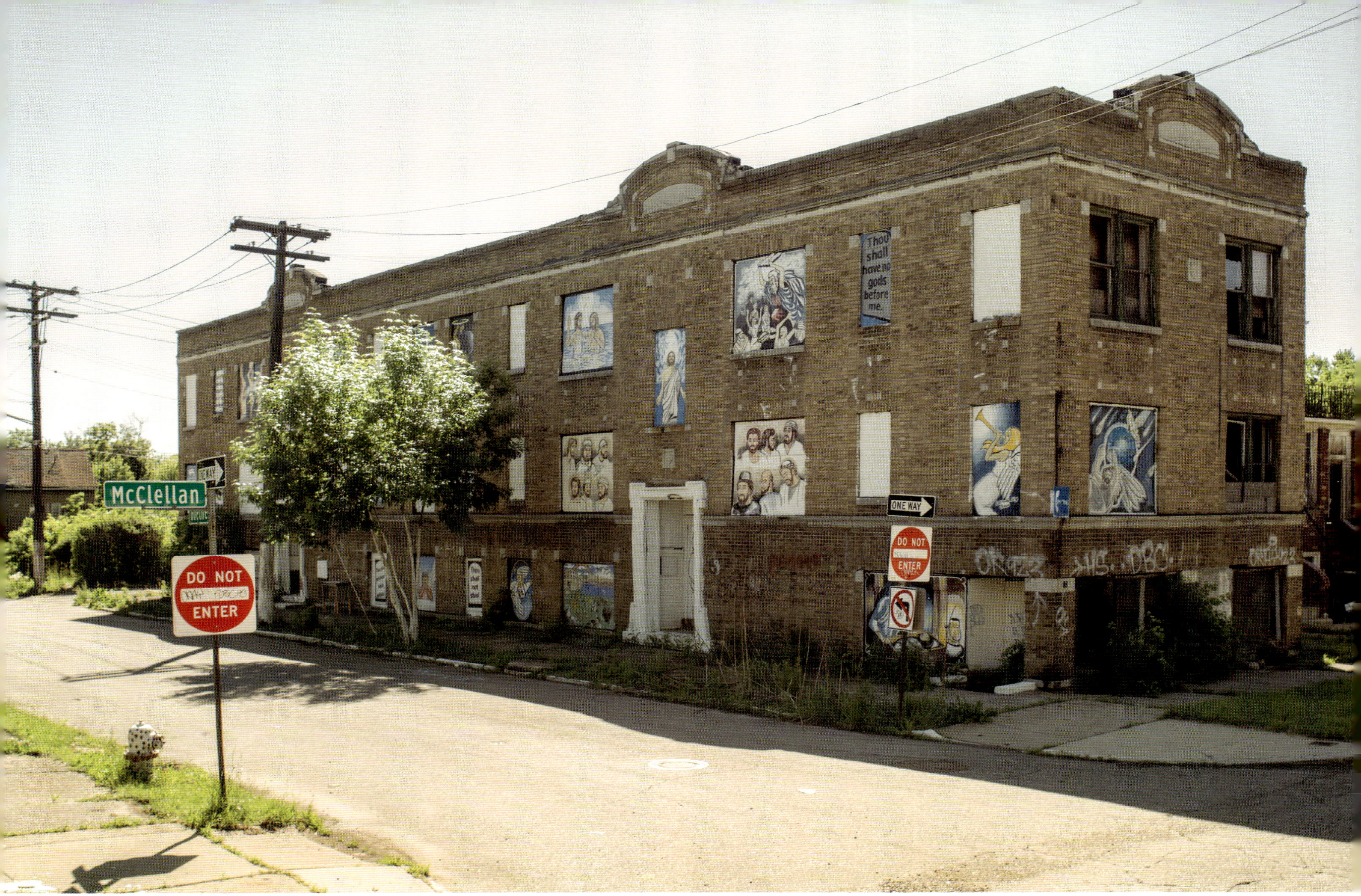

Ruins of the Goethe apartment building of 1924. McClellan Avenue at Goethe Street, Detroit, 2014. Historian Tim Samuelson commented that if an upscale coffee house opened on the dangerous street across from the Goethe Building, it would not last long.

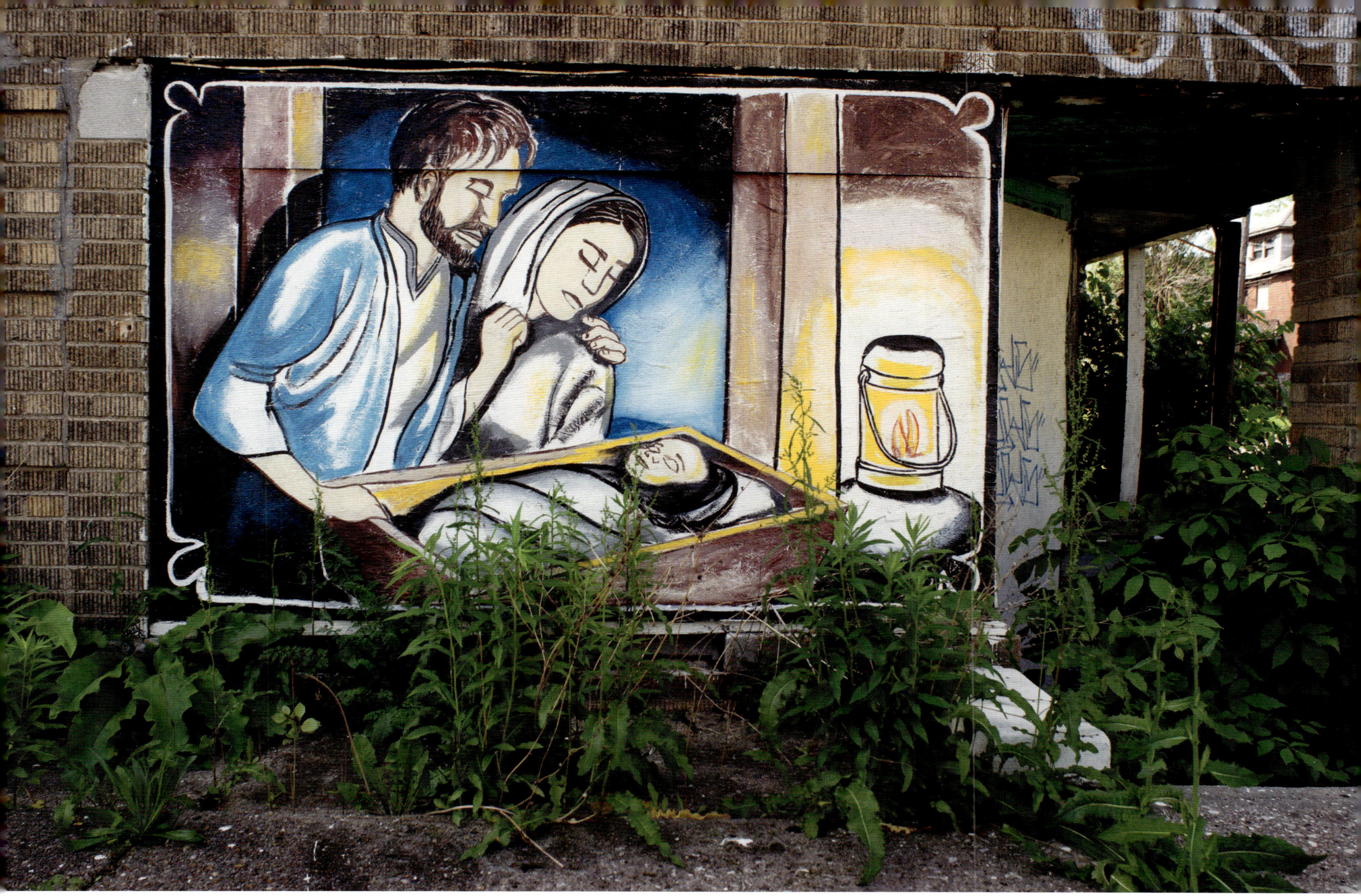

Nativity scene commissioned by Kat, painted on the ruins of the Goethe apartment building. McClellan Avenue at Goethe Street, Detroit, 2014.

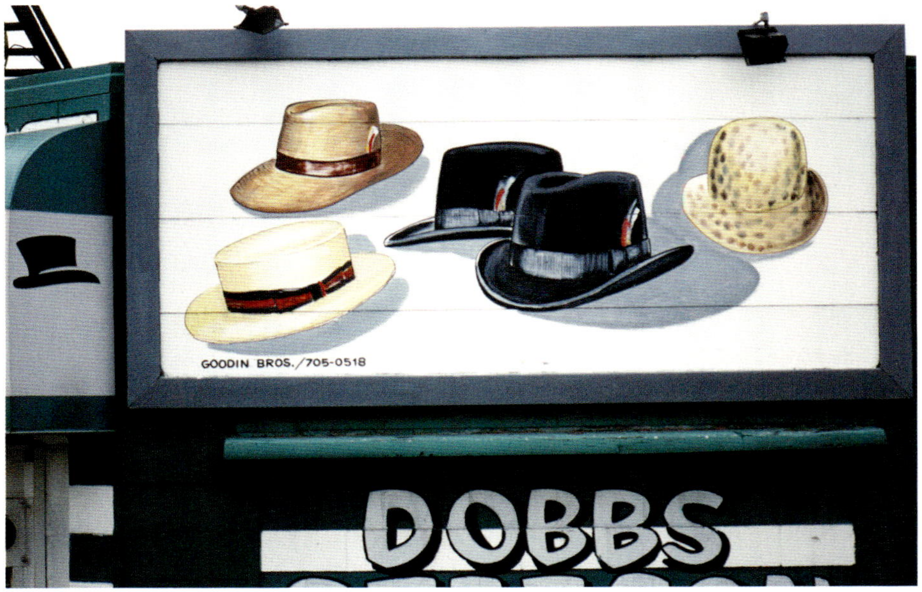

BUSINESS-ORIENTED SIGNS

The sign for Hats Galore & More, signed by Goodin Brothers, has been in place for twenty-three years. Bob, the owner of the store, proudly referred to the depicted hats as 1920s "classics." (The aesthetics of the store sign is reminiscent of the paintings of cakes, toys, and other common objects by the American artist Wayne Thiebaud.) Bob showed me a newspaper clipping of Luciano Pavarotti trying on a $150 Panama hat in his store; Bob said that the singer had a big head and that he was happy to find a hat that fit. In the store, he has snapshots of Beyoncé and Lil' Kim wearing his hats. Bob told me that a producer from New York, in search of authentic headgear, would buy hats from him. He hopes that someday Bill Clinton will come to his store and buy one.

The dance studio "I Choose You" on McNichols Road has a sign with two dancers and the hours for ballroom classes. Patricia, the owner, said that she wanted a simple sign that did the job. On Michigan Avenue, a homeless folk artist approached the owner of Willie's Garage about decorating the façade. The artist painted the story of transportation, a playful arrangement of letters, vehicles, and animals, ranging from donkeys to jet planes. Willie, the owner of the garage, remarked, "It looks nice. I didn't recognize my own building. You have a lot of guys down the street, they have talent. He used paint I had here. It costs me nothing.

Hats Galore & More. According to Bob, the store owner, people in Detroit love hats, although there are few hat stores left. 10061 Gratiot Avenue, Detroit, 2001.

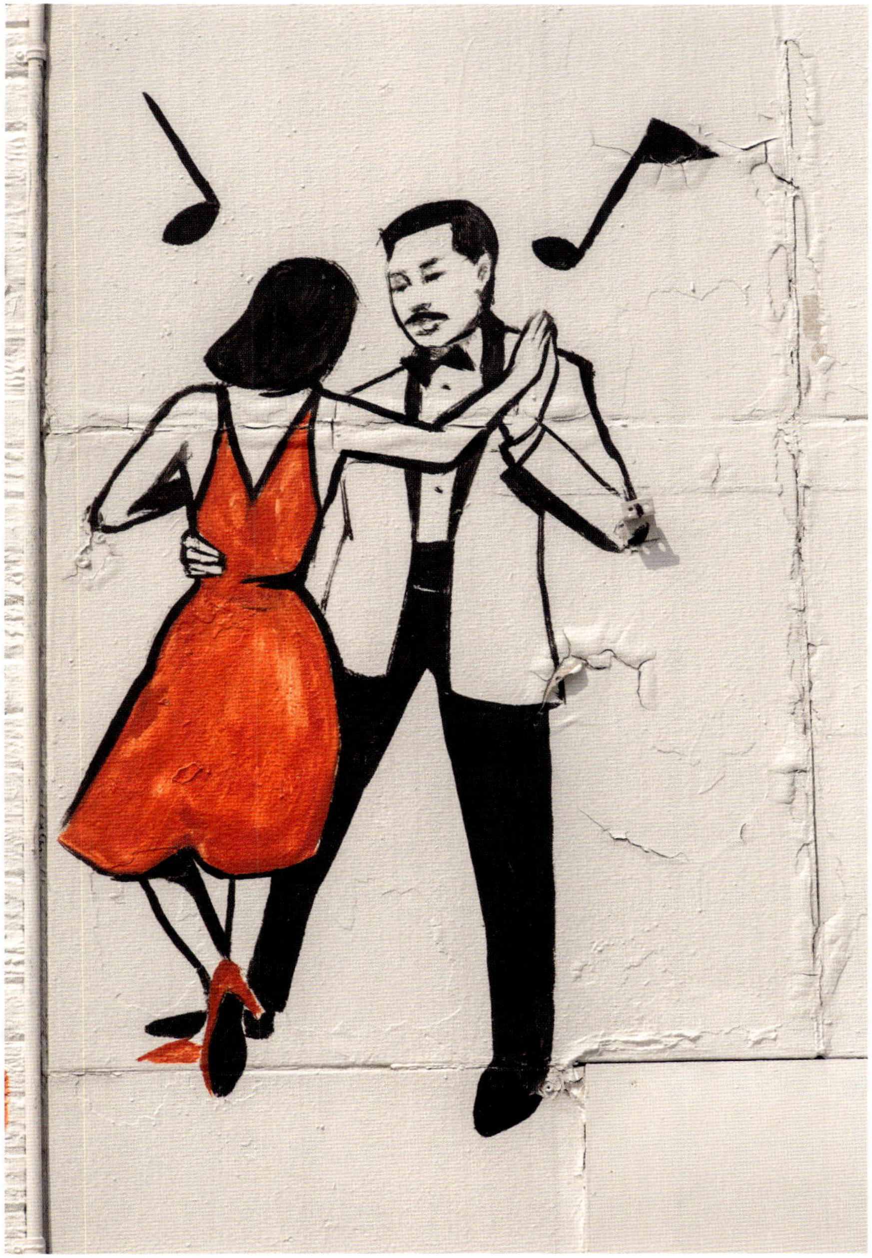

Above the image, the sign reads: “Dancing, I Choose You Presents Ballroom Classes.” 7631 West McNichols Road, Detroit, 2015.

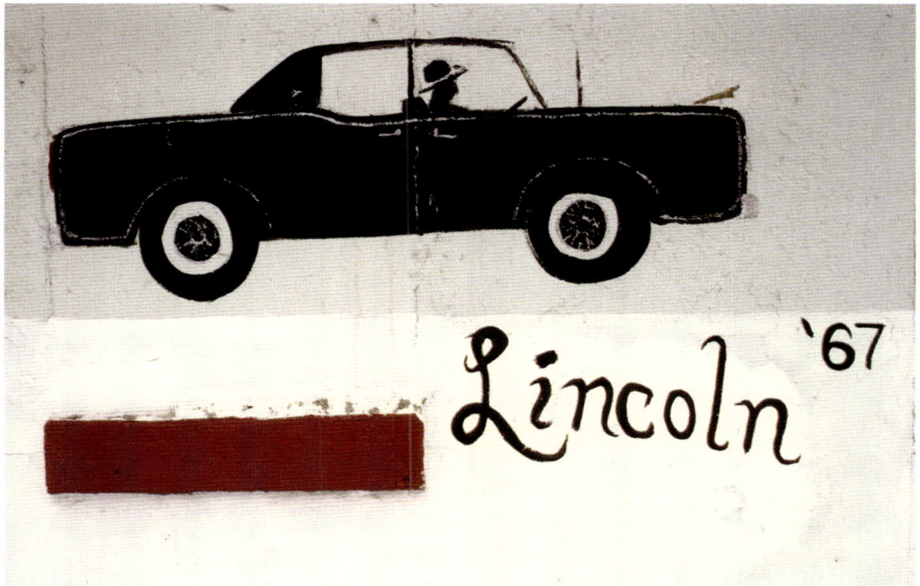

1967 Lincoln, painted on Willie’s Garage. 2250 Michigan Avenue, Detroit, 1997.

Sign showing a winged, grinning death's head wearing a motorcycle cap. People, vintage cars, and motorcycles in front of the notorious Detroit Highwaymen Motorcycle Club. Michigan Avenue at Tillman Street, Detroit, 2015.

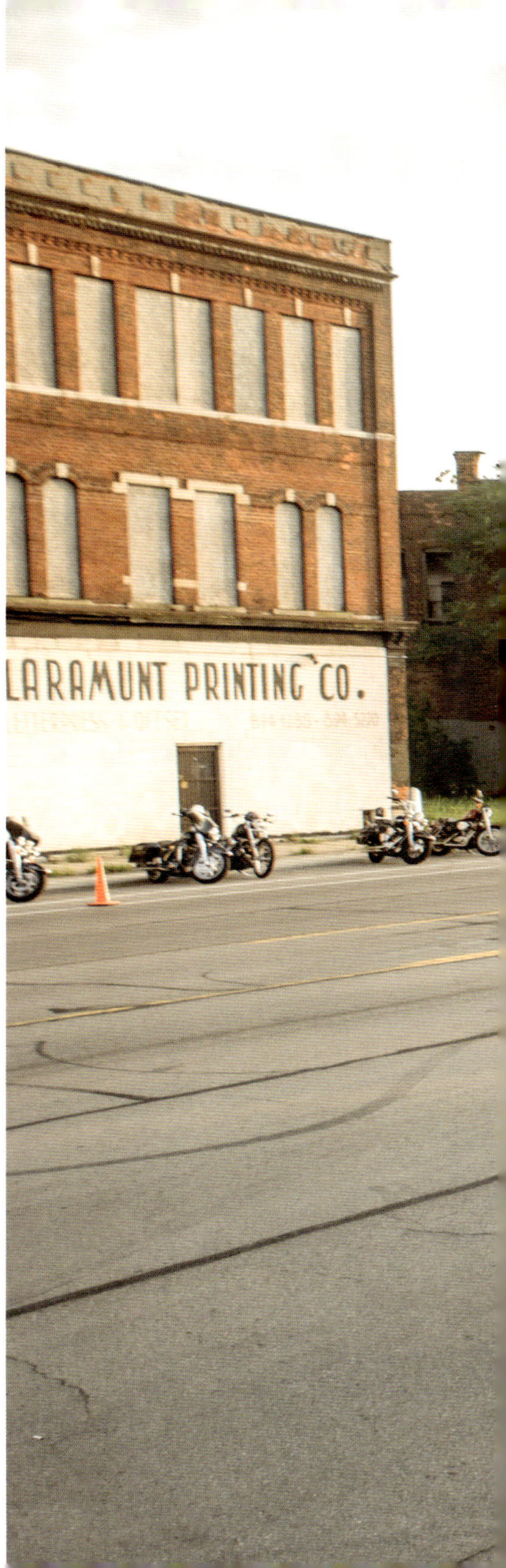

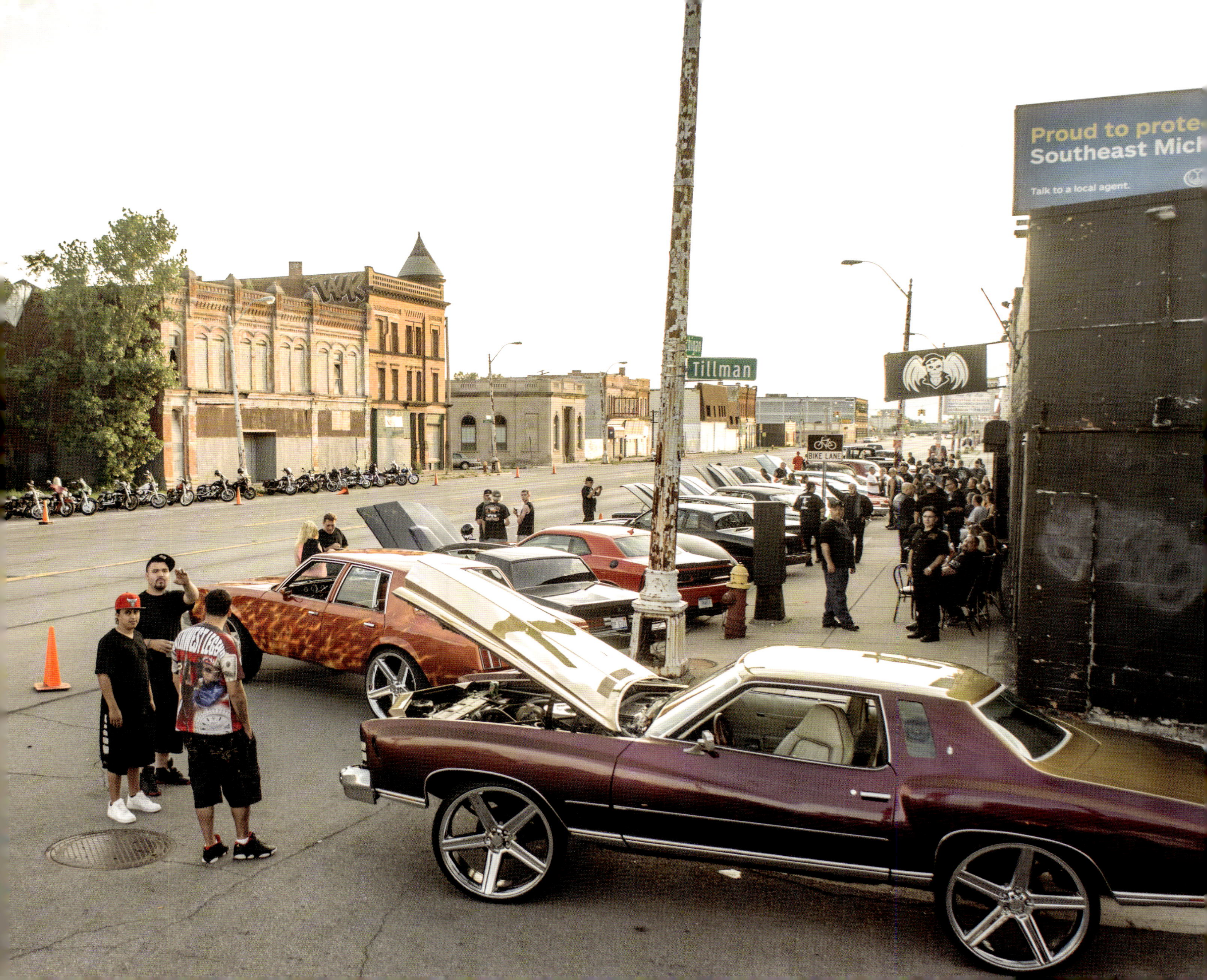
Tillman
BIKE LANE
Talk to a local agent.

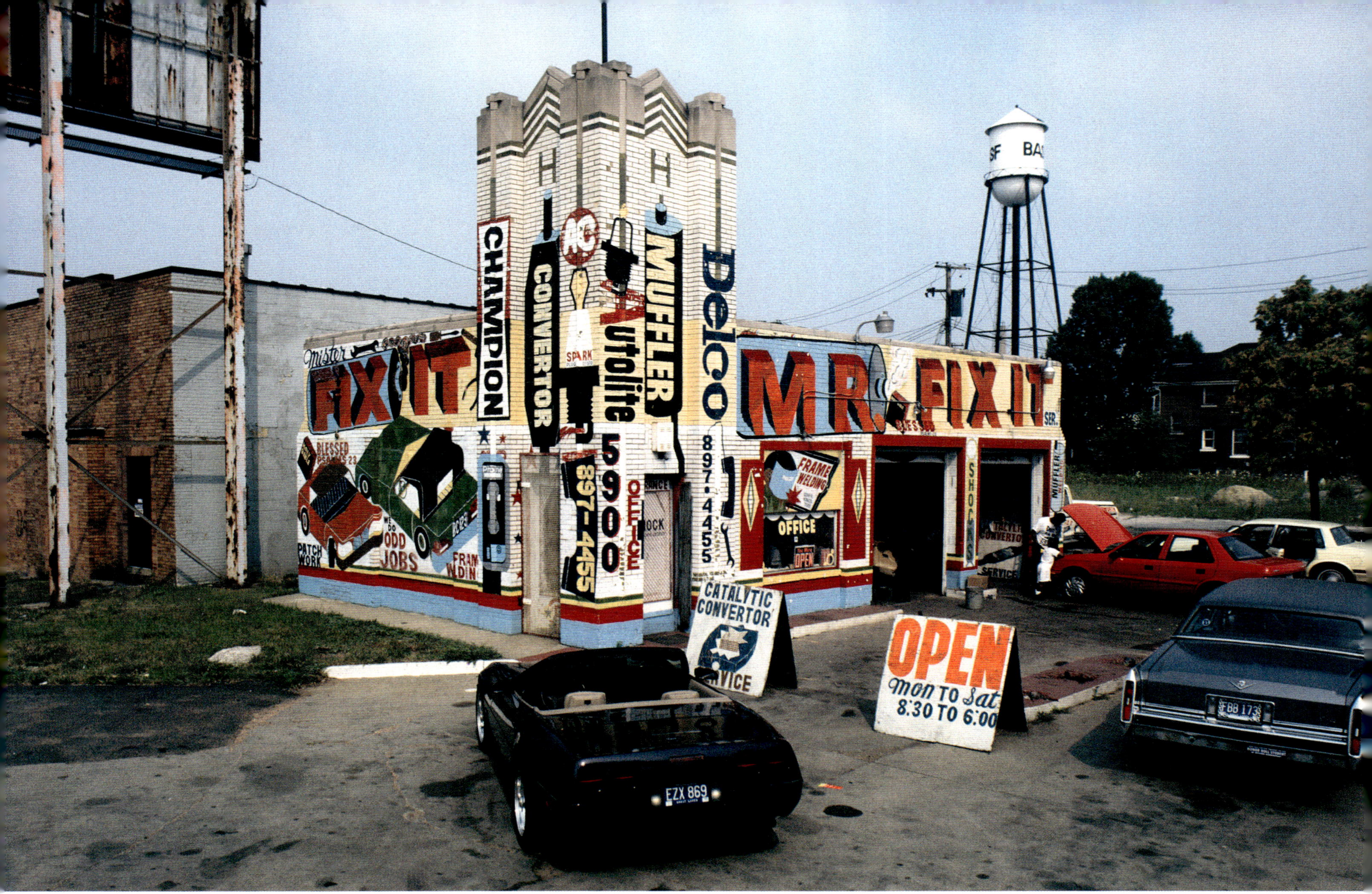

Mr. Fix It, a former 1920s High Speed Gas Station, in 1995. The artwork is by Eugene, an itinerant sign painter with a distinctive style. His fading store signs can still be seen in southwest Detroit. Epworth Street at West Warren Avenue, Detroit, 1995.

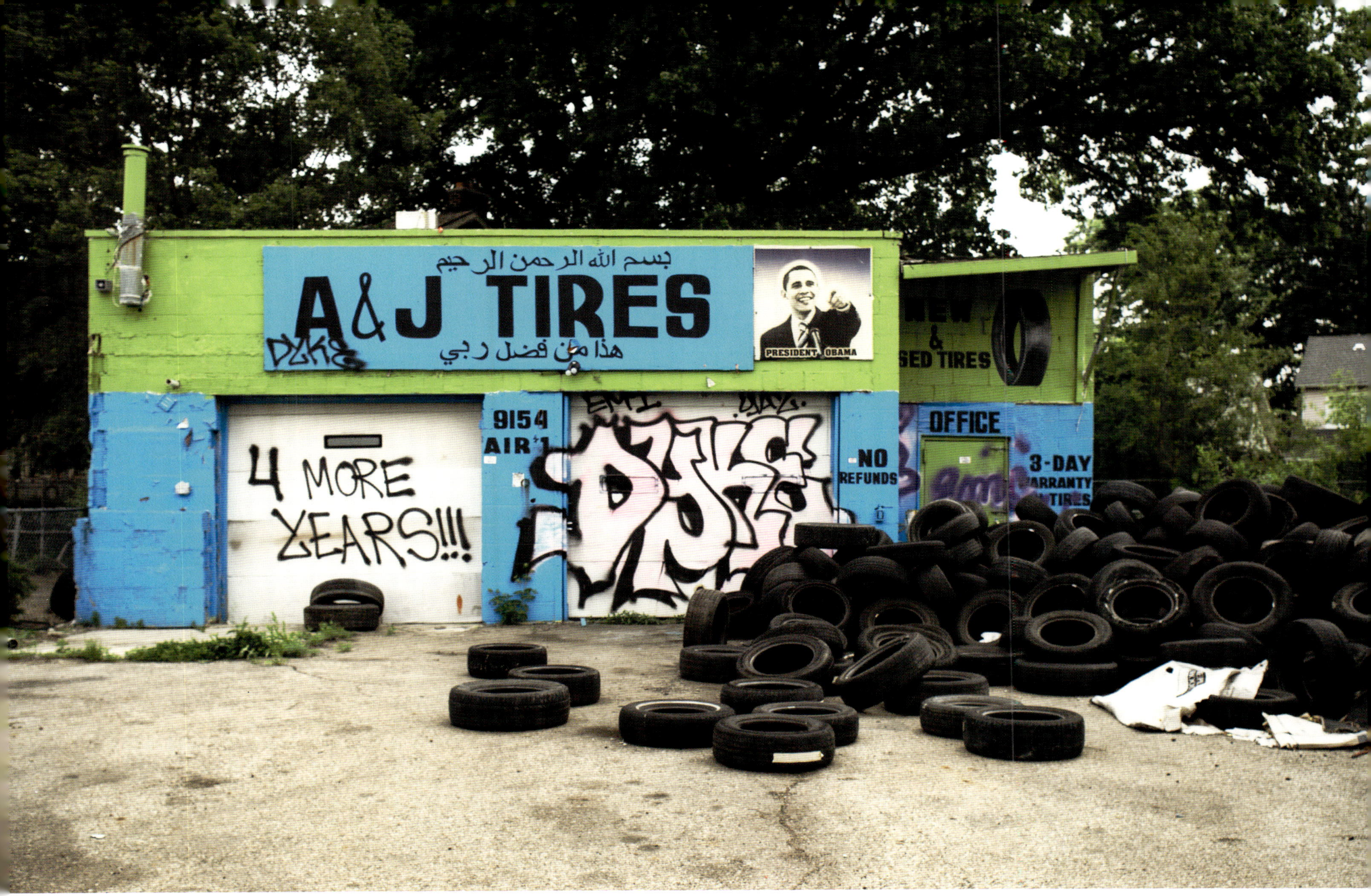

Abandoned A. and J. Tires store, with a poster of President Obama on the façade, 9154 Livernois Avenue, Detroit, 2014.

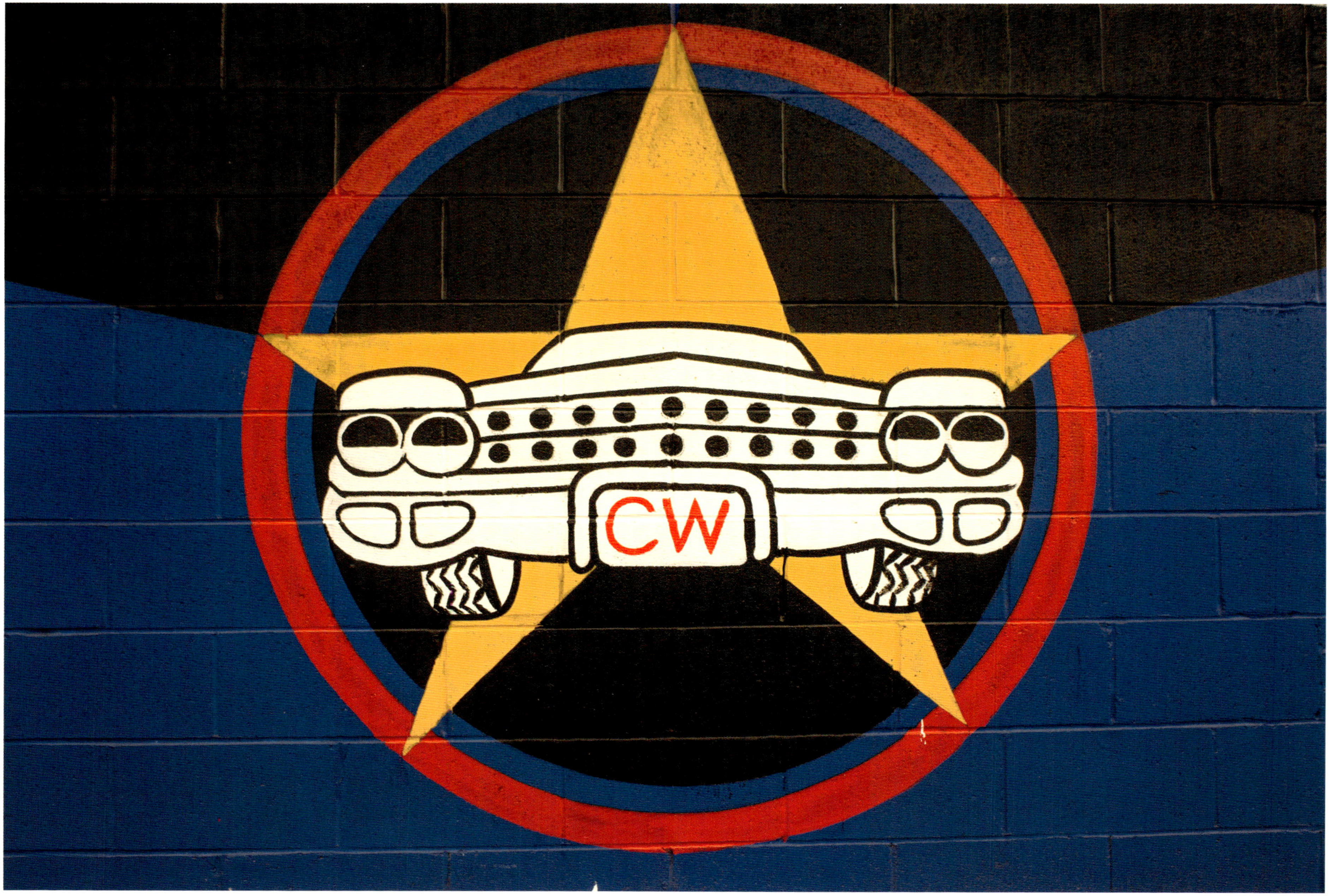

Celebrating an American "gas guzzler" at a carwash called Clean Whips.
11556 Livernois Avenue, Detroit, 2015.

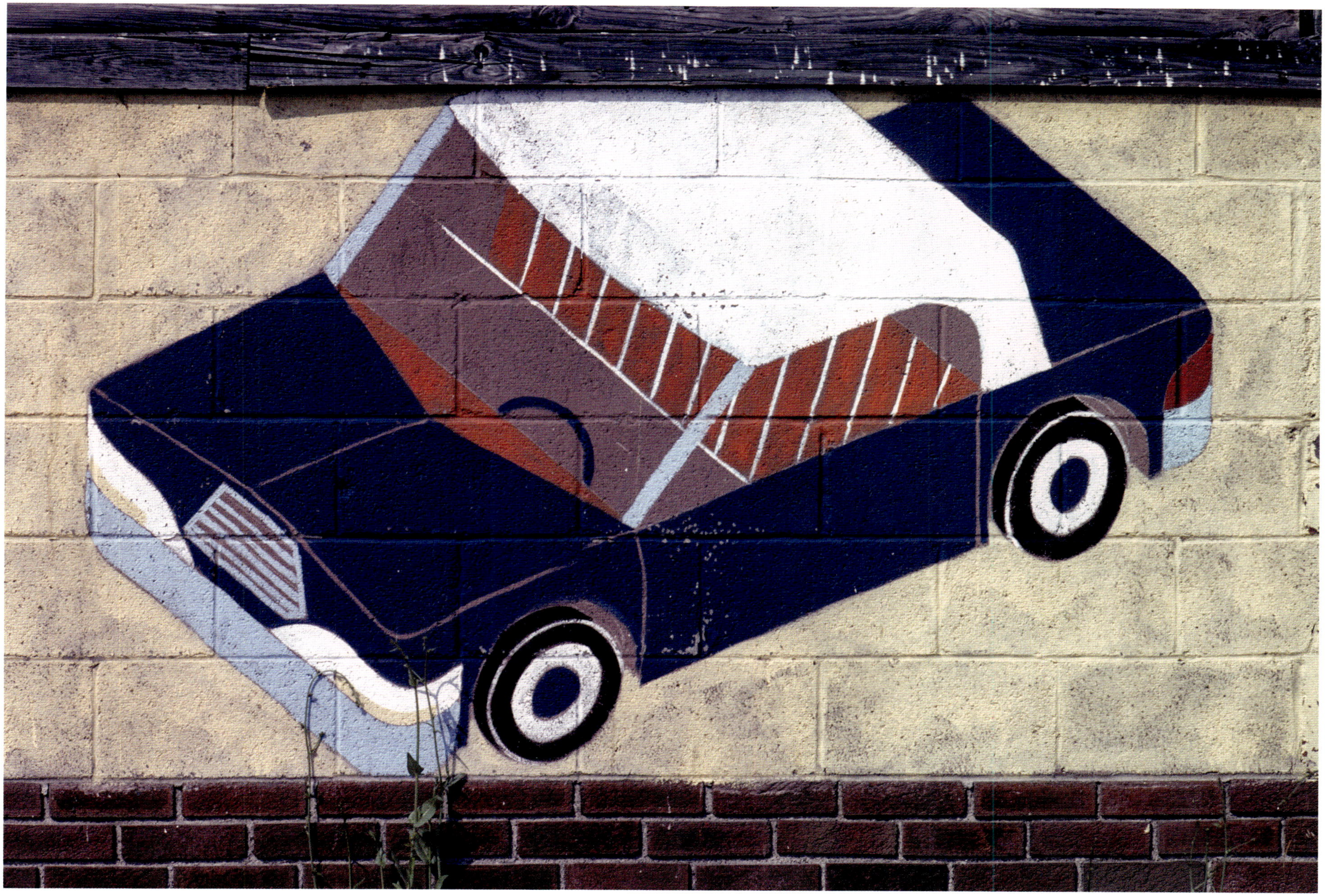

Boxy car painted by folk artist Eugene. 8081 Livernois Avenue, Detroit, 1998.

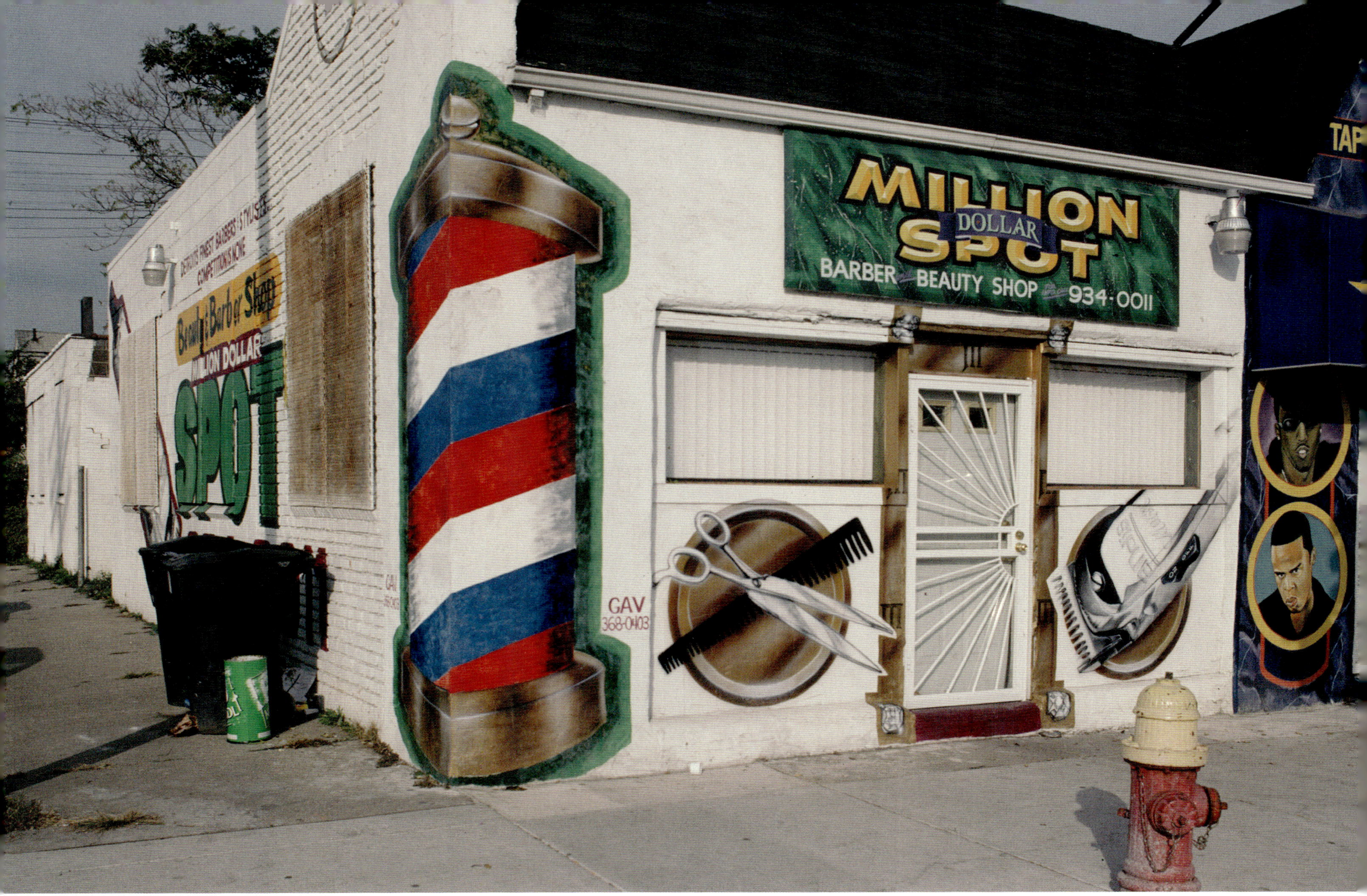

Million Dollar Spot, Barbershop and Beauty Salon, painted by artist G. A. V.
Livernois Avenue at Northfield Avenue, Detroit, 2000.

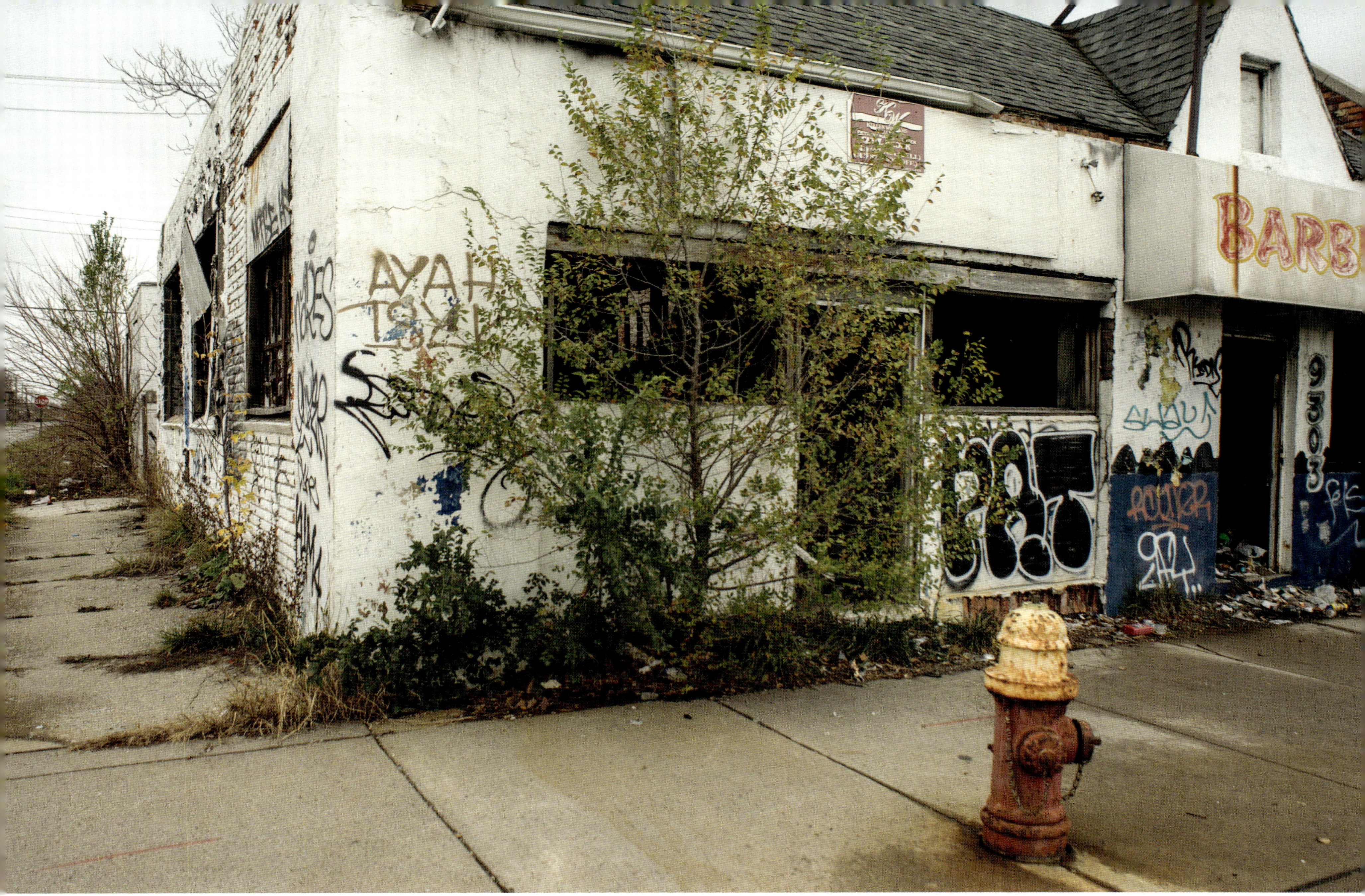

Former Million Dollar Spot, Barbershop and Beauty Salon
Livernois Avenue at Northfield Avenue, Detroit, 2015.

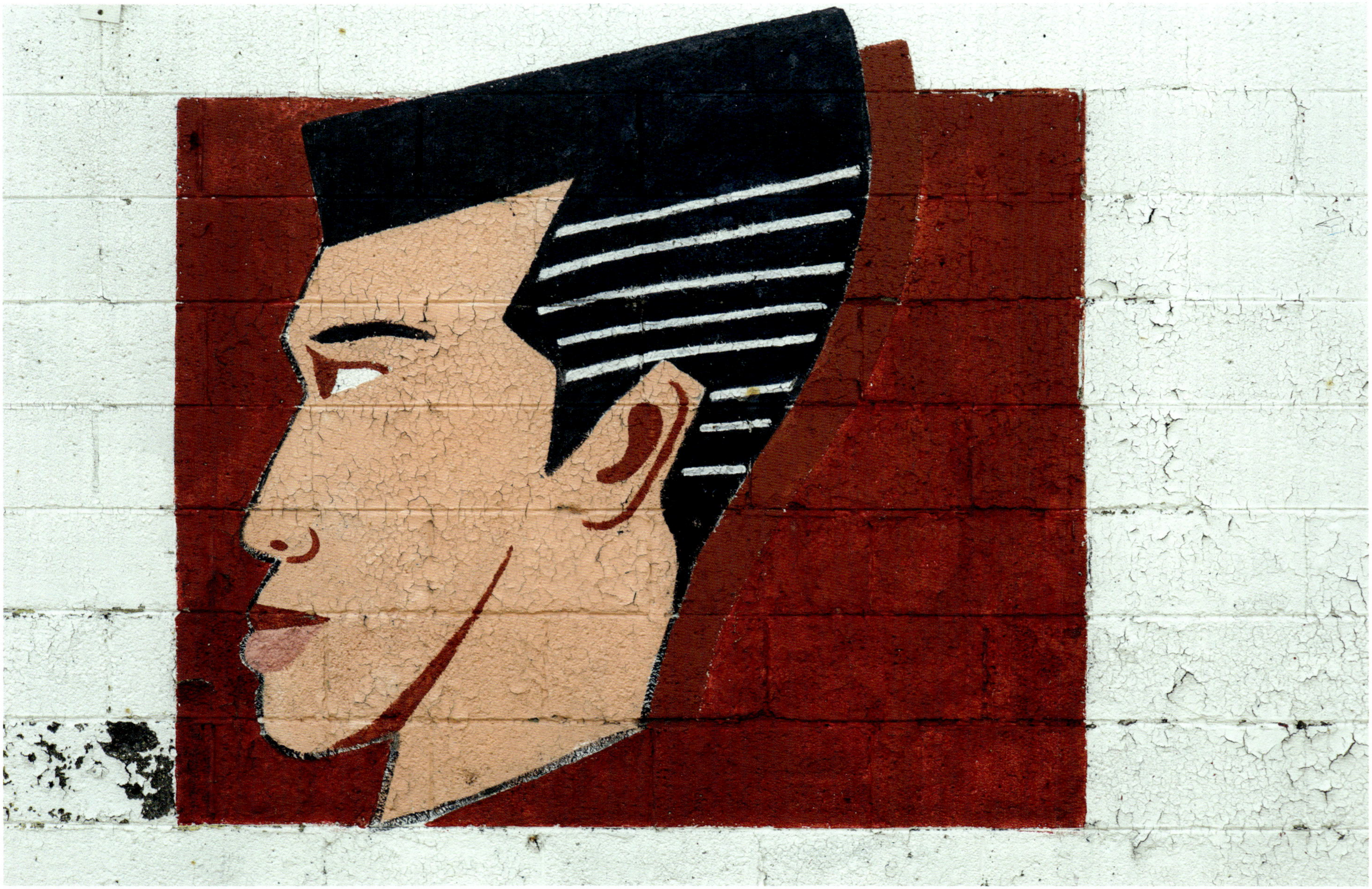

Glen's Barbershop. The haircut depicted in this boldly angular painting, signed by Ron, is called a flat top fade. 16234 Plymouth Road, Detroit, 2015.

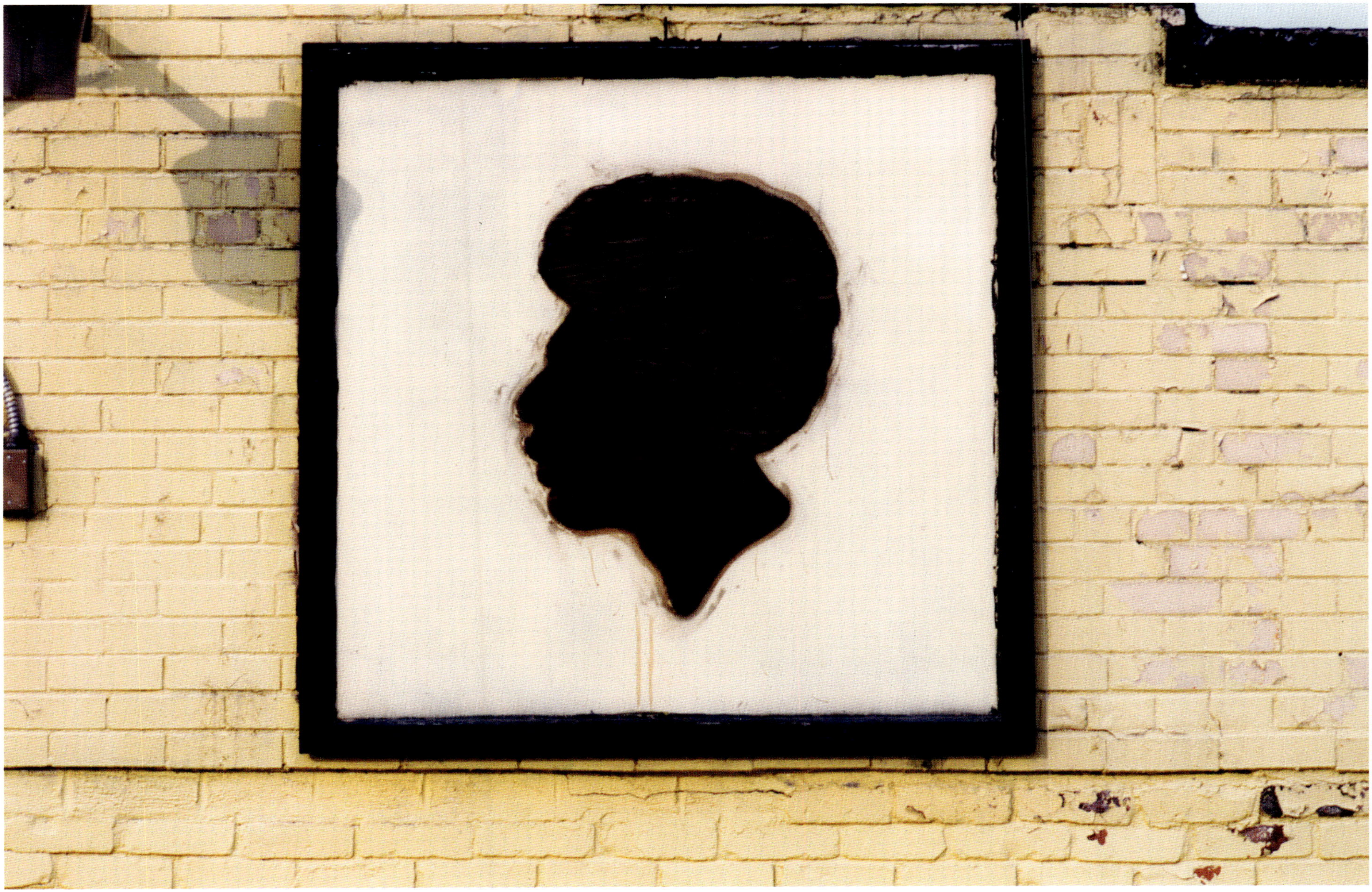

Afro sign, William Styling Barber Shop.
Grand River Avenue at Ward Street, Detroit, 2002.

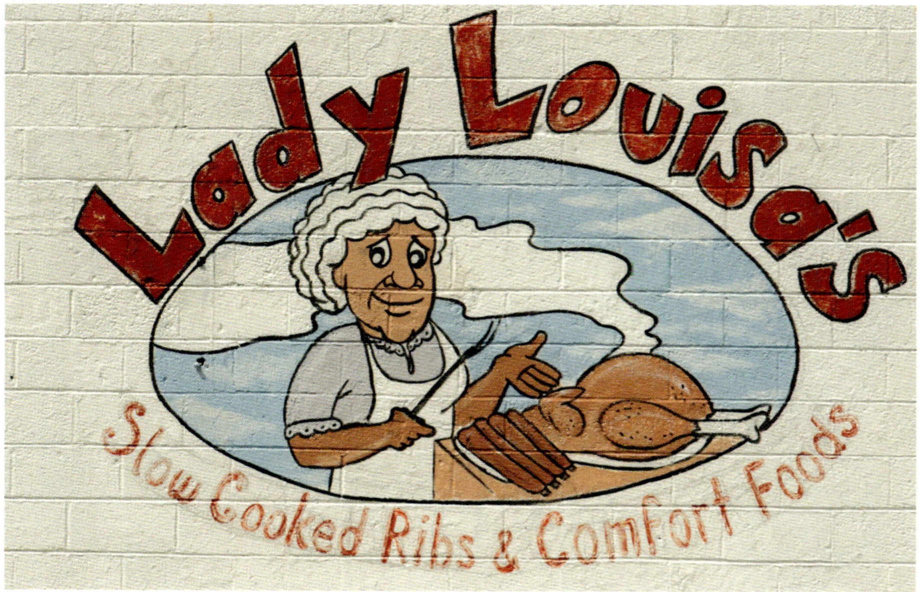

Lady Louisa's. 15535 West McNichols Road, Detroit, 2015.

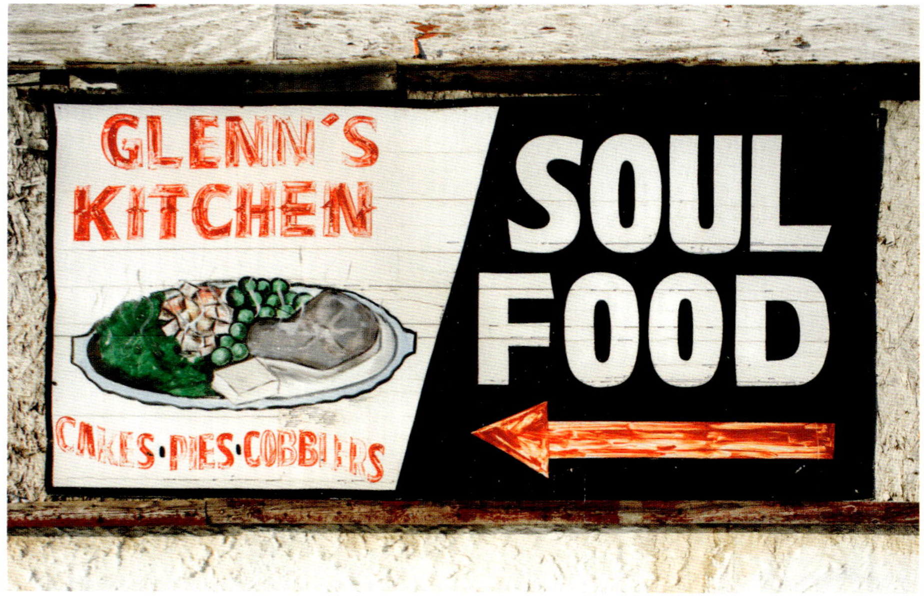

Soul food, Glenn's Kitchen. 9525 Wyoming Street, Detroit, 2014.

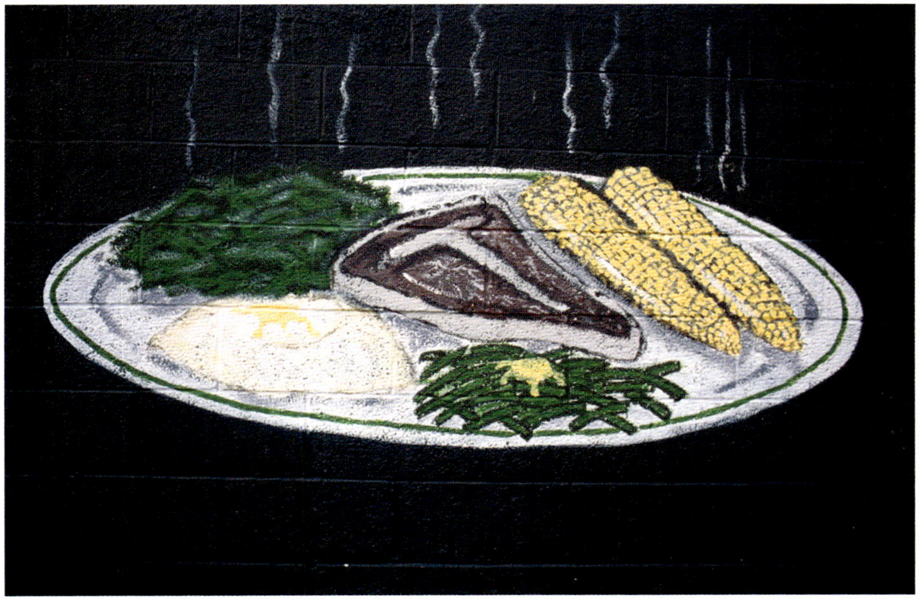

Hot T-bone steak with trimmings, R & D Soul Food. 11811 East Seven Mile Road, Detroit, 2012.

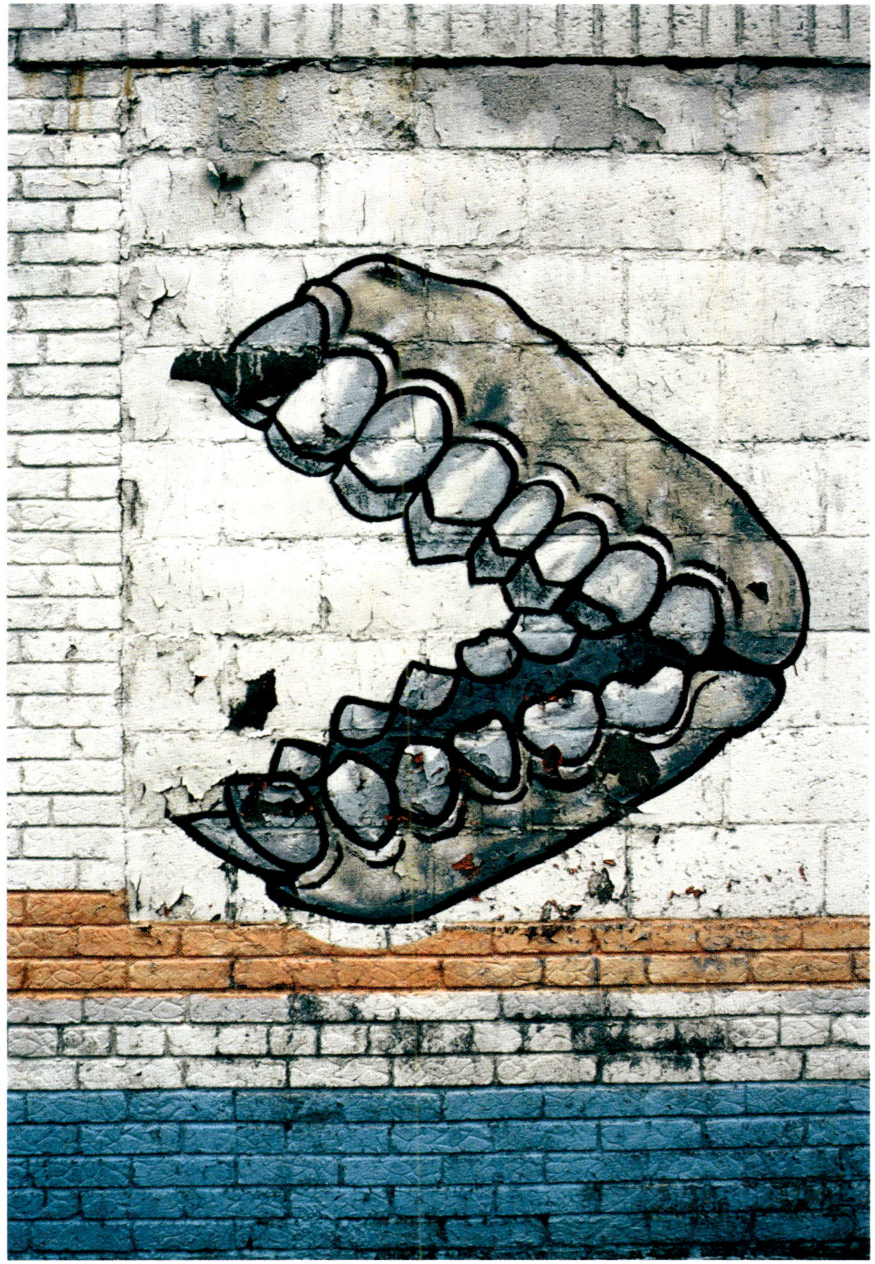

Customized Dental Laboratory. With time, the depicted dentures seem decayed. The artist Bird commented on the dentures that "when they were first painted they looked good." 2919 Mack Avenue, Detroit, 2007.

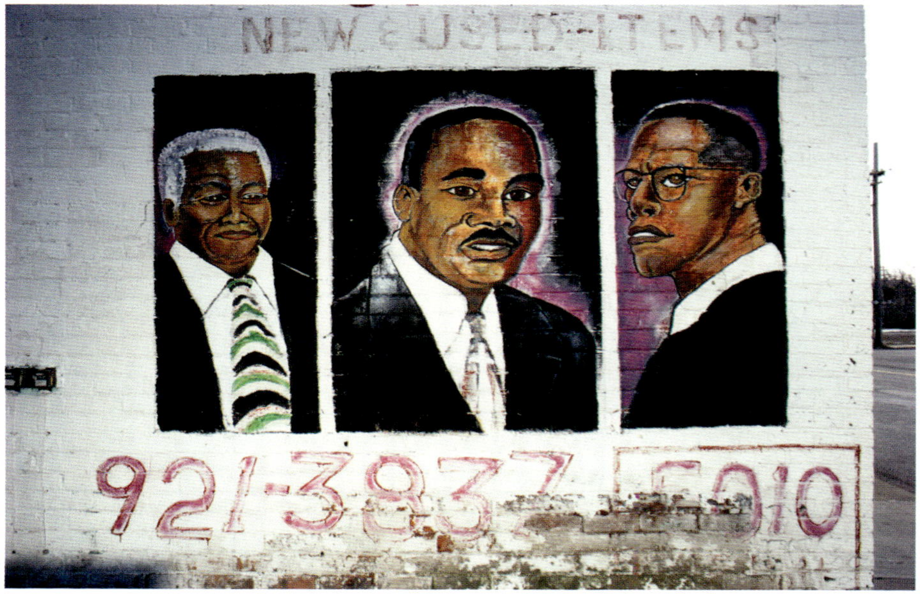

Mural depicting Martin Luther King, Jr., Malcolm X, and Nelson Mandela on a resale shop. Mt. Elliott Street at East Warren Avenue, Detroit, 1998.

CELEBRATING BLACK HEROES AND HEROINES President Obama's likeness is popular in Detroit. Sometimes he appears with the White House or the Detroit skyline in the background, or is depicted next to Martin Luther King, Jr. or the American eagle. Mrs. Lockhard, director of the Jumpstart Learning Center, explained: "We love Obama here." She commissioned a mural for $150 from a folk artist living in Oak Park, Michigan. At the Fair Party Store, Barack and Michelle Obama are painted as though protected by an eagle. Nick, the store owner, commissioned it from artist Sam Phillips to celebrate President Obama's 2008 election victory.

The mural Dare to Dream!!! employs imagery of black, civic, and national pride. It depicts Coleman Young, Malcolm X, and Martin Luther King, Jr., as well as Joe Lewis's fist and gold medalist Tommie Smith along with bronze medalist John Carlos making the Black Power salute during the 1968 Mexico City Summer Olympics. At the same time it includes the Renaissance Center, the American eagle, and the American flag, creating an unexpected amalgam of symbols in one of the most devastated areas of Detroit.

The singer Aaliyah, memorialized in another mural, attended the Performing Arts High School in Detroit, had several hit records, appeared in two movies, and for a short time was married to singer R. Kelly. She died in a plane crash in 2001 at the age of 22. The face of the young Aaliyah, her eyes wide open, above the entrance to an abandoned used-appliances store on Mack Avenue, was crude, simple, and haunting. The portrait has disappeared, leaving behind a black rectangle.

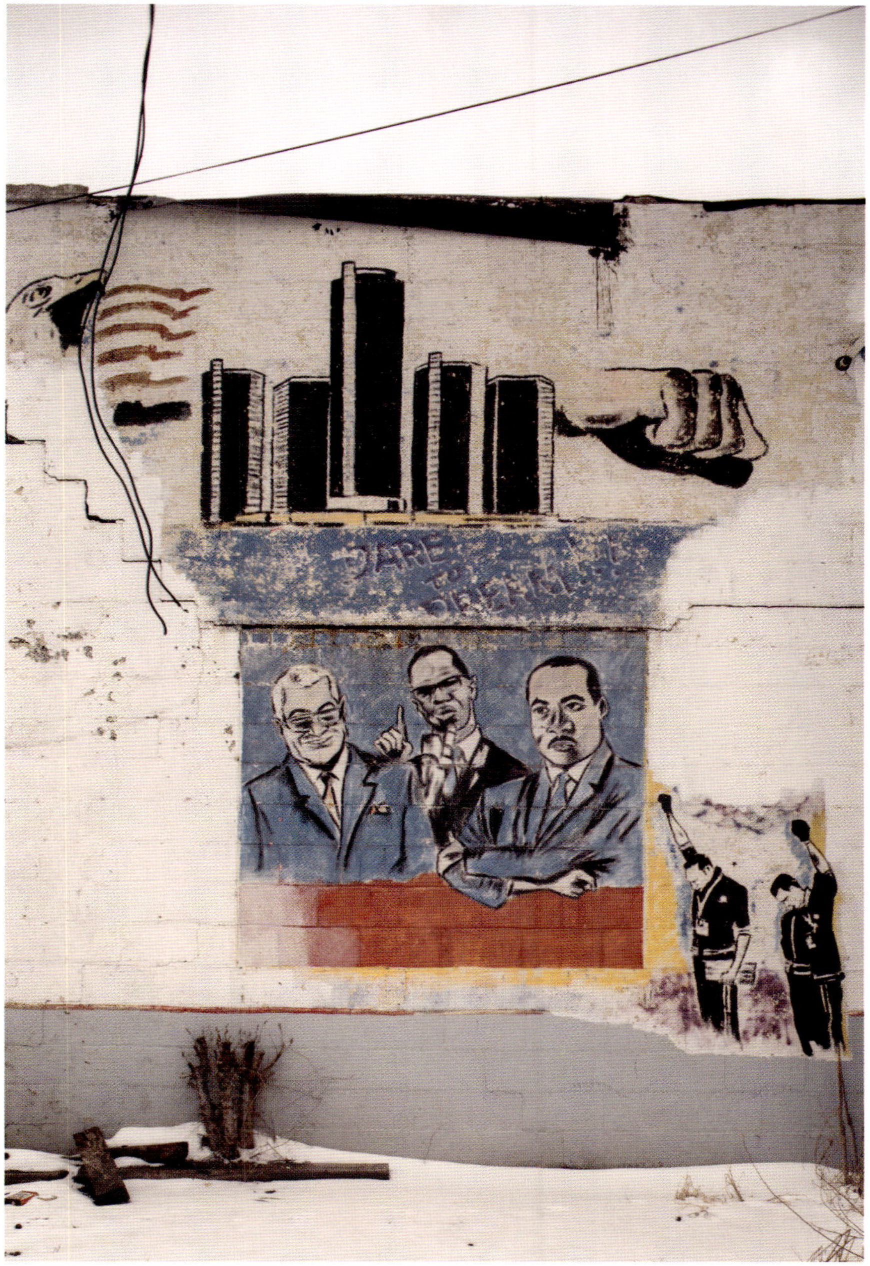

Mural, Dymin Mufflers and Car Wash. Cloverdale Street at Elmhurst Street, Detroit, 2015.

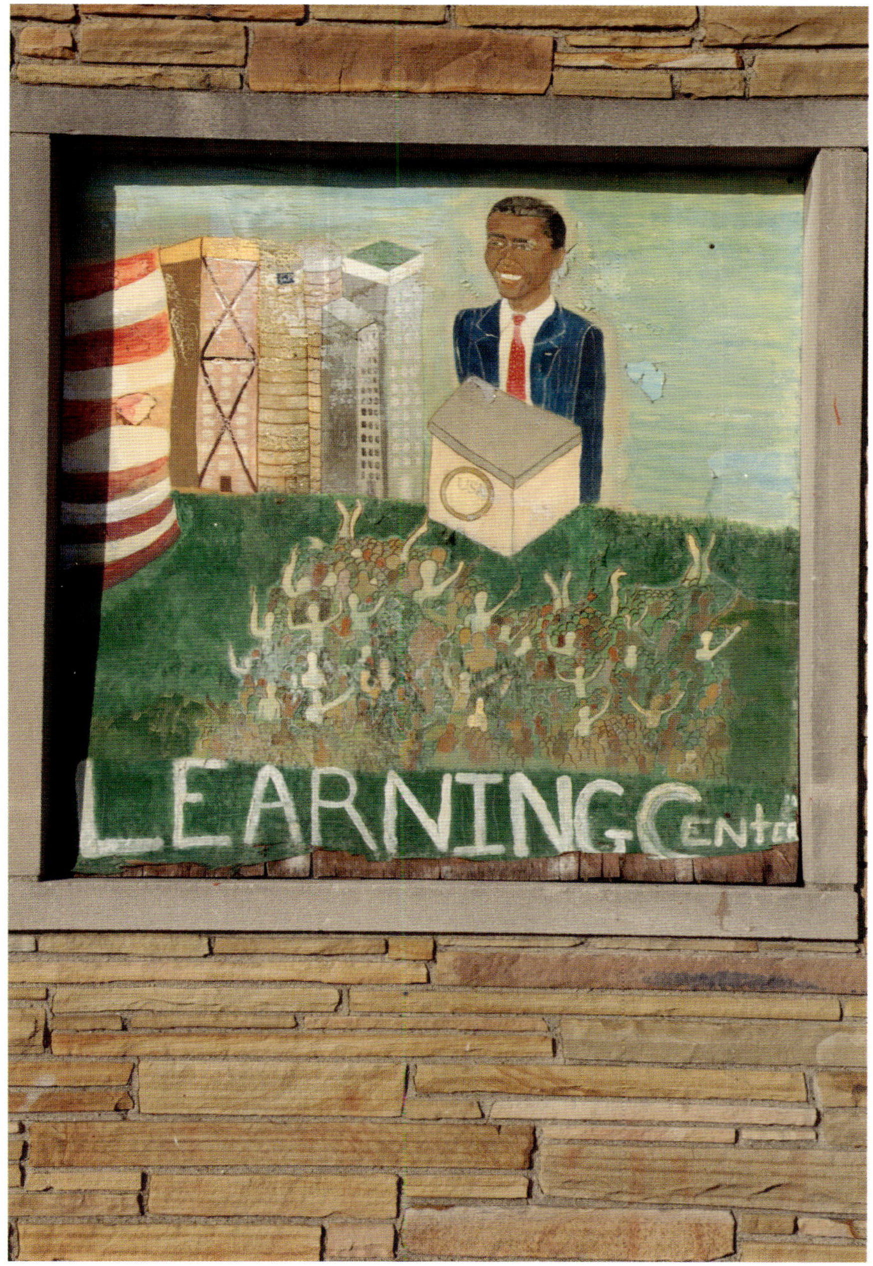

Jumpstart Learning Center. West Chicago Avenue at Birwood Street, Detroit, 2012.

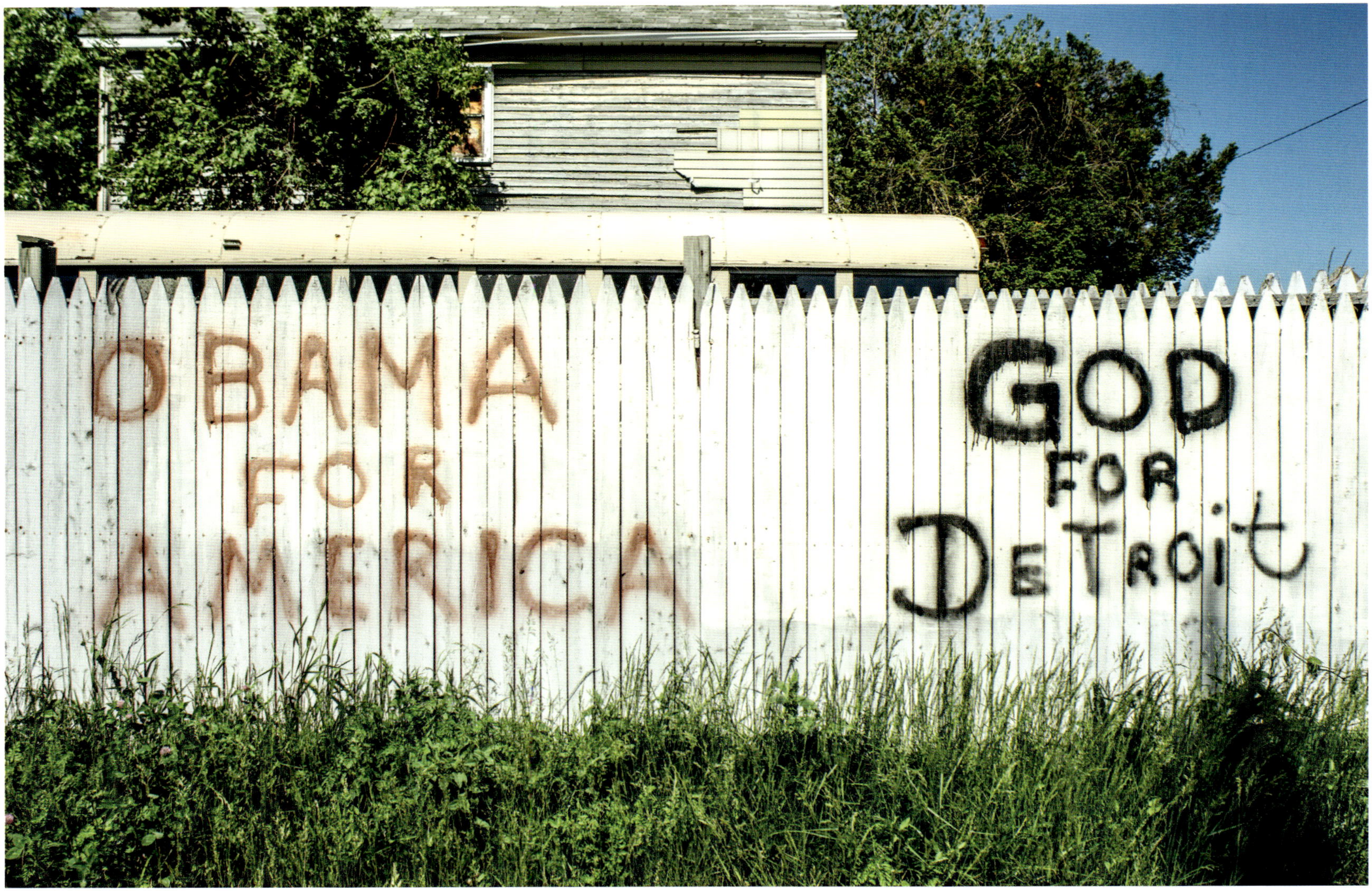

Graffiti: "God for Detroit." East Forest Avenue, Detroit, 2014.

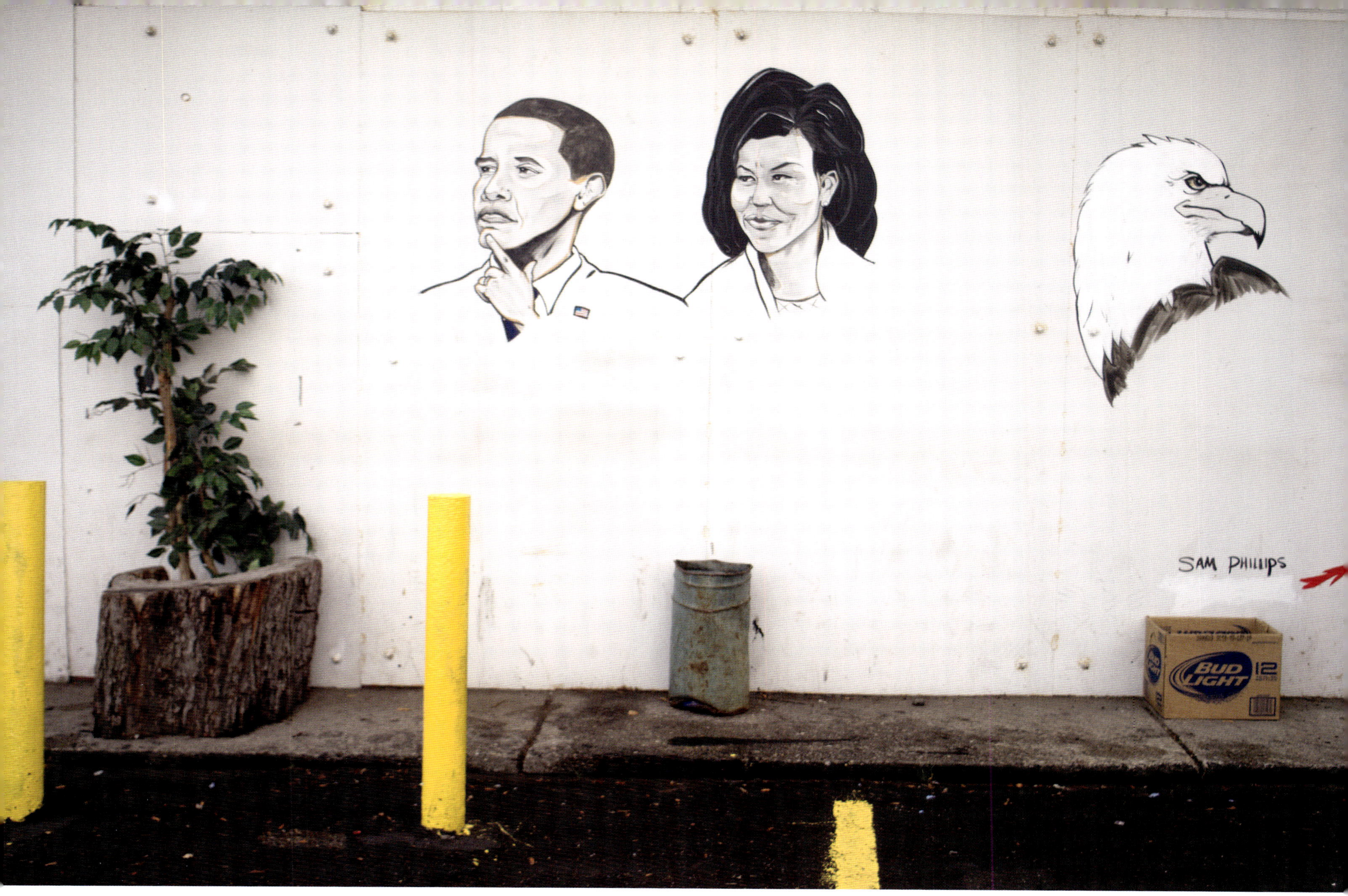

Fair Party Store. 6541 Gratiot Avenue, Detroit, 2013.

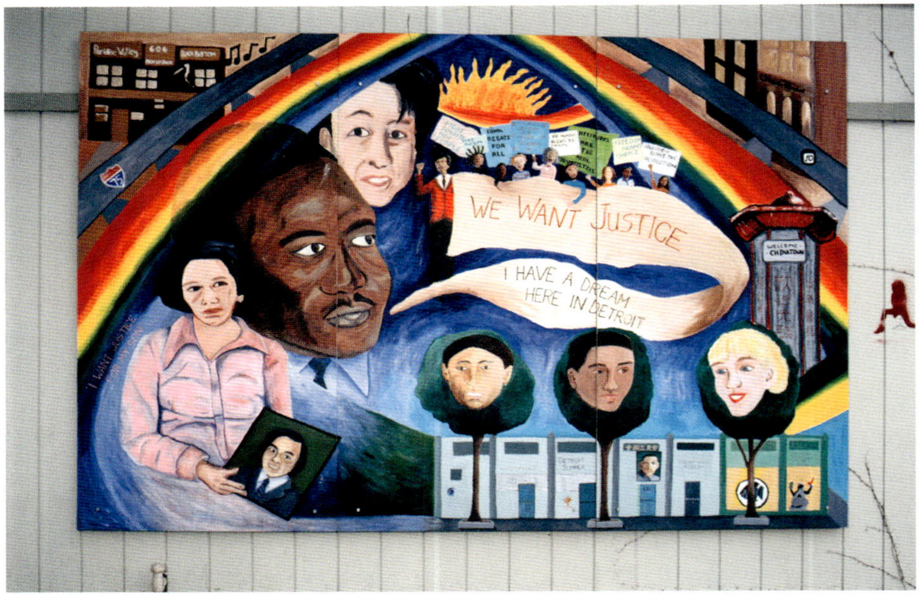

"We Want Justice," mural for Vincent Chin, a Chinese American beaten to death in Highland Park in 1982. 425 Peterboro Street, Detroit, 2008.

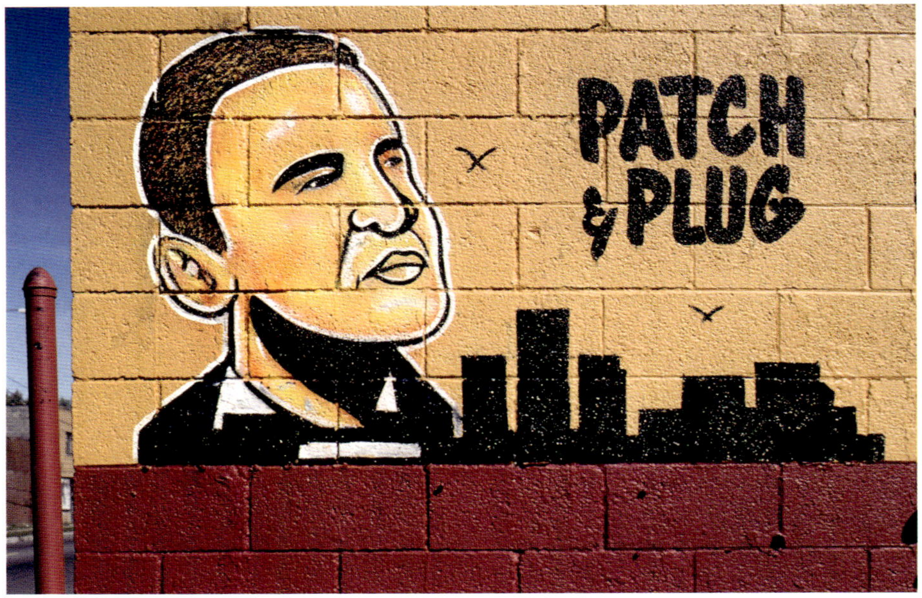

Patch & Plug, Obama, Frank Tires #1, mural by Ron. 4270 East 7 Mile Road, Detroit, 2009.

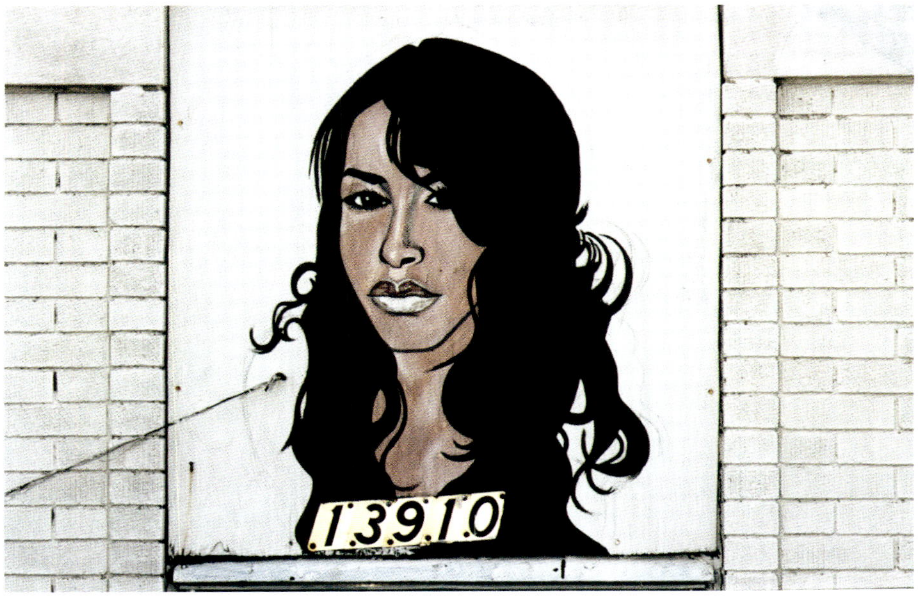

Aaliyah memorial. 13910 Mack Avenue, Detroit, 2008.

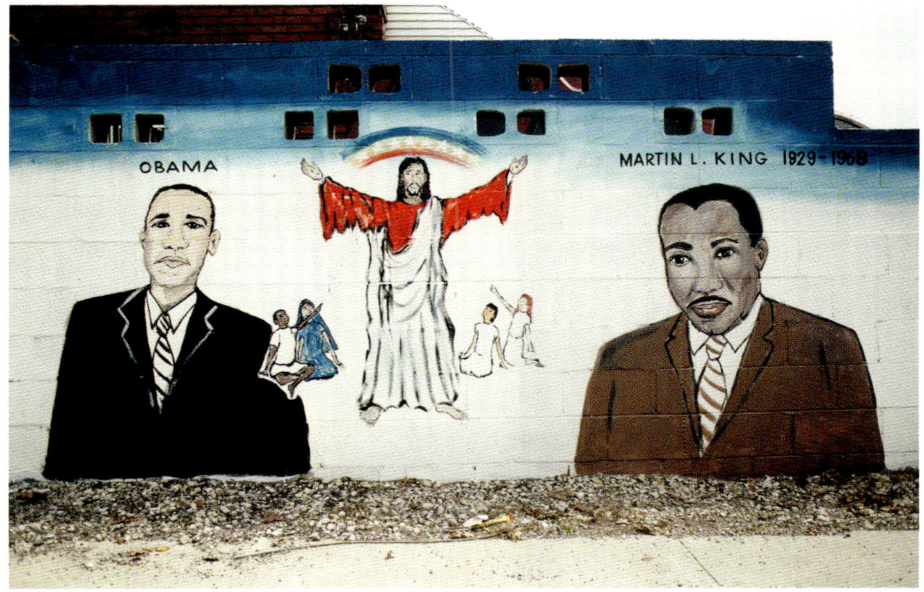

Martin Luther King, Jr. mural. Local artist Bird told me the mural was about "three powerful men, three men that changed the world." West Montana Street and Woodward Avenue, Highland Park, 2009.

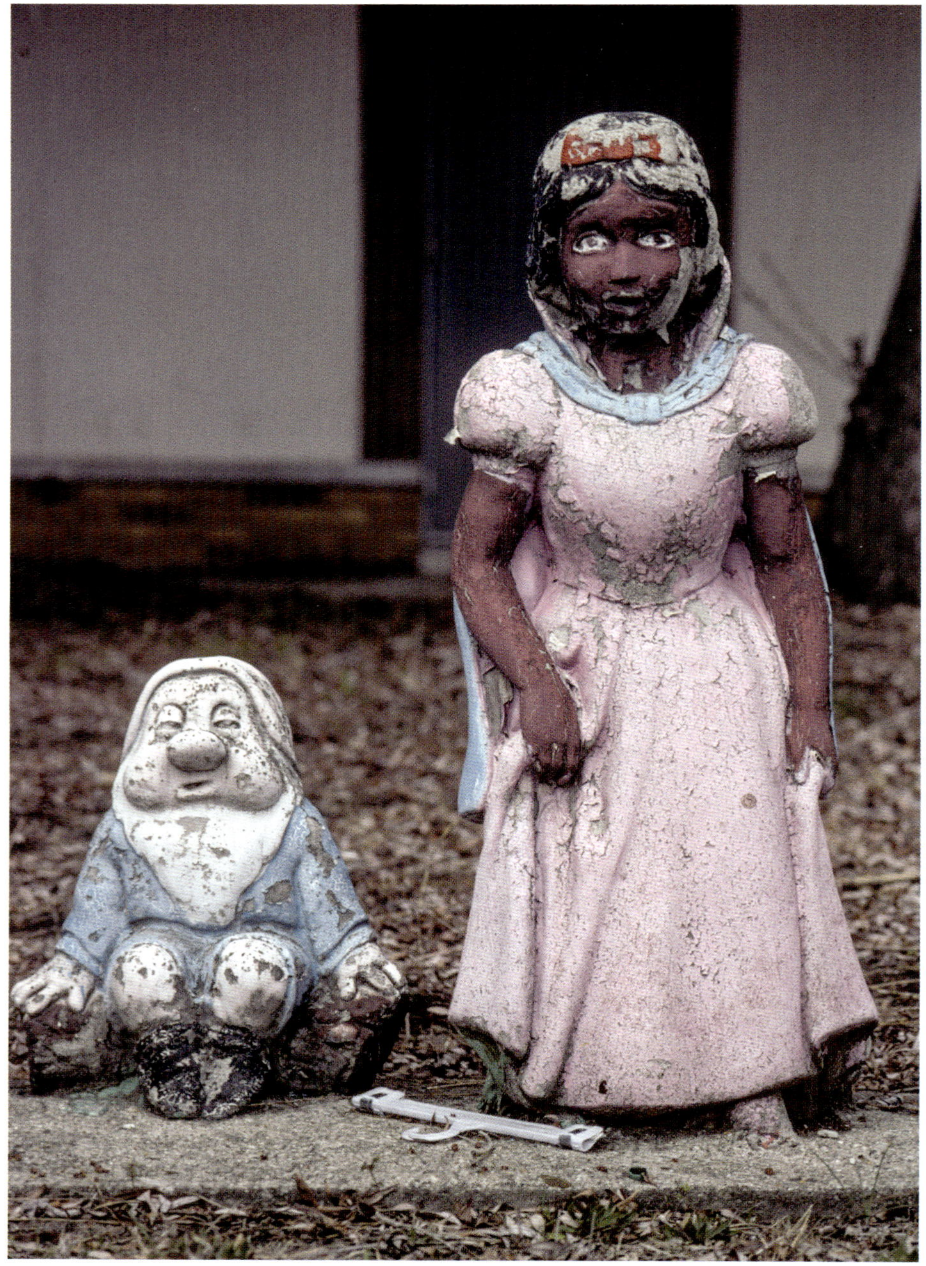

Snow White, Burns Day Care Center. West McNichols Road at Freeland Street, Detroit, 2009.

"IT HAS NOTHING TO DO WITH RACE": SNOW WHITE, SNOW GREEN, SNOW BROWN

On the lawn of Little Learners Academy, statues of Snow White and the Seven Dwarfs were at one time erected as decoration. When I visited, they had been painted. A staff member told me: "We painted them brown. The kids are reminded of chocolates. They know the names of the dwarfs. A white lady wanted to buy them for a party and paint them white." She continued, "Painting them brown has nothing to do with race," a statement that continues to puzzle me. When I asked her if any white children attend the day care center, she told me no. Upon seeing the statue, the artist Bird called Snow White "Snow Brown" and laughed.

Having much to do with race, Detroit, and America, and appealing to both black and white children, is a new item by American Girl Dolls. The concept of the African American "Melody Ellison" doll, coming thirty years after the company's founding and retailing for $115, runs like this: "Nine-year-old Melody is growing up in Detroit in the mid-1960s, a time of great energy, optimism, and change for the African American community. She is a singer and loves to perform in church, with her family, and in her community. Her stories are set against the backdrop of the civil rights movement, which was gathering momentum, and the music scene, including the success and popularity of Motown Records and its artists. As Melody gains more awareness of racial inequality and her sense of community grows from her extended family to include her neighborhood and, ultimately, all African Americans, she is inspired by Dr. King to have a dream of her own: to lift her voice for fairness and equality." Melody comes with a book telling her story and placing her in history. One can also purchase a play recording studio to go along with her love of music and the Motown Sound. The doll and the picture of the little girl on the cover of the accompanying book is brown-skinned with textured, but perfectly straight hair. Unlike the brown statues of Snow White and the Seven Dwarfs, a great deal of money and a massive campaign of research went into the creation of this American Girl Doll.

Brown Snow White and Melody Ellison represent opposite views of America. One appropriates popular symbols for cultural survival in the ghetto while the other represents a celebration of the achievements of the Civil Rights Movement and of Motown music in a nation that embraces diversity. One tells of growing up in segregation and poverty on the west side of the city, the other rejoices in black Detroiters having overcome discrimination and richly contributing to the nation.

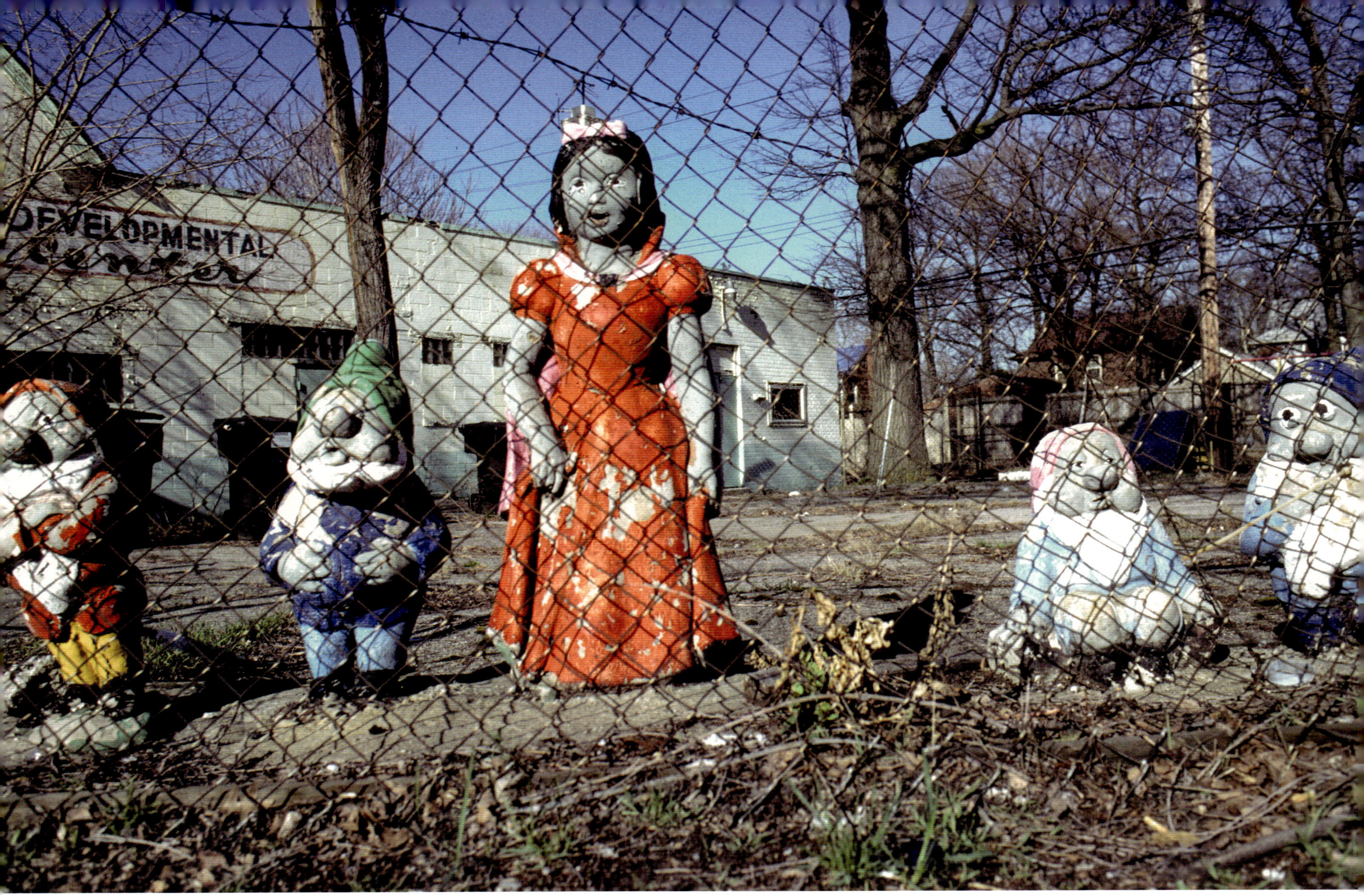

A green Snow White. Little Learners Academy, day care center.
18310 Livernois Avenue, Detroit, 2009.

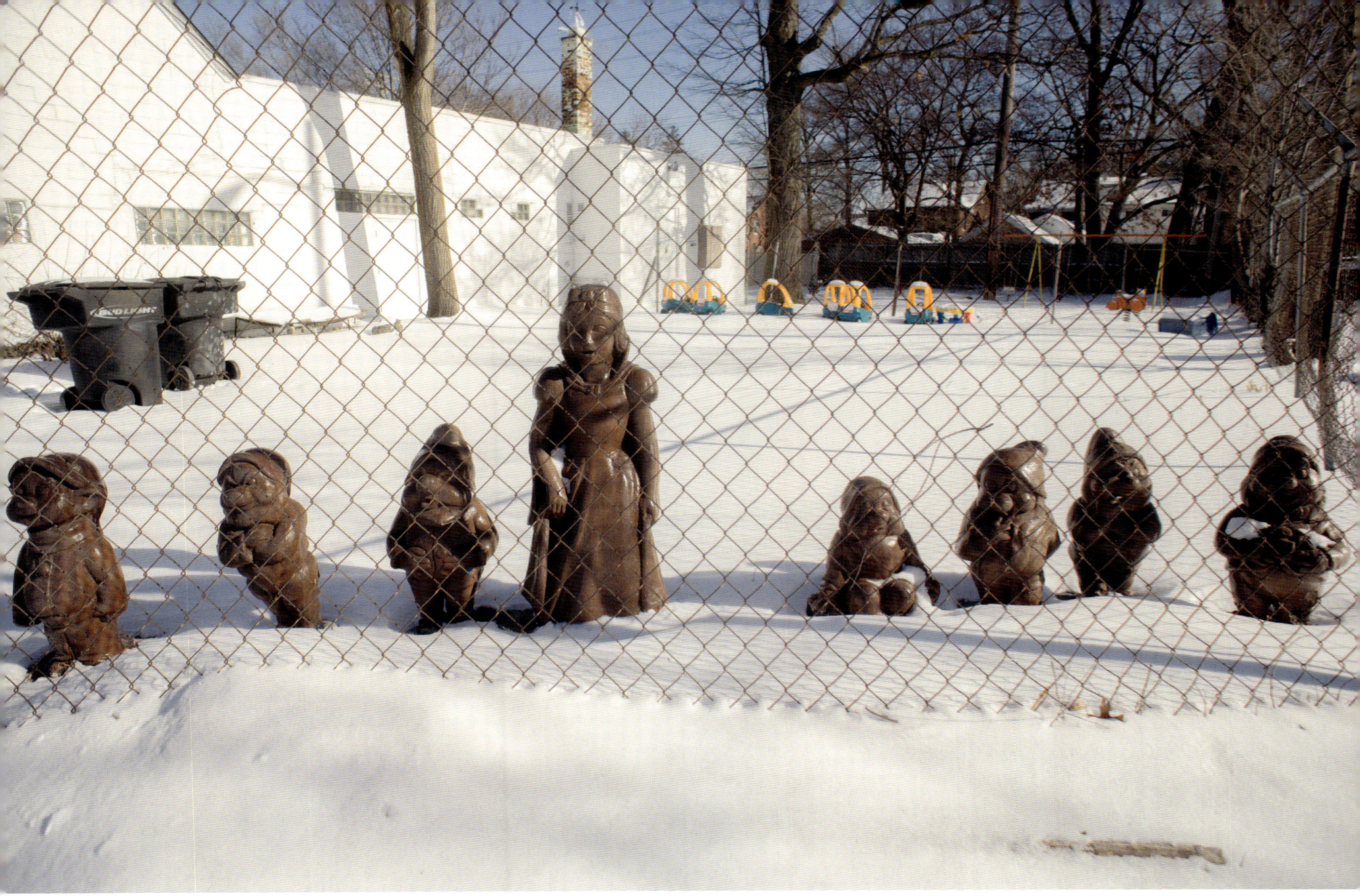

Little Learners Academy, day care center. 18310 Livernois Avenue, Detroit, 2014.

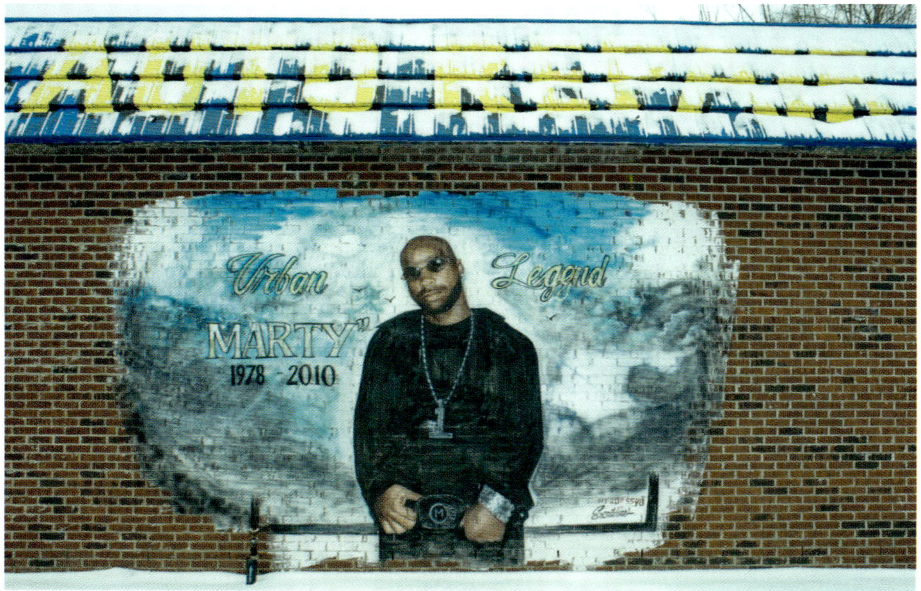

Marty, Urban Legend, East Warren Avenue at Lenox Street, Detroit, 2014.

"GONE BUT NOT FORGOTTEN": MEMORIALS Along ghetto streets are memorials to dead gang members, drug dealers, people caught in the crossfire, and others. Murals, paintings, and graffiti are the work of individual artists or family members, or are sponsored by them. Memorials often take the form of murals covering a large wall, but they can also be made of cards, photographs, and stuffed animals. Marty died of a rare blood disease that afflicted his whole family; his memorial was painted on the side of Kal II Auto Repair Shop. Mike, on the other hand, is memorialized on a lamppost. When I was taking this photograph a man passed by screaming, "Murder City, 400 homicides so far." And someone wrote on the memorial, "Sunny thoughts your way." More unusual is the memorial to Ralph on an expressway overpass, visible to thousands of drivers a day, unlike the familiar street-level memorials. The letters are made with plastic cups.

On the east side of Detroit, on a fence facing Woodlawn Avenue, there are more than twenty poster-size memorial portraits of people who once lived in the neighborhood. A resident told me, "They are all dead people. Somebody puts them up for memory." Bill, who lives on Woodlawn, does not like the display of mostly young bloods who "lived the fast life." One of those memorialized, Big Pope, was loved in the neighborhood and remembered for dressing like Santa Claus at Christmas. His poster, at the center of the display, is decorated with yellow plastic flowers.

The most moving of these paintings was a memorial for seven children killed in a house fire in the early afternoon of February 18, 1993. In the painting only three of the children have faces, the rest being represented by blank face shapes, each marked by a simple cross, and identified below with their names. A clock at the foot of the memorial marks 2:00, the time of the fire. After the fire, the house was decorated with balloons, a tricycle, and plastic flowers with a note saying "seven flowers for seven angels." Stuffed animals were lined up on the steps that led to the entrance. Fire Chief Harold Watkins called the fire "the worst loss of life of children in a single fire in my 38 years on the job." The *Washington Post* article on the fire noted that Chief Watkins "thought of his own seven grandchildren, and he cried."

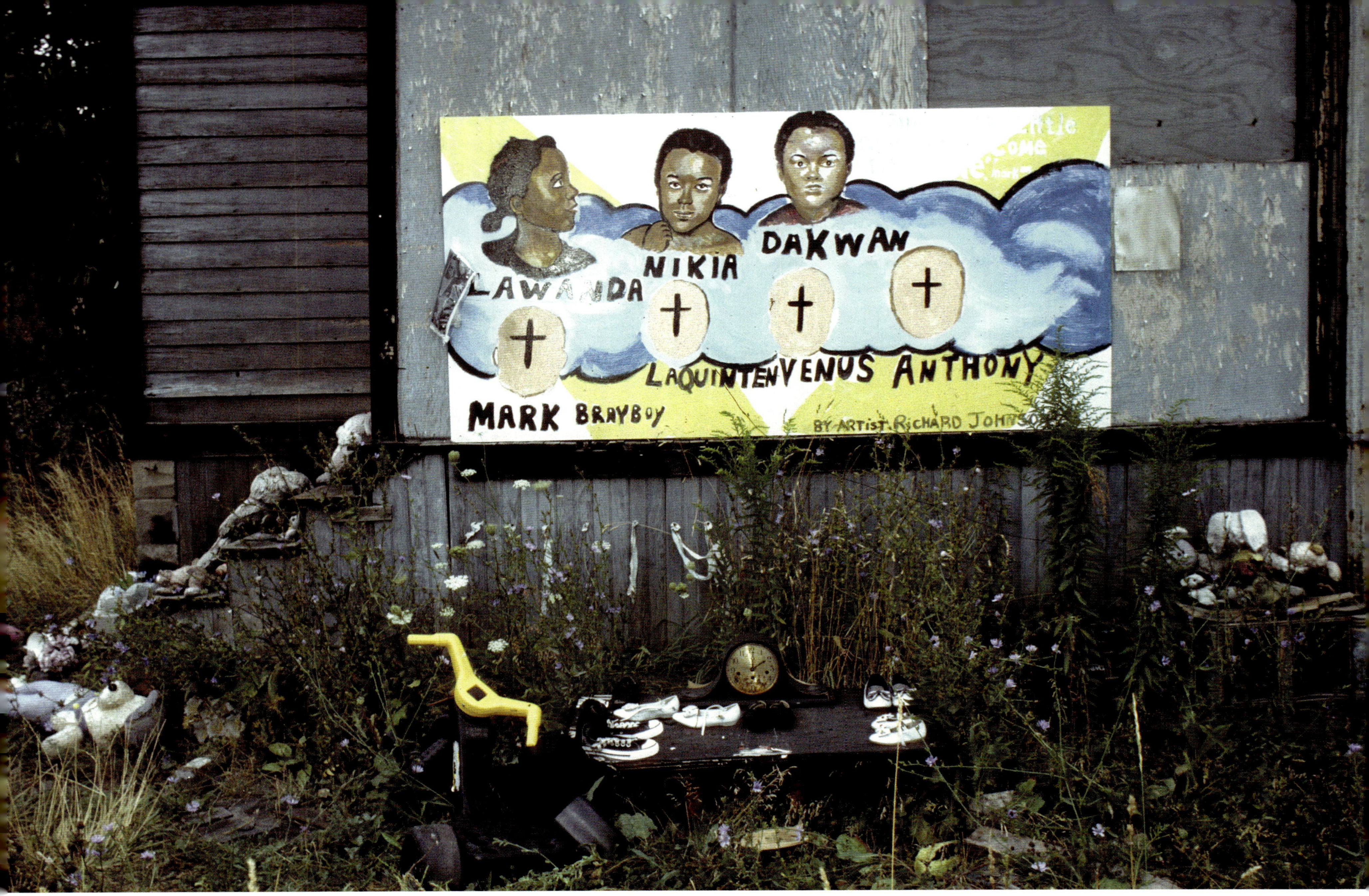

Memorial to seven children by Richard Johnson. 2258 Mack Avenue, Detroit, 1993.

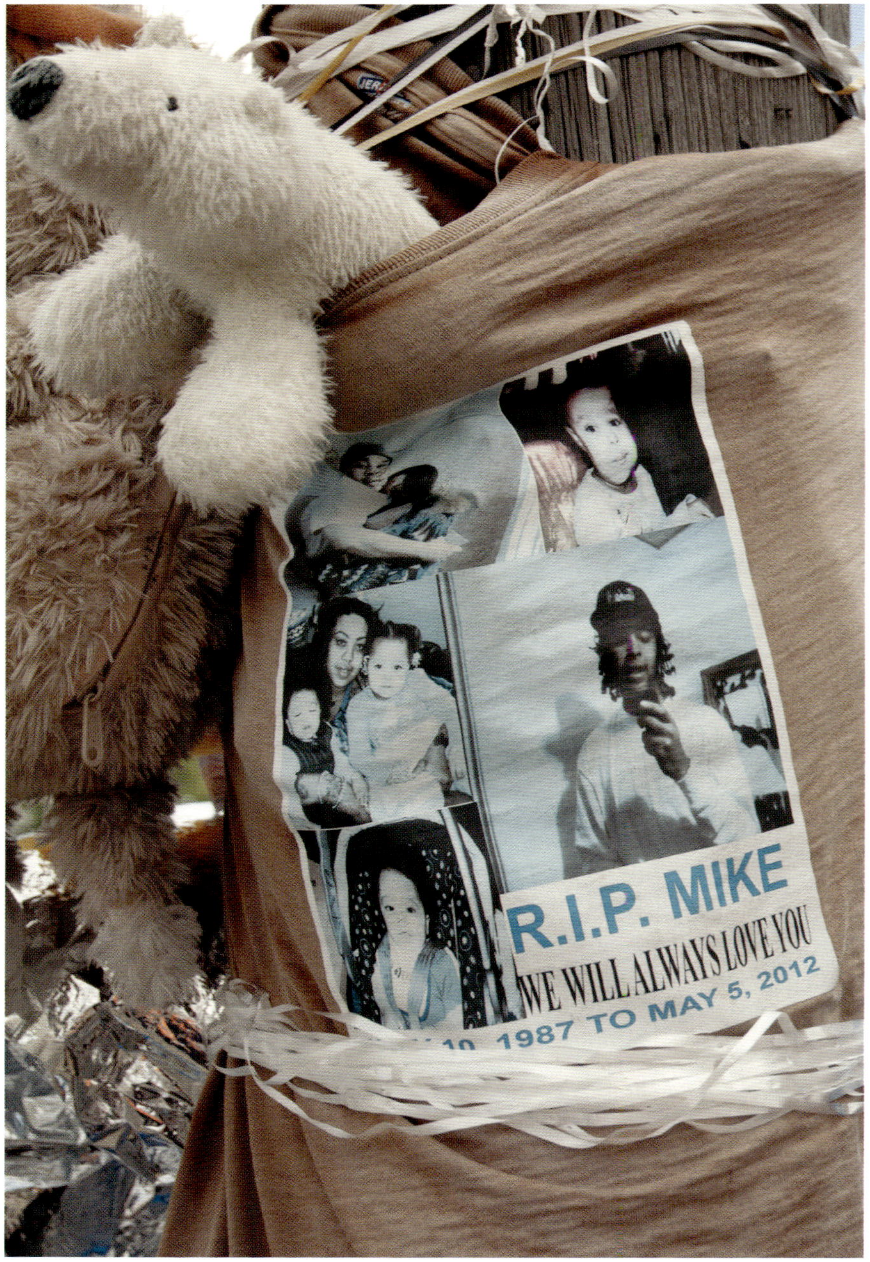

Plymouth Road at Minock Street, Detroit, 2012.

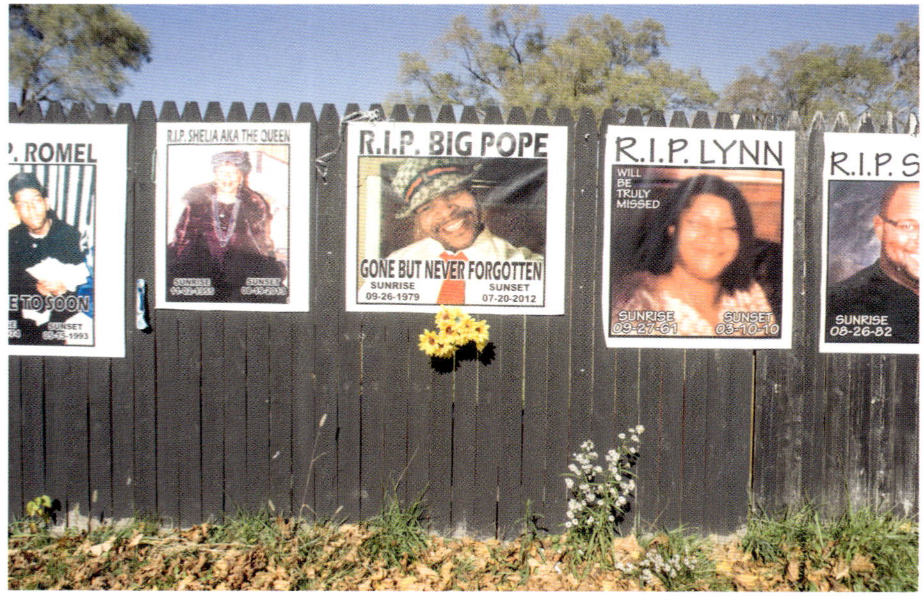

Memory Fence, portraits of the neighborhood dead.
Woodlawn Avenue and Erwin Avenue, Detroit, 2015.

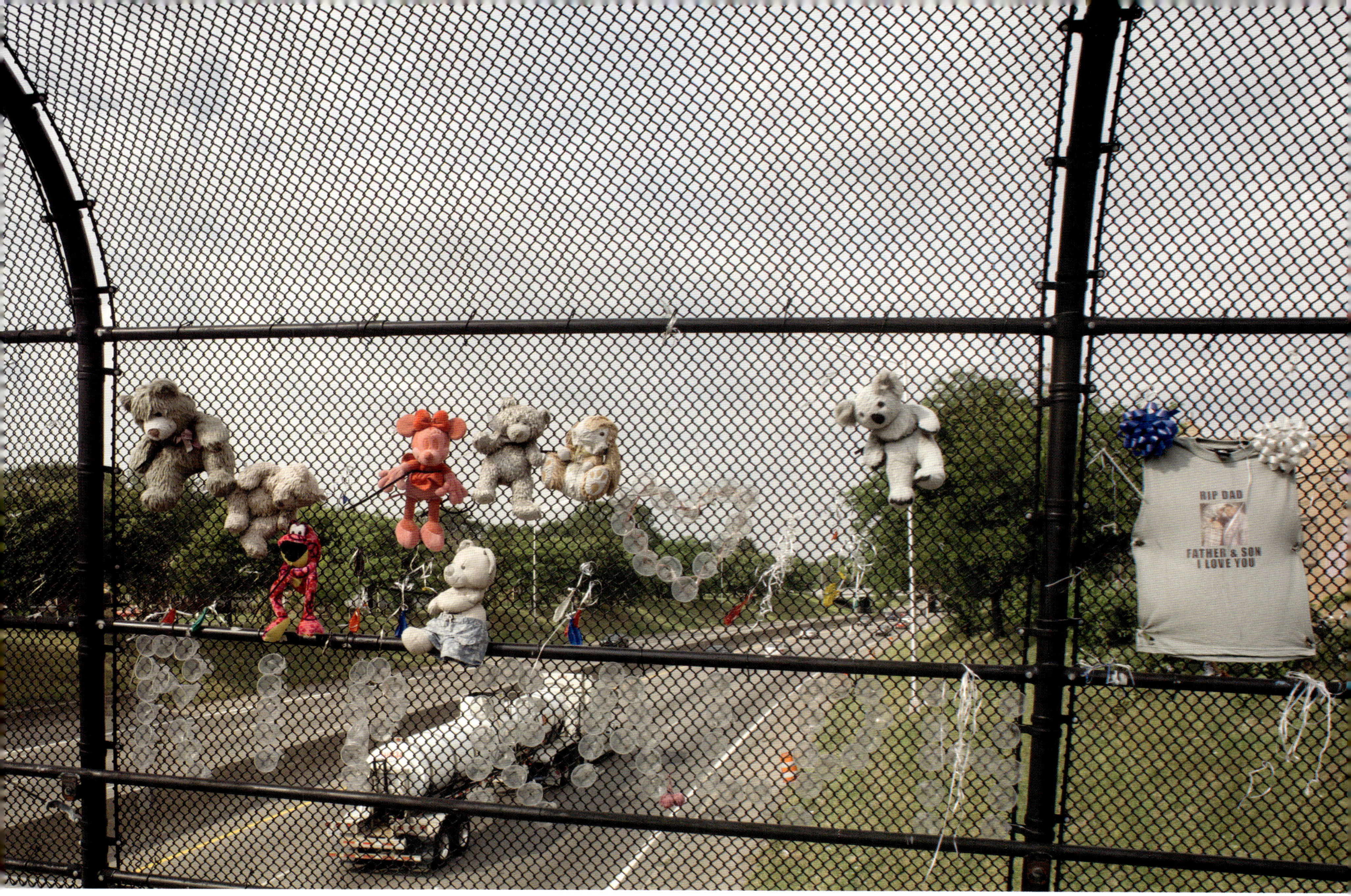

Pedestrian overpass with memorial to Ralph.
East I-94 Expressway at Chatsworth Street, Detroit, 2015.

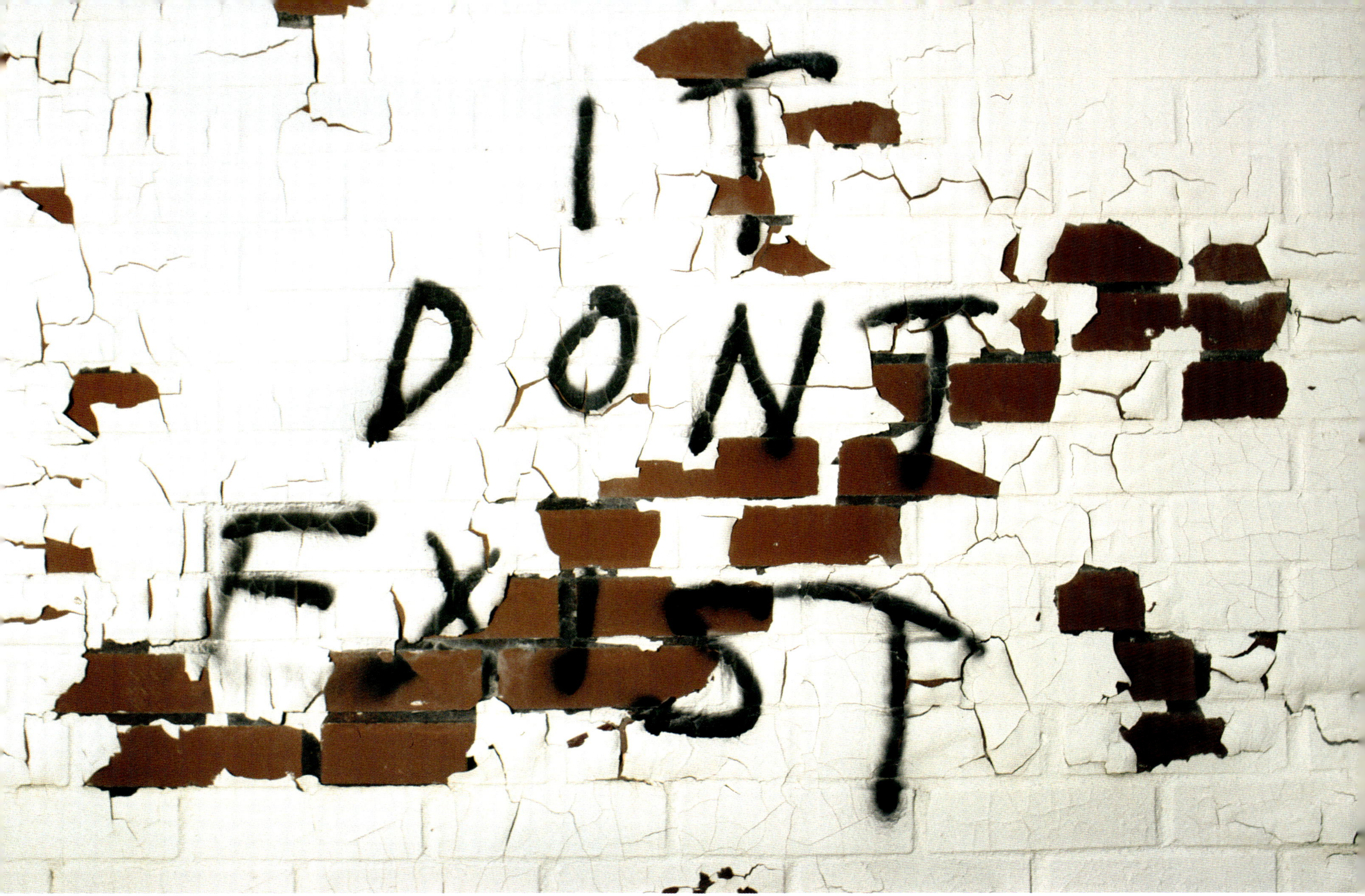

"It Don't Exist." This intriguing statement on buildings across southwest Detroit prompted the weekly *Metro Times* to declare it "Best New Tag" of 2007. Michigan Avenue at Tillman Street, Detroit, 2008.

"YOU ALL CAME HERE AND JUST MARKED UP OUR ENTIRE CITY"

Street artists, muralists, installation artists, and sculptors, from as far away as Texas, California, New Zealand, and the Netherlands, are leaving their mark along major avenues near downtown Detroit, on urban ruins, in galleries and museums, and most of all online. Their powerful online presence makes them a different breed from grassroots artists.

Taggers dialogue with Detroit as they spray paint throughout the city. I first encountered the tag "It Don't Exist" while driving along Michigan Avenue in 2008. I imagined that it expressed incredulity at Detroit's strangeness. The tag, ubiquitous throughout the southwest part of the city, was chosen "The Best New Tag" by the *Metro Times* in 2007. Another tag consists of a reversed Detroit Red Wings team logo with female breasts replacing the wheel, a commentary on the practice of female fans baring their breasts during the games. The cut-out, stenciled yellow snake once shown crawling out of a hole in the wall of The Museum of Contemporary Art and in other places throughout Detroit stood for snakes inhabiting the abandoned city.

Portraits by artist Nicole MacDonald celebrating a variety of notable Detroiters appear on the windows of an abandoned building. As local art critic Mark Stryker described the work: "The well-executed paintings include a range of homegrown political and cultural leaders and activists, among them Rosa Parks, John Conyers, Walter Reuther, Maryann Mahaffey, Helen Thomas and Grace Lee Boggs" (*Detroit Free Press*, 2015). Works such as MacDonald's contrast with the religiously oriented and memorializing works by local sign painters.

In 2004, Carl Kamulski, a local artist, felt that "Detroit could use some angels to remember and mourn what once was." He was speaking of the formerly vibrant Delray area. To get those angels, Kamulski sponsored a public art installation. He made 114 plywood angels and engaged the community to paint them. People from all walks of life enthusiastically volunteered. The angels were attached to buildings throughout the area.

There is a thirst in Detroit for highly visible places where people can put their mark. A good example is the abandoned United Community Hospital, which can be seen from the Fisher Freeway. The façade has become a magnet for large-scale tags in big block letters. Melvin Hollowell, former chief legal counsel for current Detroit mayor Mike Duggan, said of the graffitied façade: "Southwest [the hospital's former name] has been one of the biggest eyesores in the city of Detroit for more than a decade, and it's very visible from three of the major freeways." Built to serve the area's African American community, United Community Hospital was once a shiny modernist building. Who would have imagined, before it closed in 1991, that its final purpose would be that of a giant canvas for taggers?

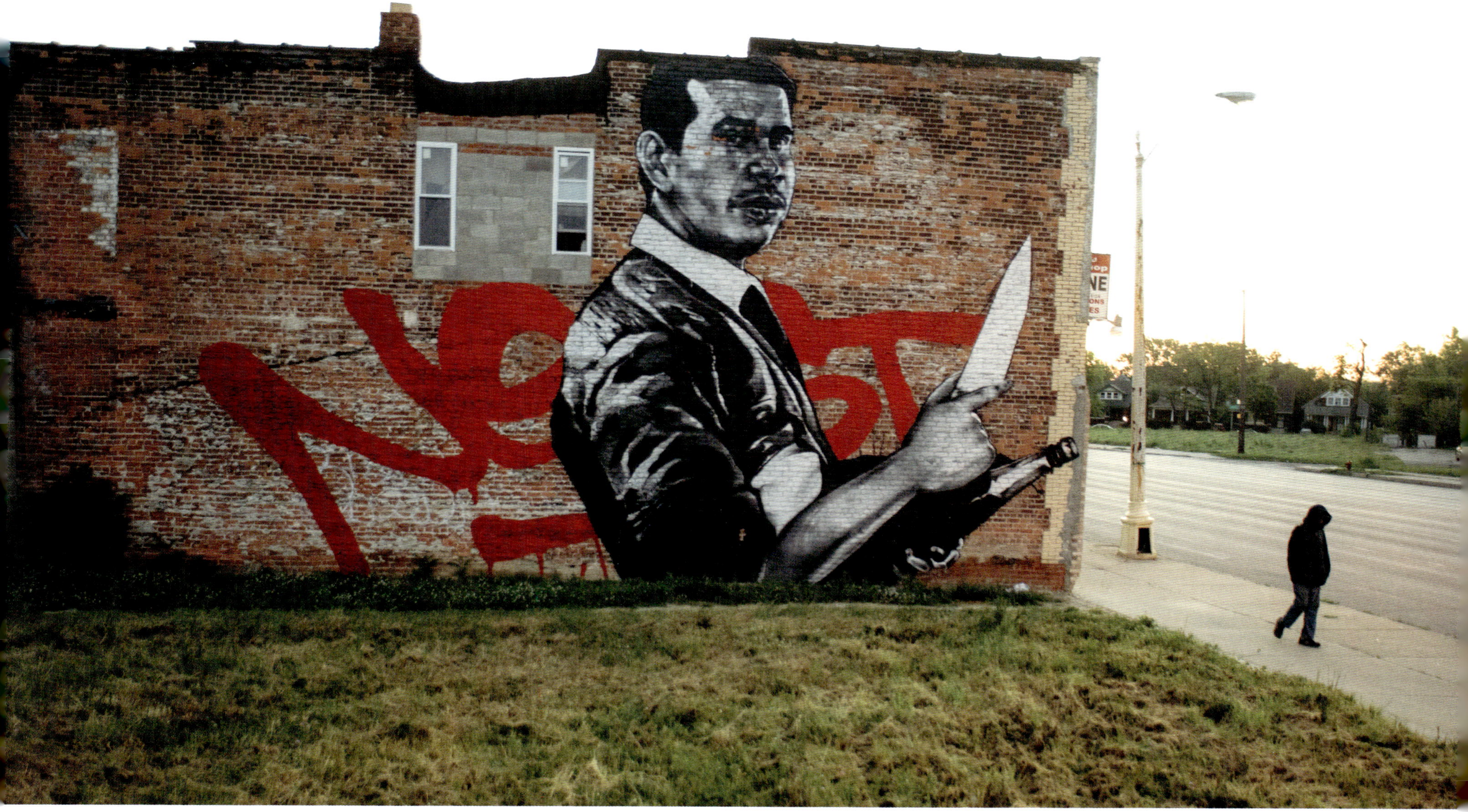

Tribute to street artist Nekst by New Zealand artist Askew One.
Monique's One Stop, Gratiot Avenue at Iroquois Avenue, Detroit, 2014.

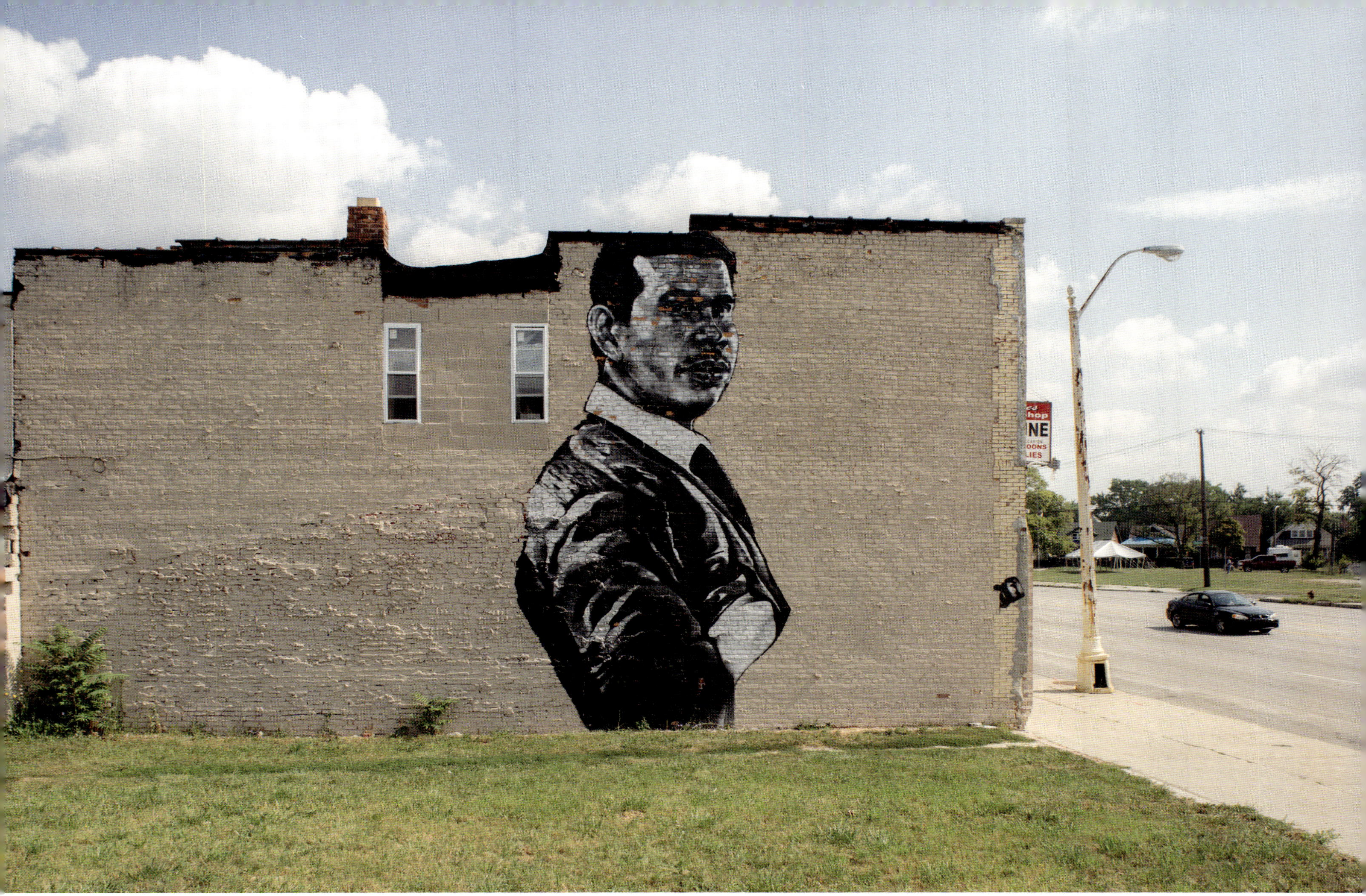

Partially erased tribute to street artist Nekst, by New Zealand artist Askew One on the wall of Monique's One Stop. Mattie, the owner of the store, was threatened with a ticket by the city—"by the one that is over the buildings"—if she did not remove the image of the knife. "I wasn't going to pay no ticket," she told me, and hired a lady to paint over the offending weapon. Gratiot Avenue at Iroquois Avenue, Detroit, 2015.

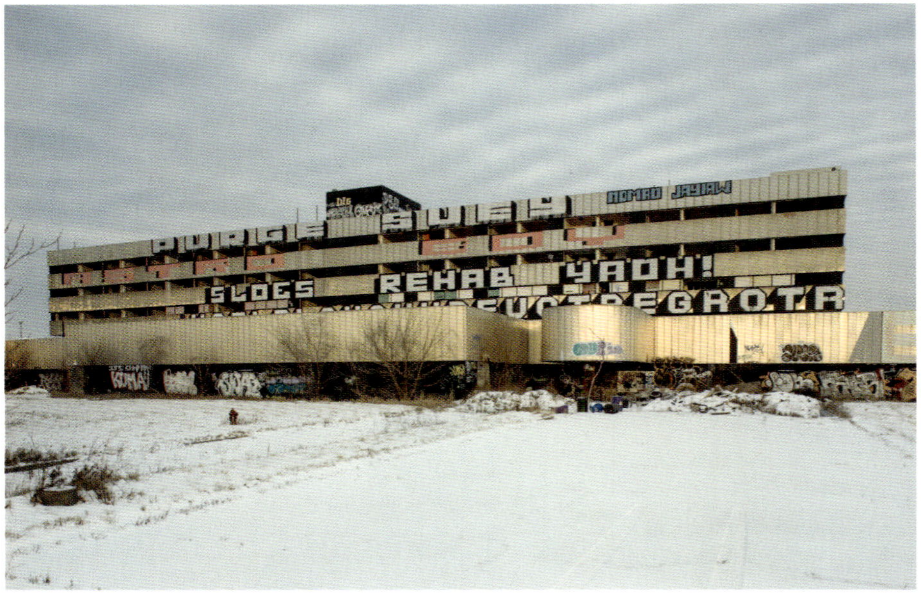

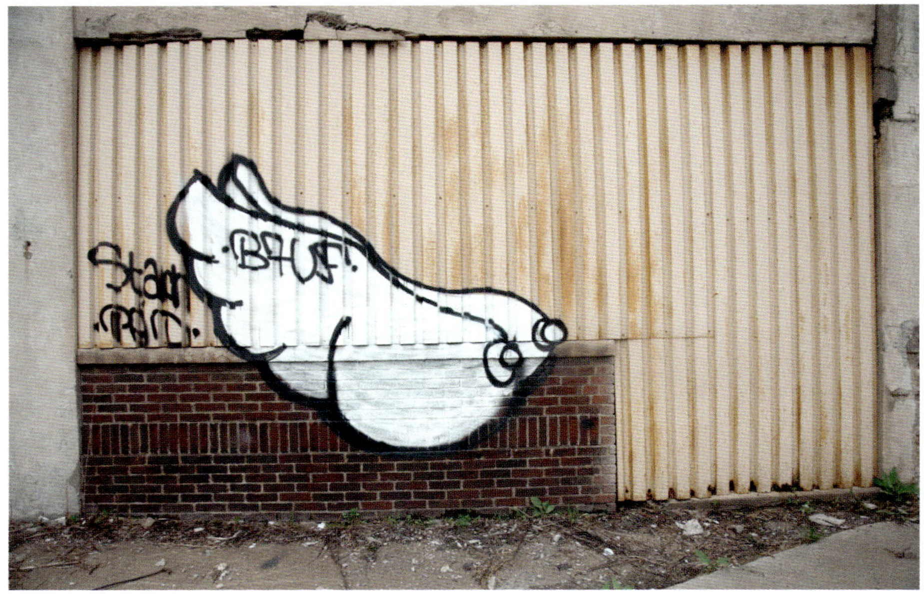

Former United Community Hospital, opened in 1974. Michigan Avenue and 20th Street, Detroit, 2015.

Sign referring to the practice of women displaying their breasts during Detroit Red Wings hockey games. Mt. Elliot Street at Strong Street, Detroit, 2012.

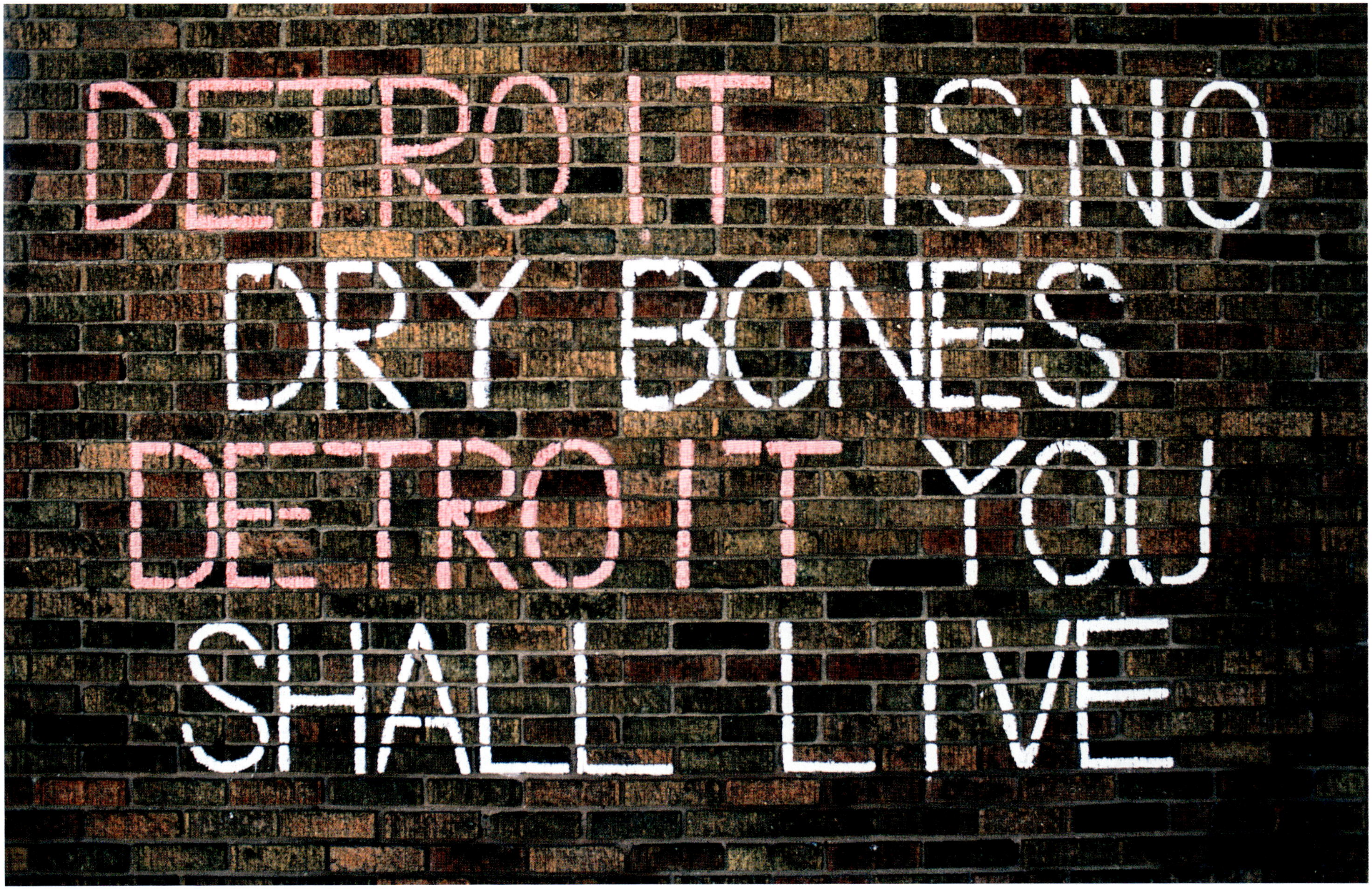

"Detroit Is No Dry Bones," Ruth Chapel AME Church. East Kirby Street at Baldwin Street, Detroit, 2012.

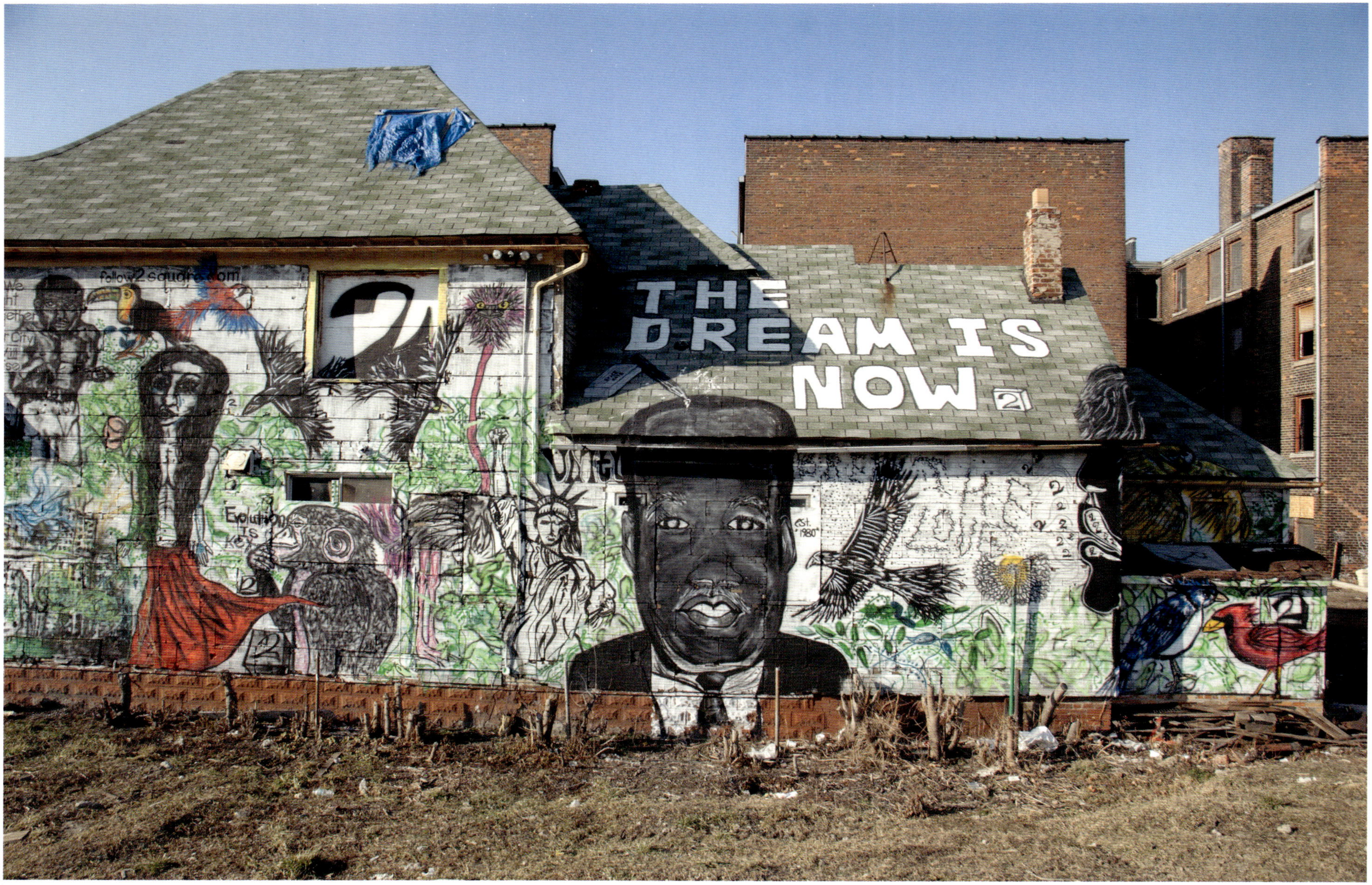

Martin Luther King, Jr. mural, "The Dream is Now." Two burned-out homes, bought for $1,000 each and located less than a block from the former Michigan Central Station, make an unlikely site for the ambitiously named "Imagination Station." Isolated but enhanced by the glorious old depot, Imagination Station supplies plenty of space for art installations and gatherings. The Henri Rousseau-influenced mural was created by the traveling artists collective 2Square. Dalzelle Street at 14th Street, Detroit, February 2012.

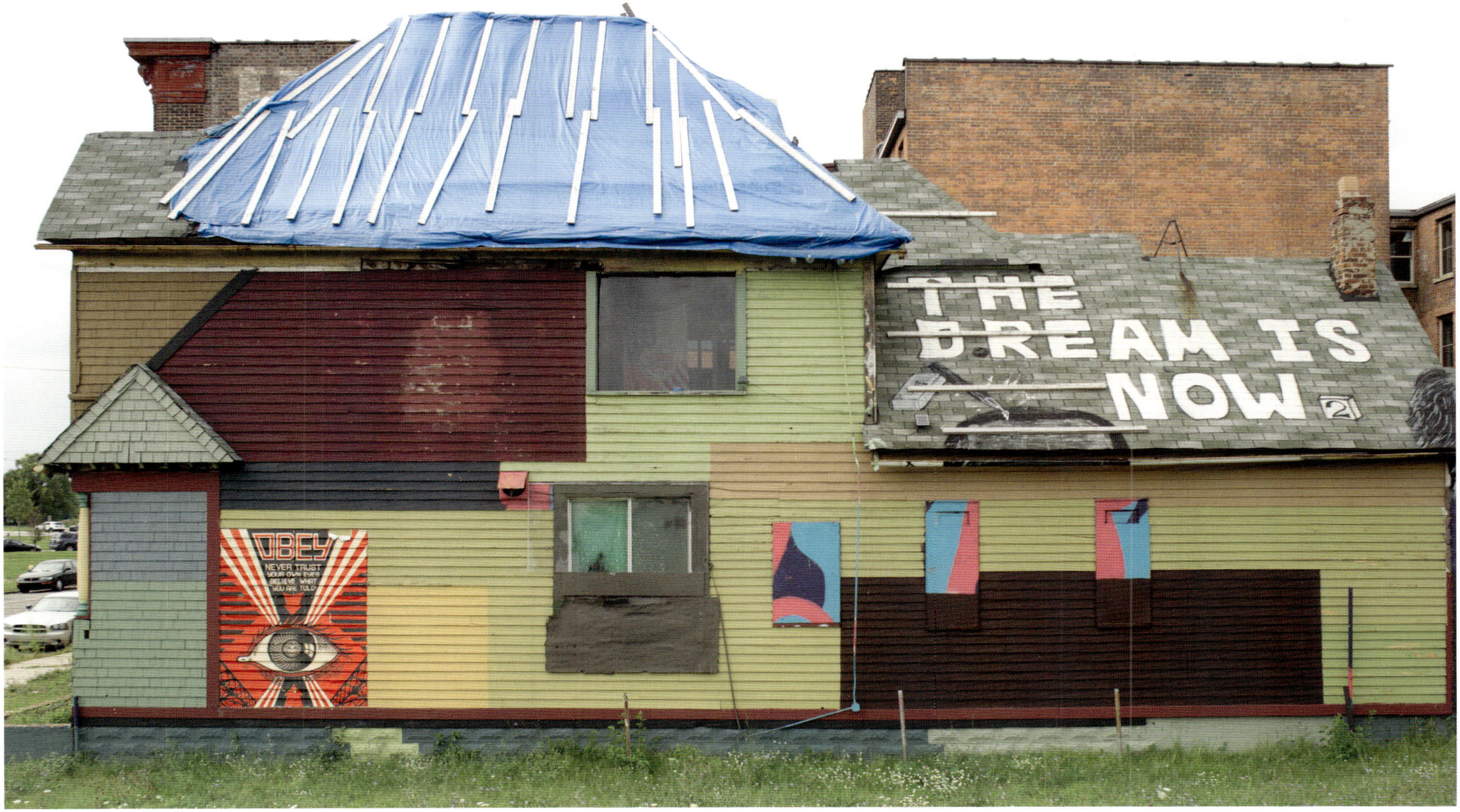

The Imagination Station, painted by Jerry Paffendorf, is patched up and still standing in 2015. At lower left is a piece by Shepherd Fairey. Dalzelle Street at 14th Street, Detroit, 2015.

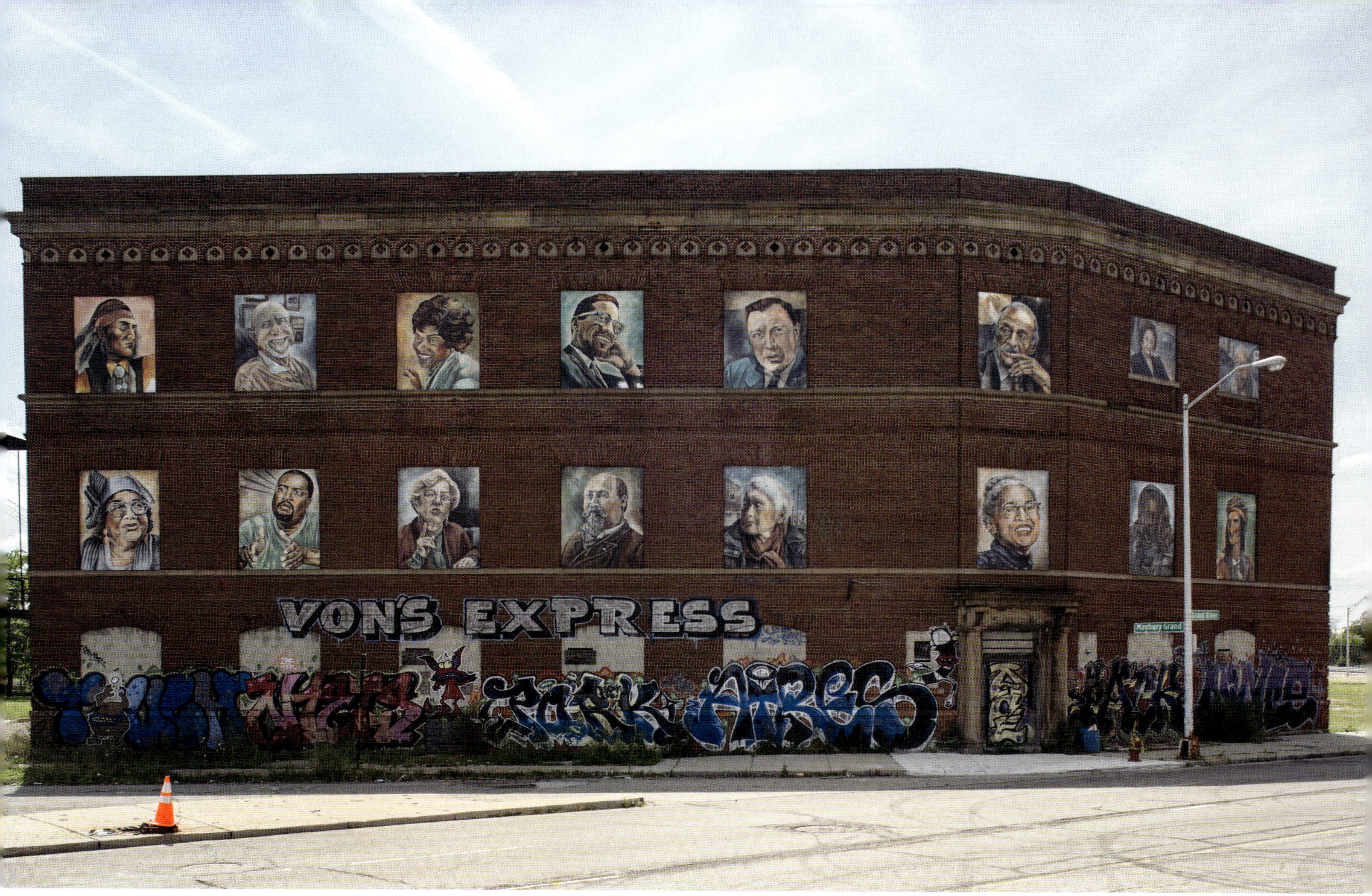

Grand River Avenue at Maybury Grand Street, Detroit, 2015.

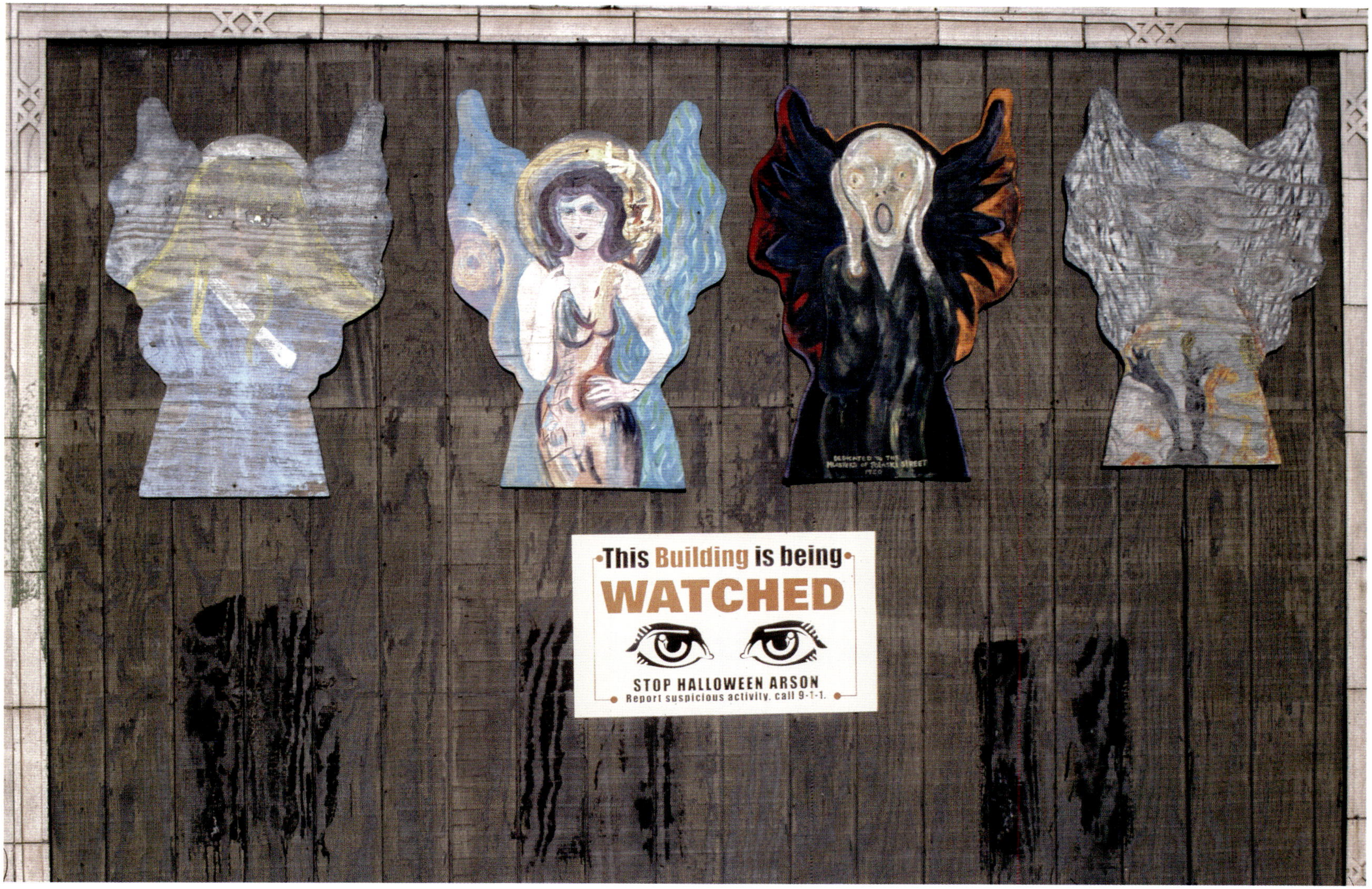

Faded angels by Carl Kamulski and "Devil Night eyes." An elderly west side resident remarked, "They have the eyes outside for Angels' Night [sic] so that people know that they have the eyes on them." I ask him: "Whose eyes?" "Well, the neighbors," he answers. Then he adds: "Mostly me. I'm the only one that takes any interest in them." West Jefferson Avenue at Cary Street, Detroit, 2008.

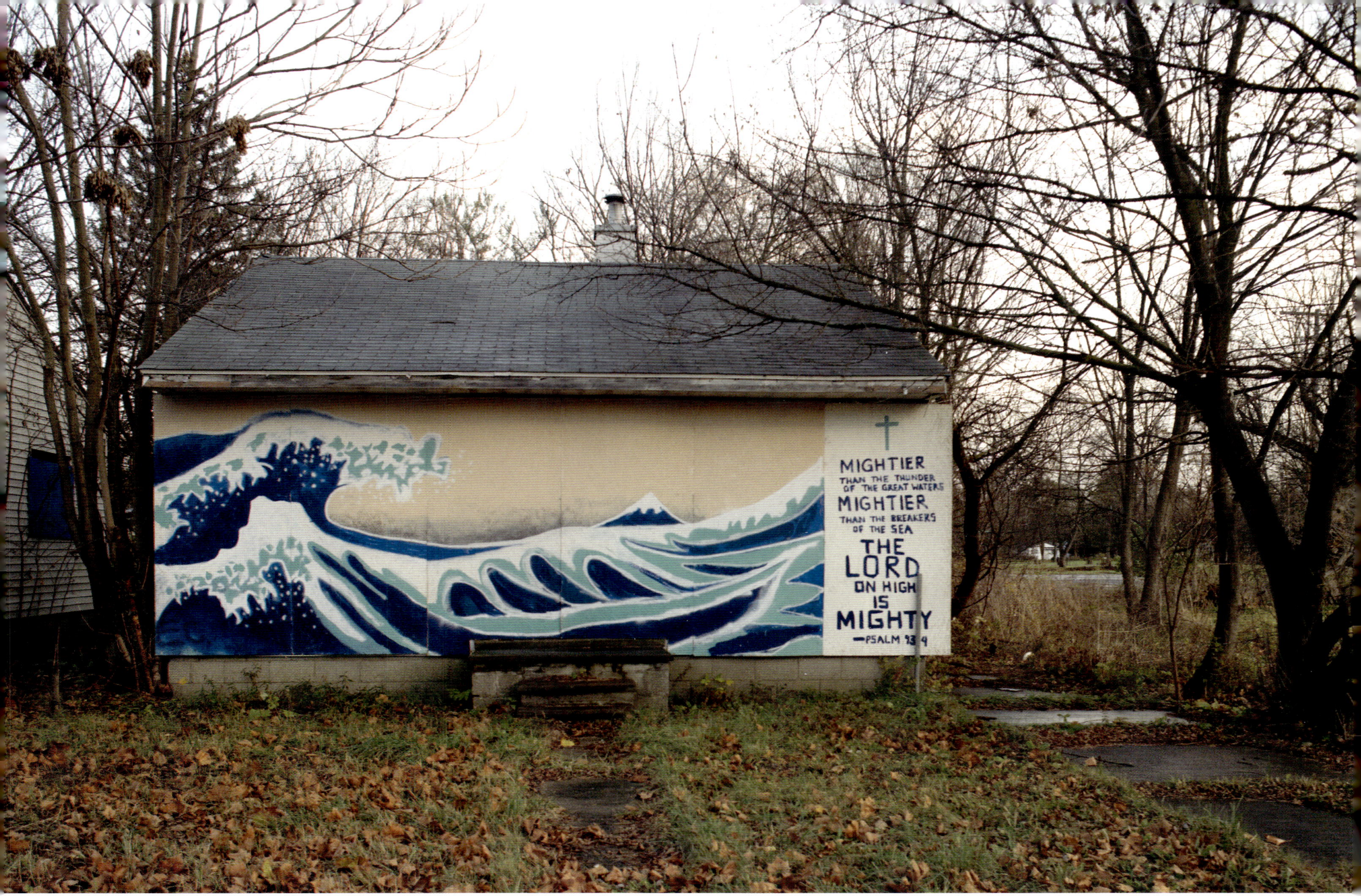

"Great Wave" house, design after Hokusai. Bentler Street at Acacia Street, Detroit, 2015.

BRIGHTMOOR: THE SEARCH FOR A BUCOLIC UTOPIA BY THE ROUGE RIVER

Brightmoor was built in the early 1920s as a planned community, "a working's man paradise," covering a four-square-mile area of slightly rolling hills on the northwest border of Detroit. In 2015, the neighborhood has 12,000 residents, down from 31,000 in 1980, and its population continues to decline. This modest development, one of the more integrated neighborhoods in Detroit, was built to house migrants coming from the southern United States to work in the city's automobile plants. In 2015, the neighborhood is poor, depressed, depopulated, and dangerous, with over 1,600 vacant buildings and 1,163 at risk of being foreclosed in 2016. Brightmoor is one of the eight neighborhoods in Detroit most affected by foreclosures. But with a surprisingly strong online presence, and a group of media-savvy activists committed to its future, Brightmoor is one of the communities with the most visibility in the city.

I had visited Brightmoor in June 2014 looking for a herd of eighteen baby goats brought there by Mark Spitznagel of Idyll Farms as an "urban farming experiment . . . to help clean up the overgrown area." After driving for more than an hour around a desolate section of Detroit, I finally got to the location where the goats had been grazing, only to discover that the city had denied permission for them to stay, and they had been taken back to the farm.

I returned to the area in the fall of 2015 to encounter many boarded up houses with their façades brightly painted, often with religious texts. Before my visit, I had studied the streets online, where I learned that the artwork had been done after 2013, the last date Google Streets had been there. I was surprised to now see such motifs as trees, butterflies, stars, hearts, hand prints, flowers, the sea, and ice cream, intermingled with such words as rebirth, faith, hope, love, God, and touchdown. I saw quotations from the Bible written on the façades, attesting to the church volunteers' Christian beliefs.

On the front of a Grayfield Street bungalow is written: "For God did not send his Son into the world to condemn the world, but to save the world through him." And on a house on Burgess Street we read: "This is the day that the Lord has made so let us rejoice and be glad in it." Also on Burgess is the biblical "Let Your Light Shine!!" (Matthew 5:16). A big painting of waves on Bentler Street, inspired by the famous Japanese print by Hokusai from the 1830s, is paired with: "MIGHTIER than the thunder of the great waters. MIGHTIER than the breakers of the sea. THE LORD on high is MIGHTY." In July 2014, artist Maggie Hubbard, while on a mission trip with the First United Methodist Church of Palatine, Illinois, led a small team that included two neighborhood children to paint the waves and inscription. Maggie wanted to "bring color to a fairly desolate neighborhood." In the week she spent in Brightmoor, she "was eager to bring the vitality back to the streets." The words on the right, she explained, "are from Psalm 93:4, chosen with the hope of saying that though circumstances are difficult, there is a loving God who controls things we cannot."

My interest in the decorations surprised local community organizers who regard the art work and boarding up as a temporary way to deal with vacancy, not central to the redevelopment of the neighborhood. I was nevertheless attracted to the images and texts for the beliefs and values they expressed. Unlike images I encountered in other Detroit neighborhoods, these are not black-oriented; they do not include cultural motifs such as the pyramids, black sports figures, or portraits of Martin Luther King, Jr. The imagery instead consists of generalized, feel-good symbols. "It is hard to disagree with kids, colors, nice flowers, and stars," remarked Nick Tobier, a landscape architect at the University of Michigan. In contrast to the cheerful signs, a small yellow tax foreclosure note is attached to two of the façades. References to the Lord are absent in vacant dwellings along Burgess Street painted with red warnings, saying "STAY OUT," or "TRESPASSERS WILL BE SHOT!!" Yet another house, untouched by the "Brighten Brightmoor" project, has a crude image of an eye outlined in black and an American flag.

Joe Rashid, an official at the Brightmoor Alliance, explained that the work done by volunteers is a morale booster for the residents, giving them "the impression that people do care." The city provides the boards for free to some of the 17,000 volunteers who come for a day during the summer from outside the city. Many of them, sponsored by the Lutheran and Methodist churches, select the designs in collaboration with local neighborhood organizations. Since they bring no resources of their own, the "supplemental workforce" of volunteers is limited mainly to boarding up houses, decorating vacant dwellings, picking up trash, and mowing lawns. Among the sponsors of this art and employment project are the Knight and Skillman foundations and the city. Rashid refers to managing volunteers, dealing with foundations, residents, the city, and other community organizations as struggling to "create social capital," "leveraging resources," and "creating a local economy."

Brightmoor was never a good neighborhood. Its flimsy houses, resembling those found in Appalachia, fall apart easily, and a small fire means the end. In 2015, the Knight Foundation described Brightmoor as an "area devastated by the mass exodus from the city [that] has quietly transformed itself into a utopia of urban gardens, public green spaces and a community determined to do better for itself in the absence of much help from outside." "Transformed . . . into a utopia" is far too optimistic an assessment. More people are leaving Brightmoor than are staying. But with news of the developments undertaken by the urban pioneers spreading far and wide online, a true transformation might eventually take place. The neighborhood is now surprisingly punctuated by property where a few "Mad Max artist types," "white hippies," and eco-tourists, attracted by the area's tall trees and quiet open spaces and fueled by a desire to raise farm animals, grow food, and congregate, are trying to build a bucolic utopia by the Rouge River.

Still, at dusk, under tall trees, Brightmoor's painted bungalows look doomed; some are already burnt. The cheerfulness of the decorated façades reminds me of corpses in funeral homes prepared for viewing, yet unlike those bodies, the houses are left to rot and to be swallowed by nature. Their bright colors are fading, the boards are coming unscrewed, and the houses will collapse. The open land will turn Brightmoor into a rural village for the residents who remain and for white pioneers. Online, at least, the area's desolation becomes a space of hope and innovation as the neighborhood lures homesteaders and visitors from as far away as Sweden, the Netherlands, and Germany, as well as from all over the United States. "External influences," they are called, pioneers on a mission to be self-sufficient and to live a more authentic life. "People are very intrigued," says Joe Rashid.

Powerful companies that define America are partnering with organizations like Blight Busters. I was surprised to see a video at Myfordmag.com of John George of Blight Busters in a shiny new 2016 Ford 150, which Ford had provided, tearing down a dilapidated Brightmoor garage. The garage resisted at first, then tilted and collapsed. The neighbors cheered, and John George remarked: "I believe we're on the front porch of one of the greatest urban comeback stories in this nation's history." The message is: back to square one and starting over in this beautiful land. The world may buy overpriced carrots, eggplant, honey, and artisanal goat cheese produced by Brightmoor enterprises as it does with the "authentic" watches and bicycles made in Detroit by Shinola or soft leather jackets by John Varvatos.

Other attractive communities—such as Corktown, a revived Indian Village, and a refurbished downtown with the formerly ruined skyscrapers fixed or torn down—reflect Detroit coming back. This is not the case of Brightmoor. No tycoon cares to overwhelm this former shantytown with his projects, and its racially-mixed residents are not struggling to create great examples of urbanity similar to others found throughout America. "Farm city," is unique; it is developing organically into a new, diverse, and democratic community.

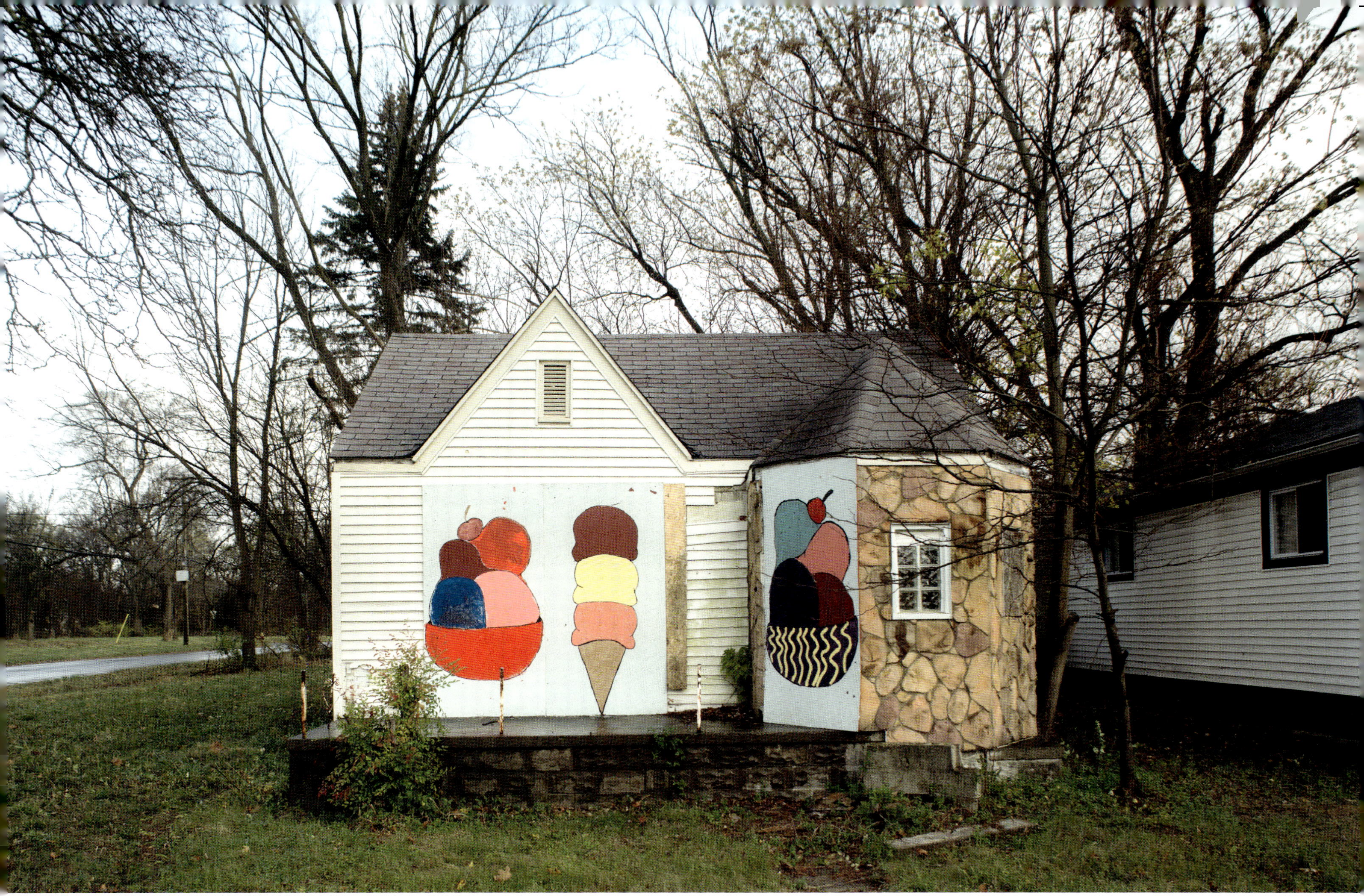

Jumbo Ice Cream House. Burgess Street at Kendall Street, Detroit, 2015.

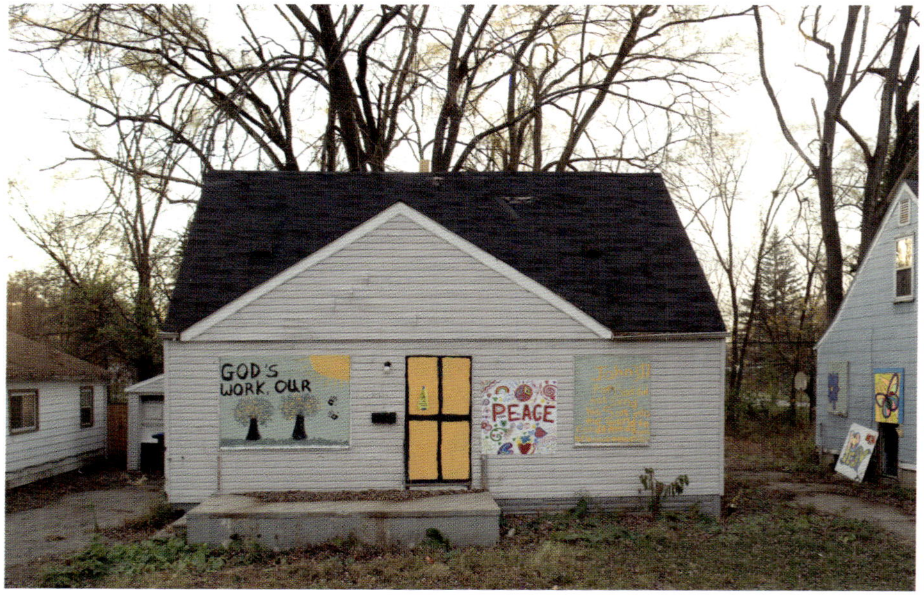

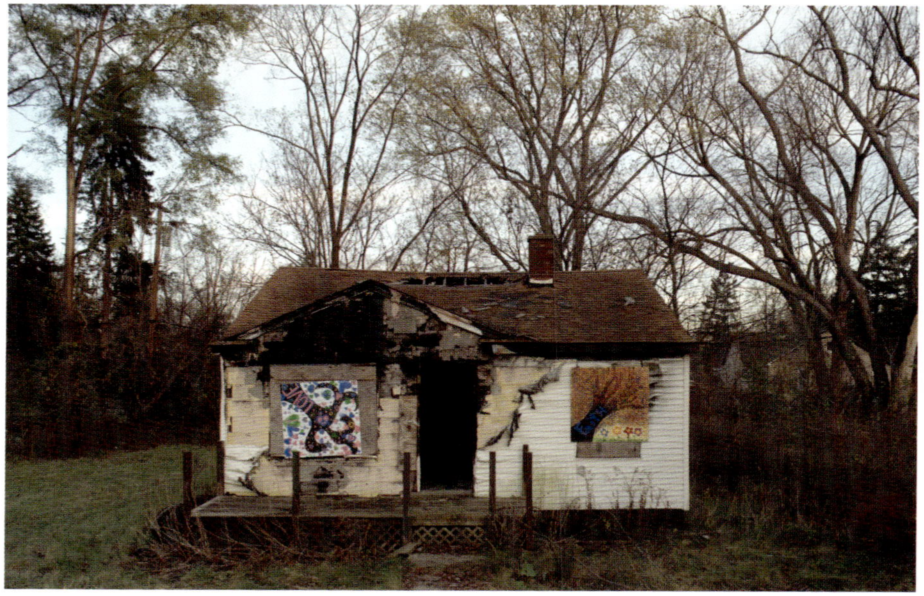

"God's Work Our" and a tax foreclosure notice. 15501 Greyfield Street, Detroit, 2015.

Love and Faith bungalow. 15830 Virgil Street, Detroit, 2015.

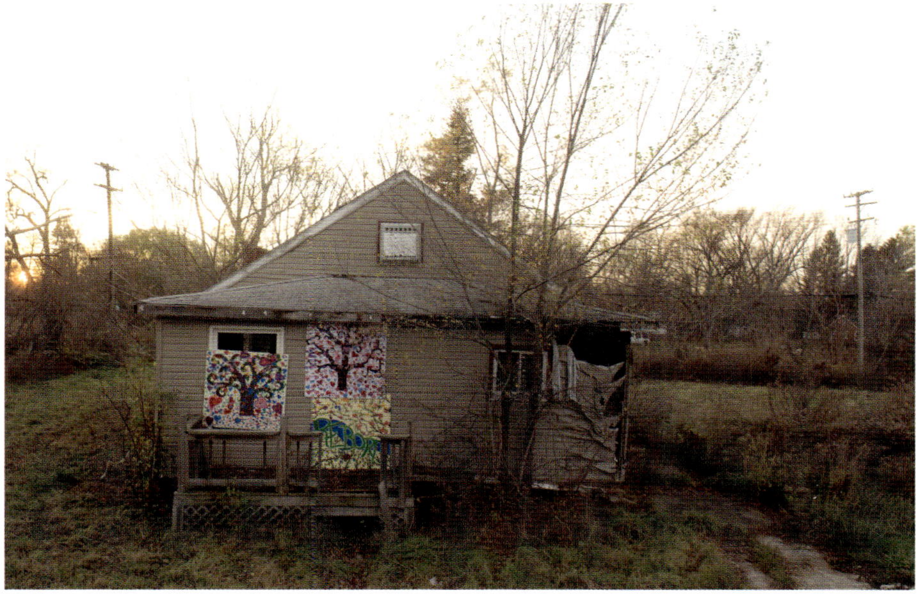

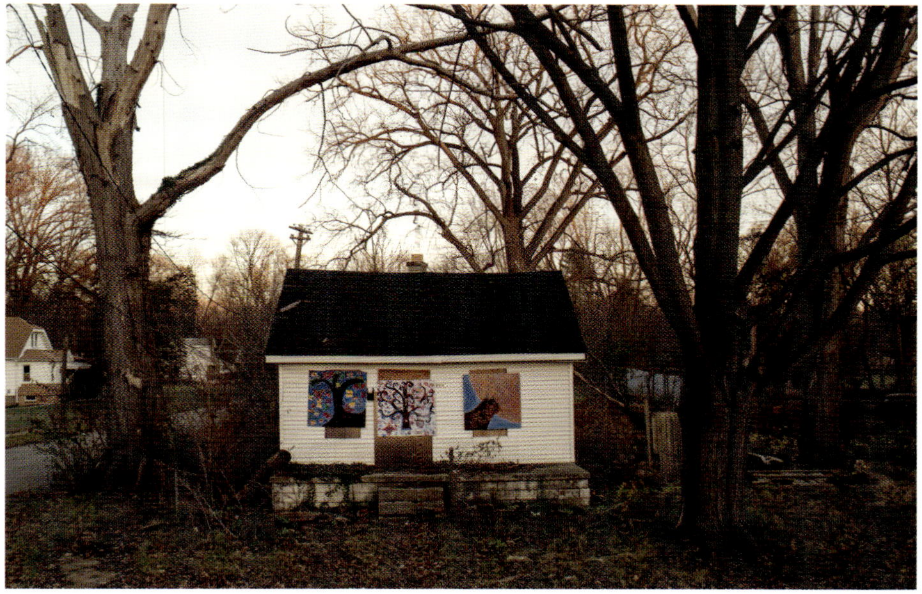

Twilight House with the word “Reborn.” Riverdale Avenue at Midland Street, Detroit, 2015.

Bungalow with “Love, Faith, Hope” and butterflies. 15880 Illiad Street, Detroit, 2015.

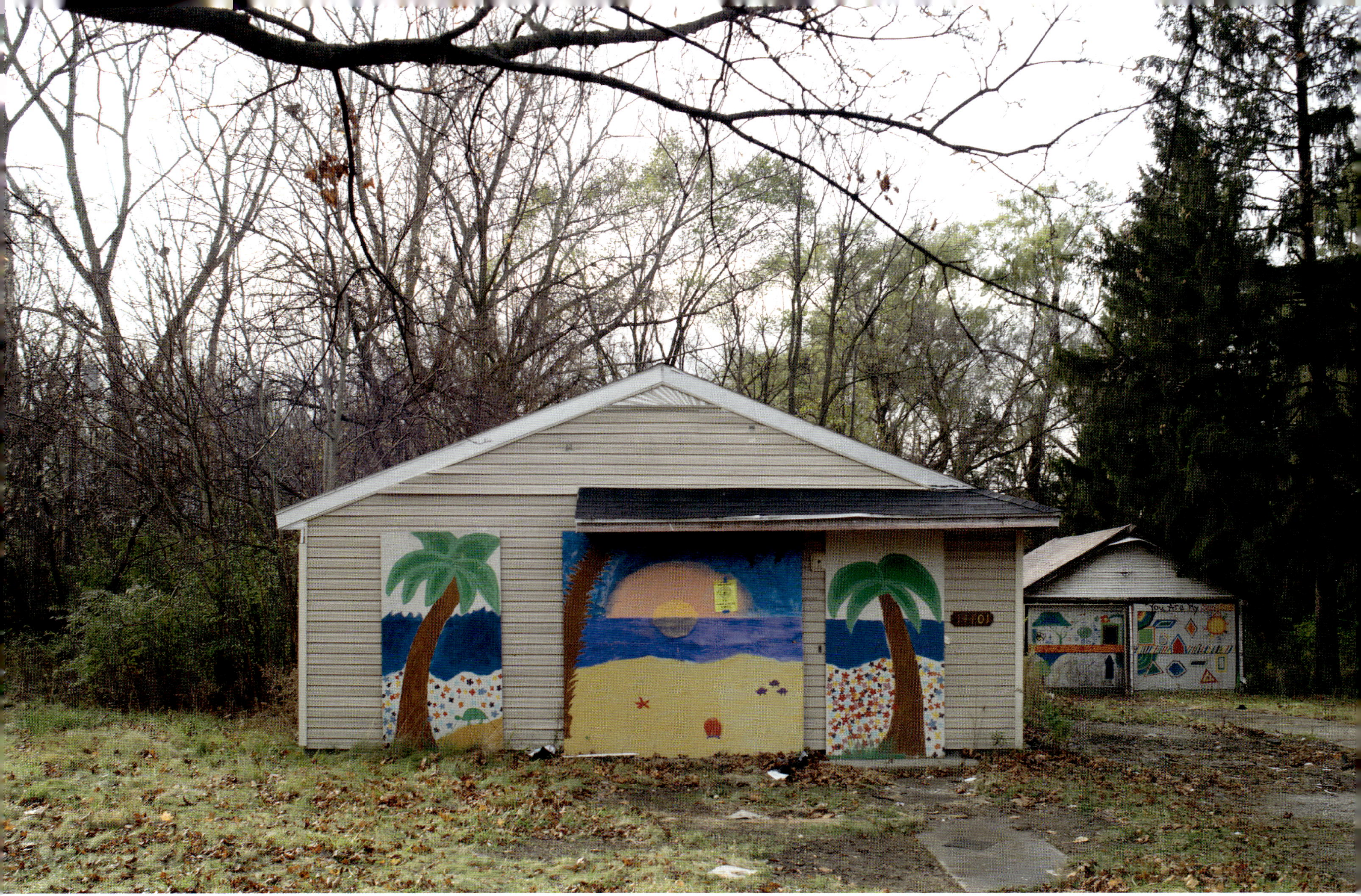

Bungalow with paintings of palm trees and stars, and a tax foreclosure notice on the door. Burgess Street at Kendall Street, Detroit, 2015.

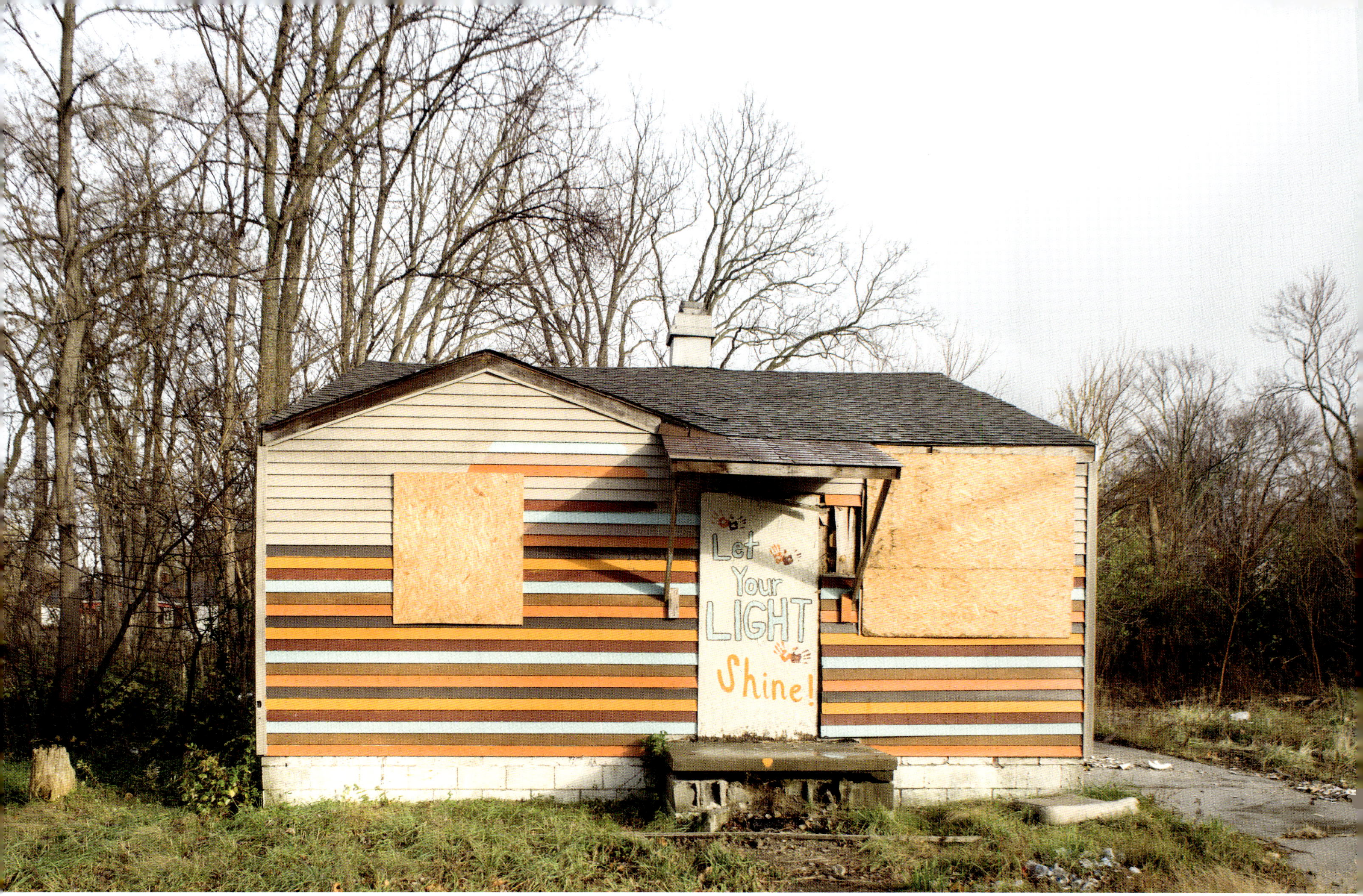

"Let Your Light Shine," sponsored by Community Arts Project, CCA.
14390 Burgess Street, Detroit, 2015.

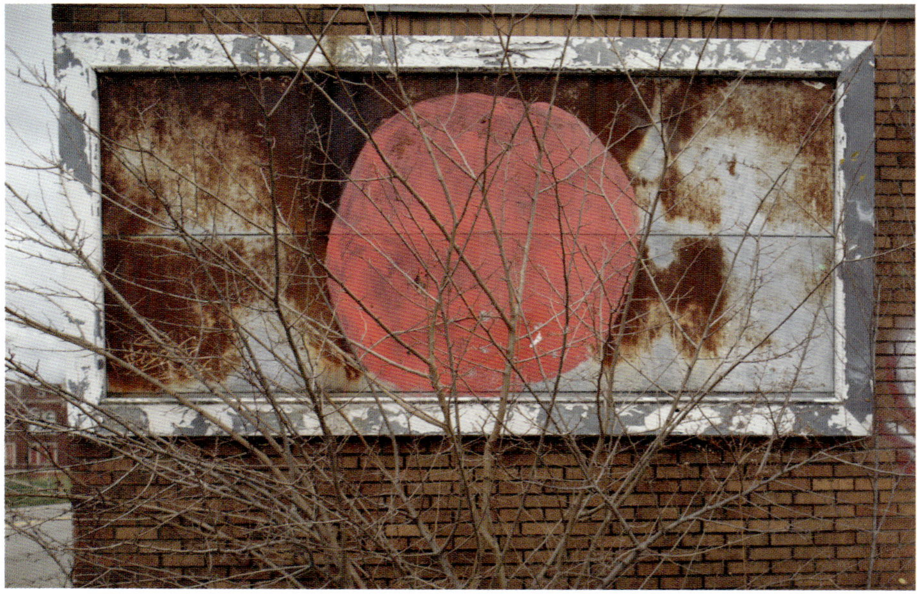

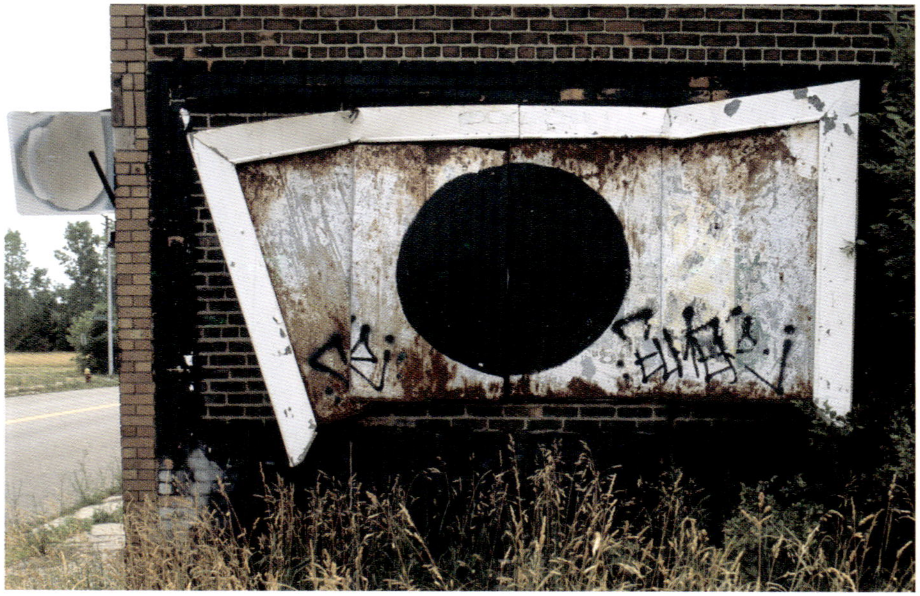

Tyree Guyton's signature dot, Detroit's simplest and most ubiquitous art image. Guyton painted the dot on thousands of abandoned buildings, including the former Michigan Central Station. Chene Street at Garfield Street, Detroit, 2015.

Tyree dot, Chene Street north of Garfield Street, Detroit, 2012.

AFRICAN AMERICAN ARTISTS: HISTORY, REMEMBRANCE, TURF Curtis Lewis, in his African Amalgamation of Ubiquity (1985), represents a sweeping view of the history of black people. The imagery starts with the Egyptians at left, followed by slave ships sailing on the ocean, then the presence of African Americans in Detroit, and culminates in the portrait of Coleman Young next to the Renaissance Center and the People Mover, both built during his administration. Slavery is central, embodied by an enchained, kneeling African facing the distant slave ships. Behind him, masses of Africans await the same fate. Having just broken his chains, a muscular slave holds a sign that reads: "Behold! My people Arise . . . Stand strong & proud for ye come from Pharaohs, Emperors, Kings and Queens." The figures in the mural are exclusively black. The panorama provides a stark contrast to the widespread use of tags by white artists.

Tyree Guyton is by far Detroit's most famous artist. Born on Heidelberg Street, he created The Heidelberg Project, an open-air art environment. Almost three decades ago he began covering the exterior of abandoned houses in his neighborhood with ordinary objects he collected throughout the city. Among them were children's toys, street signs, clocks, kitchen chairs, sofas, stuffed animals, shoes, and car parts. He also displayed these objects on derelict vehicles and shopping carts, hung them on trees, and arranged them in vacant lots. In Detroit, Tyree's work stands alone in its ingenuity, scope, and resilience. His folk celebration of Motown, with its colorful objects given prominence and dignity, has a joyful strain. Using mannequins, dolls, shoes, flags, and the ubiquitous word "God," Guyton's work also speaks about absence, memory, and the indifferent higher powers that allow so much waste and suffering.

In addition to his work in his neighborhood, Guyton painted dots on thousands of abandoned buildings throughout Detroit, thus becoming the unofficial certifier of ruins. Officials disliked his work because it drew attention to decay and taught viewers who had grown used to dereliction to take a fresh look at their surroundings. Bulldozers demolished his most important houses in 1991 and 1999. He lost additional houses to arson in 2013 and 2014. When his "Party Animal House" was torched in 2014, Tyree used the brick base left behind as a platform on which to display an art piece consisting of a dining room set with stuffed animals sitting on the chairs. "I want to be part of the great comeback of the city of Detroit," he said.

Guyton painted a 1955 Detroit bus (from the same year as the Montgomery Bus Boycott) with colorful polka dots and crosses and passengers of all races looking out the windows. It stood parked in a huge east side empty lot. The Rosa Parks Bus was a homage to "the first lady of civil rights," challenger of "move to the rear" oppression, who at the time was a Detroit resident. This art installation was both a moving memorial and the best piece of outdoor sculpture in the city. But by 2007 it had lost all its passengers including its blonde driver and its Rosa Parks sign. The stripped bus became another piece of junk and was removed from its site, yet the marks left by its tires are still visible on the ground.

The memorial to Malice Green portrayed on the wall by artist Bennie White in 1992 attracted wide attention. Green, a 35-year-old addict, was beaten to death for no reason by two white Detroit police officers, Walter Budzyn and Larry Nevers. In a *Detroit Free Press* interview, White said that it was God's work that led him "to paint the mural on a rainy day, leaving a portrait that seemed to be shedding tears." The painting was effective, gathering to it people who posted protests against police brutality and injustice and brought objects to form a shrine. The building served as a crack house and place of prostitution until it was demolished in 2013.

The notorious Sintex (Brian Glass) is the youngest of the trained black artists. He wrote of his mural, Rosa Parks, in 2014: "The beauty i provide to the real people of Detroit is my voice . . . my divine ambition is to revive the minds of the lost n dead in my community . . . this just is not just painting some bullshit ass mural about what you think my city is." By "some bullshit ass mural" he is referring to giant tags painted by out-of-town artists. He painted Rosa Parks over the mural that had been made in honor of Vincent Chin by Gaia, a famous white artist from Baltimore. Although this act provoked criticism, Sintex warned that a race war would break out if anyone dared to paint over his own mural.

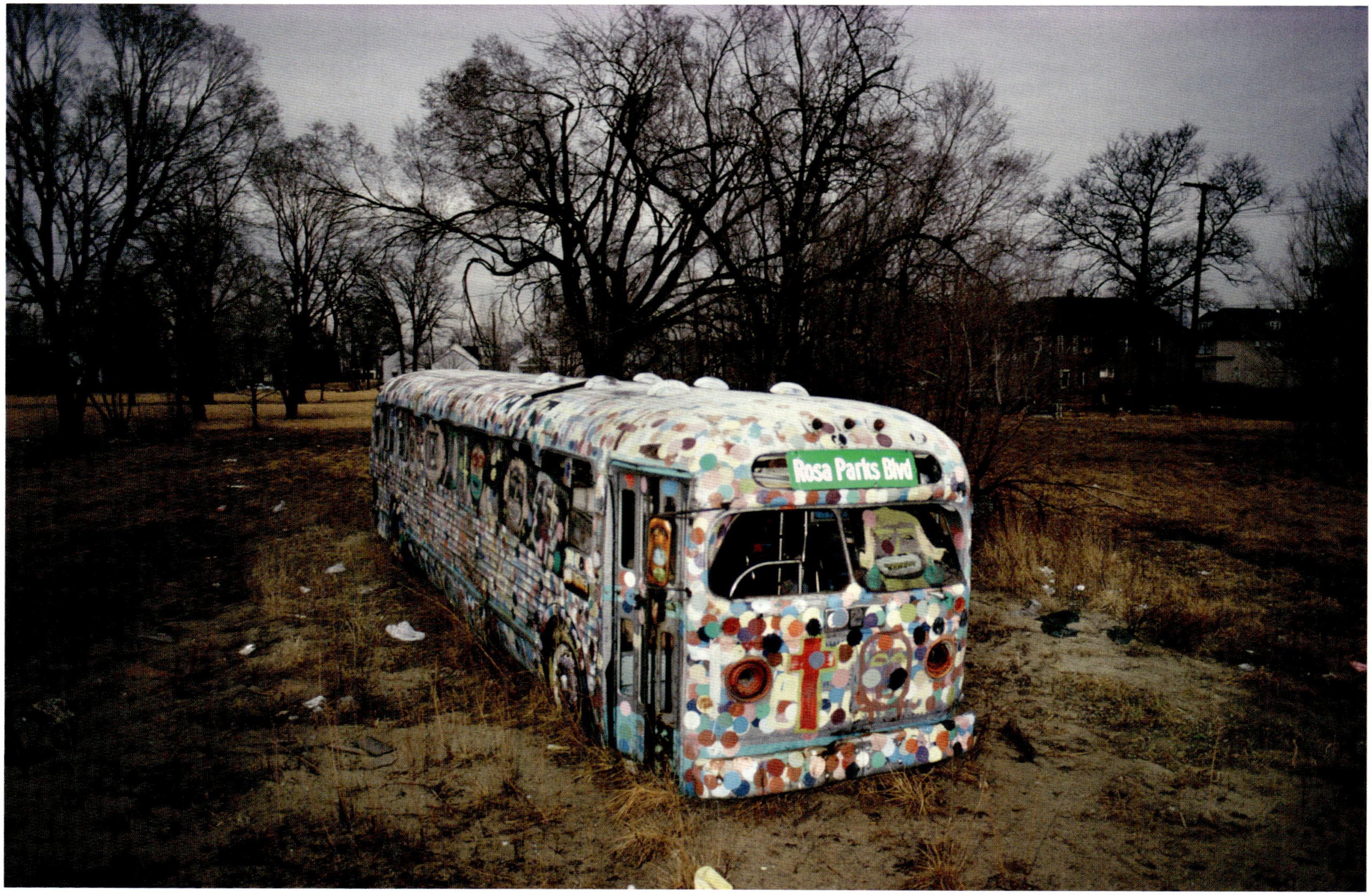

Rosa Parks Bus. East Canfield Avenue, east of Chene Street, Detroit, 2003.

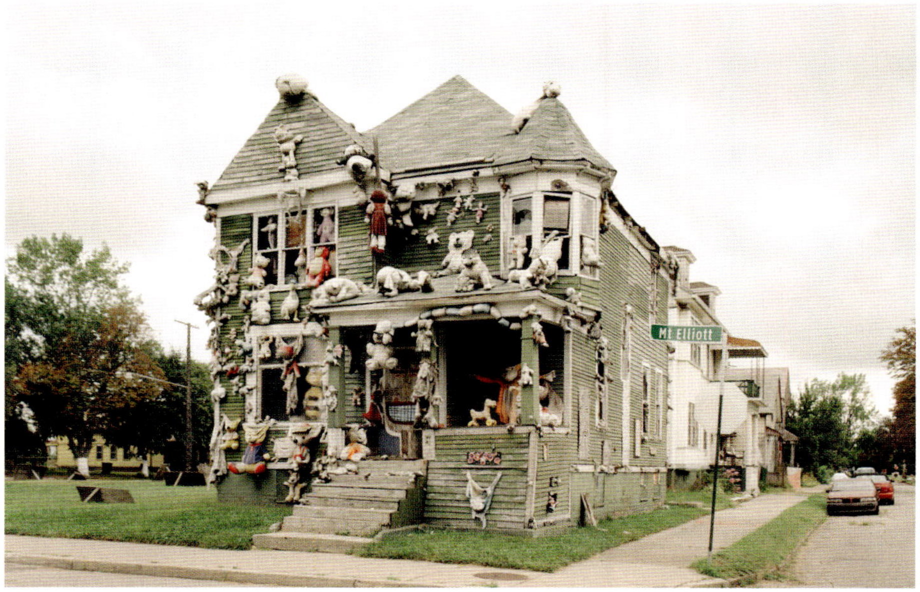

Tyree Guyton's surreal Party Animal House, part of his Heidelberg Project. The house was consumed by a fire in 2014. Mt. Elliott Street at Elba Place, Detroit, 2010.

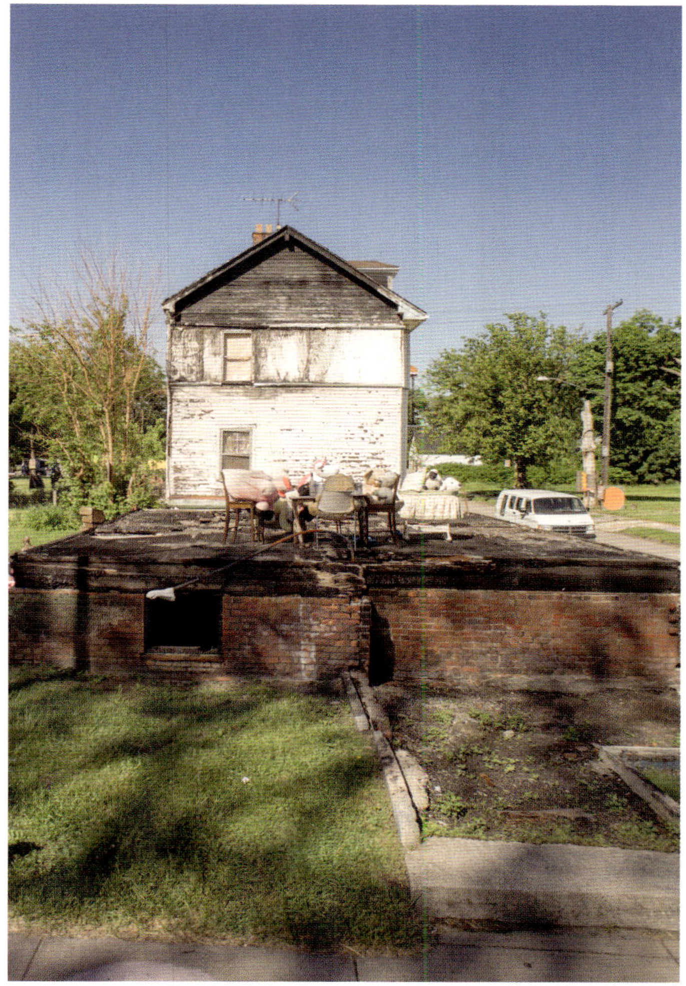

Ruin of the Party Animal House, part of the Heidelberg Project. Tyree put a dining room set on the remaining platform. Mt. Elliot Street at Elba Place, Detroit, 2014.

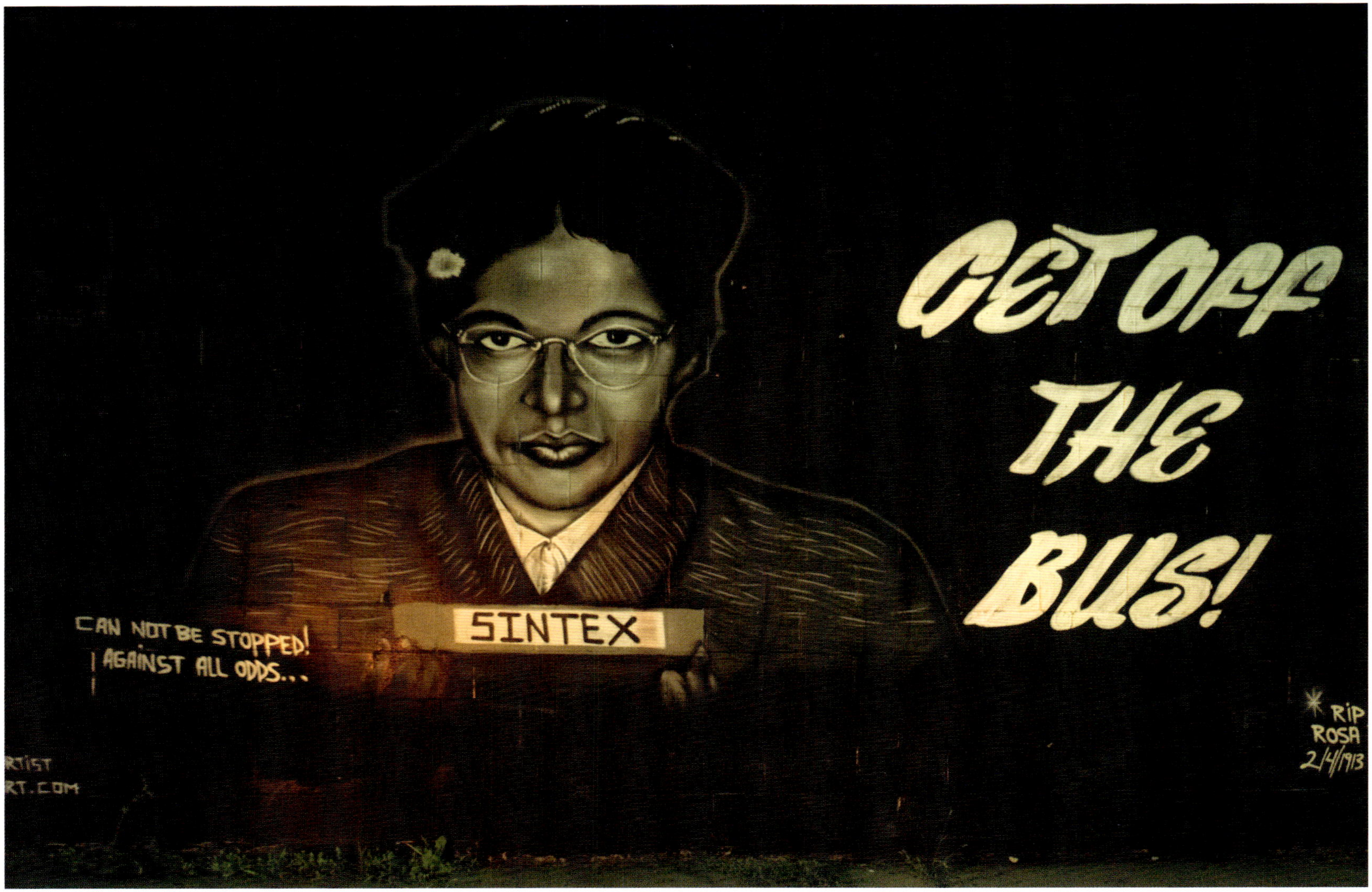

An intense, short-lived mural depicting Rosa Parks, by Sintex (Brian Glass).
14th Street at Grand River Avenue, Detroit, 2015

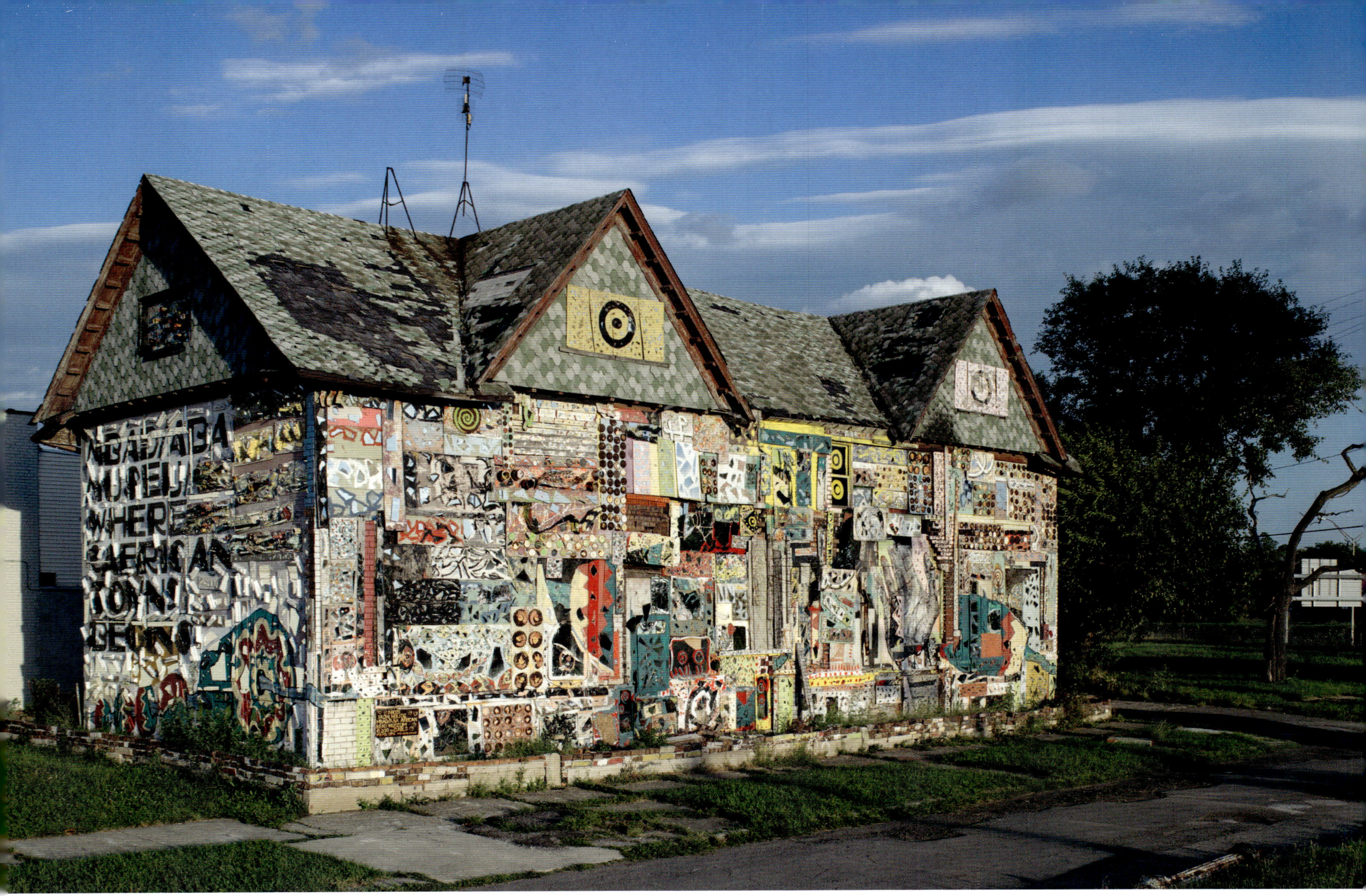

N'kisi Iron House, part of MBad African Beads Museum, Where African Towns Begin. Taft Street at Grand Fiver Avenue, Detroit, 2015.

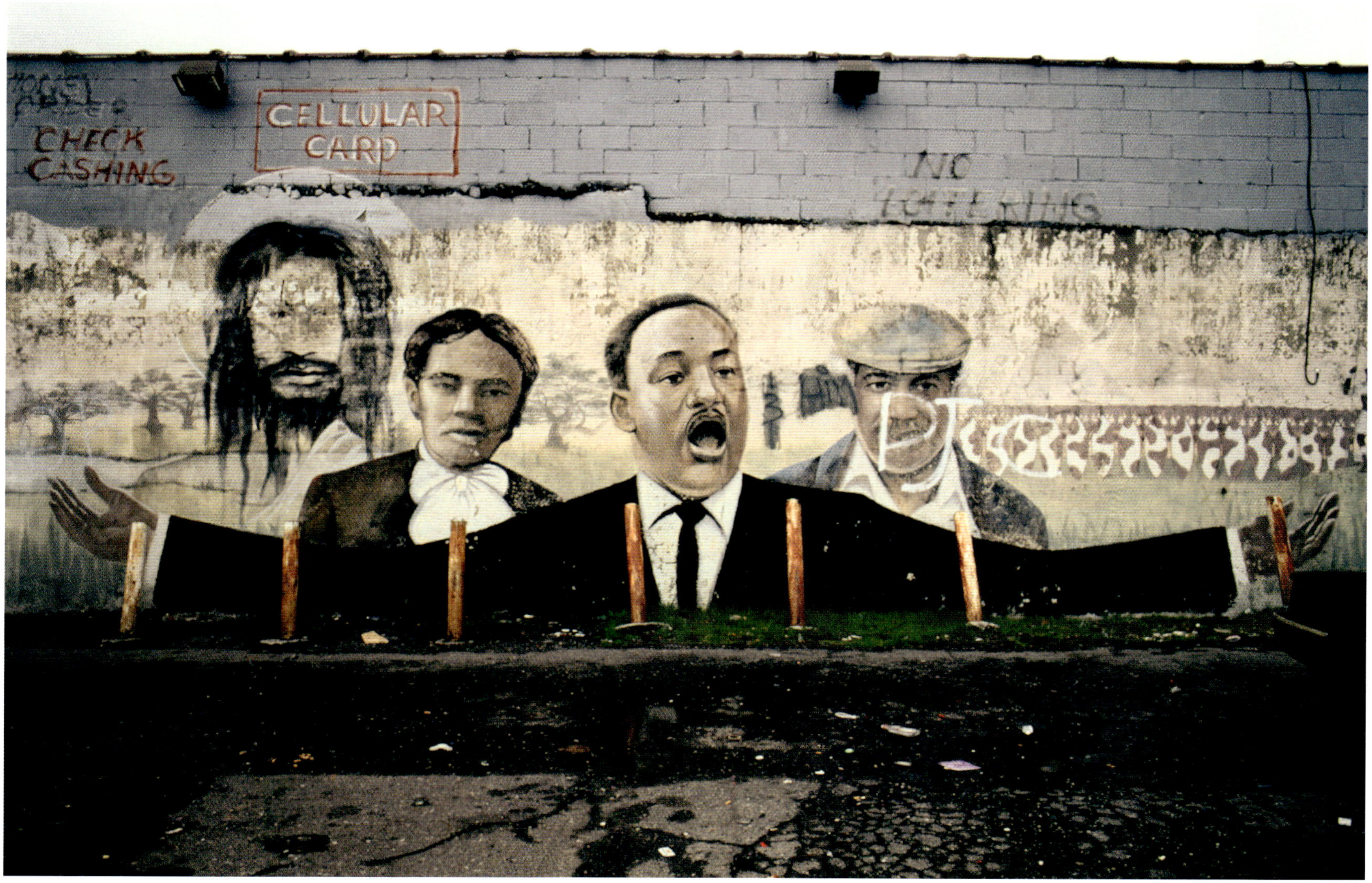

Martin Luther King, Jr. mural at AAA Party Store, painted by Bennie White, 1993. Behind Dr. King are Jesus Christ; a boyish looking Harriet Tubman; and Ivie Shelton, the store founder, portrayed wearing a cap. East Warren Avenue at Lenox Street, Detroit, 2009.

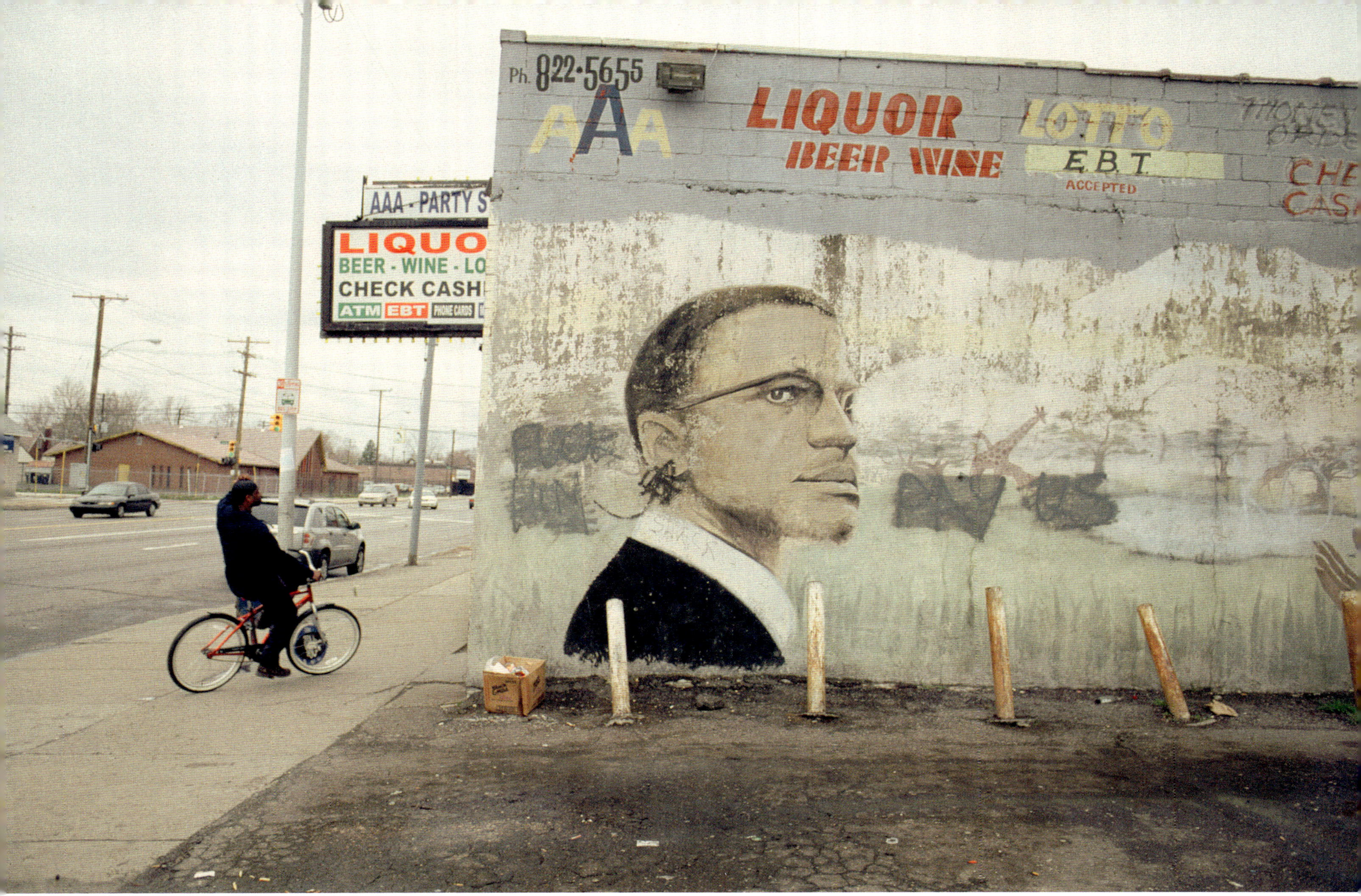

Malcolm X, AAA Party Store, painted by Bennie White in 1993. East Warren Avenue at Lenox Street, Detroit, 2009.

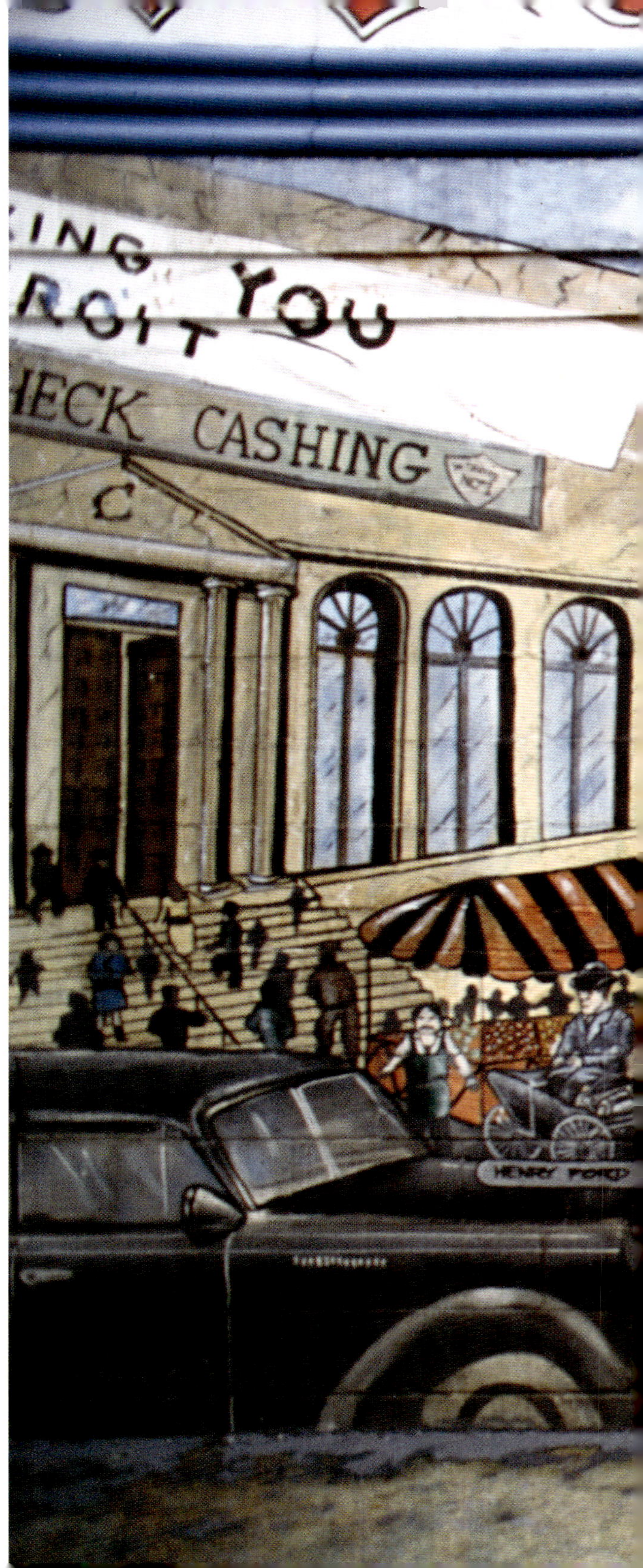

The exterior of this check-cashing business is covered with a whimsical mural depicting an Afrocentric vision of Detroit in its 1920s heyday: the blue ghost of former mayor Coleman Young (served 1974–94) contemplates a thriving downtown from the skies and a tiny Henry Ford is shown driving one of his early automobiles. The largest building in the mural is Hudson's Department Store, which was second in size only to Macy's in New York City before being demolished in 1998. East McNichols Road at Alcoy Avenue, Detroit, 2011.

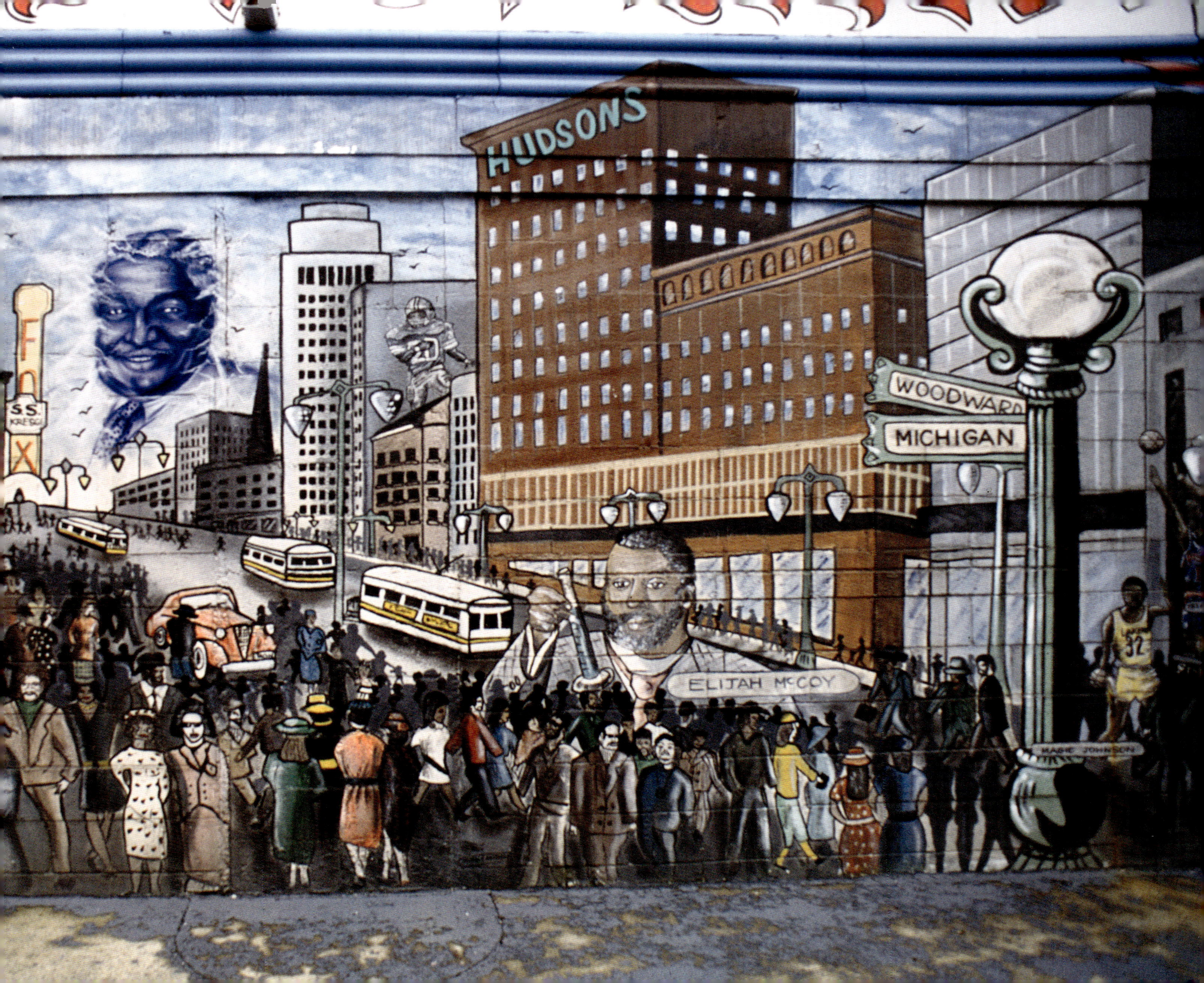

HUDSONS
FOX
S.S.
WOODWARD
MICHIGAN
ELIJAH McCOY

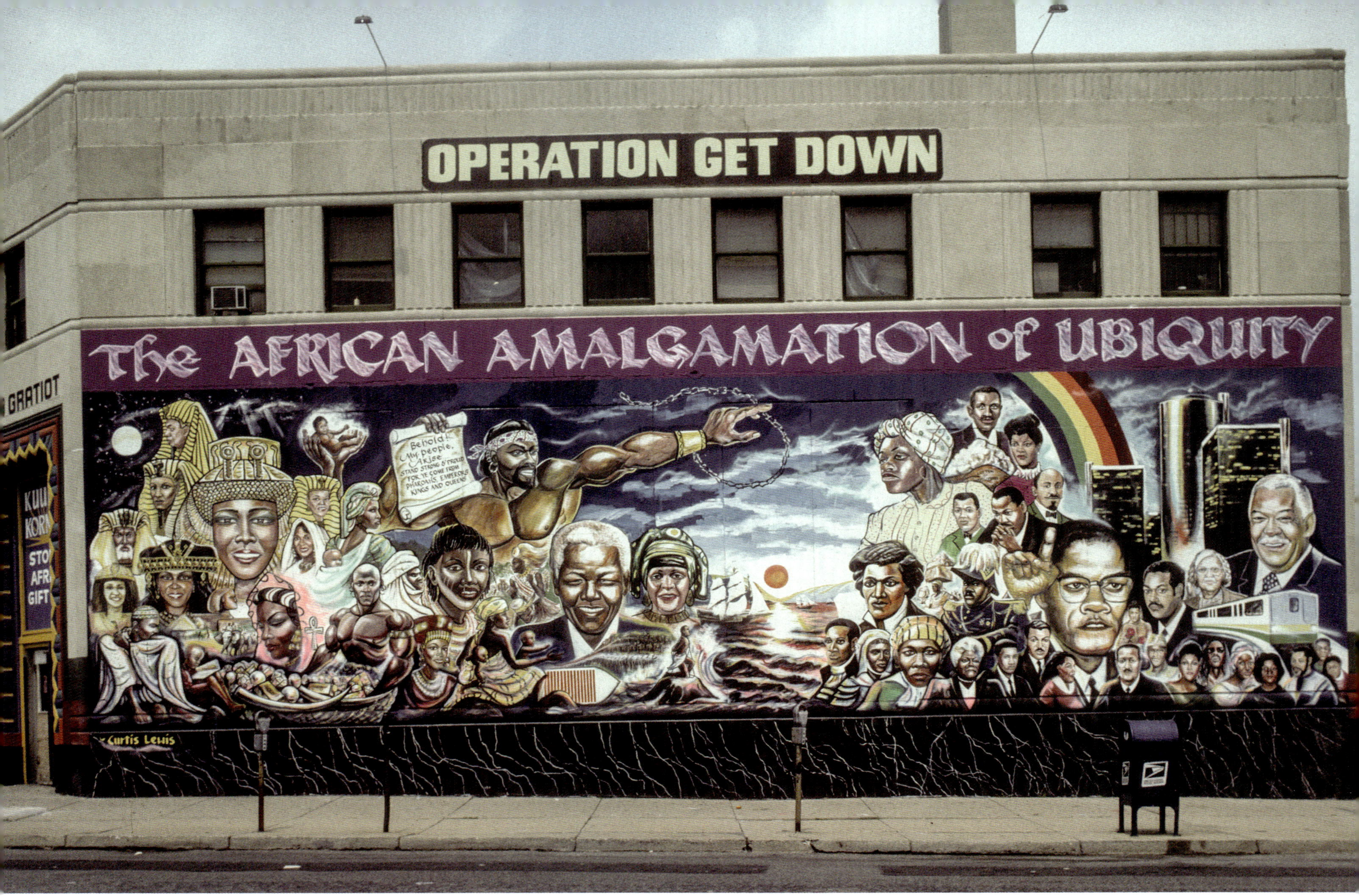

The African Amalgamation of Ubiquity mural was painted in 1985 by Curtis Lewis on a substance abuse treatment center called Operation Get Down. This former bank building later became part of Timbuktu Academy of Science and Technology and is now abandoned. 9980 Gratiot Avenue, Detroit, 1995.

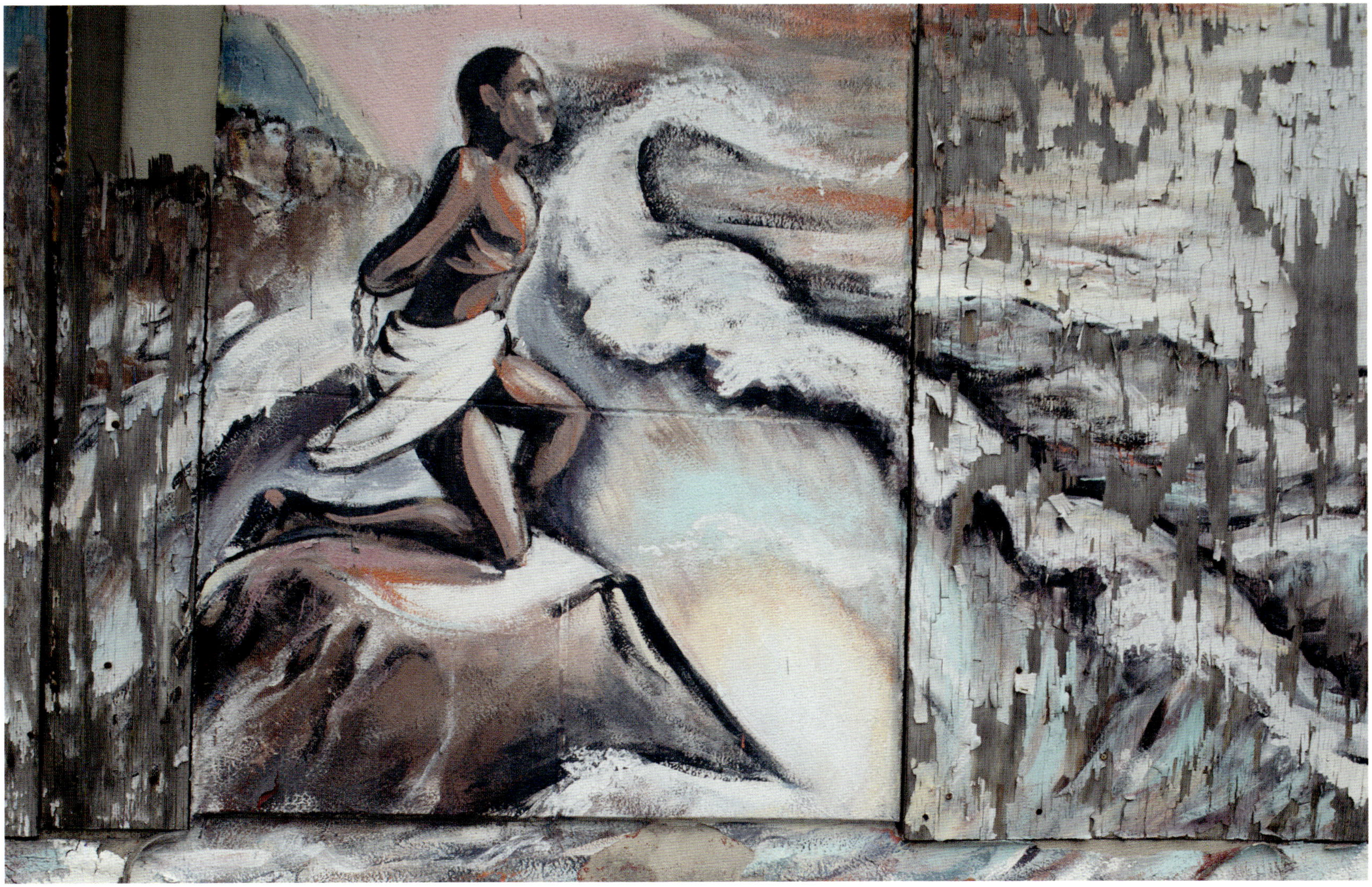

Detail from The African Amalgamation of Ubiquity mural painted in 1985 by Curtis Lewis on a former substance abuse treatment center. 9980 Gratiot Avenue, Detroit, 2015.

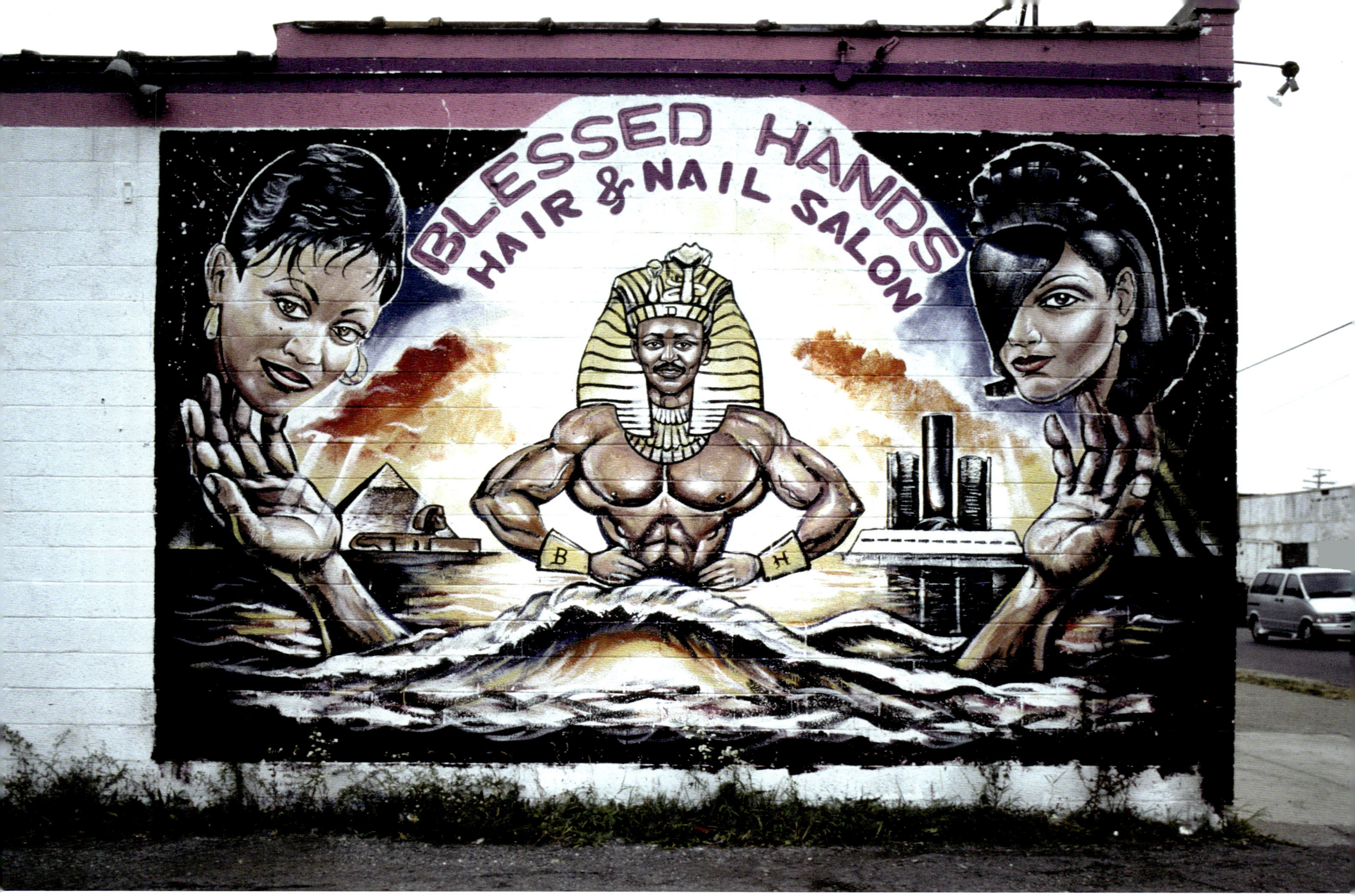

Blessed Hands Hair and Nail Salon. Fantasy figure at center, flanked by, among other imagery, Egyptian monuments at left and the Renaissance Center at right. Helen Street at 7 Mile Road, Detroit, 1999.

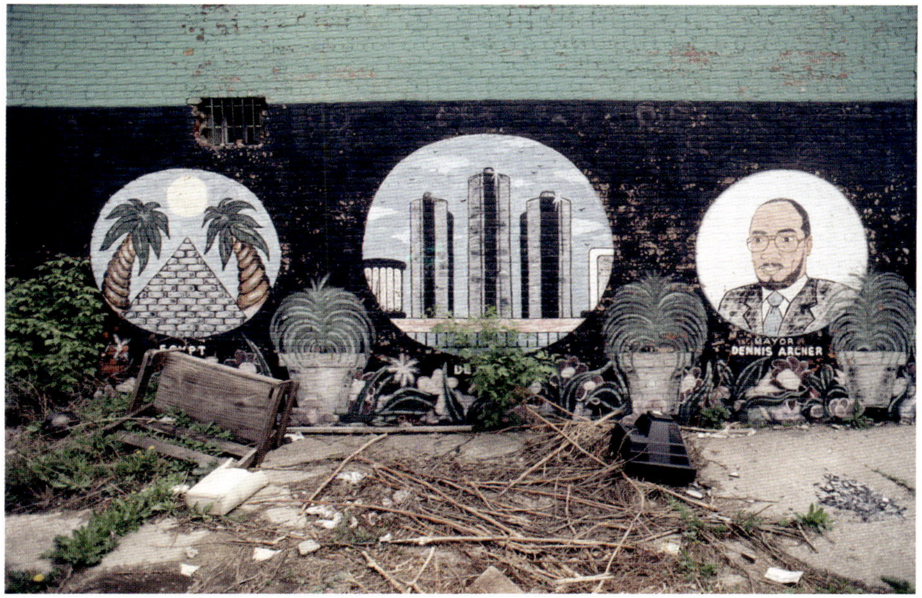

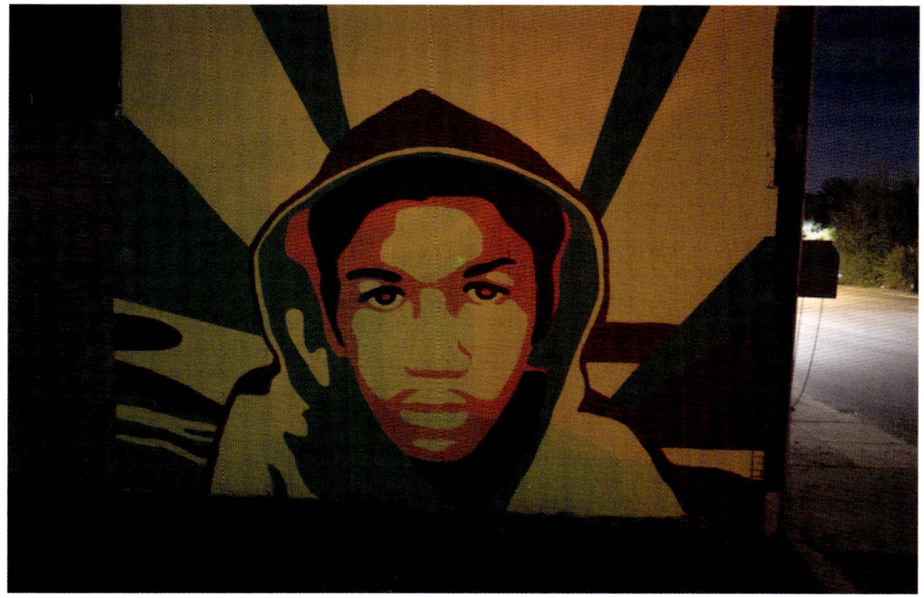

Curtis Lewis, mural depicting an Egyptian pyramid, the Renaissance Center, and a portrait of Mayor Dennis Archer, honoring the African American identity of Detroit. The mural has disappeared along with the former Canfield Market, whose back wall it once graced. East Canfield Street at Philip Street, Detroit, 2008.

Trayvon Martin memorial by Sean Marshall in the style of Shepard Fairey's Obama "Hope" poster. "Everybody loves it, they love the colors," remarked Dorothy, the owner of Sheps Barber and Beauty Shop who gave permission for the mural to be painted on her side wall. Hamilton Avenue at Tuxedo Street, Highland Park, 2013.

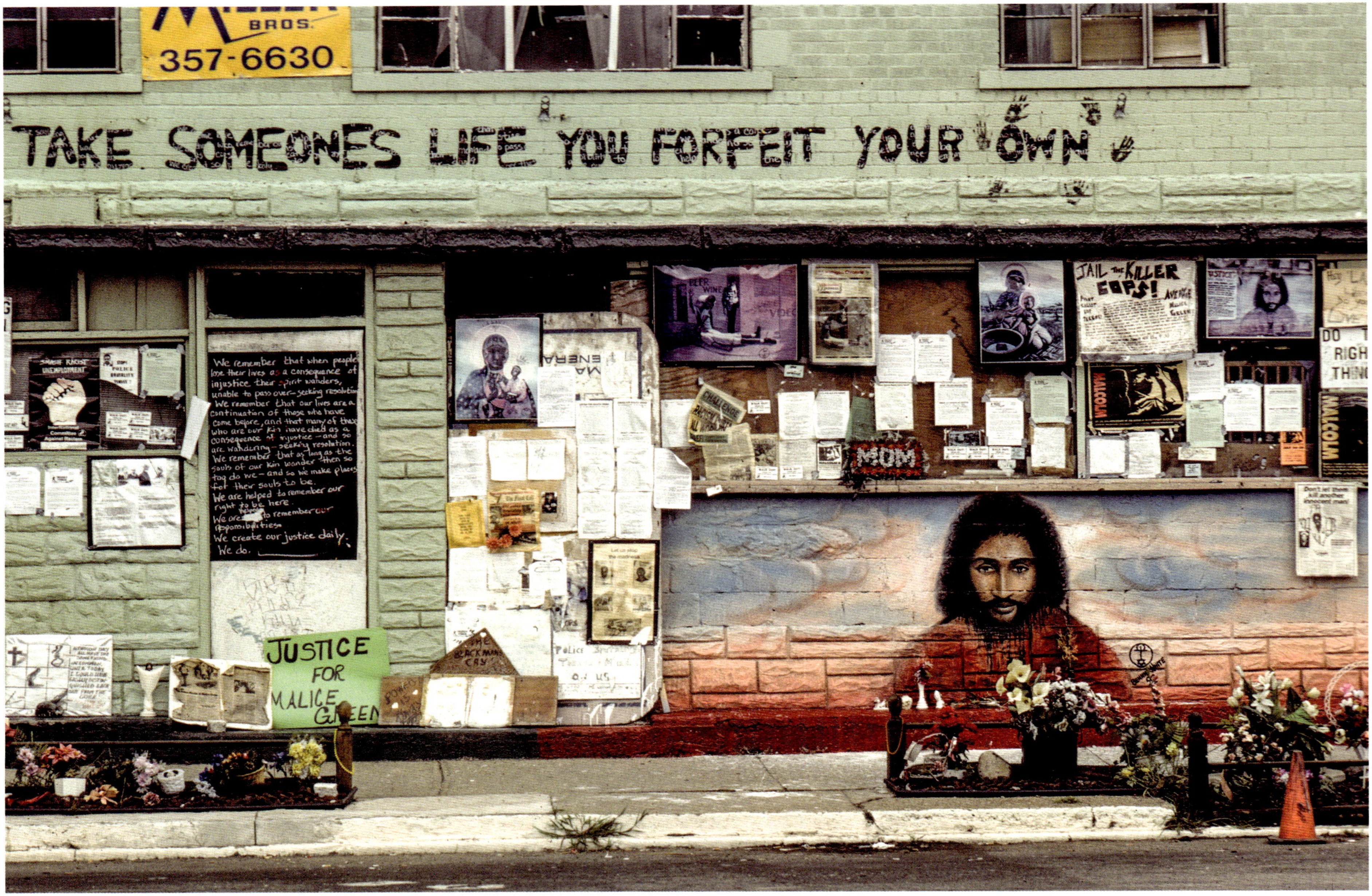

Malice Green memorial. 23rd Street at West Warren Avenue, Detroit, 1993.

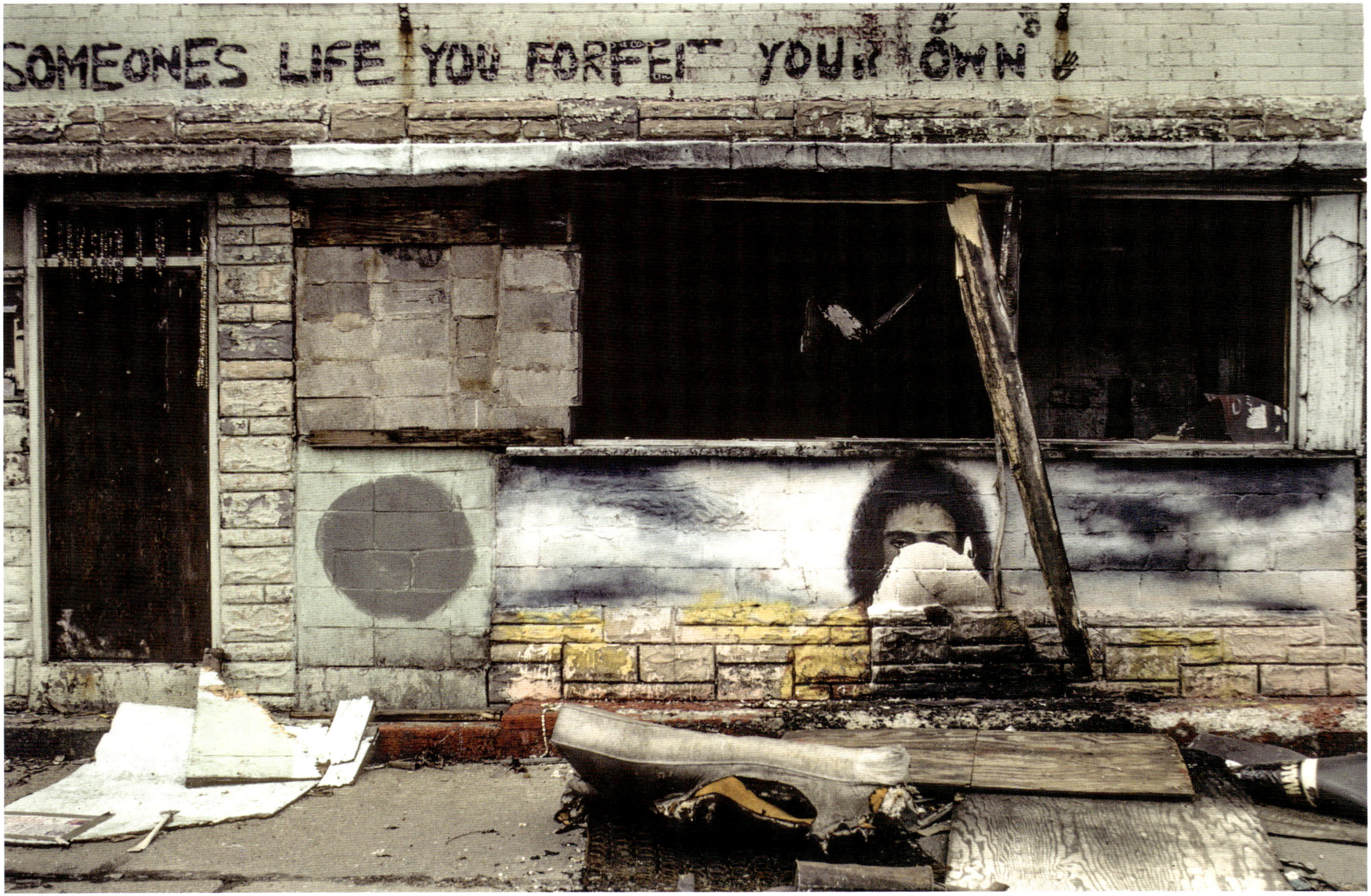

Malice Green memorial after a fire, 23rd Street at West Warren Avenue, Detroit, 2001.

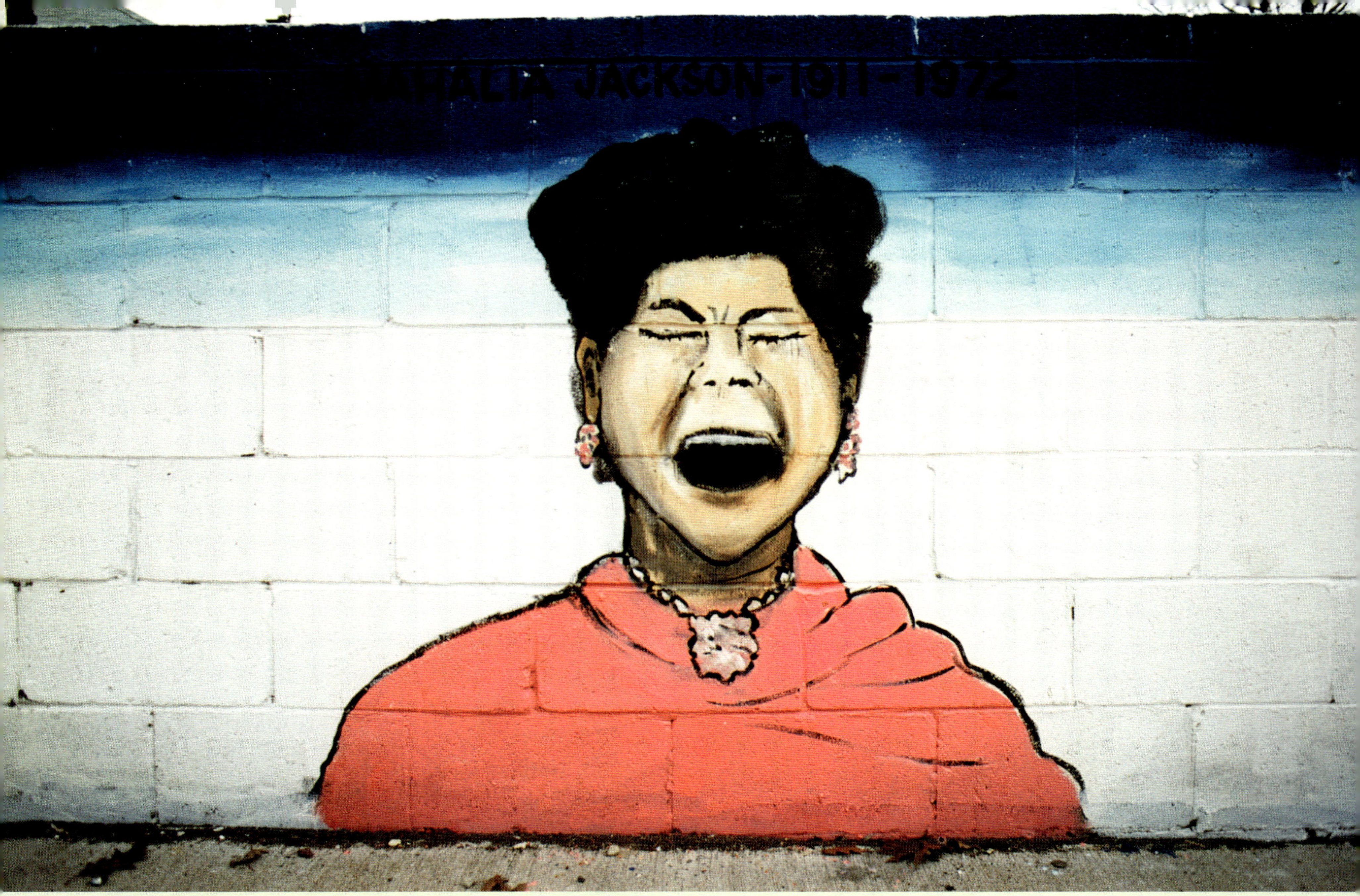

Mural memorializing Mahalia Jackson. West Montana St. at Woodward Avenue, Highland Park. 2009

PERSISTENT BLIGHT, CONCENTRATED

AN ABBREVIATED STREET GUIDE

IN 1989, THE *DETROIT FREE PRESS* PUBLISHED "Survey of Vacant and Abandoned Property," which contained a list of the city's most blighted intersections; chief among them were:

Livernois Avenue at Fenkell Avenue
Livernois Avenue at Fullerton Avenue
Joy Road at Grand River Avenue
Grand Boulevard East at Grand River Avenue
Lillybridge Street at East Jefferson Avenue
Mack Avenue at McClellan Avenue
Mack Avenue at Seyburn Street
Mack Avenue at Chalmers Avenue
Harper Avenue at Chalmers Avenue
Harper Avenue at Van Dyke Road

"Survey" also included a mile-long stretch of mostly vacant lots and abandoned houses along Charlevoix Street between Fischer Street and Conner Street. Many buildings at these intersections were beyond rehabilitation. Motivated and directed by this study, I have regularly photographed these intersections and streets since 1991.

Then, in 2007, the *Detroit Free Press* similarly published a series called "Driving Detroit, Every Street Covered: A Once-In-A-Lifetime Snapshot of a City" by award-winning journalist Bill McGraw and a team of photographers and other journalists who worked for the paper. In a segment entitled "Nature Reclaims Urban Wasteland," McGraw wrote, "Some of the streets themselves have been obliterated by decay and vegetation.... When you drive along Georgia Avenue, west of St. Cyril, you enter a vast, decomposing zone of tall grasses, weeds, trees, dozens of piles of loose refuse and numerous mounds. One of the mounds, off of Huber Avenue east of Mt. Elliott, is more than two stories high." McGraw tells how the mounds in the zone came into being: "Trucks illegally dump piles of heavy-duty materials such as cement, drywall, used soil or rusty metal bars. As the piles sit, nature gradually takes over. Grass, weeds, trees and soil swarm over the piles, transforming them into green mounds. Before long, the mounds look as if they've been sitting there forever. There are hundreds of mounds across the city. Some are knee high; others are big as a garage." McGraw goes on, describing "weird mounds that dot the landscape, the result of old dumps alchemizing with weeds and soil. Inside the zone, which extends for several blocks, there are no homes, no factories, no parks, no people and no street signs." (Might the crumbled remains of Hudson's Department Store, of the Statler Hilton Hotel, and other Detroit skyscrapers be pushing up trees through these mounds, just as the remains of New York's old Penn Station were found in the unregulated dump of the Meadowlands swamp?)

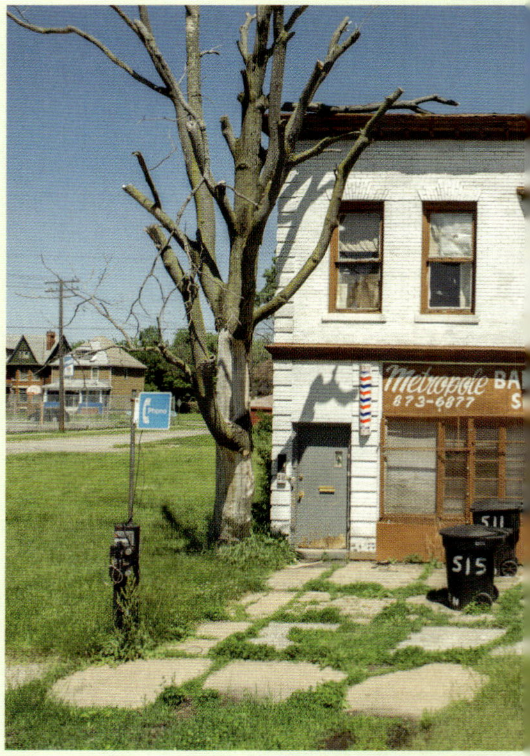

If McGraw were to do this kind of inspiring work today, he would be accused of "dumping" on Detroit and of creating "ruin porn." But one might also link McGraw with the sentiments of eighteenth-century philosopher Denis Diderot. Writing about Hubert Robert's painting *Le Port de Ripette a Rome* (1766), Diderot stated: "The ideas ruins evoke in me are grand. Everything comes to nothing, disappears, perishes, passes. Only the world remains, only time endures."

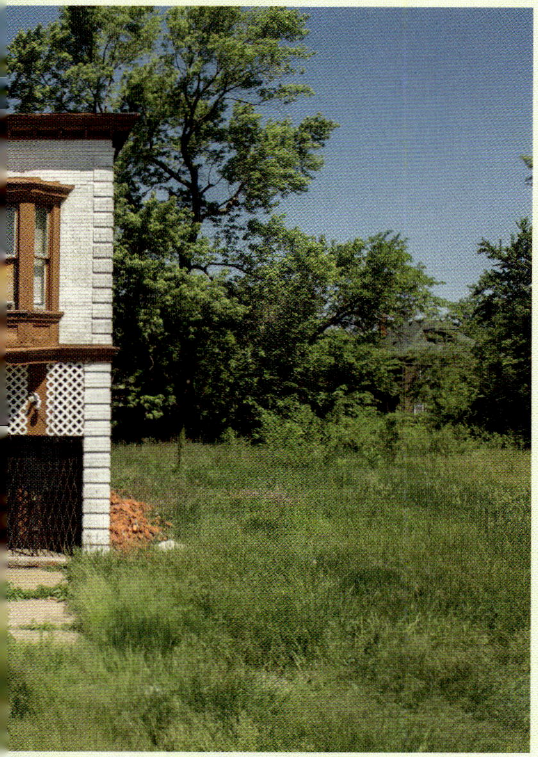

While McGraw was conducting his survey, Google Streets was also taking a snapshot of the city, and has continued to do so up to the present. I used the two *Free Press* surveys (1989 and 2007), Google's biannual surveys, and my own documentation to study Detroit at its most decayed. I got addresses for the most blighted parts of the city from "Survey of Vacant and Abandoned Property" and "Driving Detroit," and then, looking them up on Google Streets, I continued to trace changes online. Just as with my own time-lapse photography, through the time feature of Google Streets I am able to see these parts of Detroit change on my computer screen. Between 2009 and 2013, for example, a stretch of sidewalk at 17144 Hawthorne Street became so overgrown that it disappeared. And in 2013 the Google Streets car stopped recording at the intersection of East Dakota Street and Hawthorne Street after it became impassable. Such occurrences are frequent. If Detroit's revival were measured by the condition of its most blighted locations in 2015, one would have to conclude that the city has gotten worse. There were some small revivals, however; for example, a garden with a picket fence sprang up on East Jefferson Avenue at Fairview Street. At Ellsworth Street west of Livernois Avenue, I was surprised to see three new houses. And I admired the tenacity of the resident of 4235 Pennsylvania Street who managed to keep up his house while the three next door were abandoned and one of them demolished.

Former Metropole Barbershop, a once-comfortable example of Americana until the side wall fell down. 511 East Bethune St., Detroit, 2014.

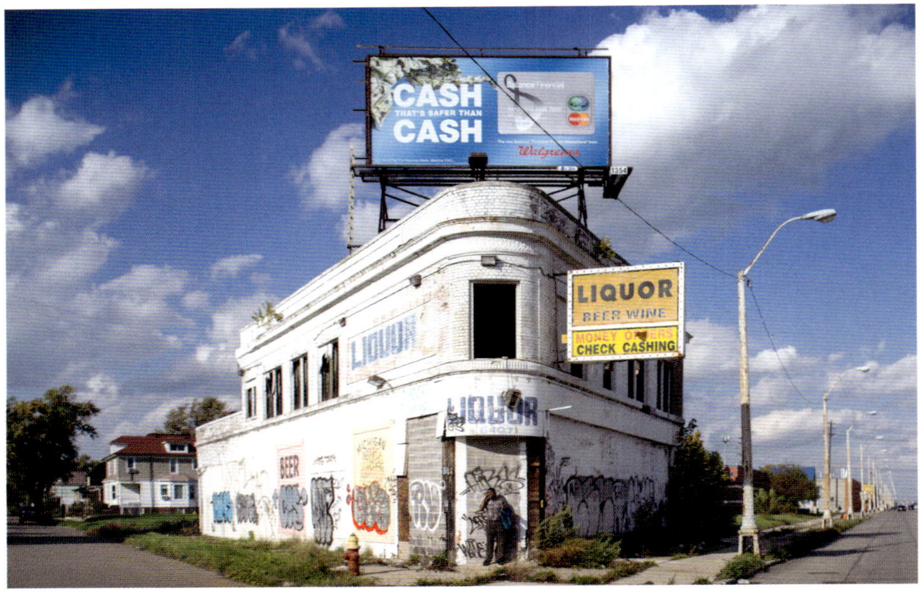

6407 Gratiot Ave., Detroit, 2013

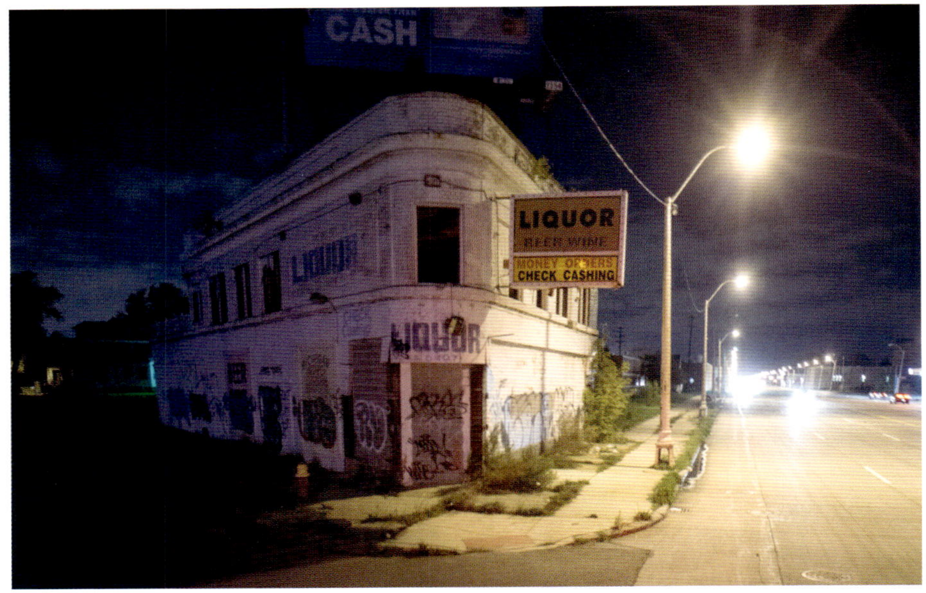

6407 Gratiot Ave., Detroit, 2013

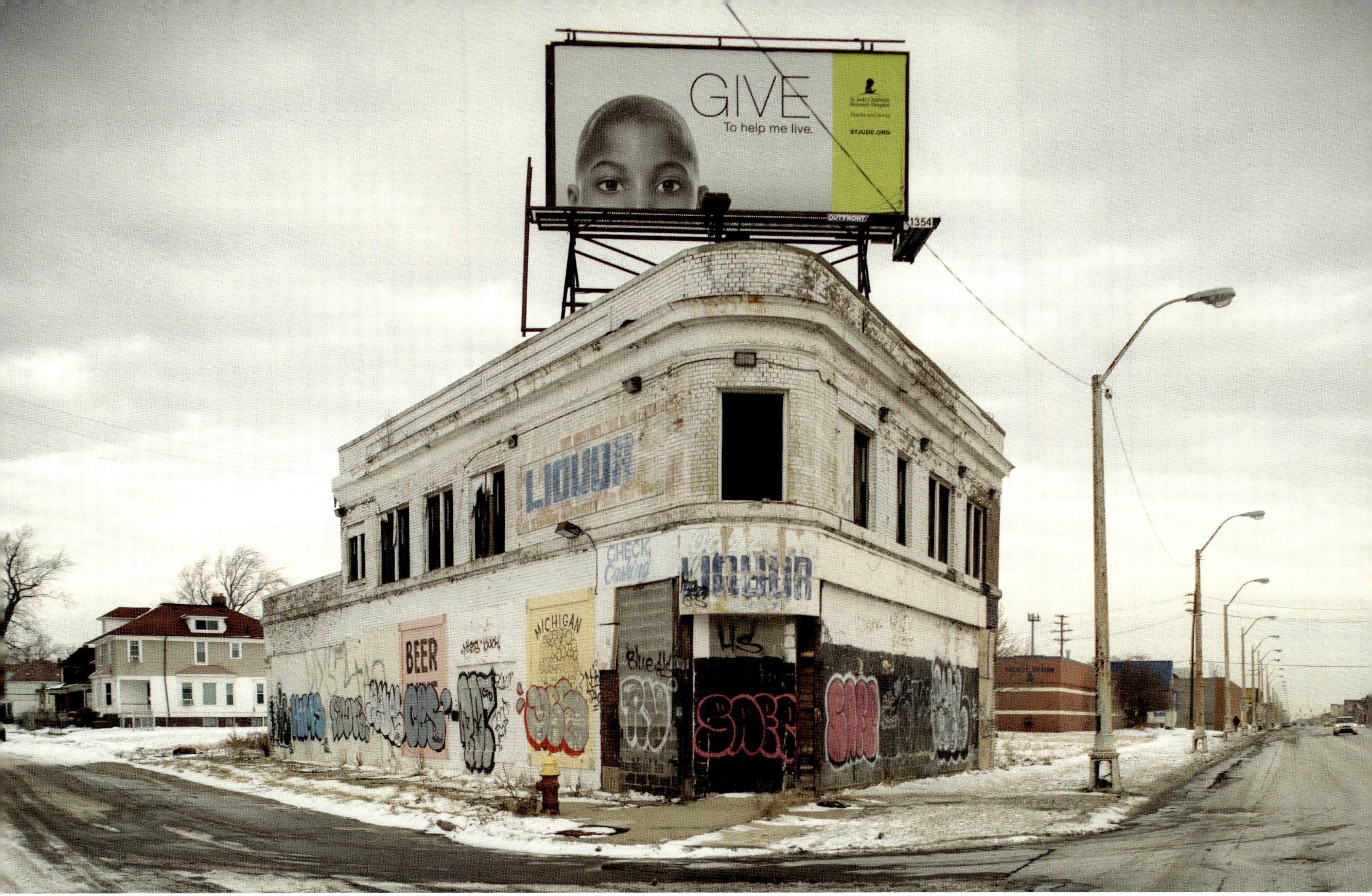

6407 Gratiot Ave., Detro t, 2015

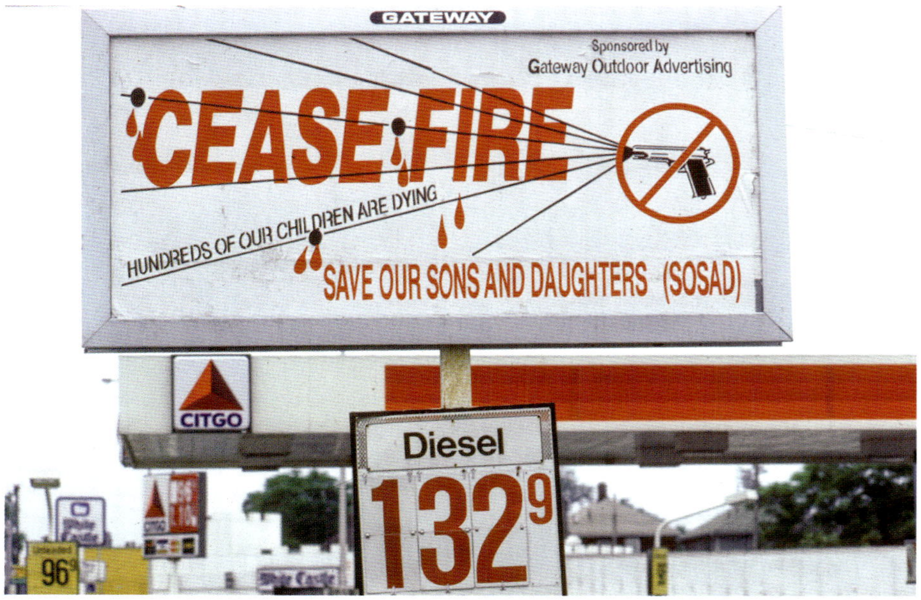

Cease Fire billboard. Livernois Avenue and West Warren Avenue, Detroit, 1992.

INNER-CITY BILLBOARDS Billboards are banned as visual clutter from middle-class neighborhoods and affluent communities. But public service billboards often crop up in the bleakest cityscapes, becoming a familiar sight to residents of ghettos and barrios. These are billboards that, because of their location, outdoor advertisement companies find difficult to sell to paying clients. As a result, the companies are willing to lend them at no cost to churches, community organizations, and public agencies. The messages on them are written in spare, straightforward, sometimes tough language, with images to match. Many deal with dangers—of drugs, guns, abusive partners, sexually transmitted diseases, and insurance fraud—while others stress the need for God, compassion, and self-esteem. While photographing a Crime Stoppers billboard on East Warren Avenue, which showed a large photograph of crime victim Lorenzo Glenn, I encountered Clyde, once a neighbor of Glenn. As if, upon seeing the billboard, he had seen the real Glenn, Clyde said: "I didn't know he was here. . . . He was shot inside his house during a robbery. He was a real nice guy. He had a daughter." Some billboards are left empty, their frame and metal backing rusting. A car wash at 7734 Mack Avenue adapted an abandoned billboard, attaching to it a much smaller sign advertising their services.

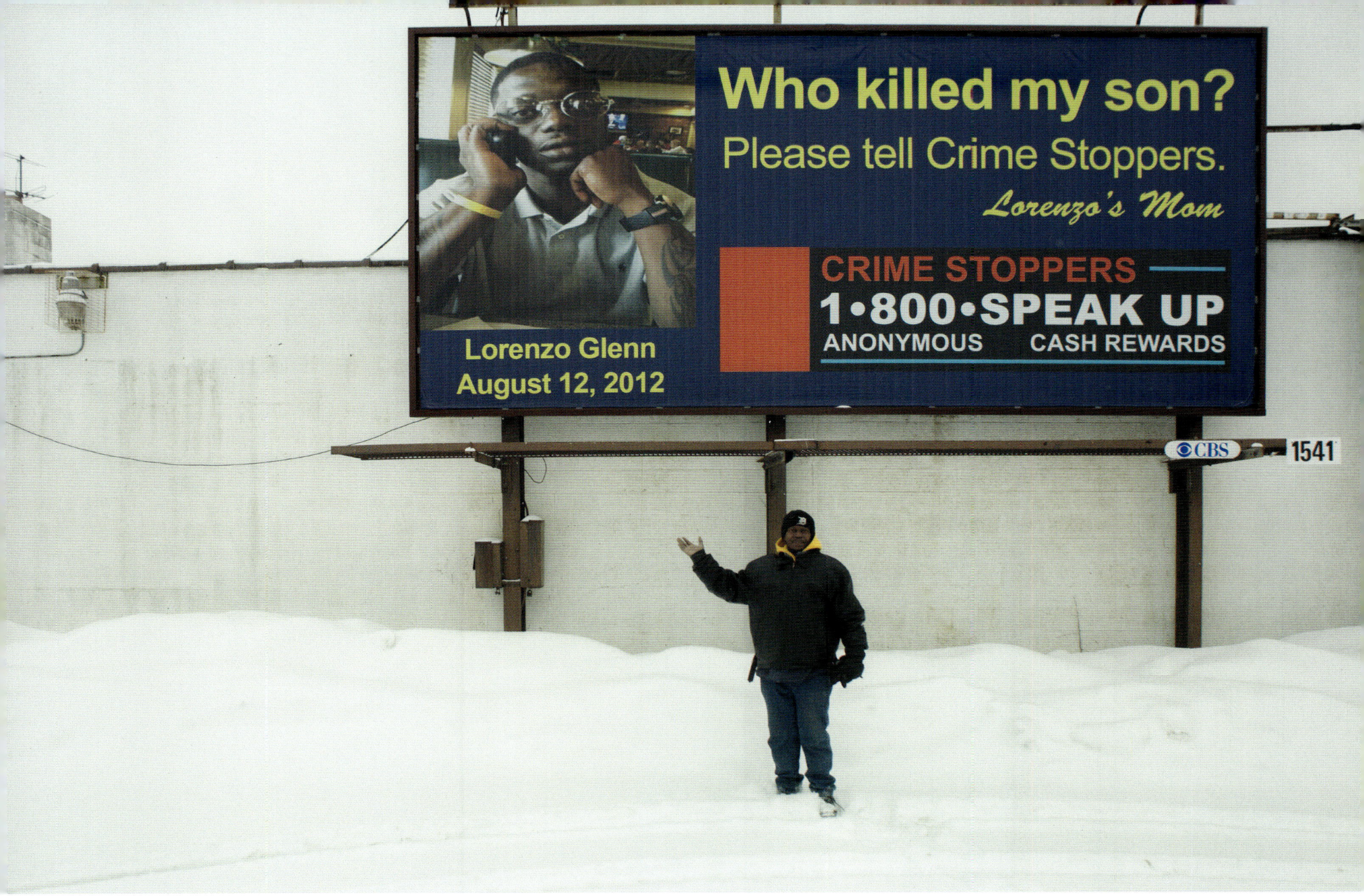

Crime Stoppers. 12800 East Warren Avenue, Detroit, 2014.

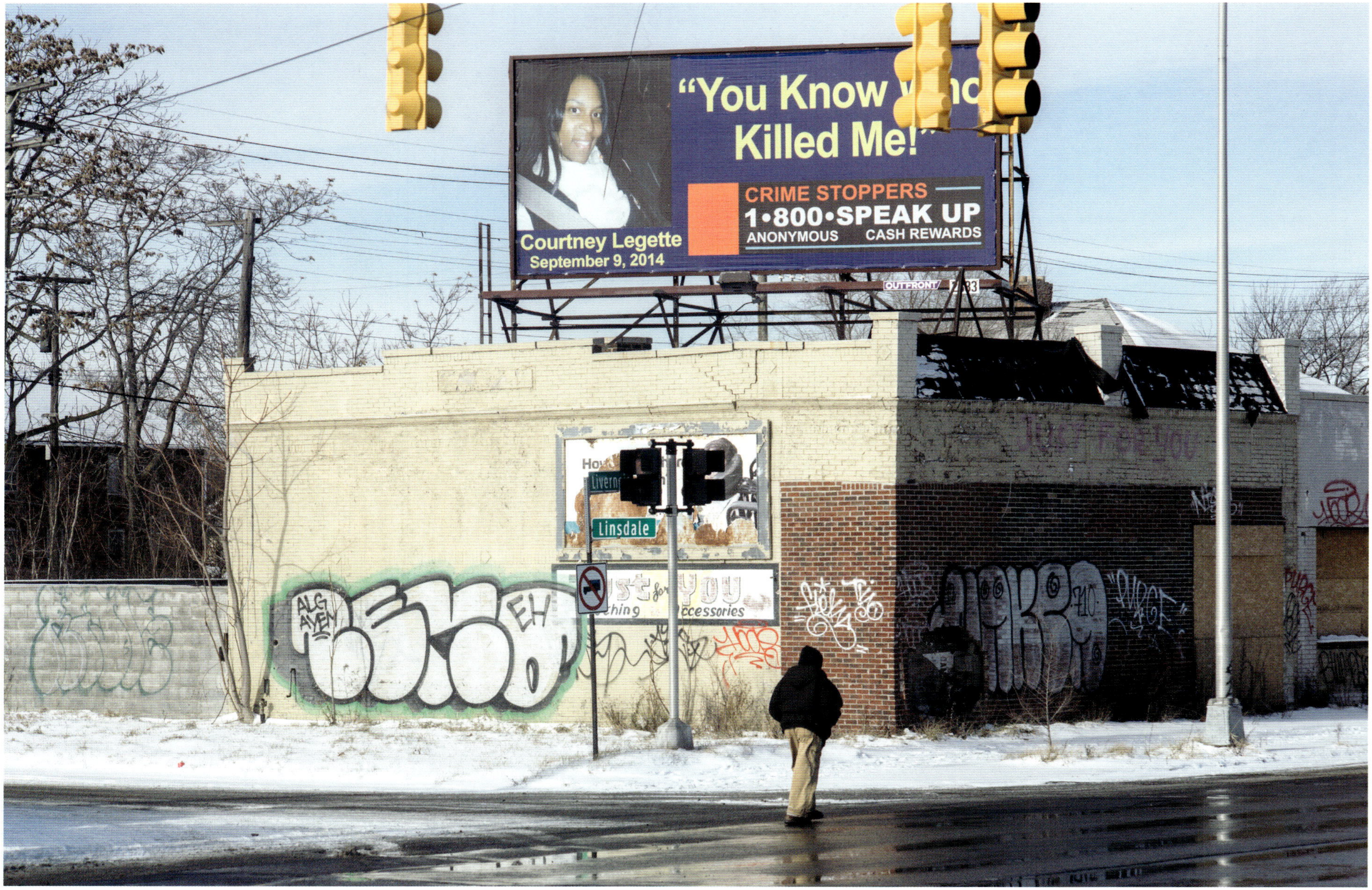

Crime Stoppers. Livernois Avenue at Linsdale Street, Detroit, 2014.

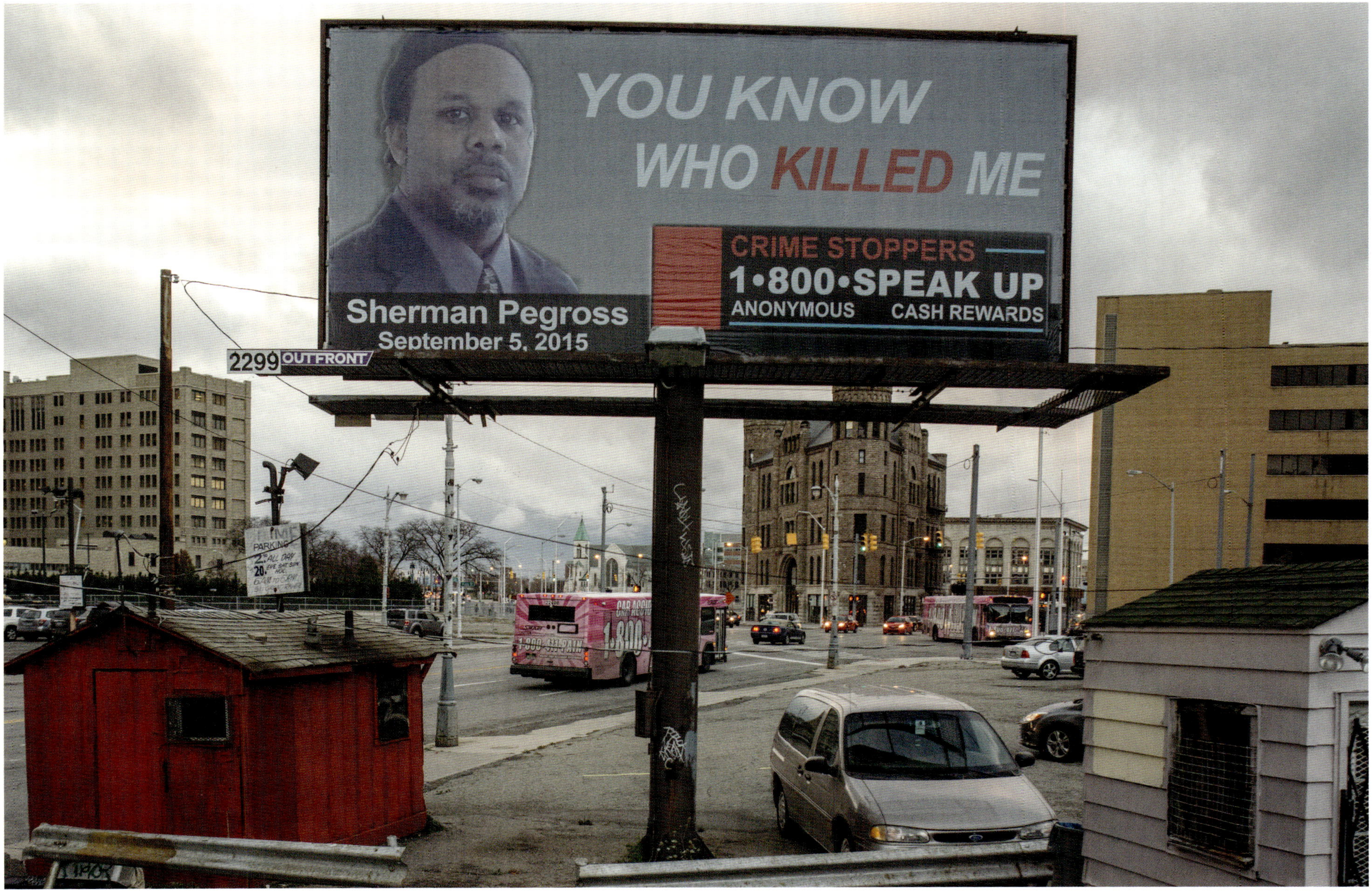

A prominent billboard depicts a homicide victim and the words, "You Know Who Killed Me," and offers a cash reward for information. The billboard was formerly used by a group of personal injury lawyers and thereafter by an energy drink, a Subway restaurant, and Doritos. This latest public-service use, so different from the previous commercial messaging, comes as a surprise in a city that is becoming increasingly image-conscious. Bagley Avenue at Cass Avenue, Detroit, 2015.

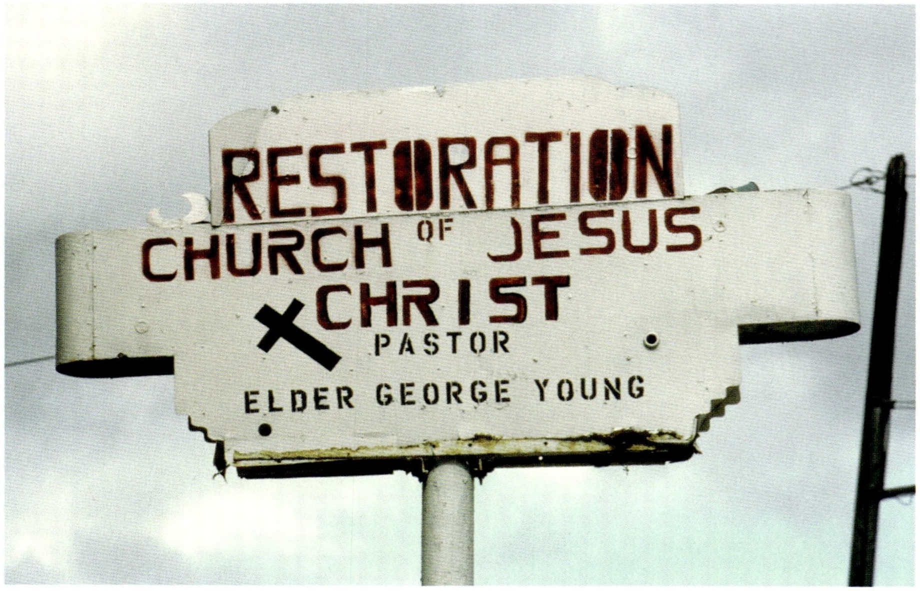

A commercial sign adapted for the Restoration Church of Jesus Christ.
7611 Miller Avenue, Detroit, 2001.

EXTINGUISHED NEON SIGNS Extinguished neon signs, their tubes broken, hanging from rusty supports, remain after the businesses they advertised are long gone. On windy days they swing, making creaking noises. Youngsters pelt signs with stones; sparrows build their nests inside them. City officials try to remove them before they crash to the sidewalk. Some get a second life by being painted over; for example, a commercial sign was adapted for the Restoration Church of Jesus Christ on Miller Avenue. On Oakland Avenue, a tall sign in the shape of an ice-cream cone becomes rust-covered. Once upon a time, signs like these told us where we were and gave a sense of place to commercial streets. Today, they function as historical markers, nostalgic reminders of the businesses that once lined the streets. At night they cast sinister shadows. Bob, of Hats Galore & More on Gratiot Avenue, would like to fix his neon sign in the shape of a top hat but it would cost him about $2,000.

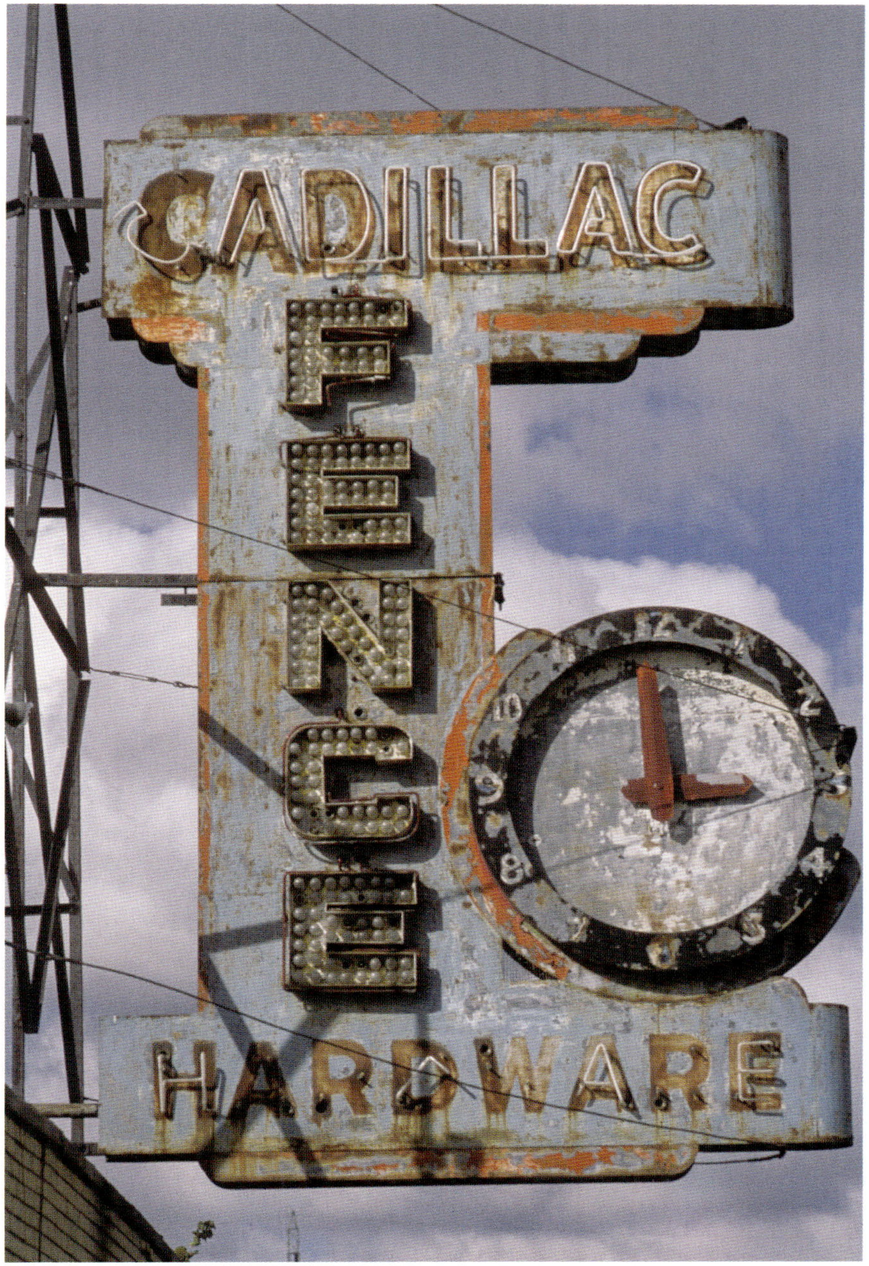

Cadillac Fence and Supply. This large, heavy, once-colorful sign is a reminder of stable, optimistic times. Plymouth Road at Schaefer Highway, Detroit, 2012.

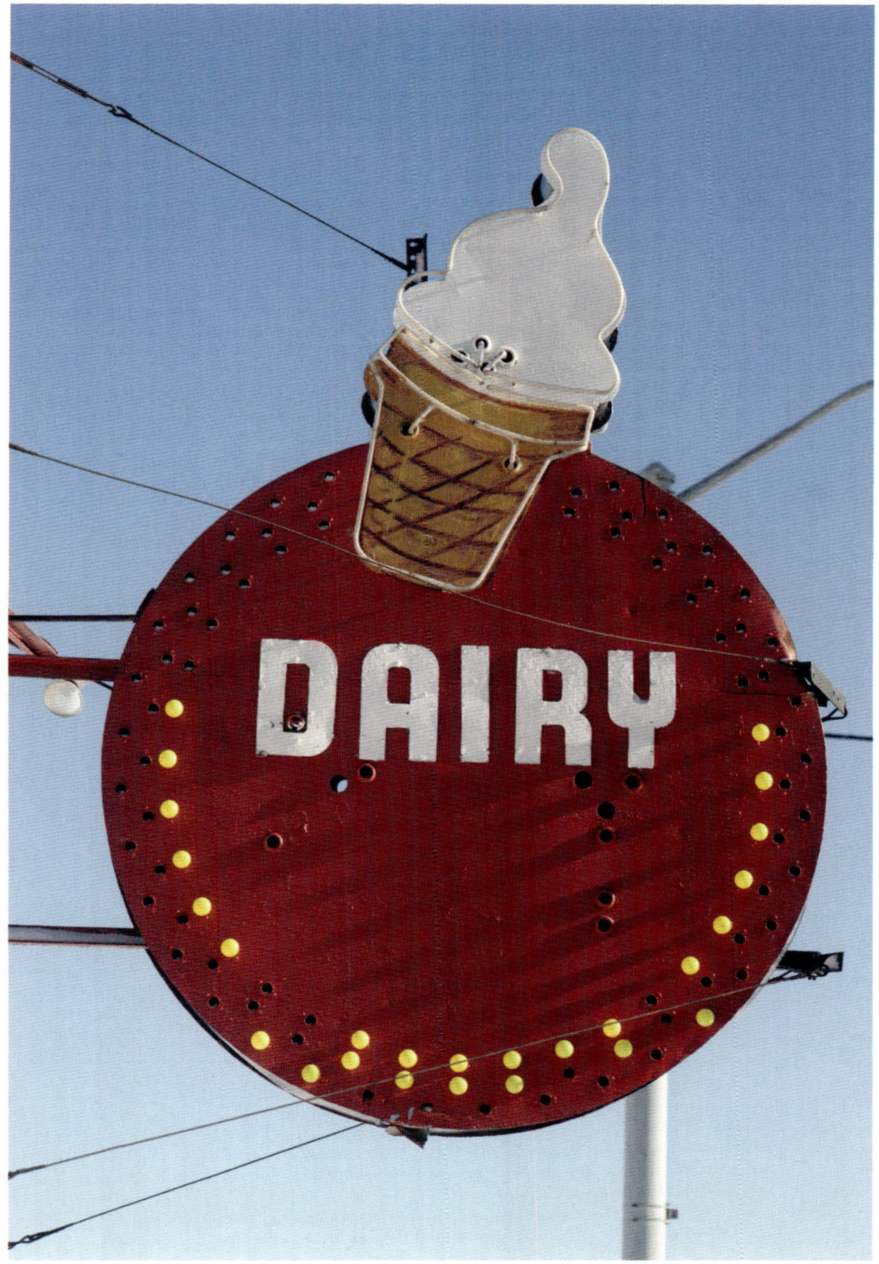

Dairy Queen sign. Mack Avenue at Iroquois Avenue, Detroit, 2014.

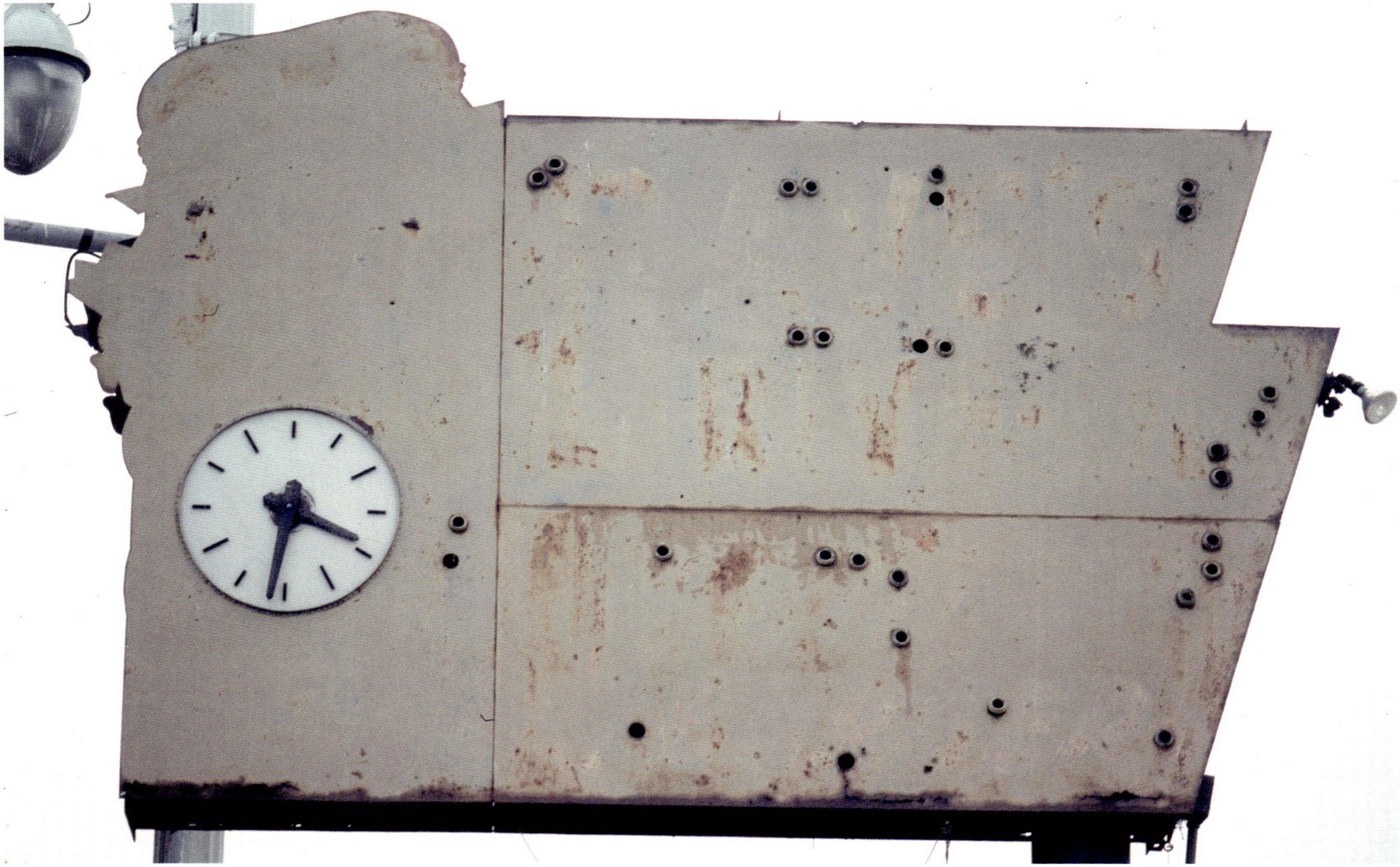

Former neon sign, the neon gone but with traces of "Dave's Drive-In" still visible.
Piquette St., at John R, Detroit, 2006

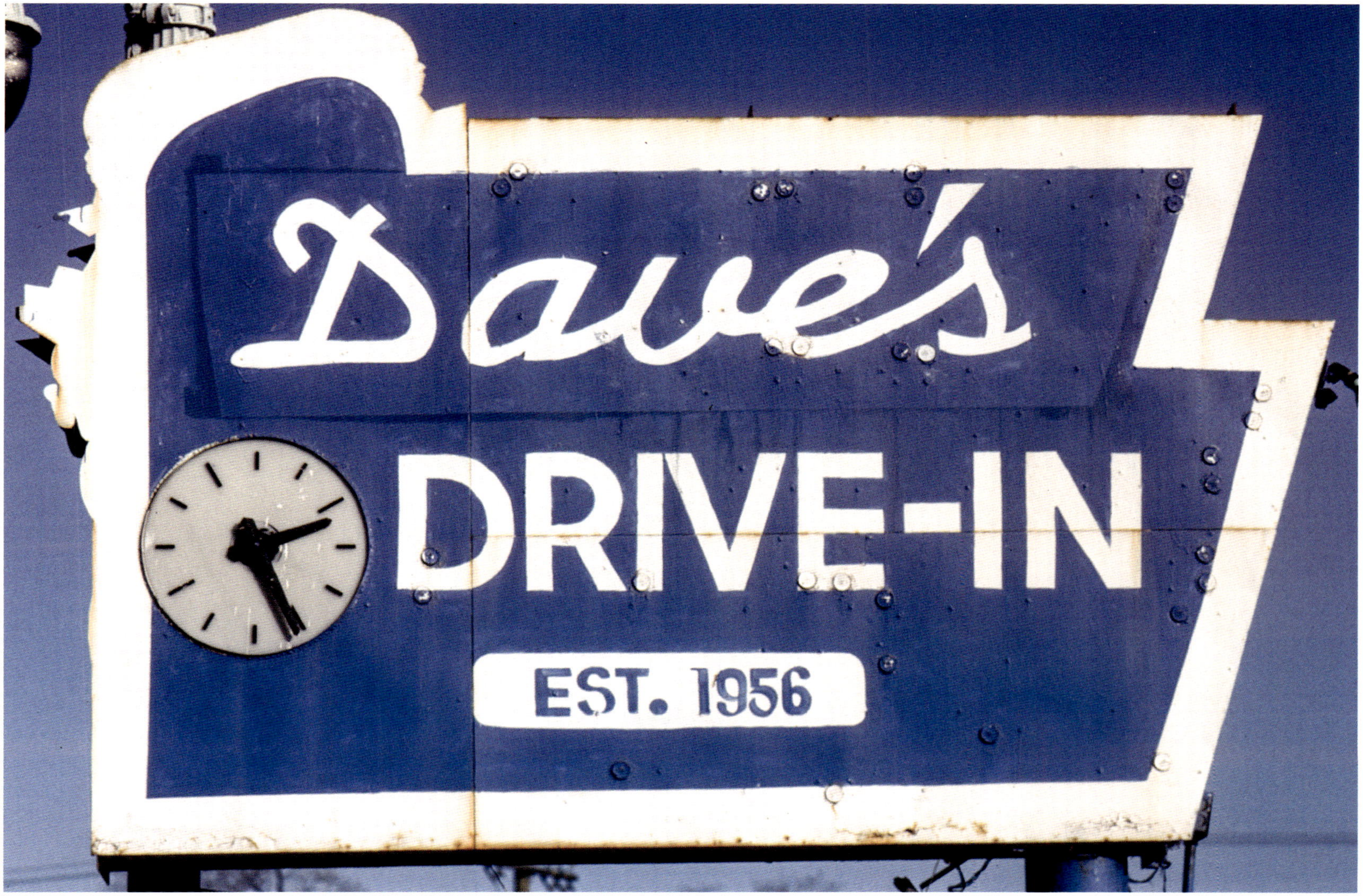

"Dave's Drive-In" sign painted over with same message. This sign was short-lived, made too early for the eventual revitalization of the neighborhood. Piquette St., at John R, Detroit, 2009

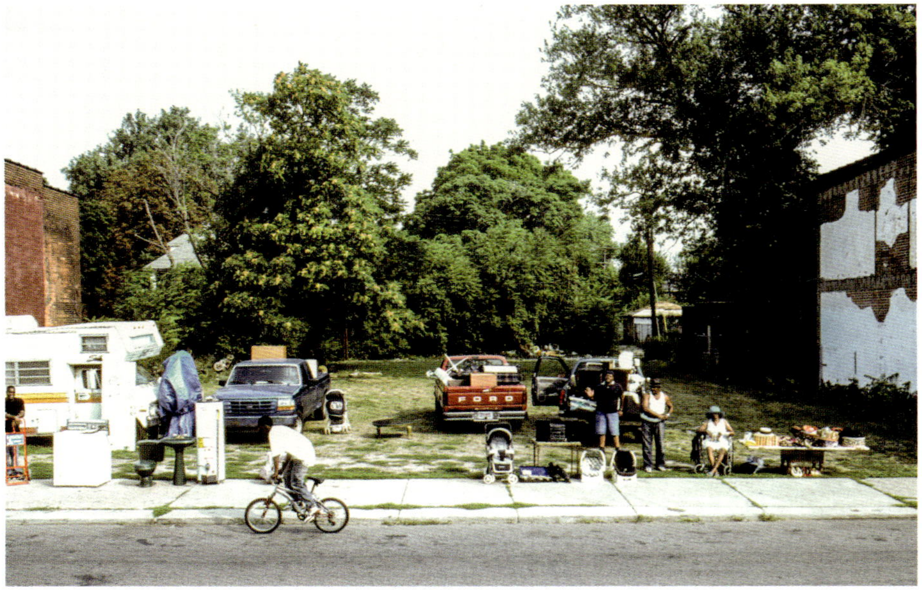

STREET VENDORS On vacant lots throughout Detroit, street vendors sell clothes, car seats, bicycles, furniture, and other objects that they bring in pick-up trucks and park nearby. On East Warren Avenue, a vendor, fearful of having to pay taxes on his sales, asked me: "Are you with the government?" When I explained my documentation project, he responded angrily: "I don't care who you are, I don't want you taking my picture." Parking lots, too, are abundant. They afford places to sell barbecue, for example; vendors just set up a drum, a table and some chairs, and the smoke begins to rise. Often the markets are fundraising efforts of a local church. I saw the extraordinary sight of used clothes hanging on a cyclone fence; they were being sold by Norma Sutton and Mabel Farmer for The Heavenly Mission Baptist Church along busy Harper Avenue. When I asked where they got the clothes they answered, "From my closets, out of her closets, from our friends," adding, "We don't charge people an arm or a leg. And we don't sell junk."

Yard sale. Theresa and family bring some life to this desolate neighborhood.
Mack Avenue at Townsend Street, Detroit, 2007.

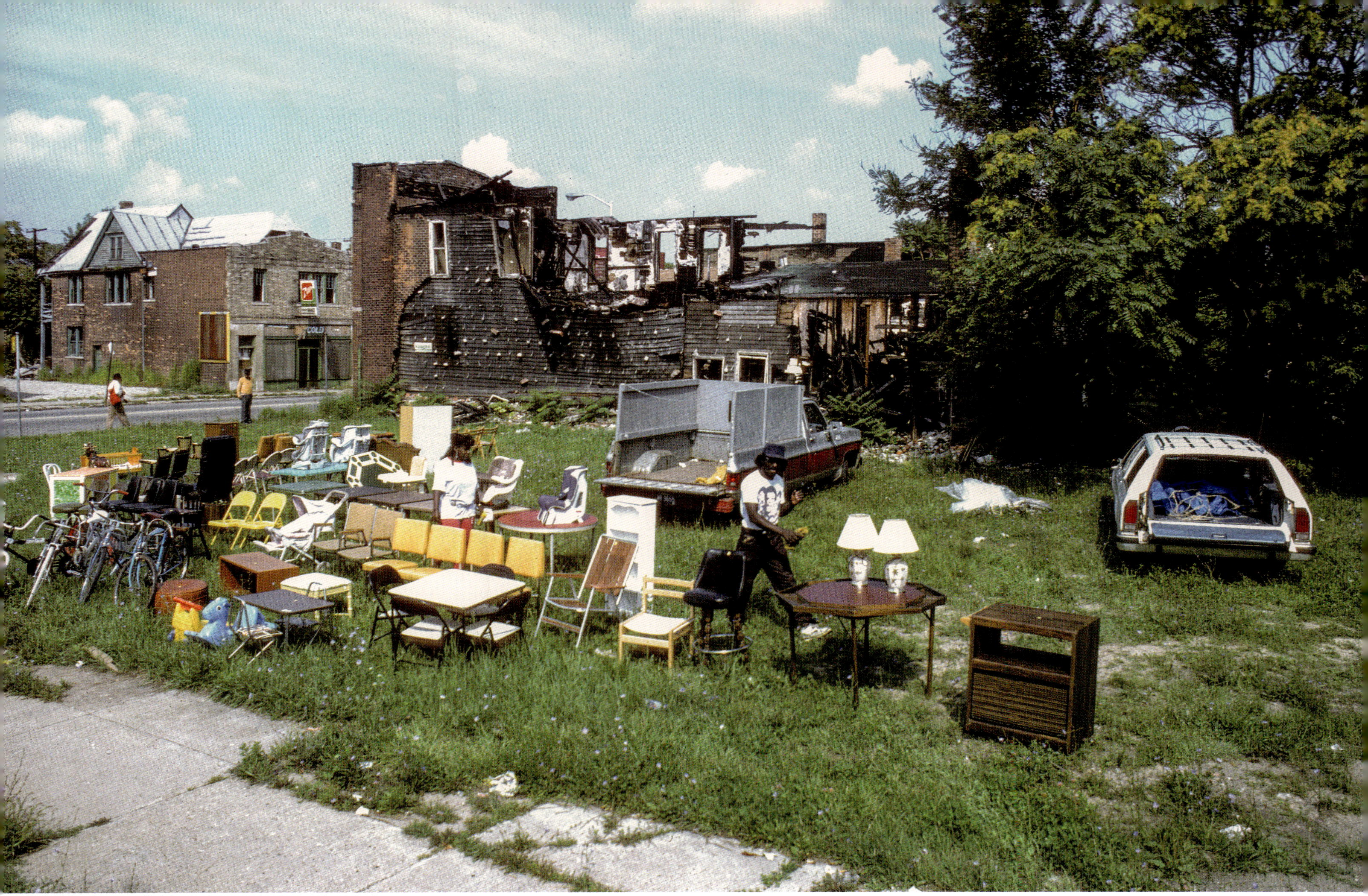

Outdoor sale. East Warren Avenue at Chene Street, Detroit, 1994.

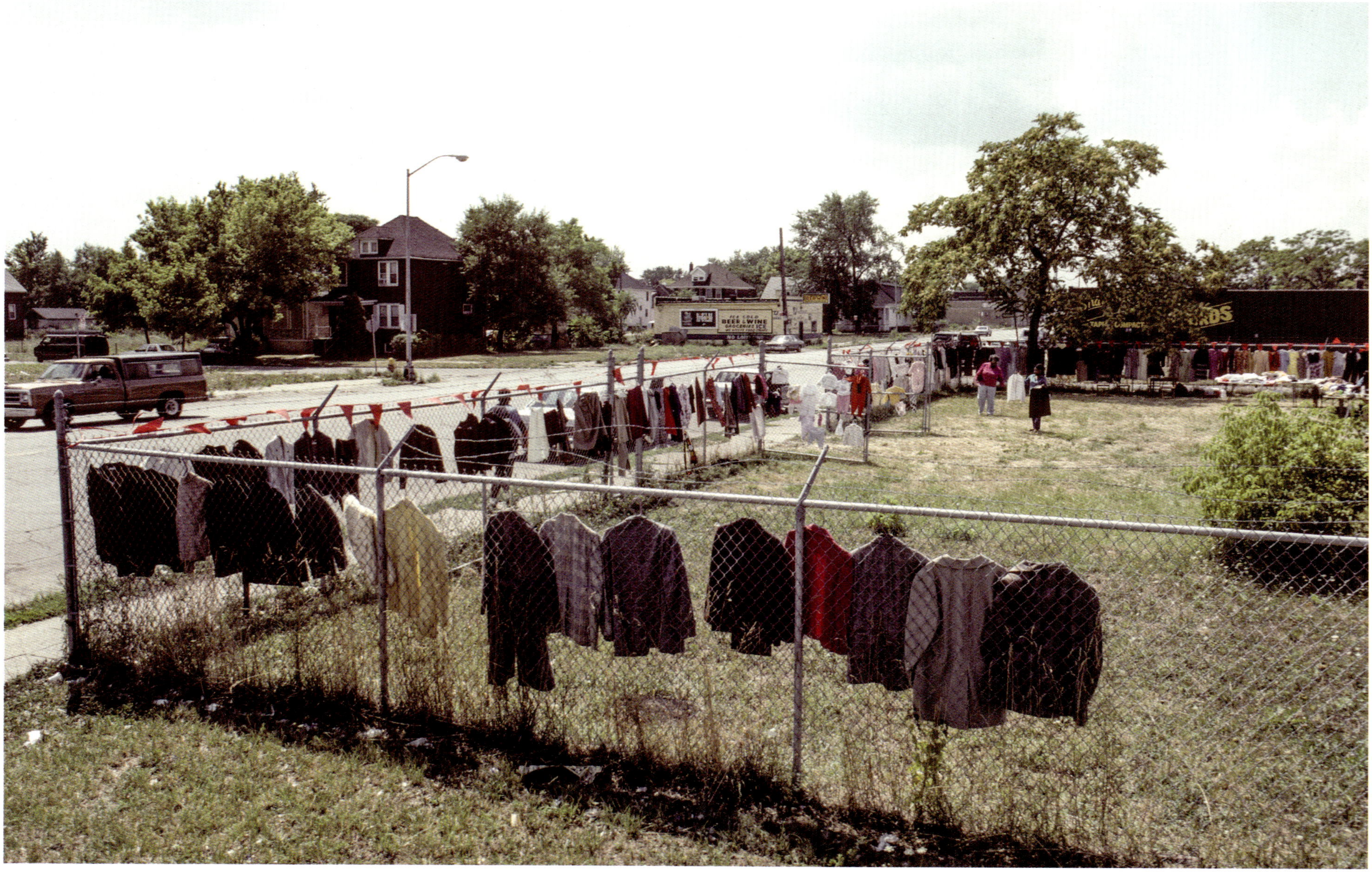

Flea market sponsored by The Heavenly Mission Baptist Church.
Harper Avenue at McClellan Street, Detroit, 1991.

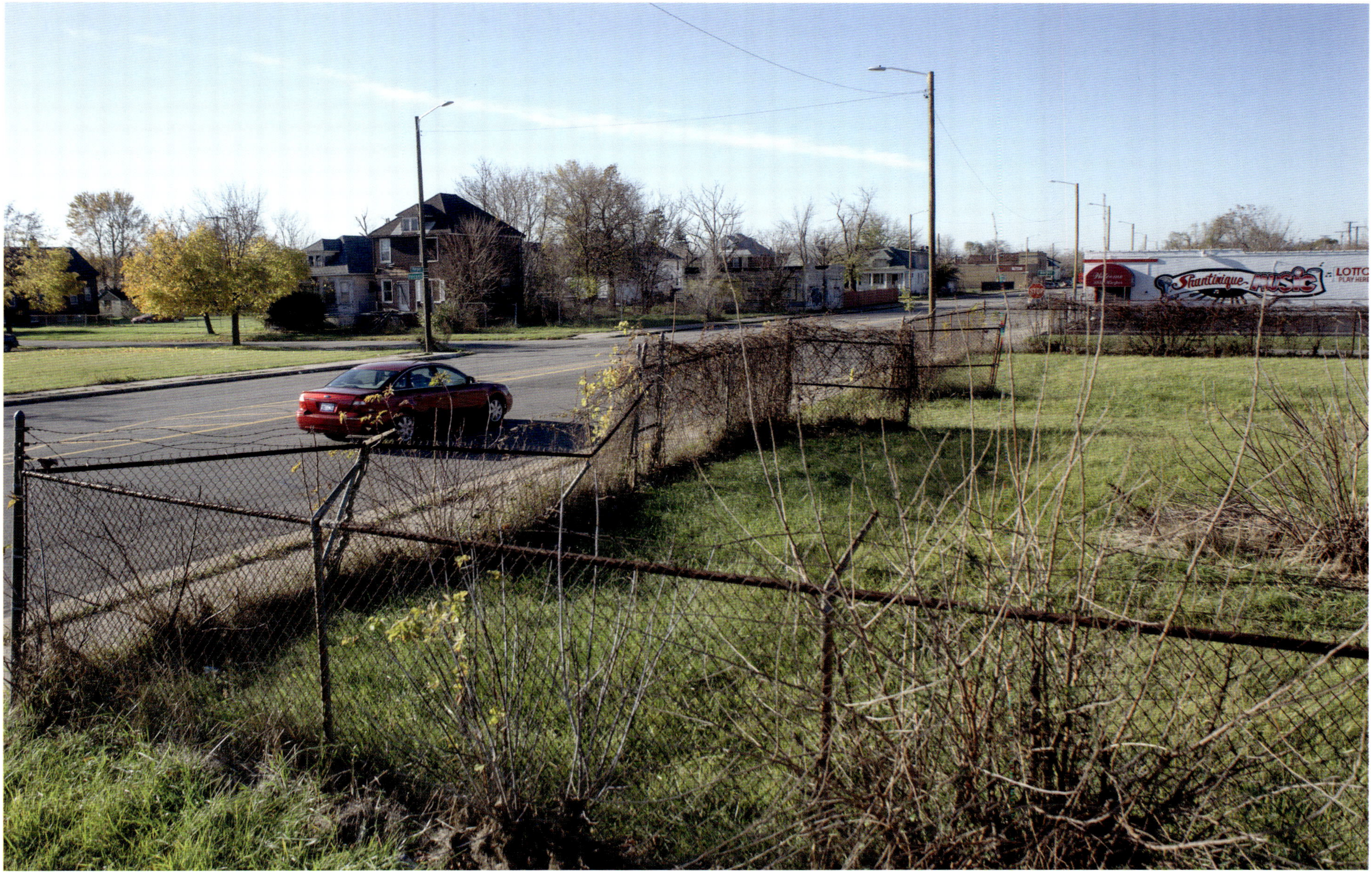

Vacant lot, Harper Avenue at McClellan Street, Detroit, 2015,

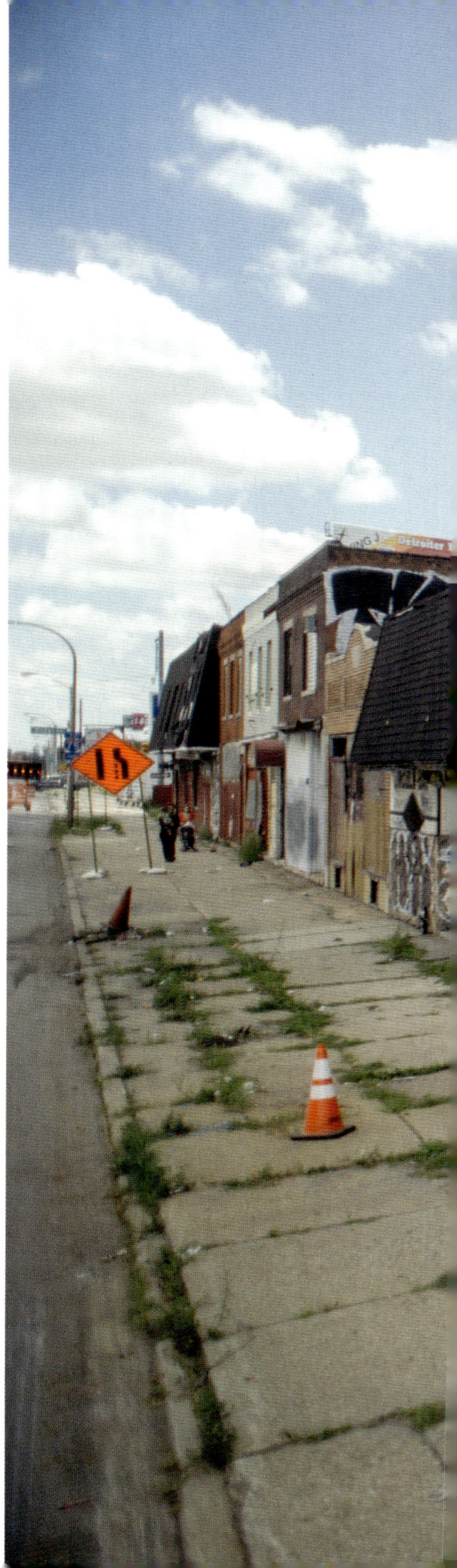

A sex worker waiting for customers at a well-travelled intersection near the Ambassador Bridge. 6100 West Fort Street, Detroit, 2015.

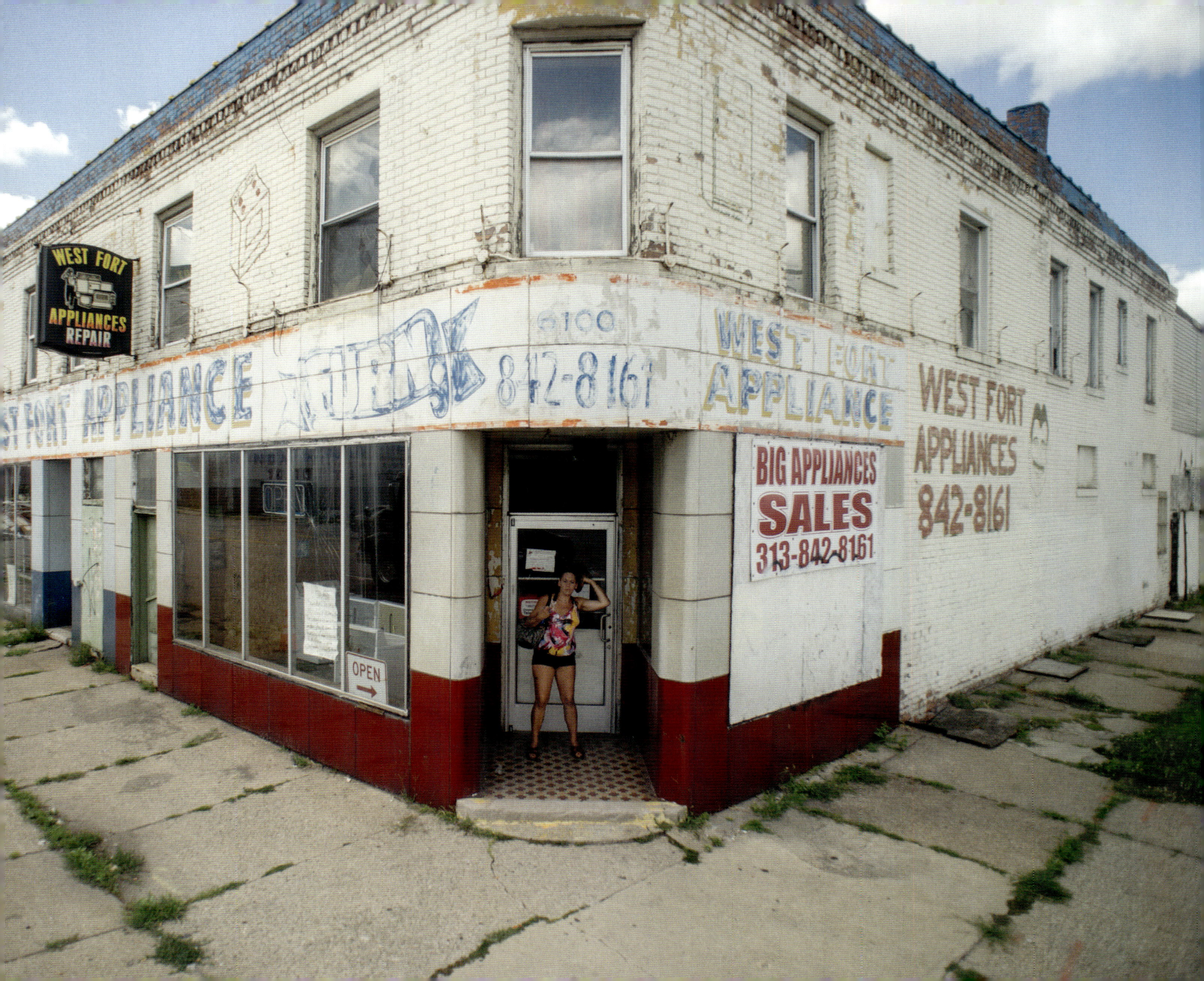
WEST FORT
APPLIANCES
REPAIR
ST FORT APPLIANCE
842-8161
WEST FORT
APPLIANCE
BIG APPLIANCES
SALES
313-842-8161
WEST FORT
APPLIANCES
842-8161
OPEN

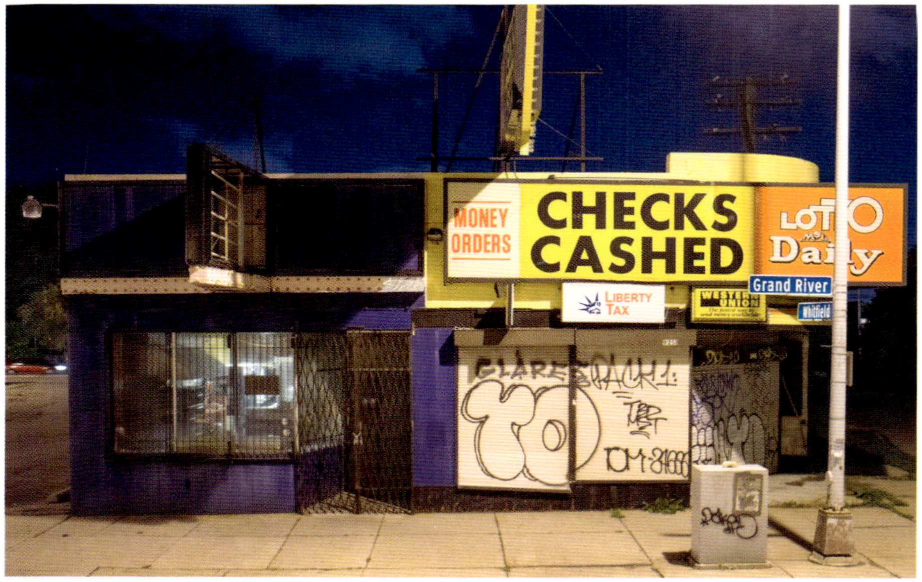

Check-cashing place and former Famous Pizza. 9051 Grand River Avenue at Whitfield Street, Detroit, 2013.

DOING BUSINESS BEHIND PLEXIGLASS

Former stores are prepared for another possible incarnation, graffiti gets cleaned, the outside is brightly painted, a few racks are bought and products arranged on them. The greater the variety of products and services and the less expensive they are, the greater the chance of making a sale. Among services, the most common are tax preparation, notary public, car wash, check cashing, hair salons and barbershops. Popular products include cell phones and, more recently, medical marijuana. New businesses are built of cinderblocks, but some are never completed and fall into ruin. Sometimes signage gets out of hand, as in the case of the LA Insurance corner store on West McNichols Road. The business manager gave a sub-lease to a tenant who, according to her, "was special," and he put up the signs. Someone with authority was upset and complained to the city, saying that it was not appropriate; as a result, the city required that many of the signs be removed.

Fear of stores being robbed and vandalized is widespread. On the front of the West Front Appliance Repair a handwritten sign reads: "RING BELL, REMOVE HOODS, HANDS OUT OF POCKETS THANK YOU!" The police encourage store managers to install video cameras connected to the police. To get a clearer image they advise illuminating the store's perimeter with powerful lights. White folks rarely patronize these stores. When I asked the waitresses in a coney island on Gratiot Avenue when she had last seen a white customer, she replied, "Yesterday, a white woman came running in. She had to piss."

Mattie, a store owner, told me that in a dream God told her to sell the things that people want. Accordingly, she sells beer, cigarettes, and sodas in her store on Gratiot Avenue. Darnell, another store owner, has been on East Grand Avenue for six years. He thinks that his three stores two blocks east of the Packard Plant are "something that stands out, a Christmas tree to our neighborhood." And being in such a dark and desolate place, his stores, painted red and blue and decorated with flags, are a sign of life.

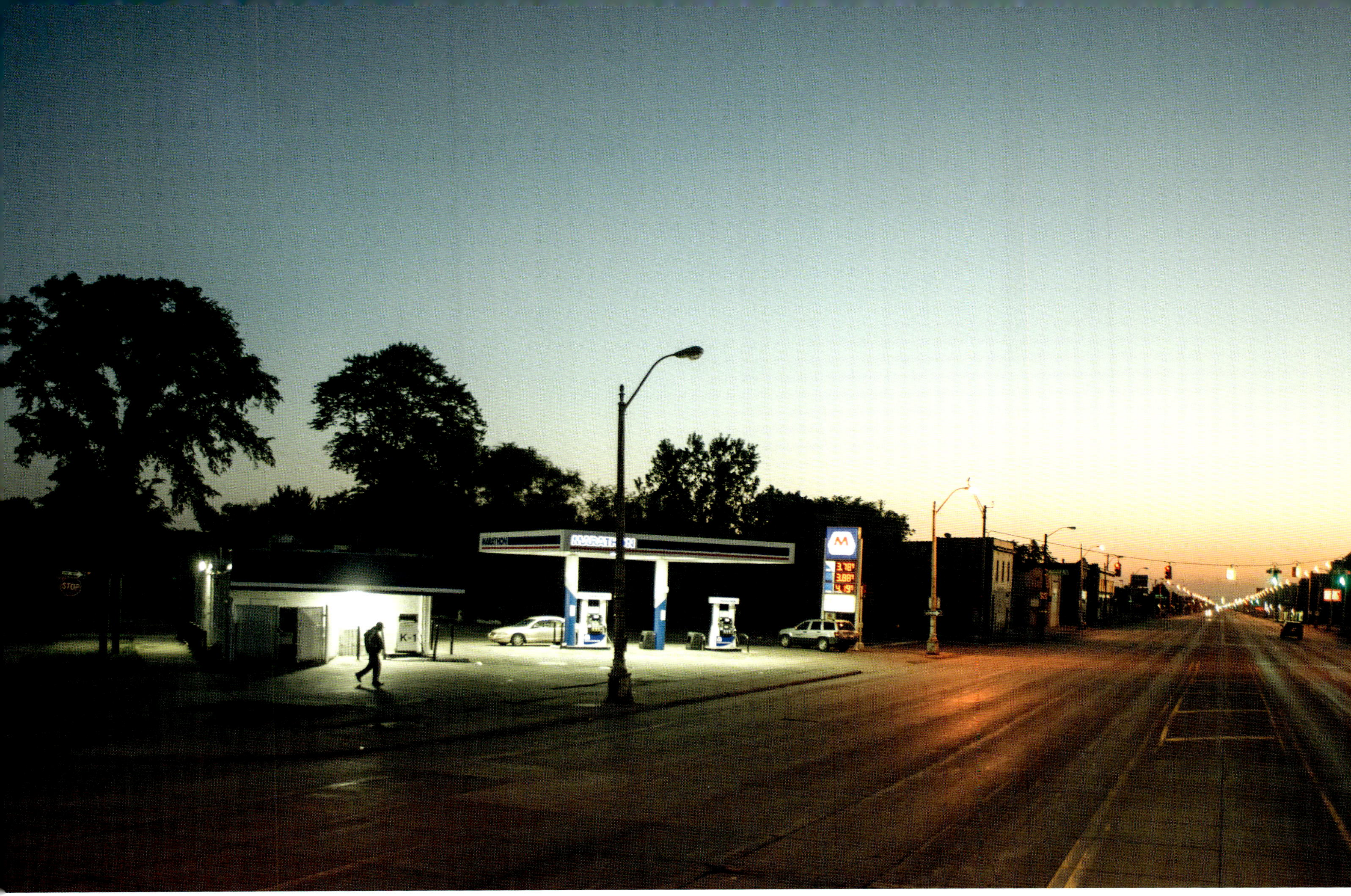

View east toward the rising sun. Residents, fearful of being carjacked, are reluctant to get gas within the city limits. Gratiot Avenue at Concord Avenue, Detroit, 2014.

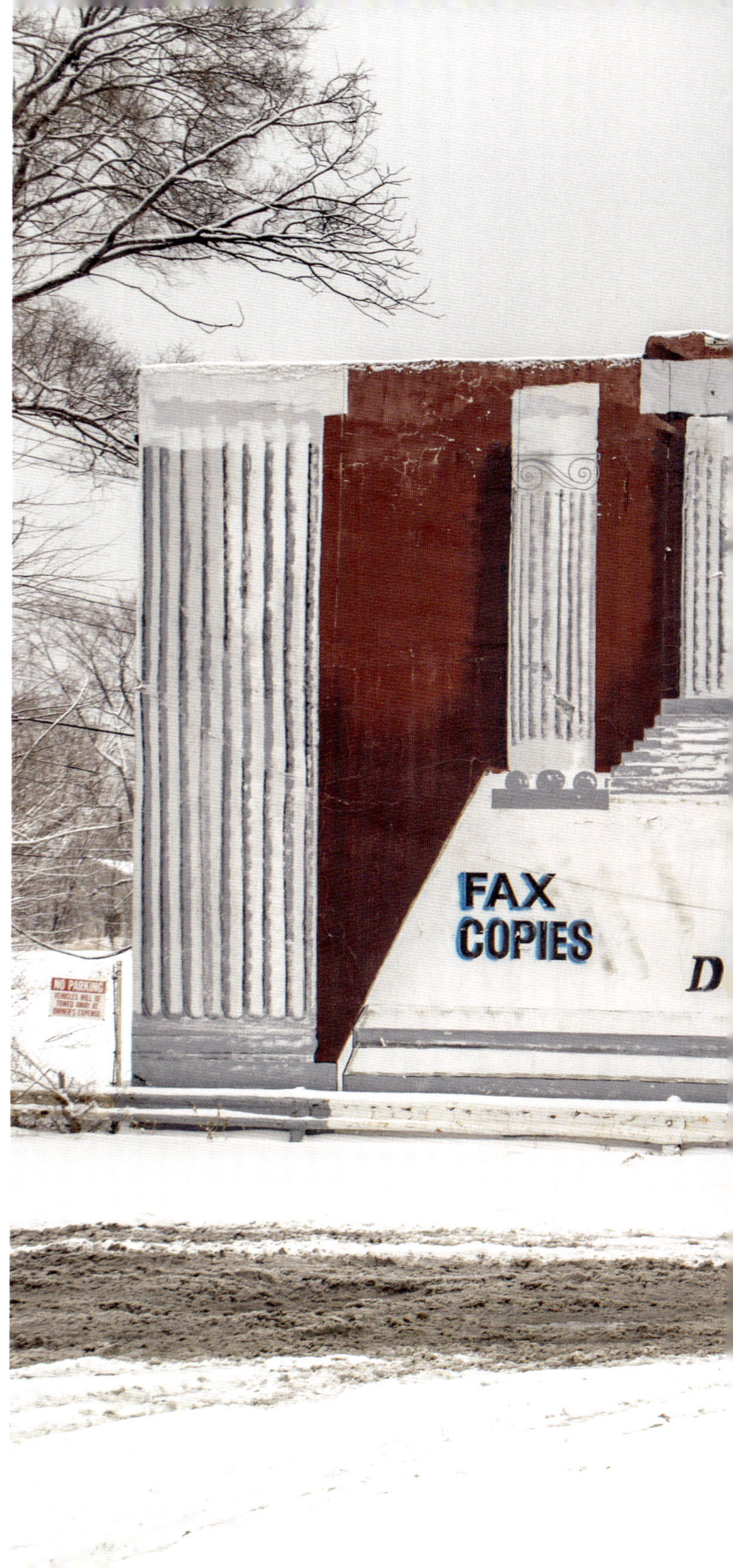

Greek mural on the side wall of a burnt liquor store.
Mack Avenue at Chalmers Street, Detroit, 2015.

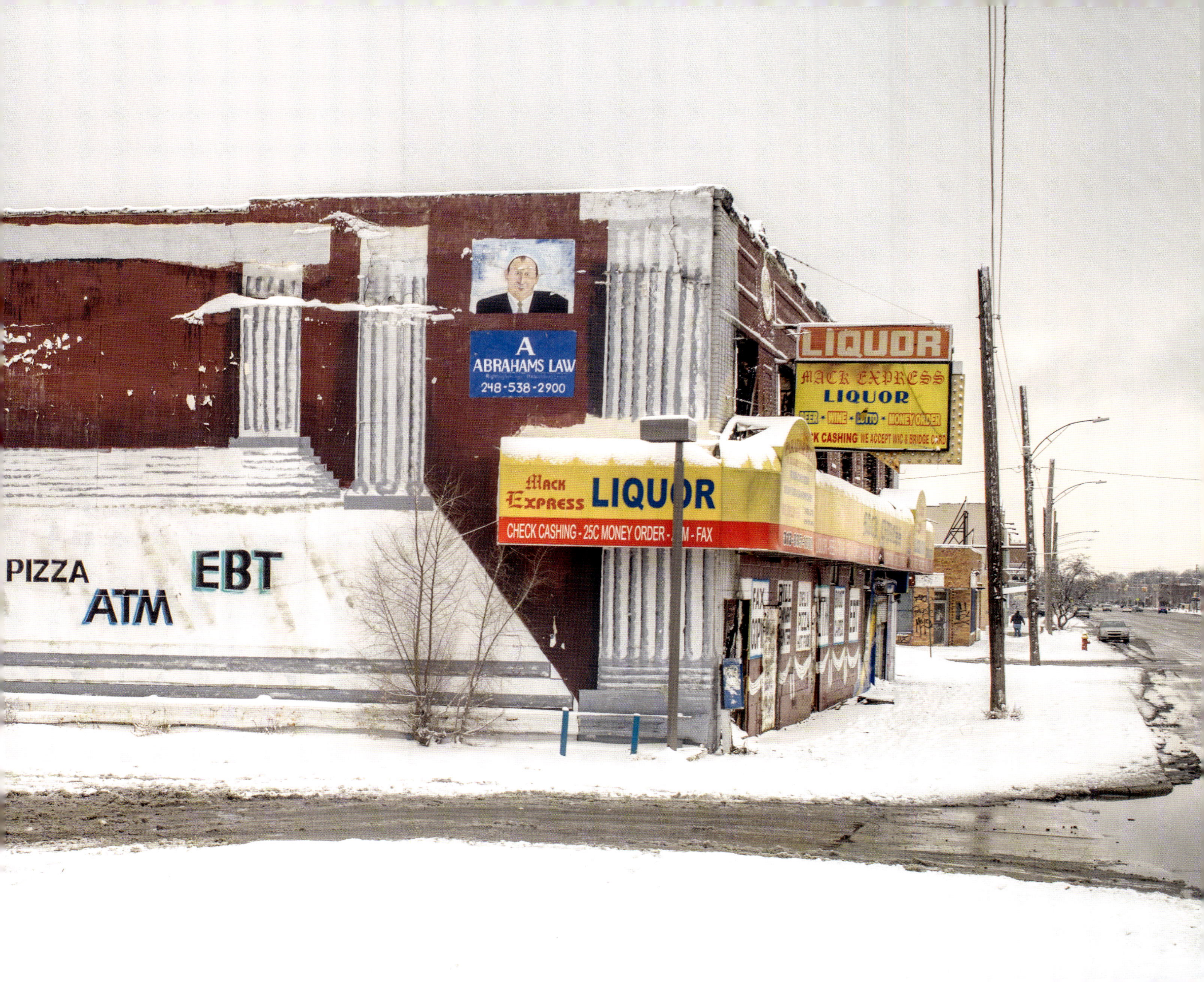
A
ABRAHAMS LAW
248-538-2900
PIZZA
ATM
EBT
LIQUOR
MACK EXPRESS
LIQUOR
BEER • WINE • LOTTO • MONEY ORDER
WE ACCEPT WIC & BRIDGE CARD
Mack Express
LIQUOR
CHECK CASHING - 25C MONEY ORDER
FAX

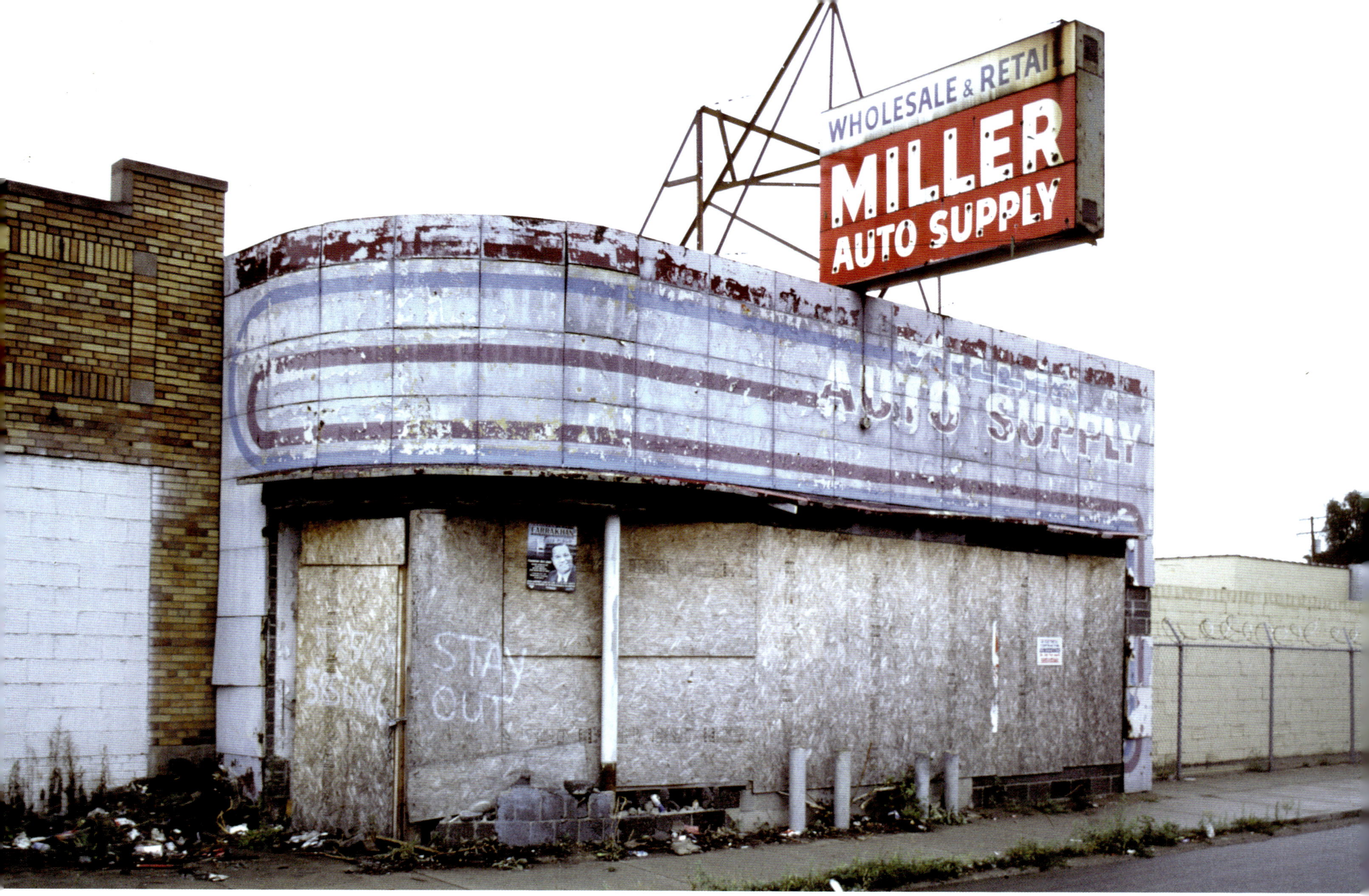

Former Miller Auto Supply. Wyoming Avenue at DeSoto Street, Detroit, 2007.

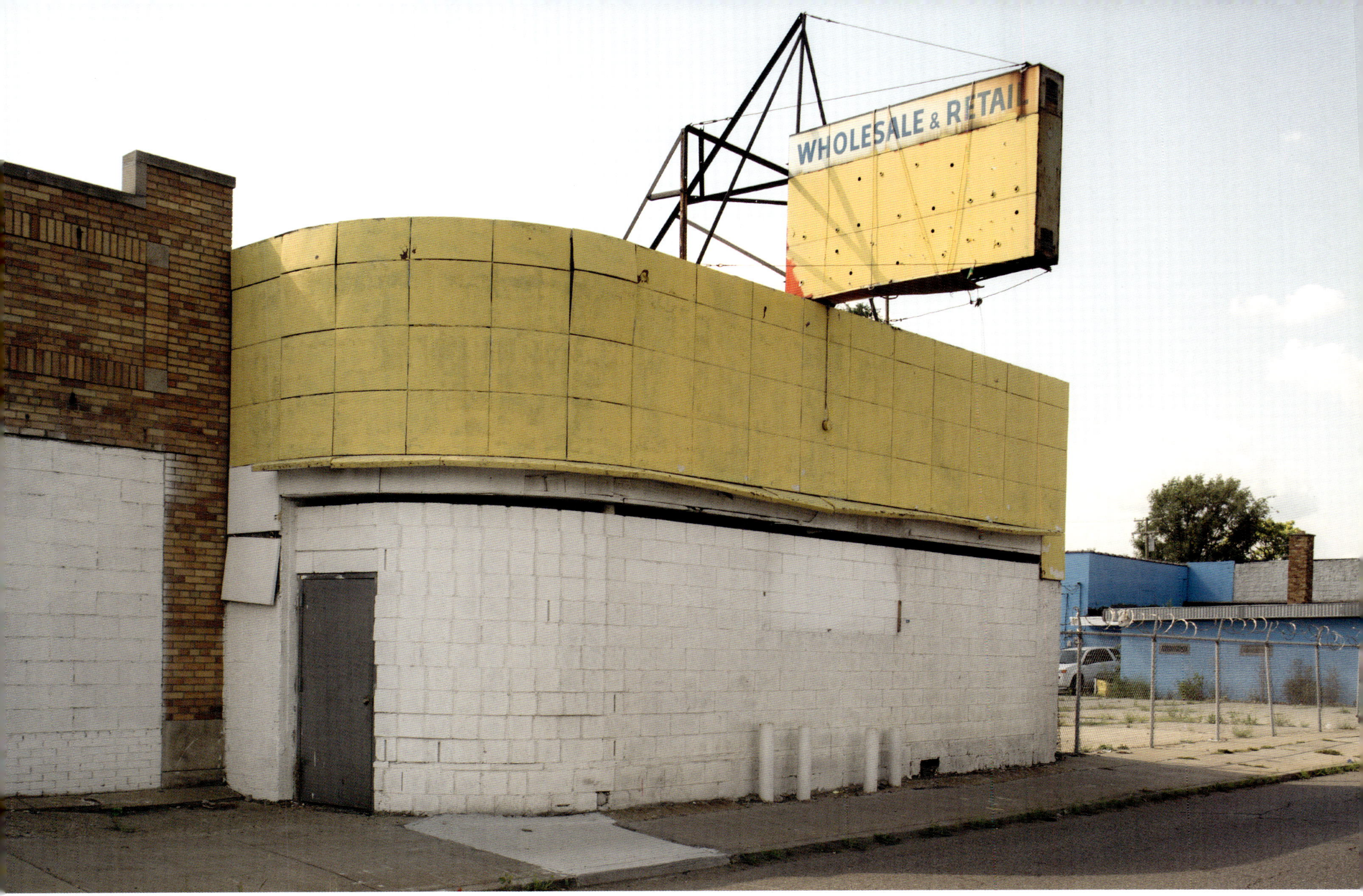

Former Miller Auto Supply. Someone felt it was worth the effort to mask the rundown state of the building. Wyoming Avenue at DeSoto Street, Detroit, 2015.

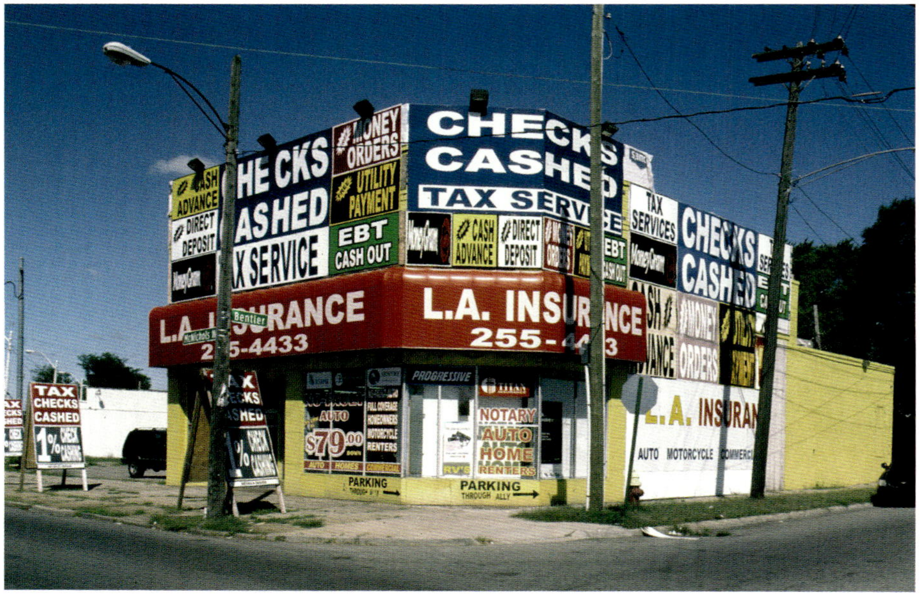

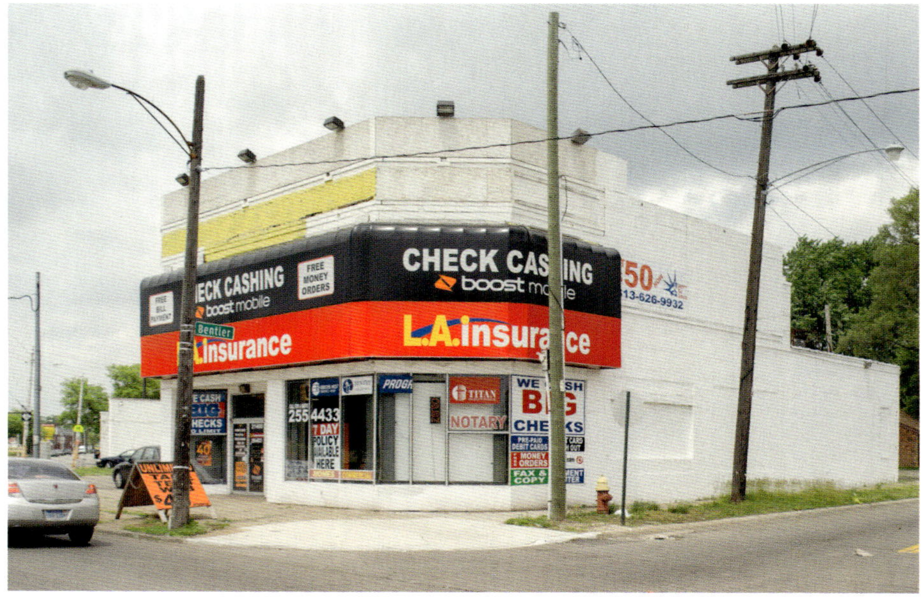

Check-cashing, taxes, insurance—an example of over-signage.
West McNichols Road at Bentler Street, Detroit, 2010.

A place with check-cashing, tax, and insurance services, its signage reduced.
West McNichols Road at Bentler Street, Detroit, 2014.

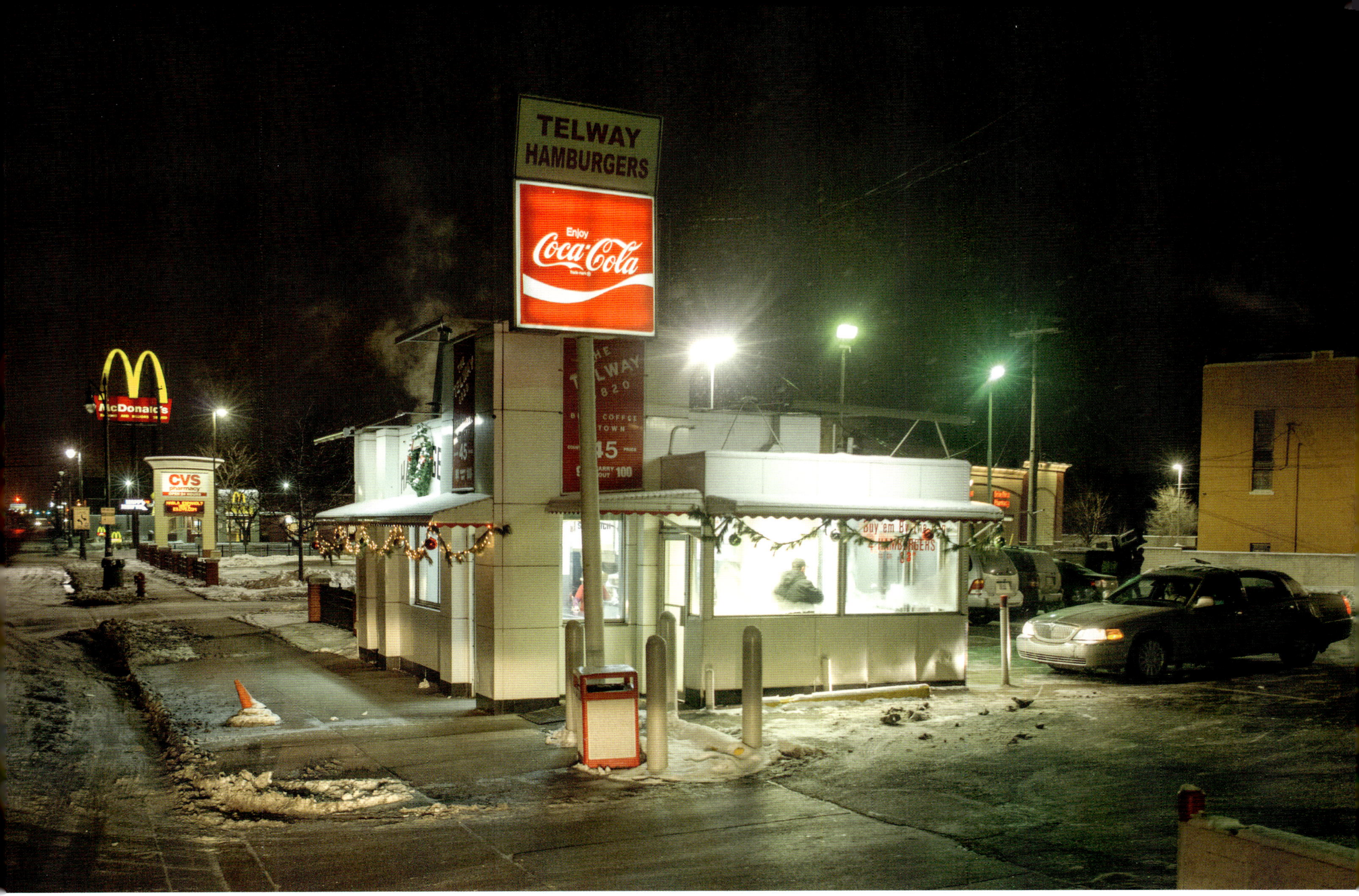

Night view of Tellway Hamburgers, formerly a White Tower restaurant, and now a popular 24-hour spot and local landmark. Michigan Avenue at Martin Street, Detroit, 2015.

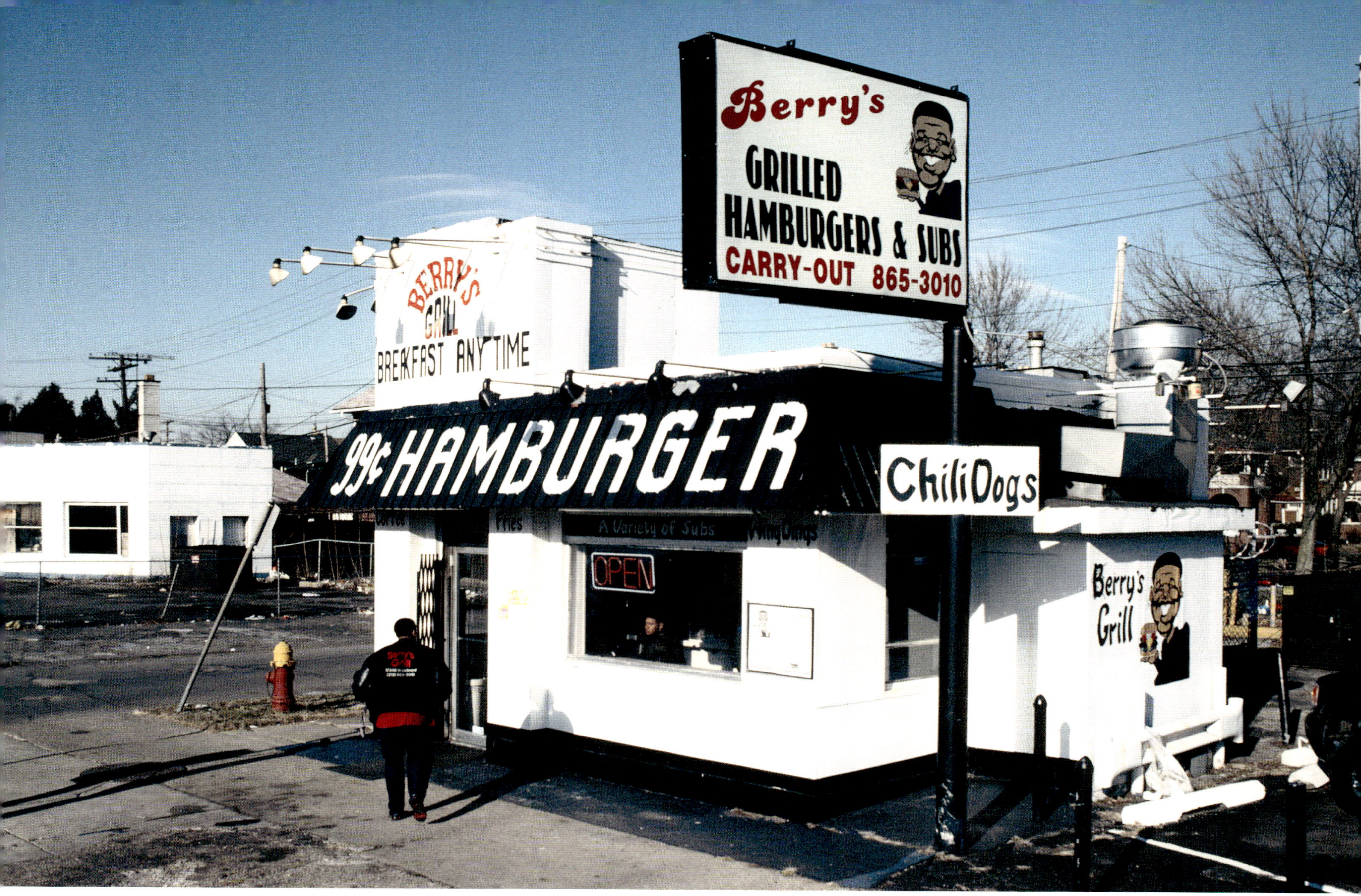

Berry entering Berry's Grill. Woodward Avenue at West Dakota Avenue,
Highland Park, 2001.

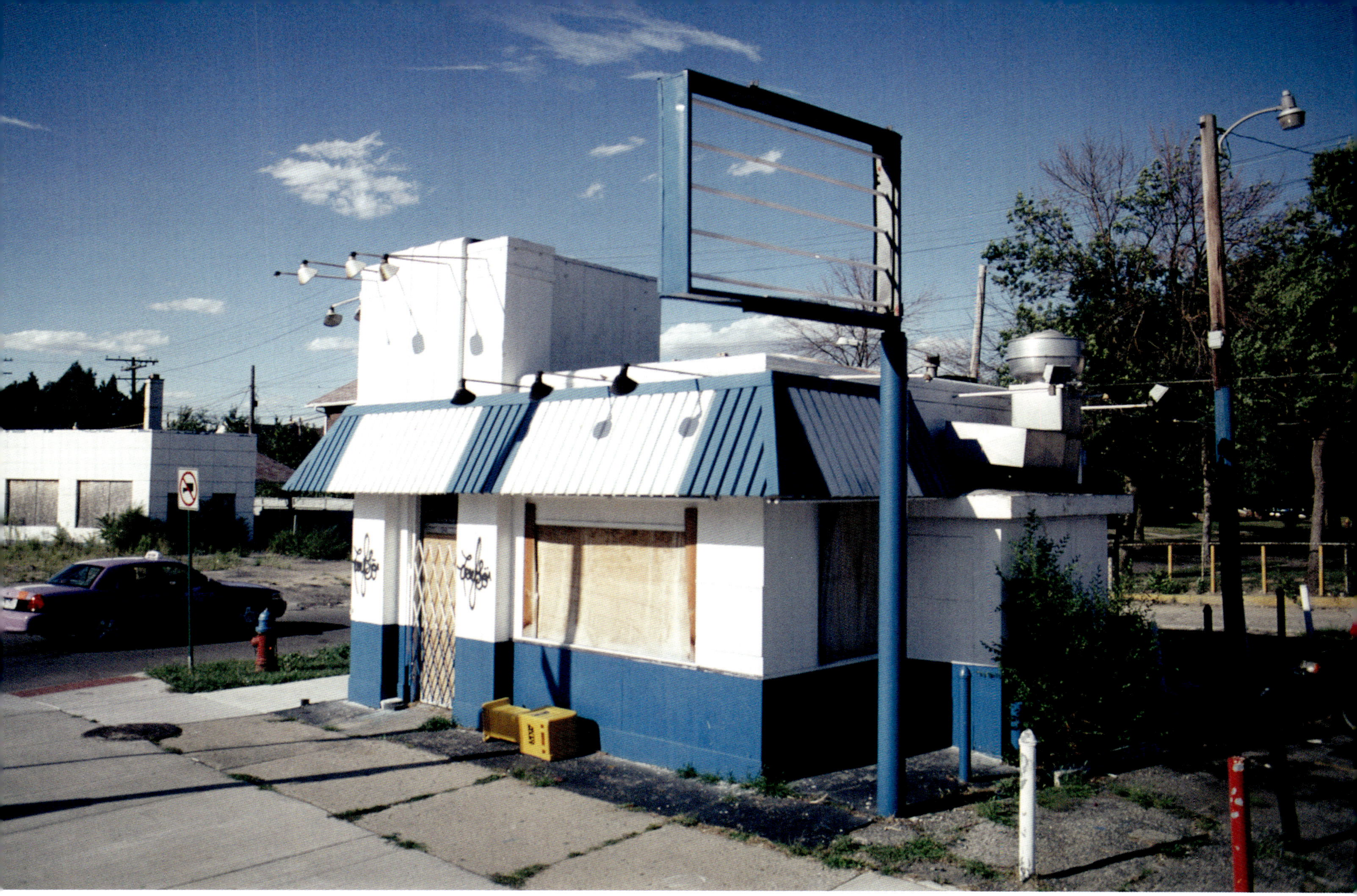

Former Berry's Grill. Woodward Avenue at West Dakota Avenue, Highland Park, 2007.

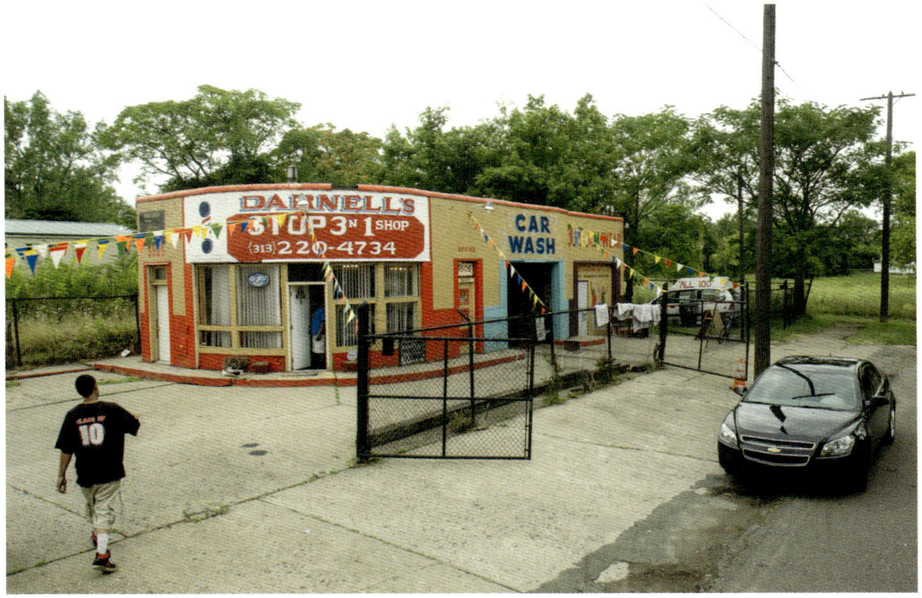

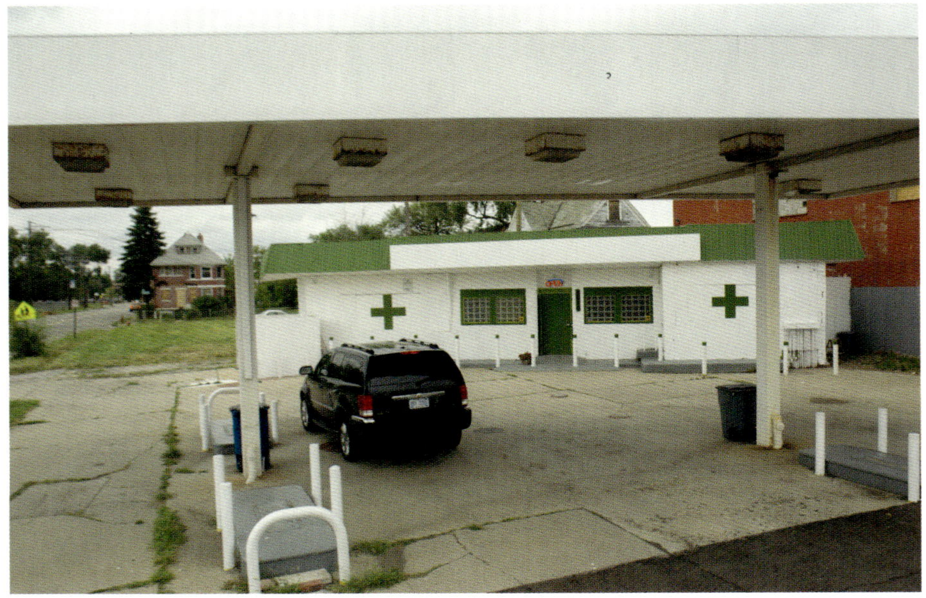

Darnell's 3 n 1 Shop, including a barbershop, a car wash, and the Dreamwear store that sells t-shirts. Darnell, the owner, has been there for six years. East Grand Boulevard at Helen Street, Detroit, 2015.

Marijuana dispensary in a former BP gas station. Beaubien Street at East Grand Boulevard, Detroit, 2015.

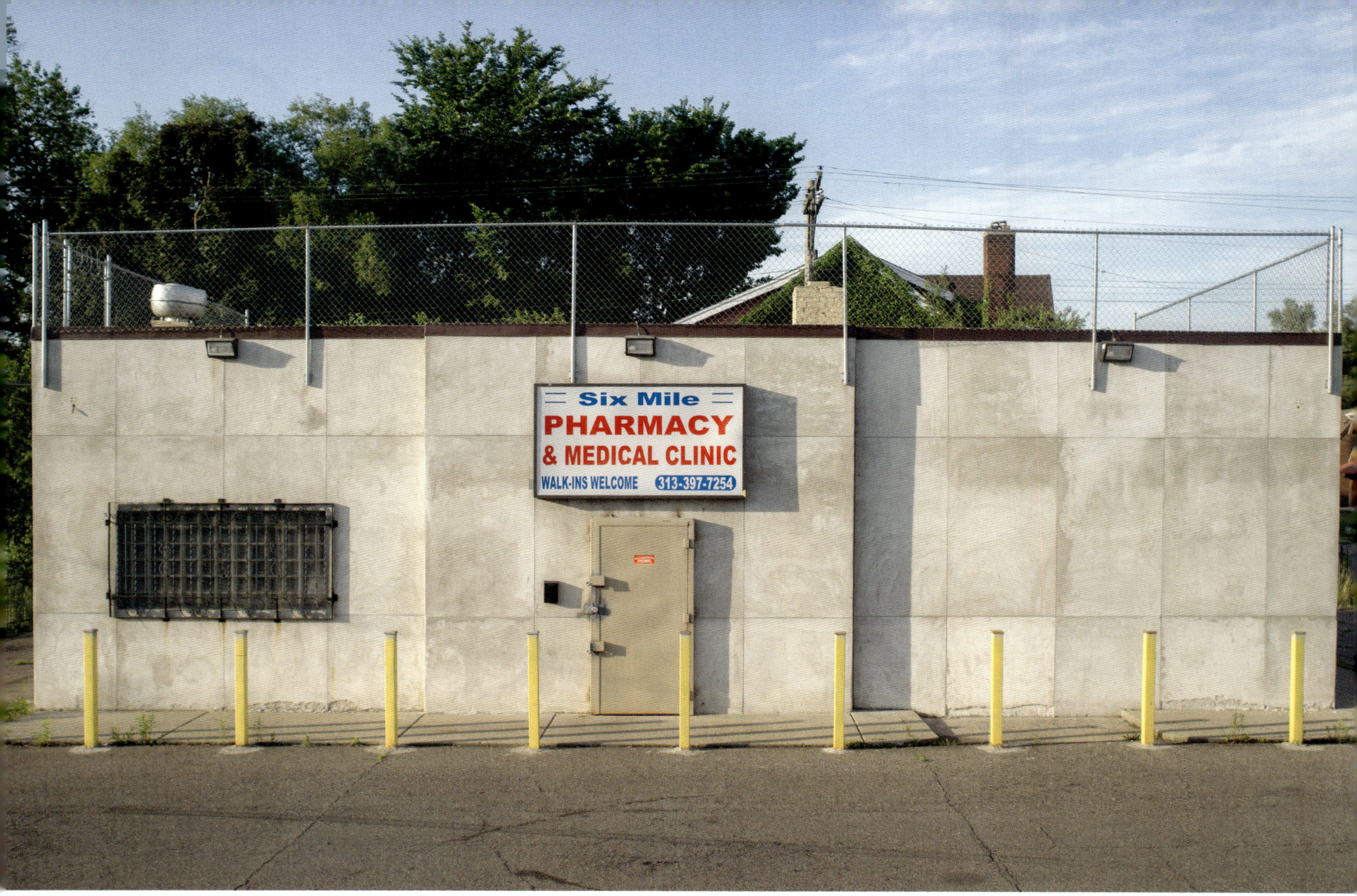

The fortress-like Six Mile Pharmacy and Medical Clinic.
West McNichols Road at Monica Street, Detroit, 2014.

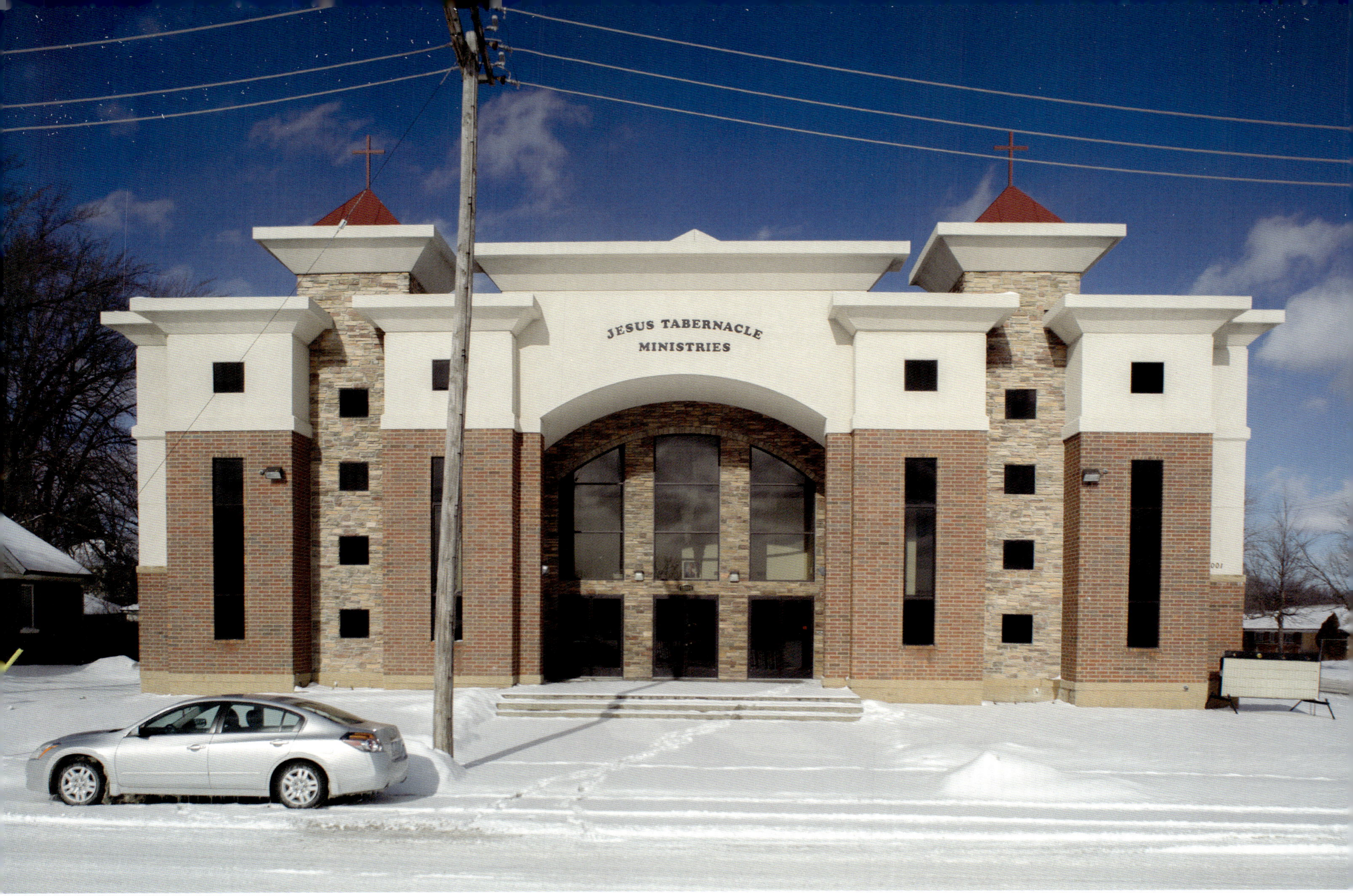

Jesus Tabernacle Ministries. "The anointing is real," remarked a congregant.
11001 Chalmers Avenue, Detroit, 2014.

OASES AMIDST DESOLATION: DETROIT'S NEW ARCHITECTURE

Detroit abounds with a certain kind of fantasy architecture that is practical, clean, well lit, safe, comfortable, and usually in good repair; such buildings were not to be seen ten years ago. Brightly colored cladding made of Dryvit, a pliable, inexpensive material, allows builders to create arches, cantilever roofs, and shape building contours into ornamental forms. New and refurbished fast food franchises, gentlemen's clubs, churches, liquor stores, marijuana dispensaries, and convenience stores, dressed up in foam with a shell surface, are covered with strange, exaggerated shapes. On the exterior, large planes of color and flashing screens designed to catch the eye attract drivers to these businesses and organizations.

At night, brightly lit 24-hour fast food places called "coney islands" resemble the painting *The Nighthawks* by Edward Hopper. With customers illuminated behind the glass, these eateries seem like oases, unlike the ubiquitous silhouetted, bunker-like buildings with their small, barred windows, metal doors, and concertina wire running along the roof. Competing with national chains such as Subway, KFC, Little Caesars Pizza, and White Castle, these coney islands are mostly owned by families of Greek and Albanian descent.

Simon, originally from Albania, purchased Universal Coney Island from an owner who had bought the palm trees and was responsible for the overall design: Motown's version of Southern California style, with patio furniture and bright colors. Simon explained the popularity of these colorful façades, saying, "When somebody does something and makes some money, they have followers who copy them." Yet he is no fan of Dryvit because "it is real soft." Instead, he likes brick because "it lasts a real long time." He attributes Universal's popularity not to the design but to "the best quality" food.

Nicky D Coney Island, on Grand River Avenue, was originally a White Castle. Its shape and landscaping has changed little with the change of ownership, but its color scheme went dramatically from white and blue to orange, red, and maroon, and the outside texture was so transformed with brick and stone facing that its origin as a White Castle is no longer discernible. Morris, the manager, calls this "the Vegas look," attributing the redesign to Ziggy, the Albanian owner of the Nicky D chain. Most of the customers are African Americans who come because they like the bright building and the freshly prepared food. The restaurant is open, with bullet proof glass windows that allow light to come in during the day and for the interior to be seen from the outside at night.

Churches also use Dryvit on their façades, but less flamboyantly. Jesus Tabernacle Ministries, with its stressed symmetry, was built in 2005 before Detroit's bankruptcy, when more people had jobs. Pastor Elaine Billy would like for the church to revitalize the neighborhood, but now "there is no money." She nevertheless believes that God is good and that "money is going to come." The church, on the site of a former apartment complex, cost about $3 million. Pastor Billy wanted the church to resemble Noah's Ark, and remarked that she wished for columns as well but they were too expensive. The architect presented her with a drawing she liked.

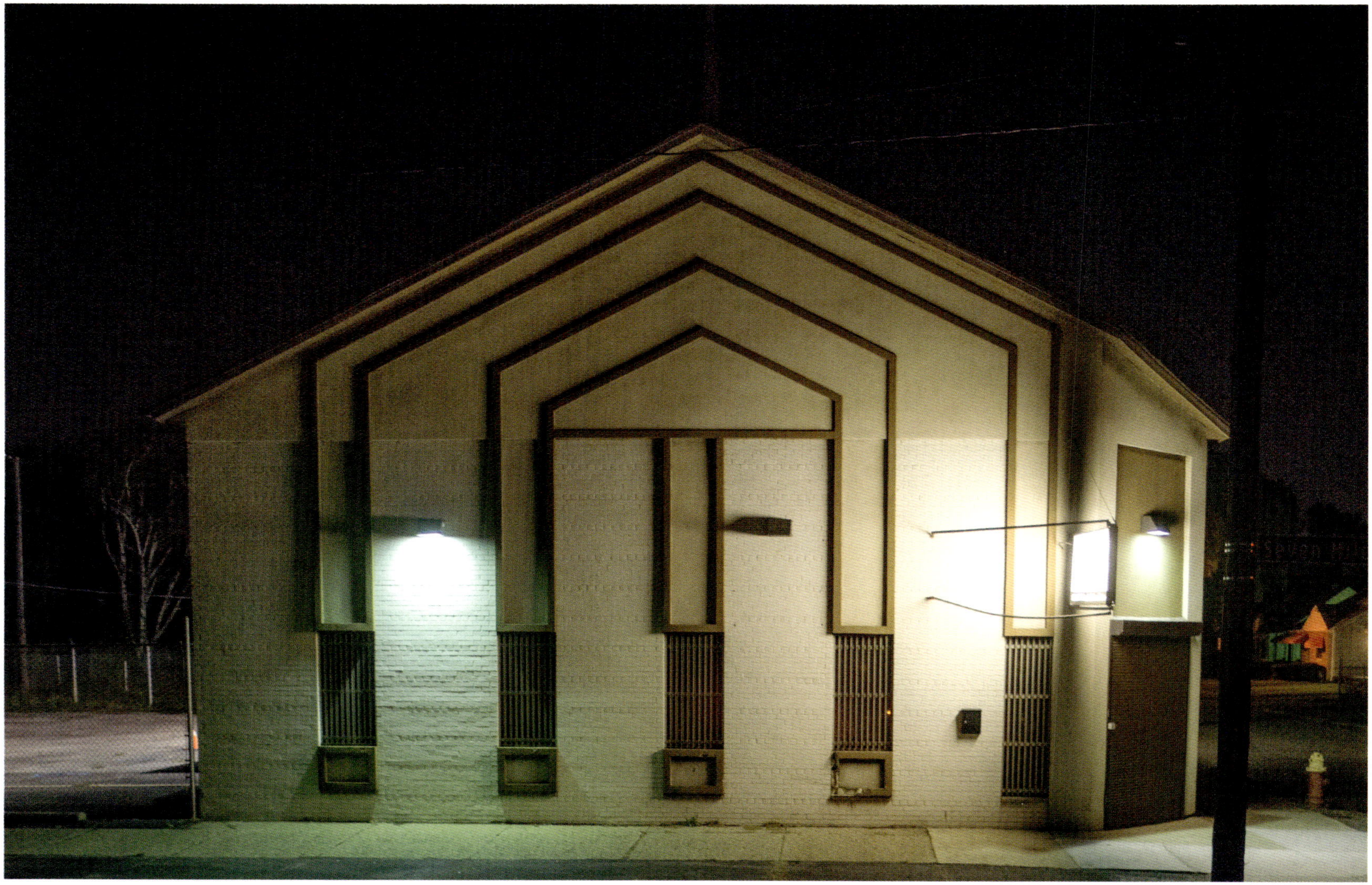

Good Hope Missionary Baptist Church of Detroit, located in a former industrial building; Jimmie Jackson is the pastor. 12051 East Seven Mile Road, Detroit, 2013.

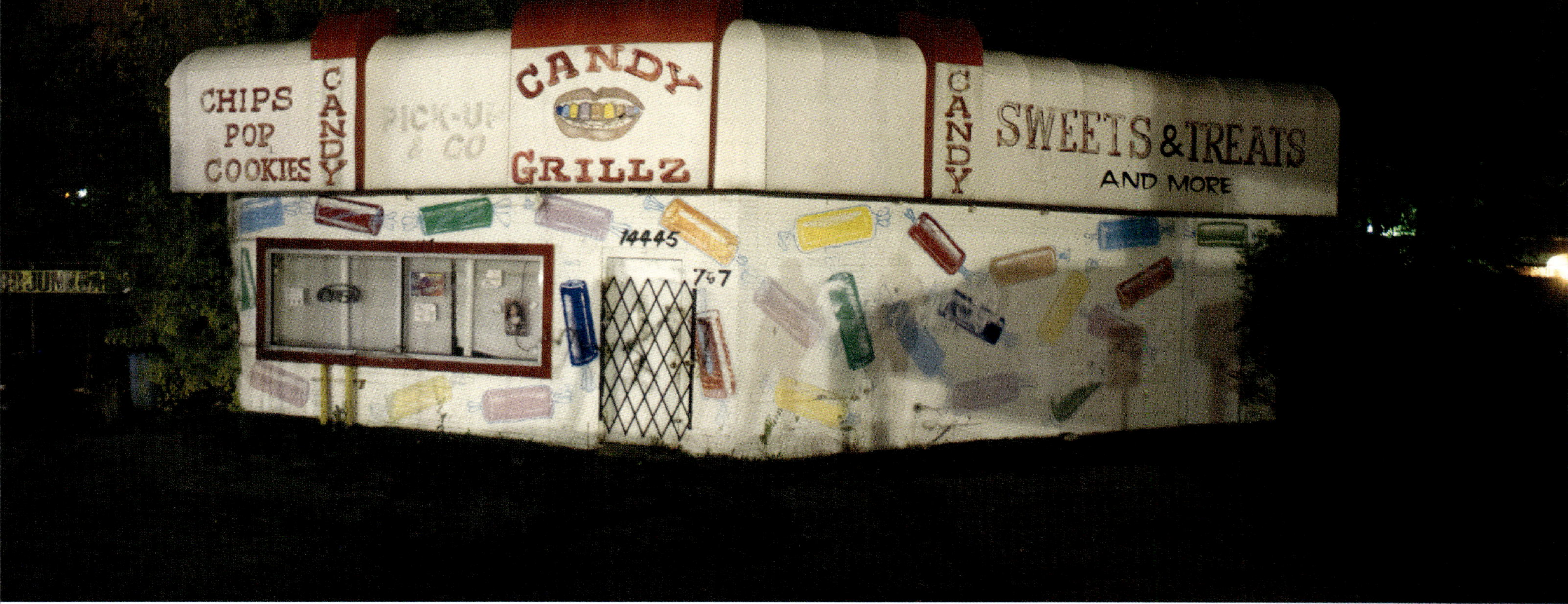

Candy Grillz. At night, its black base makes it seem to float.
14445 Fenkell Avenue at Strathmoor Street, Detroit, 2013.

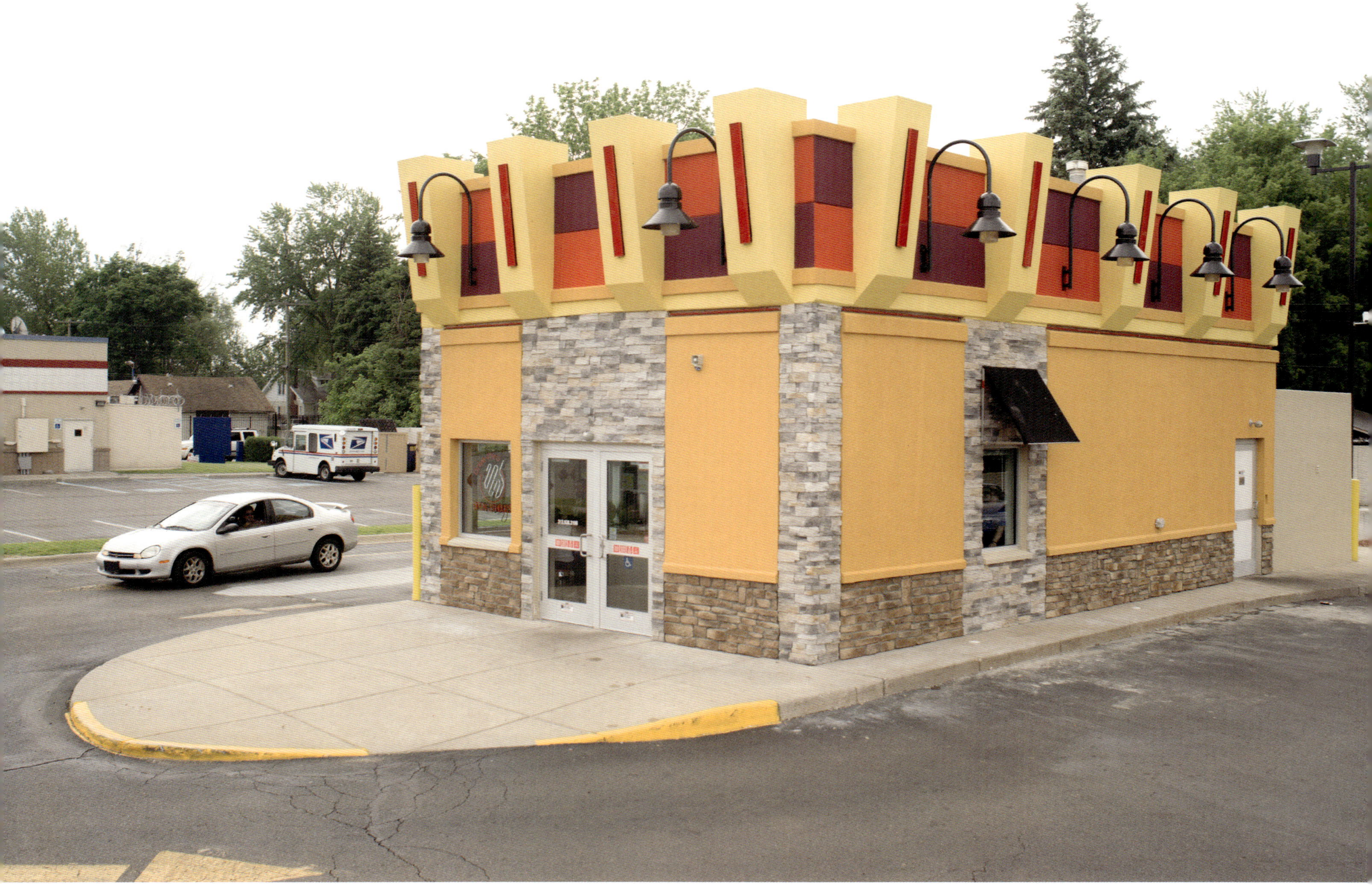

Drive-through for Nicky D Coney Island, formerly Rio Grill, and before that a White Castle. Grand River Avenue at Northrop Street, Detroit, 2014.

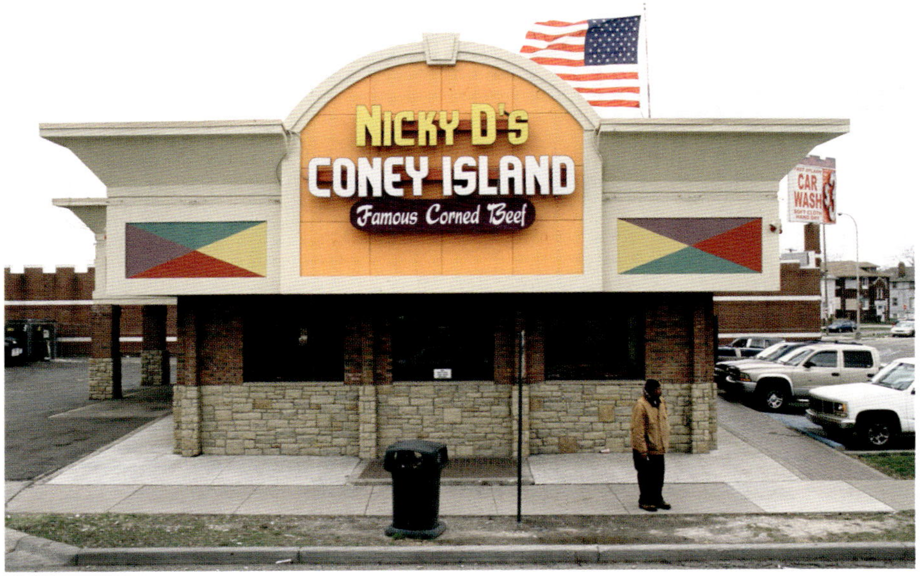

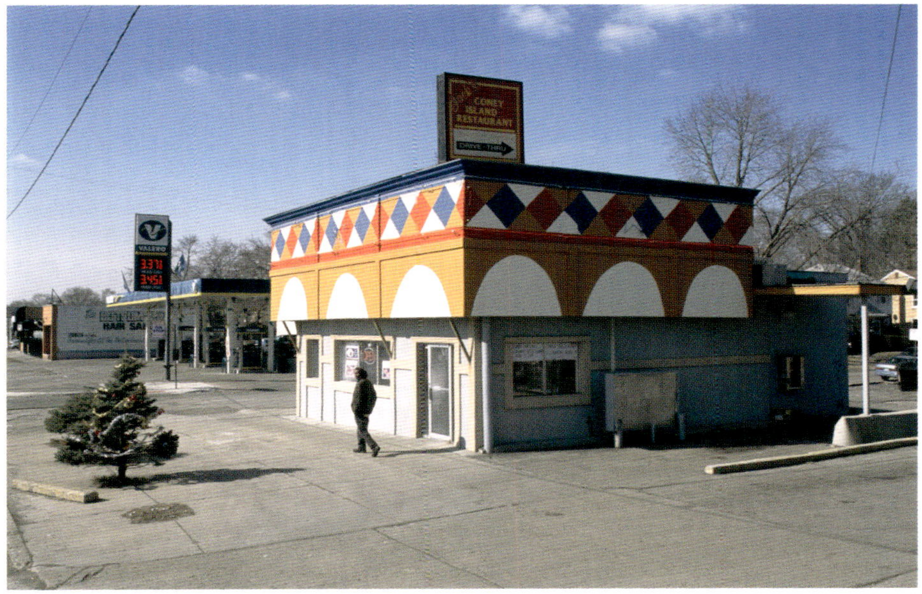

Nicky D Coney Island. Rehabilitated building decorated with Dryvit siding—taken to the extreme—and painted in Tex-Mex colors. West Warren Avenue at Livernois Avenue, Detroit, 2011.

Jack's Coney Island Restaurant. West Seven Mile Road at Pierson Street, Detroit, 2012.

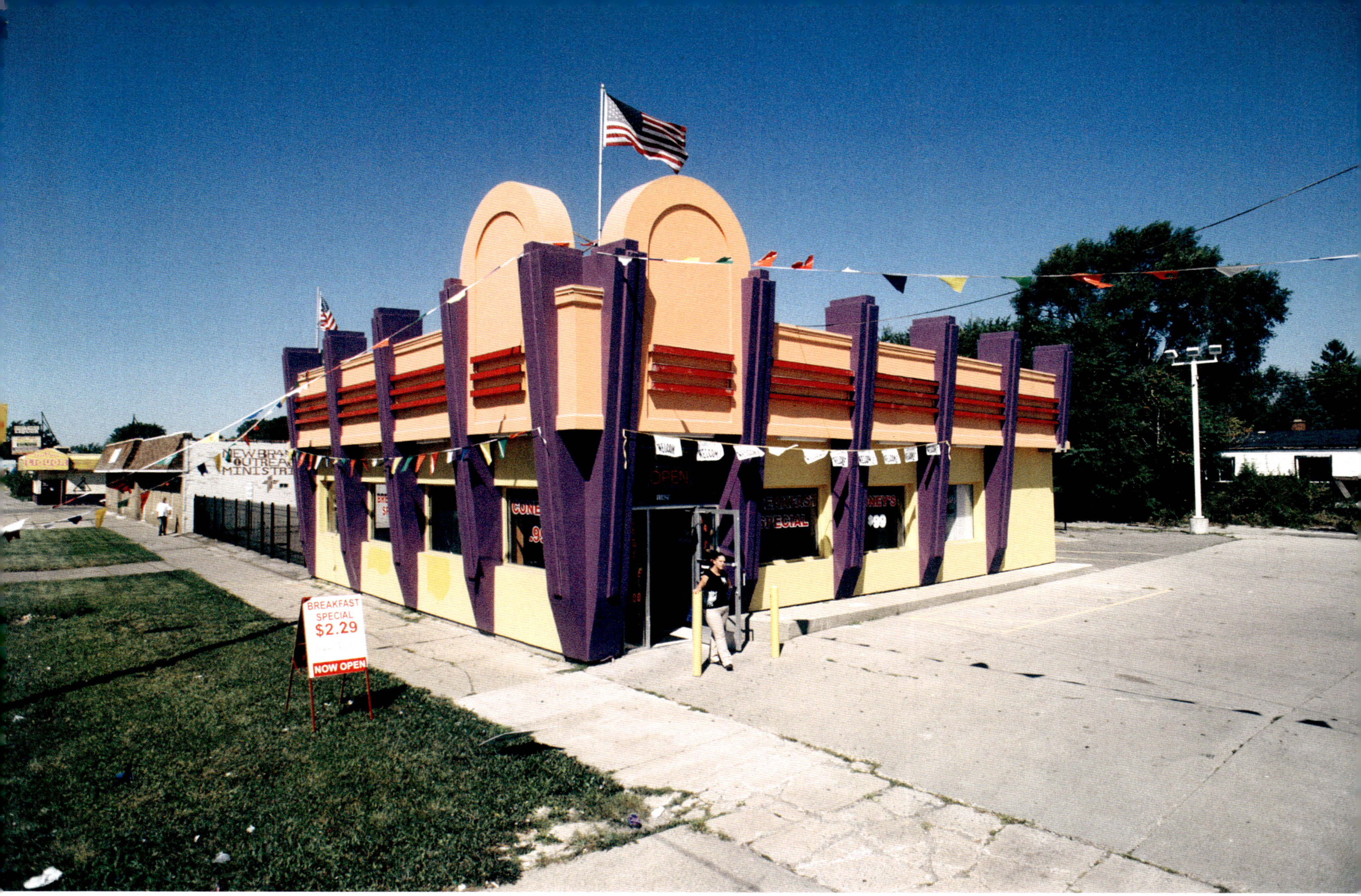

2 Brothers Soul Food. East Seven Mile Road at Albion Street, Detroit, 2010.

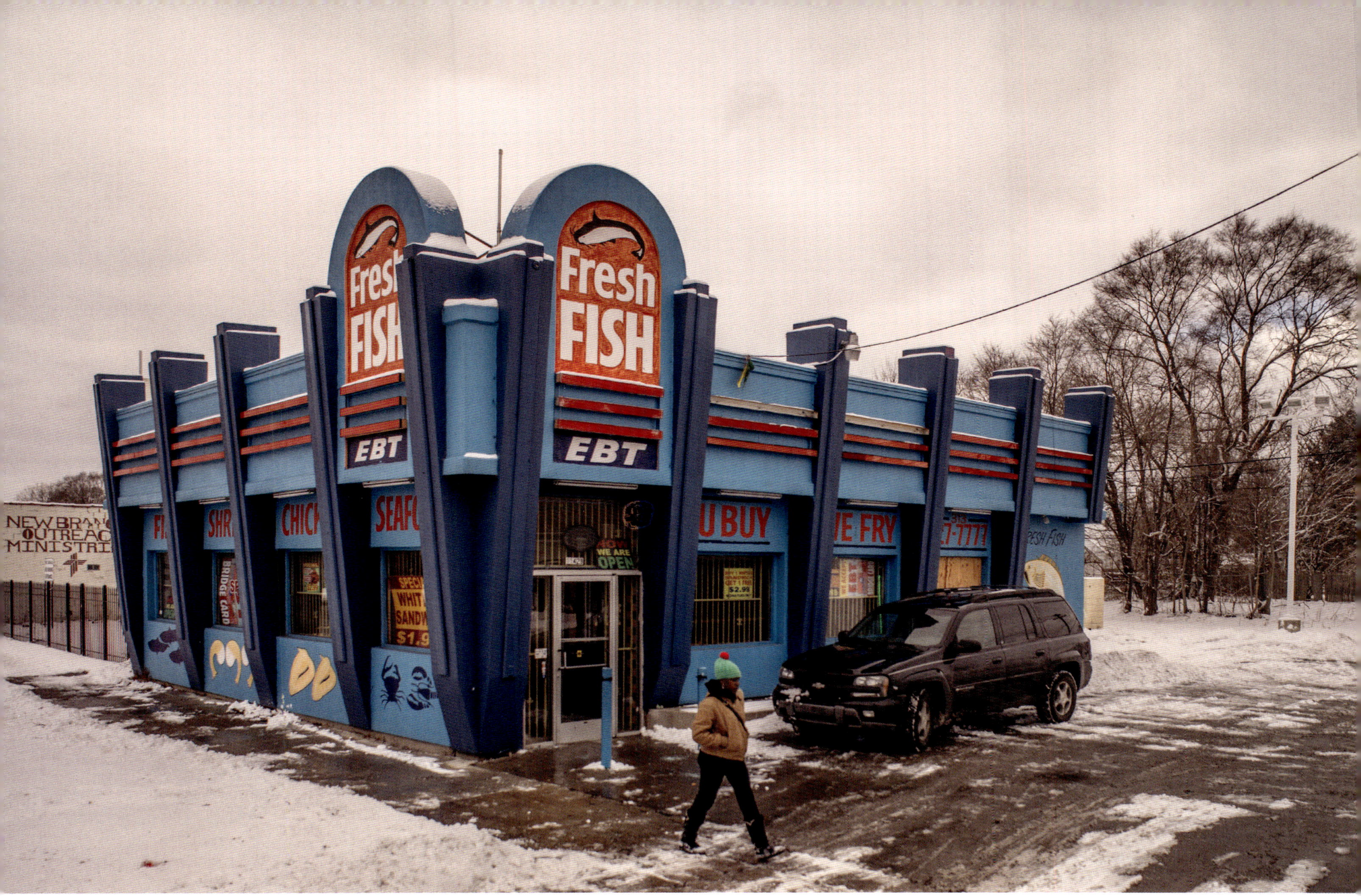

Royal Fish and Chicken. East Seven Mile Road at Albion Street, Detroit, 2015.

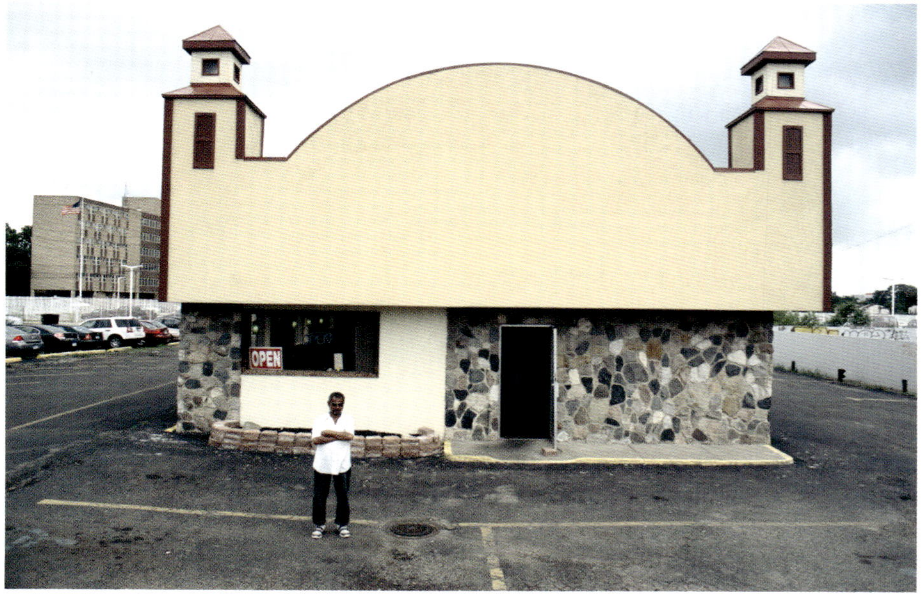

Pauly's Grill: "We are not the best, just the greatest." 1008 East Warren Avenue, Detroit, 2011.

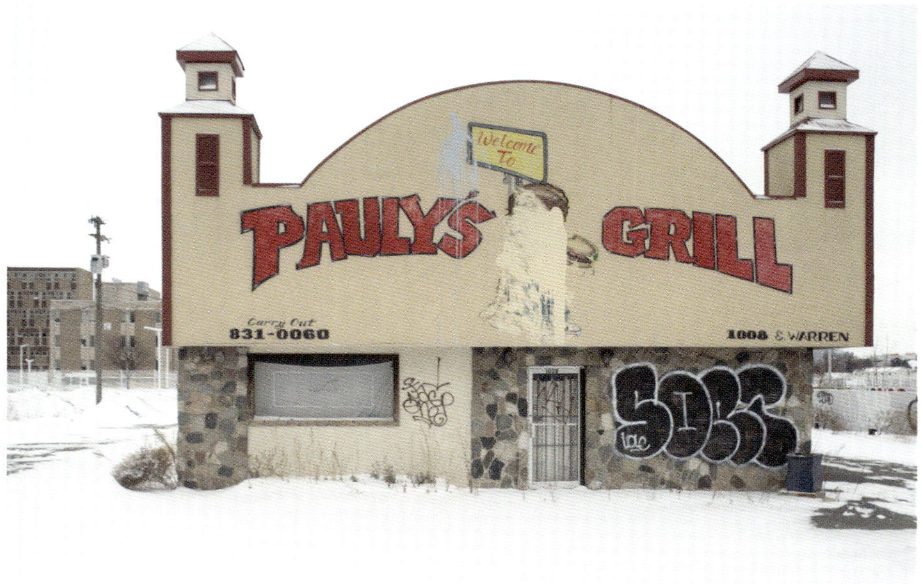

Pauly's Grill, vacant. 1008 East Warren Avenue, Detroit, 2014.

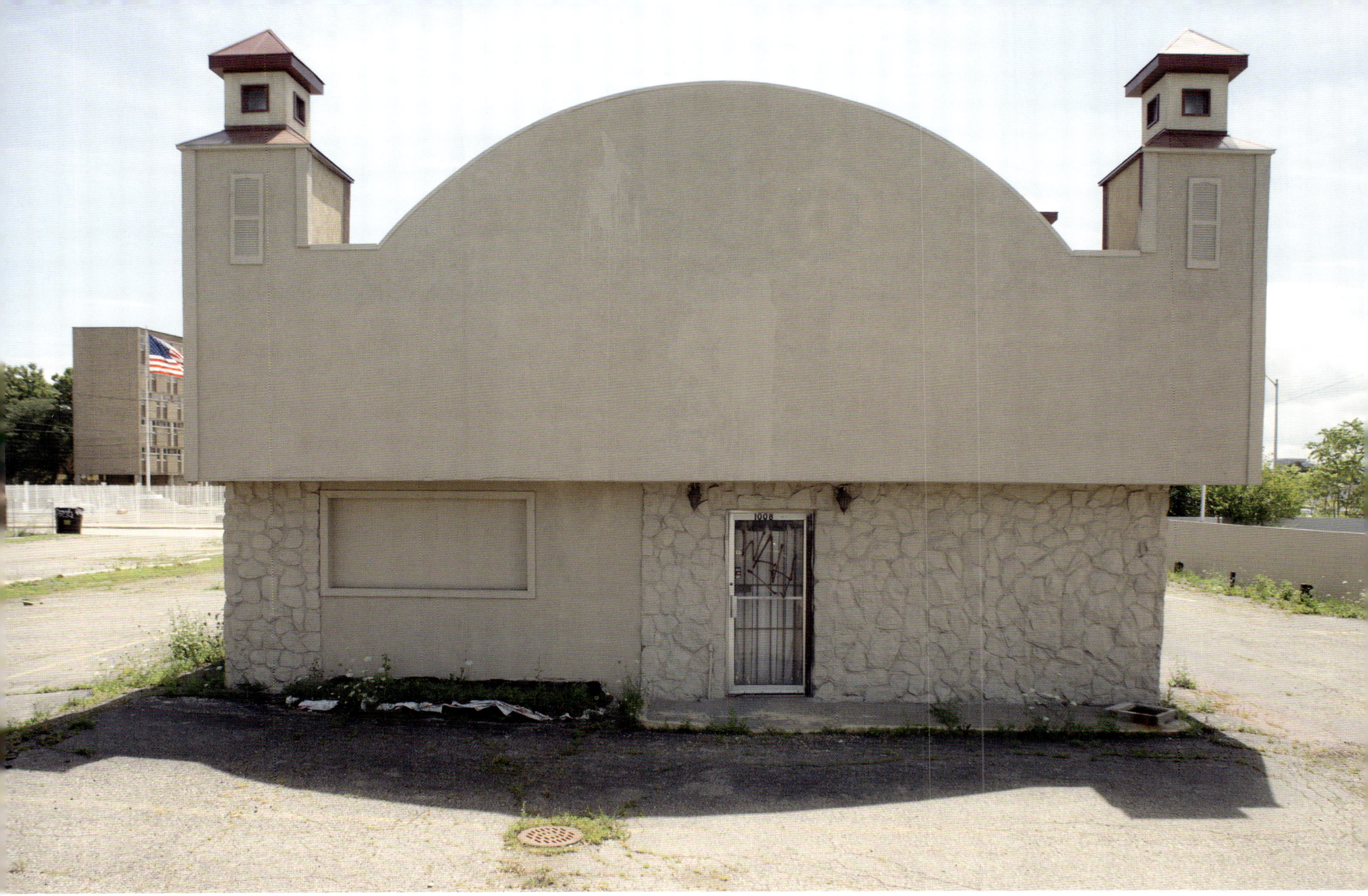

Former Pauly's Grill. 1008 East Warren Avenue, Detroit, 2015.

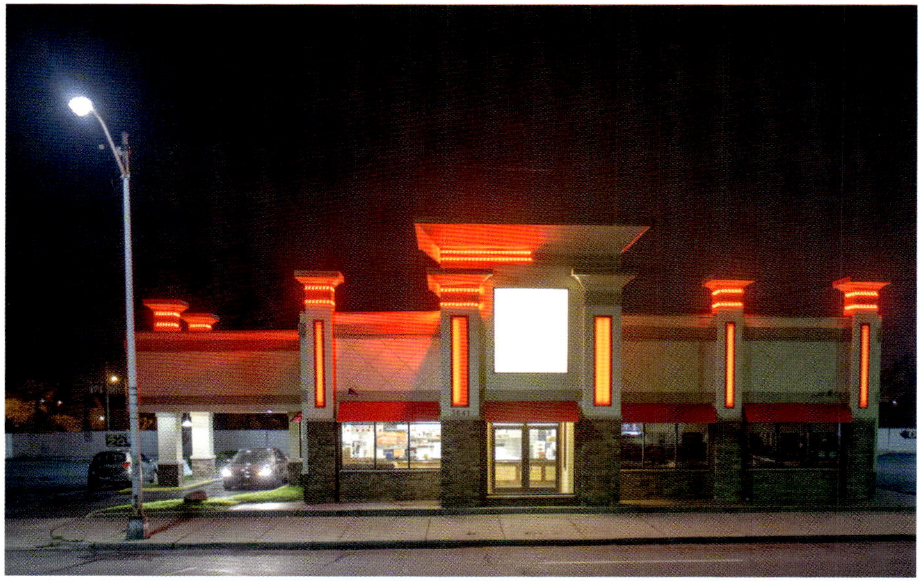

Motor City Grill and Restaurant at night. A man asked me: "Hey man, what do you do? Why are you taking pictures?" Grand River Boulevard at Magnolia Street, Detroit, 2013.

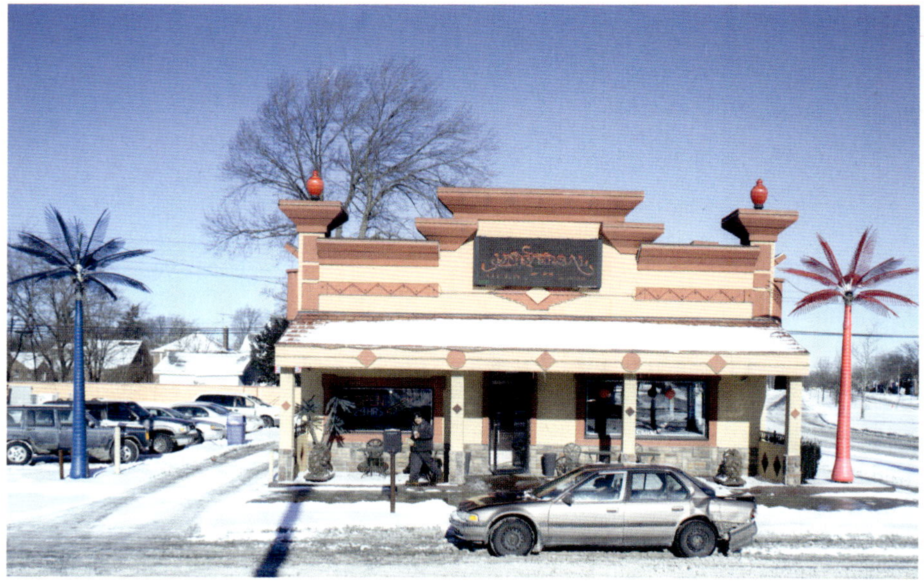

Universal Coney Island. Harper Avenue at Outer Drive East, Detroit, 2014.

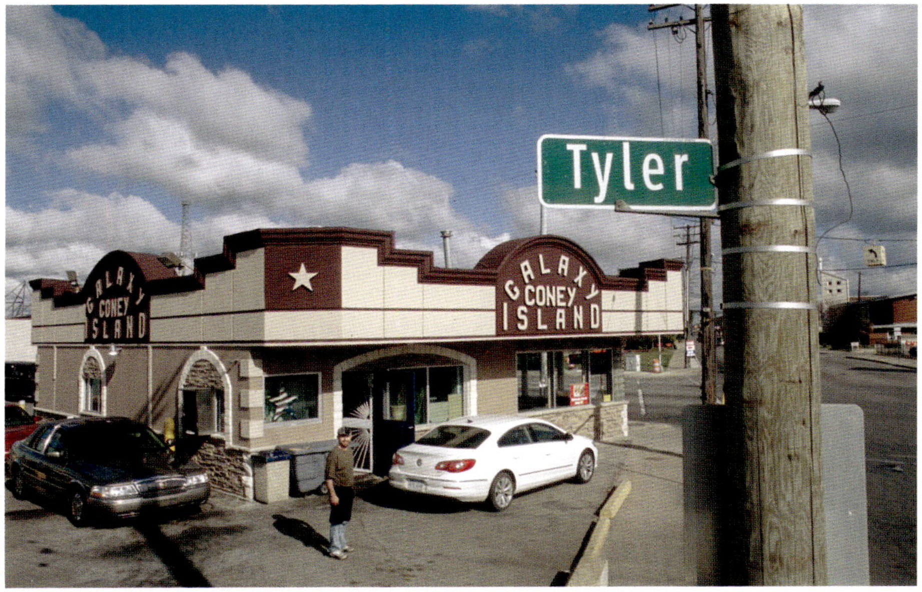

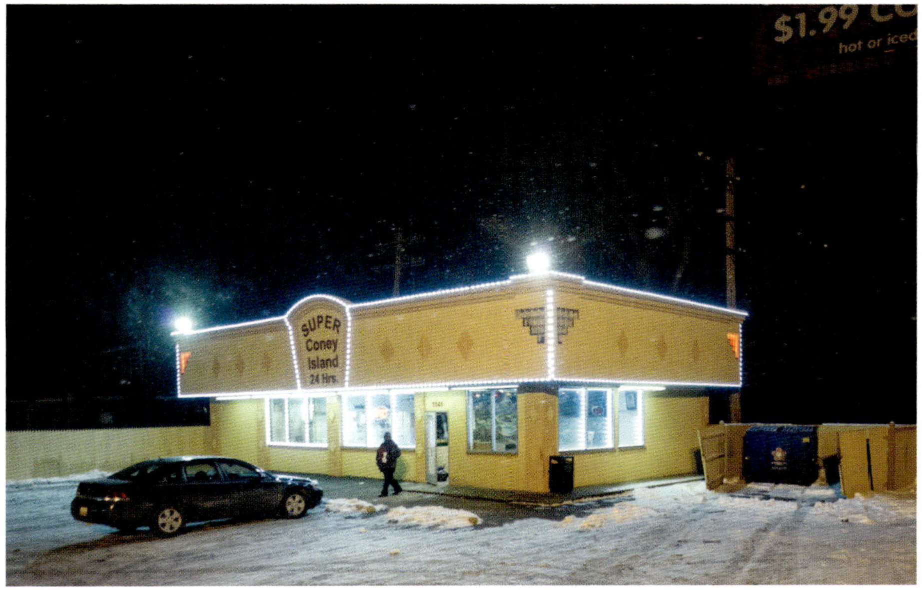

The Albanian-owned Galaxy Coney Island. Schaffer Highway at Grand River Boulevard, Detroit, 2012.

Super Coney Island. A remark on Yelp: “Food here is great! But once in awhile the crowd can get a little wild, mind the bullet holes on the outside.” 1141 Clay Street, Detroit, 2015.

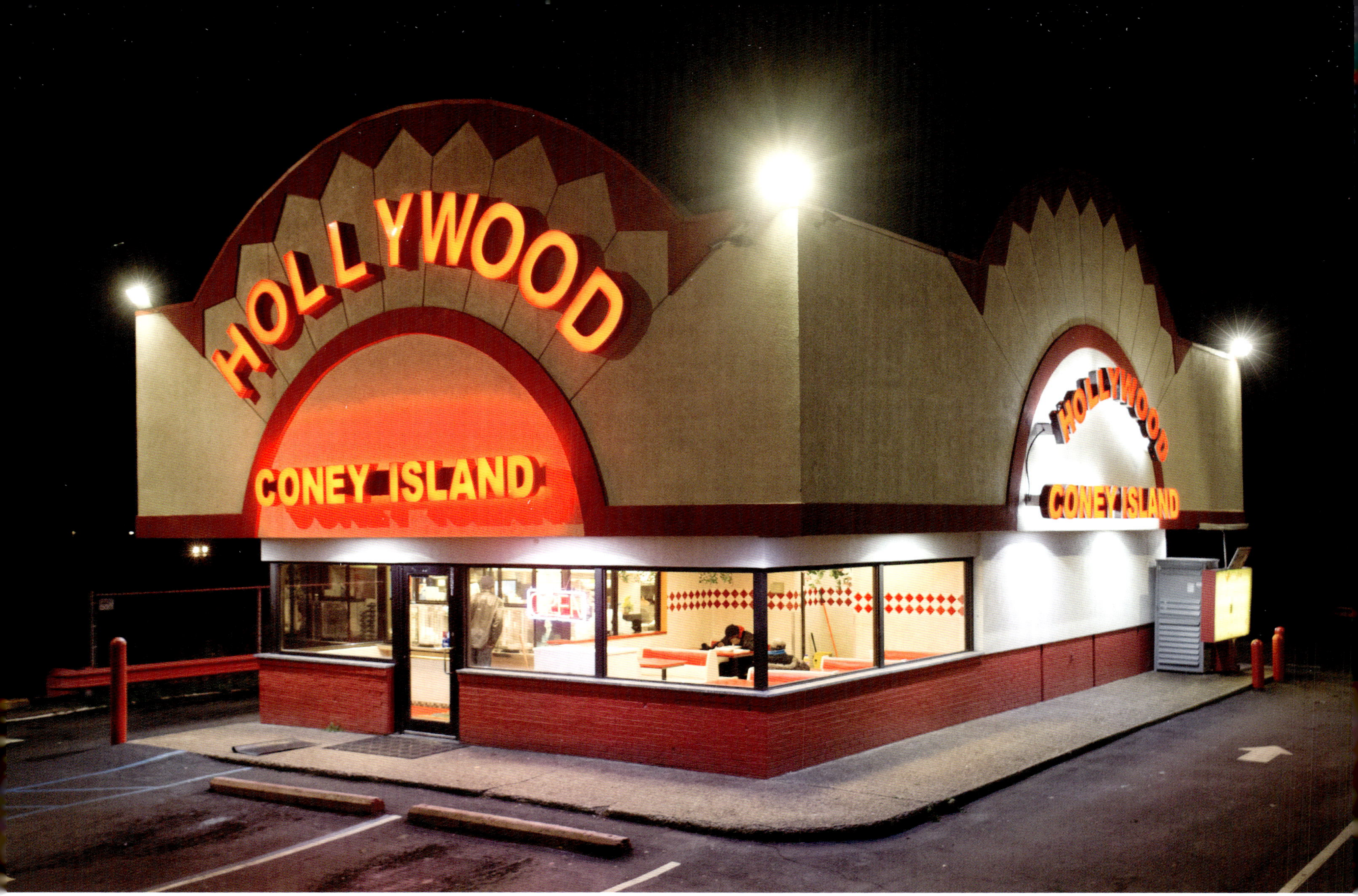

Hollywood Coney Island, formerly a Church's Chicken outlet. Upon seeing the man seemingly asleep in my night photograph of the restaurant, Rail, who sells videos there, commented: "Anybody could have gotten him in his sleep. It is very easy to get you in your sleep." Gratiot Avenue at Harper Avenue, Detroit, 2013.

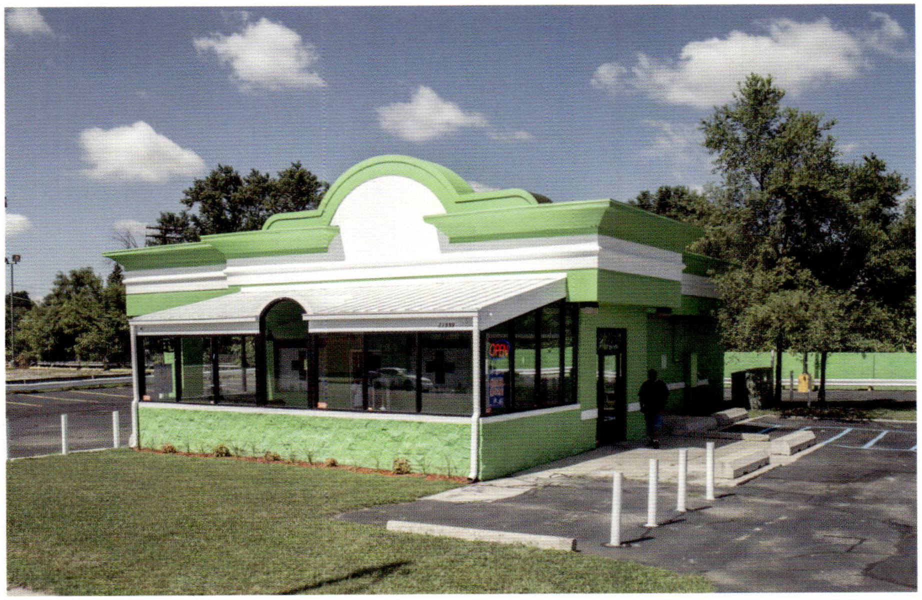

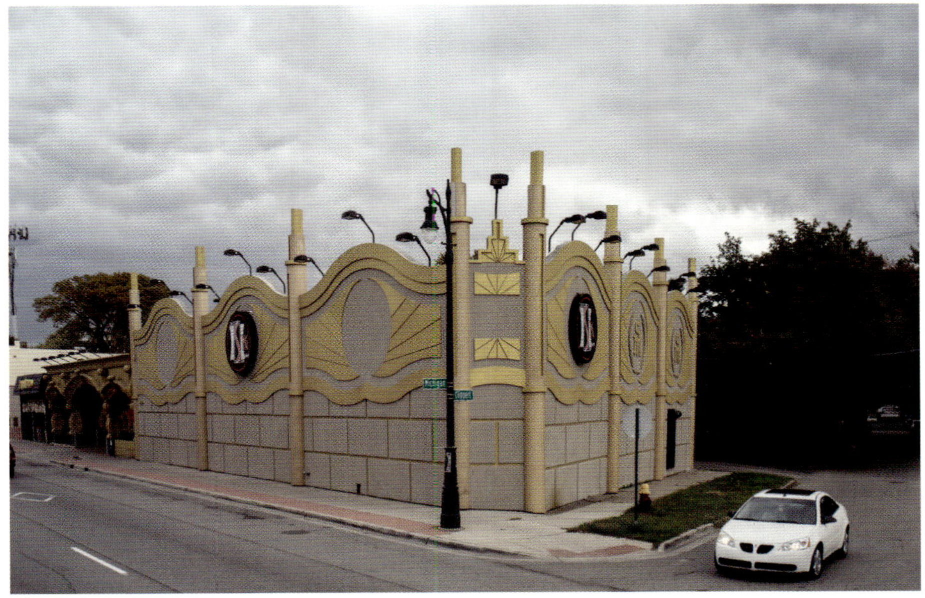

Marijuana dispensary, formerly R. S. Soul Food and a coney island.
11999 Gratiot Avenue, Detroit, 2015.

Sting, gentlemen's club, formerly Vegas Strip Club. Michigan Avenue
at Clippert Street, Detroit, 2013.

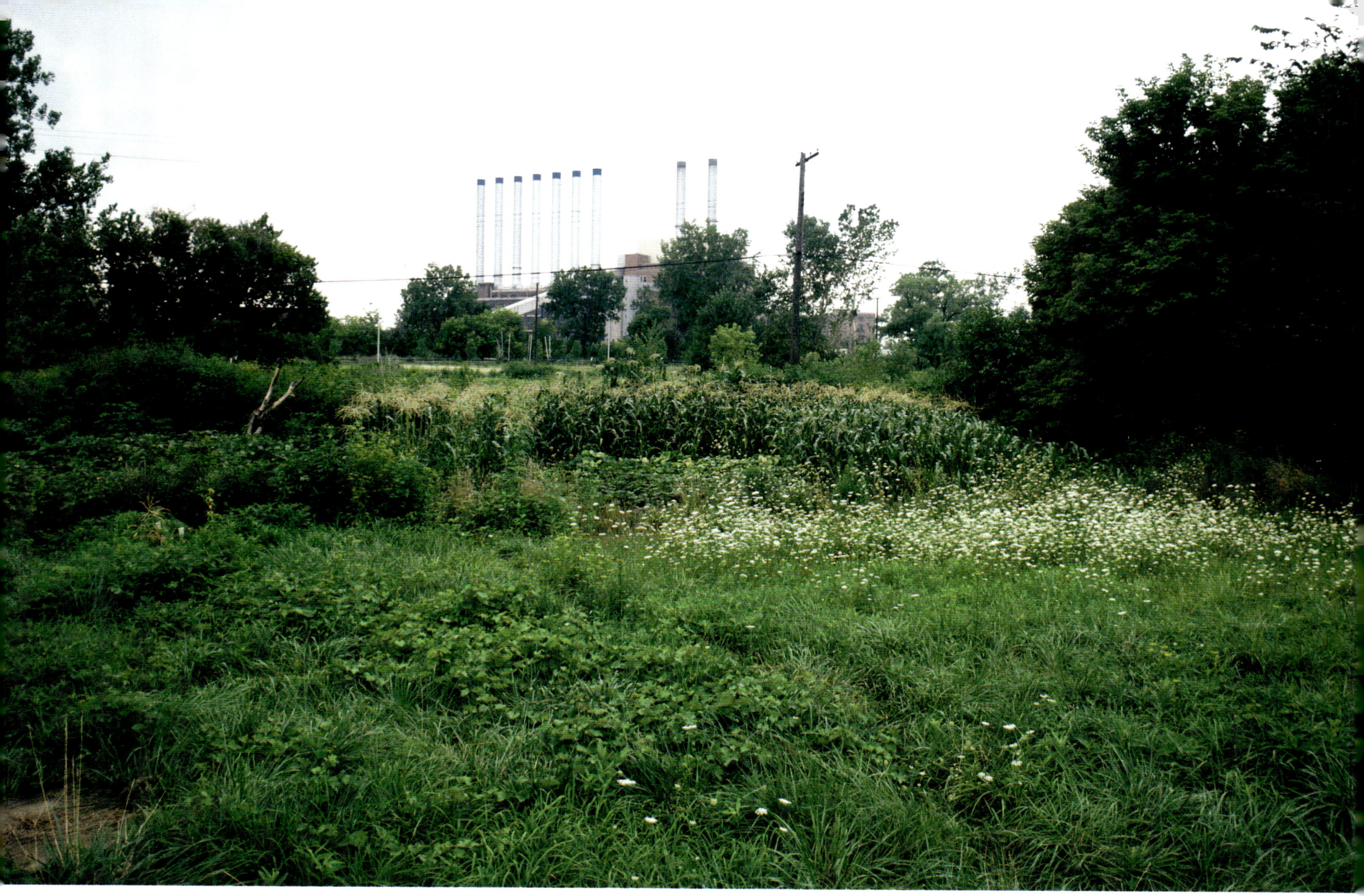

Cornfields in front of the "Seven Sisters" Power Station. The seven original smoke-stacks were built in 1915 and demolished in 1996. The larger "two brothers" remain. Near Clairpointe Street and Essex Avenue, Detroit, 1987.

"FARM CITY": REPLACING BLIGHT WITH BEAUTY

Abandoned buildings in Detroit are expensive to refurbish and dangerous if left standing, and, with a declining population, they are not needed. As they get in the way of development, they have a "negative energy." Accelerating the transformation of the once continuous urban fabric into a cluster of villages has become a mission in Detroit, bringing together different groups of people and foundations. The leader of this mission is John George of Blight Busters, who elevated blight to the city's #1 problem. The need to rehabilitate abandoned structures has been transformed into a resolve to "replace blight with beauty"—that is, to demolish vacant properties and to cultivate the cleared land. In numerous videos, vacant structures are shown being demolished, with images of rows of corn, tomatoes, and flowers, the sun shining, and smiling children, a new America rising. In contrast, clearing abandoned buildings in Cleveland, Gary, or Camden goes on unremarked.

Among the pioneers are young suburbanites for whom growing vegetables and raising farm animals has the magic of the real, and Christian evangelists who equate blight with sin as well as local residents with roots in the rural South who never forgot their origins. To these one must add the Capuchins, who are growing food at their Earth Works Urban Farm and have been feeding the hungry since before the Great Depression. There is also John Hantz, a businessman who in a for-profit enterprise is farming and planting "high value trees" on one square mile of the city near Indian Village, "the world's largest urban farm."

In 2008, Mark Covington, finding himself out of work, started the Georgia Street Community Collective where with the help of volunteers he raises goats, pigs, bees, chickens, and flowers. Mark knew little about farming; his initial interest was to stop people from dumping garbage on the empty land across from his grandmother's house. His office and community center is in a former liquor store with a sign saying "Plant a Seed Watch it Grow" on the wall. The Georgia Street Community Collective has attracted international attention. In addition to Detroit school children, visitors and volunteers come to his urban gardens from as far away as Nigeria, Kenya, Brazil, Korea, Germany, and England.

Bill Walton is a recently retired bus driver who in 2013 bought a greenhouse, with funding from the USDA, from a farmer on Acacia Street and installed it in a lot he owns across from his house on Woodlawn Street. "My dad was a farmer," said Bill, adding, "I was interested in things that grow. I was raised on a farm in Georgia . . . I liked the idea of growing lettuce, peppers, tomatoes, flowers, and swiss chard." He is now able to sell produce to distributors in Eastern Market.

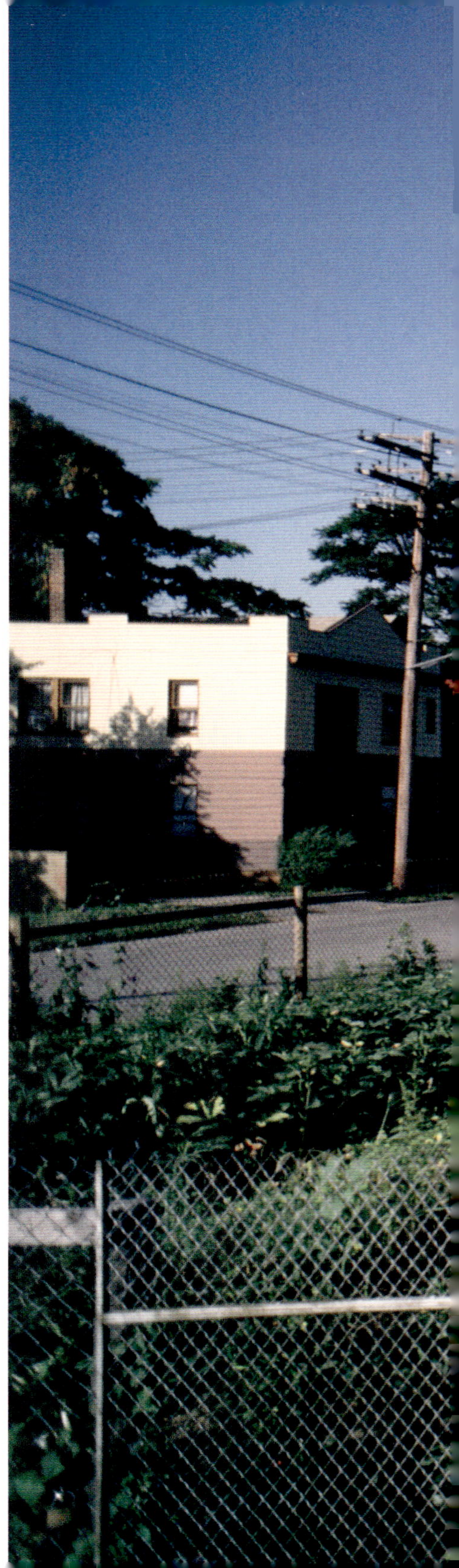

Hutchins Cole, retired construction worker from Bufford, Georgia, in Detroit for forty years. Rosa Parks Boulevard, Detroit, 1987.

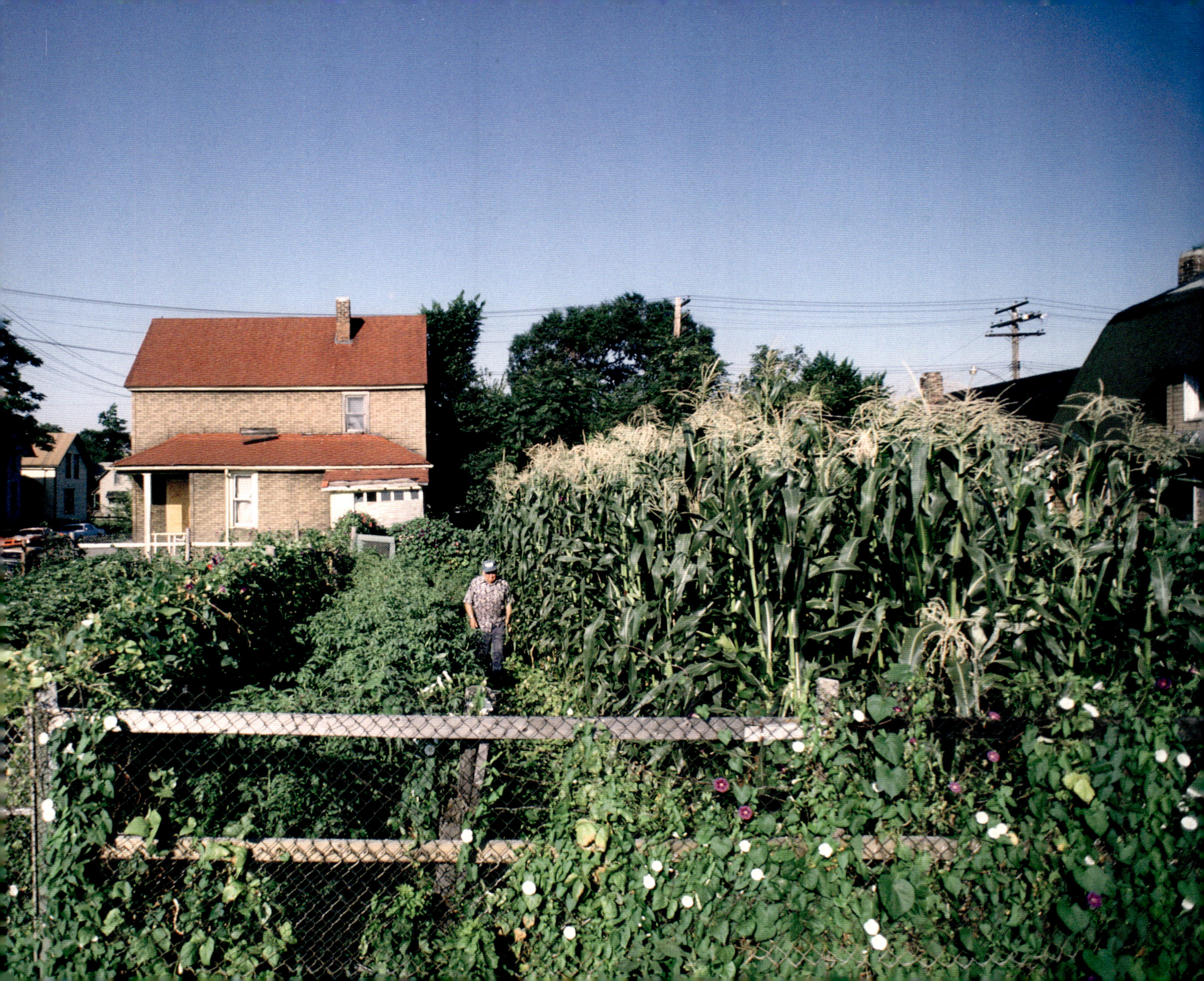

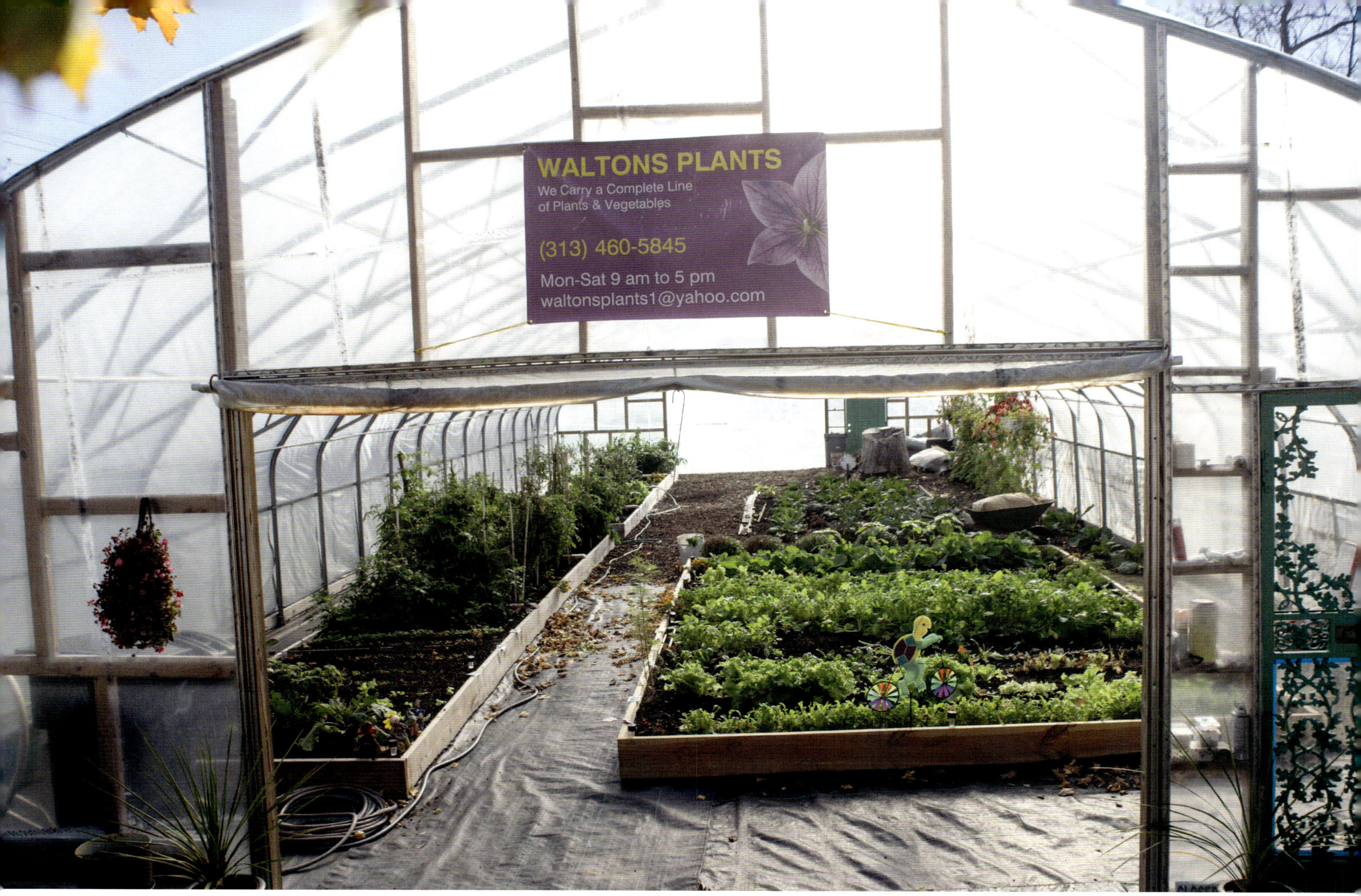

Bill Walton's greenhouse, Woodland Street at McClellan Avenue, Detroit, 2015.

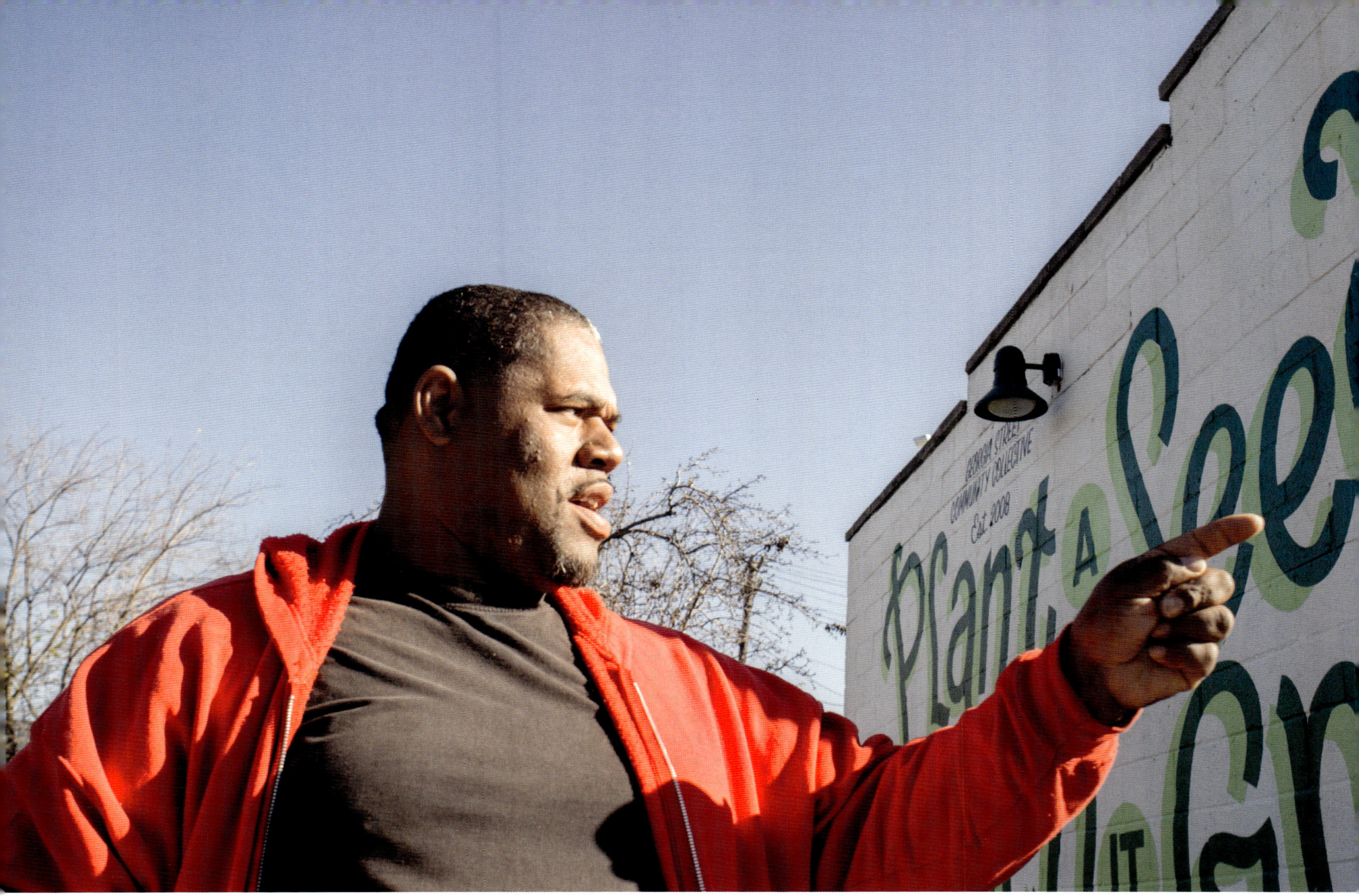

Mark Covington, Georgia Street Community Collective.
Georgia Street at Vinton Avenue, Detroit, 2015.

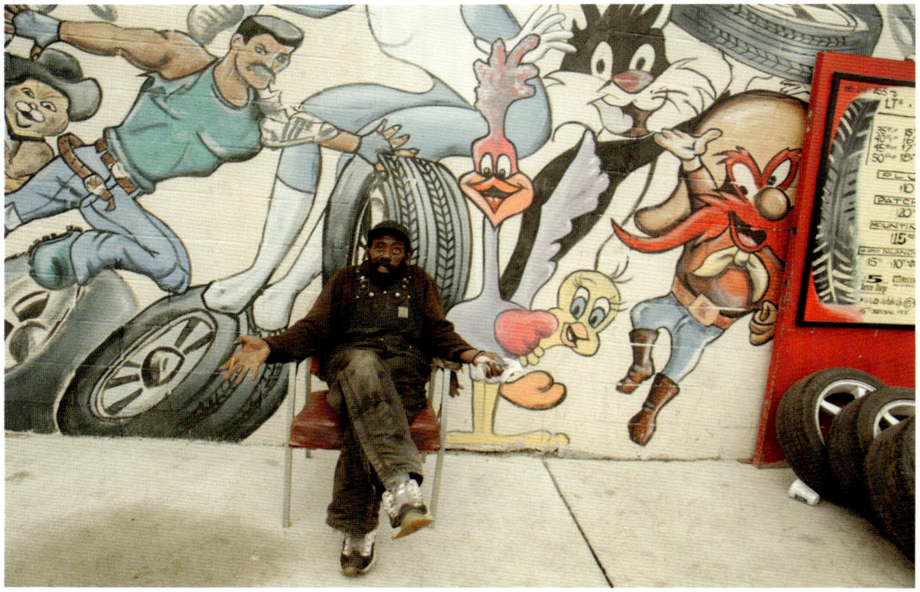

What Is Up Doc? DOT Tires, Made in Detroit. 8500 Van Dyke Avenue, Detroit, 2011.

DETROITERS Without speaking to residents, I could not understand the evolving urban fabric of Detroit. I approached homeless people in downtown to ask their opinion about the vacant skyscrapers and ruins. I stopped people in motorized wheelchairs to ask them what it was like to ride the streets of Detroit, and how far they could go on a charge. Hookers waiting for customers along desolate streets came to talk to me at night as I was minding my camera. I talked to church members preaching and sometimes offering food to passersby. I spoke to Terry at a garage as he was drinking pink Remy Martin Cognac from a plastic cup. He offered me a shot.

I had brief conversations with people on their way to classes, talking on their cell phones, walking in the middle of the street, or when my car broke down and I needed help. I met an eighth-grader selling newspapers in the rain on a corner of Grand River Avenue. On the same street, years later, I met Devin on a freezing January day as he stood holding a sign advertising “Tax Service.” Some of these encounters were extraordinary, as when Catfish showed up silently in the waiting room of the Michigan Central Station. So, too, the self-appointed caretaker of the Packard Plant who, knife in hand, showed my friend Tim Samuelson the proper way to kill.

But all in all I was surprised by the small number of people I found while documenting the city’s great desolate expanses. I thought that emptiness could be expected in zip code 48205, an area of much abandonment. But I also experienced the streets devoid of people in well-populated Corktown. One difference, though, is that in the area of zip code 48205 people often must walk in the streets because the sidewalks are so overgrown.

Online, I had encounters with people whose faces were blurred by Google as they waited for a bus or crossed a street. Sometimes the person disappeared as I clicked on a directional arrow to take a better look. On the corner of Grand River Avenue and Vancouver Street in 2015, for example, a young man wearing an orange t-shirt vanished as I turned on Vancouver to take a closer look; the year I was traveling in had automatically changed to 2011. I thought how this paralleled the disappearance that constantly occurs as streets become impassable or buildings become vacant, and the mood of the uncanny feeling that this creates.

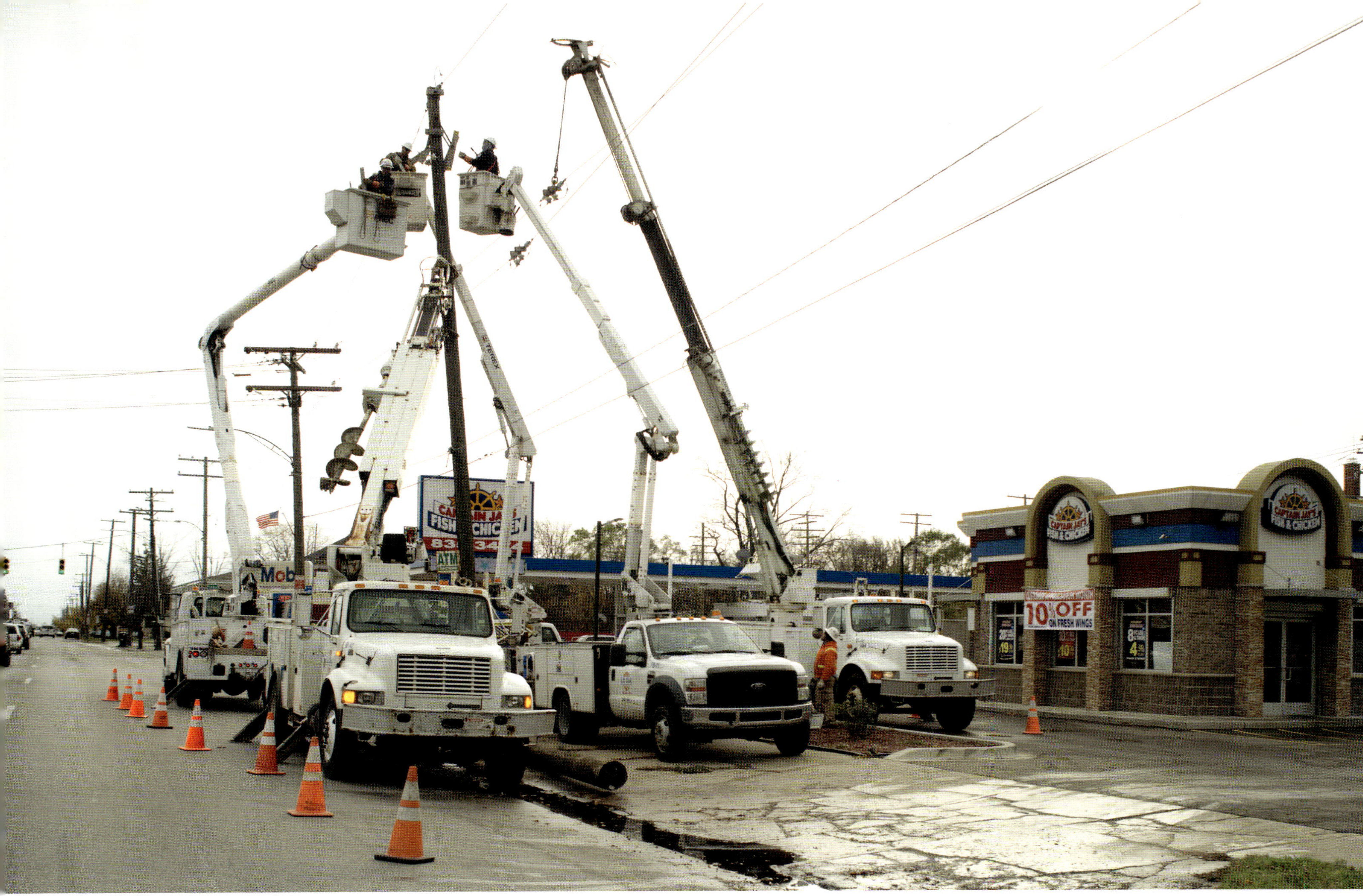

Installing new LED lights. Until a year ago, miles stretching along the city's main avenues were dark at night; 40% of the street lights were not working. Now, according to Mayor Mike Duggan, "The city is making progress." Fenkell Road at Greenfield Road, Detroit, 2015.

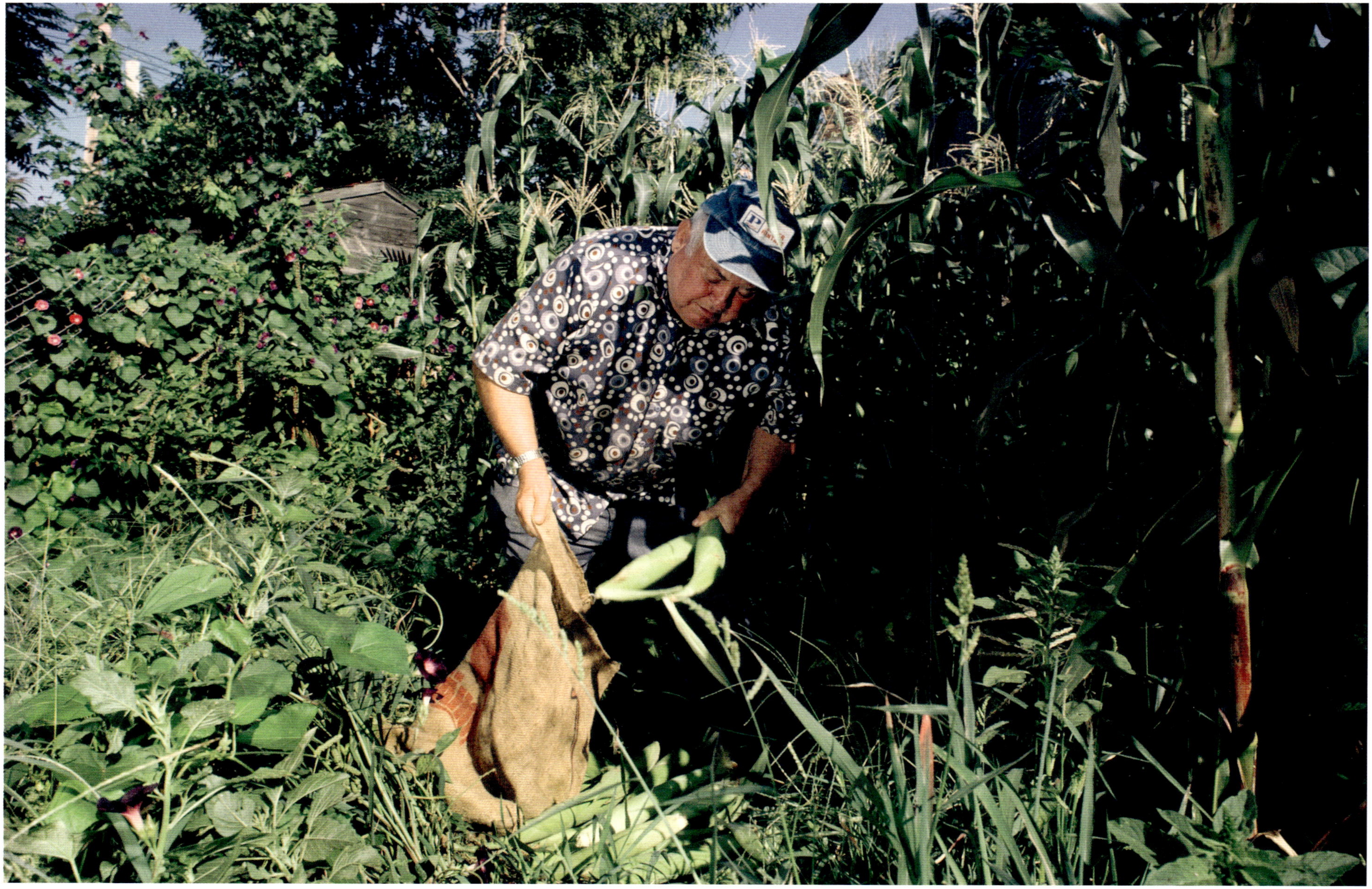

Hutchins Cole, retired construction worker from Bufford, Georgia,
in Detroit for 40 years, Rosa Parks Blvd., Detroit, 1987

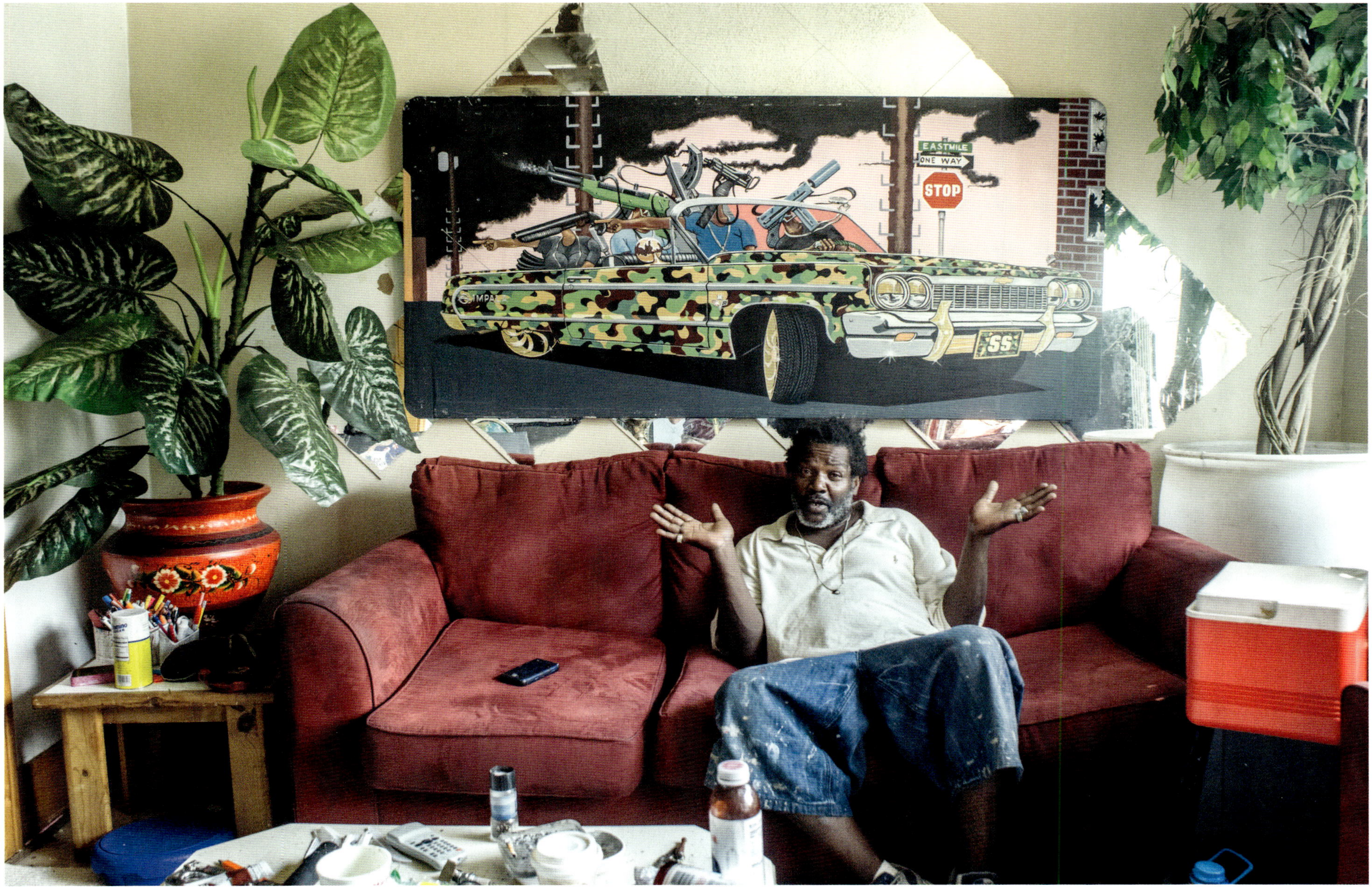

Lee Walker, aka Bird, an artist and sign painter at his house and studio. Bird complained, “How come people from all over the world are coming to Detroit and making it and people from here can’t get shit? How come the foreign guys are not coming here and collaborating?” 12731 Flanders Street, Detroit, 2015.

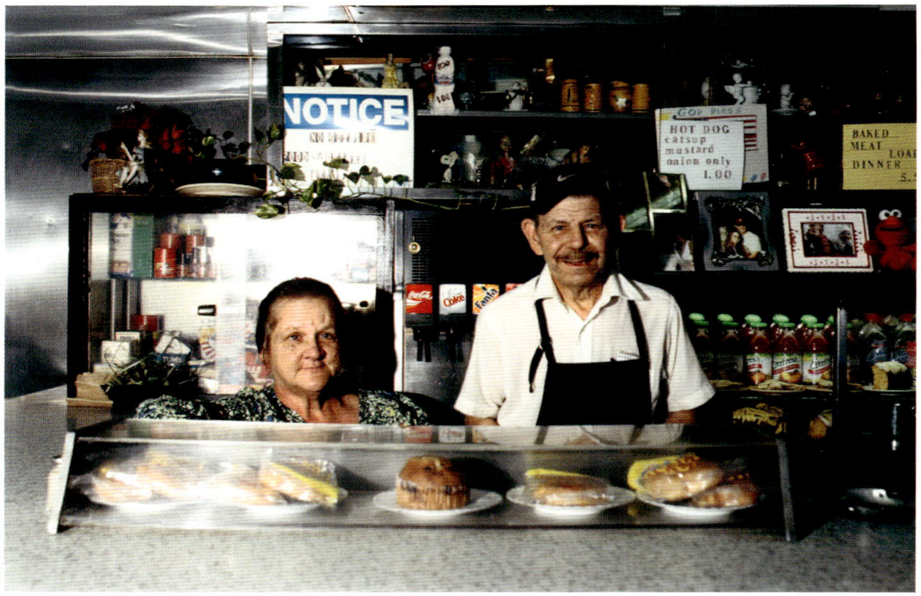

Helen White and Bob, owners of White Grove Restaurant, now closed but largely intact. 3131 2nd Avenue, Detroit, 2008.

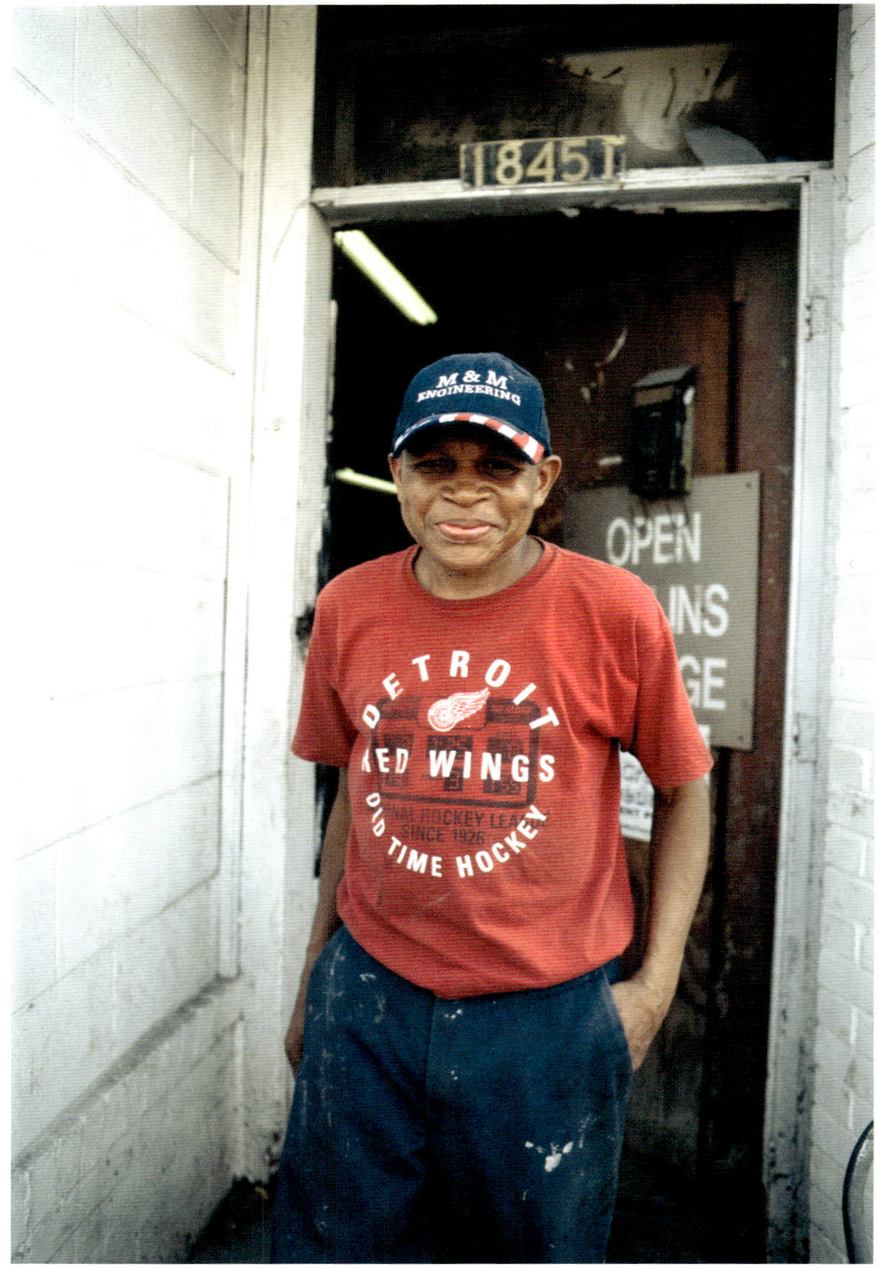

Terry, at Collins Garage. 18451 Conant Street, Detroit, 2012.

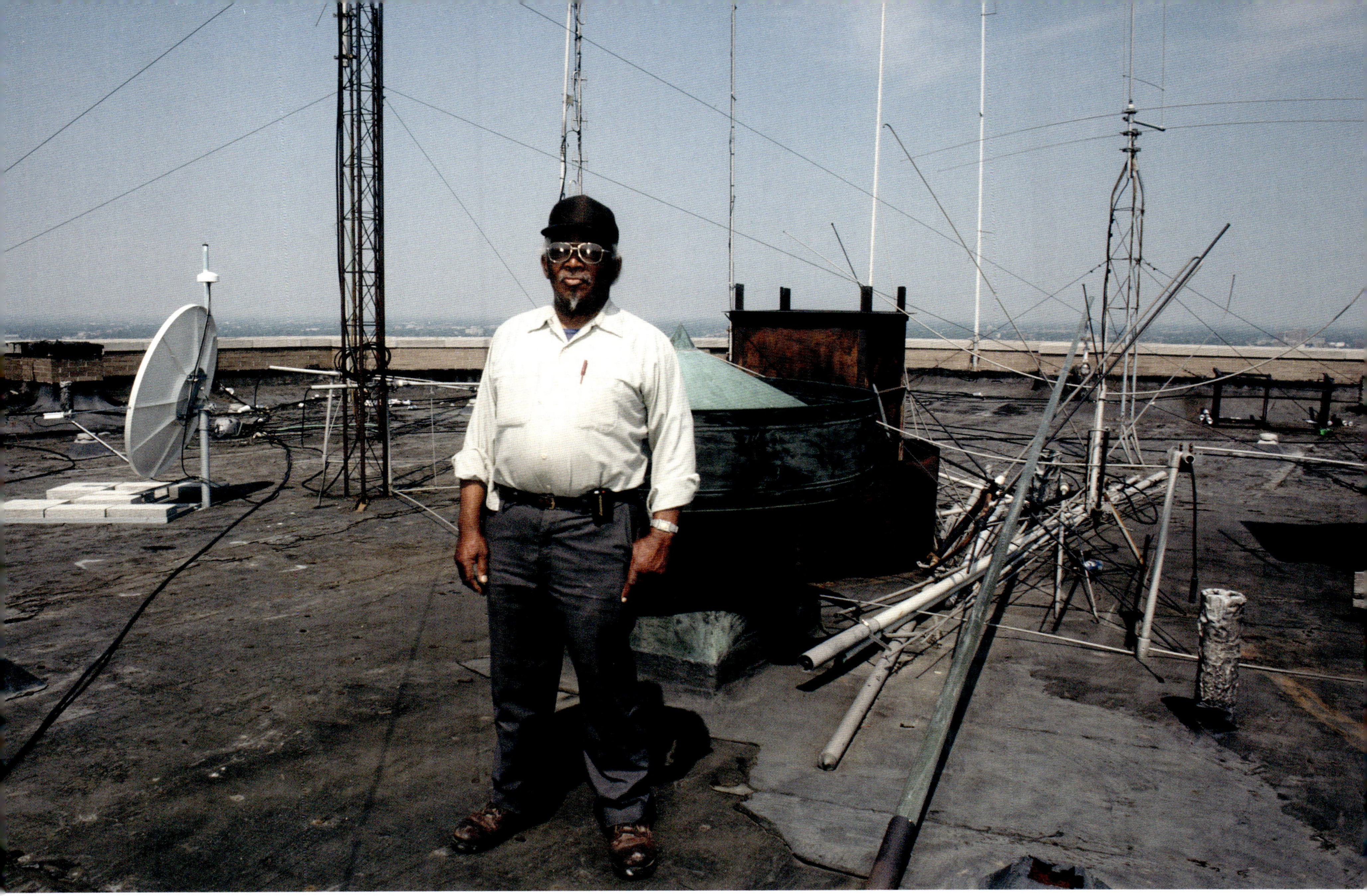

Jessie Willie standing on the roof of the David Broderick Tower, surrounded by antennas. In its heyday, the Broderick had a maintenance staff of fifteen, but here Jessie was the only caretaker left. Grand Circus Park, Detroit, 1995.

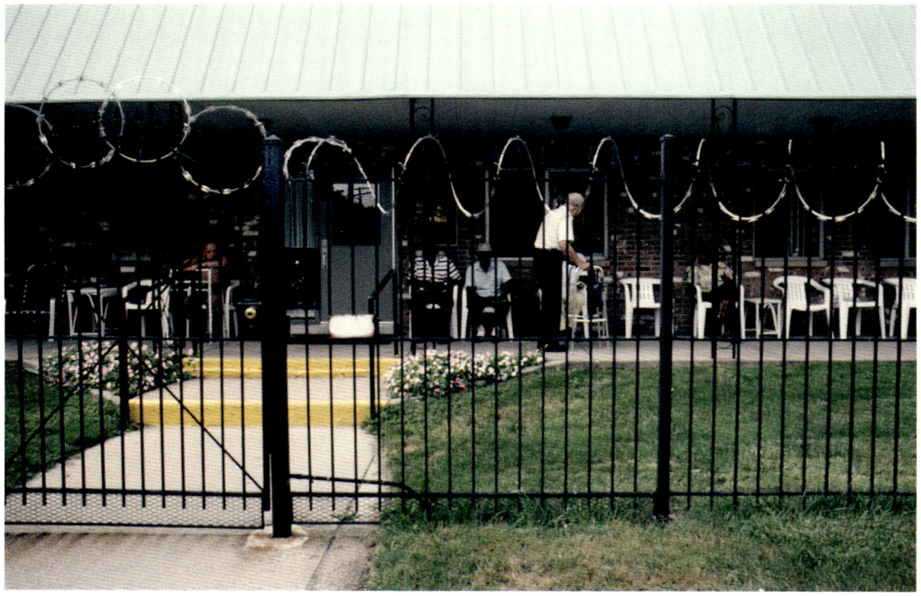

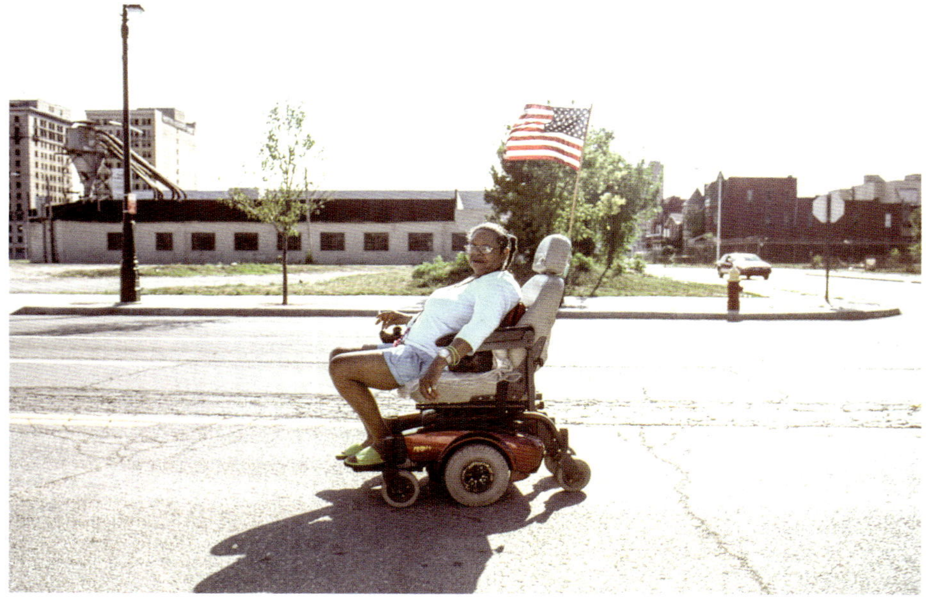

Seniors relaxing behind razor-ribbon wire at the Stapleton Center retirement apartments. A teenager told me that the jail-like security fence was there "to keep people from going in, robbing them or something." He added, "They got everything they need in there. They take care of these old people, the churches do."
Agnes Street at Parkview Street, Detroit, 1993.

A common sight, people riding motorized wheelchairs on the city's main street.
Woodward Avenue by Sproat Street, Detroit, 2007.

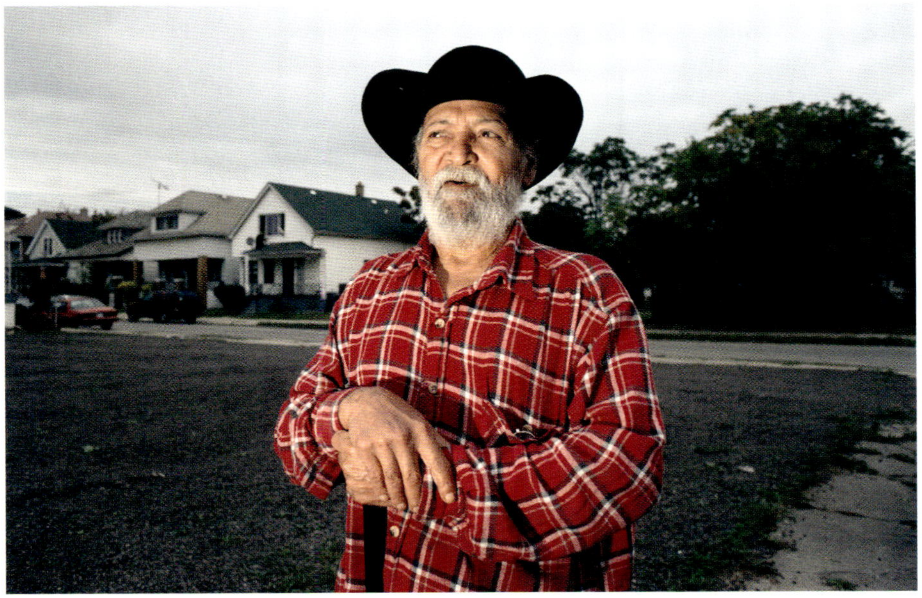

Andres, originally from Texas, came to Detroit in the 1980s to work as a landscaper. Florida Street at Wagner Street, Detroit, 2009.

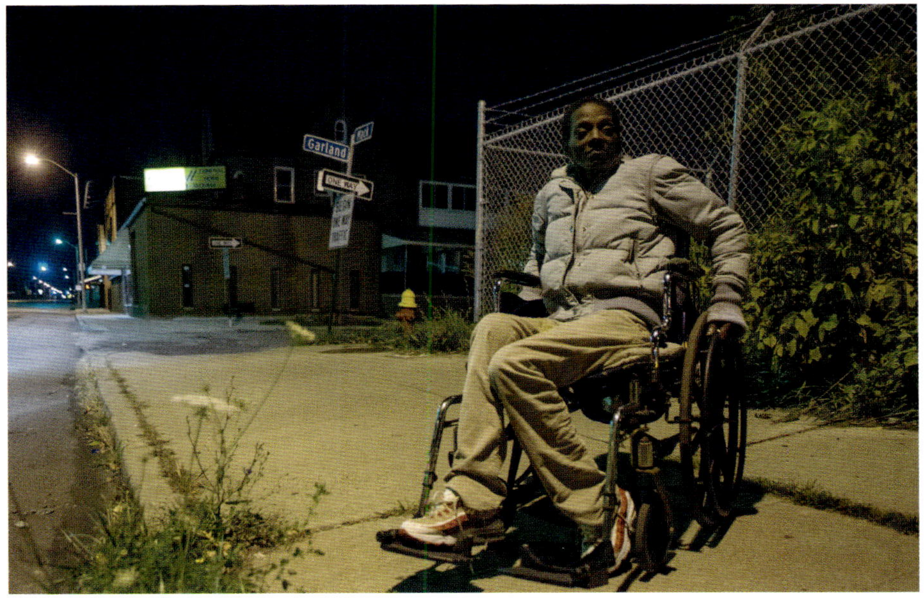

Kim, "going to get cigarettes" at 4 a.m., "hoping to find out someone to hang out with or something." She tells me she needs a hip replacement operation. Mack Avenue at Garland Street, Detroit, 2013.

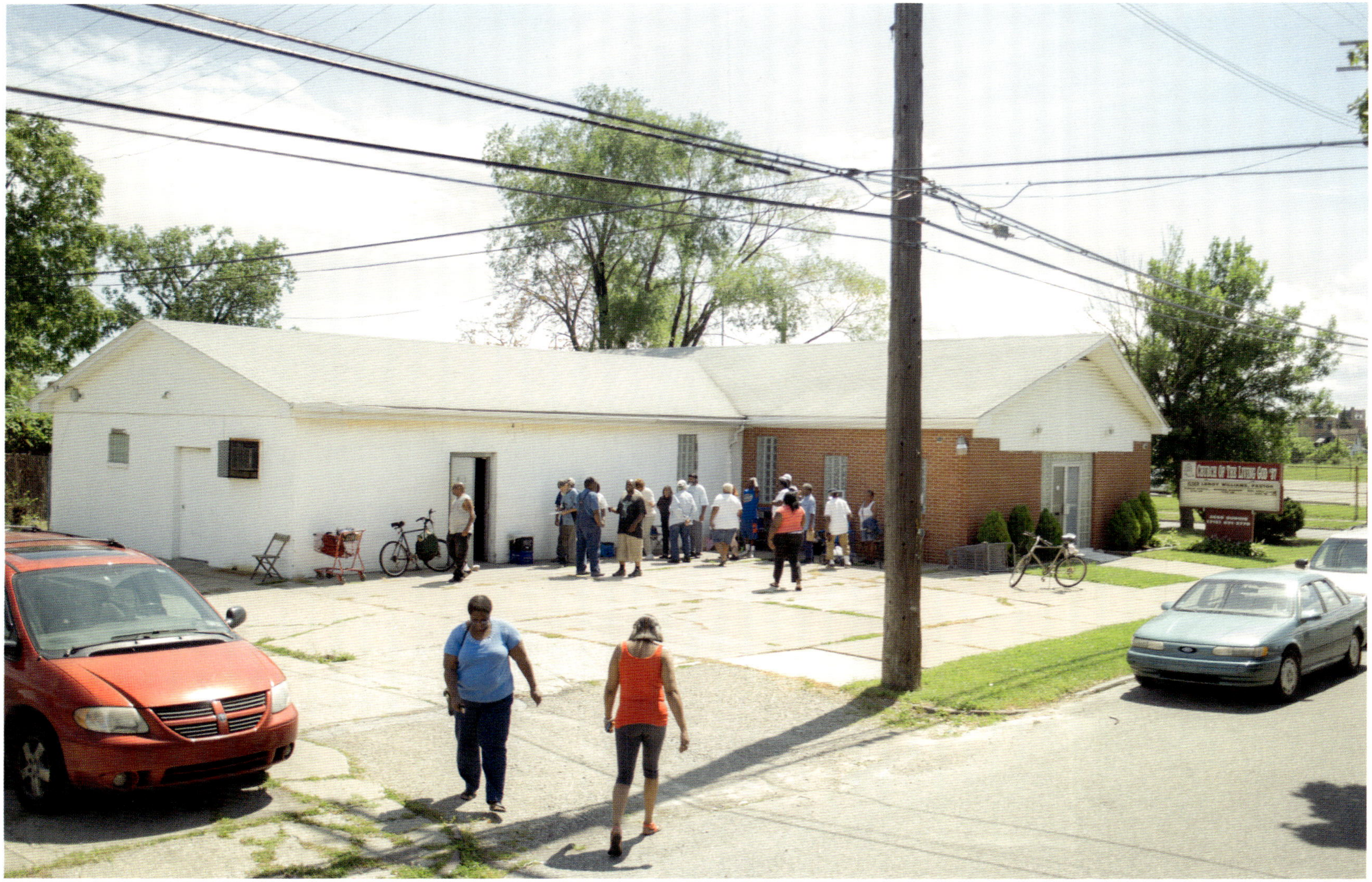

Food Line, Church of the Living God #37. Dubois Street at Hale Street, Detroit, 2015.

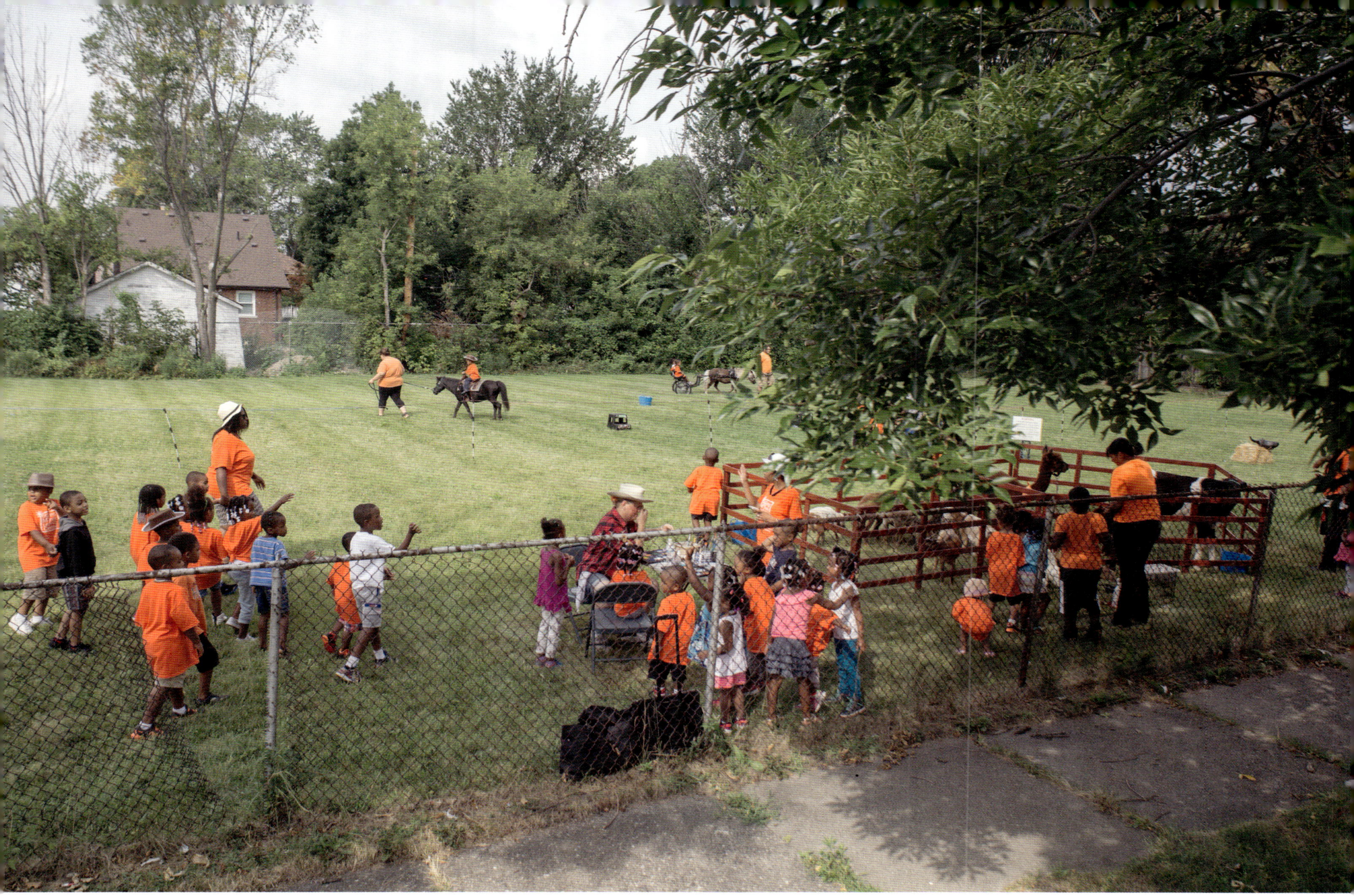

Children being entertained by Chamberlin Pony Rides and Petting Zoo, hired by Growing Minds Learning Center, a child day care facility. Chatsworth Street at Outer Drive East, Detroit, 2015.

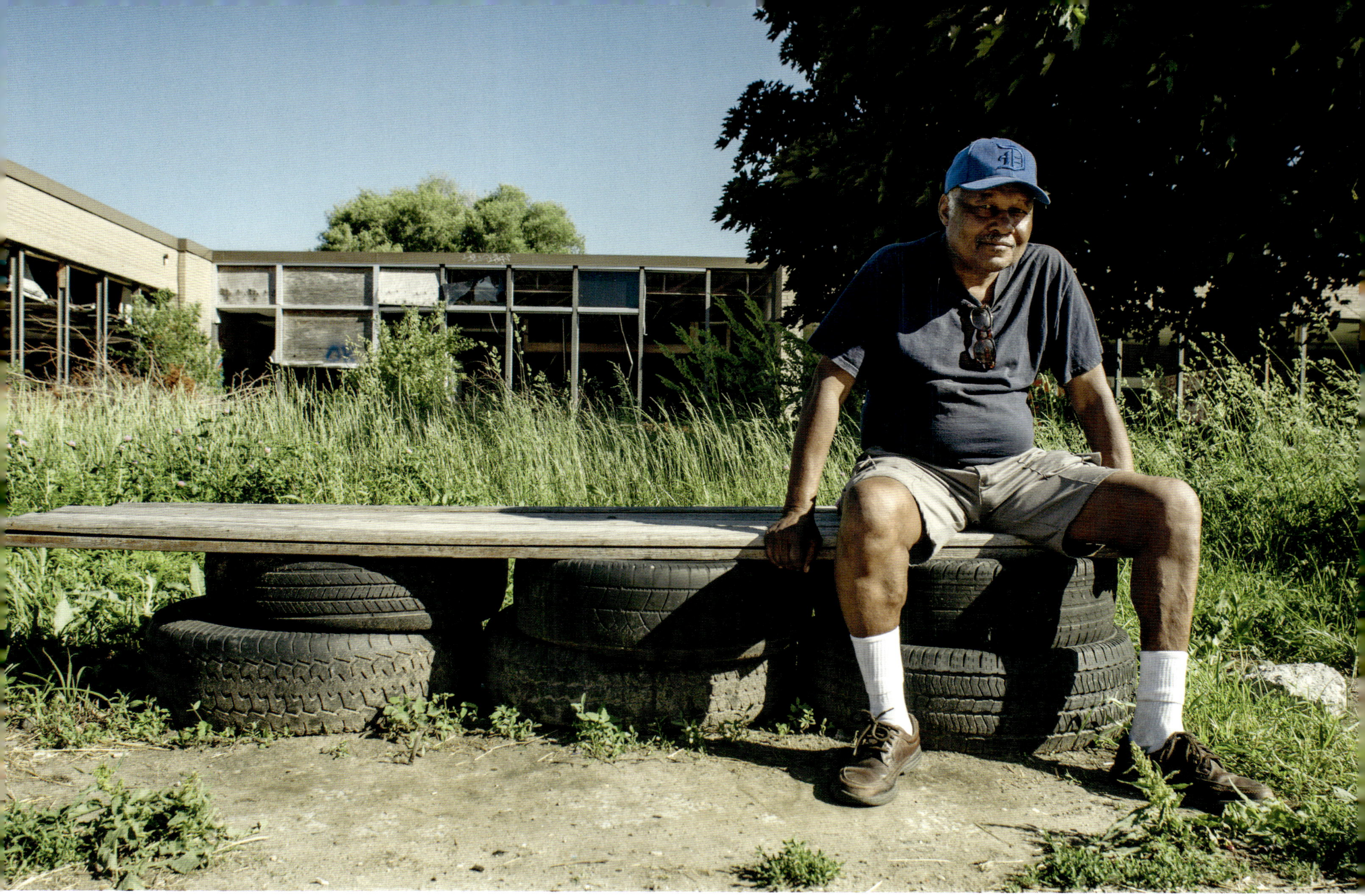

Improvised bench at bus stop. Mack Avenue at Elmwood Street, Detroit, 2014.

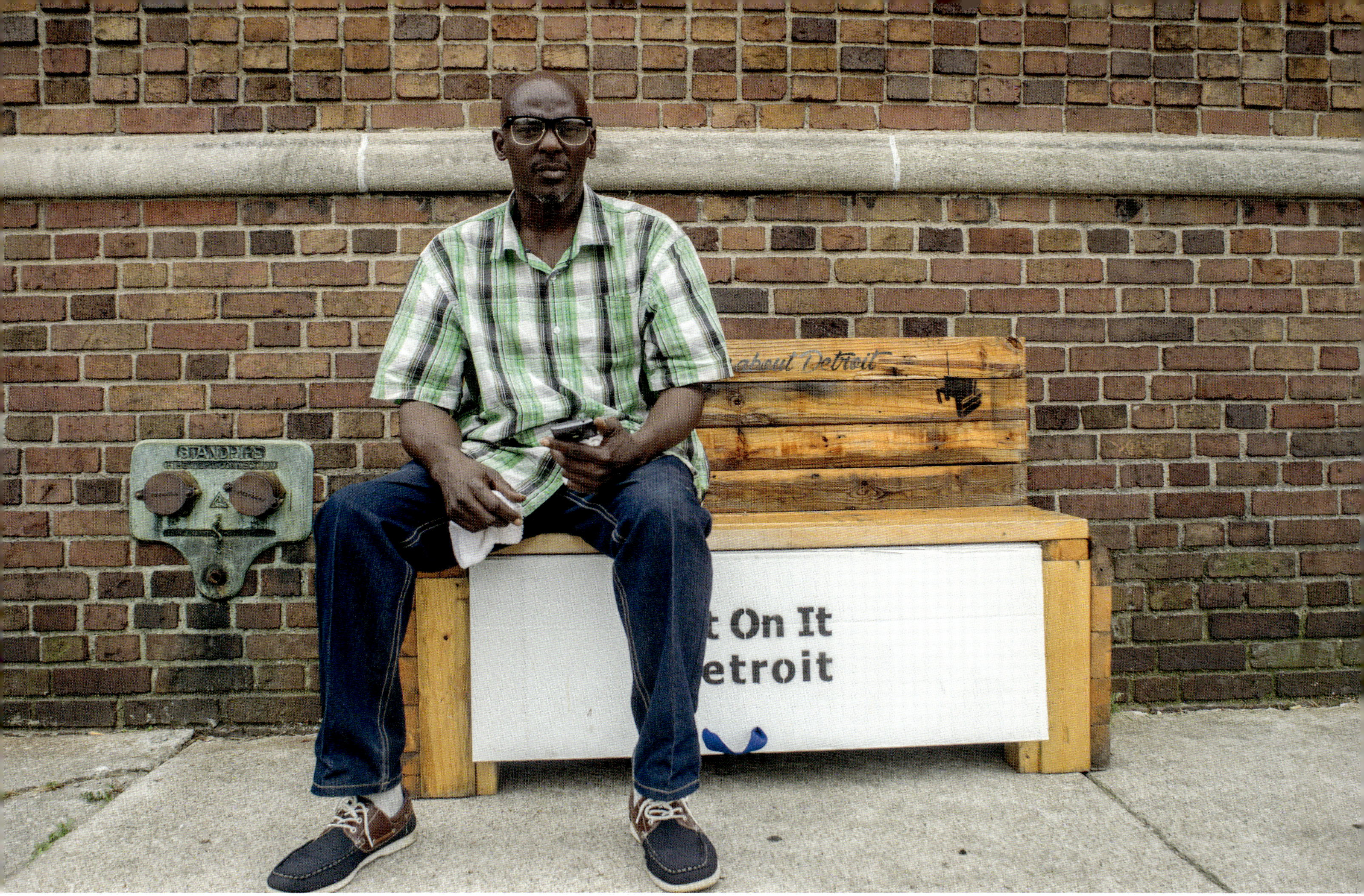

"Say Nice Things about Detroit" bench. Driving down Seven Mile Road on the east side, though, you notice that such basic amenities as bus stop shelters and benches are typically absent. People waiting for the bus must sit on trash cans or anything they can find. Rick, shown waiting for the bus, gave up and called his brother to pick him up. Harper Avenue at Hurlbut Street, Detroit. 2015.

"IN THE GHETTOHOOD": THINGS GET BETTER SLOWLY

When I asked people in the neighborhoods if they live in the ghetto, about half said no, choosing instead to call their areas poor, dangerous, or desolate. All but one agreed that there were ghettos near them. I was surprised that people seemed to take for granted the segregated character of their surroundings. I often ask people to define the ghetto or to tell me if they think they live in one. Pastor Kennard Pettaway of Wings as Eagles Church was articulate on this point: "It just happens that I am in an area called the ghetto, a poor impoverished area of torn-down houses, trash in the streets, people standing on the corners in front of liquor stores, where prostitution is high because women prostitute themselves to buy drugs. If you see some Caucasians down here, it's because they got hooked on drugs, and drugs are readily available here."

Dorothy, the owner of Sheps Barber and Beauty Shop in Highland Park, operates the only business on the block. She remembers when "there were candy stores, Dairy Queens, resale shops." "Now," she remarks, "the older people who cared about the properties have died and their children have moved away." She does not think that the neighborhood is going to come back during her lifetime. When I asked her if the area is a ghetto she replied, "That is what it is." When asked the same question, Deacon Jacob Smith of the Heavenly Mission Baptist Church on Harper Avenue answered, "They do call it the ghetto, but it is getting better . . . they are building houses two blocks away, it is coming back slow." I asked Jason Dean if his liquor store, called Jaye Dee's Market, was in the ghetto. "We are in the ghettohood," he replied, adding that Jaye Dee's Market is located two blocks away from Berry Gordy's mansion in Boston Edison. Jason believes that his neighborhood has space and that development, slowly trickling down from downtown and midtown, may one day reach it. Reverend Kevin Dean, who is white, strongly objected to calling his east side neighborhood a ghetto, a term that many people find offensive. He preferred to describe it as "difficult." Bob, owner of a hat shop on Gratiot Avenue, says that the ghetto outside doesn't bother him, and commented, "The store itself is not ghetto; it is a destination; people come here looking for the store." Moreover, he said, people who "want to stay with the roots" know that his hats are authentic.

And Nick, a liquor store owner, opined: "Without volcano eruptions and earthquakes and with plenty of water, Detroit is a land of opportunity... it is going to come back in four or five years." Patricia of "I Choose You Dancing" on West McNichols Road has never had a problem with her business; she told me that two new stores are getting ready to open a couple of blocks away and that the city is tearing down abandoned houses in the neighborhood.

As far as improving life in the ghetto, the billionaires, philanthropists, and young entrepreneurs are not visibly contributing. Nor are creativity, hard work, and investment in greater downtown fostering racial harmony; on the contrary, they seem to be reinforcing existing patterns of segregation and pushing blacks into the background. Accounts of interesting and well-designed outdoor cafes, bakeries, and micro-breweries in the greater downtown area can easily be matched by depressing news from the neighborhoods. Urban gardeners do provide nutrition and advice but cannot bring prosperity, security, and jobs to the neighborhoods. The contributions of volunteers are appreciated by local residents, some of them believing that churches and community organizations will continue to fight blight, yet they doubt that the improvements will last.

Amidst the rawness of Detroit, billionaires and hipsters who migrated from the suburbs have found a unique, safe place to achieve and to increase their fame and fortune. The world media flocks to the city to show capitalism working under the most difficult circumstances. But reporters, unable to develop stories of their own on a short timetable, construct shallow narratives based on what savvy public relations people feed them. Press releases and suggestions to the media do not include dwelling on the hopes and aspirations of ghetto residents, developments in churches or memorials, nor do they mention the new forms of coney islands or the porn industry boom. And when a voice from the neighborhoods is needed, that voice will most likely be one recommended by a city official or a foundation executive. An example of this is Phil Cooley's "Welcome-to-Detroit, it's-more-than-just-grit" tour that he gives to celebrities and VIPs.

In a 2015 *New York Times* opinion piece, "The Spirit and Promise of Detroit," Frank Bruni wrote about Sister Pie, a trendy bakeshop on Kercheval Avenue: "Even more noteworthy is its location: a stone throw from dozens of the deserted houses and decrepit lots for which Detroit is notorious. Sister Pie shouldn't be here." But Sister Pie is on the north end of Indian Village, and if instead of walking along Kercheval Street, Bruni would have turned along Parker Street, he would have seen hundreds of substantial houses, several of them mansions in different states of gentrification. Sister Pie straddles two very different Detroit neighborhoods. Several attempts at getting the newspaper to publish a clarification were ignored.

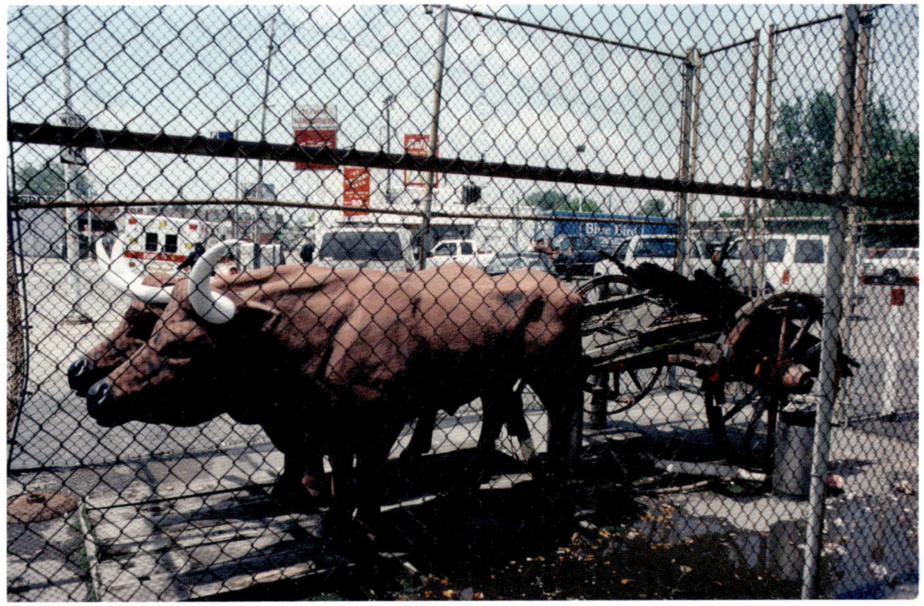

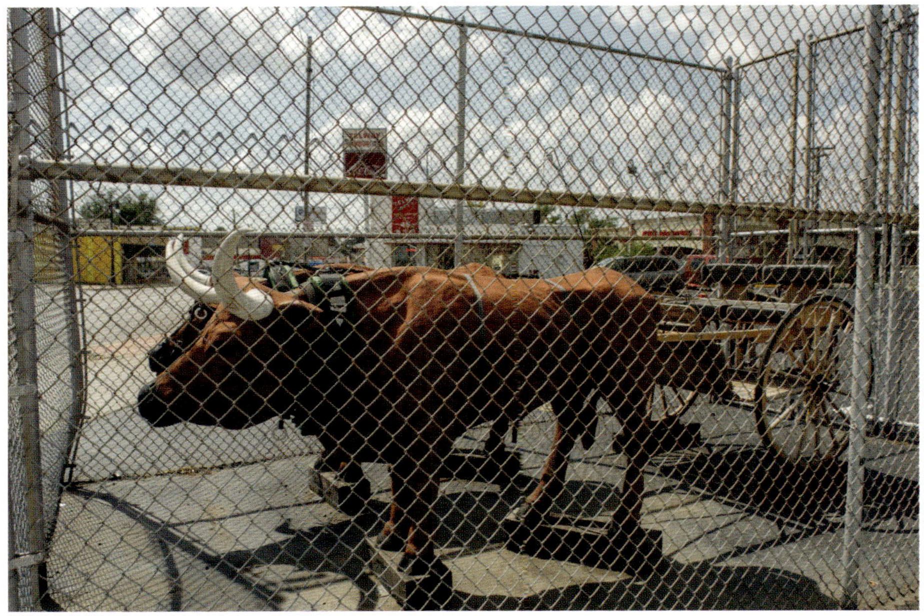

Above Parking lot of Tellway Hamburgers with sculpture of bulls pulling a cart. Michigan Avenue at Martin Street, Detroit, 2001.

Below Refurbished bulls and new cart in parking lot of Tellway Hamburgers. Earl, the owner of Tellway since the 1940s, put the bulls there several decades ago. Recently he had them restored and a new cart made. According to his grandson, the sculpture group was part of Tellway and it was restored so that the bulls "could remain a legacy." To one of Tellway's patrons, "the bulls were his landmark"; another customer remarked that his wife had "wanted to jump the fence and ride the bulls." Michigan Avenue at Martin Street, Detroit, 2015.

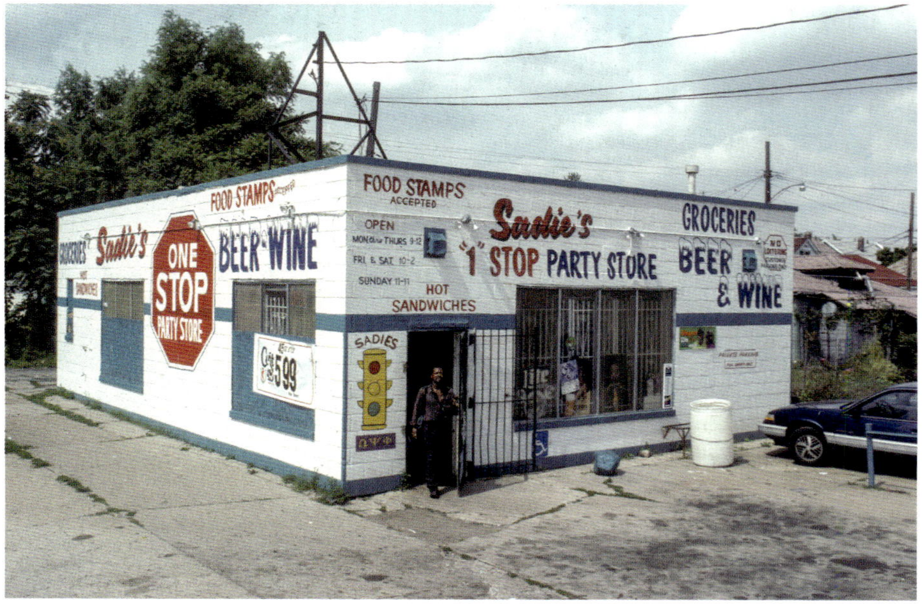

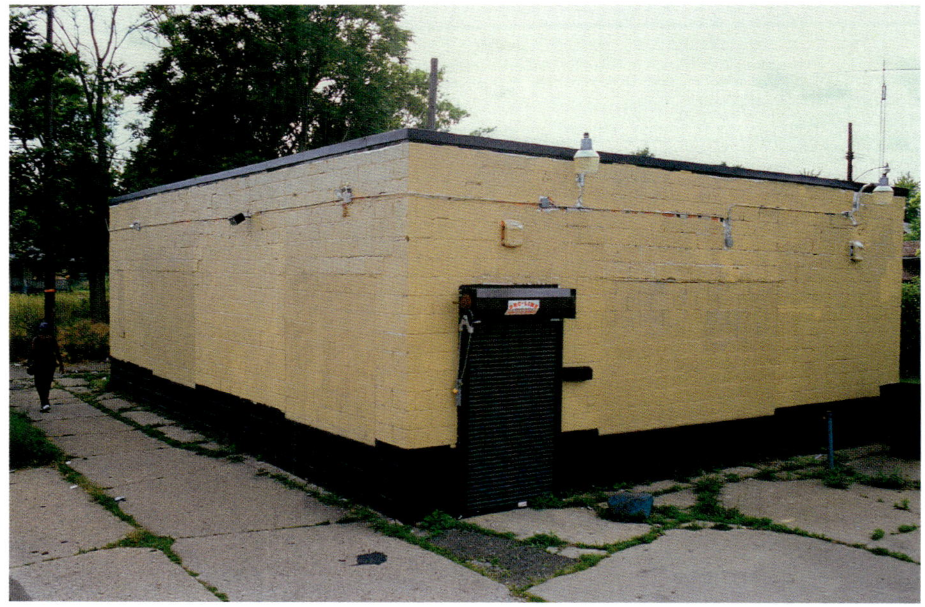

Sadie's "1" Stop Party Store. East Warren Avenue near Cooper Street, Detroit, 1994.

Former Sadie's "1" Stop Party Store. East Warren Avenue at Pennsylvania Street, Detroit, 2011.

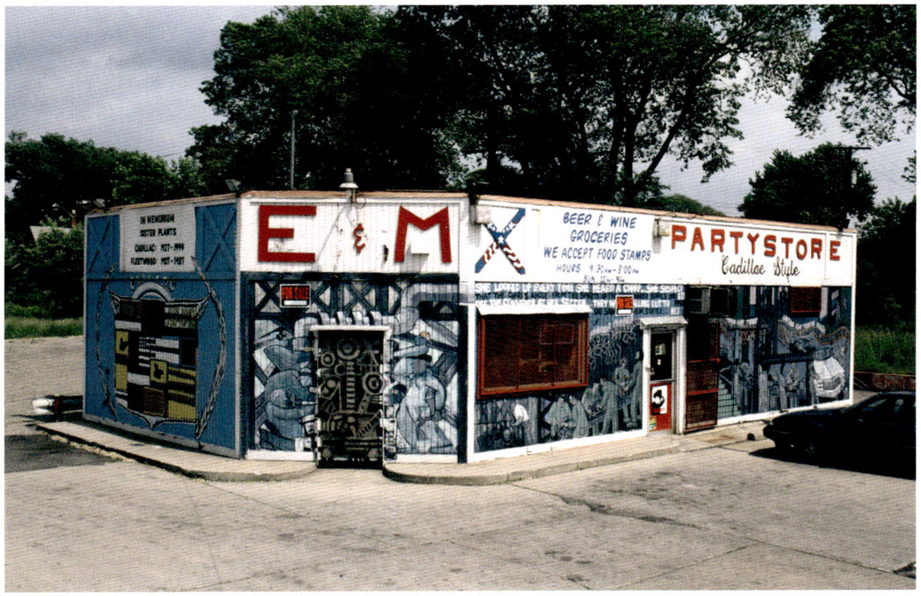

E and M Cadillac Style Party Store with Diego Rivera-influenced assembly line mural and a memorial to closed auto p ants. Scotten Street at Toledo Street, Detroit, 2001.

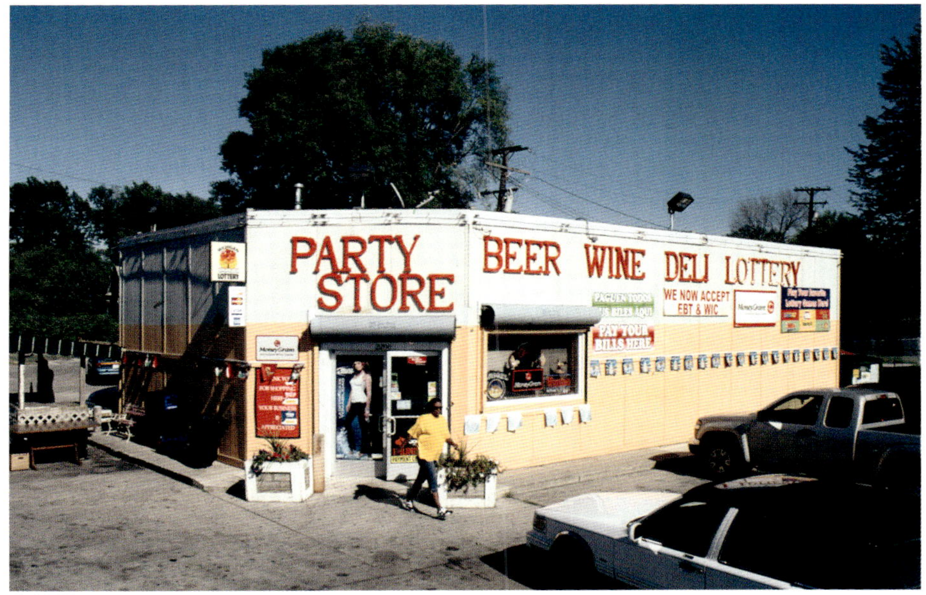

Party store. Scotten Street at Toledo Street, Detroit, 2010.

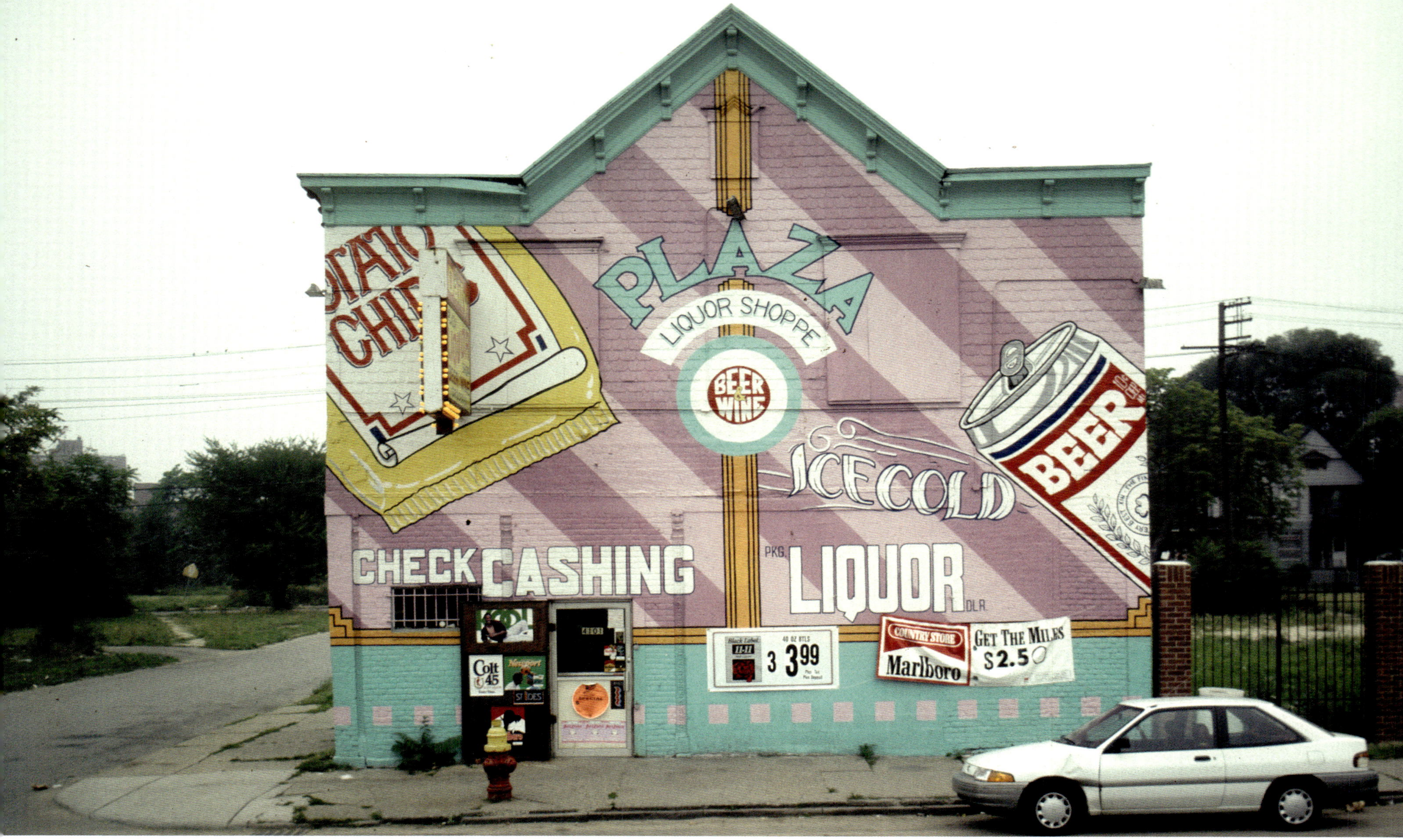

Plaza Liquor Shoppe, once the most distinctive party store in Detroit.
4101 Third Avenue corner of Alexandrine Street, Detroit, 1994.

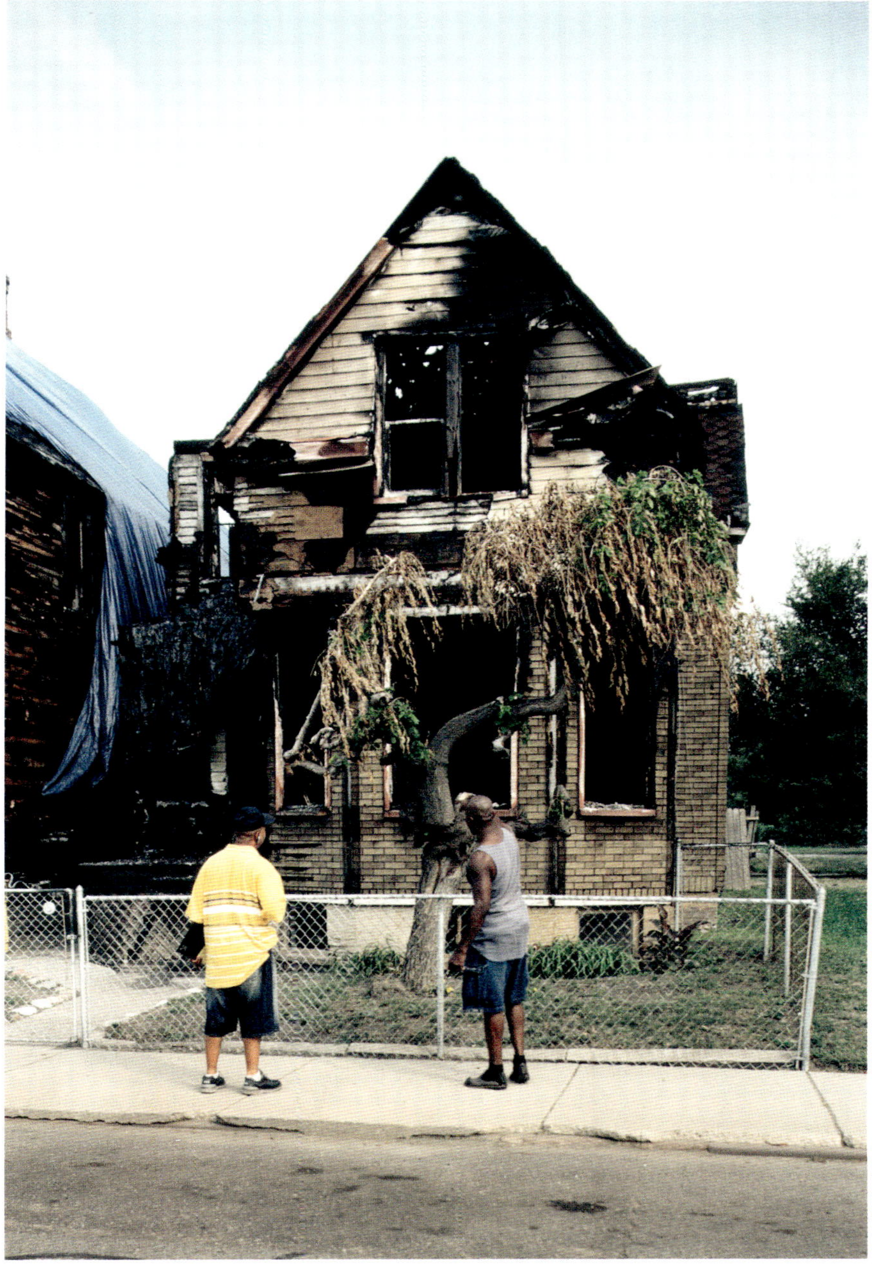

Burnt house and tree. The two men in front were comparing the tree in front of the house to a moose. 3497 Mack Avenue, Detroit, 2007.

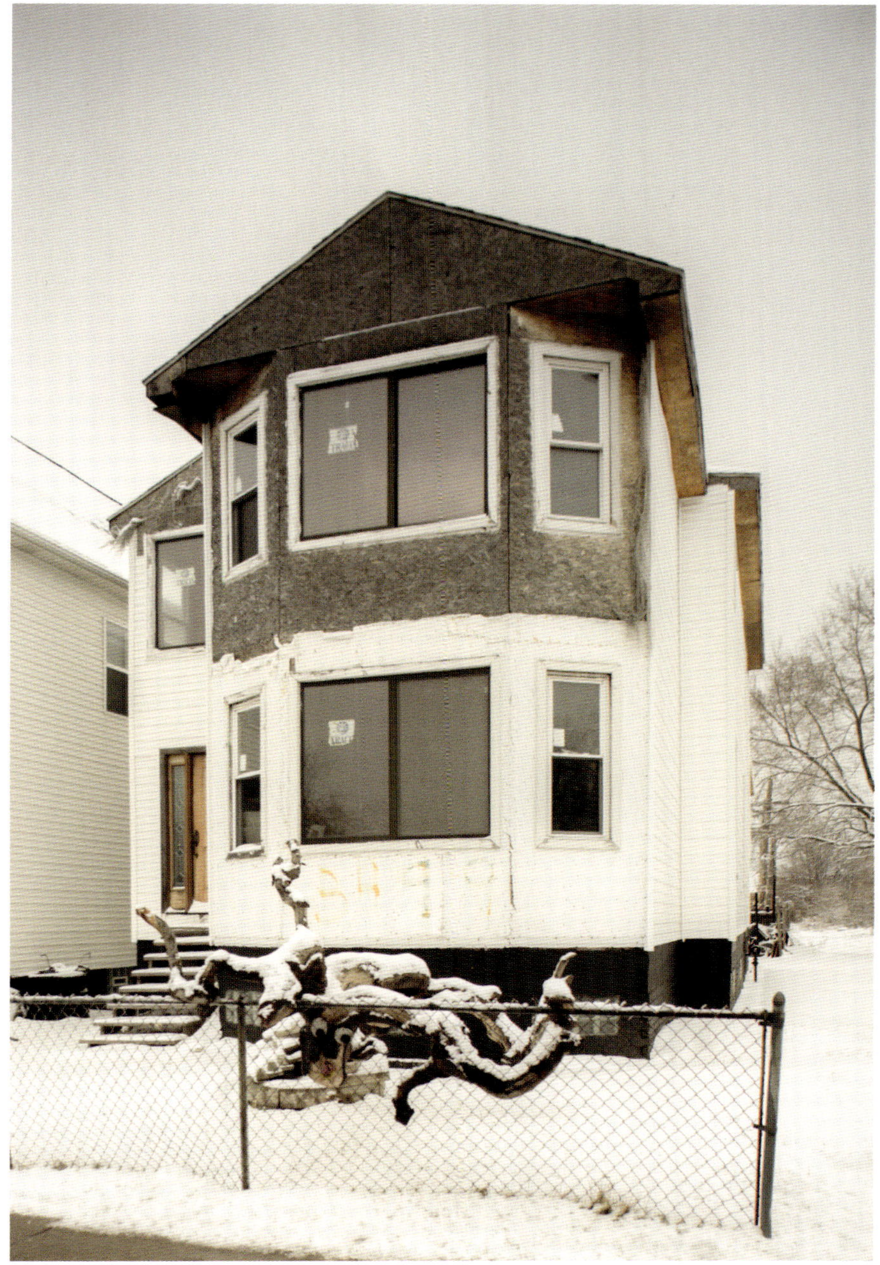

Remarkably, the owner of the burnt house is slowly rehabilitating it. Other houses on the block belong to the same family, and they wish to stay together. 3497 Mack Avenue, Detroit, 2015.

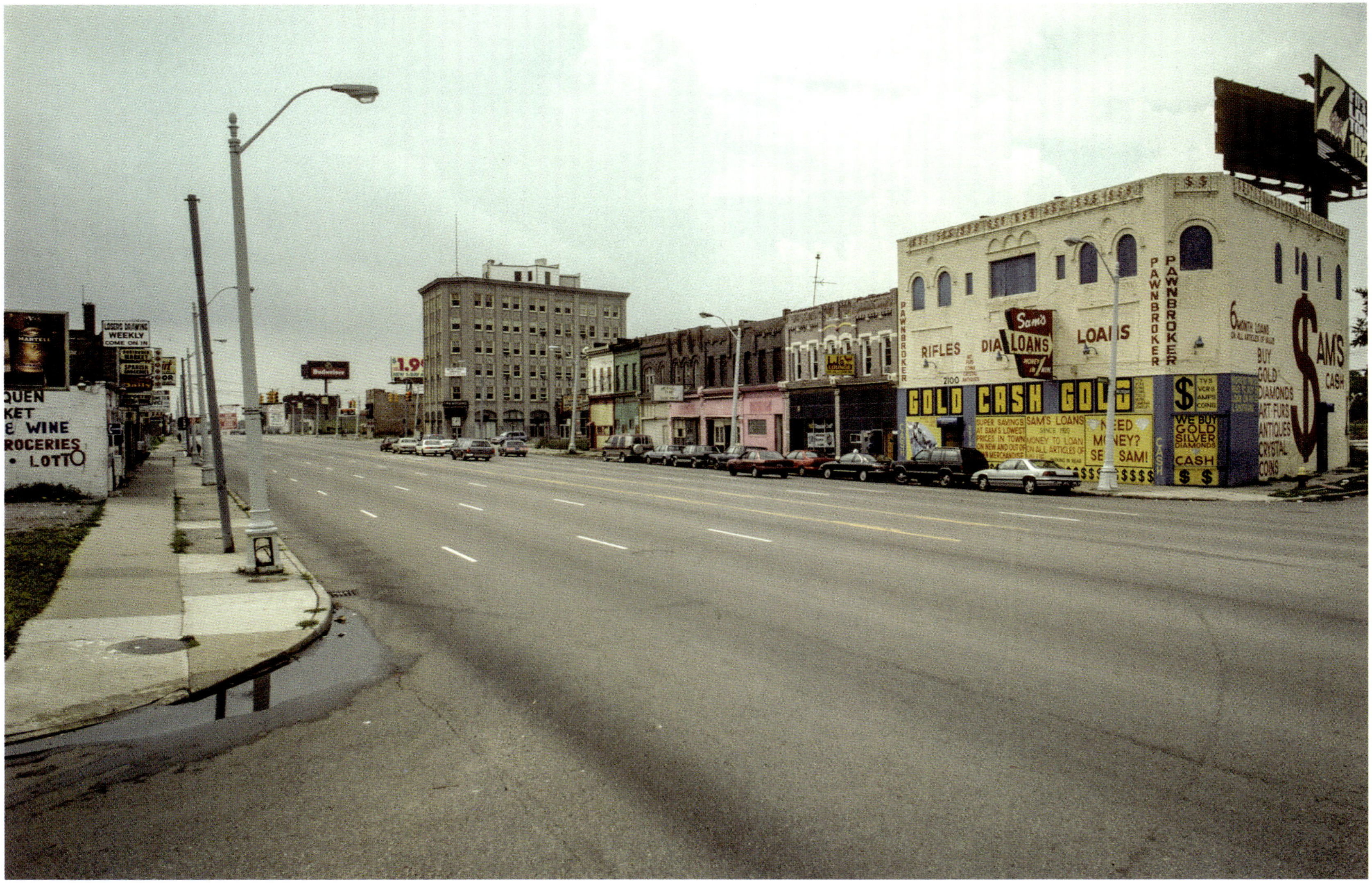

View northwest along Michigan Avenue from Wabash Street, Detroit, 1993.

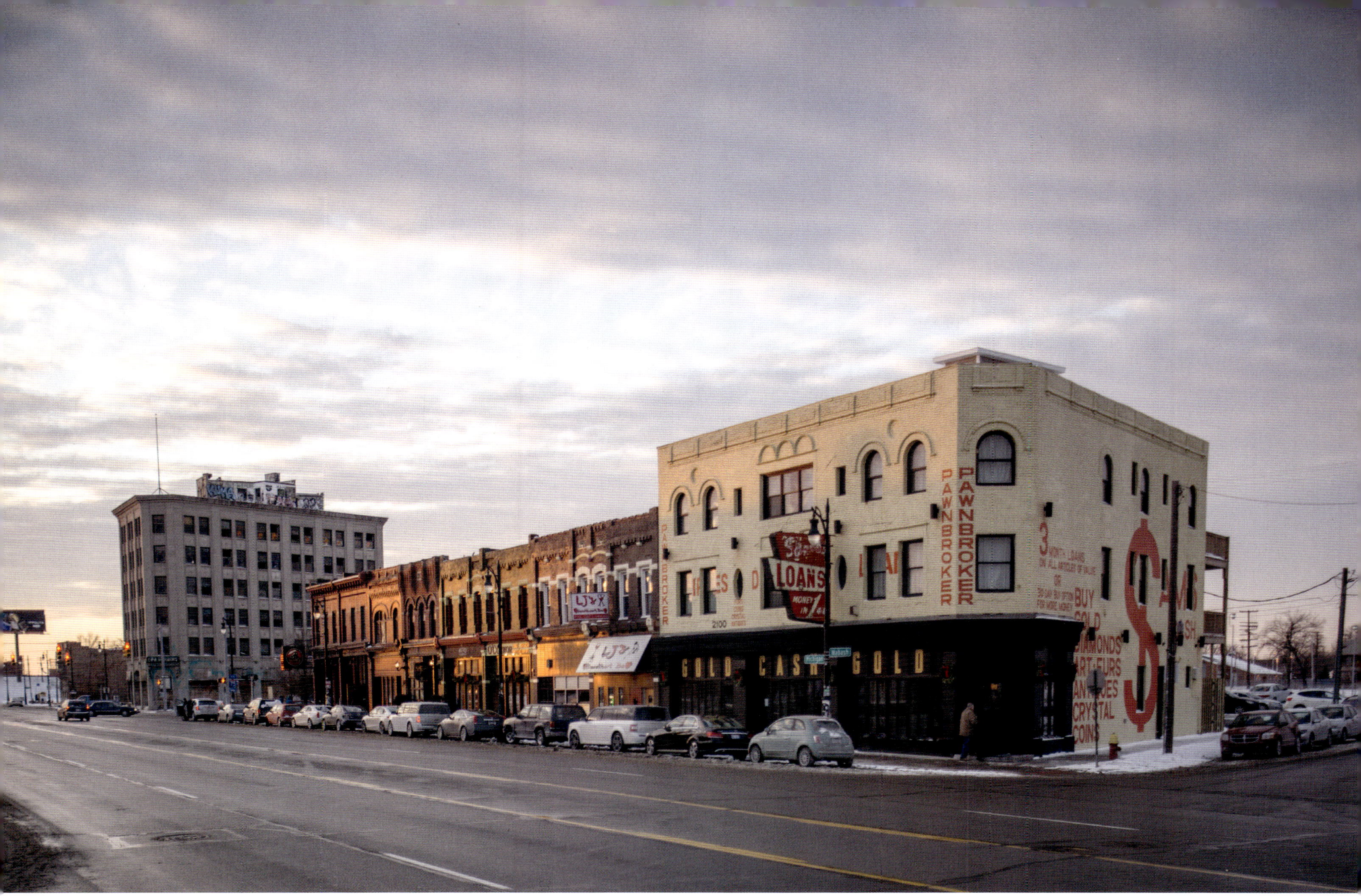

Three of the most popular venues in the city, all located on a once run-down block: Slows Restaurant, Astro Coffee, and Gold Cash Gold. Gold Cash Gold is actually a restaurant that took the place and name of the corner pawnshop, linking itself with the city's past. View northwest from Wabash Street along Michigan Avenue, Detroit, 2015.

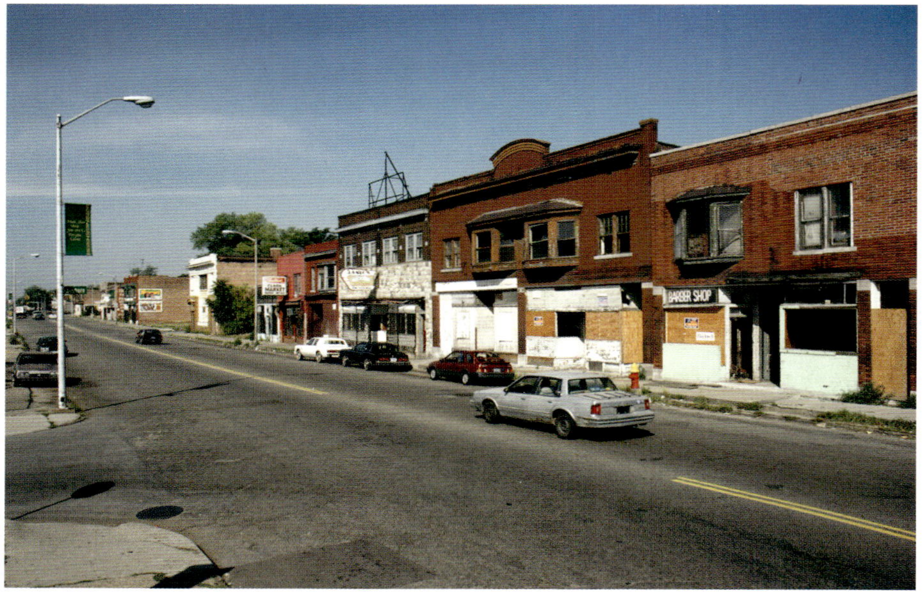

In 1993, there were banners hanging from the lampposts proclaiming "Mack Alive with you and I . . . Everyone Counts." Today, they are gone, but one finds banners with similar sentiments in other, more hopeful neighborhoods. Mack Avenue seen from Seyburn Street, Detroit, 1993.

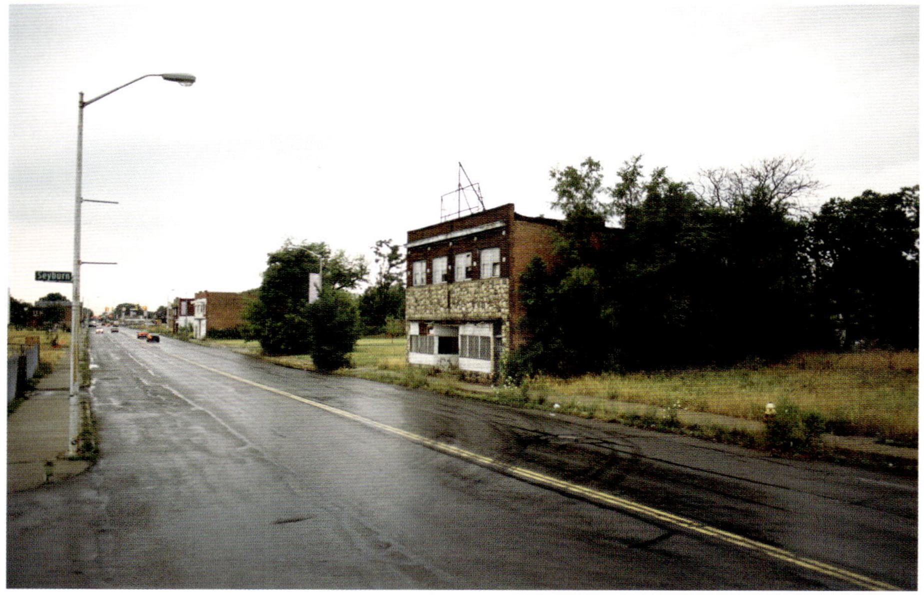

Mack Avenue from Seyburn Street, Detroit, 2012.

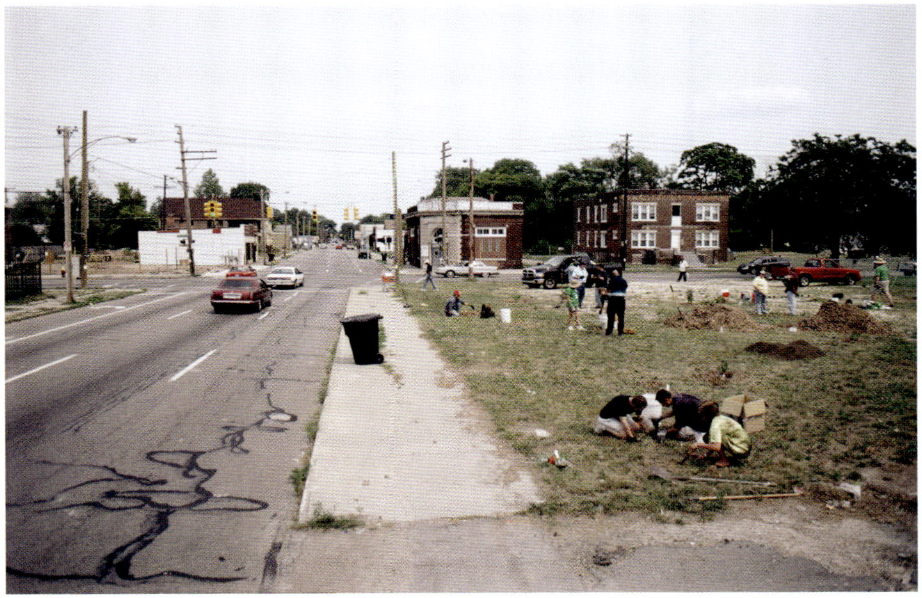

Volunteers from Friends of Detroit gathered to create a "Dream Garden," a "Peace Zone for Life," in the shape of a butterf y in an east side empty lot. East Forest Avenue at Van Dyke Street, Detroit, 2007.

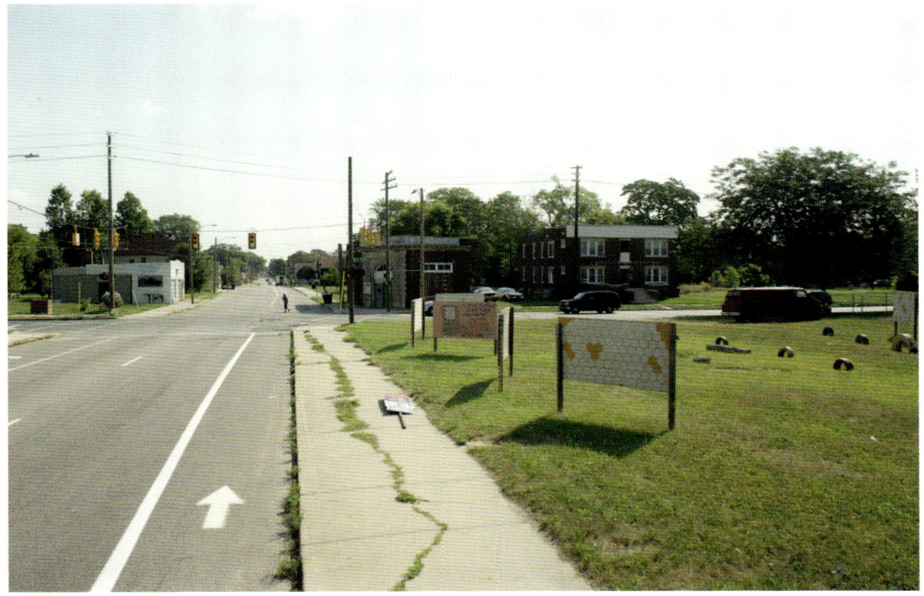

Dream Garden eight years later. Where I expected to see grown trees, I found decorated tires. East Forest Avenue at Van Dyke Road, Detroi:, 2015.

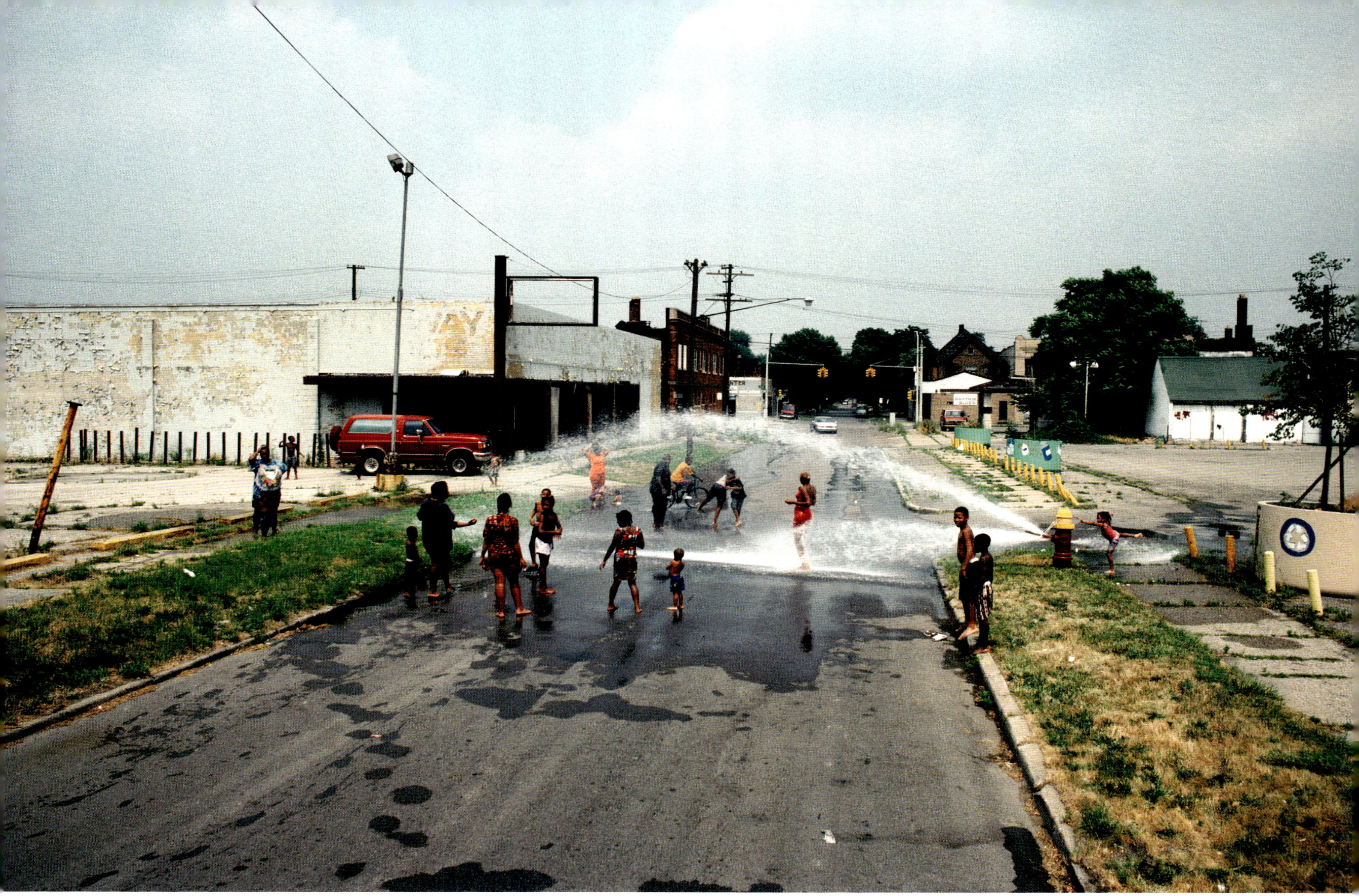

On a 95-degree day, view east along East Palmer Street toward Chene Street, Detroit, 1995.

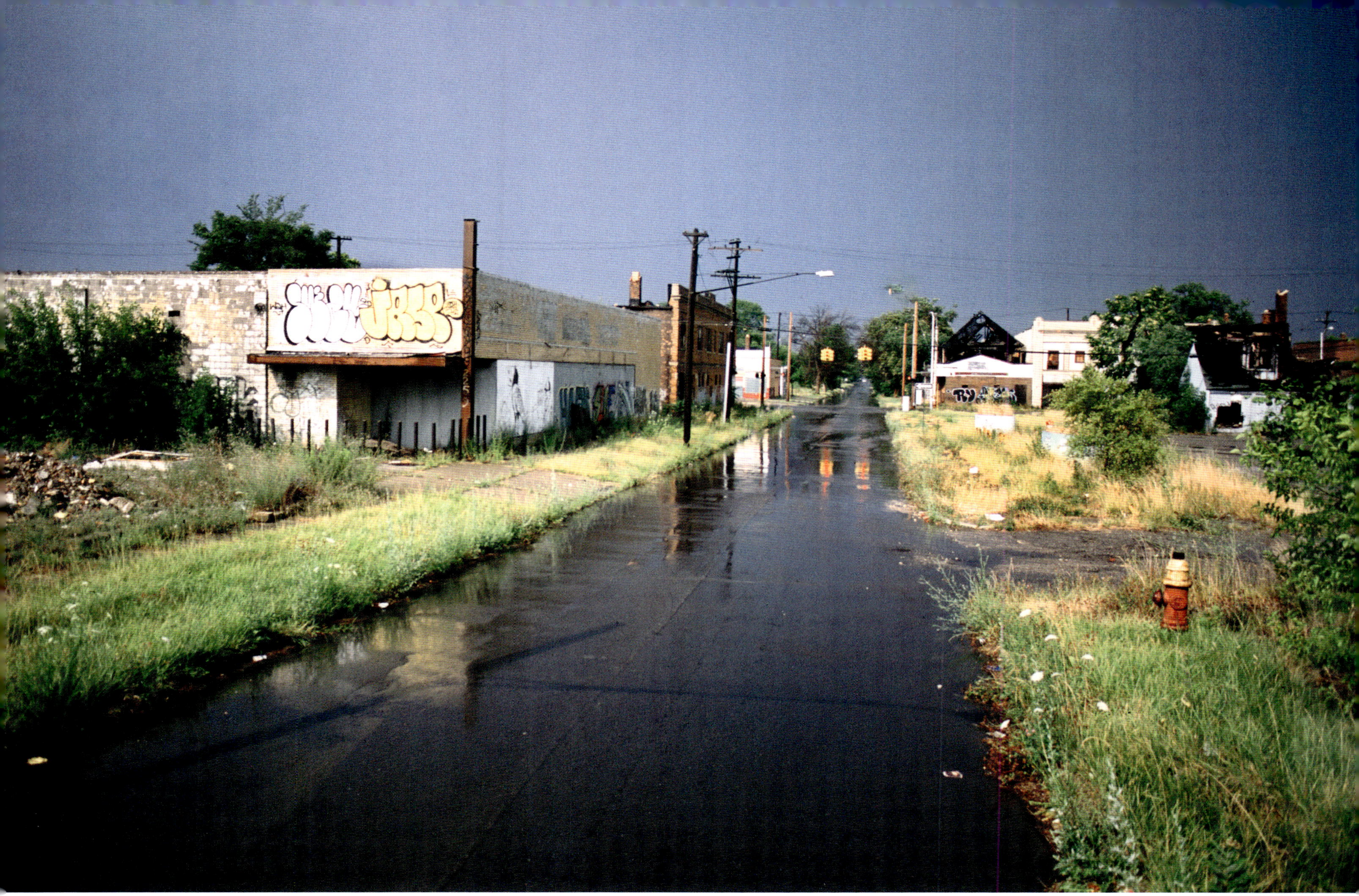

View east along East Palmer toward Chene Street, Detroit, 2012.

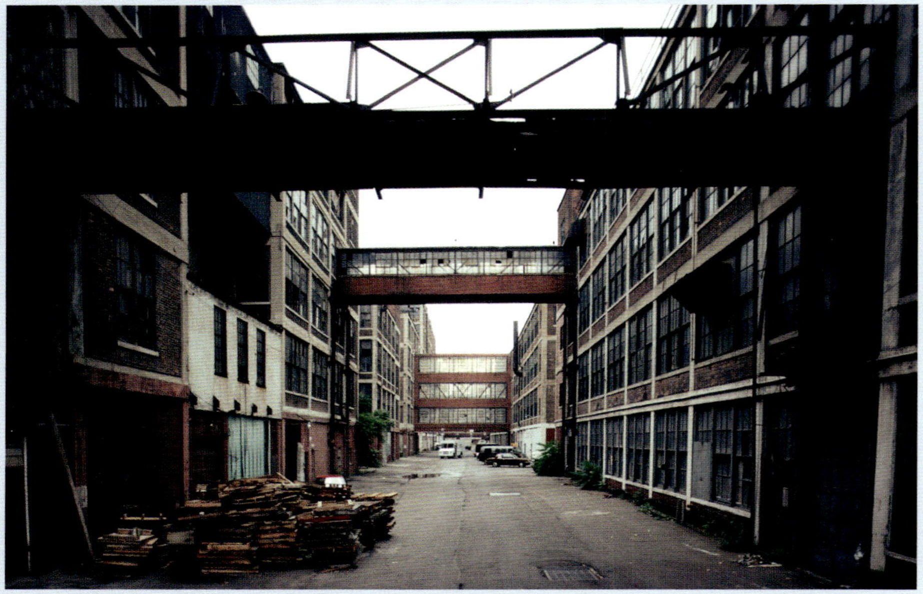

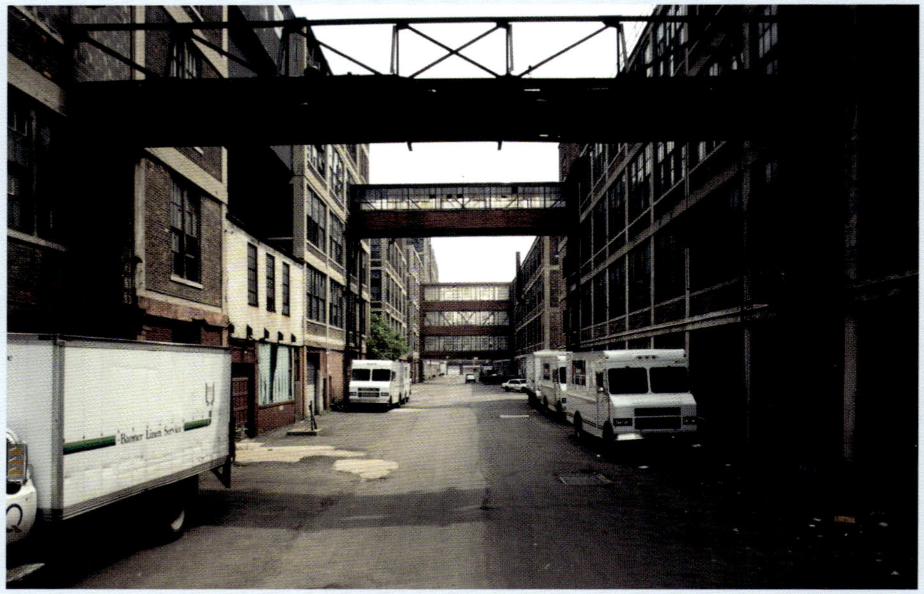

Former Packard Plant. The defunct automotive plant had become a site for stripping cars and a warehouse for paper and used clothing. An industrial laundry was still operating here at this time. East Grand Boulevard at Concord Street, Detroit, 1993.

Former Packard Plant. The building is visited by urban explorers, graffiti artists looking to make their mark, and by scavengers seeking metal to recycle. It also became a popular place for raves and paintball battles. East Grand Boulevard at Concord Street, Detroit, 1996.

CONCLUSION

DETROIT'S EVOLVING RUINS After a quarter century, I distrust the idea of "improving" the city's grand ruins. For me, it is not possible to create a place more beautiful and desperate than the Detroit of the early 1990s. The Michigan Central Station had never looked better and will never look better than when it was at its most neglected. Eminem in his video *Beautiful* (2009) captures the magnificence of the old depot. We see him walking into its monumental waiting room at its most decayed as if it were a sacred space. Inside he encounters the ghost of an elderly black woman, wearing a blond wig and carrying a beat-up suitcase as she passes by without looking at him. The artist raps while sitting on a church pew as heavenly light shines down. In this phenomenally popular video the rapper sings the refrain: "But don't let 'em say you ain't beautiful oh." The video was watched by 245 million viewers on VEVO by 2015.

On the façade of the Michigan Central Station someone wrote: Isa 23 (referring to Isaiah 23: "Howl, ye ships of Tarshish; for Tyre is laid to waste, so that there is no house, no entering in"). As writer Geoff Dyer remarked about the Michigan Central Station: "Ruins do not encourage the viewer to dwell on what they were like in their heyday. The Colosseum in Rome or the amphitheater at Leptis Magna has never been anything but ruins. They are eternal ruins. And it's the same here. This building could never have looked more magnificent than it did now. Rather than make you think of the past, ruins direct you toward the future. The effect is almost prophetic. This is what the future will end up like. This is what the future has always ended up looking like" ("Detroit: Where The Wheels Came Off... ," *The Observer*, July 8, 2000).

Some of Detroit's ruins are being sanitized, however. I dislike the elaborate garden of reeds that was planted in front of the Michigan Central Station. I dislike even more the replacement of the old window frames, which made something authentic look fake. And the clock on the Packard Plant, Detroit's second most famous ruin, has been recreated in plastic. Below, a billboard depicting vintage Packard cars has been put in front of the building, a reminder of the elegant cars that the factory once made. The ruin is a popular setting for movies and photo shoots. In August 2015, a tiger brought into the plant by British photographer David Yarrow got loose and climbed the stairs to the fourth floor of the ruined factory.

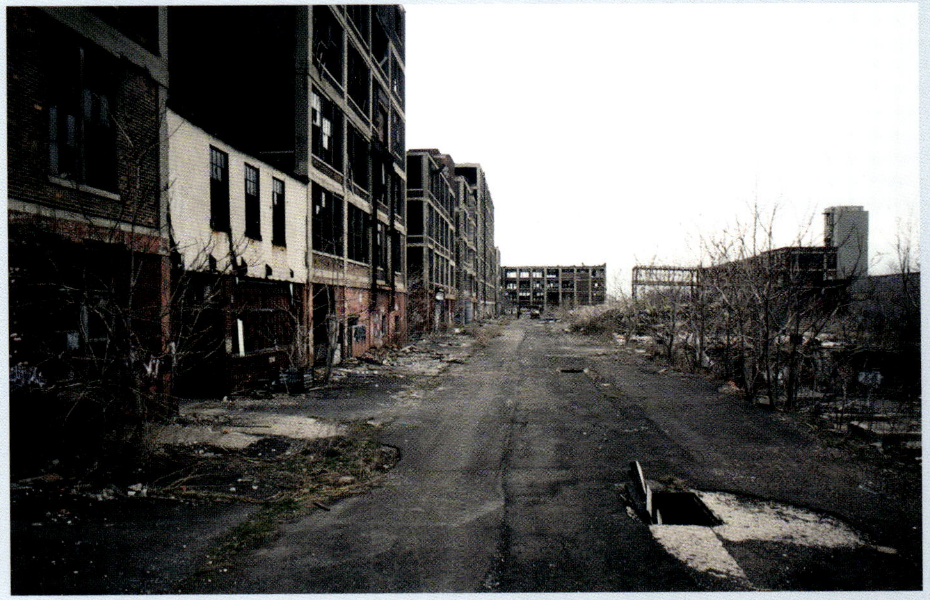

Former Packard Plant. One wing has been demolished.
East Grand Boulevard at Concord Street, Detroit, 2000.

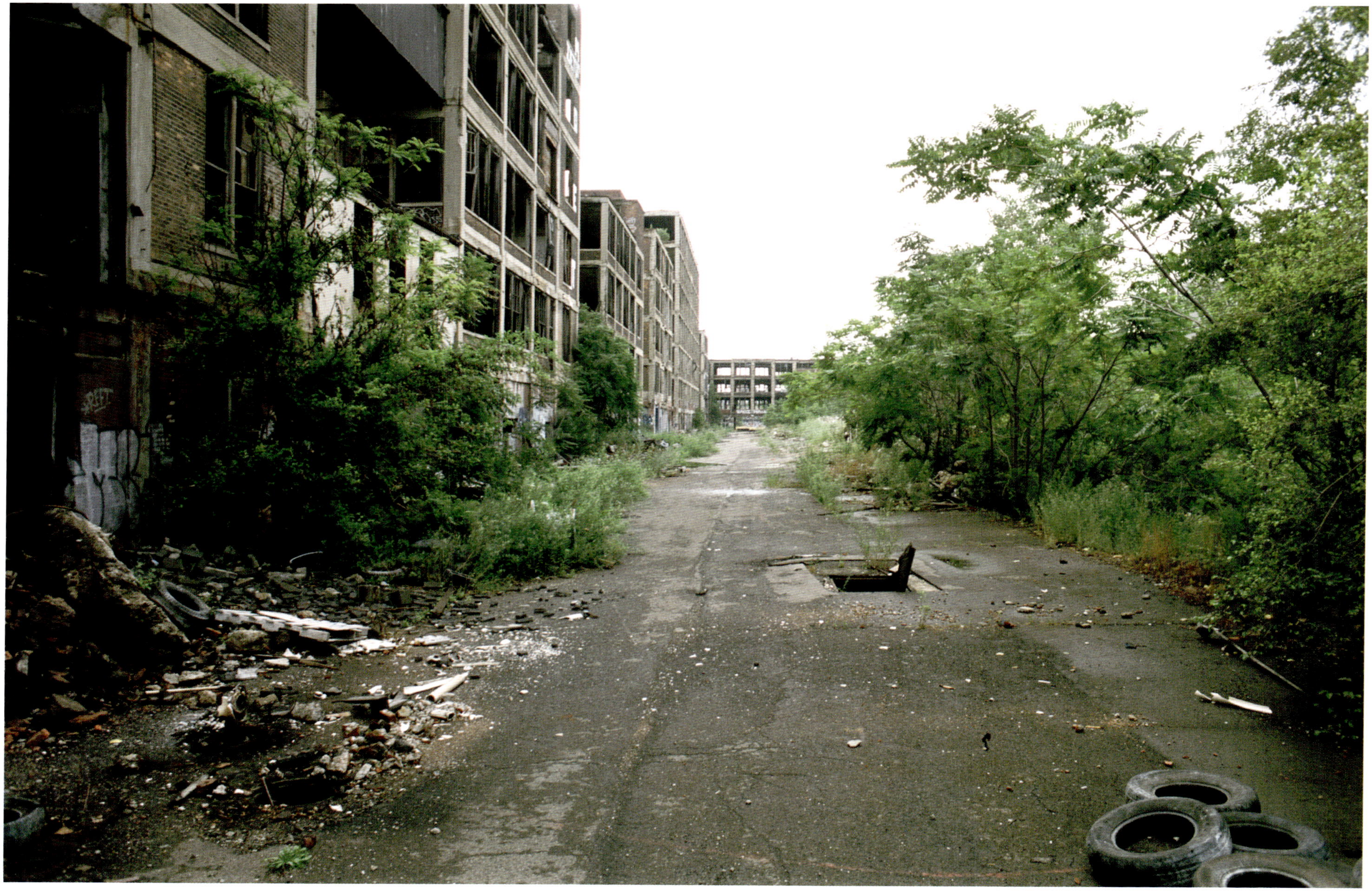

Former Packard Plant visited by tourists, graffiti artists, and scavengers. Around this time filmmakers looking for apocalyptic settings became interested in the plant. East Grand Boulevard at Concord Street, Detroit, 2012.

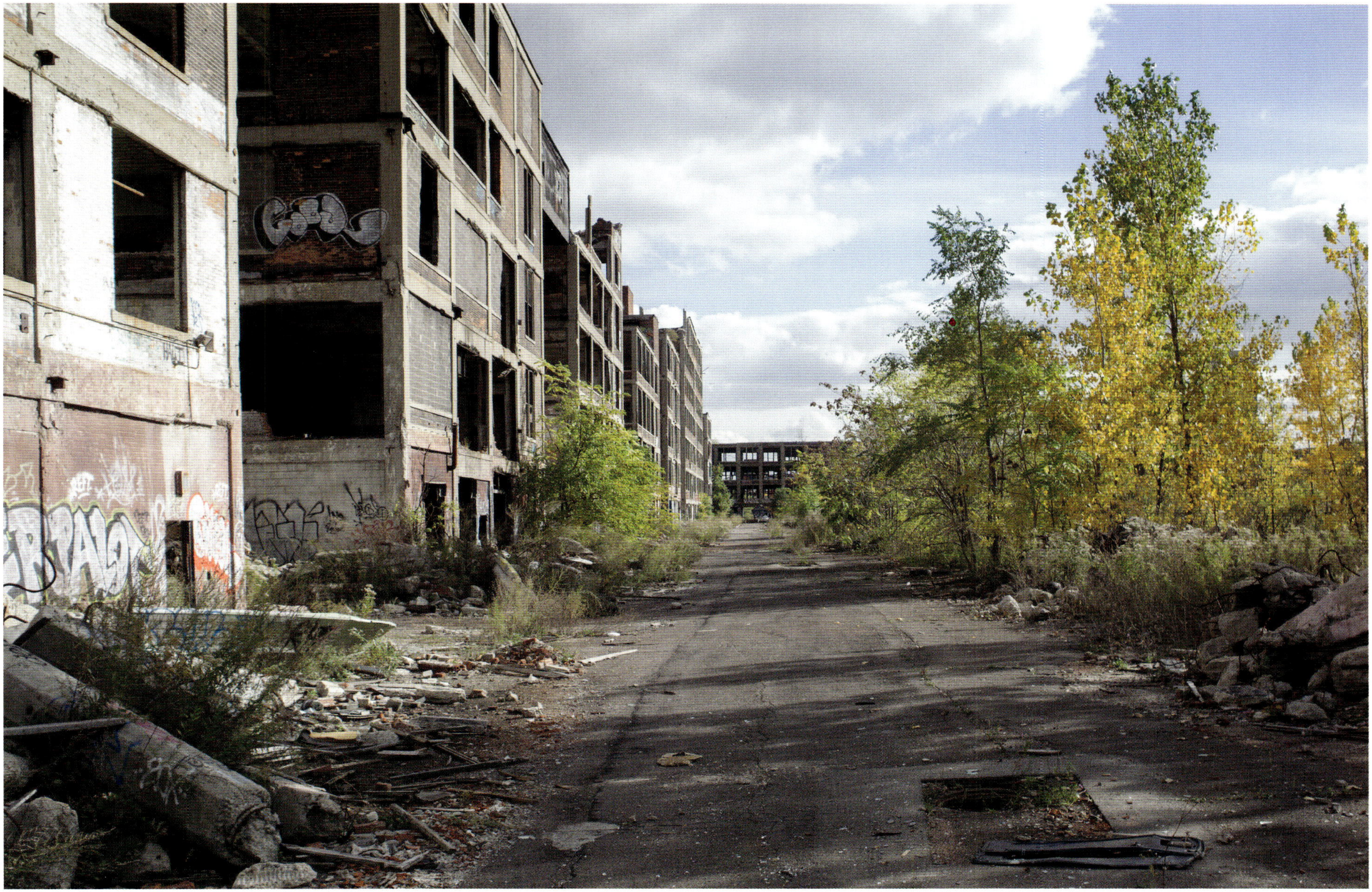

Former Packard Plant, view toward East Grand Boulevard from road parallel to Concord Street, Detroit, 2013.

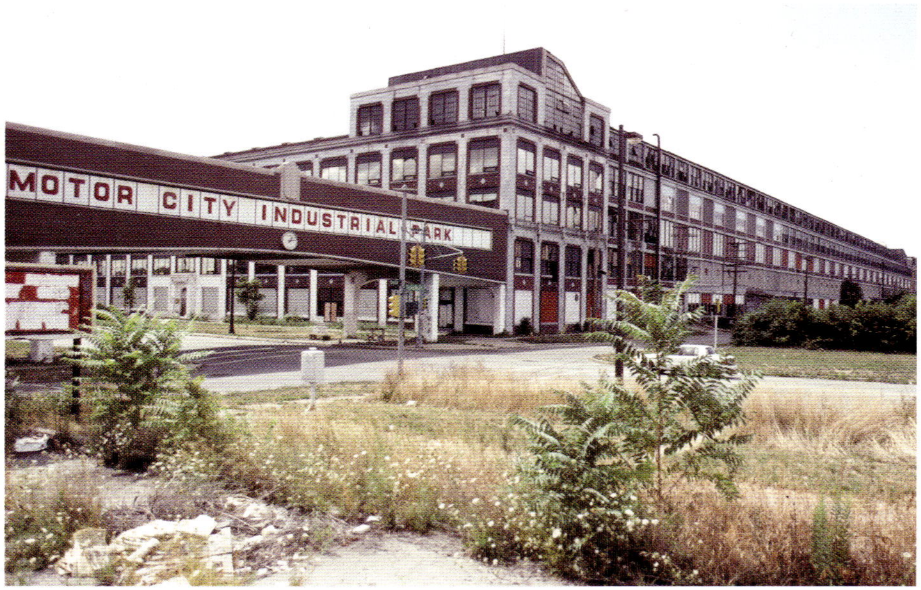

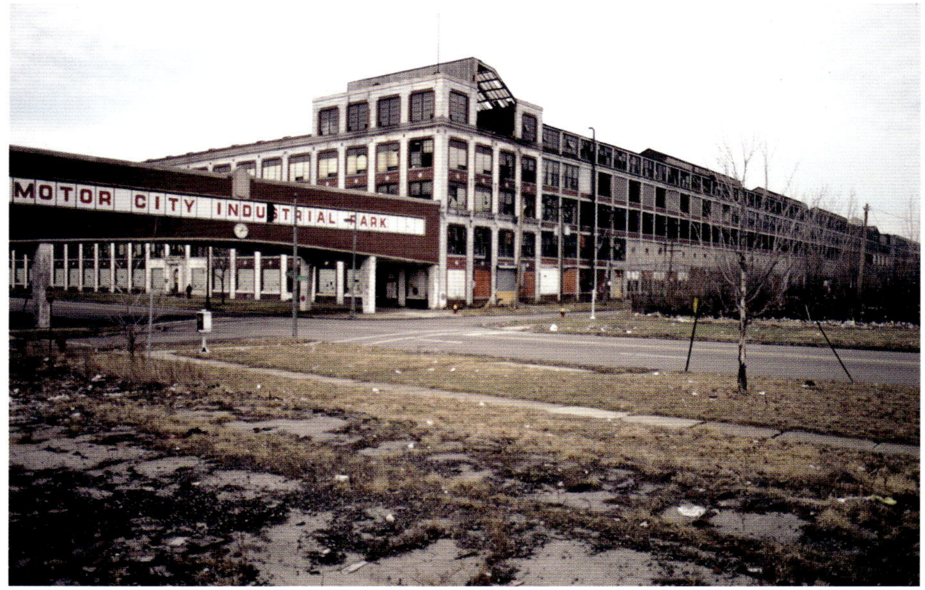

Former Packard Plant. Albert Kahn designed the early buildings of the Packard Automotive Plant, in operation from 1903 to 1958. Later renamed Motor City Industrial Park, the building became an incubator for about two hundred small businesses, including auto repair shops, an industrial laundry, warehouses, and recycling centers. East Grand Boulevard at Concord Street, Detroit, 1991.

Former Packard Plant. East Grand Boulevard at Concord Street, Detroit, 2003.

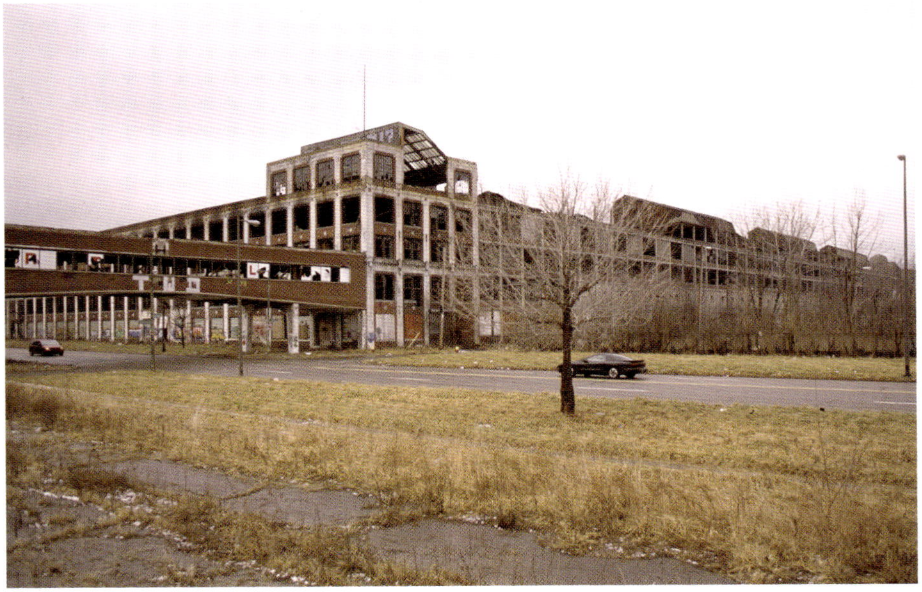

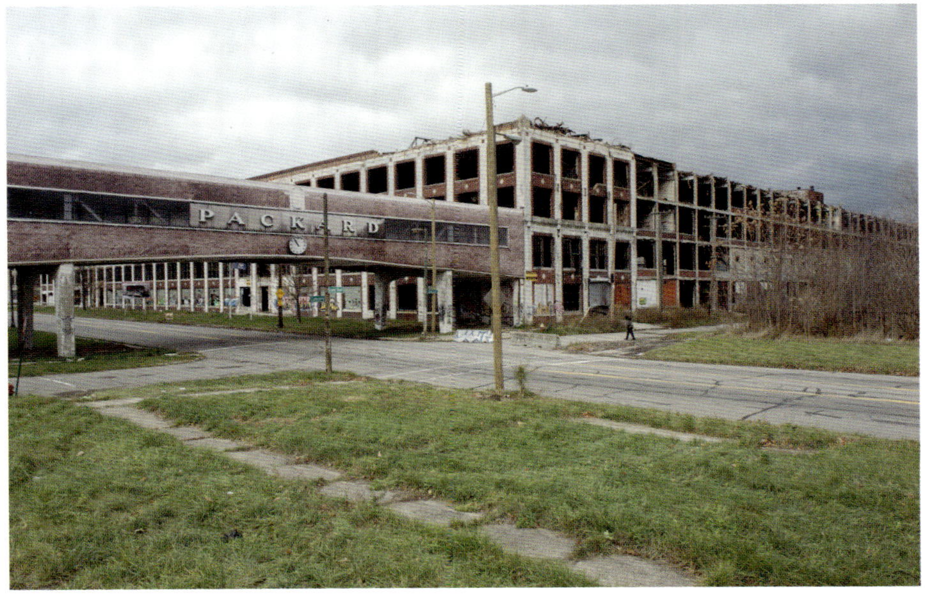

Former Packard Plant. East Grand Boulevard at Concord Street, Detroit, 2012.

Former Packard Plant. East Grand Boulevard at Concord Street, Detroit, 2015.

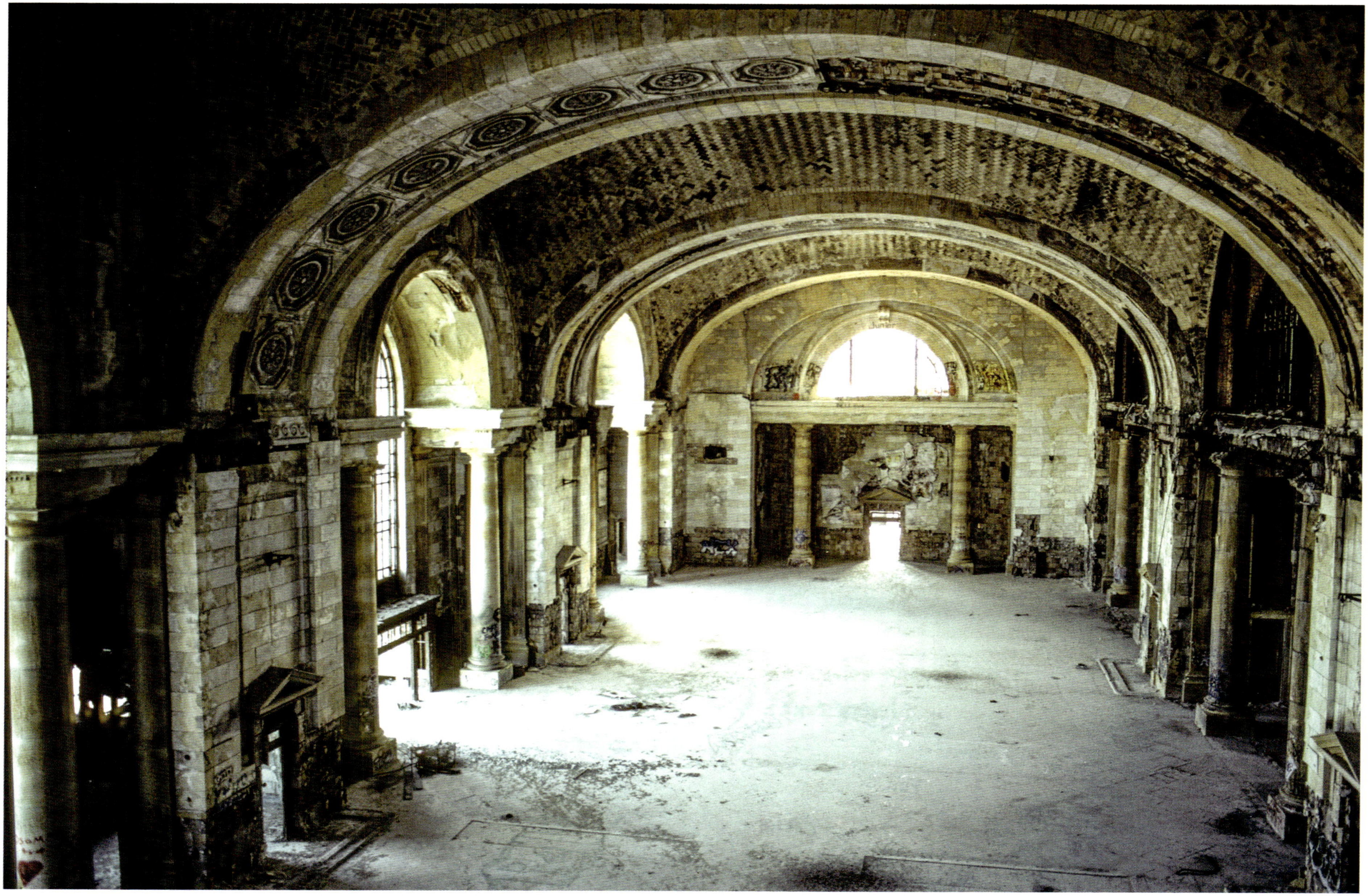

Waiting room interior, Michigan Central Railroad Station, inspired by the Baths of Caracalla. The station was added to the National Register of Historic Places in 1975. Detroit, 2009.

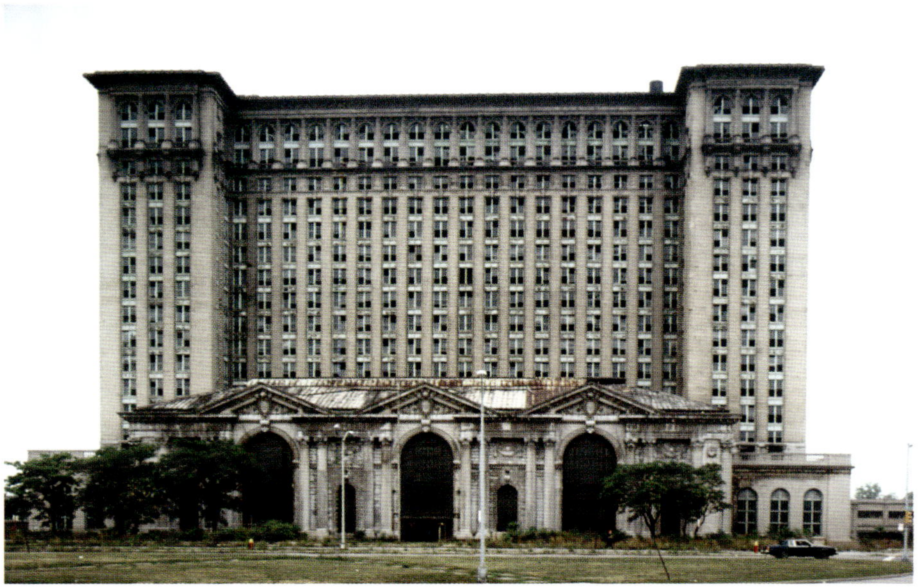

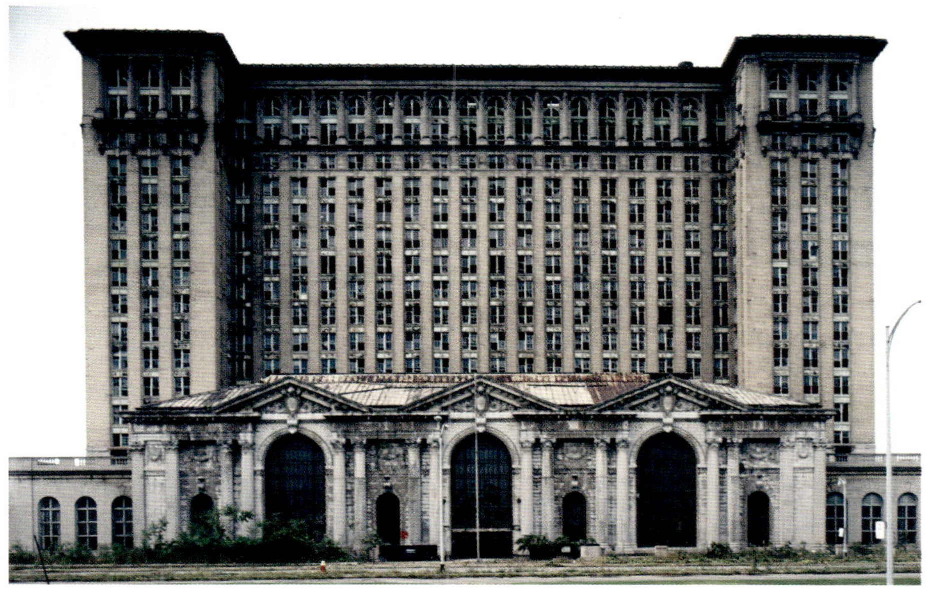

Former Michigan Central Railroad Station. Designed by the New York firm Warren and Wetmore for the Michigan Central Railroad, the station opened in 1913 and was closed completely in 1994. Detroit, 1993.

Former Michigan Central Railroad Station. Detroit, 1997.

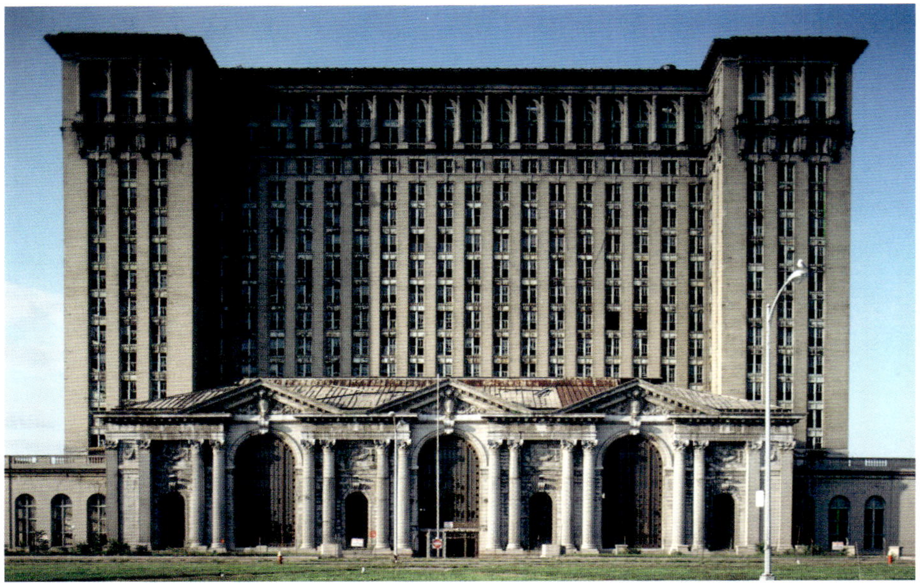

Former Michigan Central Railroad Station. Detroit, 2000.

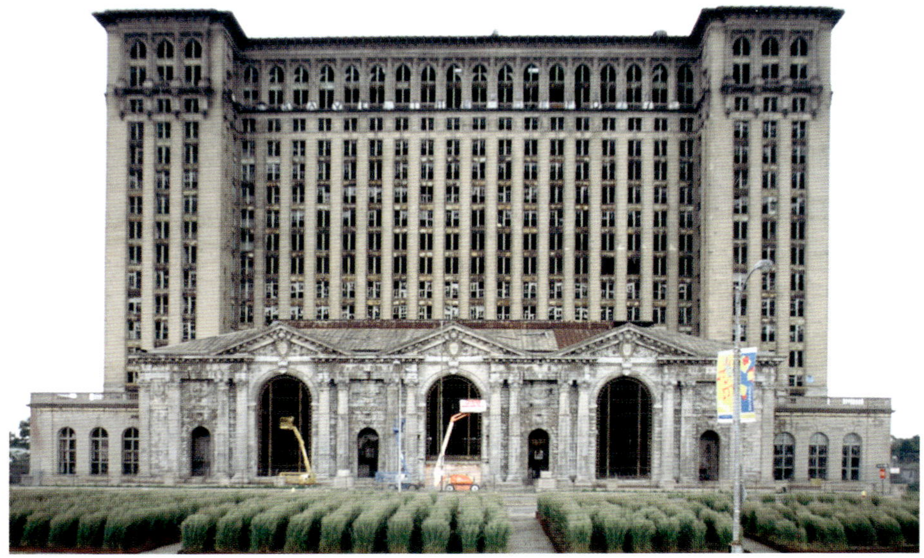

Former Michigan Central Railroad Station. Raised beds of grasses were planted in front of the station. Detroit, June 2011.

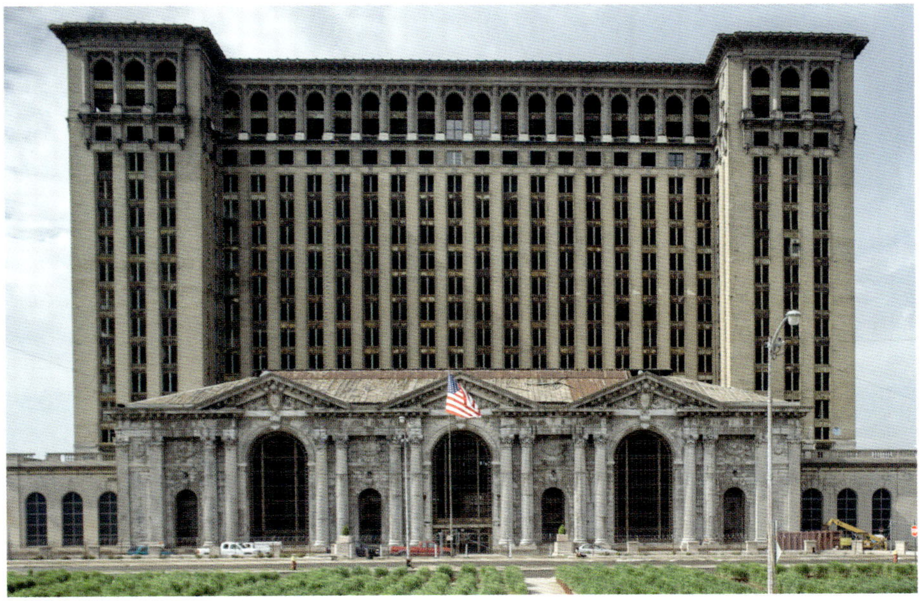

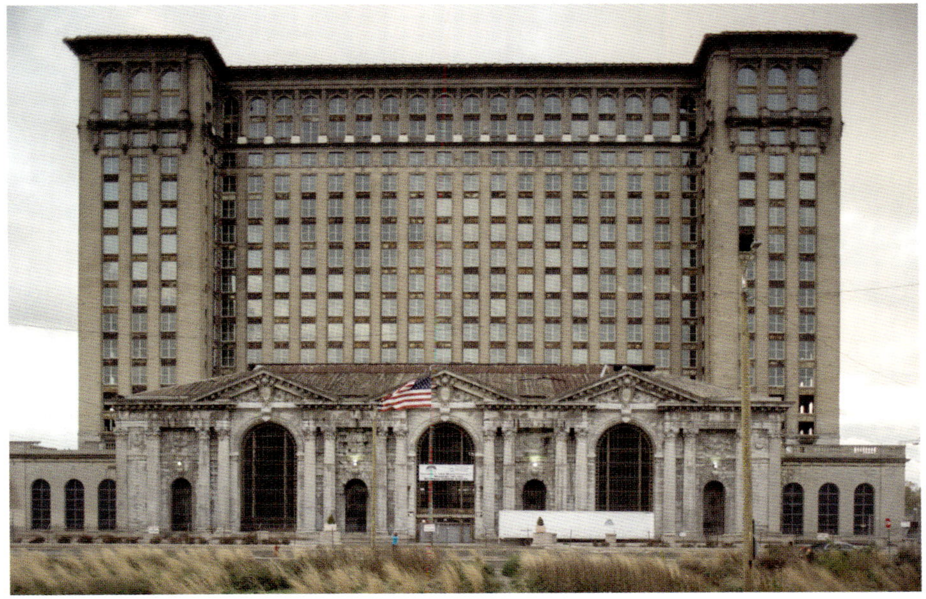

Former Michigan Central Station. Three new windows have been added to the façade. Detroit, 2014.

Former Michigan Central Railroad Station. Historian Tim Samuelson remarked that the new fenestration "is totally destroying the subtle vertical emphasis established by the original window frames and sash. What you have now is a big piece of glass and a fake criss-cross placed on the front with no vertical emphasis at all." Detroit, 2015.

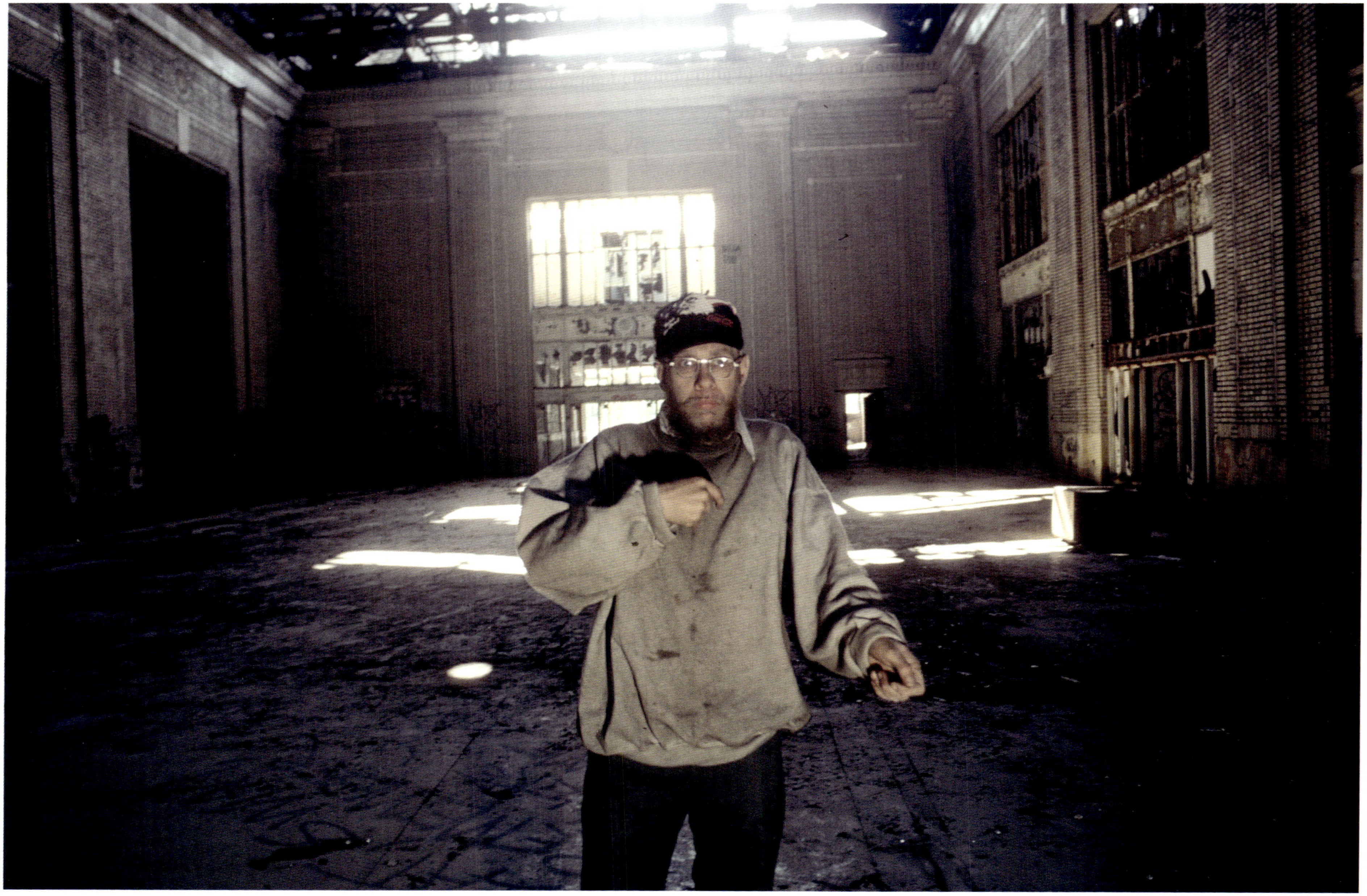

Gerald Williams, aka Catfish, a Detroit legend. Catfish, who lived inside the station in the 1990s, was recorded in a video saying: "I lost my job. I became homeless, and I settled down around here. I have nowhere else to go. I am home, I live in this building. I have been here for a couple of years. We have water and everything, there is plenty of room.... Most of the damage you see around here is from the gang kids who come in here, they get bored, and start smashing shit up." Michigan Central Station, Detroit, 1998.

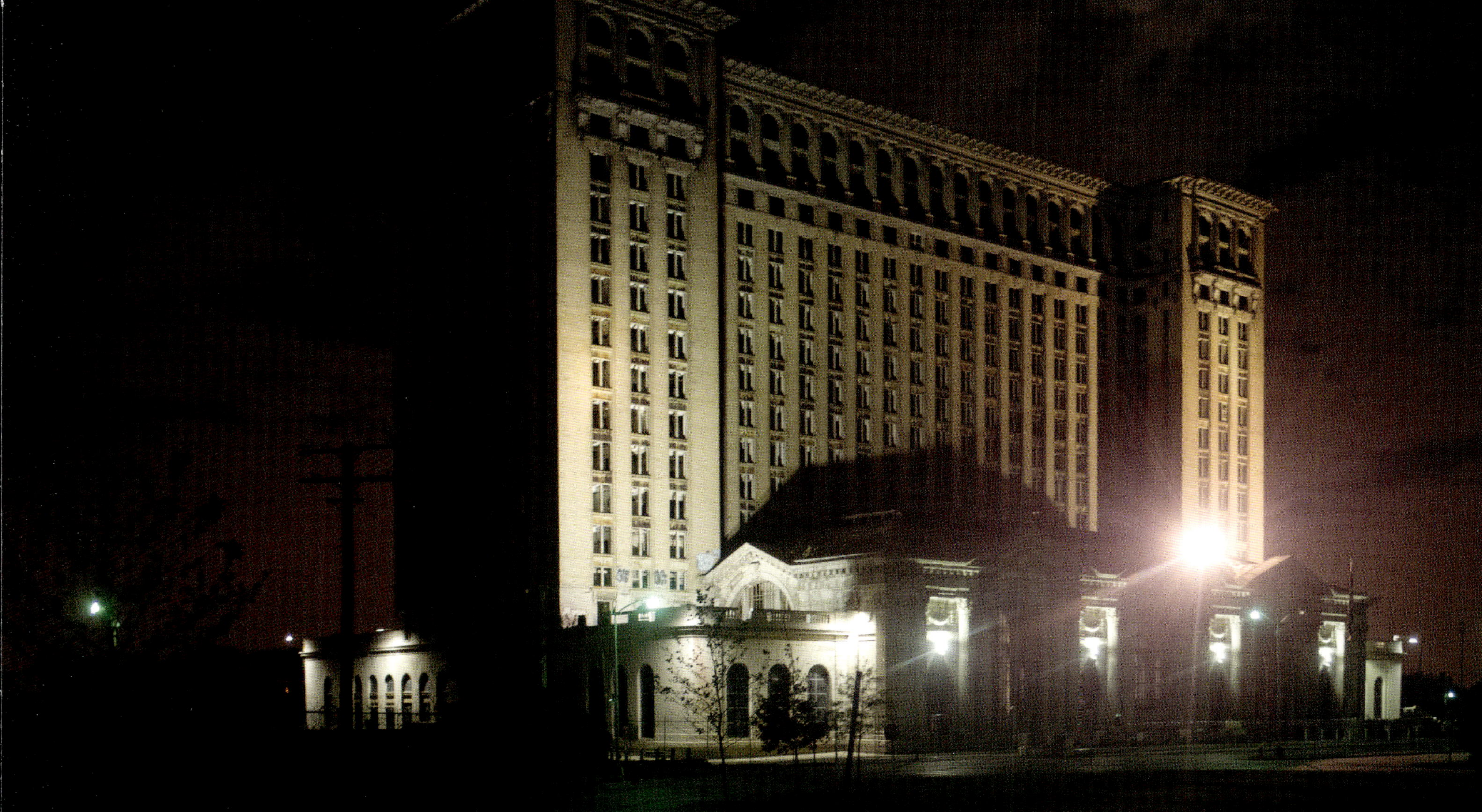

The majesty of ruins: former Michigan Central Rail Road Station. In 2011, John Leary called this Detroit landmark "the Eiffel Tower of ruin photography." Detroit, 2013.

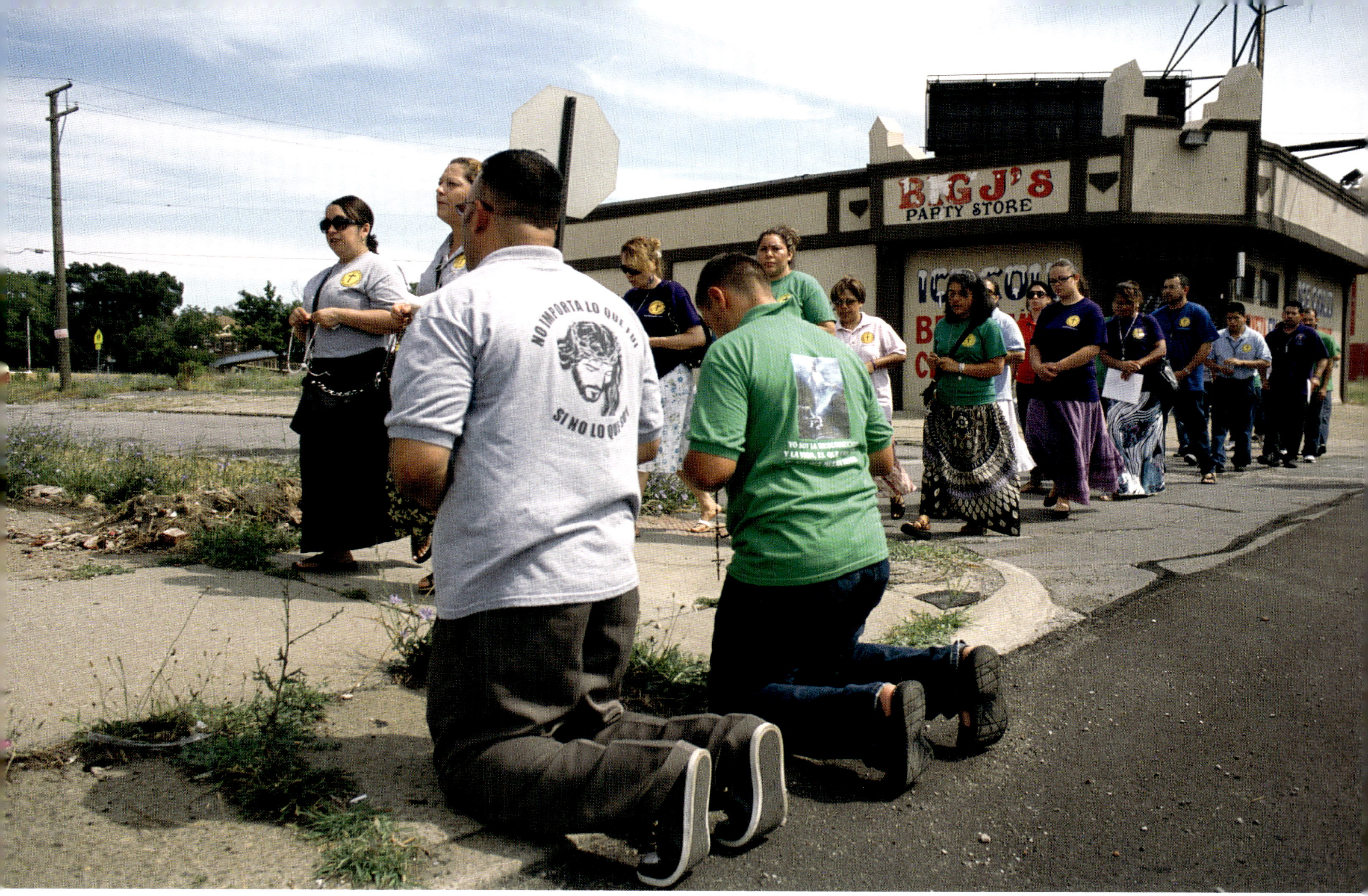

A Catholic pilgrimage organized by Movimiento Juan XXIII. West Fort Street at Rademacher Street, Detroit, 2012.

GIVING BACK TO THE COMMUNITY

Detroit has become a city to believe in, a magnet for people of good will, and a testing ground for good intentions. In a reversal of the city-suburb antagonism of the Coleman Young era (1974–94), when it was common to hear former residents boast, "I haven't been in Detroit in 20 years," there is a growing desire among suburbanites and white citizens of Detroit to participate in rehabilitating the city. They want to tell the world that "everybody is coming to make our city a better place to live." Detroit is not alone anymore; it has become "our city," its desolate neighborhoods part of "our communities." People who fled to the suburbs and for decades refused to visit Detroit are now joining Arise Detroit, Life Remodeled, Habitat for Humanity, and other organizations. Some of the largest corporations, foundations, and religious groups in the nation are participating in this movement. Guided by up-to-date surveys and maps, volunteers go to areas of "significant need" to transform "depressing neighborhoods" into better places. They expect to create communities where people want to live, that will give them pride, and that will grow stronger and stronger.

Philanthropic activities are organized with the precision of a military operation. They involve tens of thousands of people. Schools are painted; cafeterias, libraries, labs, and gyms get new floors; roofs and fixtures are repaired; cheerful murals are painted. The equipment they use—saws, lawnmowers, power drills, even bulldozers and backhoes—look new. Engineers and technicians go into some of the worst high schools in the nation, taking on hefty projects that they must finish in a day or two.

Volunteers get great personal satisfaction from helping out. They form teams wearing matching t-shirts. In many videos made of their activities, a diverse group of middle-class folks are seen having fun carrying old tires to strategically placed dumpsters. They gladly climb stepladders to board up abandoned houses, and with power saw in hand they remove dead trees and feed them into a wood chipper. They crouch to plant flowers, remove debris, and mow the grass in front of abandoned buildings. A few buildings beyond repair are demolished, and a small number refurbished. One of the organizers remarked that they were making a "life-changing impact on the neighborhood."

For decades church groups have been driving into the city to distribute food to the homeless. Volunteers come to the Cass Corridor, an area with a large concentration of SROs, shelters, and drug treatment facilities. Others go to the bus station downtown, where they give out free coffee and donuts. Neighborhood churches have their own weekly or monthly programs distributing food from food banks and government surpluses to those who come for it. But now the effort is much larger, contributing to a consensus that Detroit and its neighborhoods constitute a single organism. The idea is that if the surrounding neighborhoods continue to deteriorate, even as the downtown and midtown boom continues, then the effort to rebuild the city will have failed.

On the corner of East Forest and Van Dyke Avenue, I happened upon a strange scene that made me think of a southern plantation reversed. A group of thirteen white men and women were planting trees and shrubs on the empty corner lot. Of the thirteen, five had their hands in the dirt while three black men stood watching, one of them leaning on a shovel. A black woman and a boy were sitting inside a brand new pick-up truck, which the boy was pretending to drive. One of the white men told me that they were starting a Dream Garden, which was going to be in the shape of a butterfly. "We come from all over the country. There are people who come here from Los Angeles for the day. Some of us work for Ford or GM," he said. A banner they had put up on the lot's eastern fence read, "God, Hope and Love."

After preparing for three years to worship and volunteer in Detroit, members of the Evangelical Lutheran Church of America (ELCA) came to Detroit in huge numbers in August 2015 with the intention of "alleviating injustice." "We are doing God's work right here with our hands," said Jimmy Sandborn, age 17, of the Fresno, California, ELCA. Jeremy Smith, another teen from Fresno, remarked, "It feels good to get out and help the community, help people." Smith and Sanborn, with 10,000 other Lutherans, worked across metro Detroit to help the needy. Another 20,000 arrived to work the following two days. As noted in the *Detroit Free Press*: "Wearing orange-colored shirts, the ELCA members have been a big presence in downtown Detroit this week, holding nightly gatherings at Ford Field."

"What you need to do with blight is to attack it right away," said Steve Ogden of Rock Ventures. And Glenda D. Price of the Detroit Public School Foundation remarked, "Once the blight is removed, all sort of potentials and possibilities will exist." The implication is that job creation and economic development will follow upon the boarding up of buildings and the mowing of overgrown lawns. According to Rock Ventures' Sean Jackson, the idea is that children will be able to walk to school without having to worry about that abandoned house next to them. This assumes that no more houses will burn down or become vacant.

I was pleased to watch the volunteers in one of the videos and felt a desire to join them (https://vimeo.com/136152298). The video showed Sharon Jackson, resident of the blighted neighborhood, speaking first. Then Mary Barra, CEO of General Motors, appeared, stating: "Detroit is our home." I was left wanting to believe that for a minute the two women, one representing the Osborne neighborhood and the other a powerful corporation, had indeed met, shaken hands, and talked. One of the organizers remarked: "They're coming up to us and saying, 'Whatever you do next year, we're in.'" Charles, a member of Free Indeed Outreach Ministries, called the volunteers' help "truly a blessing," predicting that the community will continue their work.

The areas of revitalization amount to some 7.2 square miles. So we must ask whether that revitalization will trickle down to Detroit's most desolate corners. Will the abandoned houses, their front yards with a new set of cast-off tires, broken television sets, and discarded mattresses, be waiting for the volunteers when they return next year? Will a new crop of memorials, signs of violent crimes, be attached to the neighborhood lampposts? Will the planter boxes used to designate safe routes for students to follow still be there? And will the schools they attend improve? How many new jobs will be created? Will communities grow "stronger and stronger" even as the black population continues to decline? And what if this largely one-sided endeavor continues to increase, what if the number of volunteers doubles? What would the effect be? Will the visual culture that developed for over a half century in Detroit's ghettos continue to be ignored? Will businesses needing to appear "real" come to the city to take advantage of its boundless wells of authenticity? I will continue to investigate what happens, what new activities emerge.

NO DRY BONES

There is a growing belief that Detroit will prosper again, but as a different city. Perhaps the complex of events necessary to make a revival possible will not depend as much on the entire southeast Michigan region as it did in the past. If Detroit is defined through social media as a fascinating place that survives amidst adversity, that attracts creativity, and that is filled with neighborhoods where people can live interesting lives, then the world might take a chance and Detroit might leap over its suburbs.

But it is difficult for me to imagine a Detroit without its magnificent ruins, miles of decayed avenues, vacant land, and struggle for survival. For half a century, these things have been a major part of the city's aura and authenticity. With the Michigan Central Station neutered and the Packard Automotive Plant falling apart, increasing urban farming, and a significant reduction of perceived blight, Detroit will need new images. Identity, once monolithic as in "Motor City" or "The Arsenal of Democracy," might in the future consist of several identities. These are being negotiated online by the automobile industry, gentrifiers, billionaires, foundations, advertising people, volunteers, urban farmers, artists, and bicycle-riding hipsters as they struggle to understand, imagine, and remake all 139 square miles of Detroit.

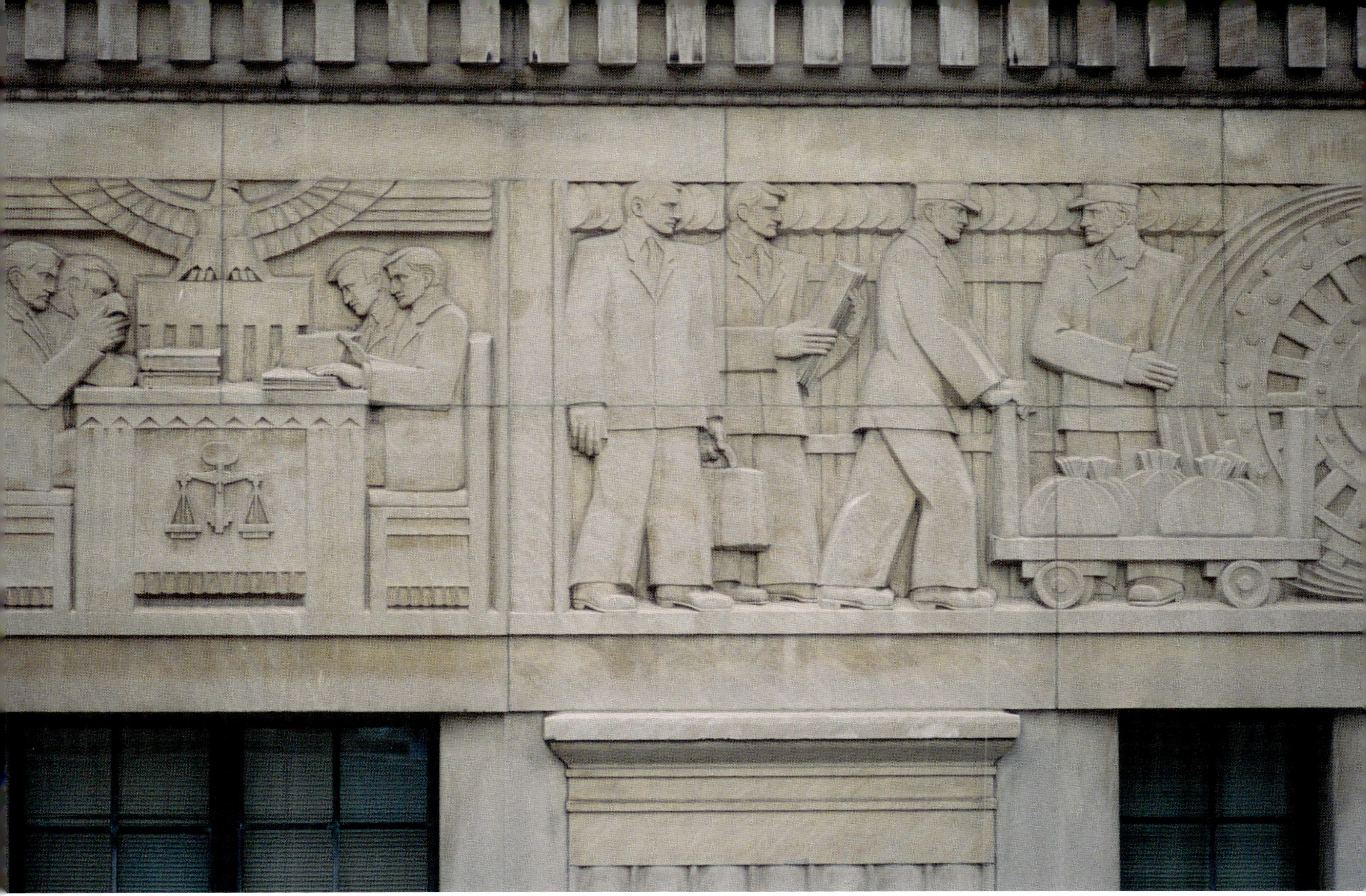

Theodore Levin United States Courthouse (1934), detail of exterior frieze representing the law and the treasury, by Corrado Joseph Parducci. Today many people looked nostalgically upon such idealized visions of Detroit's former order and wealth.

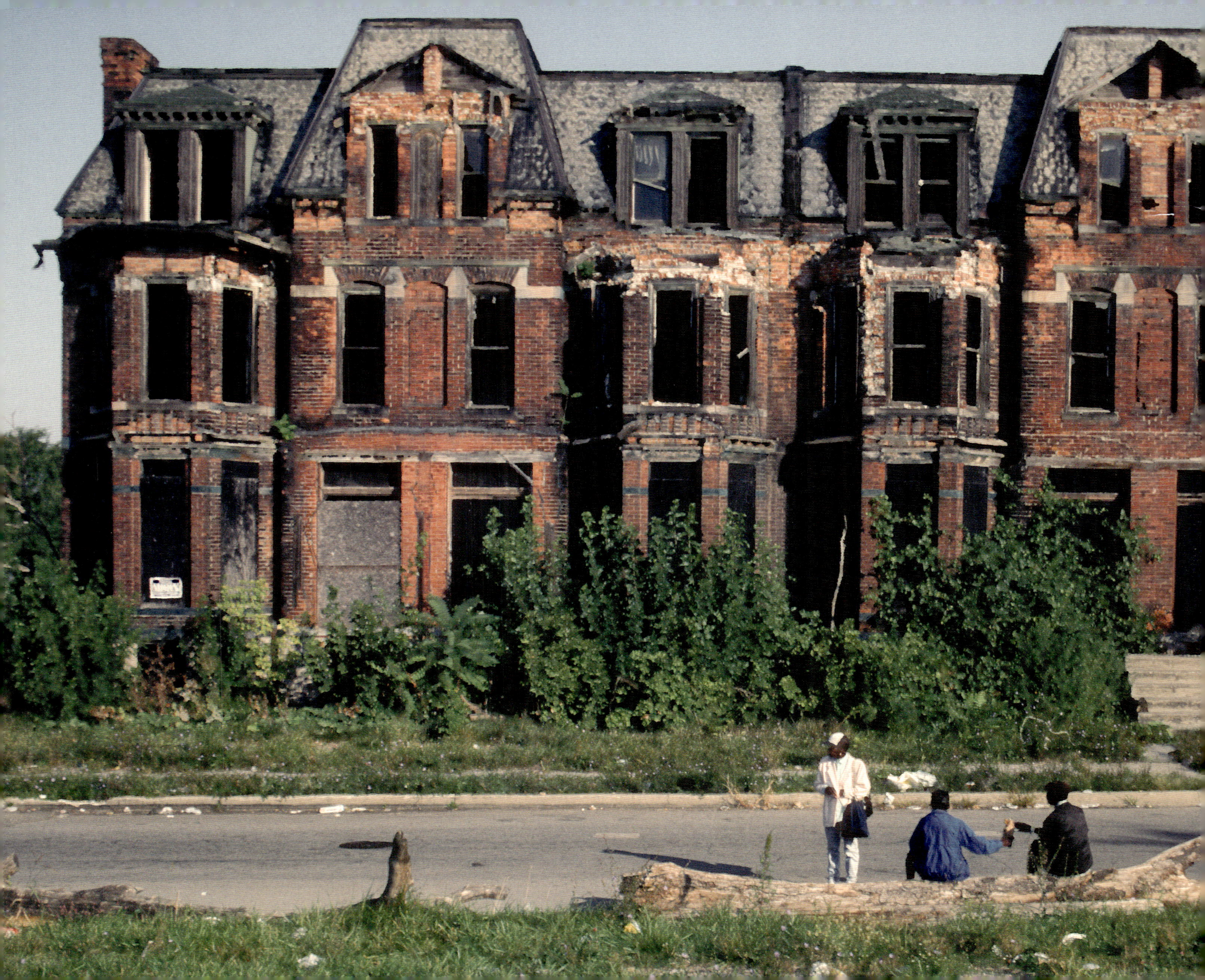

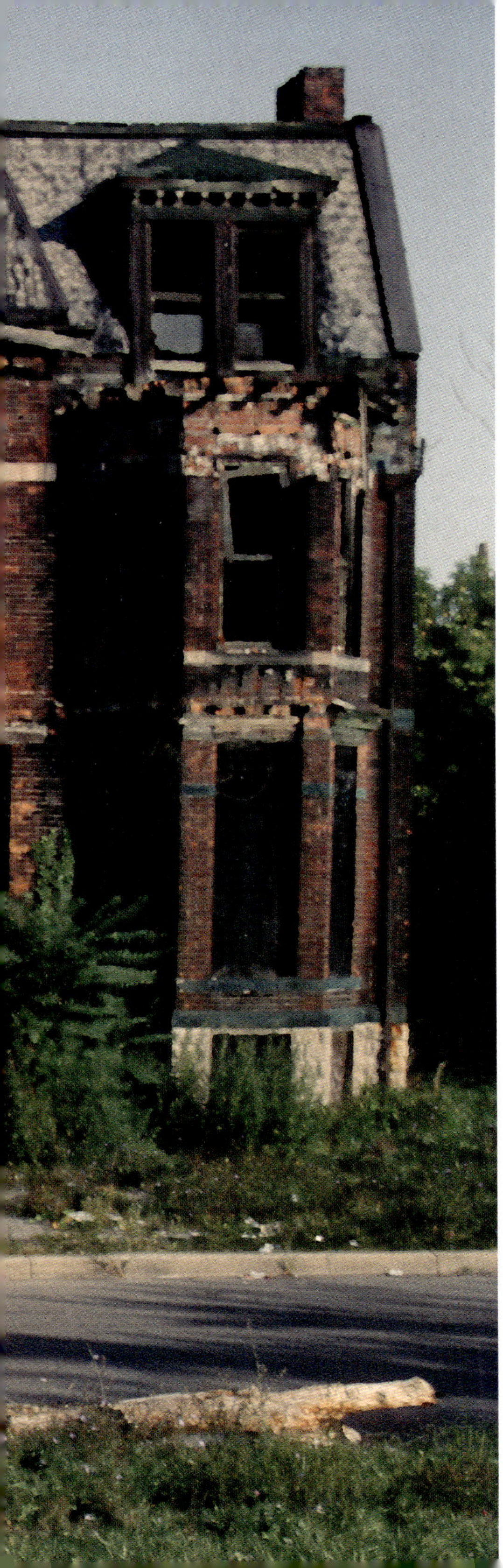

ACKNOWLEDGMENTS

Since 2010, Tim Samuelson, Cultural Historian of Chicago, has helped me immensely by engaging in an uninterrupted dialogue about Detroit. Tim and I often interviewed people together and compared impressions. When curious about a building, a sign, or anything that caught our attention, I asked for his interpretation. When I could not adequately express an idea, Tim was often able to complete the thought. Our conversations expanded seemingly unique observations into larger categories, such as "Detroit's New Architecture" and "Giving Back to the Community."

Over the years, being invited to present my Detroit project to planners, architects, and historians at various universities has been crucial in shaping my understanding of Detroit, and I thank these hosts for the generous opportunities they offered to me: Anne Whiston Spirn of MIT; Wendy Griswold of Northwestern University; and Christian Mair of Freiburg University.

Robert Beauregard, Professor of Urban Planning at Columbia University, arranged for me to talk with students and faculty several times and made many valuable suggestions that conceptually enriched the way I witnessed Detroit. Professor Robert Fishman, who wrote a piece in this book, brought my exhibition "Detroit Is No Dry Bones" to Ann Arbor, toured Detroit with me, and arranged for a public discussion at Taubman College of Architecture and Planning of the University of Michigan in 2015. Over nearly a decade, my many conversations with Professors Beauregard and Fishman greatly helped to shape this book. Both kindly read a draft of the manuscript as well.

I also benefited from having many discussions and field visits with journalist Bill McGraw, blogger Jim Griffioen, cinematographer Geoff George, and architect Steve Vogel, all of whom share a profound interest in understanding Detroit. We reflected on such issues as the thaw between the city and the suburbs, widespread dumping of refuse, ruin porn, and forms of ruination. Sometimes we seemed to want to outdo each other in our enthusiastic selection of places to visit. Art historian Dennis Nawrocki, landscape architect Nick Tobier, and urban planner Joe Rashid were always quick to answer my questions or to direct me to people who could do so.

Matt Pieroni and his father Anthony Pieroni were generous hosts during my visits to Detroit. And I am grateful to Lisa Vergara for her editorial help. She listened to me in various states of incoherence, asked questions, demanded answers, and read several versions of this manuscript.

Detroit residents such as Lee Walker, a sign painter, Mark Covington, an urban farmer, and Mattie, a storekeeper, played an invaluable role by sharing with me how they interpreted the images of their city that I showed them.

Producing a beautiful book takes talent, dedication, and passion. I was lucky to find these qualities in my friend, Detroit-raised designer Lorraine Wild, and in her colleague Amy Fortunato. Working with them was a pleasure. And I am grateful to editor Scott Ham and his colleagues at The University of Michigan Press for all they did to make this book possible.

Victorian townhouses, torn down in 2001. It became an icon, even appearing in such movies as "Beverly Hills Cop" (1984). Alfred Street at Brush Street, Detroit, 1998

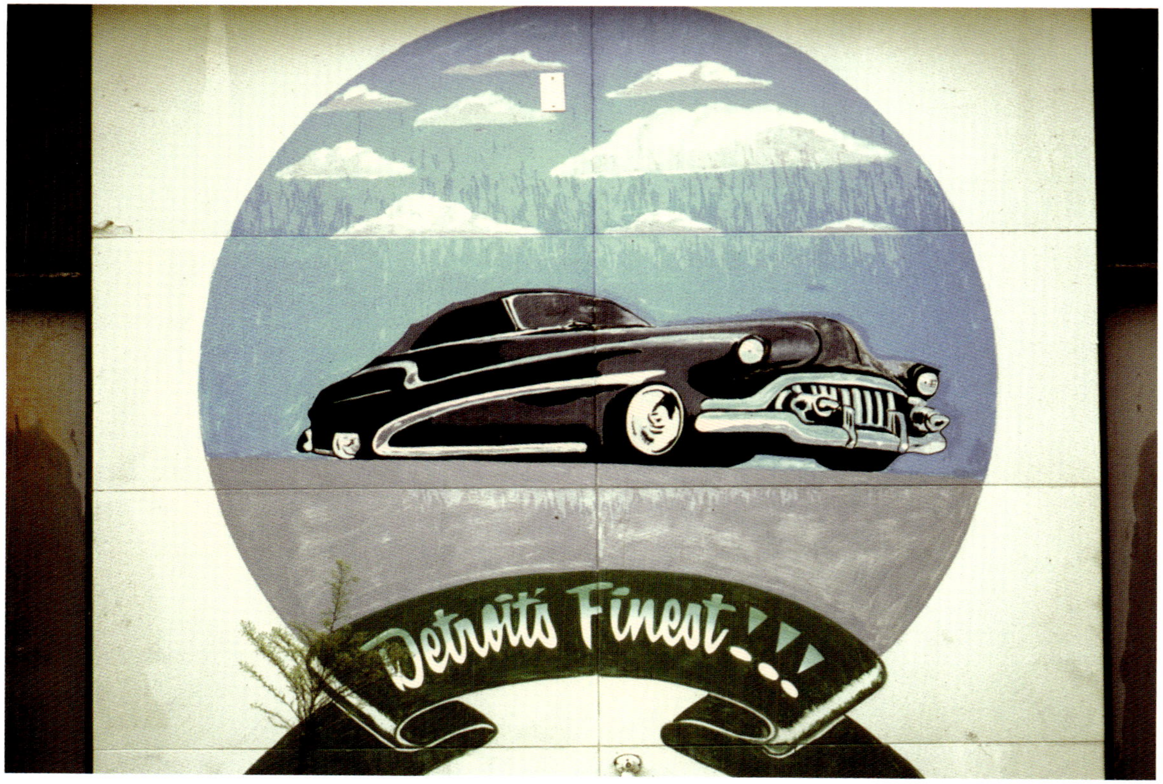

Detroit's Finest, picturing a splendid 1952 Buick, at Hand Rinses Car Wash. John R Street at East Grand Boulevard, Detroit, 1999.

The University of Michigan Press gratefully acknowledges subventions from the University of Michigan's Office of Research and Taubman College of Architecture and Urban Planning in partial support of the costs of production of this volume.

Design: Lorraine Wild and Amy Fortunato,
Green Dragon Office, Los Angeles
Typeset in Plan Grotesque, Workhorse, and Alegreya Sans

Published in the United States of America by the
University of Michigan Press
Manufactured in China
Printed on acid-free paper
2019 2018 2017 2016 4 3 2 1

A CIP catalog record for this book is available from the British Library.

Library of Congress Cataloging-in-Publication Data

Names: Vergara, Camilo J.
Title: Detroit is no dry bones : the eternal city of the industrial age / Camilo José Vergara.
Description: Ann Arbor : University of Michigan Press, 2016.
Identifiers: LCCN 2016007766 | ISBN 9780472130115 (hardcover : alkaline paper)
Subjects: LCSH: Inner cities—Michigan—Detroit—Pictorial works. | Detroit (Mich.)—Social conditions—Pictorial works. | Detroit (Mich.)—Buildings, structures, etc.—Pictorial works. | Detroit (Mich.)—Biography—Pictorial works. | Historic buildings—Michigan—Detroit—Pictorial works. | Buildings—Remodeling for other use—Michigan—Detroit—Pictorial works. | Urban renewal—Michigan—Detroit—Pictorial works. | Social change—Michigan—Detroit—Pictorial works. | BISAC: PHOTOGRAPHY / Subjects & Themes / Architectural & Industrial.
Classification: LCC HN80.D6 V47 2016 | DDC 307.7609774/34—dc23
LC record available at http://lccn.loc.gov/2016007766